STUDIES IN ARCHITECTURE

Edited by Anthony Blunt and Rudolf Wittkower

Volume IX

Sir William Chambers

John Harris

Sir Joshua Reynolds. Sir William Chambers (Royal Academy)

Sir
William Chambers

Knight of the Polar Star

by John Harris

with contributions
by J. Mordaunt Crook and Eileen Harris

A. Zwemmer Ltd
London 1970

Copyright © 1970 by A. Zwemmer Ltd
Published by A. Zwemmer Ltd, 76–80 Charing Cross Road, London, WC2
SBN: 302 02076 4
Designed by Graham Johnson/Lund Humphries
Printed in Great Britain by Lund Humphries, London and Bradford

To my Wife

Contents

List of Plates

List of Text Illustrations

With the exception of Fig.16, all plans have been reproduced drawn to a sixteenth inch to one foot scale by Mr Keith Blanchard.

Photographic and Line Illustrations Acknowledgements

Her Majesty The Queen: 40, 111, 121–124, 126, 129, 130, 132–134, 196

Avery Library, Columbia University: 185–7

Lionel Bell (for photographs): 1–11, 18, 21, 24–5, 28–31, 33–7, 39–41, 51, 56, 60, 63, 65, 68, 69, 74–7, 79, 80, 91, 94–100, 104, 109–23, 126, 128, 131, 133, 134, 138–44, 146, 147, 149, 150, 153, 155, 164, 165, 169, 170, 176–81, 192, 193, 196–8

Bodleian Library, Oxford: 148

Bruce Bailey: 81

Duke of Buccleuch: 72

Chichester Photographic Services Ltd: 48

Major C. R. Compton: 76, 77

A. C. Cooper Ltd: 124

Country Life: 46, 49, 66, 71, 72, 87, 88, 136, 137, 159, 171, 183, 189; Fig.3d

Crowther: 188

Dublin, Office of Public Works: Fig.7

John Freeman: 67, 126

Greater London Record Office: 67

Grosvenor Estate Office, London: 177

F. Jewel-Harrison: 90

Hans Huth: 42

Earl of Harewood: 43–5

Iveagh Bequest, Kenwood, London: 199

Miss Lambart John: 51

A. F. Kersting: 47, 89, 156, 160–3

Kunstindustrimuseet, Copenhagen: 12–17, 20

Mrs Phyllis Lambert: 19

London Museum: 135

Mr and Mrs Paul Mellon: 125, 167

Metropolitan Museum of Art, New York: 22, 23, 27, 32, 184

Ministry of Public Buildings and Works, London: 26, 157, 168, 172–5; Fig.15

National Gallery of Scotland, Edinburgh: 194, 195

National Museum, Stockholm: 127

National Monuments Record, Edinburgh: 62, 85, 86

National Monuments Record, London: 55, 82, 83, 101, 102, 166, 190, 191

National Portrait Gallery, London: frontispiece

Bernard Pardoe: 61

Alistair Rowan: 53, 54

Royal Academy, London: facing p. xvi of preliminary pages, 182

Royal Botanic Garden, Kew: 38

Royal Commission on Historical Monuments: 64

Royal Institute of British Architects: 1, 8, 24, 35, 79, 94, 104, 109–10, 112, 119, 139, 152–53, 179

Sanssouci Archives: 42

John Sarsfield: 50, 52, 84, 93, 151

Tom Scott: 105

Slatkin Galleries Inc: 19

Sir John Soane's Museum: 4, 74, 96, 98, 100, 131, 155, 165, 178

Austin Underwood: 78

Bertram Unne: 43–5

Victoria & Albert Museum: 2–3, 5–7, 59, 65, 69, 80, 92, 97, 99, 128, 142–7, 180

Ben Weinreb: 61

Westminster Public Library: 114, 116, 120

Marquis of Zetland: 106–8

The author: 34, 73, 92, 185–7

Abbreviations

Add.MS	Additional manuscript, British Museum
Avery	Avery Library, Columbia University, New York
APSD	Architectural Publication Society's Dictionary
BM	British Museum
Bull	Bulletin
C.Life	Country Life periodical
Charlemont Letters	Historical Manuscripts Commission, Charlemont MSS, 12th Report (1891), I; 13th Report (1894), II
Coll.	Collection
CRO	County Record Office (prefixed by name of county)
DML	Delaware Memorial Library, University of Delaware, U.S.A.
EXHIB	Exhibited, cf. Appendices
FD	Farington's Diary
GLC	Greater London Council
HMC	Historical Manuscripts Commission
HWC	Horace Walpole's Correspondence (ed. W. S. Lewis and others)
IOL	India Office Library
LCC	London County Council
MPL	Minet Public Library, Lambeth and Camberwell Surrey Collection
MMA	Metropolitan Museum of Art, New York
MRO	Middlesex Record Office
MS	Manuscript
NMR	National Monuments Record
PML	Pierpont Morgan Library, New York
PRO	Public Record Office
RA	Royal Academy
RCHM	Royal Commission on Historic Monuments
RIA	Royal Irish Academy, Dublin
RIBA	Royal Institute of British Architects
RO	Record Office
RS	Royal Society
Sale	Sale catalogue, cf. Appendices
SOC	Society

ABBREVIATIONS

s of A	Society of Arts
s of Antiq	Society of Antiquaries
Soane	Sir John Soane's Museum
St MPL	St Marylebone Public Library
V & A	Victoria and Albert Museum, London, Print Room
VCH	Victoria County History
WC	Sir William Chambers
WCRL	Windsor Castle, Royal Library
WPL	Westminster Public Library (Buckingham Palace Road)

Sir Joshua Reynolds. Sir William Chambers (National Portrait Gallery)

Preface

Several incentives led me to write this monograph, not the least being the paucity of published writings about one who dominated the professional and official architectural scene in a way that more fashionable architects, such as Robert Adam, never could. Although it may seem paradoxical, I think this was due to the daunting mass of original documents, so large that they defy inclusion in one book. To sift through all this meant intolerable delays, and I owe a great debt to Desmond Zwemmer for his patience at my delay in sending in the manuscript. In 1962 my wife began to work with Professor Wittkower on their bibliography of English architectural writings and theory. As her knowledge in this field is more profound than mine, it seemed appropriate that she should contribute the chapter on the *Treatise on Civil Architecture*; she also persuaded me – quite rightly, as it turned out – to write about the 'Chinese' books. I then found Dr J. Mordaunt Crook patiently working through the Office of Works's papers in the Public Record Office for his contribution to the *History of the King's Works*, and it only seemed fair that he should be the author of the chapter concerning Chambers and the Office. I owe both these historians a debt of gratitude, the extent of which will be evident to all who read their contributions.

With Chambers I was faced with the problem of bringing together the unusually wide range of his interests, covering not only architectural design, but landscape gardening, architectural writing and theory, the foundation of the Royal Academy, the Swedish East India Company, and the architectural profession. I therefore decided to present a series of self-contained articles, prefaced by a synopsis of his life's events. The first part of this volume is concluded with a group of appendices. The second part is a catalogue of his projects and executed buildings, by which means I was able to release the chapters in the first part from much otherwise necessary footnoting. As I have hinted, I was sorely tried by the mass of documentation, particularly the letters and the thousands of drawings. It was quite prohibitive to catalogue fully all these, but I have referred to every letter and drawing relative to a building. When it comes to acknowledgements, over the past seven years I enquired from a host of kindly scholars, librarians, friends, and owners of houses. From all I received help and courtesy. I would like first and foremost to thank Her Majesty The Queen for gracious permission to reproduce drawings and documents in her collections at Windsor Castle. Of the owners I would like to thank the Duke of Richmond and the Duke of Abercorn; the Earl of Pembroke; the Earl Fitzwilliam and Earl Spencer; the Earl of Bessborough and the Countess of Midleton; the Baron Boston; Sir William Worsley; Mr George Howard and Mr Marcus Worsley. There have been many who have been generous in providing me with information, advice, and correcting my errors. I thank all and sundry, but I would particularly like to mention Mr Geoffrey Beard, Mr Geoffrey de Bellaigue, Colonel John Busby, Mr Anthony Clark, Mr Howard Colvin, Dr Maurice Craig, Mr Edward Croft-Murray, Miss Kitty Cruft, Mr Svend Erikson, Desmond Fitz-Gerald, Knight of Glin, Mr John Fleming, Mr Brinsley Ford, Mr Hugh Honour, Mr Francis K. Kelly, Mrs Lesley Lewis, Mr T. McCormick, Sir Nikolaus Pevsner, Mr and Mrs John Gurney Salter, Miss A. Scott-Elliot, Miss D. Stroud, Sir John Summerson, Mr P. Reuterswärd, and Mr F. J. B. Watson. I have a special debt to the late Sir Albert Richardson, one of the custodians of Chambers's letters and manuscripts (now bequeathed to the Royal Academy), and to the late Rupert Gunnis, whose great library was always available for my use. Finally to Professor Rudolf Wittkower, who pushed me through this task, to the Swedish Institute for Cultural Relations, who gave me a grant to pursue Chambers in Sweden, to Mr James C. Palmes, always lenient when I wanted to leave the RIBA on a Chambers jaunt, to Mr Keith Blanchard, who redrew the plans for my text and, last but by no means least, to my wife, for without her there would have been no honouring the Knight of the Polar Star.

Glin Castle, April 1968

Chapter 1

Biography

On 23 February 1723, William, the first child of John and Sara Chambers, was christened. The event took place in Gothenburg where the Chamberses, a Scottish couple descended from the families of Chalmers and Forbes on one side, and the Elphinstones of Glack on the other, had settled in the early eighteenth century.[1] There John Chambers was established as a merchant in partnership with William Pierson, godfather to his son. Though little is known of the firm of Chambers and Pierson, its success can be measured by its accounts with King Charles XII of Sweden for supplying stores to the royal armies.[2] The royal patronage of the elder Chambers may well have contributed in some small way to the far greater honours bestowed upon his son. As the Chamberses prospered, so they grew in numbers. Within seven years there were four more children: Sara born in 1724, John in 1726, Elizabeth in 1728, and Mary in 1731. William, however, had little time to enjoy the intimacies of family life. Being their eldest son, he was soon sent off to be educated in England, presumably at the local grammar school in Ripon where he would be under the eye of his father's cousin, Dr William Chambers.[3] When he arrived and how he fared in this market town in the North Riding of Yorkshire we do not know. These years must have been happy ones, for in 1774 he could write nostalgically about the 'lovely bowers of innocence and ease, seats of my Youth, where every sport could please', confessing, however, that 'Rippon has now no charms for me, those I once knew and

[1] I have in this monograph purposely avoided enquiry into Chambers's ancestry. What has been discovered is complex and questionable on several points, and it belongs to the realms of genealogy rather than architectural history. It is essential to consult the correspondence between Dr William Kelly of Aberdeen and A. M. Munthe of Sweden. This correspondence, known as the Munthe Letters, is in the possession of Dr Kelly's son, Mr Francis C. Kelly of London, who very kindly made it available to me. Another principal source of enquiry is Dr John Gurney Salter of Abbots Bromley, Staffordshire, a descendant of Thomas Collins, Chambers's friend and executor. Dr Heather Martienssen used the Munthe Letters in her unpublished doctoral thesis on Chambers, submitted to London University in 1951. Another source is the now well-known 'Autobiographical Note', a *curriculum vitae* written in January 1770 when Chambers was knighted by the Swedish king. The original of this Note, sent personally to the king, is missing, but a copy exists in the archives of Uppsala University (location no.x222). It was first published by Arvid Baeckstrom in 'Nagra notiser rörande William Chambers', *Rig*, 1948, 25–9; and was englished and used by Osvald Sirén in *China and the Gardens of Europe*, 1950, 62–3.

[2] Munthe found a balance sheet for debts owed to the firm for stores supplied to the armies of Charles XII, a monarch notorious for not paying his debts. Munthe also discovered an attestation made out by John Chambers in favour of Theodore Innes, a merchant, who may have been the father of William Innes, Jamaican merchant, who married Chambers's daughter Selina.

[3] The reference to this Chambers is contained in Add.ms41135, 45–46v. He was a surgeon who married a cousin of Charles Turner of Kirkleatham Hall. His name also occurs in the Chambers correspondence in the Royal Academy archives, ex. coll. Professor Albert Richardson.

loved, are dead or dispersed, and the town is a melancholy desert, where I know not a soul but my physical cousin, and two old women, famous for telling long storys.'[4]

In 1739 a young man of sixteen returned home, ready, in the eyes of the family, to begin the long and difficult preparation for a mercantile career. Hence he entered the service of the Swedish East India Company, and in April 1740, only a few months before the death of his mother, he set sail on the *Fredericus Rex Sueciae* bound for Bengal. As a newcomer he would have been given the junior rank of cadet, apprenticed to the Assistants and Assistant Supercargoes[5] who were responsible for marketing the Company's goods and investing money in the various ports of call – Lisbon, the West Coast of Africa, Cape Town, Bombay, and Colombo. Although we know nothing at all of his experiences on this first voyage, there can be little doubt that two and a half years at sea thoroughly convinced him that he would never be a merchant. Looking back on these early years he recalls that even then he felt 'the strongest inclination' for architecture, and so on 'these voyages studied modern languages, mathematics and the liberal arts, but chiefly architecture.'[6]

The first voyage was completed on 18 October 1742, and after a brief leave of six months in Gothenburg (and presumably Stockholm) he was off for another two and a half years, this time on the *Riddarhuset* destined for the mysterious splendours of Cathay. This second trip gave him several months in Canton where within the confines of the European quarter of the city he diligently observed whatever he could of Chinese arts and manners. By the autumn of 1745 he was home again to enjoy a hard-earned and long-awaited respite of two years. His precious freedom was not to be wasted in Sweden. In these years he returned to England and Scotland, presumably to Ripon and London, travelling through the Low Countries to northern France and perhaps even to Paris. Looking at buildings doubtlessly occupied a good portion of his time. Indeed, there is reason to believe that the hastily-drawn sketches of Amsterdam Town Hall, buildings in Antwerp, and English Palladian houses, including Narford, Holkham, Houghton, Combe Bank, Highclere, and Tottenham Park, pasted into his Franco-Italian Album in the Victoria and Albert Museum, were made in these years. They are certainly immature in comparison with his drawings made in 1750. But there was still a year and a half before he would be free really to give himself over to architecture.

On 20 January 1748 the *Hoppet* sailed out of Gothenburg with Chambers as the 3rd Supercargo, a rank of some standing in the Company. Of his three eastern voyages this last one is the best documented and was doubtlessly the most pleasurable. For one thing he had the company of David Sandberg, an agreeable friend who was later to marry his sister Mary and for whom he built a villa at Partille Slot (Pl.73) on the outskirts of Gothenburg – his only work in Sweden. Furthermore, as a senior officer he no doubt enjoyed the same comforts and privileges as those described by his brother John in 1773: a fine accommodation and a 'table of my own for six or seven persons, which was plentifully

[4] BM Add.MS op. cit.

[5] The functions of these merchants are discussed by H. B. Morse in 'The Supercargo in the China Trade', *English Historical Review*, XXXVI, 1921.

[6] Autobiographical Note, op. cit.

and elegantly supplyd.'[7] More important, however, his rank must have afforded him more time to pursue his architectural studies and to explore and sample Chinese culture. Reports of his observations aroused interest and excitement among learned scholars in Sweden, and soon earned him a considerable reputation as an amateur sinologist. Indeed, in 1748 and 1749 his Chinese studies must have reached the ears of Count Scheffer, a Confucian scholar who was to befriend Chambers in Paris and eventually obtain him his knighthood, and also to Frederick, Prince of Wales, in London, then dallying with chinoiserie. Olof Toren, a fellow merchant in the Swedish East India Company, informed the great Linnaeus that drawings of the 'Chinese method of raising water' and of 'the proportions of the parts' of the columns in Chinese houses had been sent to the 'First Commissioner Baron Harleman', Sweden's leading architect.[8] Notes and drawings were not all that Chambers brought back from China. A perquisite of his post allowed him to fill the hold of the *Hoppet* with, amongst other things, twenty-three chests and forty-eight tubs of tea, many cases of silks and cloths, glasses, a bedstead, and a writing case.[9] From these items he no doubt earned enough to finance the professional training to which he looked forward.

Canton disappeared over the horizon for the last time in the autumn of 1748. After seven months at sea – calling briefly at Madras where Chambers managed to make a plan (Pl.1) of the nearby temple of Chidambarum – the *Hoppet* docked at Gothenburg on 11 July 1749. For Chambers this was the end of merchant adventuring and, before the summer was out, farewells also to the surviving members of his family, whom, except for John, he was never to see again.[10]

The events leading up to his arrival in Paris in the autumn are left to speculation. England beckoned him first, and during August and September he must have made the acquaintance of the two people who were to alter the course of his life – Catherine More, of Bromsgrove, Worcestershire, his future wife, and Frederick, Prince of Wales, his first and most important patron. It is hardly likely that Chambers would have arrived in London without introductions, and the Prince with his flair for the exotic could hardly fail to be attracted by the presence in England of the young Anglo-Swede with his rare first-hand knowledge of oriental architecture. Their meeting at Kew seems to have resulted first in the House of Confucius (called the India House) (Pl.23) on which building began later in the year, and then in a design for an Alhambra which though sent to the Prince by Chambers in 1750 was in fact made not by him but by Johann Henry Muntz on a recent excursion through Spain.[11]

When this happy and eventful summer drew to a close Chambers said farewell to Catherine and left for Paris to begin his architectural training in J. F. Blondel's famous Ecole des Arts. Here he made lasting friendships with those young 'habiles artistes' who

[7] RA Archives, John Chambers to William in 1773, returning from China.

[8] Olof Toren, *An East Indian Voyage*, Stockholm, 1757, 352.

[9] MS journal of Christopher Braad. Kungliga Biblioteket, Stockholm (location no.I.b.59).

[10] For the descent of his family cf. Appendix 10. I do not know the source for Munthe's statement that Chambers's sister Elizabeth died prematurely. In the RA letters is one written by an Elizabeth to her 'dear Brother' dated from Ripon in 1782. Others from her are addressed from Belle Vue (? Essex), and Cuffnels (Hants).

[11] Cf. John Harris, 'Exoticism at Kew', *Apollo*, July 1963, fig.3, p.104, and Muntz's *Proposals for Publishing By Subscription A Course of Gothic Architecture*, published 12 April 1760.

were to be the leaders of French neo-classic art and architecture in the 1760s and 1770s: De Wailly, De Chefdeville, Peyre, Greuze, Robert, Caffieri, Le Roy, and Potain, as well as the slightly older generation of architects, such as Le Lorrain, Jardin, Challe, and Le Geay, who were establishing a canon of Franco–Italian neo-classicism. In addition Chambers was almost certainly befriended here by the Swedish Minister, Count Scheffer.

In the late autumn of 1750 Chambers was ready to make his way to Italy. Inclement weather would have forced him to forgo the sublime experience of the Mont Cenis Pass and to travel instead by sea from Marseilles to Genoa or on to Leghorn, a route that would have enabled him to stop first at Lyons to see Soufflot's latest additions to the Hôtel Dieu (Pl.154) – a river wing to figure prominently among the precedents for Somerset House. Having spent over a year in Rome – a year in which his activities are unrecorded – he returned to Paris in the summer of 1751 to meet the future Lady Chambers. Here the amorous couple, unmarried as yet, spent two or three months, part of the time in the company of Joshua Reynolds who painted Catherine (Pl.199)[12] and possibly the romantic portrait of her beau as well (Frontispiece). In November[13] the two lovers left for Italy. Nothing is known of their route or activities until 21 January 1753 when Chambers was in Florence to receive a letter of introduction to Cardinal Albani from Horace Mann.[14] Florence is an unexplained lacuna in Chambers's Italian travels. It is unthinkable that he did not spend some time in the city, in the eighteenth century, as now, socially almost as congenial as Rome.

In Rome they were hurriedly married on 24 March at their lodgings in 73 Strada Felice (now Via Sistina), the house of Signor Conte Tomati.[15] Here they lived for the next two years under the same roof with the star of the Roman art world, Piranesi, who had established a shop in the Tomati house as early as 1750.[16] Added to the excitement of daily proximity with Piranesi (which could hardly fail to affect Chambers's achievement in Rome) was the birth of two daughters, Cornelia on 5 July 1753,[17] and Selina late in 1754 or early in 1755.[18] In March or April 1755 William, Catherine, and Cornelia returned to England leaving infant Selina in the care of her nurse Rosa Maccetti Giagnoni until May 1759 when she was old enough to make the trip with a Mrs Irvin.[19]

---

[12] The portrait is now in the Iveagh Bequest at Kenwood. Although related to a payment in Reynolds's Sitter Books for 1763, it was engraved by J. McArdell in 1756.

[13] Fridrik Sparre Correspondence, Sparre to Tessin, 10 November 1752.

[14] Albani had received this letter in Rome by 10 February. Haus-Hof – und Staatsarchiv (Vienna). Gesandtschafts-archiv Rome/Vatikan. Fas. 154. Mann to Albani; PRO London, SP 105/310 f 19r, Albani to Mann. Draft F 154. I am indebted for these references to the kindness of Mrs Lesley Lewis.

[15] A copy of the marriage certificate is in the possession of Dr John Gurney Salter. Christopher Golding, Presbyter of the Church of England married them, and witnesses were Dr James Murray, the principal physician to the Old Pretender, George Potter, J. A. Oughton, and Peter Grant.

[16] A number of Piranesi's etchings are so inscribed, for example, the *Veduta di Piazza di Spagna* dated 1750.

[17] RIBA Letters, Henry Willoughby (later 5th Baron Middleton) to Chambers, 23 October 1755. Willoughby was Cornelia's godfather, and it was to him that Chambers dedicated a temple in the *Treatise*.

[18] According to information derived from the Parish Registers in the Archivio del Vicariato (Stato delle Anime, Parish of S. Andrea delle Fratte), for four successive years Chambers's age is recorded as thirty-five, when it should have been thirty. His wife's age is noted as twenty, but she is named Angela. Mr Brinsley Ford kindly provided me with extracts from the Vicariato archives.

[19] RA Archives. Father Murray to Chambers, March 1759; and RIBA Letters, Rosa Giagnoni to Chambers 16 November 1756.

Five years in Rome, in the vortex of neo-classical ideas emanating from the French Academy there, had transformed Chambers from a young man of the world interested in architecture to an already respected architect, albeit one who had not yet built anything. His reputation is best described by Robert Adam, who, in fear of his advantages, unwittingly etched for posterity his Roman character. On 25 February 1755 he described his rival as 'superior to me at present as I am to Deacon Mack for greatness of thought and nobility of invention, drawing and ornamentation',[20] and again on 18 April he wrote to John Adam that 'All the English who have travelled for these five years (in Italy) imagine him a prodigy for Genius, for Sense & good taste.' He thought 'that he in great measure deserves their encomium. Though his taste is more architectonick than Picturesque, as for Grounds & gardens Boutcher can't be more Gothick. But his taste for Bas relieves, Ornaments, & decorations of Buildings, He both knows well & draws exquisitely. His Sense is middling, but his appearance is gentell & his person good which are most material circumstances. He despises others as much as he admires his own talents which he shows with a slow and dignified air, conveying an idea of great wisdom which is no less useful than all his other endowments and I find sways much with every Englishman; nay, he is in such great esteem; so intimate and in such friendship with most of the English that have been in Rome that they are determined to support him to the utmost of their power, amongst whom are Tylney, Huntingdon and others of great consequence and even reckoned of great taste. Was I conscious to myself of having superior genius for drawing as well as grand designs finished, finely drawn and coloured, as he had to show away with, it would be a different thing. But that can only come with time – and time alone can determine whether I am meet to cope with such a rival . . . it will require very considerable interest to succeed against Chambers who has tolerable Friends & real merit.'[21]

Adam's fears were not without foundation. Though time did indeed hold a rivalry in store, it was not for the immediate future. The impressive reputation which Chambers had enjoyed in the international art circles in Rome was in itself no guarantee of immediate success in London of 1755.[22] Six years of travel and study along with the added expenses of a wife and children had depleted the fortune he had earned at sea and probably most of that he had inherited from his parents. This left him little means for an impressive establishment in London. It was surely a relief, if not a pleasure, to Adam to learn that his competitor was 'drawing in a poor mean lodging up a long dark stair' at number 16 or 18 Russell Street.[23] Though far beneath the ostentatious *ménage* of the Adams, Chambers's Covent Garden lodging nevertheless had its compensation in Tom's Coffee House

[20] John Fleming, *Robert Adam and his Circle*, 1964, 192.

[21] Fleming, op. cit., 160. Not Boucher, but probably the Scottish gardener W. Boutcher of Edinburgh who published *A Treatise on Forest Trees* in 1775.

[22] For example, neither Tylney nor Huntingdon patronized Chambers in England. They both subscribed, however, to the *Designs for Chinese Buildings*.

[23] Fleming, op. cit., 249. There is one reference to Chambers immediately preceding his return to England. In the Franco-Italian album in the V & A is a scribbled note that Chambers returned to England in company with William Hall. It refers to 'share of expences at Custom House', 'coach for antequarian', and 'For his share of chest'.

next door.[24] This was the convivial meeting place of an artistic, literary, and noble coterie that included Johnson, Goldsmith, James Paine, Lord Clive, and others who were soon to become friends, colleagues, and patrons.

1756 was a busy but not very prosperous year with a stock of drawings and ideas to be sorted out, the architectural climate to be judged and assessed, the right patrons to be found, and friendships to be made. Having no other commitments, he decided – with the encouragement of the Prince of Wales – to publish *Designs for Chinese Buildings*. This involved considerable work, for not only did engravers and draughtsmen have to be organized, but, more important, designs had to be made. A rather nervous letter to his brother John in Gothenburg in June 1756[25] asking where drawings of Chinese houses could be found leads one to suspect that a good deal of what he finally published had to be made up from memory or even invented. Time was also available in this year to tour Scotland with Lord Bruce, an event which was observed with some interest by the Adam clan: 'We are not very uneasy', wrote John Adam to his mother on 14 September, 'neither at the progress Mr Chalmers may have made by then as his traversing Scotland in the manner he did shows he cannot yet be in high demand, and a book of Chinese affairs he is publishing cannot raise his reputation high among the truly learned in architecture';[26] and Robert thought a month later, that 'this jaunt sounds but badly for him for was he well employed in England he'd never find time for visiting Scotland.'[27] Although one detects a note of envy beneath this careless bravado, Robert was absolutely right. Not only were commissions slow in coming, but what was worse, the project (Pls 43–45) that Chambers had offered Edwin Lascelles for Harewood was a momentous failure that convinced him into abandoning his Franco-Italian neo-classicism for a more conservative and hence more acceptable form of Palladianism.

The lean years of 1755 and 1756 gave way in 1757 to the first fruits of royal favour and sky rocket to success. *Proposals for Publishing by Subscription, Designs of Villas, Temples, Gates, Doors, and Chimney Pieces*[28] – in other words, a pattern book rather than a treatise – were issued in April just in time to announce his classical skills before the publication in May of the *Chinese Buildings*, dedicated to the Prince of Wales. By no mere coincidence this was followed in the summer by his appointment as architectural tutor to the Prince and architect to his mother, the Dowager Princess Augusta, at Kew, Leicester House, Carlton House, Clivedon and Hedsor, in Buckinghamshire.

These favours are certainly the subject of the letter of congratulation sent to Chambers by Robert Wood on 22 August: 'I heartily congratulate you upon the compliments paid you by the Prince & upon Lord Bute's friendship.'[29] How and when Chambers first attracted royal attention and the circumstances of his introduction to Bute are not entirely clear. According to James Gandon, Joshua Kirby (tutor in perspective and drawing

---

[24] The exact position of Tom's is a matter for dispute. Beresford Chancellor in *The Annals of Covent Garden and Its Neighbourhood*, 1930, plate f, p.176, purports to show it. If so, then Chambers lived in a plain early-eighteenth-century three-bay brick house with a broad cornice below the attic story in which windows lit his room.

[25] RA Archives.

[26] Fleming, op. cit., 359.

[27] Fleming, op. cit.

[28] Munthe Letters, quoted by Martienssen, op. cit.

[29] RA Archives.

to the Prince) recommended John Gwynn as architect to the Prince, but he declined in favour of Chambers 'whose accomplished manner rendered him the most eligible person to be selected for the purpose.'[30] Gwilt, on the contrary, claims that Bute offered the post to John Carr who also declined in favour of Chambers.[31] Neither of these conflicting explanations is really satisfactory. It seems much more likely that Chambers having been patronized by Frederick, Prince of Wales at Kew in 1749, and having made the elaborate designs for the ill-fated Prince's mausoleum (obviously intended for Kew) in 1751–2, was remembered by the Princess Augusta when she decided to carry on with the embellishment of her husband's gardens at Kew. Chambers's appointment, however it came about, was neither a sinecure nor an immediate source of income. 'My hands are full of work,' he wrote, 'but my pockets are not full of money. The prince employs me three mornings in a week to teach him architecture; the building (and) other decorations at Kew fill up the remaining time. The princess has the rest of the week which is scarcely sufficient as she is forever adding new embellishments at Kew, all which I direct the execution (and) measure the work. I have also the care of the house there, Carlton House in London with three other habitations occupied in different parts of the town by her attendants, for all which I am rewarded with fifty pounds a year punctually paid by the prince and one hundred by the princess.'[32] With a building programme at Kew involving nearly thirty temples it is no wonder that he could find little time to establish his own practice. Judging from the portfolios of amateurish drawings made by the Prince, his tutelage was a laborious task that must have demanded incredible patience from Chambers.[33] This was, however, immensely influential, for it persuaded him completely to re-read architectural theory and to change his proposed pattern book to the learned *Treatise on Civil Architecture*.

There were many other reasons why 1757 was an auspicious year. Proposed by Grignion – soon to engrave plates for the *Treatise* and *Kew* – the Society of Arts elected Chambers a Fellow on 16 January. Could he have looked into the future, in 1759 he would have seen himself chosen architect for the Society's Great Room, and in 1760 as one of the dissenting artists who formed the rival Incorporated Society of Artists of Great Britain. However, despite Kew and the public recognition he was earning, his key achievement at this time was the foundation of his own private practice. The Duke of Richmond employed him at Goodwood and in Whitehall; he may have designed the related monuments to John Sharpe and Sir Hans Sloane in the respective churchyards of East Barnet and Chelsea Old Church; and he was introduced to Lord Pembroke at

[30] Thomas J. Mulvany, *The Life of James Gandon Esqr*, Dublin, 1846, 162.

[31] J. Gwilt, edition of *Treatise on Civil Architecture*, 1862, 3.

[32] RA Archives. The punctuation is the author's own, as the draft is curiously ungrammatical.

[33] The drawings are in the Royal Library, Windsor Castle. Chambers set the Prince to copy the Kew temples, the draw out orders, gateways and arches, and to copy designs from the books by William Kent and Colen Campbell. After 1759 there are many designs based upon the *Treatise*. The results are amateurish, but nevertheless painstaking. Elmes was rather over-praising when he described them as 'correct' in detail, and 'for their day and style of arts, tasteful and elegant' (*Civil Engineer and Architect's Jnl*, 1847, 271–3). Oppé in *English Drawings . . . at Windsor Castle*, 1950, illustrates a 'house with a colonnade' drawn in 1760 and published by Joshua Kirby in *Perspective of Architecture*, 1761, pl.LXIV. In the Worsley Collection at Hovingham Hall (Yorks) is a design for a door in Buckingham House, inscribed by Thomas Worsley, Surveyor General of the Board of Works, 'done by the King and given me to execute at the Queens House'.

Wilton and Lord Charlemont in Dublin – two lords with whom he was to spend long and happy hours unclouded by differences of rank.

So to 1758 and 1759 and to the completion of the stables at Goodwood (Pl.48) and the Casino and Triumphal Arch at Wilton (Pls 46–47) as the best advertisement. Equally were his decorations at both patrons' town houses in fashionable Whitehall. At Osterley, Francis Child commissioned Chambers for a new garden front (Pl.49) masking a handsome Gallery. And in Dublin, Charlemont began to build the Casino at Marino (Pls 50–54) and to enlarge his house there. Charlemont must have been the touchstone of what was to grow into a thriving Irish practice, albeit Chambers never crossed the Irish sea. At Castletown, however, it was probably through Thomas Conolly's wife, Lady Louisa Lennox, the sister of the Duke of Richmond, that Chambers got the job of finishing that vast Italianate Palladian mansion.

In these key establishing years he moved in 1758 from the 'mean lodging' in Russell Street to the more fashionable Poland Street, at number 58 on the west side near Oxford Street.[34] In 1759 Drummonds Bank[35] received 200 pounds as the first deposit of what would eventually grow into a very rich account indeed. George the Third's accession in 1760 meant the substitution of old factions by what might be called the Kew set of Princess Augusta and her son. As a result, Chambers's star was in the ascendent. Almost immediately he was commissioned to design the new State Coach (Pls 134–137) – most surprisingly a design of Kentian, rococo gaiety. Then on 18 November 1761 he was made one of the two Architects of the Works, an appointment roughly the equivalent of the French *architecte du roi*. Mystery surrounds the creation of this new Board of Works title, and if the suggestion came from the francophile Chambers, then Lord Bute saw to it that his favourite, Robert Adam, shared the honours. It may have been due to Chambers's connivance that no more kingly favours were ever granted to Adam, although his brother James succeeded as Architect of the Works in 1769 when Robert became M.P. for Kinross. For Chambers, however, the post was the first step towards the coveted Comptrollership of the Works and finally to the Surveyor-Generalship in 1782. In 1761, therefore, Chambers took the first steps on the road towards the titular head of his profession in England.

Private practice in 1760–1 rose from six commissions to fifteen. James Gandon had been articled to Chambers for seven years from 1758, and in 1760 it was necessary to employ the young Edward Stevens.[36] Although Chambers had lost the competition for Blackfriars Bridge (Pl.140) and York House (Pl.94), he must have been amply satisfied by the development of his special brand of villa at Duntish Court (Pl.60), Roehampton (Pl.55) and Duddingstone (Pl.62).

By the mid-1760s, at forty years of age, Chambers must have been keenly aware of his success. On 22 July 1762 he had been elected with Jardin (in Copenhagen), Petitot

34 Rate Books, Westminster Public Library. The house was first rated at £25. Chambers was here from 1758 until 1766. He was followed by Paul Sandby from 1767 until 1772, and Sandby was followed by James Malton from 1772 until 1780.

35 Cf. Appendix 3.

36 PRO IR/22. 18 January 1760. Edward Stevens, 7 years at £100. For these, and the following apprenticeship records, I am indebted to Dr J. Mordaunt Crook.

10

(in Parma), and Le Jolivet (in Dijon) an Honorary Corresponding Member of the *Académie Royale d'Architecture* in Paris.[37] 1763 saw the appearance of his splendid folio on Kew Gardens – the consummation of his work there – and in 1765 he must have been very much in the public eye as architect of the rebuilt and splendidly-furnished Buckingham House, renamed the Queen's House (Pls 116–117). His personal loss of twin sons[38] in 1763 was leavened by the increasing demands for his professional services. With Charlemont House in Dublin in 1762 and Gower House in London in 1764, town building vied with that in the country. By 1766 the bank account had soared comfortably beyond £5000.

Such affluence needed matching with a more public display of personal wealth and position. It was not good enough to live in a small family house in Poland Street. As he had buried his twin sons in Twickenham church he must have had a country house or cottage nearby. As it is never mentioned, it may well have been small and undistinguished. In July 1765 the Duke of Argyll's estate at Whitton was sold to a Mr Gostling, who, perhaps by pre-arranged treaty, leased the palatial Palladian villa (Pl.198) designed by Roger Morris, and the greater portion of the pleasure grounds, to Chambers. Gostling retained for his own use an Orangery designed by Gibbs. Chambers was now living in the manner of a grandee, and he spent the next quarter of a century embellishing the already famous gardens, and furnishing the interiors of the house with trophies of his friendships, travels, and collecting. He is pictured by the sale catalogues,[39] as a typical, tasteful *cognoscente,* collecting objects that took his fancy rather than following the fashions or dictates of art.

Once established at Whitton, Chambers moved from Poland Street, across the road to the undeveloped Berners Street. Here in partnership with Thomas Collins he built twenty or more dignified houses, all stamped with his restraint, and distinguished only by their masculine rusticated doorways, prophetic of the court doorways in Somerset House. His own house at number 13 (Fig.11) was planned like the rest, except for two specialities: the rear elevation was modelled in papier mâché in a style described as 'fanciful', presumably chinoiserie, and at the end of the garden was a Venetian-windowed Drawing Office opening at the back to Berners Mews. Here in Berners Street, son George was born in 1766 and Charlotte in 1767,[40] an aggrandizement of family matched in the office by the addition of John Yenn in 1764 and Thomas Hardwick in 1767.[41]

[37] *Procès Verbaux De L'Académie Royale d'Architecture*, VII, 1762, 96, where Chambers is described as an 'Elève de Blondel'.

[38] This loss is referred to in a letter from Mary Sandberg to Chambers, 13 May 1763 (RA Archives).

[39] Cf. Appendices 4 (the 1790 Inventory) and 5–8 (the Sales).

[40] George's birth is referred to in a letter from James Kennedy of Wilton, on 23 December 1766 (RIBA Letters), and Charlotte's in Add.MS 41135, a letter dated 15 April 1774.

[41] PRO IR 1/24. 14 August 1764. John Yenn, 7 years at £100; 1/25. 25 August 1767. Thomas Hardwick, 7 years at £200. Further apprenticeship records for Chambers occur in 1771: 1/26. 22 January 1771. John Rudd, 7 years at £106; and 1/27. 12 July 1771. Richard Ripley, 7 years at £161. Other and later assistants were Willey Reveley, Richard Brown, Thomas Whetton, John Read, Archibald Alison, and possibly J. B. Papworth. Thomas Telford may have assisted Chambers at Somerset House. He relates his impression of Chambers and Adam: 'In the year 1782 . . . I made my way direct to London . . . and I was fortunate in getting employed at the quadrangle of Somerset place buildings . . . and I became known to Sir W. Chambers and Mr Robert Adam . . . the former haughty and reserved, the latter affable and communicative; and a similar distinction of character pervaded their works, Sir William's being stiff and formal, those of Mr Adam playful and gay' (*Life of Thomas Telford*, ed. J. Rickman, 1838, 19).

In a paradoxical way the Swedes singled out Chambers for his worth as much as the English did. He was almost regarded in Sweden as one of their sons in foreign fields. He was elected to the Swedish Academy of Sciences in 1766, and in 1767 Queen Louisa Ulrica gave him a gold box 'imagined à la grec' and ornamented with buildings and gardens.[42] These marks of respect were prophetic of the honours to come. In return for the honours paid him by European courts and academies, Chambers was always attentive upon friends and colleagues who visited England. In 1767 and 1768 respectively, Belanger and Le Roy came from France,[43] and during these years that manic genius Le Geay was probably sheltering under Chambers's roof; from Sweden in 1768 came both Elias Martin the painter and Georges Haupt the cabinet-maker; and from Denmark in 1769 his old friend Jardin accompanied the sculptor Johannes Wiedewelt.[44] What an event it must have been for these Danes to be perambulated around Kew Gardens by its creator, and then to walk across to Richmond Gardens to see the Fête Pavilion designed to entertain their king.

Chambers's architectural practice grew apace as the years of the 1760's slipped away. Between 1766 and 1768 he was building the Town Hall at Woodstock (Pl.141), the German Lutheran church in the Savoy (Pls 142–143), and Moses Franks's villa at Teddington. By 1769 the number of his concurrent commissions had reached a peak of twenty. Extensive works were in hand at Ampthill (Pl.68), Woburn (Pl.71) and Blenheim; in Richmond Gardens upon the Observatory (Pl.125) and the ill-fated Richmond Palace project (Pl.110); and in town his biggest town-house alteration was for the Duke of Buccleuch in Grosvenor Square.

In the last two years of this decade his authority as the paternalistic head of his profession was confirmed by two honours. In December 1768 the King signed the Instrument of Foundation of the Royal Academy, and appointed Chambers its Treasurer. Some even thought him 'inclined to the President', but whatever his aspirations may have been — and he had done more than any other to found the Academy — his power as Treasurer lay in his responsibility only to the King. It enabled him to discipline the Academicians

[42] Horace Walpole, 'Book of Materials' (1771+). W. S. Lewis Coll., Farmington. 'One day last week his excellency baron Noleken, envoy extraordinary from the Swedish court, delivered to Mr. Chambers, architect to his majesty, an elegant gold box of considerable value as a present to him from her majesty the queen of Sweden; the design is finely imagined a la Grec, and the ornaments are executed with taste in gold of different colours. In the compartments are represented various magnificent structures of the Corinthian, Ionic, and Doric orders; and also several decorations of gardens after the Italian and Chinese manners. This elegant work, executed in Stockholm by Swedish artists, shews how speedily arts arrive at perfection, when encouraged by royal favour' (taken from a newspaper cutting dated 9 December 1767). About this box Chambers says in his Autobiographical Note, 'Two years ago I took the liberty of sending to her Majesty the Queen of Sweden a book of both kinds (the *Treatise* and *Kew*) which were graciously accepted; and I was honoured with a magnificent golden box, with a command to Count Gyldenstolph to let me know that the books had pleased her, and this present was sent to me as a mark of Her Majesty's favour.'

[43] For a trophy of Belanger's visit, cf. the design for the Hôtel de Brancas, dedicated in manuscript to Chambers (RIBA Drawings). Le Roy's visit is chronicled in RIBA Letters, Le Roy to Chambers 12 October 1769.

[44] Jacob J. Bjornstahl, the Swedish orientalist, writes in a letter of 19 May 1775 that 'Mr William Chambers . . . considers himself a Swede and also speaks Swedish quite as fluently as any Swede, born as he was at Gothenburg, though of English parents. He really is a great credit to our nation, has a very nice house, receives Swedes and regales them in a princely manner' (*Travels in France, Italy* 1780–4, vol.2, 180). In a letter of 29 February 1776 (vol.2, 217) Bjornstahl described a Christmas party given by Chambers to Swedes in London. He also refers to 'our Swedish painter Mr. Martin here in London: he distinguishes himself and is greatly patronised by Knight Chambers' (vol.2, 228). For the visit to London of Jardin and Wiedewelt, cf. P. Weilbach, *Dansk Konstlerlexicon*, entries under the artists.

with the same stick of moral integrity wielded at the Board of Works. It was not for nothing that Reynolds could complain about his Presidency that 'Sir Wm was Viceroy over him.'[45] The second honour for this comparatively young man of forty-five occurred in February 1769 when he succeeded Flitcroft as Comptroller of the Works. An 'old gentleman who has kept me out of a very good place for these eight years past is at length advanced to sing hallelujahs in heaven and has resigned his earthly post of comptroller general of the board of works to me',[46] Chambers wrote smugly to Lord Charlemont. He held this ultimate of professional honours until elevated to the Surveyor-Generalship of the Works in 1783.

On the occasion of the Academy's inaugural 'summer' exhibition in May 1769 the King knighted Reynolds, as an act of respect for the first President rather than a gesture of friendship. The King would certainly have preferred to dub Chambers, a congenial acolyte at his court. However, on 28 April 1770 Gustav III of Sweden knighted Chambers 'Chevalier de l'ordre d'Etoile Polaire'.[47] 'Stars and Garters for you' congratulated David Sandberg in July,[48] and Chambers has 'Sir Williamized himself' wrote Walpole when the King had later granted Chambers permission to adopt the address of English knighthood.[49]

By 1770 when Milton Abbey (Pl.64) had been begun for the irascible Lord Milton, or Melbourne House (Pl.103) for the amenable Lord Melbourne, Chambers had achieved all that he could have hoped for. In consequence he allowed the pace of his practice to drop into lower gear. During 1771, 1772 and 1773 he accepted less complicated and more pleasing jobs, like the Chinese Temple for the Duchess of Queensbury at Amesbury (Pl. 78) or the handsome Doric doorway for Lord Fauconberg in George Street, Hanover Square. Unlike Robert Adam, Chambers had never followed the 'ton' of the town. Apart from Lords Pembroke and Charlemont, his relations with his noble clients were formal and correct. 'I cannot tell when I shall be at Blenheim', he wrote in July 1772 to his friend the Reverend Weston of Witney, for 'the transition from a Palace to a Cot, as you call your habitation, is more agreable to me than you can well imagine. I shall enter your door with a jovial heart, which I seldom have in the mansions of the Great. With you I shall consider myself as a welcome Guest. With them I am like the Egiptian Bird who picks the teeth of the Crocadile, admitted and cherished while there is any work to be done, but when that is over the doors are shut and the farce is at an end.'[50] The quietus that he now preferred enabled him to return in 1772 to more literary pursuits with his *Dissertation on Oriental Gardening*, a chinoiserie polemic against Capability Brown's stereotyped view of nature.

[45] Farington's Diary, 10 December 1804.

[46] HMC *Charlemont*, I, 292.

[47] RIBA Letters. Count C. F. Scheffer to Chambers, 4 May 1770.

[48] RA Archives. 18 July 1770. Cf. *Horace Walpole's Correspondence*, ed. Lewis, Cronin and Bennett, vol.28 (1955), 28–9.

[49] The permission is referred to in a letter from the Marquess of Carmarthen to George III, 22 September 1784. Cf. *The Later Correspondence of George III*, ed. A. Aspinall, I (1962), 94 (Letter 127).

[50] BM Add.MS 41133, 76, 18 July 1772. As Professor Wittkower has pointed out, the reference to the Egyptian bird is amusing. This bird is the Ichneumon and the story is reported in the *Physiologus* and by Pliny. This only underlines how immensely well read Chambers was, for one would not have expected him to have used such books.

When Chambers confided to Vesey on 2 April 1774 how 'heartily tired of the profession'[51] he was, he wrote as an architect bent on retirement. Little did he know that he was only halfway through a busy career. The unexpected decision to build public offices at Somerset House could have become known to him late in April or early in May 1774. He was stung into action. With no warning he set out for Paris 'where many great works have been done which I must examine with care and make proper remarks upon'.[52] His words to Worsley, written from Paris on 23 May, that he was sick of French civilities 'which make an eternal festival, that neither agrees with my health, nor my pursuits in Paris, where I come with a view to Observe and not to eat',[53] reflect a new-found purpose. To Godfroy de Villeneuse he might nostalgically remember Le Roy, Doyen, Pajou, Vernet, Robert, Caffieri, and Greuze as among the 'habiles artistes avec qui j'ai vecu à Paris',[54] but he would have affirmed that his main purpose was to study the most recent public building. When he wrote this he had just been to the York Races 'dancing betting and feasting with Lord Mayors & Archbishops.'[55] He was with his old friend the Marquis de Voyer d'Argenson, who despite a 'life of dissipation' he described as 'one of the ablest officers of the french army', an 'Excellent Architect', and one who understood 'Painting and Sculpture better than most men of his time.'[56]

Underneath this veneer of pleasure lay a determination to prevent the unfortunate William Robinson from planning Somerset House. Chambers knew quite well that he had no mandate for the job, and although he set about Robinson's downfall with gusto, the outcome of all this is open to speculation. The course of events might have been otherwise had Robinson not conveniently died in October 1775. From this moment on Chambers's new career had begun. His administrative obligations at Somerset House severed his practice neatly into two parts. In this second half he had no time for private practice. New domestic works are rare indeed, and only friends seem to have prevailed upon him, such as Richard Jebb for his *petite* neo-classic lodge at Trent Place (Pl.74), or Lord Boston for an elegant Thames-side villa at Hedsor. For the King he designed the enormous utilitarian Queen's Lodge at Windsor between 1777 and 1780 (Pls 121–124). In his private life he was perhaps happiest when Cornelia married John Milbanke, Lady Melbourne's brother, in 1775, or when the Royal Society made him a Fellow in 1776[57] – an appropriate gesture to the architect of their future apartments in Somerset House.

It was also appropriate that when he finished the Strand apartments and the Royal Academy moved in in 1780, he should have been painted by Reynolds (Pl. facing p. 16). No doubt relations between the President and the Treasurer were strained, but

---

[51] BM Add.MS 41136, 16v.

[52] BM Add.MS 41135, 26–26v. Chambers to Thomas Worsley, 20 May 1774.

[53] BM Add.MS 41135, a letter before folio 27.

[54] BM Add.MS 41135, of 15 September 1774. Doyen and Pajou had been remembered on an earlier occasion when Chambers wrote to the Countess of Boufflers-Roverel, 17 December 1769, thanking her for a copy of Laugier's *Observations sur l'Architecture*, and asking her to remember him to Blondel, De Wailly, Doyen, Peyre, Pajou, Soufflot, Cochin, and John Ingram the engraver. Cf. BM Add.MS 41133, 2–2v. The Countess had a *Jardin Anglais* laid out by a Mr Prescott an English gardener, at Auteuil.

[55] BM Add. MS 41135, letter dated 20 August 1774 to Richard, later Sir Richard, Jebb.

[56] BM Add.MS 41135, 37.

[57] He was proposed by Robert Mylne, William Smeaton, James Stuart, William Hunter and Joseph Banks, in April 1776.

their respect for each other was never questioned – and it was fitting that this portrait should be Reynolds's Diploma piece. Here is Chambers's 'Official' portrait, the proud face of 'genius rising in opposition to circumstances.'[58] It is perhaps less preferable than the romantic-featured Chambers painted in Reynolds's earlier years (Frontispiece). In 1780 there was an unexplained visit to Flanders, described in gossip by Walpole[59] as a 'mystery, which time, which establishes truth, but most oftener falsehood, must settle'. However, rather than being an 'epuipée of gallantry', it was probably connected with John Chambers's business affairs.

In the eighties as year after year passed, Somerset House demanded almost constant attention from Chambers. In 1783 the political post of Surveyorship of the Works was abolished and so were the joint Architects of the Works. In their place Chambers was appointed the first Surveyor-General and Comptroller. It was the ultimate honour. In this year too he was painted by Rigaud in a group portrait with Reynolds and Wilton.[60] Behind the calm face is a man racked with gout and asthma. Death was now a very palpable conclusion. Capability Brown, that 'gentleman in the black perriwig', died in 1783, Cipriani in 1785, and in 1788 when both Stuart and Gainsborough[61] died, a new generation of architects was astir with anti-classical ideas. This was the year of Soane's first Bank rooms and of Dance's Indo-Gothic façade to the Guildhall.

Marriage was breaking up the Chambers's family circle. In 1784 at the age of eighteen, George, who was no 'chip of the old block', married Jane the daughter of Lord Rodney. They were both to dissipate their lives.[62] In 1788 Selina married William Innes, a Jamaican merchant, and although she was apparently happy in the West Indies, her absence annoyed the unbending Chambers.[63] Then in 1791 Charlotte married Charles Harwood, and about this time Lavinia married Josiah Cottin. In his later correspondence, Chambers reveals his straight-laced, moralistic attitude to a child's upbringing. It must have contributed not a little to George's diametrically opposite behaviour. Chambers was furious at his son's wish to join the army in 1784, and in conveying his contempt in a letter to Cornelia – his first and favourite child – he unwittingly conveyed to posterity his professional philosophy. He writes, 'In my profession there is a very extensive power of doing good to others, as well as to ones self, which to me, as I know to you also, is a

[58] James Northcote, *Memoirs of Sir Joshua Reynolds*, 1813, 30.

[59] *Horace Walpole's Correspondence,* op. cit., vol.29, 37–8, 42, 47. Walpole to William Mason, 19 May 1780. This story was first reported in the London *Courant* on 18 May: 'A subaltern in the royal works, who a few years ago was the hero of a celebrated Heroic Epistle, is reported to have disappeared, with a considerable sum of money in his pocket.' On 23 May the London *Courant* admitted that there had been no embezzlement on Chambers's part, and Walpole wrote again to Mason on 24 May (*Correspondence*, p.42).

[60] National Portrait Gallery, London.

[61] Gainsborough's relations with Chambers are not known, but in the Fitzwilliam Museum, Cambridge, is an album containing twenty-four drawings of urns, architectural details, etc. made by Chambers in Rome. Some may be copies of originals by Petitot and Saly. The title page is wittily inscribed 'SubLiME sCRAtChES FoR MisTgA InS BorOUGh bY miSTEr chAMBers Ao 1764'. He was a pall bearer, with Reynolds, West, Cotes, Sandby, and Bartolozzi at Gainsborough's funeral at Kew (W. H. Whitley, *Thomas Gainsborough*, 1915, 309).

[62] The sequel to George's life is related by Farington (*Diary*, 7 December 1808, BM typescript) who described him as a vagabond and as a successful claimant for damages of £2120 from the Marshal of the King's Bench Prison for allowing Captain Caulfield, a prisoner, to live and commit adultery with Jane Rodney. Cf. also *Diary*, 23 July 1817: 'Yenn spoke to me of Sir Wm Chambers family. He said his son to whom he left a handsome property is now a vagabond, where he is Yenn knows not.'

[63] A number of letters to this effect are to be found in the RA Archives, and cf. also Chambers's Will.

luxury of the highest sort. Whenever I see, as I do very often, five or six hundred industrious fellows supporting themselves and their familys, many of them growing rich, under my command; I feel such a pleasure as no General ever felt in War, be the Victory what it might. My troops conquer their difficulties and carry wealth & plenty to their habitations. His conquests are the purchase of blood, rapine, murder, desolation, maimed bodies & distracted minds. His business is to destroy, mine to create; his to ruin the world & rob mankind of every blessing, while mine is to enrich, to beautify it, and to supply its inhabitants with every comfort'.[64]

1790 marks the closing chapter in Chambers's life. He was frequently 'under the tuition' of Dr John Turton and must have sensed the impending. There is some evidence that Whitton was leased back[65] to the Gostling family, and from Berners Street the aged Chambers moved to 75 Norton (now Bolsover) Street. The great *Treatise on Civil Architecture* was augmented and renamed the *Treatise on the Decorative Part of Civil Architecture*, in a third edition dedicated to the King in 1791. The fastidious learning that it embodied was to be seen by all at Somerset House. By 1795 so many were his infirmities, that on 12 March he wrote poignantly to the King that 'your Majesty was graciously Pleased, among many other marks of royal favour, to confer upon me the honour of planning and conducting the execution of the then intended new publick Offices at Somerset Place. These under the Authority of Your Majesties Sign Manual, were accordingly designed, ever since carried on, and brought nearly to a conclusion; having, more effectually to proceed, relinquished all other business, but such of the Crown, as appeared compatible with the said great work flattering myself, by these means to have succeeded in the Attempt. But unfortunately, from a variety of unexpected delays, from age and infirmities incident to old age, which of late have come fast and severely upon me. I am now rendered totally unable to manage such a work, and am constrained to entreat your Majestys permission to resign its future conduct, into hands now more able to bring it to a proper Conclusion. It would be presumptuous even to hint at fit persons into whose hands that conduct might safely be consigned were it not that Gratitude to Your Majesty, and an earnest desire of seeing the whole satisfactorily finished for the publick, induced me, humbly to Suggest, that Mr Yenn and Mr Brown who Twenty Years, have under my direction conducted, measured, brought to account, and settled with the different persons appointed by Treasury for that purpose, latterly some years with Mr Dance, are the only persons thoroughly conversant with the business; as well with the whole executive part, as with all other parts belonging thereto, and that if it should be judged proper to appoint them my successor under Mr Dances inspection, as before; there will be all certainty of settling the whole Property, as it would proceed in the same train, while, if it should be thrown into the hands of strangers, there would be constant difficulties, of mistakes, & confusion. Finding my infirmities crouding on very fast I humbly hope the burthen already over heavy to support, will soon as may be convenient, be consigned to proper management. May every blessing attend your Majesty, Your Royal Consort and family, will be the last and fervent prayer of William Chambers.[66]

[64] RA Archives. Letter dated 9 December 1784.
[65] This may have been why the 1790 Inventory (cf. Appendix 4) was taken at this time.
[66] Archives, Royal Library, Windsor Castle.

By November 1795 he was obliged to be carried from room to room in Norton Street,[67] and on 7 March 1796, sensing death's imminence, sent for Thomas Collins who was both his old friend and executor. In 'conversation expressed with the utmost calm and recollection'[68] he asked Collins to care for his wife and family, and two days later on 10 March at 9.30 in the morning, the Knight of the Polar Star 'resigned his earthly post to sing hallelujahs'.

On 12 March a procession was to be seen along Whitehall to Westminster Abbey of 'master workmen belonging to the Board of Works, who attended, unsolicited, to testify their regret for the loss, and their esteem for the memory of a man who by their claims had ever been examined with attention, and decided with justice, and by whom themselves were always treated with mildness, courtesy, and affability'.[69] He lies[70] in the south transept, appropriately neighboured by Robert Adam and James Wyatt. There were many epitaphs, but none more sincere or just than Lord Charlemont's:[71]

TO

Sir William Chambers, Knight, Etc.,
Fellow of the Royal Academy,
And Professor of Architecture,
The Best of Men, and the First of English Architects,
Whose Buildings, Modelled From His Own Mind,
Elegant, Pure, and Solid,
Will Long Remain the Lasting Monuments
Of That Taste,
Whose Chastity Could Only Be Equalled
By The Immaculate Purity of The Author's Heart,
James Earl of Charlemont, His Friend,
From Long Experience of His Worth and Talents,
Dedicates This Inscription
To Him And Friendship

[67] Farington *Diary*, 26 November 1795.

[68] Farington *Diary*, 27 November 1796.

[69] *Gentleman's Mag.*, March 1796.

[70] The slab is simply inscribed 'Sir William Chambers Knight of the Polar Star Architect Surveyor General of His Majesties Works FRS, FAS & RA Died March 8 1796.' At the Royal Academy in May, T. Papworth the sculptor exhibited a 'Mausoleum to the memory of Sir William Chambers'.

[71] Chambers's Will is, appropriately, Harris 115. Selina, Charlotte, and Lavinia had earlier gifts topped up to £5000 each; the 'two sons of my much lamented daughter Cornelia' received £1000 each; George's children 'lawfully begotten', £1500 each; and his wife received an annuity of £700 plus 25 'Marybone' bonds worth £100 each. John Hurst, his gardener, received £40, 'downstair' servants £10, George Errington 'my servant' £30 and 'my wearing apparel & linen'. Robert Browne, an executor with Thomas Collins, received 'all my plaister casts and models which are at Somerset House' to be shared with John Yenn, and Browne had in addition 'my silver instrument case made by old Adams', and William Rose 'my brass instrument case made by the same hand'. Lady Catherine did not long survive her husband. She died in March 1798 aged about sixty-five years. Her will (Walpole 163) is enlightening only in that Selina Innes in Jamaica would be disinherited if she did not reside in England within two years.

Chapter 2

France and Italy

'. . . Travelling to an Artist is what the University is to a Man of Letters, the last Stage of a regular Education, which opens the Mind to a more liberal and extensive way of thinking, diffuses an Air of Importance over the whole Man, and stamps a Value upon his Opinions, it affords him Opportunities of forming Connections with the Great, the Learned, and the Rich, and the Friendships which he makes when Abroad, are very often the first Causes of his Reputation, and Fortune at Home.' Royal Academy Lecture notes 1770.

After bidding farewell to Gothenburg and renewing acquaintances in London, Chambers was ready to prepare himself for an architectural career. He was then a worldly man of twenty-six, well read, widely travelled, adequately financed, accustomed to an international milieu, and, most important of all, unfettered by national prejudices or parental ties. Then, unlike most young students, he was mature enough to know exactly what sort of education he required and entirely free to select the best.

Time at his age was too precious to spend on an apprenticeship in England, which in any case would have given him an unbalanced training weighted towards practice at the expense of theory. Paris on the other hand was the academic centre of Europe and the only place where he could obtain a truly systematic course of instruction in a limited time. No doubt his decision was also influenced by the experiences of his Swedish friends, Count Harleman, Linnaeus, and Count Gustav Tessin, as well as by the presence in Paris of Count C. F. Scheffer, who shared his oriental interests, encouraged his architectural activities, and was later the moving force behind his knighthood. The choice of a Parisian education underlines Chambers's European character. For an Englishman born and bred this would have been unthinkable, for Paris, at least to those interested in architecture, was only a fashionable stepping stone to antique and Renaissance Rome.

Paris in 1749 offered the architectural student two schools from which to choose[1]: the Académie royale d'Architecture and J. F. Blondel's Ecole des Arts. The Académie, although the official institution, was no longer the stimulating intellectual centre it had been in the days of François Blondel, Perrault, and Desgodetz. The curriculum was stifled by petty and pedantic controversies, and the new professors, Jossenay and Loriot, were second-rate

[1] The following information is based upon Peter Collins, *The Architectural Doctrine of Jacques-François Blondel (1705–1774)*, RIBA Silver Medal essay 1954; Robin Middleston, 'Blondel and the Cours d'Architecture' in *J. Soc. Architectural Historians* (USA), xviii, Dec. 1959; Blondel's own *Cours* and his *Discours sur la manière d'étudier l'architecture*, 1747, and *Discours sur la nécéssité d'architecture*, 1754.

architects and dull teachers. Indeed, it was to remedy these shortcomings that Blondel established his Ecole in the Rue de la Harpe in 1743. The new school was undeniably Chambers's best choice for it was uniquely equipped to hold classes simultaneously at different levels and to offer regular lectures on fortification, mathematics, perspective, quantity surveying and theoretical stereotomy (science of cutting solids). Furthermore its attractions included a well-stocked library and a room reserved for fencing, dancing, music and communal activities.

If Chambers was a conscientious student, as he no doubt was, the Ecole would have kept him fully occupied. Tuition was offered from eight in the morning until nine in the evening, six days a week. Mornings were generally devoted to discussions with Blondel or one of his *professeurs* and afternoons to a thorough grounding in geometry, mechanics, perspective, water-supply, and drainage. There was the history of architecture to be learned, sketching to practise and perfect, and long sessions of stereotomy to attend. During the months of April and May the strenuous grind was relieved by bi-weekly visits to notable buildings in and around Paris. These pleasurable field trips were a unique and immensely important aspect of architectural training in the Ecole. The critical examination and dissection of works of architects of all periods was regarded by Blondel as a major source of knowledge. 'Il faut réflechir sur l'ordonnance des façades, il en faut parcourir les dedans, repasser dans les dehors, se rappeler le motif qui les a fait élever, envisager de quelle espèce est l'édifice le genre d'appartement, par qui il doit être habité.'[2] Training at the Ecole provided the student with 'une profonde théorie, une très grande pratique, une longe suite d'expériences.'

Blondel's teaching, although not revolutionary, offered the student a sound course of instruction geared to current architectural thought. In preaching the classical rules he was patently aware, as were many of his contemporaries, that rules alone were not the essence of perfection. 'Le goût réuni aux règles, forme le bon Architect; il faut savoir que l'Architecture, ses précepts à part, est un art de goût, de génie et d'invention.[3] Quelquefois on peut et l'on doit s'affranchir de certaines règles. Ne vouloir jamais s'en écarter c'est risquer de tomber dans la sécheresse et la stérilité.'[4] These teachings may well have been the foundation of Chambers's eclecticism. They were certainly the model for his pedagogical activities as tutor to George III and as author of the *Treatise* in which he promises the student 'a series of sound precepts' arrived at by judiciously weighing all that he had read or seen in the light of reason, fact, and experience, unbiased 'by particular times, nor by general reputation of particular persons.'

Out of Blondel's safe and sensible Ecole came some of the most revolutionary architects, artists and theorists of the succeeding generation, men like Peyre, Ledoux, Gondoin, Rondelet, de Wailly, Mique, Cherpitel, and perhaps even Boullée. Many of these *avant-garde* Frenchmen like Ledoux, Rondelet, and Gondoin were later *écoliers* whom Chambers did not meet until his second visit to Paris in 1774. Although we know very little about the Blondelian students of 1749 and 1750, Peyre and de Wailly were probably the most outstanding. Both followed Chambers to Rome and remained his lifelong friends.

[2] Blondel, *Cours*, I, 1771, 443.

[3] Blondel, *Cours*, IV, 1773, xlvi.

[4] Blondel, *Cours*, I, 1771, 132 ff.

His regard for his Parisian colleagues is affectionately expressed in a letter to the Marquis de Voyer D'Argenson in 1774; 'Le roy, De Waillie, Doyen, Peyre Pajou et tous les autres habiles gents de votre capitale sont toujours dans ma mémoire.'[5] Gabriel François Doyen the painter followed him to Rome in 1750 and Pajou the sculptor joined them in 1752. Vernet, Hubert Robert, and Greuze were also among his friends in Paris and Rome. In many ways these young artists were more influential upon his immediate future than Blondel's *cours*. Of all his French acquaintances, however, the most inspiring were the slightly older pioneers of neo-classicism: Louis-Joseph Le Lorrain (1715–1759), Charles-Michel-Ange Challe (1718–1778), Nicholas-Henri Jardin (1720–1799), Gabriel-Pierre-Martin Dumont (1720–1790), and Ennemond-Alexandre Petitot (1727–1801), who had recently returned to Paris from the French Academy in Rome intoxicated with Jean Laurent Le Geay's extraordinary new approach to antiquity and composition. As we shall see, each of these architects contributed something to Chambers's remarkable project for a mausoleum for Frederick, Prince of Wales, but none was so influential upon him as well as the whole succeeding generation of Parisian designers as Le Geay and Le Lorrain.

Although the reaction against the rococo had been anticipated by Servandoni's revised design for the façade of St Sulpice, in 1739 his classicizing style was not noticeably related to antique sources, but rather to his experiences of English Palladianism. The crucial moment was 1748, the year of the Peace of Aix-La-Chapelle, the departure of the Marquis de Marigny, Soufflot, and Cochin on an archeological tour of Italy, and the announcement of the competition for the proposed Place Royale. To Chambers and his Parisian colleagues these events clearly spelled the impending fate of the rococo style. Yet in 1750 and 1751, or even in 1755 when Chambers said goodbye to Paris, the change was still invisible. Gabriel's Ecole Militaire had only been begun in 1751 and his Place Royale in 1753, and neither progressed very rapidly. While Chambers may well have seen and discussed the designs for these buildings, he was not to experience the full flowering of French neo-classicism until 1774.[6] The new public buildings that had been put up in his absence, notably Gondoin's Ecole de Chirugie and Antoine's Monnaie (Pl.153), were to be the lodestones for Somerset House. Paris in 1749 and 1750 had precious little to offer in the way of new buildings and nothing that would appeal to an Englishman. Adam as a result seems to have spent his time in laying in a stock of useful acquaintances and frilly clothes.[7] Chambers, on the contrary, acted upon Blondel's belief that there was something to be learned from virtually every work of art. His taste and diligence as an observer are uniquely recorded in his Franco-Italian sketch book, now in the Victoria and Albert Museum. Here we find drawings of the Porte St Denis, the Val de Grâce, the Château de Maisons, and the east front of the Louvre esteemed by Blondel to be one of the four wonders of French architecture, as well as numerous sketches of decorative details from a host of lesser-known buildings. Like Blondel he could also appreciate the best of rococo design in the interiors of the Oppenord apartments in the Palais Royale (Pls 2–3). Above

---

[5] BM Add.MS 41134, 7v, a letter dated 20 October 1774.

[6] Cf. John Harris, 'Sir William Chambers and his Parisian Album', in *Architectural History*, 6 (1963), 54–90, where all Chambers's Paris drawings are reproduced and discussed.

[7] John Fleming, *Robert Adam and his Circle*, 1962, 113–15.

all the sketch book reveals his native gift as a draughtsman, a skill that he had doubtless perfected before he reached Paris.

After a year of intense studies Chambers was ready to approach Italy, the mecca of architecture. He left Paris in November 1750 and by the New Year was in Italy where, apart from a brief visit to Paris in 1752 to meet Catherine More, his wife to be, he remained four years.

Unfortunately this precious period, probably the most important and eventful in his life, is shrouded in mystery. Unlike Adam he left no account of his social and artistic activities other than the sketch book and miscellaneous drawings. The picture that we can piece together from these documents and from the few comments of other people is an incomplete one, full of tantalizing lacunae and perplexing problems. Florence, for example, is a complete blank. It is impossible to believe that his only meeting with Sir Horace Mann was to obtain a letter of introduction to Cardinal Albani in 1753. Surely he must have been present at some of the many gatherings at the Casa Manetti where Mann welcomed artists of all nationalities, including Wilton and Cipriani. Under that cordial roof he could have met future patrons like Pembroke, Tylney, Brand, or Hollis.

After the probably convivial pleasures of Florence came the exhilarating but arduous task of surveying ancient and modern Rome. What interested him most he immediately recorded in his sketch book. Whether the multitude of treasure to be seen and the fascinating people to be met left no time for words, or the carelessness of future generations have lost or destroyed them, no written account of his experiences has survived. His thoughts and impressions are known only from a letter of advice written in 1774 to his foremost pupil Edward Stevens on his departure for Italy.[8] The passage of twenty years seems neither to have dimmed his memories nor altered his convictions. His counsel on both the methods and objects of study, though more dogmatic than it would have been in 1752, is nevertheless founded, like most of his opinions, on experience and reason.

'Our students at Rome are right to make a better use of their time now than they formerly used to do, for unless they study hard and acquire superior talents, they will do little here; this country swarming so with artists of all kinds, that unless a man does much better than his neighbours, he will have but an indifferent chance of making his way.

'It gives me great pleasure to hear of your perfect recovery; you will now be able to prosecute your studies properly, not by sending people to study for you, as some of our famous architects here did, but by drawing, measuring, and observing everything upon the spot yourself. Always see with Your own eyes, and though it is right to hear the judgement of others, yet never determine but by your own, not rashly, but after repeated observations, for our perceptions are not always just. It is vulgarly said that taste has no rules, but this, like most vulgar opinions, is erroneous; it has many; some pointed out by books, but more that are not mentioned, which You must find out, if You would work with certainty at all times. It is only by repeated and careful observations that you can arrive at this knowledge, common fame indeed will lead you to the works that have stood the

---

[8] Sir John Soane's Museum. The letter is titled 'Sir William Chambers to M. Edward Stevens, Architect, Au Caffé Anglois, Place D'Espagna, Rome', and is addressed from Chambers's house in Berners Street, 5 August 1774. Chambers gave this letter to Soane when he too was setting out for Rome. Cf. A. T. Bolton, *The Portrait of Sir John Soane*, 1927, 10–12.

test and been the admiration of many ages, but your own penetration must discover their true beauties and the secrets by which they were produced.

'Do not, as some have done, begin Your studies where they ought to be left off, and instead of forming your self upon these noble remains, whence the great masters of the 15th and 16th Centuries collected their knowledge, trifle away Your time, in collecting little poor ornaments and extravagent forms, from the remains of barbourous times. Our taste here has already been sufficiently poisoned by this unlucky mistake. Work in the same quarry with M. Angelo, Vignola, Peruzzi, and Palladio, use their materials, search for more, and endeavour to unite the grand manner of the two first, with the elegance, simplicity, and purity of the last'.

'Observe well the works of the celebrated Bernini, at once an able architect, painter and sculptor; see how well they are conducted, how artfully he took advantage of circumstances, and sometimes made even the defects of his situations contribute towards the perfection of his work; his compositions are not in the sublime style of antiquity, but they are always ingenious, graceful, and full of effect. Pietro da Cortona was in the same road with Bernini, but by no means his equal, excepting in painted decorations for ceilings, and other interior works, though even there Bernini was a very great master, as you will perceive by the vault of a Jesu, composed and executed under his direction.

'You will see nothing of Palladio's at Rome, nor elsewhere, excepting in the Venetian State, and particularly the Vicentine, where his works and those of Scamozzi, which are numerous, require Your particular attention. Study them carefully, and correct that luxuriant, bold, and perhaps licentious Style, which you will have acquired at Rome, Florence, Genoa, and Bologna, by their simple, chaste, but rather tame manner; form if you can a style of Your own in which endeavour to avoid the faults and blend the perfections of all.'

'Naples has never been famed for architects, they are now I apprehend worse than ever. You will see some execrable performances there, and there about, of Vanvitelli, Fuga, and some blockheads of less note, avoid them all, as you must Boromini with all the later Architects of Rome, excepting Salvi, who had indeed no general principles to guide him, yet sometimes fortunately hit upon the right, as appears by parts of his fountain of Trevi, and parts of his Dominican church at Viterbo'.

'You will find great advantage in the decorative part by sketching or drawing accurately, many of the fragments which lie scattered in all the villas about Rome, and in the environs of Naples. Draw in the Academy the human figure with the same view, correctly if you can, but at least with spirit and taste. Converse much with artists of all Countrys, particularly foreigners, that you may get rid of national prejudices. Seek for those who have most reputation, young or old, amongst which forget not Piranesi, who you may see in my name; he is full of matter, extravagent 'tis true, often absurd, but from his overflowings you may gather much information. Study painting and sculpture thoroughly, you cannot be a master in Your own art without great judgement in these, which are so intimately connected with it. Study them with regard to the knowledge of masters, as an ornamental and profitable science, but for your own use study them in a higher light. I have neither time nor paper to write any more at this time, but if You think my advice can be of any use call for it freely on all occasions, and believe me to be Most sincerely, d^r S^r, Your Obed^t humble serv^t Wm Chambers.'

One can be certain from Chambers's Blondelian background and ever righteous character that he practised what he preached. Indeed, the judgements he expresses here echo those in the *Treatise* and are fully endorsed by his drawings in the Franco-Italian Album and elsewhere. For example, Michelangelo, Vignola, Peruzzi, are drawn upon. Likewise his numerous drawings of antique bas-reliefs, sphinxes, griffins, urns, cartouches and so forth support his advice to Stevens to enrich his decorative vocabulary by sketching the fragments and ruins of Rome. That works by Borromini, Fuga, or Vanvitelli should be omitted is consistent with Chambers's tastes, but the limited number of Palladio's works – a few measured drawings of the Basilica, the Teatro Olympico, and the Villa Capra – and the total absence of any building whatsoever in Venice, Bologna, Padua, Verona, and Florence (except the Palazzo 'Armini') suggest that there was at one time another album or albums and perhaps many more loose drawings.

Oddly enough, the principal source of information[9] about Chambers in Italy is Robert Adam, whose jealous ear was alert to the activities of potential competitors. It is to him that we owe what little we know of Chambers's relationship with C. L. Clérisseau and L. Pecheux who are reputed to have tutored him in the art of drawing. Adam reports hearing from Wilton when in Florence in 1755 that Chambers owed all his 'hints and notions' to Clérisseau,[10] to whom he 'behaved ungratefully'. Thomas Hardwick's claim that the association began in Paris can be discarded as false for Clérisseau had left for Italy early in 1749 while Chambers was still on the high seas. The period of tuition must have been either between January 1751 and the summer of 1752 or between early 1753 and the spring of 1754 when Clérisseau left Rome in a huff for Florence where he took up with Robert Adam.

Owing perhaps to his employment by Adam, Clérisseau's role in the history of neo-classicism has been grossly over-extolled. There is no evidence whatsoever that he initiated a new style or that he led other architects to do so. On the contrary, most of his time in Rome was profitably spent as a drawing master, a cicerone, and maker or purveyor of views. He was undoubtedly an extremely agile draughtsman trained by Panini, from whom he inherited his overwhelming passion for drawing Roman ruins which he sold in endless and sometimes boringly repetitive sets to interested Englishmen.[11] Collecting Clérisseau's views does not, however, seem to have interested Chambers, for, unlike Adam, he had no frantic dreams of recording all of Rome. His approach was far more realistic and selective in accordance with his Blondelian training. Furthermore, he set great store on learning by experience and was opposed, as he later told Stevens, to employing 'other people to study for you, as some of our famous architects here did' – meaning, of course, Adam. He never overly worried as Adam did about competition, nor was he eager to make a scintillating debut or an ostentatious display of his skills. What then did Clérisseau give to Chambers who, to judge from his drawing of the Palais Royale in 1750, was already an accomplished

[9] I am indebted for this to John Fleming's invaluable and entertaining *Robert Adam and his Circle*, perhaps the most useful printed source to date for English artistic activity in Rome in the mid-1750s.

[10] For Clérisseau, cf. Thomas J. McCormick, 'Virginia's Gallic Godfather' in *Arts in Virginia*, v.4, no.2, 1964, 3–13; and the relevant pages from Fleming, op. cit.

[11] Natoire wrote to Marigny 23 August 1753, 'ce garçon a été gâté en dernier lieu par des ouvrages qu'il a fait pour des anglois de ses dessains de ruine; cela luy procuré quelques sequins et se croit en état de se passer de tout' (*Correspondence Des Directeurs De L'Académie en France à Rome*, x, 1900, 462).

and elegant draughtsman? Was he simply a cicerone or did he give Chambers 'all his hints and notions', and if so, what were they? These questions remain unanswered. Had Clérisseau instructed Chambers to the extent that he did Adam, then surely there should be at least a few drawings by him among the several thousand made and collected by Chambers. There is, however, only one, and that, according to the Whitton inventory,[12] was drawn by Chambers and finished by Clérisseau.[13] It is possible that the novel idea of representing an architectural design in a pictorial manner, since it is used by both Chambers and Adam, could have come from Clérisseau. The first-known example of a standard elevation in a landscape setting is Chambers's design of 1751–2 for the mausoleum of Frederick, Prince of Wales (Pls 4, 6). The notion of presenting a new project as if it were an existing building in a picturesque view is not entirely new as it was used on occasions by that great pictorial artist William Kent, but Kent was singular, and it was left to Chambers and Adam[14] to set standards in this mode of presentation. This was carried to extremes by Chambers in a section for the mausoleum where the timelessness of antique Rome is implied in the depiction of the building as a decaying ruin (Pl.6). This attractive pictorial style, that was to become *de rigueur* by 1800, was fully developed in Chambers's work in the late 1750's – in the Sherborne gate (Pl.79) in its parkscape, or in the York House section (1759) with its crumbling, flower-strewn cornice (Pl.94).

It is again from Adam that we learn of Chambers's studies with Laurent Pecheux,[15] an obscure French master of figure drawing who arrived in Rome in December 1753 with a letter of introduction to Clérisseau. After Chambers's departure as his first pupil in 1755 Pecheux cleverly managed to appeal to Adam's jealousy and vanity, assuring him that in three or four months 'he would do infinitely better than Chambers ever did or will ever do.' Encouraged by the promise of supremacy, Adam diligently applied himself, as Chambers had done, to the study of landscape painting, to mastering Le Brun's *Méthode pour apprendre à dessiner les passions*; and to copying 'feet and hands and noses and lugs' by which means 'a design in itself neither immensely ingenious nor surprising may appear excessively so.'[16] Nevertheless, for all his efforts and Pecheux's praises, he had in the end to concede that 'Here Chambers excelled'.

In March 1751 Frederick, Prince of Wales, died. Before the year was out Chambers, far away in Rome, had begun designs[17] (Pls 4, 6, 7 and Fig.1) for a proposed mausoleum – eight designs in all, the last dated February 1752. Why should an Anglo-Swede, a merchant turned architect, take it upon himself to design a monument for a member of the English royal family – and to be the only architect who did so? The answer must surely lie in a

---

[12] Cf. Appendix IV, a drawing in the library entered in the Inventory as *S W Chambers Finit Cleriss*, valued at 10 guineas.

[13] RIBA Albums, volumes said to have been put together by Thomas Hardwick when he travelled through France and Italy in 1776–9.

[14] Adam designed a ruin for Kedleston in 1758, cf. Fleming, op. cit., fig.80.

[15] The only full account of Pecheux is by L. C. Bollea, *Laurent Pecheux*, Turin, 1942. But cf. John Fleming's account of this painter.

[16] Fleming, op. cit., 169.

[17] These designs form the crux of a hypothesis presented by the author as 'Le Geay, Piranesi, and International Neo-Classicism in Rome 1740–1750' in *Essays In The History of Architecture Presented to Rudolf Wittkower*, eds. D. Fraser, H. Hibbard, and M. J. Lewine, 1967.

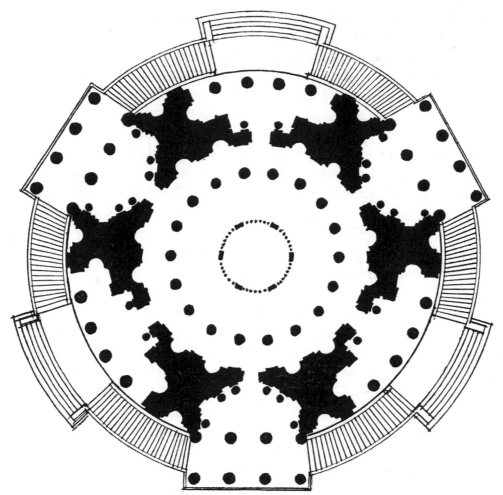

Fig.1 Mausoleum for Frederick, Prince of Wales

meeting between Chambers and the Prince and Princess in 1749 when, as is discussed below (pp.33–35), Chambers probably designed the House of Confucius at Kew built in 1749–50 (Pl.23).

In all of Chambers's work there is nothing so splendid as these mausoleum designs composed in the spirit of an antique monument, of elements borrowed from ancient and modern Rome. Here he pays homage to the tomb of Cecilia Metella and to the interior columnar elevations of the Pantheon, as well as to such modern architects as Serlio, Vignola, and Peruzzi. Although the mausoleum remained a paper dream, seven years later Chambers was able to convey something of its spirit in the Casino at Marino (Pl.50).

To explain the origin and significance of these two advanced neo-classic designs we must return to Rome and the years 1740–50, just before Chambers's arrival. Here we will find the germs of the new style that permeated the whole of Europe from the 1760's onwards. Here too we will discover, or rather rediscover, the forgotten master of the revolution, Jean Laurent Le Geay, whose bizarre genius sparked a kind of chain reaction that passed from Piranesi to Le Lorrain, Challe, Jardin, Petitot, Dumont, and finally to Chambers and Peyre. We shall then see that Peyre's mausoleum[18] (Pl.5) designed in Rome

[18] Published by him in his *Œuvres d'Architecture*, 1765, a compilation of designs made mostly between 1753 and 1757.

in the mid-1750's and long regarded as a forerunner, is, in fact, a late-comer to a style that had been developing for more than ten years.

In 1732 Le Geay was awarded the Grand Prix of the French Academy which took him to Rome, somewhat belatedly, in 1737, and kept him there for four years. On 9 June 1742 his return to Paris was announced by the Director of the Academy in Rome, François de Troy, who gave the following report of his achievements: 'il emporte une quantité de fort beaux desseins, tant des études qu'il a fait d'après les édifices publics que de sa propre composition; dans ces derniers; il y a du feu et du génie.'[19] This in itself would hardly excite any further interest in a man who (after all) achieved little else and seems thereafter to have pursued a most unsuccessful career. Fortunately, however, there are other commentators who provide a more explicit and far more exciting picture of Le Geay. C. N. Cochin, that discerning critic and acolyte of neo-classicism, applauded him in terms verging upon adulation: 'On peut donner pour première époque du retour d'un meilleur goust, l'arrivée de Legeay architecte, qui avoit été pensionnaire à Rome. C'étoit un des plus beaux génies en architecture qu'il y ait eu; mais d'ailleurs, sans frein, et, pour ainsi dire, sans raison. Il ne pouvoit jamais se borner à la demande qu'on lui faisoit, et le grand Mogel d'auroit pas été assés riche pour élever les bâtimens qu'il projettoit . . . Quoiqu'il en soit, comme le gousts de Legeay étoit excellent, il ouvrit les yeaux a beaucoup de gens. Les jeunes architects le saisirent autant qu'ils purent, peut etre plutost parce qu'il leur parut nouveau que par un véritable sentiment de ses beautés. On vit changer sensiblement l'école d'architecture au grand étonnement de tous les architects anciens de l'Academie.'[20] Though the extravagance of Le Geay's imagination may well have been his downfall as a practising architect, it nevertheless made him something of a hero to the impressionable young architects who fell under his spell. The memory of his influence was still very much alive when Joseph Lavallé and Andrieux came to write their obituaries of Charles de Wailly in 1799 and 1801 respectively. According to Lavallé, de Wailly had discovered in Le Geay's drawings some idea of the true perfection of architecture: 'ce ne fut que chez l'architecte le J'ai qu'il parvint à decouvrir, à travers les exaggérations de ce nouveau maître, le véritable point de perfection dans l'architecture dont il avait le pressentiment.'[21] Andrieux goes even further in attributing to Le Geay 'la renaissance du bon goût dans cet art; il a commencé à donner à la composition des plans une disposition plus grande que l'architecture n'avait plus depuis longtemps; d'ailleurs il dessinait avec de goût que de précision. Ce maître forme une nouvelle école d'où sont sortis plusieurs des architectes les plus célèbres de notre temps, Boullée, Moreau, Peyre l'ainé et de Wailly . . . autrefois et jusqu'au de L'ecole de Legeay les architectes se continaient de fixer des lignes et tout au plus de tracer des plans, mais ne dessinaient ni les contours, ni les corps avancés, ni les ornements; ils ne savaient pour ainsi dire pas leur langue tout entière.'[22]

Unfortunately very little of Le Geay's work has survived to illustrate these provocative eulogies. His suites of etchings – the *Fontane* published in 1767, the *Rovine* and *Tombeaux* of 1768, and the undated *Vasi* (Pl.10) – all brought together in 1770 as a *Collection de*

[19] Wittkower 'Festschrift,' op. cit., 190, n.6.
[20] Ibid., 190, n.7.
[21] Ibid., 190, n.8.
[22] Ibid., 190, n.9.

*Divers Sujets De Vases, Tombeaux, Ruines, et Fontaines Utiles aux artistes Inventée et Gravée par
G. L. Le Geay architecte* have hitherto been cast aside as being too late to throw any light
upon his activities in the 1740's. The recent discovery, however, of copies of published
and unpublished Le Geay designs in Chambers's Franco-Italian Album, compiled, as we
have seen, between 1749 and 1755, proves beyond a doubt that the original drawings for
the etchings were made no later than 1755.[23]

The *Divers sujets* are characterized by a perverse dissolution of the Vitruvian vocabulary
reminiscent of sixteenth-century mannerism and bordering upon the lunatic fringe. Rome
to Le Geay is a weird dream world where man is dwarfed by the overwhelming presence
of nature and antiquity. Such wild fantasies could hardly have failed to attract the attention of the theatrically-minded Piranesi who arrived in Rome in 1740 when Le Geay was
in his heyday at the French Academy. Indeed, it takes but a brief glance to recognize the
relationship between Le Geay's etchings and the anti-classical, anti-Vitruvian theories of
design expounded and illustrated in Piranesi's *Parere su l'architettura* of 1765 (Pl.11).
Following Le Geay, Piranesi wantonly reverses the meaning of structural forms and
pleads for an architecture freely and imaginatively embellished with quasi-archaeological
ornaments.[24]

Le Geay's etchings are neither the only nor the most important souvenir of his sojourn
in Rome. Far more exciting and informative is Chambers's copy (Pl.8) of one of those
infamous 'exagérations bizarres' labelled simply 'A plan Composed by Mons Legay'.
Here at last is an explanation of what De Troy meant by 'fait d'après les édifices publics'
and what Cochin found so startling. Beginning with Peruzzi's plan of St Peter's published
by Serlio, Le Geay evolved a vast and fantastic columnar composition in which relics of
ancient Rome – the inner ring of columns and the various shapes and motifs from the
Baths – mingle with elements of modernity in the lateral rotondas also taken from Serlio.
To judge from the comments on his work, this megalomaniac plan is not a singular, but a
typical example. In fact, it may well have been such 'exagérations bizarres' that kindled
the obsessive interest in columnar themes and mausolea that captivated Piranesi, swept
through the French Academy in Rome, and ultimately took hold of Chambers as well.

In the *Prima Parte d'architettura* of 1743, his first volume of etchings, Piranesi, though
still much attached to the scenographic traditions of Juvarra and Galli-Bibiena,
already demonstrates a devotion to Roman archaeology, an eagerness to incorporate
antique fragments into his own conspectus of designs, and a sense for the monumental.
This, however, is only a partial display of his work at this date, for there were other designs
made in 1743 which were not published until 1750 when he re-issued the *Prima Parte as
the Opera Varie* with numerous additions. The most interesting of these additions, the
Mausoleo Antico (Pl.9), is unfortunately undated. If it belongs to the earlier period, which
seems likely, then it may be regarded as a perfect elevational expression of Le Geay's

---

[23] Ibid., 191. Chambers owned a set of Le Geay's etchings (now in v & a 27737, A.I.24) that must have been given
him by Le Geay. According to an inscription on them, Chambers gave them to an anonymous friend. He must also
have owned etchings of vases by Saly and Petitot, for a volume of them at the RIBA is inscribed as having belonged
to Thomas Hardwick, who acquired many effects from his old master. These vases, as do those by De Wailly
published in 1760, display the characteristics of Le Geay's erotic neo-classic version of mannerist forms.

[24] Discussed by R. Wittkower in 'Piranesi's' "Parere su l'Architettura" ', *J. Warburg Inst.*, II, 1938–9, 147 ff.

fantastic plan. But if, indeed, it was made shortly before 1750, it provides us with a *terminus* rather than *post quam*.

Another pioneer of these early years was the painter and architect Louis-Joseph Le Lorrain (1715–1759), who after years of neglect is now recognized[25] as an important *avant-garde* neo-classical designer. Le Lorrain's earliest and most interesting contribution to the development of the neo-classical idiom is his fête and firework displays for the *festa della chinea* celebrated bi-annually on 28 June and 8 September.[26] These displays in the form of painted backcloths or temporary timber and plaster structures were erected in front of the Palazzo Colonna until the late 1730's when they were moved to the Palazzo Farnese, an event that caused the displays to be renamed *fuochi Farnesiani*. The engravings[27] of all the eighteenth-century decorations provide a unique survey of Roman design at a time when building activity was at a low ebb.

The importance of Le Lorrain becomes clear if we compare his designs (Pls 13–15) with what architects unattached to the Academy were producing at the same time or even ten years later. A design (Pl.12) by the Spaniard Francesco Preziado made for a *fuochi* in 1746 is entirely characteristic of the mass of conservative designs submitted by Italian artists who remained fully entrenched in Fuga's late-Baroque Classicism. They only help to underline the novelty and invention of Le Lorrain, Piranesi, and other associates of the French Academy.

Le Lorrain, having witnessed the homecoming of Le Geay in the summer of 1742, arrived in Rome in December to take up his *Prix*, not as an architect but as a painter. His first contribution to the *fuochi* was a painted *scena* in a traditional style of rococo-laced classicism. This was displayed on 8 September 1744. Towards the end of the month the students of the Academy jointly designed a festival decoration to commemorate the return to health of Louis XV. In terms of neo-classic decoration it could be described as a transitional piece, and the most likely candidates for its authorship are Le Lorrain and Challe.[28] By September of 1745 Le Lorrain, for some unknown reason, had withdrawn from painting and devoted himself entirely to architectural subjects. His display in this year was a triumphal arch (Pl.13), which, although as a design was not especially remarkable, did incorporate two advanced neo-classical motifs: oval panels draped with plaited rope-like swags and set in open spaces of wall, and 'Capitoline' openings borrowed from Michelangelo, who was to become a major quarry for neo-classic designers in the succeeding decades.

In the next two years – 1746 and 1747 – Le Lorrain went on to produce two compositions of outstanding originality, steeped in romanticism by virtue perhaps of their festive

[25] The key articles in the Le Lorrain reinstatement are Svend Erikson 'Lalive de Jully's Furniture "à la grecque" ', *Burl. Mag.*, Aug. 1961, 340–7; his 'Marigny and "Le Goût Grec" ', *Burl. Mag.*, March 1962, 96–101; and his 'Om Salon pas Akero og dens Kunstner Louis-Joseph Le Lorrain', *Sartryck Ur Konsthiskorisk Tidskrift*, 1963, 94–100. Cf. also C. Elling's pioneer *Jardin i Rom*, Copenhagen, 1943.

[26] The *Festa della Chinea* has hardly been treated as an architectural manifestation of the highest importance. Cf. G. Ferrari, *Bellezze architettonchie per le Feste Della Chinea in Rom nei secoli XVIIe*, xviii, Turin, and H. Tintelnot, *Barocktheater und barocke Kunst*, 1939; and R. Wunder, 'A Forgotten French Festival In Rome', *Apollo*, May 1967, 354–9.

[27] I know only of the complete set of the engraved *Chinea* in the Museum of Decorative Art, Copenhagen. For a microfilm of these I was indebted to my friend Svend Erikson.

[28] Wunder, op. cit.

function, and prophetic of almost all that was to appear in the mainstream of Parisian design in the 1750's and 1760's. The first of these, in 1746, was a square Temple of Minerva (Pl.14) rising above clouds with standard porticoes on two sides and on the two others open semi-circular colonnades screening smoking altars. While these parts may be considered characteristic of eighteenth-century scenography, what happens in the upper regions is quite a different matter. Here, instead of a dome, there is a giant pedestal surrounded by a sculptured freize *à l'antique* depicting a pagan sacrifice from which bellows smoke to envelop both the pedestal and the crowning figure of Minerva.

In 1747 Le Lorrain's *macchina* (Pl.15) was an even more remarkable invocation of pagan rite. Peripheral obelisks flanked by bowed and shrouded figures; smoking altars; and female goddesses on pedestals surround a composite colonnaded open temple whose upper parts are again markedly neo-classic. The drum is decorated with swags suspended by *putti* and oval openings framed by reclining female figures and, with its stepped dome terminating in a pagan deity, is what one might expect in the mid-1750s from someone like Peyre, but not from an architect working ten years earlier.

Like Le Lorrain, the painter Charles Michel-Ange Challe (1718–1778) may also have met Le Geay in Paris before coming to Rome in November 1742. Although we know less about Challe's Roman activities than about Le Lorrain's, his fantastic composition of monumental buildings and a triumphal bridge – drawn in 1746 (Pl.19) – reveals him to be connected in some way with Piranesi. This was when the great Roman had published his *Prima Parte*, and quite obviously Challe fell under his persuasive spell. It is, however, by no means clear what the relationship was or for that matter who influenced who. As there are no dated examples of Piranesi's work between the vital years 1743 and 1750, in other words between the *Prima Parte* and the *Opera Varie*, one cannot entirely dismiss the possibility, however strange it may seem, that it was Challe who influenced Piranesi and not the reverse.

Le Lorrain was accompanied to Rome by Gabriel-Pierre-Martin Dumont (1720-1790), a promising young architect who later proved to be a follower rather than a leader of fashion. His *Temple des Arts*, presented as his *Morceau de Reception* to the Academy of St Luke in 1746, has an interesting columnar plan and an elevation (Pl.18) with 'Capitoline' openings reminiscent of Le Lorrain's 1745 *fuochi*. In 1768 Le Geay, who one suspects was then desperate for work, contributed a number of vignettes to Dumont's *Receuil d'architecture*. This, and what Dumont inherited from Le Lorrain, Piranesi and others in Rome, is all we know of Dumont's relationship to Le Geay.

By the time Nicholas Henri Jardin (1720–1799) arrived in Rome[29] in 1744 the neo-classical scene was already set. Nevertheless, he was just in time to witness Le Lorrain's *Chinea* decorations. Indeed, the impact of these was considerable, as can be seen by comparing with Le Lorrain's designs, Jardin's *Chapelle Sépulchrale* of 1747 (Pl.17) and a *Pont Triomphal* of 1748 (Pl.16). These were probably part of a programme initiated by the French Academy, to which Petitot's *pont triomphal* (Pl.21) must also belong. Ennemond-Alexandre Petitot (1727–1801), who became a *pensionnaire* in 1746, followed Le Lorrain as a contribu-

---

[29] His career in Rome has been admirably treated by Elling, op. cit. The Roman projects were engraved in *Plans ... De L'Eglise Royale De Frederic V*, 1765.

tor to the *Chinea* in 1749. His display (Pl.20) took the form of a grandiose mausoleum, so idealized that it could just as well have been made in 1770 or 1790, by Boullée or Ledoux. This design set the final seal of approval upon the mausoleum as a neo-classical exercise.

We have seen the obsessions of Le Geay pervading the works of Piranesi, Le Lorrain, Challe, Dumont, Jardin and Petitot. Now the foundations of neo-classicism had been laid. Jardin returned to Paris in November 1748, Le Lorrain in March 1749, Challe the following September, and Petitot in 1750. Thus by the autumn of 1750 the principal participants in the Franco-Roman episode were reunited in Paris – an event of immense significance for the later history of Parisian neo-classicism. If they ever came together at all, even if only convivially, it would most probably have been at Blondel's Ecole des Arts where the impressionable Chambers was then a student.

The events of the 1740's throw new light upon Chambers's Mausoleum for Frederick, Prince of Wales in 1751, showing it to be in line of succession from Le Geay and Le Lorrain, rather than an isolated project. Chambers has brought the idea of the mausoleum from the plane of heroic fantasy or festive papier mâché to one of practicality. Had the Dowager Princess Augusta of Wales been interested, she could in fact have built it in Kew Gardens.

The activities of the first wave of French neo-classicists in Rome had only been publicized by the limited circulation of the *Chinea* engravings. The situation was radically altered when in 1765 Joseph Marie Peyre published his *Œuvres d'Architecture* including designs made in Rome between 1753 and 1757. Owing to the absence of any comparative material concerning the immediate ancestry of his early work, the Franco-Roman designs of the 1740's were not taken into account, and as a result the importance of Peyre has been somewhat overestimated. A comparison, however, of Peyre's mausoleum (Pl.5) with the one designed by Chambers (Pl.6), places it in the context of the French Academy in Rome in the 1750's – where Peyre was an intimate friend of Chambers – and as one more growth on the Le Geay family tree.

Paris was the clearing house for this Franco-Roman neo-classicism. The later careers of the coterie of architects who had flowered so brilliantly in the Roman sun, are strangely disappointing. Together they prospered, when dispersed they withered. Le Geay alone seems to have preserved his youthful fervour for which he paid dearly with poverty and disenchantment. Le Lorrain died in St Petersburg in 1759, Jardin established himself in Copenhagen in 1755 and became increasingly conservative, Petitot went to Parma in 1753, and Chambers decided to make his name in London.

Parma or Copenhagen might have provided an architectural ambience congenial to the ideas of Petitot or Jardin. London on the contrary was far too steeped in the Palladian tradition to welcome Chambers's Gallic sympathies and Le Geayesque inventions. There are, however, among his drawings a number of interesting columnar plans, e.g. Fig.5a, that may have been drawn before 1760, not to mention his unsuccessful proposals in 1756 for Harewood (Pls 43–45). In addition there was the elegant Casino at Marino (Pls 50–54) begun in 1758 for a devoted antiquarian and amiable friend, Lord Charlemont. If Chambers was deprived of the opportunity of translating his French experiences into brick and mortar, he at least had the pleasure of entertaining Le Geay in London in 1766 and 1767. What London thought of this genius *manqué* we may never know. He left no memorial save a signed view (Pl.51) of the Casino, a most appropriate monument set in a neo-classical frame[30] probably designed by Chambers. Indeed, were it not for the few records kept by Chambers, Le Geay, once celebrated as the liberator of French architecture, would now be a mere name in Thieme-Becker's lexicon.

[30] This framed picture is in the collection of Miss Lambart John, a descendant of Lord Charlemont. The inference must therefore be that Chambers had the drawing framed (to a design supplied by himself) and gave it to Charlemont who was a very intimate friend.

Chapter 3

Kew Gardens

Kew[1] has been a sightseer's mecca for the past two hundred years, or, to be more accurate, since 1763 when its splendours were announced to Europe in *Plans, Elevations, Sections, and Perspective Views of the Gardens and Buildings at Kew*, an attractive folio published at George III's expense. This book was prepared and engraved under Chambers's directions and perpetuated the six years he had spent in transforming the famous royal garden. No gardening book has received such care and attention from author, printer, and engravers alike.

When Robert Wood in August 1757 congratulated Chambers upon the favours shown him by the Prince and Princess, he was referring, as we have seen,[2] to his architectural tutorship of George, Prince of Wales, and his appointment as architect to the Dowager Princess of Wales who required an architect to take charge of Kew, as well as Clivedon and Hedsor in the country, and Carlton and Leicester Houses in town. The accounts in the Duchy of Cornwall Office are certified by Chambers from October 1757, and henceforward, almost weekly, until the Princess died in 1772.

The eighteenth-century visitor to Kew would have found two separate gardens occupying the area of the present Botanical Garden. In 1757 the road from Kew Green to Richmond followed the east flank of what were mostly fields. Then, Kew Garden extended for only a few hundred yards to the south. Where the main entrance to the gardens now is, the visitor would have found a narrow approach to the entrance to Kew Foot Lane leading towards Richmond in a roughly southerly direction, dividing Kew Garden on the left from Richmond Garden on the right. After a short while Kew Garden would have given way to fields, but Richmond Garden extended all the way to Richmond Lodge and Richmond Green. Only in 1841 were the fences of Kew Foot Lane taken down to unite the two Royal domains into the Royal Botanic Gardens.

Richmond Garden was the first to be laid out as a royal garden. In 1719 George, Prince of Wales, acquired the house that had been altered in 1694 for William III, and acquired in 1703 by the Duke of Ormonde.[3] Then in the 1730's Queen Caroline summoned Charles Bridgeman to extend the grounds and William Kent to ornament them with such conceits as Merlin's Cave and the Hermitage. After the Queen's death in 1737

---

[1] Kew is treated by the author in 'Fate of the Royal Buildings – Bicentenary of Kew Gardens', *C. Life*, 28 May 1959, 1182–4, and 'Exoticism at Kew', *Apollo*, Aug. 1963, 103–8.

[2] Cf. p.8 above.

[3] This information was given me by Mr Howard Colvin, whose account of Richmond Lodge will appear in his forthcoming *History of the King's Works*.

little was done to the gardens until the northern areas were landscaped by Capability Brown *c.*1764–8,[4] shortly before the Lodge or Palace was demolished in the early 1770's. By this time, as we shall see,[5] Chambers had become very much involved with the site, proposing at least four palaces (Pls 109–112), building the Observatory (Pl.125) in 1768, and erecting a Fête Pavilion in 1769 (Pl.126).

Kew on the other side of the Foot Lane was the domain of Frederick, Prince of Wales, who held court here from 1729 until his premature death in 1751. Kew Palace, sited at the very northerly edge of the garden, has the distinction of being Kent's first architectural achievement of any consequence. The building accounts in the Duchy of Cornwall Office, and the descriptions in Chambers's book, evoke a picture of highly gilded, tasteful splendour, where painted rooms windowed smooth lawns and statue-flanked vistas. It was not, however, a large garden, comprising only about a sixth of the acreage of Kew in 1763, and was minute in comparison to Richmond Garden – as John Rocque's survey in 1748 shows. Shortly before Kew Palace (or the White House as it was called) was completed around 1736, Kent had moved on to Carlton House to create a characteristic Kentian garden there.[6]

Between 1736 and 1749 the gardens at Kew hardly intrude upon the scene. In the few years before his death, however, the Prince seems once again to have turned his thoughts towards their ornamentation. For this new phase of activity we are indebted to the observant Vertue. In October 1750 he recorded the Prince's interest in drawings of ancient and modern philosophers as he intended to make an 'Aquaduct thro his Gardens at Kew and Earth thrown up was to make a mount which he intended to adorn with statues or Busts of all these Philosophers and to represent the mount parnassus.'[7] Most interesting of all Vertue saw the 'new Chinesia Summer hous painted in their Stile & ornaments the Story of Confucius & his doctrines.'[8] When the Summer House (Pl.23) was put up by John Lane, carpenter, Solomon Brown, bricklayer, and Andrews Jelfe, mason, it was described in the accounts as the 'India House,'[9] and in 1763 Chambers described it as the House of Confucius, adding that it was 'built I believe to the designs of Mr Goupy . . . the soffa and chairs designed by Mr Kent.' It seems very strange indeed that Chambers should be so vague about this building when he was so precise about all the others at Kew. Not only had he been working at Kew since 1757 completely remodelling all the gardens for the Dowager Princess, but he had both Lane and Brown on his staff. Furthermore, Goupy was still alive in 1763, as was the intelligent and interested Dowager Princess, either of whom could easily have supplied him with the facts. It is unimaginable that the author of *Designs for Chinese Buildings* (1757) should be so ill-informed about a building which was then one of the most important chinoiserie structures in

---

[4] Brown's first plan (in Kew Gardens Library) is dated 10 December 1764. This ties up with Joshua Kirby's report. (as Clerk of Works at Richmond) in October 1765 'that great alterations and improvements were making in Richmond Gardens by Mr Launcelot Browne' (PRO Works 4/13 11 Oct. 1756. 10 Oct. 1766. Information Mr Colvin).

[5] Chapter 6, pp.78–80.

[6] Thomas Whately, *Observations On Modern Gardening* (ed. with notes by Horace Walpole), 1798, shows Kent's work at Carlton Garden.

[7] Vertue Notebooks, I, *Walpole Soc.*, XVIII (1930), 13–14.

[8] Vertue Notebooks, VI, *Walpole Soc.*, XXX (1955), 153.

[9] Duchy of Cornwall Office, accounts Frederick, Prince of Wales, XVII (Oct. 1748–Oct. 1749).

D

Europe.[10] In fact, his description is not only vague but probably false as well, for unless the temple contained earlier furniture, none could have been designed by Kent who had died early in 1748 – and who in any case did not belong in these later years to the Prince's artistic rococo circle.[11] What is more, there is circumstantial evidence that Chambers himself designed the House of Confucius. His vagueness must therefore have been deliberately intended, to disguise what would have been regarded as a rococo indiscretion in comparison with what he published in his authoritative book on chinese architecture. The evidence for his authorship is threefold. Firstly there are the elaborate projects for the Prince's Mausoleum made in 1751 that must imply a previous acquaintance with the Kew menage. Even more important is the fact that the engraving of the Confucian house is inscribed *W Chambers architectus*. Surely this cannot be a mere slip of the engraver's burin, nor can it refer only to the substructure in the form of a bridge which Chambers designed[12] when he moved the temple from the old site. Thirdly, there is the involved question of the authorship of the first Alhambra design (Pl.24) which provides an important link between the 1749–50 phase of exotic design and that of 1757–63. This design, now in the Royal Institute of British Architects, was originally in the collection of John, 3rd Earl of Bute who was the Princess's adviser at Kew and Chambers's 'Director' there. On it are two inscriptions, the first in Chambers's hand describing it as being in 'the old Moorish taste', and beneath in another hand a note, 'this I drew in 1750 for the Prince and a model was made of it and it was built in 1758.' The artist in 1750 was therefore someone who was in touch with events at Kew in 1758 and who, although perhaps less skilled as a draughtsman, was certainly far better acquainted with Moorish architecture than Chambers, whose Alhambra (Pl.25) was a very fanciful rococo–Gothic building. The one person who fits this description perfectly is Johann Henry Muntz, the Swiss painter who was discovered by Richard Bentley in Jersey in 1753 and sent to London to work for Walpole – until dismissed his service in 1759. Not only is Muntz's drawing style identical to the Moorish design, but he can also be connected with Chambers on several other occasions. He was the architect of the Gothic Cathedral[13] at Kew, an important object in Chambers's garden; he designed an 'Egyptian' Room[14] for Lord Charlemont in 1762; and in 1768 was providing this Irish lord with further undescribed designs, encouraged, it would seem, by Chambers.[15] The final clue to his authorship of

[10] It was much larger than the Chinese House at Shugborough built c.1747 (cf. *C.Life*, 15 April 1954, 1126), said to have been based upon drawings made by Sir Percy Brett when he called at Canton in 1743 with Admiral Anson. Philip Yorke mentions the building in his *Journal* ed. Joyce Godber in 'The Marchioness Grey of Wrest Park', *Beds. Hist. Rec. Soc.* CXLVII (1968) in 1748. Thomas Anson also had a small pagoda built, 'promising greatly' according to Yorke, in 1752. Again according to Yorke, Mr Aislabie of Studley Royal was projecting a pagoda in a Chinese rock garden in 1744. In 1753 a Chinese summer house existed at Radnor House, Twickenham, and in the 1750s there was a form of pagoda at Fonthill House. Cf. E. Von Erdberg, *Chinese Influence On European Garden Structures*, 1936 and H. Honour, *Chinoiserie*, 1961.

[11] As expounded to me by Mark Girouard, whose work upon the English rococo was incorporated in three *Country Life* articles: 'Hogarth and his Friends', 13 Jan., 27 Jan., and 3 Feb. 1966.

[12] Kew accounts, Duchy of Cornwall Office, XLII, 25 Sept. 1758: 'preparing the Chineys Temple to be moved', and XLI, Nov. 1757: to Joseph Wilton 'To having made an original model in plaister of a River God's Head for Ornaments to a Bridge in the Gardens at Kew and executed the same in Wood highly finished £5 5. 0'.

[13] Chambers, *Kew*, 1763.

[14] The design is in the collection of Mr W. S. Lewis, Farmington, Connecticut. Reprd. John Harris, 'Sir William Chambers, Friend of Charlemont', in *Bull. Irish Georgian Soc.*, VIII, no.3, July–Sept. 1965, fig.26.

[15] HMC Charlemont, I, 286.

the first Alhambra design is contained in the 'Proposals' for a 'course of Gothic architecture' issued by Muntz on 12 April 1760.[16] Here he not only claims that in 1748 he drew 'some remarkable fine and curious Remains of Moresque Fabrics, still existing in the Kingdoms of Murcia, Valentia, and the City of Saragossa in Spain', but what is more he also promises to publish 'a Temple for a Garden in the Moresque Stile, of the Author's Composition, and which is going to be executed at a Nobleman's Country Seat.'

But we are still left with the problem of how and why Muntz's drawing came to be proffered to the Prince in 1750 when there is no evidence for this Swiss having visited England before 1753. In the absence of any documents we can only speculate that the Prince, noted for his rococo and exotic interests, had heard – as had many in Sweden – that young Chambers was returning from China with drawings of Chinese buildings. Whilst Chambers was in England in the summer of 1749, presumably making arrangements for his future wife to meet him in Paris, the Prince may have solicited a design for the House of Confucius from him and, being pleased with it, wrote to him in Paris in 1750 requesting another design for an exotic building. It so happens that Muntz was in Paris at this time.[17] It is therefore not unreasonable to suppose a meeting with Chambers, who certainly would have been interested in Muntz's travels and must have realized that his Moorish design could be the perfect answer to the Prince's latest demand.

When in 1757 Chambers took over at Kew as architect to the Dowager Princess of Wales he found the place unimpressive. As has been mentioned, in comparison to Kew in 1763, then nearly three-quarters of the estate was fields and only a small part cultivated garden. The gardens, Chambers wrote in his book, 'are not very large. Nor is their situation by any means advantageous: as it is low, and commands no prospects. Originally the ground was one continued dead flat: the soil was in general barren, and without either wood or water. With so many disadvantages it was not easy to produce anything even tolerable in gardening: but princely munificence, guided by a director equally skilled in cultivating the earth, and in the politer arts, overcame all difficulties. What was once a Desert is now an Eden.' This transformation is a tribute to himself, William Aiton the gardener, Bute himself a renowned botanist, the Princess with her Privy Purse, and George, Prince of Wales, the future King.

Inspired by Kent, Chambers created at Kew an inward-looking garden (Pl.22) where there were neither distant vistas nor curvaceous Brownian clumps. Around the perimeter were belts of trees and low shrubs interspersed with glades and hillocks. This frame was dotted with temples and ornaments and surrounded two rough fields contained by the *ha has*. The contrast was a deliberate one of nature simple, pictured as a bucolic scene of grazing cattle and sheep, and nature improved by art with the judicious placing of architectural features in each of the groves or glades. Beyond the northerly field was an L-shaped lake, and beyond that a spacious vista of sheep-cropped lawn bounded by Kent's palace, Chambers's Orangery, and a north-easterly area containing Aiton's greenhouses, aviary, menagerie, and botanic gardens.

Although the requirements of a modern botanical garden have necessitated the altera-

[16] 'Proposals' among the James Essex papers in the BM Add.MS.

[17] According to an album of drawings of antique vases compiled by Muntz, in Mr W. S. Lewis's collection, he was also in Rome in 1751 (where Chambers was at the time).

tion of much at Kew, the famous Pagoda, Ruined Arch, Orangery, and rebuilt temples to Bellona and Pan have survived as evocative reminders of the garden's former delight. To appreciate fully this lost elysium we must turn to Chambers's book, for just as a connoisseur may be the best guide to his pictures, so Chambers is to his garden. Led by Chambers we begin our perambulation with the royal apartments of Kew House. He takes us first through the Kent-decorated rooms, many with chimney-pieces carved by Rysbrack, then through the Gallery painted with children in theatrical dresses by Richard Ellis, and here and there commenting upon the furniture designed by Kent, and eventually leading us out into the gardens and to the nearby Orangery (Pl.26).

This *New Room*, or *Greenhouse* as it was described in the accounts,[18] was begun in 1757, but is inexplicably dated in the pediment 1761. It is the first of the Kew ornaments and the largest classical garden building there. The five arched bays and the end pavilions with their Serlian-motif openings appear to be of stone, but are in fact Solomon Brown's bricks faced with Chambers's special brand of stucco.[19] South-east of the Orangery stood the Temple of the Sun (Pl.38), built in 1761 and described by Chambers as 'of the circular peripteros kind' with a 'Salon richly finished and gilt'. If earlier than the Stourhead temple, this was the first imitation in England of the Baalbec temple of that name published in 1757 by Chambers's friend, Robert Wood. Continuing from the temple, still with Chambers as our guide, we would have found the area of Aiton's botanical pursuits. The Physic or Exotic Garden, 'not begun before the year 1760' and in 1763 not 'yet in its perfection' would in a few years be the 'amplest and best collection of curious Plants, in Europe'. In this garden Chambers would have proudly shown us his Great Stove, 114 feet long. A most decorative entrance arch, designed by Chambers but idiosyncratically Kentian, then opened to the Flower Garden, with its fretted Aviary, and a winding walk led to the Menagery (Pl.27). This was oval, the pens of Chinese and Tartarian pheasants surrounding a basin of water in which stood a wooden pavilion designed in 1760 'in imitation of a Chinese open ting'. Then the antiquity of the orient gave way, as it were, to Rome, in the form of the classical Doric temple of Bellona (Pl.29) overlooking the ting. The Doric order also appears in the small temple to Pan 'in a retired solitary walk' and again, south-east of this, in the Temple of Eolus (Pl.28) ingeniously constructed as a revolving seat to catch the sun. Here again we experience another contrast of two antiquities, for within sight of Eolus stood the House of Confucius (Pl.23), Chambers's first contribution to Kew which he later (in 1758) moved to this spot and placed upon a small bridge. From its fretwork platform we could survey the extent of the lake, the fields within their *ha has*, and the verdant peripheral walks. Beyond the House of Confucius the gardens were Chambers's province where he could place his buildings unfettered by any botanical or horticultural requirements stipulated by Bute or Aiton.

[18] The Kew building accounts are puzzling. Although work in 1757 is accounted for as fully paid, none of the otherwise complete vouchers for work in the early 1760s mentions the new Kew buildings. The inference is that there must have been a separate Privy Purse account in the Princess's name.

[19] Chambers wrote to William Seward (RIBA Letters) on 15 November 1790 about the 'Receipt for my Stucco which in the Green house at Kew and even in some Corinthian Capitals of a temple has already stood the weather thirty years and seems likely to last a century longer.' Indeed, Chambers was perfectly right, for his stucco can still be found on the Orangery 200 years after it was put on.

Today the eastern perimeter of Kew is all that remains of Chambers's peripheral walk, where the rebuilt and resited Temple of Bellona and the Ruined Arch (Pl.31) are its only surviving ornaments. A flagstaff now stands upon the mound that once vaunted the noble Temple of Victory (Pl.30) built to commemorate the victory at Minden in August 1759 and modelled upon Perrault.[20] This temple, overlooking the two pastures, marked a midway point in the perambulation of the gardens on this flank. We would already have passed the Theatre of Augusta (Pl.37), a Corinthian semi-circular colonnade[21] intended for the Princess's theatrical parties, and could either cross to the west side of the gardens, or, better still, take a path aligned upon the Ruined Arch to the south. This arch (Pl.31), really a picturesque bridge[22] to bring sheep and cattle from Kew Road into the pastures within the *ha has*, was built 'to imitate a Roman antiquity'. In fact, the allusion was a light-hearted one, for old Rome was there only by virtue of broken fragments of capitals and cornices embedded in good London stock bricks.

Although the senses may already have been satiated by the pleasures of the Flower Garden, Menagery, the House of Confucius, or the ornamental diversity of the walks, there was even more in store for the unexpecting tourist as he passed through the Ruined Arch and entered an area called the Wilderness (Pl.32). Here he would have been treated to the colourful, exotic trilogy of Alhambra, Pagoda, and Mosque, the keys to Kew's fame.

The Alhambra has already been discussed in connection with Muntz's drawing of 1750, and it has been shown that when this colourful red, yellow, and blue pavilion (Pl. 25) was built in 1758, Muntz's much more original Moresque pavilion was changed to a more fanciful rococo Gothic design laced with eastern motifs. It was the first of the three 'exotics' and stood in a glade open to the pastures and visually aligned with the Gothic Cathedral on the west walk. Chronologically the Alhambra was followed by the Mosque (Pl.33) set in a similar glade but on the other side of the Pagoda. Although Chambers would have us believe that the Mosque was an accurate representation of the 'principal peculiarities of the Turkish architecture', it was really indebted to the imaginative reconstructions published by Fischer von Erlach.[23] In fact, it is clear that Chambers's interpretation of eastern architecture is more akin to the spirit of the rococo than the archaeological interests of neo-classicism.

Today as in the past every visitor remembers Kew by its 160 feet high pagoda (Pl.35), the most ambitious chinoiserie garden structure in Europe. Though it has unfortunately lost its glitter of glazed tiles and eighty garishly-coloured iron roof dragons, it is still a

[20] Perrault, *Les Dix Livres d'Architecture de Vitruve*, 1673, pl.xxxvi.

[21] Based upon a drawing made by Visentini of an unidentified building, and inscribed by him 'Pianta del Semicolo'. Its association with the Theatre of Augusta is clinched by the fact that it can be found among Chambers's collection of architectural drawings in the v & a (3076.35).

[22] In Chambers's portfolios at Windsor Castle is a more classical version of the arch, and Chambers proposed, or may even have built, another 'Roman' ruined bridge at The Hoo (Pl.81).

[23] Fischer von Erlach, *Entwurff einer historischen Architectur*, 1725. English editions in 1730 and 1737. Cf. Mosque of Sultan Orcana at Bursa for an elevation and the Imperial Bath at Buda for a section. Chambers's Mosque was plagiarized by William Wrighte in his *Grotesque Architecture*, 1767. A similar mosque was designed by Henry Keene and possibly intended for Hartwell House, Buckinghamshire, where one is known to have existed, and where Keene worked. Thomas Brand of The Hoo contemplated one also (cf. The Hoo in Catalogue).

concoction of the Cathay of Tan Chet Qua and the Mandarin of the Nine Whiskers[24] in the heart of suburbia. Under its fancy dress is a virtuoso feat of bricklaying and carpentry. To Solomon Brown goes the credit for the 'well-coloured and well-matched greystocks, neatly laid, and with such care, that there is not the least crack or fracture in the whole structure' and probably to George Warren the Kew carpenter, the remarkable spiral staircase. In spite of the fact that Chambers must have been familiar with several pagodas in Canton, as well as Neuhof's topographical views showing the Lintsigntschoo Pagoda in Shantung Province and the famous Porcelain Pagoda at Nanking, like the Alhambra and Mosque, the Kew Pagoda was never meant to be an archaeologically correct reconstruction. It was born of rococo invention, and indeed this is best illustrated by the interior of his Mosque where green-stuccoed palm trees (leitmotivs of the rococo) surround a heavenly dome painted in delicious blue by Richard Wilson (Pl.34).

Having experienced a variety of pagan buildings, both classical and oriental, the visitor is now conducted northwards along the western periphery that bordered Kew Foot Lane, to a Christian one, the Gothic Cathedral. This unappreciated monument of the Gothic Revival, intended to represent a cathedral front 50 feet broad, was designed about 1759 by J. H. Muntz. This faced the south pasture and it marked the end of a sweep of view that took in the Temple of Victory, the Ruined Arch, the Alhambra, Pagoda, and Mosque. This panorama was almost the quintessence of Fischer's book. Further on, hidden in a bosky grove, was the Gallery of Antiques (Pl.36), an oblong room open to the sky and consisting of a screen of eight Palladian windows richly embellished with antique-style bas reliefs and statues representing the Seasons and the Arts. As there are no accounts for the building and design of this Gallery, one can only surmise that the sculptures were the *magnum opus* of Joseph Wilton.

Continuing in the direction of Kent's palace one came upon two more temples, an Ionic one dedicated to Arethusa and built in 1758 (it is now rebuilt on the western walk of Kew), and quite near the house a domed octagonal Temple of Solitude (Pl.28). From the walk between these two temples a diversion could have been made to the lake-side and an arched timber-framed bridge 'taken from an idea of Palladio's'.[25] Finally Chambers ends his perambulation with a description of his Temple to Peace (Pl.39), fronted with a very splendid Ionic portico and planned as a cross of four apses, two of them screened with columns. The absence of this temple from Richardson's accurate survey of 1771 may be explained by Chambers's account of it as 'now erecting'. Either it was for some reason never completed, or was destroyed in the following seven years.

Few English gardens could boast of an array of temples as varied as Kew's. Here the classical Gallery of Antiques, Pan, Bellona, Sun, Eolus, Victory, Arethusa, Solitude, Augusta, and perhaps Peace, took their place alongside a Gothic cathedral, and the oriental-flavoured House of Confucius, Menagerie Ting, Pagoda, Mosque, and Alhambra. Kew established Chambers as the master of the garden temple. Their small scale suited his tastes and ability.

Although Kew was essentially an expression of the interests of the Princess brought to

---

[24] Characters in Chambers's *Dissertation on Oriental Gardening*, 1772.

[25] Palladio, *I Quattro Libri*, 1570, lib. 3, 17–18. Cf. also the bridge built for John Boyd at Danson Park.

fruition by Chambers, Bute, and Aiton, the 'Exotics' as we have now seen were a continuation of the phase initiated by Frederick, Prince of Wales in 1749. The gardens laid out by Chambers may be regarded as a kind of prelude to certain ideas propounded in his later *Dissertation on Oriental Gardening*. Here was his only opportunity to discard the fashion for the natural parkscape of Brown and return to the more formalized Kentian garden where contrast and variety could be developed to their fullest. Here he managed to unite in a relatively confined space 'all that the English taste has been capable of producing, most magnificent and most variagated.'[26]

The publication of the splendid Kew folio in 1763 was not, however, the end of Chambers's responsibilities there. On the contrary, he remained the Princess's architect until her death in 1772, and to judge from his bill submitted in 1768 for 'various Journeys to Kew'[27] was kept very busy indeed supervising the upkeep of the buildings. In that year he travelled to Kew, either from London, Whitton, or Hampton Court, twenty-three times. Even after the death of the Princess, Kew remained under his surveillance in his capacity of Comptroller of the Board of Works. The King, long discontent with the inconveniences of Richmond Lodge, took advantage of his mother's death to occupy her more elegant palace. In August 1772 the first estimates[28] for alterations amounted to £4982, and on 16 October a further £4130 was requisitioned. It is not known what this expenditure involved. There is a plan at Windsor (Pl.40) showing Chambers's proposals for squaring up the palace and so producing a 'pavilion' front to what had been Kent's north entrance. This proposed to rebuild the north front 18 feet out and to provide in one wing a library and in the other a music room. A late eighteenth-century view of Kew by a Bishop of Salisbury[29] shows what must have been a three-storied clock tower.[30] As far as we know Chambers made no further designs for Kew. When the Court was there he attended his King weekly, but after 1774 architectural supervision was probably entrusted to Thomas Fulling, Clerk of the Works at Richmond and Kew.

[26] P. J. Grosley, *A Tour to London*, II, 1765, 117.

[27] Windsor Castle, Royal archives 55537: 'To various Journeys to Kew Viz. Feby 6th, 27th, March, 19th Apr 9th, Apr 23rd, May 7th, May 14th, June 4th, June 25th, July 5th, July 11th, July 16th, Aug 6th, Aug 13th, Aug 27th, Sept 5th, Sept 10th, Sept 25th, Octob 22nd, October 29th, Nov 7th, Dec 24th, Jan 7th 1769 (to 1770 *sic*) £9 4. 6'.

[28] PRO Works 4, Minutes and Proceedings, 14 Jan. 1767–Oct. 1772; and Oct. 1772–April 1778. On 12 March 1772 Chambers wrote to Kirby at Richmond (BM Add.MS 41133, 69) about work required by the King on the Dairy at Kew, saying 'It is His Majesty's pleasure that all her late Royal Highnesses workmen be employed in the works to be done at Kew House . . . to be in readiness'. These workmen included George Warren, carpenter and joiner of Kew, Elizabeth Hillman, plumber and glazier of Brentford, Thomas Hardwick, mason of Brentford, Francis Engleheart, plasterer of Kew, Samuel Cobb, painter of London and Shepheard's Bush, Thomas Westcott, slater of Grays Inn Lane, and Sefferin Alken, carver of Dofars Court, Broad Street.

[29] In the collection of Mr L. R. Paton of Barnes.

[30] Drawn in a ruined state by G. E. Papendick (Kew Gardens, c.1820) and described as a clock tower. This tower is referred to on 29 Jan. 1773 (PRO Works 4/15) in 'an Extra for Richmond and Kew Tower'.

Chapter 4

Country Houses

As a country-house architect Chambers is relatively unknown. He is neither remembered by splendid sequences of rooms like Adam's at Syon, nor by the astonishing range of houses that James Wyatt designed. In a measure reflecting his personality, his achievement is academically discreet rather than flamboyant. It is unfair to judge his country house output over the forty years of his practice with Adam's thirty-four years and Wyatt's forty-five, for with Somerset House the private practice that he had built up for twenty years virtually ceased. What he achieved in these two decades may be discussed under seven headings: (1) *Establishing Years 1756–60*; (2) *The Casino at Marino*; (3) *Villas*; (4) *Villa Types*; (5) *Villa Plans*; (6) *Alterations and Additions*; (7) *Milton Abbey*.

ESTABLISHING YEARS 1756–60

Few architects can have begun their career as inauspiciously as Chambers did. He had hardly settled in London when in November 1755 his friend John Hall Stevenson intervened with Edwin Lascelles to persuade him to consider Chambers's designs (Pls 43–45) for his projected new house at Harewood, the biggest plum of the year for the country house architect. This glorious opportunity ended in a momentous failure, and in June 1756 there was 100 guineas from Lascelles to sweeten the bitter pill. Although Chambers's proposals would have been very much appreciated at the French Academy in Rome, they were obviously alien to Palladian tastes in London, and especially to Lascelles's adviser, Lord Leicester of Holkham, the great patron of Kent. Chambers's plan (Pl.45) was a jumble of disparate elements, ill-grasped notions, and ingenious ideas, sacrificing domestic practicality to a few immature Grand Prix conceptions. His 'Louvre' portico would have been splendid, and his terminal pavilions, prophetic of the Dublin Casino, showed his characteristic skill in handling the small scale unit of design. The Harewood fiasco was a hard lesson which thoroughly convinced him of the need to 'establish a body of Sound Precepts' built as much as possible upon a rational basis and 'Adapted to the Customs & Fashions of our Time, to the Climate and Manners of our Country, and to the wants & Feelings of its inhabitants.'[1] To achieve this he erased all memories of the French Academy and concentrated instead upon refining the villa models of Isaac Ware and his Palladian predecessors.

After this dismal beginning, the lean year of 1756 gave way to an extremely promising future in 1757 when *Designs for Chinese Buildings* was published, ideas for a *Treatise* were

---

[1] RIBA, RA Lecture Notes, II, 4.

being collected, and the first hint of an establishing practice could be communicated to his Parisian friend Barreau de Chefdeville.[2] Barreau replied to Chambers on 5 May 1757 that he was 'enchanté de la reputation que vous vous faite en Angleterre. Il ne vous faut que ce la pour faire une grande fortune . . . il me pouvoit que vous avez beaucoup d'ouvrage un Pont de pierre des ecuries et remises pour 60 chevaux et un Casin cela laquelle bien commencer . . . Pajou et doyen vous fait mille compliments.' The Casina and the Bridge were for the Earl of Pembroke at Wilton and the stables for the Duke of Richmond at Goodwood.

Henry Herbert succeeded to the title of 10th Earl in 1749 at the age of fifteen. He made his Grand Tour between 1751 and 1755 when he may well have met Chambers in Florence if not in Rome, and was married in 1756. It was in all likelihood this succession of circumstances that inclined him in 1757 to turn to building. His embellishments were not to the great Jonesian house but to a small seventeenth-century formal garden laid out on a hill overlooking the south front. Chambers's first task was to replace the existing triumphal arch,[3] presumably a simple brick and timber structure, supporting an equestrian figure of Marcus Aurelius, with a stronger and more impressive stone arch in the Corinthian order and in a rather Gallic taste. This arch remained on the hill until 1801 when the garden fell into disuse and the 11th Earl requested James Wyatt to re-erect it as a triumphal entry (Pl.47) to the north forecourt and to add the necessary lodges. The only entirely new addition which Chambers made to the gardens at Wilton was the Casina, (Pl.46), a loggia with an order inspired by Vignola. Time has fortunately dealt mercifully with this little temple enabling it to survive in the neglected gardens. Now it has not only been restored but its vista down to the house has also been opened out again. Chambers's other works for the Earl at this time, terminating in 1762, were of a miscellaneous variety. He proposed a plain, substantial 'Saw-Mill' bridge, built the Rock Bridge down river as a cascade of two arches faced with rock-work, fitted up a library, and built a Tennis Court of timber.[4]

In contrast to the magnificence of Wilton, the 3rd Duke of Richmond's Goodwood was little more than a grand hunting lodge, and indeed that was its main function. Both Lord Burlington and Roger Morris had advised the 2nd Duke on embellishments, and if Campbell had had his way, Chambers would have found a 'Rotunda' house here. As it was he found an early eighteenth-century gabled house of modest proportions,[5] and to it added one of his grandest stable blocks (Pl.48), built of local knapped flint with stone frontispieces to the arches and a white-painted wood cornice. Needless to say the appearance of the new stables must have underlined the need for improvements to the house. While there is no evidence that Chambers attended to this, his bills[6] do refer to 'finishings' for the 'great room'. This was then the entrance hall from the garden, and is now the Large Library in the middle of the south front which forms a right angle with

[2] RIBA Letters. De Chefdeville was Lalive de Jully's architect for his celebrated neo-classic cabinet designed by Le Lorrain.

[3] Cf. Colen Campbell, *Vitruvius Britannicus*, III, 1725, pls 57–8. The equestrian figure must date to a period soon after the Restoration.

[4] For the Tennis Court q.v. Catalogue.

[5] RIBA Campbell Collection. A plan and measured elevation of the old house.

[6] Richmond Papers, West Sussex CRO, Chichester, contain only partial bills for work.

the east front of the stables. It is surely significant that we have here a villa elevation of one-three-one bays in a quietly modulated style typical of Chambers. In the Small Library and Tapestry Drawing Room there are further Chambersian touches, but as Chambers was the Duke's friend for many years, these, and indeed the south front, could have been designed in the 1760's or 1770's. The Goodwood commission turned out to be extremely profitable for it brought in its train the works at Richmond House, Whitehall, and commissions from the Duke's sisters: Lady Louisa Conolly at Castletown, Lady Sara Bunbury at Great Barton, and Emily, Duchess of Leinster at Leinster House, Dublin. Furthermore, Chambers, as tutor in architecture to the Prince of Wales, was summoned in March 1758 to do likewise for the Duke, one of the Prince's courtiers.[7]

There is some likelihood that had Chambers written to Barreau a year later he would have mentioned a front and a gallery. Chambers's work at Osterley for Francis Child is somewhat problematic owing to lack of documents. Nevertheless there is enough circumstantial evidence to establish his presence here before the appearance of Adam in 1761. Firstly, Adam's plan of 1761 indicates that by that date the front (Pl.49) and gallery had been rebuilt, and this is confirmed by a close examination of the house itself.[8] Secondly, among Adam's drawings there is a design for a Chambersian chimney-piece signed by Joseph Wilton – Chambers's friend and colleague – intended for the pre-Adam hall. And thirdly, the splendid pair of 'therm' chimney-pieces in the gallery are in Chambers's style. Lastly, there is the style of the front that relies for its effect not upon orders or sculptural embellishment, but upon the arrangement of its openings in the plain surfaces and the fine quality of the brick. Some may call it dull, it is certainly not enlivening, but it is entirely characteristic of Chambers's restraint and taste.

THE CASINO AT MARINO

Except for the King, Chambers had no patron who employed him as much and for as long a period of time as the 1st Earl of Charlemont. An Irish peer whose political aspiration was to settle in Ireland and to identify himself there with a town and country house, Charlemont was also a noted connoisseur and one of the leading characters in Reynolds's *Parody of the School of Athens*. For this genial friend Chambers altered Marino House and built the splendid Casino at Marino (Pls 50–54) and Charlemont House (Pl. 93) in Dublin. Although he made numerous additions to Marino House, including elegant gate piers supporting benign dragons[9] designed by Cipriani, and a temple-like structure built against the house in which to exhibit sculpture, these were all overshadowed by the new Casino, a large temple situated in the park.

We have already traced the pedigree of the Casino back to those Franco-Roman studies made by Chambers between 1749 and 1755. The exact date of its inception needs, however, further examination. The legend that there is a foundation plate bearing the date 1761 or 1762 has neither been proved, nor does it agree with the other evidence. As early as 1755 Charlemont was corresponding with Luigi Vanvitelli about designs,

---

[7] Richmond Papers Box 36/7, March 1758, 'Attendance on his Grace to teach him Architecture', five guineas.

[8] Visual evidence for this may be seen in unequal string courses, and the very obvious structural fact that Adam's staircase was not built coevally with the front.

[9] These dragons are still in the gardens of the college adjacent to the Casino.

but owing to the latter's exorbitant demands nothing came of them. It must therefore have been around late 1756 or 1757[10] that Charlemont approached Chambers, who by 1759 was able to publish his design as 'now erecting'. It was not until the end of his immensely successful career that Chambers had the courage to resurrect the ghost of his dismal failure at Harewood as the source of the Casino, which he described in the third edition of the *Treatise* as 'originally one of the end pavilions of a considerable composition, made soon after my return from Italy, for Edwyn Lascelles Esq.' The plan of the Harewood design (Pl.45), composed around October 1756, shows that the Casino had been intended as one of the terminations adjacent to the quadrant colonnades on the entrance front.

The Casino[11] stands within a sunken area balustraded on the north and south sides and on the east and west covered by broad sweeps of steps that arch across to the podium. At the diagonals are narrower arched bridges formed as pedestals supporting restored copies of Borghese lions *couchant*. Also of antique derivation are the exquisitely carved reliefs on the front of the pedestals. In the *Treatise* Chambers pays tribute to Simon Vierpyle, the sculptor brought back from Rome by Lord Charlemont, who he says executed the building with 'great neatness and taste'. Subtle proportions and an ingenious plan tend to make the Casino appear much smaller than it actually is – a cube of 48 feet to the columns or 40 to the walls. The plan (Fig.2) is a Greek cross encircled by a Roman Doric colonnade. From the elevation, it can also be seen or regarded as a square with columnar frontispieces pedimented on the north and south, and on the other two fronts with attic cornices, one with statues of Ceres and Bacchus, the other with Apollo and Venus.[12] Although the raised attic gives the temple the appearance of being only one storey high, in fact the balustrades at the angles disguise windows to four rooms locked together above the ground floor: Vestibule, Zodiac Room, Saloon, and Boudoir. In addition there are eight rooms in the basement.

As the building programme of the Casino was erratic, the decoration is difficult to date, and therefore great caution is necessary in using it as a barometer of his style. No drawings for any part of the decoration have survived, but presumably these would have been supplied by *c.*1760. On the whole the decoration matches Chambers's other recorded works of 1760–5: Duntish, Richmond and Pembroke Houses, and Charlemont House. Indeed, the ceiling of an upper room in Charlemont House (*c.*1764) must be by the same plasterer as, for example, the coved and coffered Saloon at Casino. On the other hand the finishing of the Vestibule is lighter and more elegant than the China Closet ceiling (Pl. 84) ornamented with baskets carrying implements of the garden and farm.

The building of the Casino was painstakingly accurate, but painfully slow owing to Chambers's supervision from London. Described as 'now erecting' in 1759, it was still far from complete in August 1767 when Chambers wrote to Charlemont reminding him 'that the pattern head and also the pattern for the cove, cornice etc. of the casino were

---

[10] Chambers was acting for Charlemont from at least 1757, for scribbled on the back of a letter (RA Papers) from John Chambers to WC dated 4 January 1757, is a note referring to the purchase at a sale (on 28 January) of architectural books by Kent, Wood, Desgodetz, Blondel, and Perrault. There is a memo 'To Mr Roper at Portland abt Ld Charlemont's lot', Portland being the port from which they would have been shipped to Dublin.

[11] I recommend Maurice Craig's account of the Casino in his excellent *The Volunteer Earl*, 1948.

[12] Statues are now on one front only, for the Apollo and Venus have disappeared.

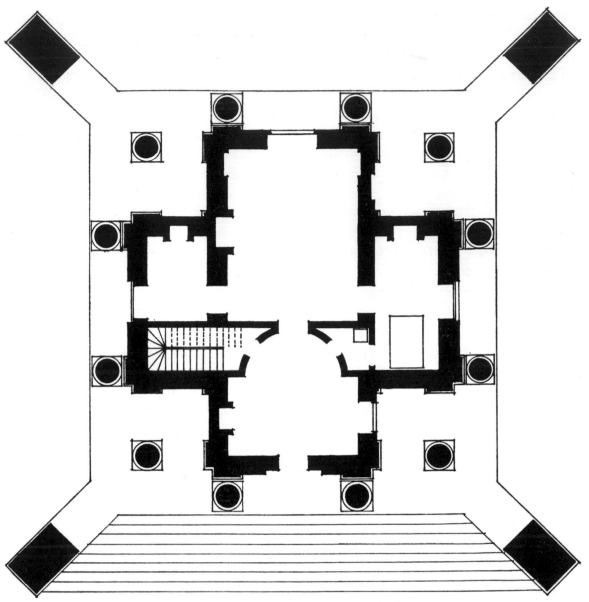

Fig.2 Casino at Marino, Dublin, Ireland

sent off a good while ago', and warning that 'the want of air always making a very considerable alteration in the colours before they arrive in Dublin.'[13] Only in 1768 was it
decided that 'the top of the Casino may be flatt'[14] to make a 'pleasant gazebo', and the
statues and chimney vases were still not in position in 1771. Chambers's instructions for
their placement bear witness to his devoted concern for the perfection of this building.
Accompanying his designs for the chimney vases were detailed directions for them to be

[13] HMC Charlemont, I, 283 (WC to Charlemont 25 August 1767).
[14] HMC Charlemont, I, 286 (WC to Charlemont 15 April 1768).

'drawn correctly on board to the full size, then cut out, and put in the place, by which means you will be able to judge of the proportions.' And with regard to the statues came a brief statement that 'they are proportioned to the columns, and cannot be made less; their heads now reach to the underside of the attic cornice and they will when seen from below, particularly if the spectator be near, appear higher than the attic, but that will have no bad effect.'[15] Charlemont must have been as much a perfectionist as Chambers to have spent his time and money so willingly. It is often said that the Casino cost him £60,000. Although this is rather exaggerated, his building activities here and at Charlemont House did in fact strain his finances to the limit. For all the expense and delay Charlemont was repaid with a perfect gem which he was able to fill with the treasures of his connoisseurship and to enjoy for more than a quarter of a century. Oddly enough the Casino, one of Chambers's first country houses, was also the last to be completed before he abandoned this branch of his practice to devote himself to Somerset House. We must therefore return again to 1760 to examine the most satisfactory phase of Chambers's architectural development, namely his preoccupation with the English villa.

VILLAS

Today the term 'villa' generally denotes a small suburban house with picturesque connotations – a moderate-sized garden, barge-boards, and twisted brick chimney-pots. This, however, is a far cry from the first use of the words by Palladio whose *Casa di Villa* was a country house surrounded by the estate or farm; and a long way too from the Imperial Roman buildings in vast country parks described in 1728 by Castell in his *Villas of the Ancients*. But surprisingly enough the past and present notions of the villa have at least one point in common – a suburban situation on the outskirts of the city. It was only in the early eighteenth century, and in England, that the term 'villa' came to mean a moderate-sized house, usually the secondary country seat of a nobleman, and more often than not situated in the environs of London. When Colen Campbell surveyed the Thames from the Claremont Belvedere c.1724 he could remark upon the 'adjacent villas';[16] when Sir John Clerk of Penicuik spoke of Lord Burlington's new house at Chiswick in 1727 he called it a 'villa';[17] and when James Gibbs presented his designs for Whitton Park and Sudbrooke House in 1728 he described them in italics as *villas*.[18] We know that what these gentlemen saw were small rather than great houses, proliferating in the Thames Valley. Size, however, is not the only common denominator. The most important characters too are their Palladian style and the articulation of their main front into a pattern of 1-3-1 windows. Villa development may be divided into two phases, the first initiated and popularized by Colen Campbell well before 1730, and the second around the middle of the century led by Ware and Taylor. Chambers, entering the field in 1760, synthesized the best of the earlier efforts to create what may be regarded as the

[15] HMC Charlemont, I, 304 (WC to Charlemont 30 Jan. 1771).
[16] Campbell, op. cit., 8.
[17] John Fleming, *Robert Adam and his Circle*, 1962, 26.
[18] James Gibbs, *A Book of Architecture*, 1728, xi, xvi.

ultimate and ideal in villa design before the picturesque transformations.[19] The death of Lady Bessborough in January 1760 provided Chambers with the opportunity to begin his highly successful refinement of earlier villa models. Lord Bessborough, grieved by his loss, decided to move from Ingress Abbey in Kent – a house later altered by Chambers for John Calcraft – to an estate called Parksted at Roehampton. Nothing could have better suited his retirement amidst his collection of antique sculptures and *virtu* than a villa. He was not far from Chiswick, his father-in-law, the 4th Duke of Devonshire's villa, where Lord Burlington's collection could then still be seen. Parksted was probably planned late in 1760 for ceiling designs are dated 1761. By the end of September 1762 it could be described as 'not yet covered in', and sometime soon after 1768 finishing works had still to be done. The front (Pls 55, 57 and Fig.3c) with its striking hexastyle portico raised upon a high perron, can be seen both as a paraphrase of the Villa Rotonda and a derivative from Foots Cray (Pl.56) in Kent, itself a Rotunda said to have been designed by its owner Bouchier Cleeve. The success of Parksted lies in the eliding of elements and refining and chiselling of Foots Cray's heavier forms. Parksted has a front 76 feet wide, Foots Cray's front less the projecting porticoes was 70 feet. As Foots Cray was published only in 1767, in the fourth volume of *Vitruvius Britannicus*, it must have been seen and recorded by Chambers in the course of a tour of new houses in the environs of London, a tour that would have been essential to any young establishing architect hoping to entice the *beau monde* with his designs.

Having visited Foots Cray he would not have failed to see nearby Danson Park, a villa that had been built *c*.1759 by Sir Robert Taylor for John Boyd, but for which Chambers was later to supply interior decorations (Pl.184), and to design a Palladio Bridge and a temple in the park. Just as Foots Cray supplied the ingredients for Parksted, so Danson contributed its share to Duntish (Pl.60 and Fig.3a) (then called Castle Hill), Walter Fitz-Foy's Dorset seat, said to have been built 'about 1760' and destroyed, quite unnecessarily, in 1965. Fitz-Foy is a mysterious figure of whom little is known, let alone how he came to commission Chambers. To be precise about the source for the three-bay centre-piece of this house we must go beyond Danson to Campbell's Stourhead, one of the key villa models of the first generation Palladians. Like Danson, Duntish was astylar, and was a villa with wings, the wings being detached and set on a lateral axis. It was also a villa of remarkably high quality with finely chiselled ceilings and Wilton-styled chimney-pieces in almost every room.

The next episode in the villa sequence is an undocumented and unexecuted project (Pl.61) for John Lewis at Llanaeron, a patron who remains even more obscure than Fitz-Foy. This design can be dated stylistically in the early 1760s and compared with another Campbell villa, Newby. Chambers's adaptation of Newby involved several significant changes. Not only did he transform its attached portico into a free-standing one but, even more important, he also eliminated the basement and covered the stylobate under the portico. These last two steps herald the appearance of the temple-form of villa that was to reach its maturity at Duddingstone (Pl.62 and Fig.4) designed for the Earl

[19] Sir John Summerson, 'The Classical Country House in 18th-c. England', *J. Roy. Soc. Arts*, July 1959, to which article I am heavily indebted for this introductory villa statement.

46

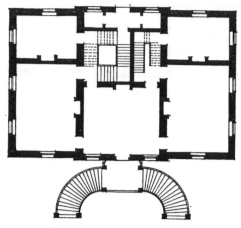

Fig.3a Duntish Court, Dorset

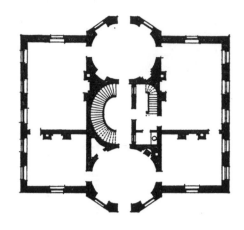

Fig.3b Hedsor, Buckinghamshire

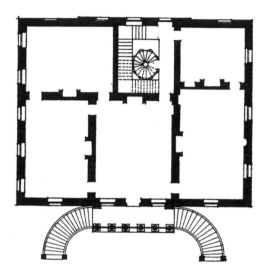

Fig.3c Parksted, Roehampton, London

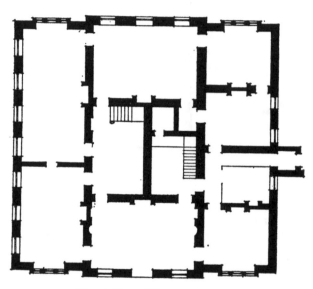

Fig.3d Peper Harow, Surrey

of Abercorn in the summer of 1762. Duddingstone, with its giant portico raised on a single step and its windows opening to the ground, is in essence a temple blown up to a villa. This ingenious fusion of forms initiated by Chambers, and attempted a year later by Adam in his alterations to the front of Shardeloes,[20] constitutes a major step in the history of the European house.

Parksted, Duntish, Llanaeron, and Duddingstone, all conceived between 1760 and 1762, are in effect the rapid and complete development of a single theme. There was only

[20] The almost identical portico at Shardeloes, Buckinghamshire, has sometimes been pointed out as a precursor of the Duddingstone one, as the house was begun in 1758. However, it is quite clear from accounts in the Bucks CRO, Aylesbury, and Adam's designs in the RIBA, that Stiff Leadbetter supplied designs for a house, with perhaps four towers, in 1758, and he was superseded by Adam c.1760. Adam did not project his portico until 1763 and it was built in 1764. It is almost certain that Adam would hardly have failed to look at Duddingstone on his own home ground.

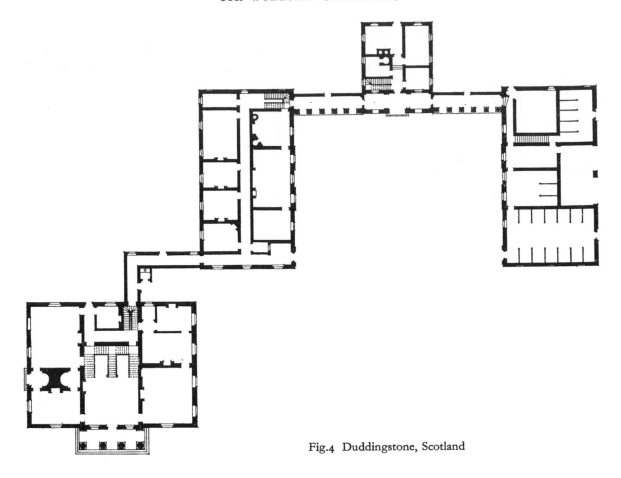

Fig.4 Duddingstone, Scotland

one other occasion on which Chambers returned to the English Palladian villa – that was at Peper Harow (Pl.59 and Fig.3d) designed for the 3rd Viscount Midleton in 1765. The architectural history of this Surrey house is exceedingly complex. Although Chambers was supplying Midleton with designs for chimney-pieces as early as 1760 and 1761, it is not clear whether these were intended for Peper Harow or for a London house. In 1762 he designed the quadrangular stables, whereupon Lord Midleton decided to rebuild the old house as well. Designs[21] were requested from both Capability Brown, then employed on the park, and his rival Chambers, who proposed a nine-bay, two-storey front with a widely-spaced, attached Ionic portico. For some reason neither of the projects appealed to Lord Midleton and in 1765 he decided to make a clean sweep of the old house and to build a villa on a new site close to the stables. Chambers's designs though approved on 11 March 1765 may well have been conceived around 1762 when he was fully engrossed in the Palladian villa. The main front of Peper Harow is based upon Ware's Wrotham Park (Pl.58) from which he abstracted the octagonal cupola, the portico, and most of the basement. Owing to the death of Lord Midleton a few months after the house was begun, the interiors may not have been completed until the maturity of his son in 1775.

21 Both Chambers's and Brown's designs are in the Richardson Collection at Ampthill.

VILLA TYPES

The smaller country houses designed by Chambers after 1765 are villas only by implication. They no longer follow Palladian or neo-Palladian prototypes, and while a few of their façades may be articulated in the villa pattern the majority have little in common with the villa apart from their small, compact size. Although there were not many of these miscellaneous commissions, and they do not greatly enrich our knowledge of Chambers, there are, nevertheless, a few that are interesting enough to merit brief discussion.

In the Victoria and Albert Museum is a drawing (Pl.63) of a villa loosely modelled upon Palladio's *Quatto Libri* project for a Villa *Gaozadore*, and is inscribed 'Franks', undoubtedly Moses Franks whose house at Teddington has long since disappeared. Although we know that Chambers did in fact build his friend a house on the banks of the Thames, a deliberate evocation perhaps of one of the villas on the Brenta, to judge from Loudon's description of Teddington in 1839 it was not the Victoria and Albert design, but another one that was executed. Among the few surviving documents are payments of £160 to Chambers in 1766, and further payments in 1767 for visits to Teddington and for designs for the Greenhouse and Temple. When Chambers visited the house in 1769 the work was completed and only the bills remained to be paid. Five years later in 1774 he was still pressing Franks for payment. The eventual settlement brought a warm reply typical of Chambers's generosity: 'Nothing is more affecting than the loss of an old friend, so nothing is more pleasant than the recovery of one supposed to be lost.'[22]

Our knowledge of what Chambers achieved at Teddington is based solely upon Loudon's description[23] of the house as a 'square mass, completely isolated, without the appearance of offices of any kind, and with nothing in it, or about it, not even a servant's window in the basement which requires to be concealed. We could fancy it a temple in a wood', aided by the 'temple-like effect' of a portico projecting from the lawn front to a double flight of steps. The beauty of the gardens was also admired by Loudon 'for though scarcely any variety of surface naturally, yet they have been hollowed out in some place and raised in others, so as now to indicate some beautiful inequalities, greatly heightened by the manner in which the trees and shrubs are disposed on them' – principles that Chambers had, of course, embodied at Kew.

The founding of the Royal Academy in 1768 and his appointment in 1769 as Comptroller of the Works in succession to Flitcroft meant an increasing involvement in London and a slackening of the country house practice. For the commissions he did accept after 1770 he was often content to provide the designs and relegate the execution to trusted pupils like John Yenn and Edward Stevens. One of these exceptional commissions was Partille Slot, a villa (Pl.73) on the outskirts of Gothenburg designed in 1770 for his brother-in-law David Sandberg, but only built from 1775 by C. W. Carlberg. Although all of Chambers's subtleties were lost in Carlberg's interpretation, and despite later alterations, Partille Slot is still immediately recognizable as a red-brick English villa in the Swedish countryside.

[22] BM Add.MS 41136, 4.
[23] J. C. Loudon, *The Gardener's Magazine*, 1839, 424–6.

E

Chambers's withdrawal from the country house round after 1770 was as much a matter of choice as necessity, for he was, after all, approaching fifty, and was, as he wrote to Vesey in 1774, 'heartily tired' of the profession. Of course at the time he had not the slightest idea of what the future and Somerset House had in store for him. This monumental task severed his career in exactly two parts, killing what remained of his country house practice and, after nagging him for twenty years, virtually killing him as well. It is not surprising, therefore, that time and inclination allowed him to design only two more houses – Trent and Hedsor – villas that depart from the Palladian mould to concentrate on what Middleton called 'Elegance, compactness and convenience'[24] on the Enfield Chase in 1777.

The first one, Trent Place (Pl.74), was built for Chambers's friend Sir Richard Jebb. Topographical views of the house in the early nineteenth century – long after Jebb had died – bear no resemblance to the 'elegant villa in imitation of an Italian loggia' described and admired by the compiler of the *Ambulator* in 1811.[25] The description fortunately complements a drawing in the Soane Museum made by Willey Reveley before 1783 and inscribed 'Sketch of a lodge on Enfield Chase altered by Sir W Chambers for Sir R Jebb.' The inscription suggests that Chambers merely rebuilt an existing hunting or keeper's lodge. Here, in contrast to the staidness of his normal elevational compositions, the paired giant Ionic order framing a central bay, the domed Music Room, and the termination ornaments, add up to a little neo-classic essay spiced with memories of what he had seen in the *cahiers* of Neufforge's books.

Unlike Trent, Hedsor had a rather conventional elevation. Before its rebuilding it was 'an old stragling low house upon the side of the hill'[26] which Chambers remembered as one of the royal lodgings of nearby Clivedon that came under his jurisdiction at the outset of his career when he was architect to the Dowager Princess Augusta. It was bought by the 1st Baron Boston in 1764 and was finally rebuilt by his son in 1778. Mrs Lybbe Powys, seeing it in July 1780 just after it had been completed, thought it 'not to be styled large or magnificent', but nevertheless, 'altogether the most elegant one I've seen for a vast while . . . my lady's dressing room octagon, the corners fitted up with the cleverest wardrobes in inlaid woods'. Apart from her description we have only a few floor plans inscribed for Lord Boston and a view published by Farington in 1793. Farington shows that it was built on a new site on the summit of the hill, and it was undoubtedly for the magnificent view that the villa was raised to four storeys. Apart from their unusual height, the brick elevations have no remarkable features. They are typically chaste and restrained with pedimented three bays to the river and with canted bays on the secondary fronts. The plan (Fig.3b) with its fluid arrangement of oval and octagonal rooms, and a staircase contained in a half-oval, is really the most interesting aspect of the design, a major departure in Chambers's planning, and perhaps not uninfluenced by the fluidly-planned villas[27] of Sir Robert Taylor.

The new ideas incorporated in the elevation of Trent and the plan of Hedsor may well

[24] Charles Middleton, *Picturesque and Architectural Views for Cottages . . .*, 1793.
[25] *The Ambulator . . . For The Tour of London and Its Environs*, 1811, 255.
[26] RIBA Chambers Msc. MSS.
[27] A small group of his plans in the Windsor portfolios reflect these spatial, Taylorian interests (cf. Fig.5b).

be the result of a refreshing visit to Paris in 1774. Indeed this might have been an exciting turning point in Chambers's country house style were it not thoroughly frustrated by Somerset House. It is a pity and a blessing that Chambers should end his career as a country house architect with the promising notes of Trent and Hedsor.

VILLA PLANS

The variety in planning that so occupied Adam had surprisingly little or no interest for Chambers. He never explored antique sources, nor in fact did he look any further than Palladio, *Vitruvius Britannicus*, or perhaps a few English Palladian villas of the 1750s. It may be said that his clear, straightforward arrangement of rectangular compartments are an appropriate corollary to the unassuming character of his façades.

The villa plans fall roughly into two categories, the first at Parksted (Fig.3c) and Duntish (Fig.3a) has three compartments in length and two in depth with the staircase in the middle on the back front. Peper Harow (Fig.3d) is of the second type where the rooms surround the centrally-placed stairwell. In the case of Parksted and Duntish the source is Campbell's Chester Le Street or Morris's Marble Hill. Stourhead, another Campbell villa, provided the plan type for Peper Harow.

If the plans are stereotyped, the staircases are always varied, but are never so complex or inventive as those in the grand town houses. In Duntish and Peper Harow the principal and servants' stairs were placed in adjacent compartments. With the one at Duntish the principal ascended around four sides of a well, and at Peper Harow rises in two elegant flights at right angles. Parksted was something of a speciality, for here Chambers borrowed Webb's ingenious idea at Amesbury (1662) of combining two stairs in such a way that the oblong well contained the principal stair enclosing an octagonal timber-framed stair for the servants. Duddingstone (Fig.4) is not only one of the better of Chambers's villas, but also the only one with a staircase comparable to the parade ones in town houses. The stair (Pl.86), of the 'Imperial' type, is entirely open to the hall and rises by a single central flight, turning to right and left by short flights, and then returning back upon itself to narrow balconied landings. One thinks instinctively of Ware's fashionable staircase in Chesterfield House, and the more so as the one surviving preliminary design[28] for Duddingstone shows that Chambers first proposed to contain the stairs behind a screen of columns, as did Ware. Just as the elevation of Duddingstone is focused on the novel portico so the plan is dominated by the remarkably generous stairs. Indeed, they consume the greater part of the interior, leaving the bachelor Earl of Abercorn with only three reception rooms, two of which, the Dining Room and the Saloon, are separated by apsed communicating lobbies, of the York House type. cf. Fig. 6.

Naturally a few of Chambers's villas and country houses have disappeared without record of their plans. In the case of Trent or Teddington this is probably no great loss, for neither could hardly have possessed rooms and staircases of exceptional ingenuity. Nevertheless, the Hedsor plan and two unexecuted projects (Figs. 5a and 5c) prove that Chambers could be every bit as inventive as Adam. The first of the projected villas is a remarkable columnar exercise (Fig.5a) that is surely related to Le Geay's fantastic cathedral

[28] Soane Museum 43/4[24-25]. The Duddingstone staircase was altered in the nineteenth century when the upper landings were shifted and an open gallery above the first landing was filled in.

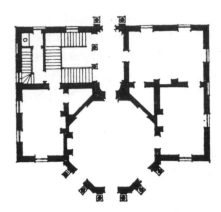

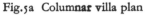

Fig.5a Columnar villa plan

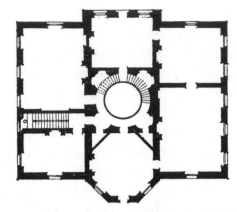

Fig.5b Plan of a villa, possibly for Hedsor, Buckinghamshire

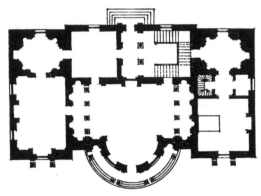

Fig.5c Roxborough, Ireland

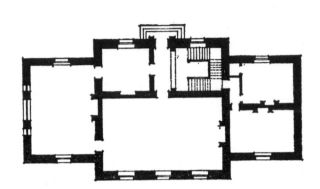

Fig.5d Roxborough, Ireland

plan. Here we find Chambers virtually obsessed with columns as wall articulation as well as porticoes. The result is a plan of movement. Although one is inclined to consider this a theoretical experiment of the Roman period of the 1750's, it could also have been intended for Lord Charlemont's unexecuted hunting lodge (Pl.69), for which there is an inscribed plan of about 1768 (Fig.5c) uniting the columnar and compartmented styles. In this plan Chambers combines square, oblong, and oval rooms with a magnificent saloon, screened at both ends and projecting into an ample semi-circular bay, which is in turn surrounded by a columned portico. Eventually, cost obliged him to reduce this plan to a simpler form (Fig.5d).

In dealing with stables and offices Chambers generally adhered to Palladian precedent, placing the block or blocks in formal relationship to the house, or, as at Peper Harow, banishing it some distance away.

Whenever offices were to be seen in visual relationship to a house, Chambers took great care in siting and proportioning them. At Duddingstone and Parksted so important did he consider this relationship that both achieved notoriety of excellence. At Duddingstone the stables (Fig.4) are arranged around three sides of a courtyard,[29] linked to the rear

[29] Shardeloes must again be mentioned in relationship to Duddingstone. Its stables *did* predate Chambers's ones, having been proposed by Adam in 1760. Although Adam's plan and linkage are similar, his buildings are rather long and low and exceedingly poor in detailing and composition.

angle of the villa. The two flanking or facing ranges are joined by a colonnaded range broken in its centre by a higher porticoed temple feature. Seen from across the park the two temple compositions were locked together in an indivisible architectural whole. At Parksted, Chambers's first villa, the temple idea was also dominant. Here, however, the problems posed by the site were solved in a very different way. As Lord Bessborough possessed a garden rather than a park, adjacent to Richmond Park, Chambers placed his villa so that it resembled a temple in a grove of trees, to be seen as such from across the open fields of the royal grazings. For this reason only the porticoed front of the villa was stone-faced. As there was no room to hide the stables, Chambers brought them into two low wings joined to the back of the villa and facing each other across a courtyard. They were therefore part of the villa yet quite invisible from the park.

ALTERATIONS AND ADDITIONS 1760–75

Documentation of Chambers's country house practice begins with drawings and bills for the period 1760 to 1769 and is then immensely enriched by the four Letter Books in the British Museum, which calendar both his work and his personal correspondence from December 1769 until late in 1775. Apart from the villas (and the Casino at Marino) which have already been accounted for, and Milton Abbey, a special case that will be treated separately, there are in the whole of the period 1760–75 only two complete country houses, Styche and Walcot, which could hardly be described as distinguished. These Shropshire houses, both belonging to Clive of India, were rebuilt in 1762 and 1763 respectively. Though the mediocrity of Clive's early commissions is underlined by the grandeur of Claremont, built for him by Brown in 1768, it must be remembered that they were distinctly secondary seats of a rather decayed family who were just beginning to re-establish themselves as country landowners.

Not only was Styche hardly lived in by Clive, but it was also considerably altered in a rebuilding of 1796 when canted bays were added to its simple brick elevations. The best that remains there is the stable range executed in a traditional style from a design now in the Victoria and Albert Museum. The principal London craftsmen mentioned in the Styche accounts are William Wilton the ornamental plasterer, his son Joseph who supplied chimney-pieces, and his assistant and former apprentice, Thomas Collins. Joseph Wilton was also employed at Walcot in company with a more distinguished group of craftsmen including the mason Sefferin Alken, the joiner Benjamin Thacker, John Gilliam (later employed at Somerset House) who executed chimney-pieces, and the sculptor Richard Hayward who supplied amongst other things two pairs of Volterra Vases. The choice of such first-class craftsmen is in character with Walcot's more sophisticated brick elevations, long and low in outline, possibly defining the old house, and accentuated only by a fine single-storey Doric portico.

Walcot and Styche belong to an unusually brisk period of country house design before 1765 that includes Kew and the villas as well as a host of miscellaneous alterations. Dedicated engravings published in the *Treatise* in 1759 swell the list of designs, but are not necessarily marks of patronage. Henry Willoughby's temple, John Ward's gateway, or Sir Thomas Kennedy's Banqueting Room were all unfulfilled hopes. There are also a few designs for friends Chambers met on the Grand Tour. Lord Bruce was probably one of these, and so indeed were Lord Charlemont and Lord Pembroke. Some, if not most of these dedicated plates may well have been intended for the proposed book of designs advertised in 1757. One suspects that The Hoo in Hertfordshire comes into this category. Whether Thomas Brand of The Hoo, like his cousin Thomas Brand of The Hyde, actually met Chambers in Italy is not known. Nevertheless, it seems fairly certain that work on The Hoo must have begun soon after 1759, for in July 1764 we find Brand writing to Chambers about an already completed gate and about the cost of building a mosque like the one at Kew. Although The Hoo has been demolished, the fascinating history of its building is fortunately chronicled in a portfolio of designs, volume four of *Vitruvius Britannicus* (1769), topographical views, and a few fragments of the house itself. Included in the portfolio are designs for a single-arched bridge, which was engraved in 1769; a sketch drawn in 1766 by S. Dawson showing the lake with the bridge as well as a nearby boathouse; and numerous studies in Chambers's hand for ceilings, gate-piers, handsome library bookcases, and, most surprising of all, for an octagonal gothic castellated dairy and tea room combined, intended as an appendage to one angle of the house. Even more surprising is a design in Sir John Soane's Museum for a chimney-piece supporting a most extraordinary overmantel with broken scrolled pediment in, of all things, a pseudo-Caroline style. This is thoroughly unlike Chambers and may be hard to believe, but the design is certainly in his hand, and is in fact inscribed by him as having been executed by 'Thacker and the carving very well done by Alken.' It was not therefore a whimsical exercise nor was it a singular one, for among the surviving fragments of the interior of the house is another chimney-piece in the same style. Here (Pl.188) the overmantel not only has a broken scrolled pediment, but is also framed by short half-pilasters lugged at the top and scrolled at the base – a characteristic motif of the phase of mid-seventeenth-century architecture that is known as Artisan Mannerism and flourished in the Home Counties, particularly in Hertfordshire. The Hoo, in fact, was one of these Artisan Manner-ist houses which in spite of considerable alterations in the eighteenth and nineteenth centuries retained a few original doorcases in that style.[30] This, of course, explains Chambers's unusual departure as a deliberate associational effort.

Among Chambers's drawings in the Metropolitan Museum is an elegant design for a pier glass inscribed 'for Adderbury', an Oxfordshire house bought in 1766 by the 3rd Duke of Buccleuch, who was also employing Chambers at 20 Grosvenor Square. Unfortunately few documents relating to this phase of Adderbury's alterations have survived. Surely the 'great things' seen here by Lady Mary Coke in June 1768 must refer to Chambers's buildings as well as to Capability Brown's landscaping. The architectural history of this fascinating house is partially illuminated by the Dalkeith archives which reveal that the early eighteenth-century house, variously attributed to Gibbs or Vanbrugh, was given an external gallery by Roger Morris, architect to its previous owner, the 3rd Duke of Argyll, and that Chambers proposed a 'Front of the intended Addition' (Pl.72). If only there were proof that this 'Addition', a saloon or banqueting room, was executed! It is a superb design, a credit to a Sangallo, and its nobility is accentuated by the all-over rustication surrounding the few windows and the crisply shadowed details.

[30] Photographs of the doorcases are to be found in the National Monuments Record.

In contrast to what may have been a considerable external addition to Adderbury, Chambers's work at Cobham for the 3rd Earl of Darnley was primarily concerned with minor, although interesting, alterations. The accounts record his visits to the great Eliza-bethan house between 1768 and 1770, which, being just after Darnley's marriage, was an appropriate moment to bring parts of the rambling mansion up-to-date. Although extensive alterations and restorations carried out by James Wyatt and the Reptons have obliterated most of Chambers's contributions, his designs in the 'Cobham Portfolio' in the School of Architecture in the University of Cambridge provide a glimpse of what he accomplished. We know for certain that he provided the attic to Peter Mills's Restor-ation west front of the cross wing. He sashed the south wing and provided it with a canted bow to a library (adjacent to a new staircase) at its west end. Eastwards of the cross wing the north wing was continued by a lower office and kitchen range. If this were, in fact, designed by Chambers, then he was responsible for its curious hooded doorway in a 'Decorated' style.

In 1761, while still engaged at The Hoo, he was commissioned by the other Thomas Brand to design a new hall and staircase for The Hyde in Essex, a pleasant red-brick house built around 1700. Like his cousin at The Hoo, Brand of The Hyde was a noted connois-seur whose collection of ancient marbles later formed the nucleus of John Disney's well-known *Museum Disneianum*.[31] This collection was amassed by Brand between 1748 and 1753 on his travels through Europe with Thomas Hollis who, on Brand's death in 1794, changed his name to Brand-Hollis. Chambers's task at The Hyde was to create a suitable setting for the display of these marbles, and to accomplish this he transformed the hall into a kind of sculpture gallery. He threw two storeys and five bays of the old fabric into one enormous space and on the inner wall opened out four bays in which he placed the staircase screened by two storeys of superimposed columns (Pl.91).

The Hoo and The Hyde are exceptionally well documented by drawings, engravings, and letters – the kind of records one would like to have of all Chambers's works. Unfortu-nately, however, there are several tantalizing references to commissions in the 1760s for which we have but the vaguest information. What, for example, did Chambers design for the politician John Calcraft at Ingress Abbey after 1760 that could have been described in 1772 as 'work of a long standing'? Brayley mentions the temple (now at Cobham Hall, Kent) on the cliffs overlooking the Thames where Calcraft housed a collection of Roman altars. Was Lord Digby's Doric Gate (Pl.79) ever built at Sherborne and what could have prompted Chambers to place Egyptian figures in its niches? Did Lord Grantham commission Chambers to redecorate Newby Park as shown by the section (Pl.75) and to design the Pheasantry (Pls. 76–77). Or later in the sixties the nature of the work for Viscount Barrington at Beckett Park in 1766 and for Lord Torrington at Southill in 1768 is equally mysterious. The very fact that nothing can be discovered about these mid-1760s projects might, of course, indicate that they were either unimportant or unexecuted. Furthermore his involvement with Kew and the villas at the beginning of the decade could not have left much time for miscellaneous country house work. The Hoo certainly repre-sents his major country house alteration at the beginning of the decade, whereas, as we

[31] John Disney, *Museum Disneianum* ... 1849.

have seen, Adderbury and Cobham were possibly the outstanding commissions of the second half.

As there was so much later restoration to Cobham it is best to suspend judgement on it. Although a visit was billed for 1770 there is no mention of it in the Letter Books which begin late in 1769, a date that can be described as a turning point in the historiography of Chambers's career. In contrast to the many insoluble problems posed by the lack of documentation for the decade of the sixties, the seventies emerge with unparalleled clarity. Thanks to the compiling of the Letter Books by Chambers and his clerk, our knowledge of Blenheim Palace, Milton Park, Milton Abbey, Woburn, and Ampthill is immeasurably enriched.

Exactly when Chambers appeared upon the Blenheim scene is not known. In 1765, Capability Brown had designed Gothic stables, but in the following year it was Chambers, not Brown, who received the commission for Woodstock Town Hall (Pl.141), a building paid for by the Duke of Marlborough. This was probably the prologue of Chambers's extensive works on the Palace and park, the bulk of which was completed by December 1769. In the four years he built the Temple to Flora; laid out the Flower Garden with a Temple to Diana and a neo-classic tripod (Pl.193), one of his most beautiful smaller designs, sculpted by Wilton; ornamented the main courtyard with pedestals tricked out with neo-classic motifs; and nearly completed Bladon Bridge. In addition he may also have decorated rooms on the south front. Between 1770 and 1774 work came, according to the Letter Books, in a somewhat slower but continuous stream. Vanbrugh's East Gate was discreetly ornamented; Bernini's reputed *modello* for the Piazza Navona obelisk was set up near a cascade above Bladon Bridge; and furnishings were being supplied to the palace interiors. Despite catastrophic sales in the nineteenth century, Blenheim is still the only country house to retain furniture designed by Chambers. The Grand Cabinet contains his pier glasses and tables – in Frenchified form – and in an upstairs room is the handsome, albeit dismantled, State Bed (Pl.183) made by a cabinet-maker named Ansell.

The respect and discretion exercised by Chambers in his additions to Vanbrugh's great baroque house are echoed in his work at Milton in Northamptonshire, a sixteenth-century house that had been partially rebuilt in the Palladian style by Henry Flitcroft. It was probably through his wife, Lady Charlotte Ponsonby, the daughter of Lord Bessborough of Roehampton, that the 4th Earl Fitzwilliam came to employ Chambers.

Neither the interior nor the exterior of Milton required drastic alteration. All that was done either to Fitzwilliam's desire or Chambers's suggestion was a re-ordering of the attic floor that resulted in the handsome attic windows, and the completion of a decorative scheme initiated by Flitcroft. Chambers's rooms, a suite on the first floor of the Palladian front and a Dining Room (Pl.87) on the ground floor below, are quiet and reserved in style, with fine but unassuming ceilings. The exception is the Great Gallery (Pl.89), a tripartite composition which Flitcroft had left as an unceiled space, and for which Chambers was given unlimited funds and complete artistic freedom to transform into an eminently successful room, shallow domed in the centre and barrel-vaulted across the ends. Turning a blind eye to the strictures of academic rules, he indulged in banded ceilings reminiscent of Borromini and in half-pilasters tucked into the angles of the walls, a practice which he himself had condemned in the *Treatise*. These contradictions to his solid academic reputation are no more surprising than the Egyptian figures in the Sherborne Castle gate, or his Artisan Mannerist chimney-pieces at The Hoo, or the Venetian confection of the State Coach, or, for that matter, the Swedish love songs he sang at Royal Academy dinners and the pornographic asides in his official as well as private correspondence.

Like Parksted and Milton, Blenheim and Woburn were linked by family relationships, in the latter case by the marriage of Caroline daughter of the 4th Duke of Bedford to the 4th Duke of Marlborough. Even before the matrimonial link the two families had, however, patronized the same architects. Stiff Leadbetter worked for the 3rd Duke of Marlborough at Langley Park in 1755 and at Marlborough House for the 4th Duke before 1766, and for the Duke of Bedford had prepared a design for rebuilding the south wing of Woburn Abbey in September 1765.[32] In July 1766, a month before his death, Leadbetter was still discussing the wing 'in danger of falling' with the Duke. It was almost certainly as a result of Leadbetter's death that Chambers was employed at both Marlborough House and Woburn, and he was bidden to the latter place in October 1767 'to consult . . . about the Rebuilding one of the Wings.'

Chambers's first and main task at Woburn was to rebuild the wing, complete by 1770 when he wrote in his *Autobiographical Note* that he had built a 'front and parade apartments' there. The correspondence reveals that from that date until the Duke's death in September 1772 he was building a bridge (Pl.80) in the park and finishing decorations in the Library and Dining Room. His 'parade apartments' must have been in the south wing, later gutted by Henry Holland. In view of the evidence above quoted, the habitual attribution of the south front (Pl.71) to Holland who created the apartments there in 1787 must be rescinded. Chambers's front was altered and adapted by Holland when he raised the ground to bring his *piano nobile* level with a new terrace. In fact to this day the thirteen-bay, two-storey expanse suffers from a monotony of repetitive motifs that is one of the flaws of Chambers's style.[33] The double-bay breaks at each end may be by Chambers, but their pedimented windows set in recessed arches are distinctly non-Chambersian motifs and were produced by Holland to give the front a little more vitality and movement. Although Holland's patron, the 5th Duke, was sufficiently stimulated by the building activities of his friend the Prince of Wales at Carlton House and was certainly extravagant enough to consider rebuilding the wing again, he did not. Nevertheless, when he replaced Chambers's Library (in the south-west tower) with the present Canaletto Room he had no qualms about destroying the new and expensive ceiling (Pl.90) painted by Cipriani and Biagio Rebecca for the considerable sum of £597, far more than was spent on any of the ceilings in the Queen's House.

Chambers's work at Woburn in the late 1760s and early 1770s was exactly contemporary with his employment by the Earl of Upper Ossory at Ampthill Park seven miles away – a fortunate coincidence which enabled him to use the same craftsmen and the same clerk of works, John Rentham, at both houses. Before Chambers arrived on the scene Ampthill was a large late seventeenth-century house similar in style to Uppark or Ramsbury. His task was to extend it by the addition of lateral flanking pavilions linked to the main block by

[32] V & A 7076, 11, from Chambers's portfolios there.

[33] For example, his project for a new Queen's House (Buckingham House) among his drawings in the Royal Library, Windsor Castle.

low corridors (Pl.68), and completely to redecorate the old interiors. Although Ampthill was stuccoed in the nineteenth century, there is enough exposed brickwork to demonstrate Chambers's painstaking attention to the matching of materials. Inside he was able to assert his own taste in a fine gallery (in one wing) reminiscent of those in Pembroke and Richmond Houses, and in a series of fine ceilings plastered by Joseph Rose. Alas, his chimney-pieces and staircase were replaced by mediocre ones in the nineteenth century.

MILTON ABBEY

Whilst Ampthill and Woburn were building, Chambers obtained the commission to rebuild Milton Abbey, a contract he regretted ever having accepted, in spite of the fact that it was his one opportunity to design a big country house. It is ironic that the largest country house by the leader of academic classicism in England should have been a neo-Gothic one. Although Chambers undoubtedly built Milton Abbey from the foundations up, did he in fact design it? There is good reason to believe that the Gothic pile was not his idea, but the child of its owner Baron Milton, and his first architect John Vardy. When Lord Milton bought the Abbey in 1752 it comprised the great Abbey Church – truncated of the nave west of the crossing – and north of that the partly medieval Abbot's Lodgings ranged around a courtyard. The architectural situation[34] before Chambers was summoned in 1769 is plainly recorded by Hutchins, the historian of Dorset; by Pococke the traveller; and by evidence in the Milton Abbey Collection at the Royal Institute of British Architects. Hutchins, who was vicar of Milton Abbas at the time, tells us that Joseph Bancks, the previous owner, began to rebuild the southern end of the west range before his death in 1737, and that this work was completed by Lord Milton. Pococke, visiting the house in October 1754, noted that 'Lord Milton is casing it all round in a beautiful modern taste', and finally there is in the Royal Institute of British Architects a 'Section Intended for the Great Room one pair of stairs at Milton Abbey' signed by Vardy and dated 1755.

Apart from completing the encasing begun by Bancks – presumably in the classical style – Lord Milton seems to have been in no particular hurry radically to improve his new estate. The first hints of what was to come were the appearance of Brown in 1763 to assess the 'capabilities' of the place, and the employment of Vardy in 1764 to alter, if not completely to redesign, his town house in Park Lane. There is every reason to suppose that this sudden spurt of activity also included designs by Vardy for a new country house. Not only are there references by Chambers in October 1771 and April 1773 to Vardy's plans, but there is a view of Milton Abbey by Edward Rooker (published by Hutchins in 1774) showing a house which differs in many details from what was actually built. From this one can only conclude that on his first visit to Milton Abbey in 1769 Chambers was handed a set of plans and elevations that had been in cold storage, as it were, since Vardy's death in 1765. If the Gothic style were alien and unbefitting to the Roman Chambers, to Vardy, brought up under Kent, it was thoroughly familiar and acceptable. Indeed the influence of Kent is readily discernible on the two fronts depicted by Rooker, and particularly on the north front (Pls 65-66) where the cupola-ed towers to the central gatehouse and the adjacent three-bay flanks echo the west front of Kent's Esher. Comparing Rooker's

[34] Cf. *C.Life*, 21, 28 July 1966.

view with the executed House, it becomes clear that Chambers did his best to classicize Vardy's 'staccato' rococo design without destroying it. He regularized the windows, simplified the roof line by removing the gables on the end pavilions and, except for the two-storey intermediate fronts, replacing the jagged battlements with a straight parapet pierced with quatrefoils similar to that on the adjacent church; and tied the whole together by adding a strongly-moulded string course above the first-floor windows. The result (Pl.64) is a much more unified and dignified composition.

The ticklish problem of revising designs of which he did not approve began late in 1769 and dragged on, no doubt to endless discussions with Lord Milton, through most of the following year. On 23 February 1771, after Stephen Carpenter, his master mason from Blandford, had ordered the bricks and the stone and flint for facings, Chambers submitted an estimate of £27,929 to demolish the old house and build the new one. Work started on the range and those parts containing kitchens and offices adjacent to the Abbot's Great Hall. The foundations were laid in March 1771 and building progressed into 1772. The north range with the gatehouse followed from April 1772 until slating late in the autumn of 1773. In December a few last-minute adjustments were decided upon to this range: blank windows were put in the angle projections of the pavilions and in the canted sides of the quadrangle turrets, and 'Alterations in the Ornaments which serve as a Battlement on the Towers of the north front both the Square and Octagon Towers.' This having been completed, Chambers wrote to Carpenter on 20 March 1773 to make preparations 'for laying the foundations of the Corner of the South front where the old Drawing room was'. In other words, the south-west pavilion on the site of the rooms begun by Bancks and completed by Lord Milton. By March 1774 the two pavilions were erected at each end of the west front and in April the foundations were laid for the connecting range containing the principal state rooms.

Walpole in his *Last Journals* described Lord Milton as 'the most arrogant and proud of men, with no foundation but great wealth and a match with the Duke of Dorset's daughter. His birth and parts were equally mean and contemptible.' After four trying years at Milton Abbey Chambers would have agreed wholeheartedly. By 29 March 1774 his relations with Lord Milton had become so unbearable that he was driven to give notice – with sarcastic humour befitting the situation: 'The laying of the new foundations must necessarily be done by me, else I should leave you in a Labyrinth which probably neither your Lordship nor your Lordship's new architect would know how to get out of ... In building as in economy, the difficulty consists in making both ends meet', and ending, 'I can serve you no longer than till Christmas next, when the whole outside of your building will be completely finished, and any other man may do the remainder without Difficulty.'

The straw that finally caused the break was Milton's obstinate niggling over travelling charges which Chambers quite rightly maintained were 'allowed to every architect of reputation here.'[35] The argument went on and on, with Milton attempting to blackmail him by insisting that his demands would not have been made by Paine. In defence of cherished professional standards Chambers replied on 30 August 1773, 'Being willing to do whatever might be most agreeable to your Lordship, I have considered the

---

[35] RIBA J., 30 June 1892, 37–73 publishes this exchange of correspondence.

conditions insisted upon, and now see in a stronger light than before, the impropriety of complying with them. I can by no means consent to an arrangement which must disgust all my other employers, and fix upon me a character which I have so long studied to avoid; I have hitherto acted upon liberal principles, and must not now fall off. The conditions I require are not of my invention. They were in use long before my arrival in England. They still continue so, and all things considered, are far from being extravagent, even in your Lordship's case. You have, my Lord, often mentioned Mr Paine as being much more moderate in his charges; as will appear by the enclosed letter from him, I ask no more than Mr Paine, or any other man of character; and there is, I presume, no reason why I should accept of less.'[36] But as he told his friend Lord Pembroke on 24 March 1774, 'It is vain to reason with Lord Milton who knows no reason but his Interest; and as vain to expect fair treatment from him, who uses everybody brutally.' He could only look back with regret at having built 'a cursed Gothic house for this unmannerly Imperious Lord who treated me, as he does everyone, ill.'[37]

In spite of the combined unpleasantness of having to deal with Lord Milton and execute a house designed by another architect in a style that he would have never chosen for himself, Milton Abbey is one of the finest Georgian Gothic houses and a special tribute to the superb quality of Chambers's stonework. The interiors, less successful, are in any case only partly his. All that he had completed before he left in 1775 were the Dining Room and Library in the west range, the staircase, modifications to the Great Hall, and the room east of it then called the Stewards Room with a ceiling which he described as 'imitated from the old part', or in other words, from one of the Tudor ceilings then remaining in the old abbatial apartments.

Except for typically Chambersian ceilings executed by Joseph Rose in the Dining Room and Library, nothing more significant survives. He also made numerous designs for chimney-pieces the more important of which were intended to be carved by Thomas Carter and were endorsed by him between December 1774 and November 1775. Only one of these designs, dated 16 December 1774, seems to have been carried out. The others were presumably doomed by Chambers's departure and the arrival of Milton's new architects, first Capability Brown, then James Wyatt.

It is difficult from the present setting of the house and church in an open undulating sea of Capability's lawns to visualize what Milton must have looked like with the medieval village clustered around the south and east sides of the church. In 1773 the autocratic Lord decided to remove the village to the other side of the hill where it would be out of sight. Although there is no doubt that Brown built the new village (Pl.197), his designs were largely based upon those submitted by Chambers and described in a letter of 7 April 1773: 'I have therefore sent a plan of a part of the intended Village & an Elevation. There will be in all 40 double houses each to contain 2 familys & each consisting on the ground floor of a Kitchen, a workhouse & a pantry & upon the garret floor of 2 rooms. The centre of each side is marked on one side by the parsonage house in which is also the school & on the other side by the almshouses. There should be little gardens behind each house

[36] BM Add.MS 41133, 109v.
[37] BM Add.MS 41136, 11–12.

& to the parsonage a larger garden than to the rest with a yard as in the Design sent.'[38]
This most perfect of model villages may have been modified by Brown, but its planning
reflects as much of Chambers's humanitarian concern for the happiness and well-being
of the working classes as does his management of the Office of Works.

[38] BM Add.MS 41133, 97–97v.

Chapter 5

Town Houses

Although Chambers's career began on a small scale with the design of garden buildings, the confidence and friendship of early patrons soon led to more imposing works. By 1760 both the Duke of Richmond and the Earl of Pembroke invited him to provide designs for the alteration of their adjacent houses in Whitehall.

The first record of work at Richmond House is a bill for a 'finished plan & Elevation for a Gate at Whitehall with an Estimate', a design that was published a few months later in the *Treatise* as 'made by order of his Grace the Duke of Richmond, for an Entrance to the Privy-Garden.' The 'grave and manly disposition' of this Doric essay seems to have had a special attraction for Chambers. It recurs around 1759 or 1760 as a similar gate, but incorporating Egyptian figures in its niches, at Sherborne Castle (Pl.79); in 1773 as the central feature of Lord Melbourne's Piccadilly screen (Pl.97), and again in 1778 in the east and west gateways terminating the cross-vista at Somerset House.[1] The Duke of Richmond's 'Entrance to the Privy Garden' may have coincided with the building of a Greenhouse in his private garden,[2] for which there is an undated and unspecified design in the Metropolitan Museum inscribed by Chambers as having been executed in part with marble brought from Carrara by Joseph Wilton. The only work on Richmond House itself was his decoration in 1760 of the Sculpture Gallery. This was prompted by the Duke's decision to allow his famous collection of marbles and casts to be studied by artists in a kind of pseudo-academy supervised by Cipriani and Wilton. Although the decision was reported in the *Annual Register* of 1758, the gallery was not officially opened until August 1760 when Chambers's ceiling was presumably completed. The design (also dated 1760) calls for a bold Palladian compartition ornamented with guilloche bands, very like the ceilings in the galleries of Pembroke House and Ampthill.[3]

On the north side of Richmond House was Pembroke House, originally a Palladian 'villa' designed by Campbell, but rebuilt in the late 1750's. Although Chambers had been recommended for this job by Lord Bruce in 1756,[4] it was just a bit too late, for Pembroke was already committed to a 'Mr Evans'.[5] Nevertheless, Bruce's favours did lead to Cham-

---

[1] There is also the 'manly' Doric doorway to Lord Fauconberg's house still existing at 15 George Street, Hanover Square (q.v.).

[2] This Greenhouse may have been intended for Goodwood, although there is no evidence of one having been built there at the time.

[3] That at Ampthill still exists – showing Chambers favouring this type of ceiling as late as 1770.

[4] RIBA Letters.

[5] BM Add.MS 41136, 13, mentioned in a letter from Pembroke to WC on 27 March 1774.

bers's employment at Wilton, which turned out so satisfactorily that he was then commissioned to decorate the Saloon and Gallery (Pl.92) at Pembroke House. Today only the Saloon survives incorporated in the 1913 Government Offices built over the site. Both rooms are documented, however, by ceiling designs dated 1760. The Palladian compartition used here, as at Richmond House and Parksted, is typical of Chambers's early style. However, in the Dining Room decorated in 1773, photographs show his style to have thoroughly changed. The prominent beams are now abandoned for a shallow Adamesque composition of rinceau, trophies, shells, and urns. According to Letter Books, this later work at Pembroke House also included the building of a Riding House described as 'near done' in November 1773 and now lost without trace.[6]

Having recovered from the Harewood fiasco of 1757, gloom descended once more when in 1759 Edward, Duke of York, rejected his designs for what would have been the grandest town house in Pall Mall. His Franco-Italian style was again his undoing. The Duke, like Lascelles, preferred the orthodoxy of an uninspired Palladian – this time Matthew Brettingham the Elder. That Brettingham got the plum is not surprising for he had gained a certain reputation from his town houses for the Duke of Norfolk and Lords Strafford, Anson, and Egremont. By contrast, Chambers's grandly-conceived façade with arcade supporting a giant attached portico would have been something of an anomaly in London. His proposed staircase (Pl.94 and Fig.6) with its domed colonnade on rusticated arcades is an equally startling breach of tradition.[7] Again his Italian experiences are in control, particularly in the dome, parts of which are based upon Bernini's Church at Ariccia and in the overmantels to the chimney-pieces inspired from decorative painted motifs in SS. Trinità dei Monti. Evidently this remarkable staircase, though too *avant-garde* and perhaps too extravagant for the Duke of York, made a lasting impression upon James Paine, who saw the design exhibited at the Society of Artists in 1761 and remembered it nine years later when he designed his own staircase at Wardour Castle.[8] Chambers, as we shall see, also returned to this abortive town house in projects for St Marylebone church (Pl.145).

In the early years town-house commissions came much slower than country-house ones. Thus Parksted, Duntish, and Duddingstone had all been begun when in 1762 Lord Charlemont, determined by political duties 'to attach himself to his native country',[9] called upon Chambers to design his Dublin house in the centre of the north side of Rutland Square. Although Chambers never visited Ireland, he was exceedingly fortunate to have in Lord Charlemont a discriminating patron with whom he was in complete agreement, and in Simon Vierpyle[10] a supervising mason and clerk of works of the highest ability.

Here, as in the villas, Chambers exploited the work of Isaac Ware to provide Dublin

[6] At Wilton is a design for a Riding House signed 'VD', reprd. *C.Life*, 28 Jan. 1944, 158, fig.4. This must surely be by the Marquis de Voyer D'Argenson, Chambers's friend, an amateur architect, and a great lover of equine pursuits.

[7] In the Windsor portfolios is a section corresponding to the centre of the RIBA section, but without the staircase. In the only surviving plan (Sir John Soane's Museum) (Fig.6) the staircase accords with the RIBA section.

[8] James Paine, *Plans . . . of Noblemen and Gentlemen's Seats*, II, 1783, pl.XL.

[9] Quotations taken from M. Craig, *The Volunteer Earl*, 1948, 126–33.

[10] There is no documentary evidence for the employment of Vierpyle on this house, but it must surely be assumed.

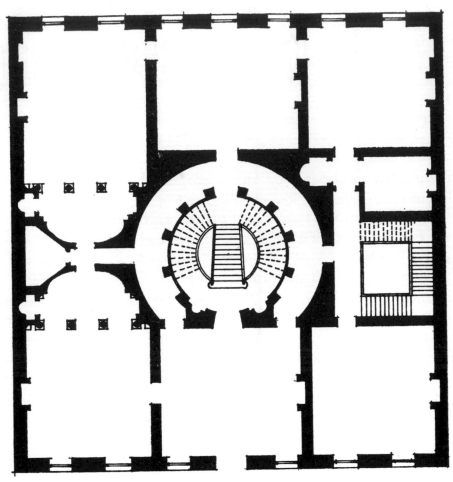

Fig.6 York House, Pall Mall

with its first truly urban house. From Chesterfield House came the five-bay two-and-a-half-storey front with alternate triangular and segmental pediments, and from an un-executed project in the *Complete Body of Architecture* (1756) came the rusticated ground-floor frontage with its sweep wings.[11] The chaste and cleanly-detailed front (Pl.93) of Charlemont House, though never slavishly imitated, stood as an example of the best of London work, excelled only by the impeccable quality of Gandon's Customs House in 1781, itself a product of the Chambers's stable.

Although there is not much to be said about the plan (Fig.7) of the house itself, the extension at the rear was a masterpiece of ingenuity. Along one side of the garden ran a passage windowed on one side and punctuated in the centre by a square vestibule which broke the ascent of the ground and provided a perfect setting for Charlemont's copy of Giovanni da Bologna's *Mercury*. At the end of this corridor, taking up the whole width of the garden, was a pavilion dedicated to Charlemont's collections of books, curiosities, and works of art – a peaceful sanctuary far from the bustle of Rutland Square. The first room entered from the corridor was the Venus Library, named after a classical statue that stood in an Ionic exhedra, lit by a glazed dome. Next came the Principal Library, the largest of the four rooms, with five windows open to the garden, giant Corinthian

11 Isaac Ware, *Complete Body of Architecture*, 1756, no.43, p.433; no.40, p.404.

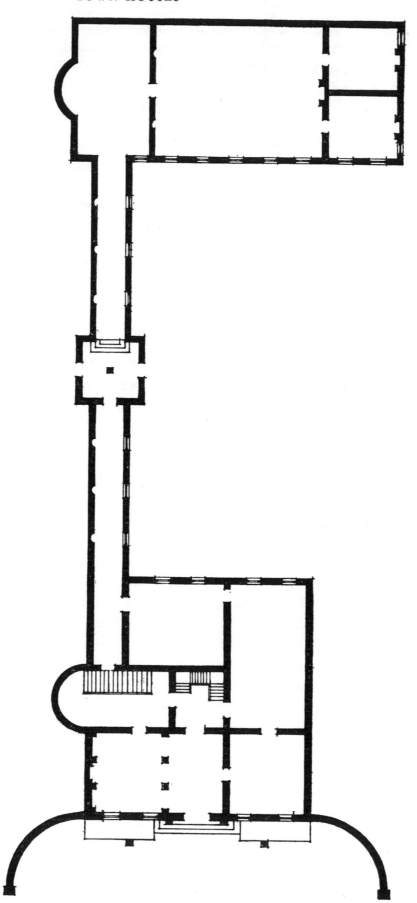

Fig. 7 Charlemont House, Dublin

F

pilasters, and Cipriani grisailles between these pilasters and above doors. At the east end doors flanking a handsome chimney-piece led to a cabinet of 'pictures and antiquities' and a cabinet of 'medals and bas-relievos'.[12] The idea of this connoisseur's group of rooms was a brilliant one that added verve to an otherwise traditional town house.

The misguided conversion of the house into a Municipal Gallery of Art soon after 1929 brought ruthless and unexpected destruction of the whole garden extension and much of the decoration in the main block. Some ceilings on the first floor, the hall now opened out to the width of the house, and by good fortune the elegantly-curved staircase, are all that remain of Chambers's interiors.

Being entirely directed from London, the building of Charlemont House required a voluminous correspondence most of which has fortunately survived to provide a detailed record of events and personalities. We learn, for example, that on 12 March 1763 the form of the sweep walls had not yet been determined, nor had Charlemont decided whether to face his walls above the rusticated ground floor with brick or stone; and that by 25 August 1767[13] the decoration of the interiors was near completion, although the library rooms may still have been unfinished. Perhaps the most interesting correspondence is that concerning the furnishings in 1767 and 1768. Accompanying Chambers's letter of 25 August 1767 were designs for the drawers of an important medal cabinet. Being carved by Sefferin Alken and ornamented with ormolu mounts by Mr Anderson, Chambers gives a full account of their progress. He reports that Anderson 'who had the bronzes in hand' is dying, therefore 'as soon as I can get the models I must employ some other person to do the work, both for the medal cases and the Tritons.' 'In his ill-health he has lost the inscriptions on the medal cases so that new copies are required' from Charlemont. As for Alken, about 'one of the little heads for the corner of the doors of the medal cases, but as he tells me he cannot do them under three guineas and a half a head, I have stopped his further progress till I hear from your lordship.' 'I think antique patteras or nails which will cost but a trifle will answer the purpose almost as well.'

On 12 September Chambers informed Charlemont that he had set Alken 'about a head of Plato, to match that of Homer' and that a design for the 'French table-feet' would soon be despatched. Three days later he wrote again promising to send designs for sideboards 'with French contours', presumably in traditional rococo style, and reporting that 'one of the tritons for the candlesticks is cast, but as I find the pair will come to £36 by the time they are finished, exclusive of the models, I have stopt farther proceedings till I hear from your Lordship. For my own part, as these things are rather for show than use, I should recommend the wooden ones well bronzed, which, at the distance they are to stand will look full as well as real bronze.' The decision to use real bronze is described in a letter of 2 October[15] notifying Charlemont of Anderson's death and satisfying him that Anderson's man would finish the medal case ornaments 'as well as he could have

[12] The Royal Irish Academy, Dublin, has photographs of the rooms before their destruction. HMC Charlemont, I, 291 is Cipriani's accounts for the decorative paintings, and including bills for the Dragon Gates at Marino. Two of Cipriani's grisailles may be seen in the photograph reproduced in Craig, op. cit., pl.VIIa. Joseph Wilton supplied two marble table tops, one of lapis-lazuli, the other of green jaspar.

[13] HMC Charlemont, I, 283.

[14] HMC Charlemont, I, 284.

[15] Ibid.

done himself.' Anderson's death seems to have left a certain amount of confusion which troubled Charlemont and necessitated a firm promise from Chambers on 19 December[16] that the ornaments would be finished exactly 'as we have found some figured sketches relating thereto.' This comforting note also brought designs for the girandoles in the Venus Library for which glasses were being considered on 9 February 1768.[17] Finally on 12 March[18] the medal case ornaments and Triton candle branches were nearly finished. The Tritons, Chambers writes, 'are finished all but the bronzing, and they are so finely executed that it would be a pity not to have them quite complete. I have therefore ordered them to be entirely gilded, for I feared that bronzing would make them appear dull, and partly gilding upon the bronze would look tawdry. This will increase the expence of them, but I think it will answer when done.'[19]

By 1770 Charlemont could boast the best town house in Dublin and one of the finest temples in all Europe. He had found in Chambers not only a first-rate architect, but also a life-long friend. Indeed, the success of Charlemont House and the Casino at Marino is due as much to their harmonious relationship as to Chambers's skills in designing and Simon Vierpyle's able execution and superintendence of the work. There can be no better expression of the depth of their friendship than Chambers's letter to Charlemont on 15 April 1775 congratulating him on the birth of a son. He begins with a description given him by Giuseppe Baretti of a Piedmontese custom of celebrating such an event. Whenever a son is born 'the father plants a thousand Poplars; which by the time the Young gentleman comes of age, are worth just a thousand pounds; and are given him as a portion: an easy way of providing for posterity, which might with great success be introduced in Ireland; where waste lands are frequent, and well prepared for the growth of poplars. By the help of this secret, your Lordship may have as many sons as King Priam, and make for them, any provision you think proper; you may then, as now, build temples upon every occasion without fear on the consequences; and I shall be your Lordship's Architect with infinitely more pleasure, when I know your fund is inexhaustible! fifty good poplars will produce a tolerable sized column; five hundred, a pretty temple; five thousand a villa; a Bridge, a triumphal arch; a Casino; a paralaia; a Boudoir; or any thing that five thousand pounds can purchase; a viva il Baretti.'[20]

Charlemont House, although it cut an impressive figure in Dublin, could hardly compare with the town houses of the grand English nobility. Chambers's first opportunity to design one of these important London houses was provided by the rich and powerful Earl Gower who in March 1764 obtained the lease of a vacant site flanked on the west by Whitehall and on the south by Whitehall Yard, adjacent to the Banqueting

[16] Ibid.

[17] Ibid.

[18] HMC Charlemont, I, 285.

[19] The original candlesticks are lost, but fortunately the model survives as a Wedgwood copy in black basalt (cf. *Apollo*, Jan. 1966, xlvi, for a pair illustrated in an advertisement) referred to in correspondence between Wedgwood and Bentley 16 Nov. and 6 Dec. 1769. Cf. *The Selected Letters of Josiah Wedgwood*, eds. Ann Finer and George Savage, 1965, 87. The 'ornamental utensils' engraved in two plates of the *Treatise* in 1791 include something for Lord Charlemont, but sadly it is not particularized. Anderson is almost certainly the Anderson who exhibited a tripod 'from an original design of Mr Stuarts' at the Free Society of Artists in 1761. Cf. E. Harris, *The Furniture of Robert Adam*, 1963.

[20] In a letter dated 19 April 1775. HMC Charlemont, original MSS in Royal Irish Academy.

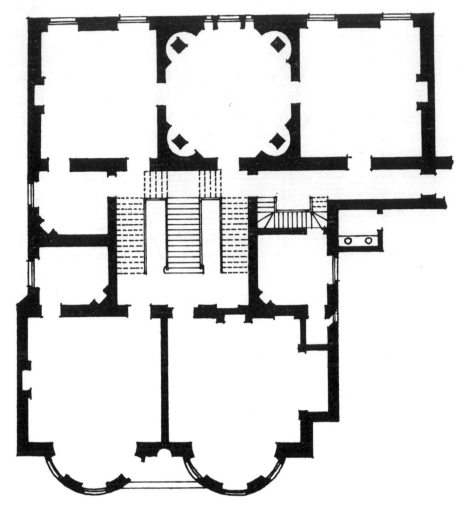

Fig.8 Gower House, Whitehall. Preliminary design

House. The Gower House commission appears to have aroused in Chambers a remark-able flair of inventiveness particularly in the design of the staircase and in the novel placement of the house (Fig.8) on the irregular L-shaped plot. Custom would have given the widest area facing Whitehall to the main entrance. Chambers on the contrary used this valuable space for a parade of reception rooms which he fronted with a brick and stone façade (Pl.95) of five bays with a two-storey tier of Palladian windows in the centre. The entrance front with adjacent Palladian openings, one the main door and the other a window to the dining room, he placed in the narrower space facing east to Whitehall Yard. Although twisting the house around meant sacrificing a grand front approach to the staircase, it enabled him to provide Lord Gower with a more splendid and interesting suite of three state rooms in the shape of two oblongs flanking an octagon.

For sheer beauty and ingenuity there was nothing in Gower House, or for that matter in any other London house outside perhaps of 44 Berkeley Square and Ashburnham House, to equal Chambers's staircase (Pls 98, 101–102). Approached through the cross-vaulted vestibule screened by a Doric arcade, a single flight ascended from the ground floor to an intermediate landing, where again it divided back right and left to an Ionic arcade and another vaulted vestibule with exits at each end giving access to an upper gallery immediately below the glazed dome. The walls of the staircase carried largish plasterwork ornaments in a Neo-classical style probably executed by either Thomas Collins or Michelangelo Pergolesi. The source of this staircase, so admired that it was paraphrased by James Wyatt at Dodington in 1798, is Longhena's seventeenth-century staircase in the Convento di S. Giorgio Maggiore in Venice.

With the exception of the staircase, the decoration of Gower House was keyed to a new note of restraint and Parisian elegance. The abrupt change in Chambers's decorative style from the refinement of heavy Palladian motifs found in the villas like Duddingstone to a fully-synthesized Parisian style in the Strand apartments in Somerset House, is perfectly illustrated in his design (Pl.100) made about 1768 for Gower's Great Room, called the Great Drawing Room, the Gallery, or the Ball Room. Here the most distinguishing motif was the ornamented pilaster (or better-termed pilaster-strip) dividing the wall into rectilinear compartments. Although Chambers had indeed used it in the Saloon (Pl.117) at Buckingham House, c.1763, here it is accompanied with painted overdoors, a French shallow-coved ceiling, and a thoroughly Parisian chimney-piece.[21] These Anglo-Gallic ensembles must be regarded as a prelude to the Somerset House interiors and to the even later Gallicisms of Henry Holland at Southill and Somerset House.

Unfortunately the building of Gower House is not well recorded. The fact that embellishments, albeit minor ones, were still being made in 1774 – seven or more years after designs had been submitted – suggests that work was carried out at a leisurely pace. Although the plasterwork can be attributed to Collins and the painted insets to Cipriani, the only other documented craftsman is Pergolesi whose responsibility for the plaster decoration in the library[22] comes as something of a surprise for he was primarily an Adam man, never employed by Chambers on any other occasion.

Gower House, even before it was complete, made Chambers's reputation as a town-house architect bringing two more great commissions in 1771: Melbourne House, Piccadilly, and Dundas House, Edinburgh. Whatever there was to see in Piccadilly in 1771 was enough to convince Lord Melbourne[23] to trust the building of his London house to Chambers instead of to James Paine then architect of his country house at Brocket in Hertfordshire.

In general layout Melbourne House followed its neighbour Burlington House with a gate and screen (Pl.97) to Piccadilly, offices flanking a court (Pl.103), and a garden stretching to the present Vigo Street. In appearance (Pl.96) it is a sedate and unpretentious essay in brick, relying for its effect upon perfect proportions rather than upon outward show. The recessed arches of the ground-floor windows and the three-bay centre projecting forward beneath a pediment are the only concessions to 'movement'. Inside and out it was a world away from the flowing ornament and variety[24] of the Adam style. Here

---

[21] The chimney-piece, some of the doors, and other decorative motifs, are incorporated in a house now belonging to the school at Wycombe Abbey. They were removed there after the demolition sales, having been bought in by Lord Carrington.

[22] Cf. his album of drawings in the Pierpont Morgan Library, New York.

[23] BM Add.MS 41134, 33–4; 41135, 21. Cf. also originals in Wrest Papers, 10597, Beds CRO.

[24] Compare Chambers's plan to that submitted by Adam to Lord Holland, for the same site. Reprd LCC *Survey of London*, XXXII, pl.112a.

(Fig.9) there were no sequences of plastically-shaped rooms, only gentle curved bows to the garden front, a few niches here and there to relieve walls, and a screen of columns in the Dining Room. It is as if Chambers deliberately immobilized the state rooms in order to effect a more startling contrast with his extraordinary staircase (Pl.99). We have already remarked on the unusual staircases at Parksted and Gower House, but these hardly compare with Melbourne House and its progeny at Dundas House and Somerset House. Leaving the hall the visitor passed under a colonnade into the stair well, and under a flight of stairs arching above his head. This disclosed the first flights rising against the farther wall to right and left up to a half-landing. From this point the arched flyer dramatically reached across and up to the colonnaded landing on the hall side of the well. After which the stairs safely returned to the walls rising, again by right and left, to side landings at first-floor level. Needless to say this spectacular feat needed little embellishment. Here as elsewhere in the house decoration was as Spartan as the interiors of Duddingstone, the only distraction being Cipriani's mythological scenes inserted in some of the ceiling compartments. Melbourne House was the absolute antithesis of the works of the Adam brothers. No one was more aware of and indeed pleased by this contrast than Chambers. In 1773 he wrote to Lord Grantham[25] defending his own achievements in the light of 'the presumptuous book' recently published by the Adam brothers. 'They boast of having first brought the True style of Decoration into England, and that all architects of the present day are only servile copyers of their excellence.' He cannot, of course, accept the blatant falsehood of 'the first of these positions' and 'can produce many proofs against the last, among others, Melbourne House, decorated in a manner almost diametrically opposite to theirs; and more, as I flatter myself, in the true Style, as approaching nearer to the most approved style of the ancients.'

The building of Melbourne House was a thoroughly satisfying experience to everyone concerned. Lord Melbourne, having spent nearly £24,000 by 1774, could cheerfully state that 'few people have had better reason than myself to be pleased with so large a sum laid out',[26] and Chambers could proudly announce to Lord Grantham that 'all the world is delighted with it; because the few that give the Ton are pleased.'[27] After the measured simplicity of Melbourne House and all that went before, it is a pleasant surprise to find Dundas House (Pls.105–108 and Fig.10) basically a country villa of the Marble Hill type, garnished with acanthus frieze, Greek key strings, and fluted Corinthian pilasters to the attached portico. This generous use of ornament was not a special display of Sir Laurence Dundas's wealth, however great that might have been, but a deliberate change of style, limited to exterior architecture, and further developed in the undated project of the late 1770s for a nobleman's town house (Pl.104), or Richmond Palace project IV of 1775 (Pl.112), and finally in the fronts of Somerset House. For all his money, which it must be noted was invested in Chambers in preference to Adam or Carr, his architects at Moor Park and Aske, Sir Laurence received a highly sophisticated house complete with a simplified version of the Melbourne House staircase (Pl.108) and a charming garden (Pl.106) like a miniature Kew, with peripheral walks around open lawns. In short,

25 BM Add.MS 41134, 34. ff. also original in Wrest Papers 10597, Beds CRO.
26 BM Add.MS 41135, 8.
27 BM Add.MS 41134, 37.

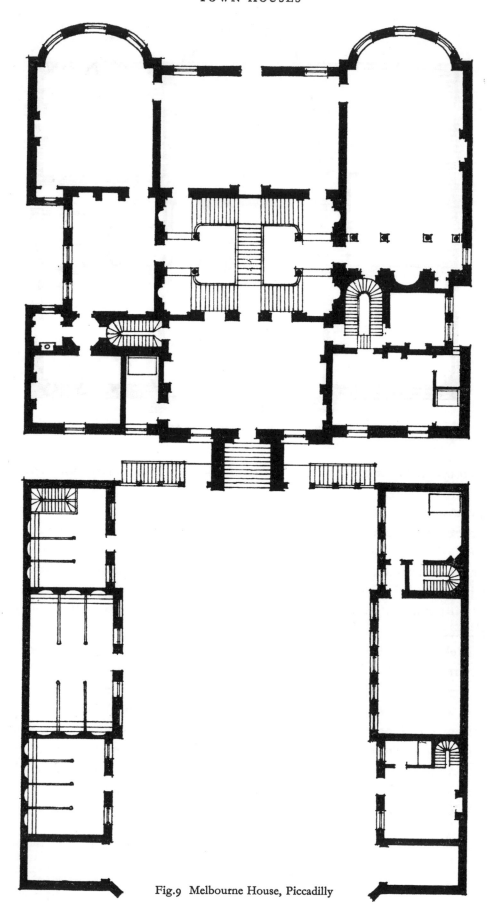

Fig.9 Melbourne House, Piccadilly

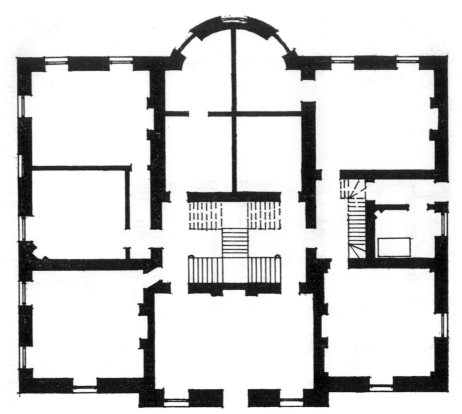

Fig.10 Dundas House, Edinburgh

Dundas House in St Andrew Square was to Edinburgh what Charlemont House was to Dublin.

As fate would have it, Chambers's success as a town-house architect was doomed to a cruel succession of tragedies that have left us precious little by which to remember him. Of a total of twenty-one commissions of consequence, seventeen, including Gower House, have entirely disappeared, and only the exterior of Melbourne, Charlemont, and Dundas houses survive more or less as built. What is more, this melancholy list of fatalities is almost doubled by the total loss of his twenty small but dignified houses in Berners Street.

Fortunately the extent and character of the Berners Street development can be fairly accurately reconstructed with the help of the St Marylebone rate books, a few surviving designs, topographical drawings and photographs. In 1764 Chambers, who was then living just south of the Oxford Road (now Oxford Street) in Poland Street, joined his friend Thomas Collins,[28] a distinguished resident of St Marylebone as well as one of London's finest plasterers, in buying leases from William Berners of undeveloped land bounded on the east by Harley's Oxford Market and on the north by Paine's Middlesex Hospital. Development began auspiciously with number 13, Chambers's own house on the east side of Berners Street, just north of the junction with Eastcastle Street. In 1771

[28] I am grateful for the researches made into the life of Thomas Collins by Col J. H. Busby, and particularly to his invaluable typescript of 1965 titled *Thomas Collins of Woodhouse, Finchley and Berners Street, St Marylebone*. Collins appears later as a speculator on a large scale, sharing responsibility with John White on the Portland Estate around the Harley Street area.

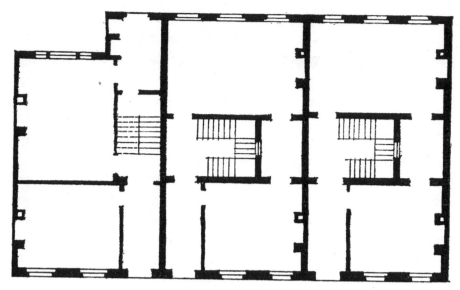

Fig.11 Berners Street, London

numbers 14[29] for James Long and 15 for Thomas Rouse were added to 13 to make a uniform group of three houses (although they were undoubtedly planned as a trilogy from the beginning) (Fig.11). Numbers 16 and 20 were building for Collins in 1770; 18 was begun in 1769 for William Green, 19 in 1770 for John Gordon, and 17, although undocumented, was probably also by Chambers. On the west side of the street number 44 was occupied by Collins who also held the leases of numbers 46, 47, 54, and 55 – all obviously designed by Chambers. Number 56 was leased by Chambers to Robert Gregory, and photographs show quite convincingly that numbers 57 and 58 were also in his style.

Regardless of when and for whom they were built, all of the Berners Street houses were well proportioned and of a uniform simplicity, their fine rusticated door surrounds – a foretaste of the courtyard doorways at Somerset House – being the only distinctive mark of Chambers's presence. Numbers 13 to 15 for which plans and records of their interior decoration have survived, can be analysed as representative examples. Each house was three bays wide, with the end one – either on the right or the left – as the entrance. The staircase was located either immediately off the entrance hall or farther along between the front and rear rooms at right angles to the wall. Decorative embellishments though simple and sparing were always of a high standard: S-scrolled balustrades to the stairs, circular bas-reliefs above the chimney-pieces and doors, and elegant Doric or Ionic screens in those rooms that had segmental bays projecting into the garden. As might be expected Chambers's own house, behind its uniform façade, had several special features. To the stables at the end of the garden he added a drawing office and studio with a Venetian opening. From here he could look back to what must have been an extraordinary garden front described by Charles Bielefeld[30] in 1850 as having been decorated

---

[29] It would appear incredible in our age of documentation and so-called preservation that this house could have survived in most of its essentials until 1964, yet have remained unlisted by the Ministry of Housing and Local Government, and to have been demolished without record or protest. The author saw its fine plasterwork one week, and lo! the following week there was but a hole in the ground.

[30] Charles Bielefeld, *Ornaments in Every Style of Design* . . . 1850, 7.

in moulded papier mâché in a 'fanciful' style. Was Chambers, we may ask, secreting a Chinese whim in the midst of London? Sadly, we may never know.

Chambers's achievement in Berners Street has for too long remained unappreciated. Although speculative, there is no doubt that each house received the most careful attention not only from Chambers, but from his principal assistant Edward Stevens (the author of many of the surviving drawings). To look at Berners Street was no match for the scintillating Adelphi. Financially, however, it was a much more rewarding speculation which brought Chambers a small fortune at the peak of his career.

The complete town house and the development of Berners Street may have been the cream, but the bread and butter came from a host of miscellaneous alterations and additions. Letters and drawings bear witness to an impressive list of clients including the Dukes of Buccleuch, Leinster, and Marlborough, and Lords Abercorn, Clive, Fitzwilliam, and Milton, most of whom were also employing Chambers in their country houses: Marlborough at Blenheim, Milton at Milton Abbey, Fitzwilliam at Milton, Northants, Clive at Styche and Walcot, and Buccleuch at Adderbury. Unfortunately this branch of Chambers's practice in town has suffered the same fate as his larger works. With the exception of a few rooms in the houses of Clive and Marlborough, which, however, do not contribute significantly to our knowledge of his style, all of his additions have disappeared. Admittedly, some of his commissions were minor ones that demanded very little attention. For example, all that was required by Lord Abercorn when he took the lease in 1762 of 25 Grosvenor Square, an Early Georgian house on the west side, was a few surface renovations. Exactly what was involved is not known, but on 18 August 1763[31] Chambers discussed the work as 'entirely finished' except for 'part of the great stair to clean and one small room on the ground floor to paper.' Similarly, when some of the old-fashioned Palladian rooms on the garden front of Leinster House, Dublin required redecoration Chambers simply sent designs to Duchess Emily for execution by Irish craftsmen. The results here, as typified by ceilings, door surrounds, and chimney-pieces, although at once recognizably Chambersian, are less distinguished and sophisticated than they might have been had Chambers supervised the work himself or commanded Vierpyle to do so.[32]

It would seem, from the little information we have, that his most extensive scheme for alteration was for the 3rd Duke of Buccleuch at 20 Grosvenor Square. The joining of this corner house, purchased in 1766, with Buccleuch's adjacent property in North Audley Street must have been a considerable undertaking. Nevertheless, the only surviving records of the great town house are Horwood's map of 1784 showing the two plans presumably as they were re-organized by Chambers, and a ceiling design possibly for the Duchess's Dressing Room, exhibited at the Royal Academy in 1768. Both houses were, of course, earlier ones, but it is likely that the conversion involved very considerable redecorations and alterations.

The more celebrated Dorchester House, the town house of Lord Milton, has also been buried in the forgotten annals of history. Here, as at Milton Abbey, Chambers succeeded

31 Abercorn correspondence, Baronscourt, Co Tyrone.
32 Cf. also his work at Castletown.

John Vardy whose 'Design for a nobleman's stable and terrace to the garden near Hyde Park', exhibited at the Society of Arts in 1764, was correctly identified by Walpole with Dorchester (or more properly, Milton) House. After Vardy's death in 1765 the irascible Milton called upon Chambers to complete the work and to make other additions as well. The payments to Chambers of £500 and £600 entered in Milton's bank account[33] on 10 October and 1 December 1770 coincide with Chambers's report on 27 October 1770 that 'the whole new building is covered in and the roof over the stairs will be done in three or four days.' The fact that this is five years after Vardy's death suggests that Chambers was responsible for the whole 'new building',[34] a wing at right angles to the house facing the park. In the following year he informed Milton that the 'carver has already done a good part of the carving in the new rooms', but that Ansell a cabinet-maker whom he had employed at Blenheim had 'not yet been able to make out his Estimates for the Gilding', which, he says, would be as good as Samuel Norman's gilding at Buckingham House.[35] To the works on Dorchester House mentioned in Chambers's correspondence we can add the entrance gateway published in John Carter's *Builder's Magazine* of 1774.

Lord Fitzwilliam's house at 79 Stratton Street on the corner of Piccadilly was made 'convenient and elegant' around 1771. This and the fact that the attics were heightened is all we know, for neither the house nor the documents have survived.

We are somewhat better informed about the work for the 4th Duke of Marlborough in Pall Mall. Having taken over at Blenheim after the death of Stiff Leadbetter in 1766, it is not surprising that he should be summoned to Marlborough House in 1771 to build another storey projected five years earlier by Leadbetter. In making this addition (which heightened the house by nearly a third) Chambers was sensitive enough to repeat the motifs of Wren's elevations and to retain the straight balustraded roof line. His commission also included extensive interior redecorations of which several cornices and door-cases, a pair of splendid chimney-pieces (Pls 186–187) by Hayward or Wilton in the Saloon, and a room in the south-west angle were preserved in Pennethorne's remodelling of 1861.[36] The elegant simplicity of the Marlborough House decorations echoed the slightly earlier work in Lord Clive's house in Berkeley Square. This Early Georgian house was purchased by Clive in 1761 and refurnished by Chambers between 1763 and 1767. Although the survival of one complete room here may be considered a major victory in the wholesale destruction of Chambers's London works, it is, however, not nearly so informative or valuable as the complete building accounts which reveal an interesting parade of craftsmen: Sefferin Alken carver, Thomas Collins plasterer, Benjamin Thacker joiner, Edward Gray bricklayer, George Mercer and Joseph Pickford[37] masons, James Palmer smith, George Evans painter and gilder, and William Chapman plumber. All of their works, including a ceiling painted in 1766–7 by Charles Catton and Augustin Brunias, were

[33] Coutts Bank archives.

[34] BM Add.MS 41133, 23v.

[35] BM Add.MS 41133, 56v, a letter following one of 18 Oct. 1771.

[36] John Yenn provided much furniture and further decoration in the late 1780s. He also installed an observatory. Cf. the so-called 'Holland' album in the University of Delaware Library.

[37] For Pickford, cf. SANDON PARK.

swept away by the neo-Georgian improvements of late nineteenth-century and early twentieth-century owners.

Considering the short duration of Chambers's town house practice, barely sixteen years from 1761 to 1777, his achievement is extremely impressive: four major town houses (Charlemont, Gower, Melbourne, and Dundas); three medium-sized houses (Weymouth, Calcraft, and Errington) of which the heightened façade of Weymouth still stands in Arlington Street; about twenty, if not more, Berners Street houses; and at least ten major alteration schemes (Richmond, Pembroke, Clive, Milton, Fitzwilliam, Abercorn(?), Buccleuch, Marlborough, Fauconberg in George Street, Hanover Square, and Turner in Grosvenor Street). His output was, in fact, greater than Adam's in thirty years, nearly twice the time. Admittedly his plans, apart from the garden appendages to Charlemont House, are unremarkable – and do not fix themselves in the memory as do those of Adam's great town houses. Nor are his façades much more exciting. Between the extremes of the Palladian refinement of Charlemont House at the outset of his practice and the ornate Dundas House at the end is a succession of unrelieved brick fronts. Where he does excel, however, is in the design of staircases. The ravishing beauty of Gower House and the ingenuity of Melbourne House are unsurpassed in English architecture. His interiors although not so inventive as Adam's were in their unpretentious way just as elegant and perhaps, because they were more masculine, more satisfying. Here his most significant contribution was the use of French trim and detailing, from which he developed an Anglo-Gallic style that culminated in the Somerset House interiors, the prototype of much of Henry Holland's similarly-styled work.

Chapter 6

At Royal Command

The Hanoverian kings inherited no palace of any consequence. Hampton Court, as large and handsome as it is, could hardly rival a Sans Souci or an Aranjuez, and, like Whitehall, St James's, or Somerset House, is a complex of varying dates lacking in architectural unity. Jones and Webb, Wren and Talman, and a host of lesser luminaries had proposed great palaces in vain; and when in 1712 Shaftesbury said 'Tis the good Fate of our Nation in this particular, that there remain yet two of the noblest subjects for Architecture: our Princes' Palace, and our House of Parliament,'[1] he was echoing the perpetual hopes of many generations of architects who saw visions on the embers of Whitehall or in the chaotic disarray of Westminster.

The palatial dreams of the Georges were focused not on London but on Richmond, where in 1719 George, Prince of Wales, purchased the red-brick lodge, originally altered in 1694 for William III, and later acquired by the Duke of Ormonde. Not long after George's succession to the throne in 1729, Sir Edward Lovatt Pearce, Surveyor-General of Ireland, submitted plans for a grand Palladian palace in the style of Colen Campbell. This was followed in the mid-1730's by Kent's pearwood model of a splendid palace in the Holkham vein.[2] Nothing came of either attempt, and there were no further projects for Richmond until George III's accession in 1760. The new reign gave rise to fresh hopes, but these, as Chambers was to find, were as false as all those in the past.

Anyone might have predicted that Chambers's appointment in 1757 as tutor to George, Prince of Wales and architect to the Dowager Princess Augusta would result in a lifetime of royal patronage and the official leadership of the architectural profession. Exactly how Chambers came to receive these favours is not entirely clear. We know that on 18 November 1761 George III created by Letters Patent a new and obviously personal 'office called Architect of Works'. It is altogether possible that the idea of an English equivalent to the French 'architecte du roi' was suggested by the francophile Chambers, but the peculiar and indeed unsatisfactory decision to have to share the office with his arch rival, Robert Adam, was almost certainly due to the powerful Lord Bute. Although Bute may have recommended Chambers at Kew, he never employed him in any private capacity, for that was the exclusive preserve of Adam. Despite Bute's influence Adam failed to ingratiate himself with George III and was given no more to do than a ceiling and chimney-piece in Buckingham House. For Chambers, on the other hand, the title of Architect of

[1] Shaftesbury, *Letter Concerning Design*, 1712.
[2] Pearce's designs are in the collection of Sir Richard Proby of Elton Hall; the Kent model is in the Dutch House at Kew.

77

Works merely confirmed his already secure position. The State Coach had already been designed in 1760, Buckingham House was put in hand in 1762, Richmond Observatory in 1768, and the Queen's Lodging at Windsor Castle in 1772. These choice fruits of royal patronage were more substantial than the paper dreams for royal palaces. The idea and ideal of a palace obsessed Chambers for twenty years and no architect could have been so unfortunate in the failure of all his schemes.

Count Frederick Kielmansegge, in his memoirs of a visit to England, reports hearing in October 1761 that the King had 'decided to begin the building of an entirely new palace in February (1762)', but that the site was still to be settled. This project can be related to the 'North front of a Villa for a particular situation near London', exhibited by Chambers at the Society of Artists in 1762, and identified by Walpole as for the King at Richmond (hereafter called Richmond I). Its fate was quickly sealed by the expensive building works at Buckingham House begun in 1762. As soon as the London expenditure began to decrease Chambers was requested to project a second palace (Richmond II). Numerous designs (Pl.111) were drawn up, an estimate was made for £89,320, and a wooden model (Pl.109), executed by Benoni Thacker, was presented to the King in 1765. There can be little doubt that all this coincided with Capability Brown's plan of 'Richmond Gardens with the proposed Alterations' dated 10 December 1764 on which is shown the block of a palace 400 by 200 feet sited towards the northern extent of the gardens as they had been extended by Bridgeman. Chambers's model and designs proposed a block 328 by 225 feet with pavilion towers at the angles, a Corinthian portico and a series of dull oblong rooms including an apsidal hall inside (Fig.12). It acknowledged Holkham, a house he greatly admired for 'being intimately well contrived, both for state and conveniency.'[3] Richmond II, however, was a grandiose but dull and ponderous design, without any of the liveliness of Kent's work, and very different too from the fluid and well-integrated plan made for the Society of Arts some five years earlier. It is perhaps fortunate that it remained unexecuted, for it would have added little to Chambers's reputation.

Although Richmond II was shelved, interest in the site remained very much alive. In 1765 Brown proceeded with his landscaping and in 1768 Chambers was called upon to build a Royal Observatory near the old lodge. This small but elegant building afforded only temporary relief from palace frustrations, for in the summer of 1769 he exhibited at the Royal Academy an 'elevation of one of the flanks' of yet another project. The progress of this Richmond III over the next four years is fully recorded by Mrs Papendiek, Lady Coke, Thomas Worsley, and Chambers himself. Mrs Papendiek, whose husband was a member of the Royal Household, recalled many years later that in the autumn of 1769 'his Majesty was greatly occupied in digesting plans with Sr Wm. Chambers for a new palace at Richmond, the lodge now occupied being too small for the increasing family.'[4] In his *Autobiographical Note* written in January 1770 Chambers states that he is 'at present engaged on plans for a Royal Palace at Richmond', and according to Lady Coke the foundation stones were laid during the summer of 1770. She says further that what was begun was really 'a Lodge (alas not a palace) in Richmond Gardens, very near

3 Chambers, *Treatise*, 1759, 82.

4 Mrs Papendiek, *Court and Private Life in the Time of Queen Charlotte*, 1, 1887, 42.

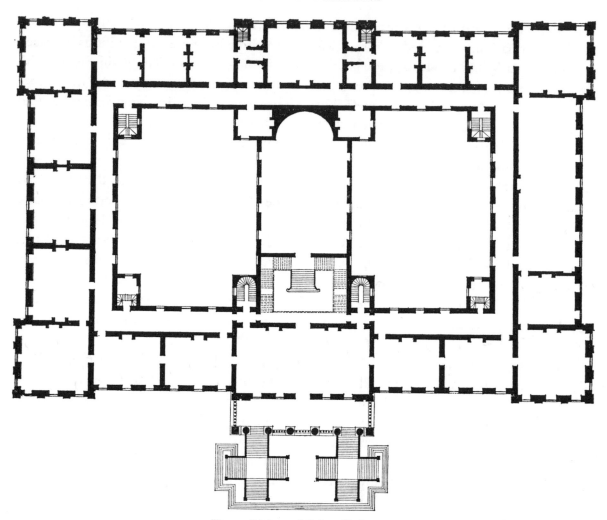

Fig.12 Richmond Palace II, Surrey

where the old one now stands' and was to be '140 ft and to be built on arches as I suppose to command greater prospect.'[5] The 'arches' to which she, and later Lysons, refers must have been either the vaulted basement, or more likely the ground-floor arcading.

The commenced palace is shown on Richardson's survey of 1771, standing roughly between the Observatory and the present Queen's Cottage. At this point the future was quite promising, but it was not long before the gloomy clouds of uncertainty began to descend. On 19 January 1773 Thomas Worsley wrote to Chambers 'pray how do you go on at Kew, does Richmond stand still? What a pity he cannot go on with so small a design. If it were a grand *Caserta* I should not be surprised, but so modest an undertaking to stop, or go on so slow is hard.'[6]

On 4 August 1775 Chambers wrote to tell Worsley about the completion of another project (Richmond IV), but confesses that 'when the building begins is not determined.'[7] As far as we know it was never begun. To judge from the model (Pl.110) (executed by a Mr Goldsmith of Covent Garden) Richmond IV (Pl.112) was a grandiose project, still

[5] *The Letters and Journals of Lady Mary Coke*, II, 1889 180–1.
[6] BM Add.MS 41134, 30.
[7] BM Add.MS 41135, 72v.

Palladian, but much more mature than Richmond II. Its plan, an oblong nine-bay block linked by quadrant colonnades from the angles to three-by-three bay pavilions, is based on Palladio's Villa Mocenigo, probably via Nostell or Kedleston. The main façade with its one-and-a-half-storey pilastered elevation above an arcuated basement is a neo-classic interpretation of either Leoni's Queensbury House, or the Jonesian New Gallery at Old Somerset House which had appeared in 1772 as a head-piece in his *Dissertation on Oriental Gardening*. The fact that the centre block of Richmond IV corresponds with the description of Richmond III as a front of about 140 feet 'raised on arches' suggests that it was an enlargement of the earlier design. Indeed, this is all the more likely as Richmond III had been built up to first-floor level. Not only does Richmond IV incorporate Richmond III but it also looks forward to the more enriched style of the Somerset House Strand block. In the interval between the two palace designs Chambers had re-visited Paris, and had gathered there a refreshing new vocabulary of motifs and ideas. His change in style is perhaps best illustrated by a comparison, only faintly to be seen in the old photograph of the Model (Pl.110), of the plain windows in the arcuated storey of the model's main block (Richmond III) with the garlanded, frenchified *œil de bœufs* in the pavilions (Richmond IV).

Taken together the four Richmond projects show a logical sequence of ideas and development of style. They are all distinctly suburban and cannot therefore be related to the pair of palace façades (Pl.179) for an urban site, presumably London, in the Royal Institute of British Architects. These, like his noble but sadly unexecuted designs for the Savoy (Pl.178), are expressive of his experiences at Somerset House and must post-date 1776. Despite their Gallic veneer Chambers is still unable to disguise his debt to English Palladianism, and more specifically to parts of Inigo Jones's Whitehall designs.[8] When all is said and done, he was perhaps more inventive for the incredible range of complicated staircases (Fig.13) proposed for these designs and for the many various palace designs now in the Royal Library at Windsor Castle.

THE STATE COACH

By the time George III came to the throne the baroque State Coach, made for Queen Anne and used by the first two Georges, was well and truly out of fashion, and indeed an embarrassment in comparison to the Lord Mayor's new coach. It is not surprising, therefore, that the *Journals*[9] of the Clerk of the Stables at the Royal Mews records that 'a very superb state coach was ordered to be built, after several designs and drawings made for the purpose and shown to the Master of the Horse were examined, and the approved parts thereof thrown into one by Mr Chambers Surveyor of His Majesties'

[8] His debt to English Palladianism is patently evident from a study of the enormous number of designs for country houses and palaces in his portfolios in the Royal Library, Windsor Castle. None is dated and few inscribed. It is therefore virtually impossible to apportion them to any specific purpose. Some were obviously made when Chambers was tutor to the King i.e. in the late 1750's but most appear to be projects for either Richmond III or IV. They may be roughly grouped into four principal schemes: (A) an oblong block with straight links to pavilions forming flanking courtyards; (B) a courtyard range continuous with and to one side of the main block; (C) a square block with a projecting portico; (D) schemes similar to Richmond IV with quadrant links. Their most remarkable aspect is the variety of staircase design, owing much to continental persuasions (Fig.13).

[9] MS. Royal Mews, Buckingham Palace.

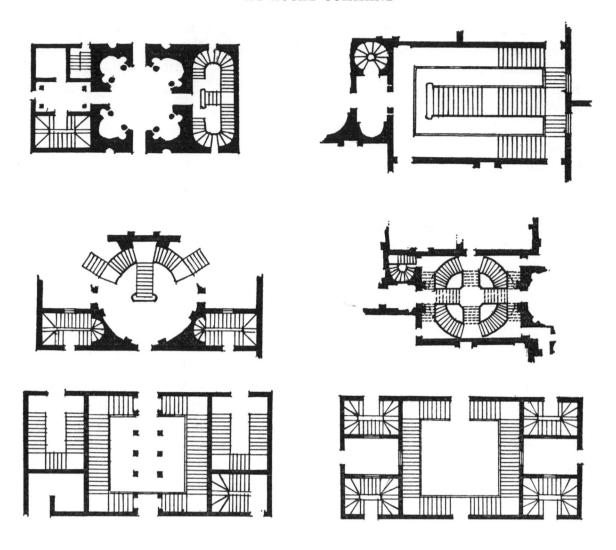

Fig.13 Six staircases proposed for royal palaces

Board of Works.' Of the 'several designs' that have survived, the most finished is one (Pl.134) signed by Chambers and Cipriani and dated 1760. This was probably the drawing shown to the King and approved by Samuel Butler the royal coach-maker. A wax model (Pl.135), now in the London Museum, was then made for Joseph Wilton who was responsible for most of the carving. J. T. Smith[10] visiting Wilton's studio with Nollekens in the 1770s described it as 'a most beautiful toy: exquisitely adorned with ornaments, modelled in wax by Capitsoldi and Voyers, the panels being painted in water colours by Cipriani.' After the carvers, painters, gilders, chasers, and other craftsmen had completed their work the parts were handed over to Samuel Butler, the coach-maker, to assemble. It was his technical skills that determined the success of the whole, and for that he received the largest remuneration. Butler, however, must have found it extremely

[10] J. T. Smith, *Nollekens and his Times*, ed. Stonier, 1949, 12. Capitsoldi was Giovanni Battista Capezzuoli, and Voyers, John Voyez. Cf. Rupert Gunnis, *Dictionary of British Sculptors 1660–1851*, 1953, 78, 410.

vexing to have to execute Chambers's design, not only because Chambers was a relative newcomer in court circles, but more annoying still because he himself had submitted a design (Pl.138) in collaboration with the carver and cabinet-maker John Linnell. Although there may have been projects by other competitors, theirs, which was engraved, is the only one known.

It will never be known just how much of the coach is Chambers's invention. It follows the precedent of French coach-builders and bears a resemblance to the Lord Mayor's coach made by Butler in 1757. There is surely no more glorious English rococo confection than this (Pls136–137), although inevitably it was laced with neo-classic trimmings. It is rich in allusions to the Monarchy and the victory of the Seven Years' War. The front tritons proclaim the approach of the Monarchy of the Ocean, and rear figures carry Imperial fasces with tridents. On the roof three cherubs, the genii of England, Scotland, and Ireland, support the royal crown and hold the Sceptre, Sword of State, and the Ensign of Knighthood. Cipriani was paid £315 for seven paintings: the front panel with Victory presenting laurel to Britannia, attended by Religion, Justice, Wisdom, Valour, Fortitude, Commerce, and Plenty; the right-hand door with Industry and Ingenuity giving a Cornucopia to the Genius of England; the right-hand panels with History recording the reports of Fame and Peace burning the implements of War; the lower back panel with Neptune and Amphitrite attended by Winds, Rivers, Tritons, Naiads, issuing from their palace in a triumphal car drawn by sea-horses to bring the tribute of the world to the British shore; the upper back panel with the Royal Arms; the left-hand door with Mars, Minerva, and Mercury supporting the Imperial Crown of Great Britain; and the left-hand panels with the Liberal Arts and Sciences protected.

BUCKINGHAM HOUSE

With Kew Gardens and the State Coach Chambers's position in the royal orbit was firmly fixed. His next task, following George III's marriage in 1761, was to provide a suitable Dower House for the new Queen. St James's Palace was inconvenient and old-fashioned, as indeed were the other royal houses in London, especially in comparison with the great town houses recently erected by the nobility. As it happened, the King's requirements fortunately coincided with a dispute over irregularities in the lease of Buckingham House. The Crown, finding that it owned part of the land, obliged the Buckingham Trustees to sell the house for £28,000. Although the Board of Works gave sanction for 'necessary works and repairs' in July 1762, the great period of alterations did not begin until the end of 1762. By 1774 nearly £73,000[11] was spent transforming old Buckingham House into the more palatial and more appropriately-named Queen's House. Being a Board of Works's job, this transformation should in theory have involved the aged Flitcroft the Comptroller; Stephen Wright the Deputy Surveyor; and the two Architects of the Works, Chambers and Adam. In effect, however, the work was undertaken almost

---

11 *Journals of the House of Commons*, xxxv, 320, recording expenses from Lady Day 1762 until Christmas 1774 of £72,627 os 1½d. To date H. Clifford Smith, *Buckingham Palace*, 1931, is still the only documentary history of the palace. However, *Buckingham Palace,* by De Bellaigue, Harris & Millar is now published, and *The History of the King's Works* edited by H. M. Colvin, will soon appear.

entirely by Chambers with Adam contributing only the design for the chimney-piece in the Saloon, and the ceiling in the Japanned Room.

A letter[12] from Chambers to Lord Abercorn in September 1762 reporting that he was busy making designs for various alterations in the Queen's House, the survival of a number of designs, and the style of the executed work, bear witness to Chambers's involvement. Precisely how the King ordered his requirements we do not know. It must be remembered that George III and Chambers, like George IV and Nash, were intimate friends who doubtless worked out their problems in discussions and who, furthermore, shared their friendship with the Surveyor General, Thomas Worsley. Indeed it may have been Worsley, well known for his equestrian interests, who designed the Riding House (Pl.120) completed by 1774 at a cost of £9757.

Buckingham House was built c.1705 by William Winde for John Sheffield, Duke of Buckingham. Although it was not the first house of its type, its conspicuous London site made it a fashionable model for country-house builders. Its giant order supporting an entablature with attic pilasters (Pl.115), and its quadrant colonnade linking the main block to office wings flanking a courtyard (Pl.113), were soon to be found in innumerable variations throughout England. The subsequent history of the house from its inception as a royal residence in 1761 is a sequence of additions, re-facings, and encasings. The changes were certainly radical, but they never destroyed the original building or its domestic character. Buckingham Palace is, and always was, a grand country house in town – a fact acknowledged by the Duke of Buckingham himself when he inscribed *Rus in urb* on one of his friezes.

Chambers, called upon to bring this baroque house up to date, encased it in new smooth brick, removed the giant pilasters from the angles, disguised the basement by raising the forecourt, and gave the roof a new balustrade (Pl.116). The results were restrained and unpretentious in accordance with both neo-classical fashion and George III's plebeian tastes. The King's unpretentious, domestic taste and the palace's informality and homeliness were further underlined in 1770 by the substitution of a low iron railing around the forecourt in place of Tijou's formal iron-work screen.

Enlarging the house (Pl.114) was largely a matter of keeping pace with the King's insatiable bibliomania. Chambers's initial intention was to extend the garden front by low seven-bay wings, one on the south for libraries and the other on the north for miscellaneous offices. The south wing housing the 'great' or 'West' Library was begun in 1762. Before it was finished it became clear that more space was needed to accommodate drawings and medals, whereupon another wing, called the South Library, was added at right angles to the West Library. This was followed in 1766–8 by the great Octagon Library (Pl.118) built at the east end of the South Library for Consul Smith's books purchased in 1763. The royal collection continued to grow at such a rate that within a few years the three new libraries were insufficient. In 1772–3 a single-storey East Library was formed in the space between the South Library and the main block. Then in 1774 a second storey was added as a Marine Gallery for the King to display his models of British ships and harbours.

The northern extensions set aside for miscellaneous offices were a very much simpler

---

[12] Abercorn correspondence, Baronscourt, Co. Tyrone, by courtesy of the Duke of Abercorn.

operation. A wing corresponding to the West Library was built between 1766 and 1768 and was plainly fitted up. Its size and importance were increased in 1778 when the Prince of Wales was given apartments in an eastern extension that terminated in a half-octagon. This may have been the work of Kenton Couse, Clerk of the Works from 1775.

The most complete visual record of the interiors of Buckingham House before they were swept away by Nash is contained in Pyne's *Royal Residences*, a collection of coloured aquatints by various artists, published in 1819, of the royal family's rooms. Of the King's rooms Pyne shows only the Octagon Library which was probably the only one with any architectural character, the others being primarily utilitarian. His emphasis is appropriately placed on the richly-decorated Queen's apartments in the main block. The new interior preserved the arrangement of the Duke of Buckingham's old rooms. From the forecourt one entered into a low hall with Laguerre's painted staircase at one end, which led to the state rooms on the first floor. Chambers, either of his own will or the King's request, preserved the greater part of Laguerre's work. Although in 1776 he proposed to transform the old well stair into an 'Imperial' one which was executed by James Wyatt in 1800, in the 1760s he did nothing more than replace the mural on the north wall with a sympathetic decoration of his own design[13] painted by William Oram. The main feature was a large *trompe-l'œil* niche around a door which he introduced to provide direct entry from the stairs to the Saloon. Within the Saloon (Pl.117) his alterations were far more drastic. He swept away the rich Venetian atmosphere created by the paintings of Laguerre and Bellucci and replaced it with a cool grey neo-classical scheme 'painted in the antique taste' by Cipriani, aided by Oram. The walls were compartmented by pilaster strips, a French motif hitherto unknown in England, used again in Gower House (Pl.100) and Somerset House (Pl.174), and Peper Harow (Pl.88). In each of the principal divisions was a Cipriani grisaille surmounting gilt oval mirrors designed by Chambers. Although somewhat subdued, redecoration of the Saloon was certainly regal enough for its use as the Queen's Throne Room.

The only other redecorations of any consequence were the Red Drawing Room, sometimes called the Japanned Room, in the centre of the garden front with a ceiling by Adam, and the Second Drawing Room (Pl.119) north of the Saloon, entirely redesigned by Chambers. It is interesting to see that both Adam and Chambers designed similar ceilings for both rooms, ornamented with neo-classical grotesques and painted insets by Cipriani in the manner of Stuart's painted decorations of 1757 at Spencer House. For both architects they were, in fact, the first fully-integrated neo-classical ceilings.

Refurnished and refaced at considerable expense the Queen's House was still no palace. Indeed, it is clear from this and the abortive Richmond projects, that a palace, however much it may have been needed to accommodate the growing royal family, was never really wanted. George III's personal interests came first – hence the numerous libraries added to the Queen's House, and the building of an observatory (Pl.125) at Richmond before the anticipated completion of the palace begun in 1767.[14]

---

13 The design for the *trompe-l'œil* exedra is among the Buckingham Palace drawings in the Gardner Coll., Westminster Public Library. It is, however, unsigned and is not in Chambers's hand.

14 I am indebted to Mrs C. Donnelly for her account of observatories in the *Mémoires* of the Académie royale de Belgique (cf. Catalogue).

There had been no Royal Observatory since 1675 when Wren built the one at Greenwich. The Transit of Venus plotted for 3 June 1769 provided an appropriate moment to build a new one. The circumstances of its building, however, are unknown. As there are no Board of Works's accounts, it must be presumed that it was financed by the King out of his Privy Purse, and that the technical installations were the combined effort of Stephen Demaimbray, the King's astronomer, Chambers, and possibly his friend, the Swedish astronomer Perh Wargentin.[15] Swedish precedent plays an important part in the genesis of the Richmond Observatory. The transition from the old open-view tower to the modern concept of a turret or cupola to house the instruments (as perfected at the Radcliffe Observatory in 1771) was initiated by Celsius at the Uppsala Observatory in 1740, and advanced at the Stockholm Observatory built between 1746 and 1753. Both buildings were designed by Harlemann, one of Chambers's oldest professional friends. There can be little doubt that Chambers knew the Uppsala Observatory and probably the one at Stockholm as well, if only from designs. In the chronology of observatories Richmond follows Stockholm. Unlike its predecessors, however, it was an adaptation of a Palladian villa,[16] and more specifically of the Tanfield Casino (q.v.). The body of the villa was only one-and-a-half-storeys high with canted bays on the north and south fronts, proclaiming an interior plan of two conjoined octagons. These octagonal rooms were both fully-walled with fret and glazed cases for the display of books, instruments, and minerals, and one was also fitted with a 'Chippendale' fret gallery. The Observatory still stands, in the midst of a golf course, as the sole reminder of the Hanoverians' love for Richmond Gardens.

The only other new or partially new building at Richmond was a fête pavilion (Pl.126 and Fig.14) for the entertainment on 24 September 1769 of Christian IV of Denmark. This ephemeral structure of wood and canvas incorporated the remains of an unused fête pavilion designed some years earlier by Robert Adam. The inside was 'elegantly painted and gilt in a whimsical but agreeable style' with a large central dome supported by eight columns wreathed with flowers; three triumphal arches decorated with 'emblems of Various Sorts'; and pedestals supporting 'figures of Rural deities with Nymphs and Satyrs holding festoons of flowers suspended from one figure to the other between the arches', all designed by Chambers and painted by Cipriani and Richards.

By 1770, only ten years after his appointment as architect to George III, Chambers had surrounded Richmond Lodge with an impressive, albeit largely temporary, group of royal buildings – the observatory, the fête pavilion, and the beginnings of Richmond Palace III. Then in 1772 Princess Augusta died and Richmond was forsaken for Kew House with its greater accommodation. According to the Board of Works's accounts enlargements and alterations began immediately; and one surviving plan indicates that Chambers intended to square up the house by repeating the pavilion plan of its garden

[15] It may be significant that Chambers had been corresponding with Perh Wilhelm Wargentin, the Swedish Astronomer Royal. His letter, however, of 23 May 1768 refers to other matters. Both were members of the Swedish Royal Academy of Sciences. Cf. N. V. E. Nordenmark, *Perh Wilhelm Wargentin*, Uppsala, 1939, 428.

[16] Today the Observatory looks even more like a villa as its flanking lower parts were raised level to the centre roof line in the nineteenth century.

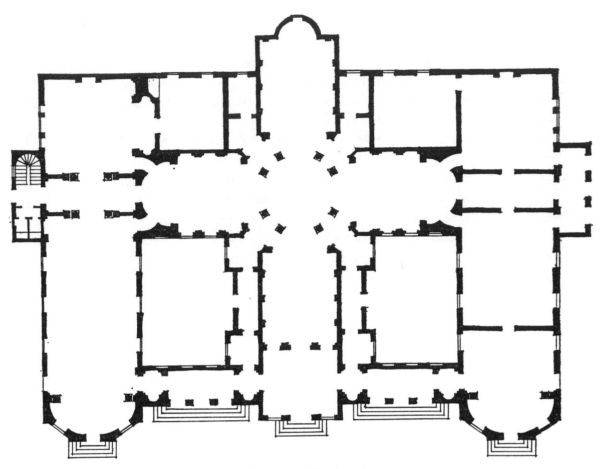

Fig.14 Richmond Gardens, Surrey

front in the rear. At this time was also built a small domed clock tower. However, although considerable sums were spent, exactly what was accomplished is uncertain.

If the move to Kew forecasts the doom of Richmond Lodge, its fate was finally sealed by the decision in 1778 to build the Queen's Lodge on the south terrace of Windsor Castle. Lodge is a gross misnomer, for what was, in fact, a huge and gloomy house to contain the ever-increasing royal family. Surprisingly for the author of the *Treatise* it was an essay in the castle style (Pls 121–124) and, like the Gothic Milton Abbey, never to be repeated. No royal house of recent centuries has been so completely forgotten as the Queen's Lodge. Pyne omitted it from his *Royal Residences*, St John Hope ignored it in his indigestible history of Windsor Castle, and Sir Jeffry Wyattville demolished it in 1823. Everyone seems to have agreed with Walpole that it was 'plain even to meaness'. Nevertheless, the stark simplicity of its arched windows and castellated parapets echoed the style of Hugh May's seventeenth-century work in the Upper Ward, and the building as a whole was sympathetic to the unrestored silhouette of the medieval and seventeenth-century castle. Considered in this light it was admirably successful. This in fact was recognized by James Wyatt when he succeeded Chambers as Surveyor General in 1796 and began restoring Windsor. What he saw of May's and Chambers's work provided the ingredients for his short-lived essays in the castle style at Shoebury (unexecuted, 1797), Norris Castle, 1799, and Pennsylvania Castle, 1800.

86

The Queen's Lodge, completed in 1782 at a cost of nearly £75,000, was Chambers's last major work for the royal family. After a remarkable record of twenty-five years as sole architect to George III, illness and old age began to take the upper hand. By 1792 he was so incapacitated that Wyatt had to take his place at Frogmore. It was, we can be sure, a favour willingly allowed, for at the age of seventy Chambers must have been 'heartily tired of the profession'.

SWEDEN

Chambers's decision in 1755 to establish an architectural practice in London could hardly have been wiser. England, however, was not the only place open to him, for, unlike most architects, he was free by virtue of his international background to settle wherever he pleased. In 1752 negotiations were afoot for his appointment as *architecte du roi* to Frederick the Great of Prussia; but they came to naught. Paris was another possibility, although there is no indication that he ever thought of working there. A much more serious consideration was Sweden, where he might have hoped one day to succeed Harlemann as principal architect, but even so, he could not have had the vast and varied opportunities that he found in England. His former association with Frederick, Prince of Wales, at Kew, his English wife and friends made on the Grand Tour, and not least the building boom, were among the many attractions that finally led him to England. Although once there he never returned to Sweden, he continued to think of himself as an Anglo-Swede and to maintain close relationships. He corresponded with his family in Gothenburg, with various Swedish scientists and men of letters, and seems to have been on friendly terms with Count Scheffer, a powerful minister who was, like Chambers, a sinophile. Towards the end of 1767, he was presented by Queen Louise Ulrica with a gold box inset with painted views of the Swedish royal palaces. This was more than a gesture of friendship or a gift in return for *Kew, Chinese Buildings*, and the *Treatise* which he had sent to the Queen. It was a prelude to the Knighthood of the Order of the Polar Star (*Chevalier de l'ordre de l'étoile polaire*) conferred upon him in 1770.

The fact that Chambers, at this time, began making designs for Swedish buildings had no bearing upon his royal honour. His first design, exhibited at the Society of Artists in 1767 and now lost, was for a fish market at Gothenburg. This was not executed, nor does it seem that it was ever seriously contemplated. Furthermore it was for a municipal rather than a royal building. His next design was a royal one for Queen Ulrica's palace at Svartsjo. Although it was exhibited at the Royal Academy in 1775, there is reason to believe that it was made before 1769, the year Adelcrantz was employed to enlarge the palace built by Harlemann. In the Tessin-Harlemann Collection in the National Museum in Stockholm is a design (Pl.127) signed by Chambers's pupil Edward Stevens and dated 1769. As might be expected, it is full of Chambersian passages, and is distinguished by a large portico based on the centre portico of Perrault's Louvre front, rising above the main body of the house. Stevens's design has several features, including the portico, in common with a design (Pl.128) of Chambers at the Victoria and Albert Museum. This may well be the drawing exhibited at the Royal Academy in 1775. It entirely satisfies Walpole's description of the Royal Academy project as 'handsome and simple'. Stylistically it is related to the 1765 design for Adderbury (Pl.72) which was also fully rusticated. In the 1791 edition of the *Treatise* Chambers confessed that his 'considerable composition' for Harewood was 'with considerable variations.... afterwards wrought to the extent of a palace for her late Majesty, the Dowager Queen of Sweden.' The Harewood composition (Pl.44), only recently discovered, has the unusual adaptation of Perrault's portico, and is, incidentally, fully rusticated. This confirms the fact that both Stevens's and Chambers's designs were intended for Svartsjo, submitted, however, more as an ideal than as a practical project.

Chambers's exhibition of his *c.*1769 palace design in 1775 may have been prompted by his re-involvement with Svartsjo in 1774. In that year he submitted to Baron Nolcken, the Swedish Ambassador in London, a 'Design for the gardens of Svartsjo wherein he has preserved the Greatest part of the old work according to her Majesties intention and introduced a Style of new, that may be executed at a Moderate Expence and be useful as well as pleasant and ornamental.'[17] It is a peculiar design, old-fashioned, and in a somewhat formal Bridgemanesque manner, and unrelated to what is known of the eighteenth-century garden.[18] Included in his plan is a large double-courtyard palace which bears no relation to the Harlemann-Adelcrantz complex or to earlier portico designs, and must therefore be either an expression of his ignorance of the current architectural situation there, or a new palace project. Whatever the case, his interest in Svartsjo was eclipsed in 1775 by the prospect of Somerset House when the government offered him the opportunity to display his talents on a scale undreamed of by English, let alone Swedish, eighteenth-century royalty.

17 BM Add.MS 41133, 126. The plan referred to exists as two copies in the V & A.
18 According to Mr Sten Karling a map of 1814 in the Byggnadstyrelsen Arkiv in Stockholm shows part of Svartsjo with curving paths and decorative buildings that could point to Chambers's work. I think, however, that this is due to the English taste in gardening in the later years of the century.

Chapter 7

Public Building

SOCIETY OF ARTS

When Chambers was elected a member of the Society of Arts in January 1757, he had neither built nor published anything. Two years later, when the Society[1] acquired a more spacious site behind 380–1 the Strand, facing Denmark Court, he was a rising star – having published *Designs for Chinese Buildings*; built the Casino and Triumphal Arch at Wilton; stables at Goodwood; begun work as the Dowager Princess of Wales's architect at Kew; and most portentous of all, having won the favours of George, Prince of Wales. It is not surprising therefore that he should be chosen by the Society to design their new room.

According to the articles of agreement drawn-up on 20 March 1759, Chambers was to provide a 'Great Room' upstairs, and a smaller 'Repository' below. Unfortunately his designs have not survived, nor are there any contemporary drawings of the rooms which were destroyed in the nineteenth century, having been vacated when the Society moved to its present home designed by Robert Adam. All that we have is a lease of 1760 describing the 'Great Room' as a double cube of 80 by 40 feet[2] (compared with 60 by 30 of the double cube at Wilton or the 110 by 55 of that at the Banqueting House) which had a 'Palladian' ceiling, probably meaning a coffered one, and lit by an oval dome raised upon four Corinthian columns – perhaps something in the manner of the Ashburnham House staircase dome. This impressive interior was one of Chambers's first, and its decoration must therefore have been in the manner of the Pembroke or Richmond House rooms. It certainly post-dates his unexecuted *Plan of a Building for the Society of Arts, Manufactures, and Commerce* (Pl.139), a grandiose conception combining elements from Burlington's Chiswick, Kent's Holkham, and Paine's Kedleston with a little of the columnar play that had fascinated him in his Roman days. This plan is surprisingly much more mature, and its parts more integrated, than those proposed for either the Richmond Palace project of 1764 or that of 1769. As the Society of Arts plan could never have been remotely feasible, it suffered from none of the practical considerations implicit in designing a palace that was to be built.

The 'Great Room' was not only designed by Chambers but was also furnished by him in 1759 with tables, seats, and chandeliers. To judge from the surviving President's Chair

---

[1] The most recent history of the Society's buildings is D. G. C. Allan, *The Houses of the Royal Society of Arts*, 1966. I am indebted to Mr Allan for providing me with much new information.

[2] There are discrepancies in the given dimensions of the rooms. According to the Baker-Arderon correspondence in the Foster Collection (V & A), in one report the room measured 51 × 38 feet in area (vol.4, 130), in another as 61 × 35 feet. The height was 16 feet with a cupola measuring another 16 feet.

(Pl.181), these pieces were of the so-called 'transitional neo-classical' type. While the upper part of the chair has S-scrolled arms and a scrolly rococo back, the lower part has a straight seat rail boldly ornamented with Vitruvian scrolls, and straight spiral-fluted legs. The search for firsts is an invidious one.[3] Nevertheless, this does seem to be one of the first chairs to incorporate the kind of rectilinear elements associated with the neo-classical style. The portraits of Marigny, like Roslin's of 1761, may include neo-classical pedestals, lyres, tables, and picture frames, but the chairs are thoroughly rococo.[4] Furniture historians[5] now agree that the earliest neo-classical furniture was designed by Louis Le Lorrain in 1756 and 1757 for a room in Lalive de Jully's house, decorated by Barreau de Chefdeville. Chambers, as it happens, was a good friend of Chefdeville and was almost certainly acquainted with Le Lorrain as well. What is more, he and James Stuart, who had designed neo-classical tables for Spencer House and Kedleston between 1757 and 1759, were involved directly or indirectly with these and other French artists in the promising activities at the French Academy in Rome.[6] It was here, under the leadership of Le Lorrain, that neo-classical architecture emerged as a recognizable style between 1740 and 1750. In view of these connections, it is not surprising to find in Chambers's Franco-Italian album of small studies, made between 1749 and 1755, a drawing of a chair (Pl.180) with lower parts strikingly similar to the President's Chair, but with a kidney-shaped back. What is surprising, or rather intriguing, is that the drawing is made on the same paper as others known to have been done in Paris, which suggests, despite evidence to the contrary, that a chair of this type may have existed in Paris when Chambers was there in 1750, 1753, or 1755.

BLACKFRIARS BRIDGE

We have seen that Chambers failed with a grandiose plan for the Society of Arts, just as he had failed two years earlier at Harewood, and was to fail again, in 1759, at Blackfriars Bridge. No doubt, his colonnaded design[7] (Pl.140) with its *Grand Prix* effects would have made an attractive addition to the Thames skyline, especially if seen, as it would later have been, as an adjunct to Somerset House. Although only the elevational design survives – and that as a photograph, for the original is lost – it is clear that structurally it was exceedingly conservative with none of the engineering skill or inventiveness that won Mylne the commission.

WOODSTOCK TOWN HALL

From the dream world of grand academies and triumphal bridges, we come to the reality of Chambers's first public building, the Town Hall (Pl.141) at Woodstock built in 1766 for the 4th Duke of Marlborough. Chambers's employment here in preference to Brown,

---

[3] Cf. John Harris, 'Early Neo-Classic Furniture', *Furniture History*, 2, 1966.

[4] E.g. the chair that Marigny is seated in when painted by Roslin in 1761 (Château de Versailles), where all the other decorative and ornamental effects in the picture are strictly rectilinear.

[5] Cf. Svend Erikson, 'Lalive de Jully's Furniture *à la grecque*', *Burl. Mag.*, Aug. 1961, 340–7.

[6] Cf. Harris, op. cit.

[7] Chambers's design is surprisingly reproduced by R. S. Mylne in *The Master Masons to the Crown of Scotland*, Edinburgh, 1893, when it was then in the possession of a W. J. Harvey. It is now lost. Chambers is said to have been encouraged to submit a design by a Mr Paterson, a city merchant who could have been the same as the T. Paterson, for whom Mylne designed a house in Norwich in 1764.

who acted in an architectural capacity at Blenheim in 1765 and probably in 1766 as well, may have been recommended by the Duchess, whose father, the Duke of Bedford, had then begun to employ him at Woburn. On the other hand he might have succeeded Leadbetter who had been employed by the 3rd Duke of Marlborough, had died in 1766, and whose project for rebuilding a wing at Woburn was posthumously being realized by Chambers. Although erected for the remarkably modest sum[8] of £497 14s 4½d, the Town Hall is a masterpiece of control and dignity, commended by Hardwick for its 'just simplicity' and 'appropriate character'.[9]

THEATRE ROYAL, LIVERPOOL

No such praise could be bestowed upon the Theatre Royal at Liverpool documented as having been designed by Chambers in 1772. It has long since been destroyed, no plan survives, and the front is known only from a rather crude engraving. If indeed this was Chambers's child, then it must have been raised by a Liverpool architect. There is no mention of the Theatre in Chambers's Letter Books, and although it repeats the size and scale of Woodstock's three-bay pedimented front, the provincial hand is revealed by solecisms like the Palladian window beneath the pediment, that would be unthinkable for Chambers.

GERMAN LUTHERAN CHAPEL IN THE SAVOY

The most auspicious year for Chambers's public buildings before Somerset House was 1766. In addition to the Woodstock Town Hall he had a commission from the German Lutheran congregation to design their new chapel in the precinct of the Savoy.[10] This commission, like his later unexecuted projects for Marylebone church (1770) reveals his dependence upon Gibbs – Gibbs of the *Book of Architecture* rather than of the Roman Baroque. At the Savoy he refined (Pls 142–143) and paraphrased both the exterior and interior of Gibbs's Harley Chapel, interpreting in neo-classical terms its handsome galleries. Although the Savoy Chapel has not survived there is enough topographical evidence to show that it was built according to Chambers's designs. The building accounts are particularly informative about the craftsmen employed in this middle period, and they reveal that several members were brought over from Clive's house in Berkeley Square, which was then nearing completion.

ST MARYLEBONE CHURCH

A chapel and a town hall by 1767 might appear to augur well for the establishment of a public works' practice. In effect, however, they were diversions to his thriving private practice in town and country. There is no stylistic development or congruity between any of the designs executed, or unexecuted. In fact he had no style specifically for public buildings before 1770. In 1772 he designed the chapel for Trinity House, Hull, a commission that probably arose from some family connections with the port and its Scandi-

---

[8] The sum is quoted from a bill by Mr David Green in *Blenheim Palace*, 1951, 282. As I have not been able to examine this I cannot tell if it represents the total amount.
[9] Chambers's *Treatise*, ed. Gwilt, 1862, 9.
[10] Cf. R. Somerville, *The Savoy Manor: Hospital: Chapel*, 1960.

navian trade. Apart from the barest hint[11] of a tall narrow pedimented front, nothing is known of this chapel, destroyed in 1844. Whatever he provided was extremely well received by the Corporation who rewarded him with ale and hams over and above his fee. This amicable exchange is in sharp contrast to the unpleasant experience with the Vestry of St Marylebone church for whom he spent two years, between 1770 and 1772, drawing and redrawing designs to no avail. Nevertheless, out of these abortive designs there emerged a stylistic pattern that passed via Woodstock Church tower and Trinity College, Dublin, to Somerset House.

Despite the rapid spread of London northwards, the Parish of St Marylebone had no church comparable to St George's, Hanover Square, across the Oxford Road. The Vestry, though they recognized the need, were for years unable to decide where the church should be, whether they had sufficient money, or indeed whether it was all worth the trouble. Into this unstable situation was precipitated Chambers, little knowing that the end would be a church built in 1813 by his pupil, Thomas Hardwick, with many of the ingredients of his rejected designs. When in 1770 Archdeacon Harley approached Chambers, he was approaching an important parish developer, literally in command of Berners Street in the centre of a favourable residential area. On 3 August Chambers supplied alternative designs for a church with a dome (Pls 144-146) or a spire (Pl.147) warning Harley that the 'Dome will exceed the sum you propose laying out considerably', whereas the 'Spire will as near as I can determine upon rough calculation amount to £16,109, inclusive of my commission of 5 p cent.'[12] By June 1772, the Vestry were still vacillating and his patience was wearing thin. 'I have', he complained, 'already made five if not six different designs, some of them very considerable ones, I have also made several estimates of this Building and had a great deal of trouble.'[13] Nor was this the end. In February 1773 he submitted a 'new plan' and an estimate of £20,000. Finally, after all his efforts, the Vestry proposed to pay him off with the paltry sum of £120. He replied with an explosive letter to Harley on 16 February 1774: 'I am sorry to find by the Discourse we had yesterday in the street, that the Gentlemen of the Vestry propose making me so trifling an offer for all the trouble wh they have given me wh regard to the intended Church & some other works wh have been executed under my direction. I will not suppose there is any intention to affront me by offering what I cannot with Decency accept of, & must therefore conclude either that the Gentlemen have forgot what has been done or are no Judges of its value, in either of wh cases it is necessary to set them right. I cannot do this myself for Reasons very obvious, but must necessarily be troublesome to some friend. Would you, Dr Sr, who have so kindly assisted me on many other occasions be so obliging to take this matter in hand, & when you have a proper opportunity represent to the Gentlemen the following Circumstances – I was appointed by the Vestry, I believe, upwards of two years ago, their Architect, & it was then agreed that I should, as usual, be allowed 5p Cent upon the works executed in Consequence of this appointment. I have by the Directions of the Vestry attended the Execution of the

11 Reproduced in A. S. Harvey, *The Trinity House of Kingston Upon Hull*, 1950.

12 BM Add.MS 41133, 20.

13 BM Add.MS 41133, 73v.

Vaults & burial Grounds, & also the Court-house, having made or examined the Estimates, settled the Bills, measured the works, & inspected into the Construction &
finishing of the whole by a regular & due attendance either by myself, my Assistants, or
Clerks, as the nature of the works required. I am consequently entitled to 5 p cent upon
the amount of the bills for these two works, wh to the best of my recollection amount
to about £3500, & 5 pr cent thereon is £175. For the Church I have made no less than
6 different Designs, all of them large & complicated, consequently very Difficult to
contrive & tedious to execute. I will not trouble you wth a Bushell of Sketches & Calculations wh were made previous to the Designs, but I have sent you the finished Drawings
to show by wh those who understood such works will judge of the rest. I have beside
made 3 Different Estimates, one of wh is sent for the Gentlemen's inspection; it fills 3 Sheets
of paper, & those who understand it know how laborious & tedious such Calculations
are, in short, Dr Sr, Upon the nearest Calculation I can make I am upwards of two
hundred pounds out of pocket by these works in wages to Clerks, measurers Bills,
allowance to Assistants, &c, &c, & there is no Architect of reputation, I am persuaded,
who would do the Designs, &c & wh I have done for the Church for less than 3 hundred
Guineas besides the sum Due to me on the other works. A vast deal of my own time has
been employed in these works, particularly in the Contrivance of the Designs, besides
the wages, &c., wh I have paid to others. I do not, however, mean to insist upon a
generous or even a just requital for my Trouble & Expences. I am too well acquainted
with the temper of the publick Bodys. If I am treated wth tolerable Kindness; tis all I
expect, & I shall be ready to submit to any terms my friends shall judge reasonable.'[14] It
would seem that 'tolerable Kindness' was not a perquisite of the Vestry, for even in
April 1776 a memorandum to 'make application to friends for Marybone',[15] with the
names of Wilton, Collins, Newton, and Mercer listed, suggests that he was rallying these
friends, who were also Vestrymen, to his support. It is indeed odd that this shockingly
unfair treatment of Chambers should be neither recorded in the Vestry Minute Books,
nor its final consequences known. In fact, although one must assume that Chambers was
speaking the truth when he mentioned designing the Court House, this too is an unrecorded event.[16]

His domed designs (A & B) are based upon Gibbs's 'first Draught' for a round church
(Fig.15) at St Martin-in-the-Fields, from which they take not only the plan of a circular
nave with a portico flanked by oval stairs at the west end, and a group of three vestries
or chapels at the east end, but also his peripteros of giant Corinthian columns supporting
the dome and carrying galleries. Scheme A, the most Gibbsian of all, has, in addition,
an elevation (Pl.144) composed of two of his temples.[17] In scheme B he reiterates the
staircase dome (Pl.145) from his own unexecuted designs for York House (1759) (Pl.94),

[14] BM Add.MS 41136, 2–2v.

[15] Sir John Soane's Museum Drawer 41/5. Others who were friends of Chambers were John Devall, Joseph Rose,
and William Greenell – all vestrymen.

[16] Chambers inexplicably appears as a vestryman on 1 May 1775, but according to the Vestry Minutes (St Marylebone Public Library) at no other date. On 24 February 1772 the 'insufficiency of the Rooms at the Court House'
were recorded in the Minutes and plans were presented on 2 May. It is uncertain if these were Chambers's plans.
What work he carried out was demolished before 1850.

[17] James Gibbs, *Book of Architecture*, 1728, pls.67, 72.

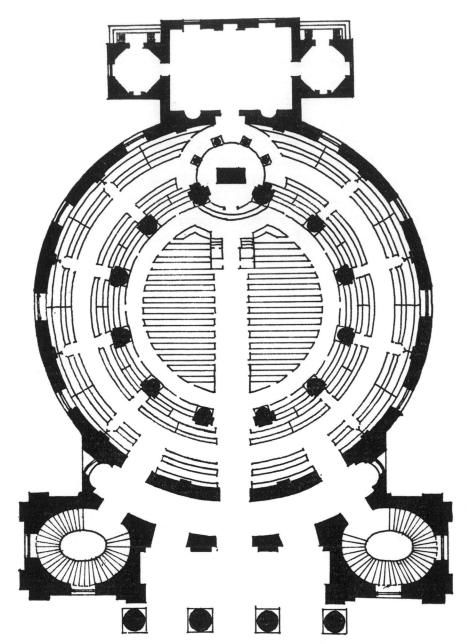

Fig.15 St Marylebone church, London

but modelling it upon that of Bernini's S. Andrea al Quirinale. Of the Spire scheme (C) only one drawing has survived (Pl.147). It shows a Gibbsian tower[18] laced with neo-classical details, and rather peculiarly placed against a bare, barn-like box of a nave. Through the Marylebone projects, Gibbs's influence is extended to the Woodstock Church tower design and to Trinity College, Dublin.

WOODSTOCK & TRINITY COLLEGE

On 29 April 1770, the Mayor and Churchwardens of Woodstock argued that Chambers, the architect of their town hall and then busy at Blenheim, was the 'proper person to

18 For the obelisk, cf. Gibbs, op. cit., pl.29, and for the circular windows under the broken pediment, pl.23.

survey the state of the tower, & if dangerous to give an Estimate of a new Tower & make good that part of the Church were [sic] the Tower now stands.'[19] It is not clear whether in fact the survey was carried out. In any case, the Vestry decided to demolish the tower on 9 October 1774. They then vacillated over the choice of an architect, and it was ten years before they finally got their new tower in 1784. Had Chambers's design (dated 1776) (Pl.148) been executed, Woodstock would have been able to boast a piece of neo-classical urbanity sired by the spire of St Marylebone. Unfortunately he had to suffer once again the indecision of a public body who in the end settled for a local builder. This, however, did not deter him from submitting his tower and spire for the third time to Trinity College, Dublin.

Trinity College can have had little difficulty in deciding upon Chambers as architect of their new lecture theatre and chapel in 1775. They had come to prefer London architects after the success of the west front designed by Henry Keene and John Sanderson in 1759, they knew Chambers's work in Ireland; and may even have been prevailed upon by one or other of his patrons, Charlemont, Leinster, Loftus, or Vesey. For Chambers, about to be inundated by Somerset House, a commission of this size cannot have been entirely welcome. Nevertheless, he agreed on 6 December 1775 'to undertake the business of drawing plans . . . to furnish all the necessary designs for the workmen of every sort, figures drawn out at large, and accompanied with such instructions as will enable any intelligent Clerk of the Works to construct the buildings with as much precision as if he were upon the spot himself'.[20] His plan was to erect two identical porticoed buildings on College Square, a Chapel (Pl.151) on the north side and a Theatre (Pl.150) on the south, each linked with Keene and Sanderson's west block by a range of lodgings. On axis with the centre of the west front, but some distance east of the Chapel and Theatre, he intended to rebuild Richard Castle's earlier free-standing arch and to raise upon it a version of his St Marylebone-Woodstock tower and spire, as a sort of campanile (Pl.149). This scheme is known only from an engraving published in March 1779 by Pool and Cash[21] who must have had access to the original designs, now lost. What they published in 1779, however, was what was intended, and not what was executed. An isometric perspective[22] (also now lost) of the college drawn by Samuel Byrom in 1780 shows that by that date only the Theatre and the southern lodging range had been built. We know, in fact, that the Chapel was not completed until 1793,[23] and that the arch, tower, and steeple, like their ill-fated predecessors, were rejected (in favour many years later in the nineteenth century) for an inelegant campanile by Lanyon. Furthermore, Chambers (as it turned out) was not even in full command of those parts of his plan that were executed. His position is made clear in a letter of 20 May 1779 to Lord Charlemont, in which he explains that he provided designs 'on the supposition that in the course of these works' he would have been able to visit Ireland, but the business of Somerset House and the 'perplexed measures sent me

[19] Vestry Minute Books, cf. H. M. Colvin, 'The Rebuilding of Woodstock Church Tower', *Oxford Arch. Soc. Rpt.*, 87, 1949, 9–14.
[20] Trinity College Minutes.
[21] Pool and Cash, *Views . . . in Dublin*, 1780.
[22] Cf. *Trinity*, I, 1949, 30.
[23] J. Payne, *Universal Geography*, Dublin, 1793, 197.

from Dublin at different times' made it impossible to give anything more than 'a general disposition of what I intended, from which I have since learnt that the buildings are now erecting. If there be any merit in the general intention I may claim some little share in it; but the whole detail; upon which the perfection of these works must greatly depend, is none of mine and whatsoever merit that has is Mr Myers, who I understand is the operator'.[24]

Chambers need not have had any reservations about the merit of the 'whole detail'. As Clerk of the Works, Graham Myers was every bit as competent as Vierpyle at the Casino. We shall never know, however, if the east side of Library Square – seen behind the obelisk tower – was also part of Chambers's design. Probably it was, for the whole scheme unifies the disparate college buildings. The Trinity blocks, though not personally supervised by Chambers, are nevertheless key buildings in his *œuvre*. They are the first fruits of his refresher course in Paris, tinctured with the Gallic sophistication of Gabriel and Antoine, and accordingly bold and assured. This indeed was the prelude to Somerset House.

SOMERSET HOUSE

The centralization in 1776 of the various offices of the English Government in Somerset House was an historic departure from international tradition which had always demanded a separate building for each department. Exactly how this idea was conceived and who was its administrative principal are by no means clear. If, however, there was any one person deserving the title of *eminence grise* it was, as we shall see, Edmund Burke. The Treasury had long been disturbed by the uneconomical and inconvenient dispersion of Government offices throughout London. Although an Act was passed in 1772 to develop Ely House for a number of offices, it was not proceeded with, and any plans that might have been drawn up were scrapped in 1774 when Somerset House was chosen as a more eligible site. This choice was doubtlessly related to an Office of Works's report on the parlous state of old Somerset House submitted on 6 May 1774. The future of the palace was discussed by the King and the Prime Minister, Lord North, on 10 May, and on 17 May the King consented to its demolition for Government offices in exchange for the settlement upon Queen Charlotte of Buckingham House as her official dower house.[25]

The next date of consequence was 28 May when Lord North and William Masterman, Clerk of the Council of the Duchy of Lancaster, agreed to embank the Thames in front of the Savoy and Somerset House. The Savoy was not part of the Somerset House scheme, but a separate project for which plans to house the offices of Salt, Stamp, Land Tax, Hackney Coach, and Hawkers and Pedlars, had already been prepared by William Robinson.

In view of Robinson's participation in the Savoy development and his Clerkship of the Works at old Somerset House, it was only natural that he should be invited to submit designs for the new Somerset House. For a moment it looked as if the greatest public building since Greenwich, and every architect's dream since Jones's Whitehall designs,

24 HMC *Charlemont*, I, 349–50.
25 For the works report cf. PRO. Works 6/19, 27. Its consequences and the subsequent act, cf. *Commons Journals*, XXXX, 299, 316, 319, 335, 340.

would fall into the hands of a decidedly second-rate member of the profession. The buzz that this must have caused can hardly be exaggerated. Chambers intervened almost at once, with the intention, of course, of capturing the commission for himself. The King would not build his palaces, but there was reason to hope the Government would. By no mere coincidence he was off to Paris just after the Savoy-Somerset agreement, not for pleasure, but to 'examine with care and make proper remarks upon' the 'Many great things' that had been built there since his last visit in 1754. The trophy of his brief excursion was a beautifully delineated album[26] of watercolour drawings of the latest Parisian *hôtels* and public buildings – Antoine's La Monnaie (Pl.153), Gabriel's Ecole Militaire and Place Louis XV (Pl.152), Gondoin's Ecole de Chirugie, and Chalgrin's Hôtel de la Vrillière – all pertinent models for a potential Somerset House. Indeed, only the prospect of Somerset House could have caused this sudden burst of activity a month after he had complained to Vesey of being 'heartily tired of the profession.'

Although Chambers had not the slightest assurance that the commission could be wrested from Robinson, he was absolutely determined to do so. He began his campaign on 22 June with a letter[27] to his superior, and friend, Thomas Worsley, in which he strongly attacked both the defects of Robinson's designs (which have not survived) and the actions of the authorities in choosing him as architect. Robinson, he complained, showed 'no mercy for poor Inigo Jones's fine front . . . nor for a great part of that extensive palace almost new, having only been built about thirty years' – referring to Kent's alterations in the 1740s. 'I could easily save both and many thousand pounds, but neither I, nor any of the Board officers are consulted, even in this vast work, which is to contain at least a dozen offices, and which the ground alone is to cost the nation seventy-eight thousand pounds.' It was, to put it politely, 'strange that such an undertaking should be trusted to a Clerk in our Office, ill-qualified as appears by what he has done at the Exise and the Fleet while the King has six architects in his service ready and able to obey his commands. Methinks it should be otherwise in the reign of a vertuoso [*sic*] prince.'

On 13 September[28] he struck again, this time taking his protest even higher, to the Prime Minister's Secretary, William Brummell. In his reply of 1 October, Brummell admitted that 'Lord North Imagined the business of the New Offices at Somerset House, lay before the Board of Works, and that his Lordship's application to Mr Robinson our Secretary in preference to any other person, was merely as considering him the Officer of the Board, and by no means the principal in that great design.'[29]

There was no further mention of Somerset House until April 1775[30] when the freehold of Buckingham House was given to the Queen by Act of Parliament. It was at this point that Edmund Burke entered the scene. North's report[31] to the King describes him as

[26] John Harris, 'Sir William Chambers and his Parisian Album', *Architectural History*, 6, 1963, 54–90. Chambers's remarks on the purpose of his visit are BM Add.MS 41135, 26–26v.

[27] BM Add.MS 41135, 28v.

[28] BM Add.MS 41135, a letter dated 13 September 1774.

[29] BM Add.MS 41135, a letter dated 1 October 1774.

[30] *Journals of the House of Commons*, 12 April 1775, 229.

[31] Burke's part is commented upon by Joseph Baretti, *A Guide Through The Royal Academy*, 1781, 3 – based upon what was said in the House of Commons. Cf. *The Correspondence of King George The Third*, ed. Sir John Fortescue, III, 1928, 207, no.1648 – a letter from Lord North informing the King of Burke's 'pressing for splendor'. Cf. also *Parliamentary History*, XVIII, 26 April 1775, and the Act of 15 May 1775 in *Parliamentary Debates* under the same date.

H

one of the 'men of taste' who desired the new offices to be 'an object of national splendour as well as convenience', an 'ornament of the Metropolis', and a 'monument to the taste and elegance of His Majesty's Reign.' Burke's demands undoubtedly turned the tide in Chambers's favour, for however sorry one might feel for Robinson, his designs for the Savoy site show him quite incapable of rising to this splendid occasion. However, the final stroke of fortune fell on 13 October 1775 when Robinson suddenly died. Without effort or embarrassment, the whole situation was resolved, and before the month was out Chambers was appointed architect. Chambers in his jubilation did not fail to recognize Burke's role in establishing the character of this grandiose project. Somerset House, he wrote to Burke, is 'a Child of your own', and ''tis but right you should see it fledged before you leave it.'[32]

However much Chambers regretted the demolition of the Jonesian parts of old Somerset House,[33] he surely welcomed the opportunity to plan anew on the spacious six-acre site. There were, however, two limitations: firstly, he had to keep to the plan of the old Strand front – a protruding neck of land enclosed on two sides by private buildings; and secondly, he was compelled to keep open Duchy Lane,[34] a public way that bisected the western parts of the site and gave access to the river gate.

In the tradition of Inigo Jones and Whitehall, he turned to the permutation of court-yard plans to solve the problems of accommodation. If he is criticized on these grounds, then the answer must be that the requirements urged upon him demanded a utilitarian strategy with the most stringent economy of planning and apportioning of space. There could be no baroque vistas as at Greenwich. In only one plan (Pl.155), presumably his first one, did he express himself in bold and unrestrained terms. It is an astonishing performance of oval and oblong courts linked in a most intricate columnar manner reminiscent of Le Geay and the Franco-Italian fantasies evocative of Imperial Rome. Reason, however, prevailed with a more mundane arrangement. Although his final plans have not survived, the pattern of development can be followed in a number of preliminary studies. There is, for example, one late scheme showing the Strand block with E-shaped wings and a court open to the river. To provide further accommodation the next scheme has the court closed to the river with secondary courts flanking it on the east and west. This comes very close to the accepted plan (Fig.16) with its great court – in essence the most splendid of London squares – open to and aligned upon a free-standing Strand block on the north, and closed to the river by a 500-feet wing raised upon Herculean terraces and vaults. Cutting across the site was Duchy Lane, spanned on the river front by a Palladian Bridge linking the centre portion of the frontage with a westerly pavilion that was the south end of a terrace of houses for the Commissioners of the Navy. Although he planned an identical Palladian Bridge and pavilion to terminate the eastern end of the wing, he was never to see it built in his lifetime.

The problem of providing sufficient accommodation was a minor one in comparison

---

[32] Burke Correspondence, Sheffield Public Library Bk 2/543.

[33] The Lord Protector's work is treated by N. Pevsner in 'Old Somerset House', *Architectural Review*, Sept. 1954, 163–7.

[34] The fine late seventeenth-century range of stables flanking this lane was eventually replaced by a terrace of houses to stable the Commissioners of the Navy.

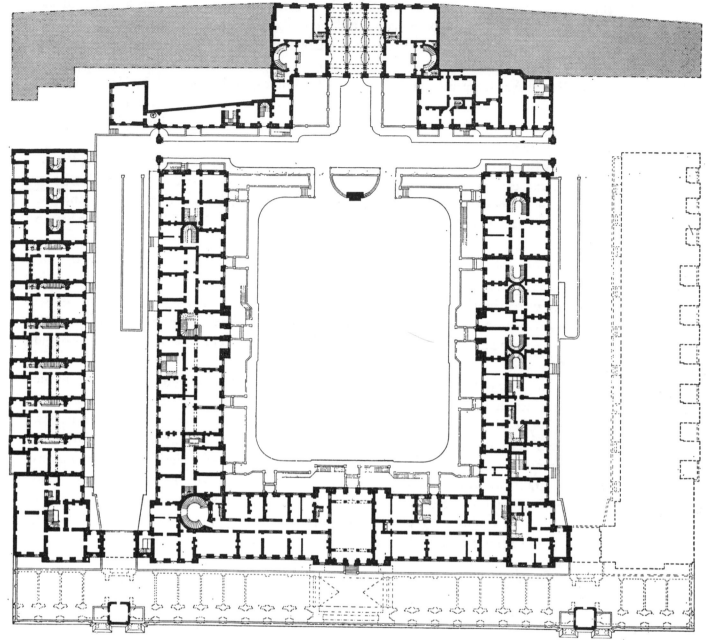

Fig.16 Somerset House, London

with the polemics over its allocation. Each office regarded itself as autocratic, and each clamoured for the best and largest space possible. Satisfying all these demands was a monolithic task that would have tried the most hardened of administrators. Chambers had not only to examine plans of the old offices, and determine the new requirements in discussion and correspondence, but also to submit each unit of the proposed plans to the office in question for its approval.[35] Some of his plans were rejected out of hand; others were returned to him for second and sometimes third amendments. Even after

[35] Cf. Soane Museum Drawer 41/4[25-30], plans of the Tax Office dated 25 March 1777 and inscribed 'Examined these Plans and found them well calculated for carrying on the Business of this Office'.

the final settlements were committed to paper there were still unforeseen and, indeed, unforeseeable, problems. Obviously a building of this size took a long time to execute. As a result, many offices found when they finally settled in that their initial requirements, made perhaps ten years earlier, had altered considerably.

The Royal Academy was housed in the Strand block to the west of the Vestibule, and the Society of Antiquaries and the Royal Society to the east. In the balancing wings that extended the block on the court side, space was found for Legacy Duty, Hawkers and Pedlars, Exchequer, Lottery, Privy Seal and Signet, and Hackney Coach and Barge Masters. Elsewhere the greater offices were given the more architecturally elevated positions. In the east court wing were Audit, Salt, Tax, Pipe, Clerk of the Estreats, and Duchies of Cornwall and Lancaster. The Navy occupied both the west wing and the river wing west of, and including, the central Seaman's Hall. East of this was the Stamp Office.

Apart from the Seaman's Hall, the Staircase, and a few Board Rooms, all belonging to the Navy, pressures of accommodation ruled out liberality of planning. The majority of offices were tightly-fitted, like pieces of a jig-saw, around a spine of cross-vaulted corridors. Only underground was Chambers free from bureaucratic demands. His great gloomy record vaults are an achievement that would certainly have impressed his old friend Piranesi.

From an office in part of the old Palace that was allowed to remain standing within the courtyard just in front of the Strand block, Chambers commanded the early stages of building while his Clerks were hard at work at their drawing boards and account books. John Yenn and Robert Browne were joint Clerks of the Works; Thomas Clark was 'superintendent of works'; and Francis Symmons was 'assistant clerk'. Under Symmons were a number of Royal Academy students anxious to gain invaluable experience; and under Samuel Saxon were Willey Reveley, Nathaniel Lindigren, and William Rose. The first tasks in 1776 and 1777 were to push ahead with the embankment of the Thames, and with the Strand block where Chambers was anxious to house the learned societies as quickly as possible.

The Strand front (Pl.156) is first and foremost a monument to John Webbs's Jonesian New Gallery, one of the choicest parts of the old palace and the first home of the Royal Academy.[36] Its nine bays of one-and-a-half storeys over an arcade are an expansion of the five-bay gallery; three-quarter columns replace the original Corinthian pilasters; and the ornamentation is spelled out in contemporary neo-classical terms. Secondly it pays homage to Ammanati, Palladio, Vignola, Peruzzi, and to Salvi, an exponent of late baroque Classicism who Chambers thought sometimes 'hit upon the right'.[37] The attic, fronted by four statues and surmounted by a coat-of-arms, is taken from Salvi's Trevi Fountain, measured[38] by Chambers, and an appropriation for which he found precedent in Soufflot's Hôtel Dieu at Lyons (Pl.154).

[36] This is why Chambers illustrated the New Gallery as the head-piece to his dedication to the King in the *Dissertation on Oriental Gardening*, 1772.

[37] Chambers's admiration for Salvi is expressed in the 'Note of Advice' to Edward Stevens (cf. p.21).

[38] Cf. his splendid drawing of the Trevi Fountain, purchased by Soane as Lot 70 in the 1811 sale; today Soane Museum Drawer, XXI, 8.

This tribute to the Jonesian New Gallery was not Chambers's first. He had experimented with the theme before in his third and fourth projects for Richmond Palace, as well as in his undated design for a nobleman's town house (Pl.104), which, if indeed earlier, is a remarkable prefiguration of the Strand façade – and, of course, if he wished for an intermediate precedent, there was Leoni's pioneer town-house front at Queensbury House in Burlington Gardens. Nor, for that matter, is Chambers's relationship with Jones limited to the contents of these designs. His ability to take a number of renaissance models and fuse them into a composition entirely his own also makes him comparable to Jones. And, like Jones, he is at his best with small-scale units of design of which the Strand block is a perfect example – a polished academic jewel appropriately set aside for the academic bodies.

The Strand block raises the curtain on a programme of sculptured decoration that extends over the whole of Somerset House, inside and out. Its particular role in the iconographic web is England's maritime resources. The nine keystones of the arcades are carved[39] with masks symbolizing Ocean and the eight great rivers of the country. Ocean, Thames, Humber, Mersey, Medway, and Tweed were carved by Wilton; and Tyne, Severn, and Dee by Carlini. Ocean is represented as a venerable old man, his beard of waves filled with fish. On his head is a crescent denoting the influence of the moon over the tides, and around his temples is a tiara of royal crowns and tridents. The Thames is a majestic head with billing swans and garlands of flowers and fruits. His hair and beard are neatly plaited to express good sense, humour, and urban perfection. Humber, in contrast, is athletic and hardy; his beard and hair disordered by the tempests, his cheeks and eyes swelled with rage, expressive of the boisterous character of the river. Mersey is crowned with garlands of oak; Dee with reeds and other forms of marine life. Medway, less urbane than Thames, bears the emblems of a ship of war as well as festoons of hops. Tweed is a rustic of strong character with a rough beard and lank hair crowned with roses and thistles. Finally, Tyne is dressed with salmon, kelp, and seaweeds, while Severn wears a crown of sedges, and cornucopia spilling forth water and lampreys.

On the attic are four venerable men in senatorial robes with the cap of liberty on their heads, representing Justice and Moderation (by Cerrachi), and Prudence and Valour (by Carlini). Above them is Bacon's Arms of the British Empire, supported by the Genius of England and Fame.

The iconography of the court front (Pl.164) of the Strand block is somewhat less complex. In the five keystones to the arches are the 'Lares or Tutelar Deities of the Place' carved by Nollekens. The four attic statues (Pl.158) by Wilton represent the Continents, America armed and breathing defiance, the others, in contrast, 'loaded with tributary fruits and treasure'. Bacon again supplied the crowning arms supported by tritons and

[39] Descriptions of the sculpture are to be found in Baretti, op. cit. The RIBA accounts are summarized by Wyatt Papworth in *RIBA J.*, 25 Dec. 1892, and 5 Jan. 1893. Cf. also *Copies of the Minutes . . . of the Board of Treasury . . . for carrying on the Buildings at Somerset House . . .* 27 May 1788. In the accounts Midsummer–Christmas 1778, Bacon's group cost £367; Carlini's pair of statues £240 and Ceracchi's £200. Wilton's six keystones cost £126 and Carlini's three cost £63. J. Fittler, who entered the Royal Academy Schools in 1778 and was elected Associate Engraver in 1800, may have planned to engrave the keystones, for in the Society of Antiquaries, Misc. Portfolios 2, Green Ports, pt. 2, is a *Head of a River God The Tyne*, a drawing from which his engraving was made – to be found in the same library, but Brit. Romana 2, 36.

festoons of nets filled with fish.⁴⁰ Few other English buildings were as iconographically decorated, nor could they boast such an impressive display of sculptured decoration by first-class craftsmen.

If the attic is the Strand front's diadem or tiara, its belly-jewel is the Vestibule (Pls 157, 160), a triple-arched entry in which the spectator is treated to a fascinating play of cross-vaults⁴¹ and coupled Doric columns. Here is Chambers acting the virtuoso. According to Baretti, the 'general idea' of the Vestibule was taken from the Farnese Palace. As one who had undoubtedly discussed Somerset House with Chambers, and used his information for the compilation of his guide book to the Academy, Baretti must, obviously, be treated with respect. Nevertheless, there are two other prototypes worth mentioning: Le Vau's Vestibule at the Louvre, and Antoine's at La Monnaie. Of greater plasticity and elegance than any of these, the Somerset House Vestibule is handled with a delicacy that is most reminiscent of the vestibule approaches to the Gower House staircase (Pl.101). Inside the passage, on the centre of each wall, is a Vignolaesque doorcase, the one on the Academy side with a bust of Michaelangelo, and the other, on the Royal Society side, with a bust of Newton, both by Wilton. These doorcases, however, are no more than ornamental deceits for which Chambers has been often and somewhat unjustly criticized. It is true central openings would have been more correct. But they also would have demanded axial entrance halls dividing the width of the block into three rather paltry spaces. Lateral entrances (with blind symmetrical counterparts) enabled him to provide each of the learned societies with an impressive entrance hall and another good room as well.

It is a great pleasure to leave the hub-bub of the Strand for the quiet of one of the most satisfying squares in London (Pls 162–164). From just beyond the Vestibule, one can fully appreciate the grand domestic character of the elevations. The scale is low, the accents muted, and the divisions calm and deliberate. There are neither baroque gestures nor great vistas. Bacon's unfortunately mundane statue of George III, rising like a mechanical *Tableau* from the Piranesian vaults,⁴² at once sets the scale. Having taken in the Strand block with its projecting wings, one's eyes light first upon the immaculate Doric gateways that frame the space between the Strand block extensions and the court wings, then continue on quietly to savour the exquisite parts of the court elevations. They are bound together, not by any ostentatious device, but by the uniform quality and elegance of their architectural and sculptural elements. They are more French than English; indeed, were this Paris one would immediately think of Gabriel or de Wailly. The Hôtel de Conti style doorways (Pl.159) and the altars with guarding sphinxes by Cheere – both on the Strand wings – or Wilton's Salyesque vases⁴³ 'enriched with Tritons and other Emblematical figures . . . allusive to the different offices' that flank the main entrances (Pl.161) from the court, bear witness to Chambers's Gallic tastes and preferences.

⁴⁰ Bacon's arms cost £367 10s and Wilton's statues £480 – all accounted for in 1778.

⁴¹ The vaults in the vestibule are constructed on a wood frame with lath and plaster. Above the entablature over the centre of each column may be seen the ventilating holes.

⁴² Cf. Soane Museum 41/1¹¹, a plan showing 'arched rooms for Keeping Records' – all cross-vaulted. In the 1789 account book Bacon's George III cost £2270 5s.

⁴³ There are eight of these vases costing £640 in 1787.

Unlike the public today, the Georgians were permitted not only to perambulate the square, but also to pass through the Seaman's Hall in the centre of the river wing, onto the great terrace there to enjoy the mercantile view, and walk and talk by the Thames. The first scheme of embanking in 1776 took in a river frontage 550 feet long; but this was later contracted to 438 feet. Securing this great terraced embankment on pile-driven foundations was one of Chambers's most significant achievements at Somerset House, and, incidentally, the most unappreciated. The Thames in his day lapped at the long parade of vermiculated arches and flowed into the Stygian blackness of the King's Barge Master's Entrance in the centre. At the ends, projecting from beneath the Palladian Bridges are his two river gates combining elements of an earlier gate[44] designed for Thomas Brand at The Hoo and Gerbier's York Water Gate a short distance up river. Here along this stretch of the Thames, in terms of Piranesian drama, Chambers had served the old Roman well.

Looking up at the river wing façade from the Terrace or along from Waterloo Bridge (Pl.164) one can appreciate the faultless proportions and detail of the sequence of bays grouped in bay units of 3–5–3; 9–5–9; and 3–5–3. One can also appreciate Chambers's masterly use of the Palladian Bridges to enliven the front by bringing light through it and at the same time creating a powerful contrast to the dark shadow of the three bay porticoes *in antis* in the centre. The similarities with the long river front of Soufflot's Hôtel Dieu in Lyons are obvious, but so too are the differences. Unlike Soufflot's tightly-knit composition, Chambers's is marked by a Kentian staccato; and whereas Soufflot triumphed with a dome, Chambers failed miserably. Before thoroughly condemning his failure one must remember that the vast discrepancy in the length and depth of the river and court fronts did make it virtually impossible to accommodate both. Thus, seen from the court, his dome and pediment decorated with Banks's 'Trophies and Naval and Military ornaments' and Rathbone's[45] 'Sea horses, Amphitrite and Tritons', are in proportion. From the river, on the other hand, they appear ridiculously small. Oddly enough, Nash was defeated by the same problems at Buckingham Palace fifty years later.

Compared with the court elevations, the apartments in the east, west, and river wings are rather disappointing. Except for some of the principal rooms with attractive 'Statuary and Sicilian Jaspar' or 'Statuary and Spanish Marble' chimney-pieces by Haywood, the majority of the offices are strictly utilitarian in character. This, however, was a matter of necessity, and had no effect upon quality which is never lacking. Nor did utility cramp the styles of the dramatic Navy Staircase (Pls 168, 170) linking the Navy offices in the river and west wings. Here, within a top-lit circular shell, Chambers presents a virtuoso display of spatial gymnastics that exceeds its predecessor at Melbourne House and at the Marquis D'Argenson's Château les Ormes[46] in Touraine. No wonder Chambers

---

[44] Published in the 1759 *Treatise* where it is dedicated to Thomas Brand. Chambers never built a gate such as this at The Hoo, although he did build some sort of gate (cf. Catalogue). In the 1791 edition of the *Treatise* he added to the text, 'I have since executed nearly the same design in the embankment of Somerset Palace with the addition of lions over the columns of the order, medallions and vases in the side intercolumniations and pedestals under the columns, which, with the steps down to the Thames, considerably improve, and augment the consequences of the composition.'

[45] Rathbone's sculpture in the north pediment cost £77 in 1784, whilst that in the south pediment cost £78 in 1785. Banks's four trophies, in two pairs, cost £248 in 1785.

[46] For the Château des Ormes stair, cf. John Harris, op. cit., fig.10, and Catalogue.

was singled out by Soane for 'the composition of his staircases' (e.g. cf. Fig.13). For ingenuity and technical skill the Navy Staircase is matched only by the pair of stairs (Pls 171–172) serving the learned societies on opposite sides of the Strand block.

The planning of the Strand stairs, like the rest of the Strand interiors, was severely restricted by lack of space. For Chambers, however, such difficulties seemed to be fuel for invention. Unable to use open sweeping flights, he devised a kind of *trompe-l'œil* composition within a semi-circular tube rising the whole height of the block to a top-lit skylight.[47] All that is visible from the Doric screen in the Hall is a two-part flight curving around the wall to disappear through the ceiling. In fact, above this is another semi-circular flight from a mezzanine to the first-floor landing where there are three doorways set beneath a barrel vault, and composite orders on the wall. The stairs then take a final turn to the upper landing with a Corinthian order and a doorway giving access to the Great Exhibition Room. This is certainly theatrical architecture – a splendid piece of deception that creates a sense of spaciousness where none exists in reality.

The sculptural decoration of the exterior of the Strand block is matched on the interior by a programme of painted allegories on the walls and ceilings. The iconography of the Royal Academy apartments was first discussed by Baretti who commended Chambers for his success in blending the arts of ornamental sculpture, paintings, plasterwork, and gilding. Alas, most of the paintings have since been destroyed or removed. The wall of the staircase mezzanine was decorated with a chiaroscuro by Cipriani of 'several Genii employed in the study of Painting, Sculpture, Architecture, Geometry, and Mechanics'; and on the second-floor wall was another chiaroscuro by him, a 20-feet long frieze of 'Minerva visiting the Muses on Mount Parnassus', considered by Baretti to be 'a noble specimen of that Gusto of the Antique, which has long secured to him (Cipriani) the esteem of the most intelligent.' In the cove of the library he supplied emblematic paintings of Nature, History, Allegory, and Fable to accompany Reynolds's grandly-composed Theory of Painting in the centre. Baretti's highest praises were lavished upon the Council Room. Here, he thought, was the perfect medium between the 'excessive luxuriance of Le Pautre and the trifling fashion' of Adam 'so universally adopted among us.' Benjamin West's five pictures of 'Nature and the Four Elements' were surrounded by Angelica Kauffman's four ovals of Genius, Composition, Design, and Painting; and in the spandrels of the ceiling were Biagio Rebecca's small medallions of Apelles, Phidias, Apollodorus, Archimedes, Palladio, Bernini, Michaelangelo, Fiammingo, Raphael, Domenichino, Titian, and Rubens.

Mounting the stairs from the Academy's first-floor apartments to the attic storey, one would have passed Cipriani's Parnassus frieze. Then into the ante-room of the Exhibition Gallery where on a wall was a large *trompe-l'œil* by Rigaud representing a Sacrifice to Minerva, a Marriage of Cupid and Psyche, an 'open window with a distant sky', and 'Painting and Sculpture supporting a medallion of their Majesties'. This was intended as a prelude to the Great Exhibition Room (Pl.176) where four huge Diocletian windows in the timber-trussed lantern allowed light to pour down upon the canvases ranked row upon row on the vast areas of wall. Here decorative paintings were, by necessity, limited

---

47 Unfortunately so complicated and compressed are these stairs that they evade photography.

to the upper regions. In the spandrels were 'Groups of Boys practicing Painting, Sculpture, Architecture and Geometry' painted by Charles Catton; and in the dome 'a very well executed sky . . . more properly introduced there, than the finest Picture would have been.'

Visitors accustomed to the Adam style of interior decoration must have been startled, perhaps even relieved, by the Parisian character of the Strand apartments with their shallow coved and consoled ceilings (Pl.175), and walls compartmented by pilaster strips. (Pl.174). Chambers, now at the head of his profession, was no longer obliged, as he had been in the 1750's, to pander to prevailing fashion. Free to exercise his own tastes, his architecture became more adventurous, and his decoration distinctly Gallic. His first attempt at a French-style room was the Saloon (Pl.100) at Gower House, c.1768–70. The results, as might have been expected, were hesitant and unresolved. Ten years later, however, the Strand apartments were completed with a fastidiousness and elegance equal to the best Parisian interiors.[48]

It was inevitable that the financing of a public building of the size of Somerset House should be the subject of Parliamentary surveillance, criticism, and parsimonious quibbling. Oddly enough, there seems to have been no overall estimate of the work after the £135,000 proposed by Robinson in 1775 for his much more utilitarian design. By April 1780, when the Strand block was finished and there were two storeys left to build on the court wings and three on the river, £90,000 had been spent.[49] By February 1790[50] no less than £353,000 had been swallowed up. Even with this enormous expenditure, the eastern end of the river wing, one Palladian Bridge, and the houses of the Commissioners of the Navy were still waiting completion. When the final account was closed in 1801 – five years after Chambers's death – Somerset House had cost £462,323. Adding the expense of Sir Robert Smirke's finishing[51] of the river front by completing Chambers's Palladian Bridge and end of the river wing, using it as the river front of King's College in 1829, the total cost to the nation would have been well over half a million pounds.

If this was regarded as excessive, it was certainly no fault of Chambers. To check on his accounting the Treasury insisted in 1781 that the Board of Works, which until then had only priced the work, should henceforth 'survey, examine, and measure' as well. This he accepted, but their attempts to appoint their own measuring clerk, he regarded as an excessive interference in his affairs. A compromise was finally worked out, and with his approval the Treasury appointed James Paine as an impartial 'architect of credit' to certify the accounts. Until his death in 1789 Paine's reports, and those of his successor,

[48] The two prominent carvers of these rooms were Richard Lawrence and Sefferin Alken. Wilton and Hayward provided the best chimney-pieces, and Collins the better ceilings. Collins's Royal Society Council Room ceiling is not only his masterpiece, but it is one of the finest neo-classic ceilings in Georgian England (cf. Pl.171).

[49] Journals of the House of Commons, xxxvii, 788–9 for 14 April 1780. John Yenn produced a fuller report on 3 May; cf. Journals, op. cit., 818–19.

[50] Journals, op. cit., XLV, 117–18. In this 1790 report are itemized payments for 'Chair-women', lamplighters, attendance upon clocks, and the cost of the demolition of old Somerset House as £5631 14s 1d. Building the 'New Watch House' in front of St Mary Le Strand cost £156 4s. The designs for this Watch House are v & A, 3390 and Soane, 42/7²⁻³. Malton engraved a view of it in 1792 (Picturesque Tour Through . . . London, I, 1792, pl.36).

[51] For the early nineteenth-century architectural history of Somerset House, cf. Dr J. M. Crook's University of Oxford doctoral thesis (1962) on Sir Robert Smirke. It is puzzling that there are no fully-drawn-out designs for Chambers's river front. Did Smirke borrow these in 1825 and fail to return them?

George Dance the younger, confirmed 'that the Money has been very properly expended; that the Materials used, and the Workmanship, are uncommonly good in their different kinds; that the Measurements and Accounts have been skilfully conducted, and with every due attention to the Interest and Advantage of the Public.'[52]

Questions about the cost of Somerset House were frequently raised in the House of Commons, obliging Chambers to present himself to the 'Bar' to explain the situation. Not only were his replies able and convincing, but he was also fortunate to have the support of powerful champions like Burke. In 1781 Burke, with all the 'liberal impulse of his mind', declared 'that no man who looked at the . . . works going on' could doubt 'the honesty and care of the application of sums that parliament had granted'. Somerset House, he continued, 'did honour to the present age, and would render the Metropolis of Great Britain famous throughout Europe.'

Somerset House did not earn Chambers a fortune. On the contrary, it killed his private practice, and involved him in colossal labour and organization. The remuneration first offered him in 1775 was the two and a half per cent that Robinson had received at the Excise Office (he was, in other words, still haunted by Robinson's ghost). In 1777 he requested that this be raised to the five per cent, normal in architectural practice, protesting that the works were 'very much to the prejudice of my own income, which, by having been under the necessity of relinquishing all other employment, is lessened by at least 1800 pounds a year.' To judge from his bank account, his complaints were certainly just. Nevertheless, his request was not granted until 1780.[53]

Unfortunately, Somerset House came too late in Chambers's life and consumed all that was left of his career. As his final triumph it is a masterpiece of Academic correctness, dignity, and perfection in its parts, and yet full of flashes of unrestrained licence. In depth and in breadth, in every major and minor part, it is a studiously thought-out design. The consistency that this imparts to it makes it unique among European buildings of comparable size and complexity. It is a perfect marriage of the principles of architecture expounded in the *Treatise* and the best (in fact *the* text-book) of Georgian craftsmanship.

THE SAVOY

As Chambers had designed the German Lutheran church in the precincts of The Savoy in 1767, he was certainly not unfamiliar with the site. He would certainly have read John Gwynn's *London and Westminster Improved*[54] – a prophetic book that had pinpointed in 1766 the importance of the site, and had suggested it be developed either with three radiating streets converging upon a |new bridge, or with a square open to the river. That nothing was done was due in no small way to the legal disputes[55] between the Duchy

---

[52] *Journals*, op. cit., xxxix, 837–8, for 1783.

[53] There were, of course, vicissitudes of building Somerset House. When five central piers collapsed in 1788 he was exonerated. When James Wyatt, John Johnson, and John White surveyed the damage they found it 'not owing to any bad construction of the plan or to any Neglect in the execution' (PRO Works T29/60, 121), and Chambers was similarly discharged from fault when the floor of the RA Exhibition Room moved slightly in 1790 due to a rent girder (cf. PRO Works T29/61).

[54] John Gwynn, *London and Westminster Improved*, 1766, 95 ff, and pl.1.

[55] I am indebted to Robert Somerville's *The Savoy*, 1960, chapter ix, for the story of the disputes.

of Lancaster and the Crown over the Savoy. These, however, were settled by an Act of 1772, and this led to the joint conference between the Treasury and the Duchy on 24 May 1774, concluded by the Act of 1775 to embank the Thames in front of both Somerset House and the Savoy.[56] It must have been around this time that William Robinson made a plan to house the offices of Salt, Hackney Coach and Hawkers, Land Tax, Stamp, and Pedlars in a terrace block facing the river[57] – and it was surely this scheme that led Lord North's office to commission Robinson for Somerset House designs. Here at the Savoy, as at Somerset House, Chambers succeeded Robinson as architect.

Gwynn's recognition that the Savoy should be linked to a new bridge and a new planning concept for the area was forgotten. A Royal Warrant on 25 December 1775 provided for new barracks. Early in 1776 Chambers prepared his first scheme[58] to house 3000 officers and men of the Foot Guards. On 2 March fire destroyed the old barracks – a calamity that may have postponed any decisions that might have been taken. In any case, Chambers must have been frantic with the opening phase of Somerset House, and he did not appear at the Duchy again until February 1777. In June pressures of work made him decline to proceed with the Savoy, and although the Duchy had contemplated plans in 1782 and 1788, and Chambers had expressed himself willing to take them up in 1783, Treasury money was simply not forthcoming for a project that boded to be as expensive as its neighbour. The last we hear of the Savoy and Chambers was on 10 August 1795 when the aged, infirm architect reported to the Treasury that he had a 'complete set of designs for Barracks at Savoy, capable of containing 3000 men, designed by him by order of (Treasury) under Inspection of Principal Officers of the Guards . . . which had laid before His Majesty, the Duke of Gloucester, & all concerned in so important a business, and had in general been approved of.'[59] The reason for this sudden re-awakening of interest in a dormant project was probably due to the declaration of war upon Britain by the Revolutionary Council of France on 1 February 1793.

It seems impossible to distinguish between what Chambers proposed in 1776 and any further revisions he might have made over the succeeding ten years. His basic idea was to build a large courtyard block closed to the river by a porticoed water gate and an arcaded terrace that must have sought to emulate the mood of the Somerset House terrace. With Somerset House arising on the east and Adam's Adelphi to the west, the commission gave Chambers a splendid opportunity for architectural display. He rose to the occasion with 'My last designs for the Savoy' (Pl.178),[60] a precious, faintly-penned perspective of an ideal, unfettered by the problems of Somerset House. At each angle are lofty belvederes – rusticated transplants of the Richmond Palace (IV) pavilions – and in the centre of the north approach, aligned on a new road, are raised a pair of domed porticoed temples linked by arcades. The channelled rustication imparts a Gallic air; it has the potency of a Ledoux. Had it been built, a monograph on Chambers would have been written many years ago.

[56] Agreements are in Soane Museum, 41/5.

[57] These designs are Soane Museum, 43/1[2-4], 43/1[24], proposing a 286-feet terrace articulated with pilasters.

[58] Chambers's schemes are Soane Museum, 43/1[7, 8-22, 25,27].

[59] PRO Works T29/56, 221.

[60] Soane Museum, 43/1[5].

Chapter 8

The Office of Works 1761–96
by J. Mordaunt Crook

Administrative history is often reckoned to be a dry subject. Human interest seems to evaporate when translated into accounts, minutes, and memoranda. But the later eighteenth century was an age of formal manners and informal government. Its administrative records are littered with comic crises and studied insults. Even so, the biographer of Sir William Chambers is more than usually lucky. Each letter to his colleagues in the Office of Works, each report to his superiors in the Treasury or Lord Chamberlain's Office, bears the imprint of a broad sense of humour, a vigorous and sympathetic personality. His correspondence reveals not the 'solid and serious' figure of architectural text-books,[1] but an urbane and knowledgeable official, witty, worldly, and humane. First and foremost he was a professional architect, nervously aware of the new-found dignity of his calling and acutely conscious of his divided responsibility to government, tradesman, and labourer. He had in turn to act the part of King's confidant, Civil Servant, and champion of the underdog. As an administrator Chambers was both diplomat and clerk, a courtier with the common touch. Peter Pindar satirized his earthy humour and popular sympathies:

> 'Therefore, Sir Knight, pray mend your manners,
> And don't choose cobblers, blacksmiths, tinkers, tanners:
> *Some* people love the converse of low folks,
> To gain broad grins for good-for-nothing jokes . . .'[2]

But in the eyes of subordinates and employees Chambers stood for a sense of integrity and responsibility seldom found in administrative circles during this period.

Chambers's career in the Office of Works falls neatly into two sections. Before 1782 he bore unofficially the heaviest burden in an inefficient organization, first as Joint Architect of the Works (1761–9) and then as Comptroller (1769–82). Between 1782 and 1796, as Surveyor General and Comptroller, he was the acknowledged generalissimo of a rejuvenated department. His architectural achievements were mostly crowded into his first period of office. The later years were memorable only for a host of petty squabbles and for the completion of his masterpiece, Somerset House. But as an administrator Chambers performed his most valuable services between 1780 and 1785. These years were crucial to the development of the department. They were also the turning point in Chambers's administrative career. It was during these years that the Office of Works was transformed, by legislative process, from a mixed collection of architects and sinecurists into a wholly

---

[1] A. T. Bolton, *The Architecture of Robert and James Adam* (1922), I, p.100.
[2] Peter Pindar [Dr J. J. Wolcot], 'The Progress of Knowledge', *Works* (1794), I, p.92.

professional body. Chambers presided awkwardly over this transition. He demanded the highest professional standards, but at the same time he refused to jettison methods and customs which he believed to be in the best traditions of the department. During the 1780s the balance between efficiency and idiosyncrasy was kept firm. Such a precarious compromise could hardly survive Chambers's death. During his fourteen years as Surveyor General and Comptroller the Office of Works maintained an unusual reputation for efficiency, common sense, and humanity. These standards were very soon upset by the incompetence and irresponsibility of his successor, James Wyatt.

Chambers entered the Office of Works as the result of a political revolution. In 1760 the accession of George III was the signal for a government reshuffle. Under the spell of his tutor, Lord Bute, the young King set about replacing the old Whigs whom he had inherited from his grandfather with new men who would repay royal confidence with loyalty. In this way the administrative Board of the Office of Works received three valuable new recruits, Thomas Worsley, Robert Adam, and William Chambers: a departmental head who was at least a dilettante as well as a politician, plus two young advisory architects already rivals for the leadership of their profession. All three belonged to the circle patronized by George III and Bute. On a 'sudden and positive order' from the King, Worsley replaced the Hon. Henry Finch, M.P. for Malton. Finch had been a Whig placeman and one of a whole flight of Finches produced by the 2nd Earl and Countess of Nottingham.[3] But the two Joint Architects were new appointments.[4] Their colleagues on the Board, survivors from the previous regime, had all been in office for some time: Henry Flitcroft the Comptroller, Stephen Wright the Master Mason and Deputy Surveyor, and William Oram, the Master Carpenter, known as 'Old' Oram.[5] Robert Adam carried his political appointment to its logical conclusion by becoming M.P. for Kinross-shire in 1768 and resigning his Office of Works post to his brother James.[6] But not Chambers. More self-consciously professional than his rival, uninterested in politico-financial projects like the Adelphi, and assured of royal favour even after his eclipse by Wyatt, Chambers remained at the Office of Works and reaped an appropriate reward. Flitcroft died in February 1769. 'I blush to . . . find myself . . . overjoyed,' wrote Chambers to Lord Charlemont, 'that an old gentleman who has kept me out of a very great place for these eight years past is at length advanced to sing hallelujahs in heaven and has resigned his earthly post . . . to me.'[7]

In 1780 political pressure once again began to bear upon the Office of Works. Out of office for many years, the Opposition to George III gambled on an administrative purge as the only means of unseating Bute's current successor Lord North. The campaign was long

[3] They reared thirty children at Burley on the Hill; seven were still-born and ten died young. For Finch's dismissal cf. 'Register of the Correspondence of the Earl of Bute', BM Add.MS 36796 f.62; Sir Lewis Namier, *Structure of Politics at the Accession of George III* (1957 edn.), pp.20, 217, 472.

[4] 'Mr. Chambers and Mr. Adam to do the duty of the Clerks of Denmark House and the Tower of London in the room of Mr. Kyniston but with such Additions that their income shall be £300 p.a. each' (BM Add.MS 33055 f.317, 24 Feb 1761; PRO Works 4/12, 24 Feb. 1761).

[5] For their respective careers cf. H. M. Colvin, *Dictionary of English Architects* (1954).

[6] PRO Works 4/14, 3 Nov. 1769; Sir Lewis Namier and J. Brooke, *History of Parliament: the House of Commons, 1754–90* (1964), I, pp.7–8.

[7] *Manuscripts and Correspondence of James, 1st Earl of Charlemont*, HMC 12th Report (1891), I, p.292, 22 Mar. 1769; PRO Works 4/14, 17 Mar. 1769.

and difficult. But in March 1782 the Rockingham Whigs returned to power after sixteen years in the wilderness. 'At last', admitted the King, 'the fatal day is come.'[8] Abroad the American colonists had triumphed at the battle of Yorktown. At home the King surrendered to the Rockingham 'clan', and the spirit of 'Oeconomical Reform', 'virtue run mad', as Lord Hillsborough christened it, was in the ascendant.[9] Among the leaders of the movement Edmund Burke was the most vociferous. Their 'good stout blow'[10] against royal influence carried a triple sting: the exclusion of government contractors from the Commons, the disfranchisement of revenue officers, and the reform of the Civil List. Burke's Act,[11] as the third of these measures came to be known, was less severe than its progenitor, the draconic Bill of 1780. Nevertheless it abolished 134 redundant offices and aimed at an annual saving of £72,368 by limiting the Civil List to £900,000, the Pension List to £90,000 and the Secret Service Fund to £10,000. This drastic diminution in what Burke called 'the cumbrous charge of a Gothic establishment',[12] was to offset an accumulated royal debt of £295,877 18s 4d at the rate of £12,500 per quarter. Strictly speaking, Economical Reform was a Parliamentary fiction. In attacking corruption the Rockingham Whigs were attacking the Crown. But several of the departments abolished by Burke's Act were vulnerable targets on both financial and political grounds. Among these the Office of Works was particularly notorious.

Lord Rockingham's death on 1 July 1782 transferred responsibility for Economical Reform to Shelburne's shoulders. Shelburne in turn delegated the task to Thomas Gilbert, M.P. As an instrument of reformation Gilbert was certainly well qualified. He was already known as an ardent Poor Law Reformer and 'Oeconomist'. He 'had formerly made laws for the poor', remarked Horace Walpole; 'now [he] was making poor for the laws.'[13] Burke's Act had been a political manifesto, more concerned with abolition than with reorganization. It was Gilbert who translated Burke's estimates into concrete economies. Out of office and quite out of sympathy with Shelburne, Burke publicly dissociated himself from Gilbert's work.[14] The reconstruction of the Royal Household was therefore almost entirely Gilbert's personal achievement. But in the process he trod on too many toes. His administrative career scarcely outlasted his patron's brief ministry. Even Shelburne had good cause to remark ruefully: 'we have had a good deal of difficulty with

---

[8] Sir John Fortescue, ed., *Correspondence of George III* (1927–8), V, no.3593, 27 Mar. 1782.

[9] Horace Walpole, *Last Journals*, ed. A. F. Stewart (1910), II, p.299, 13 April 1780.

[10] *Memorials and Correspondence of Charles James Fox*, ed. Lord John Russell (1853), I, p.316, 28 April 1782.

[11] 22 G III cap. 82: *Statutes at Large*, XIV (1786), p.262. Further details are contained in BM Add.MS 29466 ff.15, 29 and *Annual Register*, 1782, pp.180–1. For Burke's 1780 scheme cf. *Parliamentary History*, 1780–1, XXI, p.111, and *Correspondence of Edmund Burke*, ed. Earl Fitzwilliam and Sir R. Bourke (1884), II, pp.321–4. 'Some parts' of the Bill, remarked George III, 'are more revolting than others' (Fortescue, *Correspondence of George III*, V, no.3648, 12 April 1782).

[12] *Parliamentary History*, 1780–1, XXI, p.2.

[13] Walpole, *Last Journals*, ed. Steuart, II, p.492, 6 Mar. 1783. For Gilbert's career cf. Namier and Brooke: *History of Parliament*, II, pp.499–501. He is remembered as a friend of Bridgewater and Brindley, a promoter of road and canal improvements and the author of Gilbert's Act, 1783, which permitted the combinations of Poor Houses known as Gilbert Unions.

[14] 'He had aimed only at the destruction of Parliamentary influence, and of sinecures for Parliamentary men; but [Shelburne and Gilbert] aimed their blows at inferior officers of twenty, thirty and forty pounds a year' (*Parliamentary History*, 1782–3, XXIII, pp.263–4, 1070). Walpole agreed (*Last Journals*, ed. Doran (1859), II, pp.557–8; *Letters*, ed. P. Toynbee, VIII, pp.264, 396; IX, p.2).

Mr. Gilbert.'[15] Of the several departments he reconstituted none was in greater need of reform than the Office of Works and few presented greater difficulties. In brief, the department was purged of sinecures and absorbed into a reorganized Royal Household under the jurisdiction of the Lord Chamberlain. Over a period of less than twenty years, 1760-79, its expenditure had totalled £881,000.[16] 'For all this expence', exclaimed Burke, 'we do not see a building of the size and importance of a pidgeon house.'[17] Of course this was a piece of Parliamentary hyperbole. After all, Chambers's work for George III was hardly negligible. But the first two decades of the reign were scarcely years of royal extravagance. Not public works but running costs, salaries, and private allowances had been responsible for this heavy outlay. Between 1770 and 1779, departmental expenditure averaged £46,368. After reform the annual estimate dropped to £25,000.[18] Indeed, from 1783 onwards the annual estimate for the whole of the new Lord Chamberlain's Department, comprising the Office of Works, the Wardrobe, the Jewel Office, and the daily running of the Household, was only £43,000. Nor was this general estimate seriously exceeded until Chambers's replacement by James Wyatt coincided with the Napoleonic period of rising prices and royal extravagance.

Before the reforms of 1782-3 the Office of Works had been a curious mixture of the archaic and the corrupt. As the corporate descendant of the medieval clerkships of works, it was responsible for the upkeep and alteration of all royal residences. Its internal establishment was divided into two categories, Officers and Artisans, both holding office by royal patent. By the 1770s Officers were mostly sinecurists and Artisans mostly pluralists. Salaries were drawn from several sources and paid in at least two ways, daily wages and annual allowances.[19] Each post carried an official house or its monetary equivalent. Officers drew a triple income from Treasury and Exchequer salaries, customary fees, and traditional perquisites. Patent Artisans – Master Joiner, Serjeant Painter, Serjeant Plumber, etc., enjoyed two sources of income. On the one hand their traditional stipends had ossified as annual retaining fees; on the other, as contracting tradesmen, they profited from their monopoly of building commissioned by the Crown. The Master Mason and Master Carpenter had long since risen from the ranks of the Artisans into the ranks of the Officers. Thus on the eve of reform Wright's successor, Sir Robert Taylor, architect, sculptor and pluralist, drew £300 per annum as Master Mason, while Oram's current successor Thomas Sandby, a military draughtsman turned architect and landscape gardener, Deputy Ranger of Windsor Great Park and Professor of Architecture at the Royal Academy, drew £200 per annum as the nominal Master Carpenter. James Stuart, Hogarth's successor as Serjeant Painter, hovered halfway between Taylor's status as an administrator and the

---

[15] Fortescue, *Correspondence of George III*, VI, no.4144, 1 Mar. 1783.

[16] *Parliamentary History*, 1780-1, XXI, p.551. For details of Office of Works expenditure 1761-82 cf. BM Add.MS 29465 f.36; PRO Works 6/20 ff.36-8; *Parliamentary Papers*, 1812-13, V, p.329 and 1868-9, XXXV, pp. 181-9. Treasury investigations were also made in 1774 (PRO Works 4/15, 4 Mar. 1774).

[17] *Parliamentary History*, 1780-1, XXI, pp.35-7.

[18] BM Add.MS 29465 f.191.

[19] For full lists of Office of Works personnel and salaries before 1782 cf. PRO Works 1/5 ff.29, 45; Works 6/20 ff.57-61; Works 5/69; *Parliamentary Register*, 1779-80, XVI, pp.225, 322-6; *Royal Kalendar*, 1782, p.85. Until 1783 salaries were subject to a 3¼% deduction: 2½% Civil List Duty, ½% Paymaster's Fee and ¼% Deputy Paymaster's Fee. Tradesmen's bills were subject to similar reductions until 1815 (PRO Works 1/5 ff.51-2, 27 Mar. 1783, 4 April 1783; L.C. 1/40, 28 July 1783; *Parliamentary Papers*, 1812-13, V, p.363, and 1830, IX, p. 141).

status held, for example, by a mere tradesman like William Cobbett, the Master Glazier. The title of Master Smith had vanished in 1716, those of Master Bricklayer and Purveyor in 1768 and 1777. Gilbert now abolished Sandby's post as well as Taylor's and Stuart's. Away went the last of the Artisans' titular relics, and with them went their traditional stipends. The tradesmen were left in control of a rationalized monopoly.

As for the Officers, both above and below the level of the Board of Works, they became a professional body in 1783. The politicians and sinecurists were eliminated. Among these, four were outstanding. William Varey, titular Surveyor of His Majesty's Gardens and Waters, drew a salary of £800 per annum.[20] But at least he was no politician. The other three, Henry Fane, George Selwyn, and Whitshed Keene, all sat in the House of Commons as government placemen. As three of Lord North's staunchest supporters, their names headed the Opposition's proscription list. As nominal Keeper of the King's private roads, gates and bridges, and Conductor of the King's person on all royal progresses, Fane drew the enormous salary of £918 per annum.[21] As nominal Paymaster, George Augustus Selwyn, wit, rake, gambler, and multiple sinecurist, drew a salary of £400 per annum, plus an allowance for stationery upon which he seldom wrote, plus £25 6s 0d per annum in lieu of lodgings for which he had no need, plus 1s 8d per day for his deputy and administrative factotum, Gabriel Matthias. More profitable still, he received 3d in every pound issued by the Exchequer to the Office of Works. His Paymastership therefore brought him more than £1000 per annum.[22]

Less remunerative than Selwyn's post, but politically more significant, was Keene's position as Surveyor General of the King's Works. Ever since Wren's dismissal by the Whigs in 1718, the Surveyor Generalship had been a political appointment. In George III's words, it was 'a very pretty House of Commons employment'.[23] By the 1770s it carried an Exchequer salary of £45 per annum, a Treasury allowance of 13s 2d per day, an extra allowance of £400 per annum, customary fees worth £80 per annum, a livery allowance of £12 15s 0d per annum, 3s per day for a personal assistant and official houses in Whitehall, St James's and Hampton Court. When Chambers first entered government service the holder of this lucrative post had been Thomas Worsley, M.P., a civilized connoisseur, horse-breeder, and amateur architect, 'a creature of Lord Bute, and a kind of riding-master to the King'.[24] In 1778 he was succeeded by Colonel James Whitshed Keene, another

---

[20] His predecessors during Chambers's period of service were George Onslow, Lord Charles Spencer and Hon. Charles Sloane Cadogan (PRO Works 1/4 *passim*). Varey also drew £600 from his Customs sinecure as Usher in the Long Room (Fortescue, *Correspondence of George III*, VI, p.179).

[21] His predecessors during Chambers's period of service were Hon. Edward Finch Hatton and Thomas Whateley (PRO Works 1/4 *passim*). Fane had previously been a Clerk in the Treasury. For his political career cf. I. R. Christie, *The End of North's Ministry* (1958), p.201; Namier and Brooke, *History of Parliament*, II, p.413.

[22] In 1769 Selwyn put up a vigorous and successful defence of his Office of Works emoluments (PRO Works 1/4 f.82, November 1769). He was also Clerk of the Irons and Surveyor of the Meltings at the Mint and absentee Registrar of the Court of Chancery in Barbados. His electoral influence won him a secret service pension of £1500 per annum (*Gentleman's Magazine*, 1791, Pt.I, p.299; *Royal Kalendar*, 1782, pp.114, 134; *Parliamentary Debates*, 1809, XIII, Appendix p.CCLXXIV; Fortescue, *Correspondence of George III*, IV, nos.469, 3674; Christie, *End of North's Ministry*, p.93; Namier and Brooke, *History of Parliament*, III, pp.420–1).

[23] Fortescue, *Correspondence of George III*, III, no.2013.

[24] Walpole, *Memoirs of the Reign of George III*, ed. D. Le Marchant and G. F. Russell Barker (1894), I, pp.28–9, 331. 'Worsley is made Surveyor of the Board of Works, he was the King's Equerry, and passes for having a taste for architecture of which . . . the King is very fond' (Walpole, *Letters*, ed. Toynbee, V, p.9). Worsley designed his own house, Hovingham Hall, Yorkshire (*C. Life*, 1961, CXXIX, pp.1410–13). For his political career as a Treasury nominee cf. Namier and Brooke, *History of Parliament*, III, pp.659–61.

ministerial favourite, but a man of very different stamp. Keene owed his career to a series of conjugal accidents: he married the 3rd Earl of Dartmouth's granddaughter, Elizabeth Legge, whose mother chose as her second husband Lord North's father, the 1st Earl of Guildford. Keene's wife was therefore, in Horace Walpole's words, 'a kind of sister' to Lord North.[25] This made Keene himself a kind of brother-in-law to the Prime Minister. Thanks to the patronage of Lord Hertford, Lady Powis and Lord North he secured a succession of sinecures in the Lord Chamberlain's Office, the Board of Trade, the Office of Works, and the Admiralty, besides sitting quietly in the House of Commons for exactly half a century.[26] As political head of the department it fell to this 'most absurd Irishman' to defend the Office of Works against the attacks of the Rockingham Whigs.[27] Chambers's relations with Worsley had been cordial, even intimate. He had acted as his agent for the purchase of Parisian *objets d'art*, his counsellor in matters of patronage, and his comforter at times of severe illness and family bereavement.[28] While Worsley retired to Yorkshire for months on end with bouts of kidney trouble and gout, Chambers acted as Chairman of the Friday Board meetings. Between Chambers's arrival in 1761 and Keene's appointment in 1778, there were as many as 830 weekly meetings. Worsley missed more than 550, Chambers less than 120.[29] Particularly after he succeeded Flitcroft, Chambers was the linchpin of the system. His official reports to Worsley were supplemented by private letters which were copious and friendly. But communications between Chambers and Keene began badly and ended worse. In 1778 Keene had obtained the prize which by right should have gone to Chambers.[30] After 1782 Keene never forgave Chambers, first for co-operating with Burke, and then for supplanting him as Surveyor General. After losing the Surveyorship Keene managed to become the Lord Chamberlain's Secretary in 1783. In this way their old enmity managed to survive reform and to poison the new relationship between the Office of Works and the Lord Chamberlain's Office.

Besides purging the Office of Works of superfluous posts, the reforms of 1782-3 rearranged the topographical basis of the department's responsibilities. This meant restricting the size of the external establishment. The existence of separate Clerkships for Kensington Gardens and Winchester Palace had been recognized as unnecessary in 1761 and 1775.[31] St James's, Whitehall, and Westminster had long been regarded as one

[25] Walpole, *Last Journals*, ed. Steuart, I, pp.128, 258n. 'Miss Legge, smitten with Col. Keene's black eyes, has consented . . . they must indeed keep a few sheep at setting out, but I suppose . . . Lord North will enable them to enlarge their flock' (Walpole, *Letters*, ed. Toynbee, VIII, p.50; *Diaries of Sylvester Douglas Lord Glenbervie*, ed. F. Bickley (1928), pp.6-7).

[26] For Keene's political career cf W. R. Williams, *Parliamentary History of the Principality of Wales* (Brecnock, 1895); Namier and Brooke, *History of Parliament*, III, pp.3-4.

[27] *Parliamentary Register*, 1780, XVII, pp.601-3; *Parliamentary History* 1780-1, XXI, p.551; *Political Magazine*, 1780, I, p.473.

[28] Chambers-Worsley correspondence, 1769-75, RIBA MSS, 36-7.

[29] Figures compiled from Board Minutes, PRO Works 4/13-16, 1761-78.

[30] On 5 June 1777, George III told North: 'I have just heard that Mr. Worsley . . . can scarcely outlive the day . . . I know very well that Adams [*sic*] the Architect formerly applied to you for it, but if his name or any other of the profession comes in question, I shall think it hard on Chambers and shall in that case only think that he must not be passed by.' The King approved of North's nomination of Keene provided the principle of seniority was otherwise observed in departmental promotions. But Worsley, 'who was dying, and said to be dead . . . was not'. Only on 13 December 1778 was the King able to report: 'early this morning Mr. Worsley died' (Fortescue, *Correspondence of George III*, III, nos.2013, 2015, and IV, nos.2364, 2471; Walpole, *Last Journals*, ed. Steuart, II, p.31).

[31] *Parliamentary Register*, 1779-80, XVI, pp.322-6.

J

administrative unit, as had Richmond and Kew, Hampton Court and Bushey Park, and Windsor Castle and its neighbouring lodges. The same principle was now extended, by bringing the Tower, Newmarket, Winchester, and Greenwich under one Clerk of the Works, and Buckingham House, Carlton House, the King's Mews, Kensington, and the King's Private Roads under another. By this means the number of Clerks of the Works was reduced from eleven to six and the number of their assistants, known as Labourers in Trust, fell from thirteen to nine. One of those who lost by this process of contraction was Kenton Couse, who had previously held the Clerkship for Buckingham House in conjunction with the posts of Secretary and Clerk to the Board and Clerk Itinerant. By way of compensation he was given the newly-created office of Examiner (£350 per annum). Similarly Richard Ripley was compensated for the loss of his offices of Chief Clerk and Clerk Engrosser by the award of a new post, that of Resident Clerk (£170 per annum). Government compensation for dispossessed office-holders was sensible, even generous. Pensions amounting to £1188 per annum were granted to Office of Works staff. Gilbert's list included an award of £150 per annum to Chambers. This covered the loss of his official residences at Hampton Court and Scotland Yard which he had previously sublet for £233 per annum.[32] As Comptroller Chambers had received a daily allowance of 8s 8d, an Exchequer salary of £27 7s 6d per annum, 3s per day for a personal assistant, a livery allowance of £8 9s 4d per annum, travelling expenses of 6s 10d per day and an annual allowance of £60 in lieu of an official residence at Kensington. His new salary as Surveyor General and Comptroller was rather more simply calculated: £500 per annum plus £10 for stationery.

Ironically, the only casualties in this minor avalanche of reform were four professionals: Thomas Sandby, S. P. Cockerell, James Paine, and James Adam. They were perhaps the most talented members of the old establishment, apart from Taylor, who was due to retire anyway, and Chambers, who was administratively indispensable. Ripley and Couse, Whitshed Keene and even the incorrigible Selwyn, all received alternative posts. But the Treasury decided that 'Artists or Tradesmen, employed merely as such' were not fit 'objects for compensation'.[33] Sandby, Paine, and Adam were all middle-aged men at the top of their profession. But for Cockerell, a junior Clerk of the Works at the Tower and Newmarket, this dismissal was a major setback at the very start of his career. His case, like 'that of several other Ingenious Artists removed at the same time', was, as Chambers told Sheridan, 'certainly hard'.[34]

In the short run, Economical Reform was a failure. It failed to halt the accumulation of deficits on the Civil List.[35] All Burke's rhetoric and Gilbert's cheeseparing could not constrict the expanding cost of government. But in the long run, Burke's attack on royal influence began the slow process by which the Crown was removed from active politics, and his subdivision of the Civil List pointed the way to an eventual separation of govern-

[32] PRO T38/507; T29/52 f.441, 20 Oct. 1782; *Parliamentary Papers*, 1812–13, V, p.338. For details of other compensations cf. also PRO T38/221; Works 6/13, 14 Feb. 1783; Works 1/5 f.61, 14 July 1783; Works 4/16, 11 April 1783, 20 Sept. 1783, 7 Jan. 1784. For lists of Office of Works personnel and salaries after 1783 cf. PRO Works 5/71; *Royal Kalendar*, 1785, p.280.

[33] PRO T29/54 f.394, 25 Oct. 1783, and f.461, 25 Nov. 1783.

[34] PRO Works 1/5 f.70, 7 Nov. 1783.

[35] For annual figures, cf. *Parliamentary Papers*, 1868–9, XXXV, pp.181–97.

mental and royal expenditure.[36] As for the Office of Works, its status and personnel were transformed, and in this transformation Chambers played a crucial role. In essence the Office of Works had been professionalized. Instead of being, as Burke put it with characteristic exaggeration, 'a junto of members of Parliament', it had become the 'concern of builders, and such like, and of none else.'[37] By pruning the department Burke had envisaged an annual saving of £7463. Gilbert went still further. Part of the saving lay in the abolition of communal perquisites as well as individual offices: livery allowances from the Great Wardrobe; riding charges or travelling expenses averaging 5s per day for senior men; Christmas Rewards at £15 per annum; and the Officers' Entertainments at £2 per month.[38] The old salary list for administrative staff alone had amounted to £3782 p.a. The new figure, for internal and external staff at all levels, was only £3818 3s 4d.[39] On the other hand, salaries were no longer subject to archaic deductions, and personal liability for taxes was transferred to the Lord Chamberlain.[40]

As a sub-department of the Lord Chamberlain's Office, the reformed Office of Works lost all semblance of financial autonomy. Before 1782 there were too few checks upon arbitrary expenditure. After reform there were almost too many. Requests for building operations by a government department or a member of the royal family had to be made in the first instance to the Surveyor General. Minor running repairs were executed at the discretion of the Clerk of the Works by Office of Works tradesmen, on the authority of the Surveyor General and under the supervision of the resident Labourer in Trust. For specific operations costing more than £100, the Clerk of the Works's estimate had to be delivered, via the Surveyor General, to the Lord Chamberlain, as a preliminary to execution. Treasury approval and the King's Sign Manual were required for all works of more than £1000, notably for the repairs ordered in consequence of the annual General Survey, usually held in April, when the chief officers personally surveyed all the buildings in their care.[41] After execution the cost of each operation was entered by the Clerk of the Works in his quarterly account and formally checked by the Examiner and Resident Clerk. These accounts were then authorized by the Lord Chamberlain who compared them with the original estimate and then obtained Treasury warrants for payment out of the Exchequer. Finally, the annual accounts were passed to the Commissioners for Auditing Public Accounts.[42] Gilbert's Instructions had stipulated that all quarterly accounts were to be submitted within fifteen days of the end of each quarter.[43] But by the 1790s they were

[36] T. Erskine May, *Constitutional History of England*, ed. F. Holland (1912), I, pp.163–7; Sir D. L. Keir, *Constitutional History of Modern Britain* (1960 edn.), pp.387–9.

[37] *Parliamentary History, 1780–1*, XXI, p.36.

[38] PRO Works 5/69.

[39] *Parliamentary Papers, 1812–13*, V, pp.334, 393.

[40] PRO Works 1/5 f.77, 17 Dec. 1784; Works 5/72, 75, 76, 78; Works 4/18 f.282, 23 Mar. 1798; Works 6/23 f.57, 8 May 1798; L.C. 1/39 5 Dec. 1794; L.C. 3/35, 1798; L.C. 1/2 f.32, 2 April 1798; L.C. 1/4, 14 Dec. 1810; *Parliamentary Papers, 1812–13*, V, pp.492–5.

[41] E.g. PRO Works 6/33 f.204, 26 Nov. 1802 and f.207, 17 Dec. 1802; Works 4/19, 17 Dec. 1802; L.C. 1/39, 30 Mar. 1787; T29/58 f.313, 26 April 1797. Directions given in April were followed by another survey in July 'to observe the progress, and another in October, to satisfy themselves as to the execution'. Travelling expenses were repaid by the Lord Chamberlain (*Parliamentary Papers, 1812–13*, V, pp.333, 406).

[42] For details of the whole process, cf. *Parliamentary Papers*, 1812, IX, p.409 and 1812–13, V, p.360.

[43] *Parliamentary Papers, 1812–13*, V, p.357.

frequently several quarters in arrear, and tradesmen occasionally waited more than a year for payment. In all, three to four years might elapse between a demand by one Lady of the Bedchamber that her apartments might be whitewashed, and the reappearance of that demand as an item of expenditure among the declared annual accounts.

The weakness of this ritual of check and double check lay first of all in the heavy responsibility thrust upon the Surveyor General. Still more important were the difficulties involved in the production of accurate, long-term estimates. There were two dangers here: the possibility of rapid price changes, and the likelihood of arbitrary demands for reconstruction and repair emanating from the royal family. As an administrator Chambers was more than adequate for the onerous burdens of office. His successor, James Wyatt, was not. Wyatt's inefficiency, the extravagance of George III's children, and the price-fluctuations of the Napoleonic period strained the system to breaking point. The result was another investigation in 1810–12 and another reform in 1815.

Chambers accepted the reforms of 1782–3 as an unwelcome necessity. He co-operated with Burke and Gilbert in removing inveterate sinecurists. But he strongly resisted every economy which seemed to threaten the independence and efficiency of his department. His conservative temperament and his friendship with the King made him doubly averse to change. In the summer of 1782 he made a last attempt to stay the avalanche. In a letter to Burke[44] he defended the old system and laid down his minimum requirements for a new establishment. With regard to the new post of Surveyor General and Comptroller, he complained, 'I fear no single man would be able to go through with it. He should . . . have the help of two other able architects . . . with respect to the whole inferior arrangement of the intended new establishment, permit me to assure you from more than twenty years' experience, that the nearer it approaches to the old one the better it will be.' A head of department and two assistant architects, a chief clerk and three office clerks, eight clerks of works, sixteen or eighteen labourers in trust, as well as engine keepers, labourers, and messengers, all these Chambers considered essential personnel for any new establishment: 'I think it cannot be more reduced without prejudice to the service.' But reduced it was, and the story of his next fourteen years in office is one of rising costs, expanding business, and lack of staff. Moreover there was now an extra source of irritation, the possibility of regular external investigation. 'I am sorry', he told Burke in January 1782,[45] 'to find still inserted in your Bill, the Clause relative to calling in Surveyors to certify to the Treasury, that works have been fairly and properly executed: it must, I apprehend, be an oversight, as by His Majesty's plan of the Office of Works, two persons are [already] appointed as standing checks upon the Surveyor's conduct . . . I must confess to you that this clause seems to me very distressing;[46] it will subject the Surveyor, who I apprehend should be chosen from among the first of the profession, to the control of the meanest . . . ; it is calculated to keep him constantly in hot water, and to place him . . . in a very contemptible

44 Chambers to Burke 5 May 1782. Chambers made sure that a copy found its way into the hands of George III. In 1804, when reform was again in the air, the King presented this copy to Wyatt (PRO Works 4/19, 17 Feb. 1804) who took care that another copy was preserved (PRO Works 6/23 f.237). For the original letter cf. Fitzwilliam MSS, Sheffield City Library, Bk.I, f.115.
45 Fitzwilliam MSS, Sheffield City Library, Bk.I, f.149, 18 June 1782. The letter was written in response to a reminder from Kenton Couse (RIBA MSS 55, 17 May 1782).
46 '. . . that I do not like this Clause at all.' (Draft MS).

light. Besides which . . . [it] will be attended with considerable expence. I therefore flatter myself that you will have the goodness to give the clause in question its due consideration before it passes into an act.'[47]

In the attenuated department which emerged in 1783, Ripley and Couse, plus two Assistant Clerks (£60 per annum), George Horsley and Edward Crocker, made up the entire administrative staff of the small office in Little Scotland Yard which Chambers had now to direct. Of personal troubles he would have plenty. But more immediately serious were the novel administrative problems produced by reform. As his title suggests, Chambers's new position was a conflation of two ancient offices, the Surveyorship and the Comptrollership.[48] As Comptroller he had only been *de facto* head of department. Now, as Surveyor General and Comptroller, he was no longer understudy to Whitshed Keene, but rightful architect to the Crown. Unfortunately he was also a servant with three masters: the Treasury, the Lord Chamberlain, and George III.

Between 1782 and 1796 Chambers held office under three Lord Chamberlains: George Montagu, 4th Duke of Manchester, Francis Seymour-Conway, 4th Marquess of Hertford, and James Cecil, 1st Marquess of Salisbury. Dignified and not untalented, Manchester held office (April 1782–April 1783) as the Rockinghams' nominee.[49] His casual acquaintance with the principles of Economical Reform proved less of an encumbrance to Chambers than Hertford's pernickety conscience. Hertford's brief and unhappy tenure (April–December 1783) marked the limits of the Fox-North regime.[50] By enforcing Gilbert's new regulations in a narrow and unimaginative way, he provoked a series of petty crises which came near to wrecking the reorganized Office of Works. Salisbury, the third of Chambers's supervisors, was fortunately more reliable than Manchester and less inhibiting than Hertford. Holding office (December 1783–May 1804) as a Pittite, he managed to maintain a high level of co-operation and efficiency so long as Chambers was alive.[51] Under Chambers's successor relations between Office of Works and Lord Chamberlain's Office were to be rather less happy.

Burke's Act had stipulated that the Surveyor General must be '*bona fide* by Profession an Architect or Builder.'[52] Chambers was a professional to his fingertips. He was also

---

[47] '. . . that you will upon due consideration leave out the whole clause.' (Draft MS). The sanction in question (22 G III c.82 clause IX) was in fact seldom invoked.

[48] Chambers himself frequently used both titles as alternatives. So widespread was this practice that in 1796 the Royal Warrant appointing James Wyatt refers to its subject as "Surveyor *or* Comptroller' (PRO Works 6/13, 16 Mar. 1796).

[49] 'His Figure, which was noble; his Manners, affable and corresponding with his high Rank, prepossessed in his Favour: but his Fortune bore no proportion to his Dignity. Though a man of dissipated Habits, and unaccustomed to diplomatic Business, he did not want Talents' (Sir N. Wraxall, *Memoirs* (1884 edn), III, p.59, and V, p.172; *Gentleman's Magazine*, 1788, Pt.II, p.839).

[50] 'But cautious Hertford shrinks when risks are run.' (W. Combe, *The Diaboliad*, 1777). He was known for his 'niggardly avarice' (*Royal Register*, V, p.153). 'The love of money only excepted, his character was negatively good' (*Charlemont MSS*, H.M.C. 12th Report (1891), I, p.23).

[51] He owed his position at Court firstly to his wife's talent for political intrigue, secondly to the influence of the Marquess of Downshire, and thirdly to his own reputation as a staunch Protestant (*Gentleman's Magazine*, 1823, Pt.I, pp.563–4; Diary of Joseph Farington, BM typescript, p.1119, 6 Nov. 1797; Lady Gwendolen Cecil, *Life of Robert Cecil, Marquess of Salisbury* (1921–32), I, p.2).

[52] 22 G III c.82, clause VI.

eminently humane and almost excessively loyal to his subordinates.[53] His humanity, his professionalism and his loyalty soon brought him into conflict with the Treasury and, more immediately, with the Treasury's nominee, the Lord Chamberlain. Trouble began almost as soon as the reorganized system came into operation. The point at issue was the method of presenting accounts, and the battle hinged upon the Lord Chamberlain's power of authorizing, or refusing to authorize, quarterly payments. The whole episode throws a flood of light upon Chambers's personality and upon the mechanism of his department in the months immediately following reform. These were months when 'Oeconomical' principles were being painfully translated into administrative practice, months when Chambers himself confessed to being 'entirely in the Dark as to what may be deemed right or wrong.'[54]

Burke's Act had imposed upon the Lord Chamberlain a strict examination of Office of Works accounts.[55] Manchester interpreted this to mean monthly lists of wages, labour, and materials. Chambers disagreed. 'To give a full account of the monthly expence incurred in the King's Works, or in any other works', he wrote, 'is absolutely Impossible, unless all the men should strike off at the end of the month, and stand still 'till the measurements were taken, which would occasion much loss of time, a vast deal of trouble and a degree of confusion which even Mr. Burke would find it difficult to unravel.'[56] Worse still, Hertford asked for detailed annual estimates as well as fully itemized accounts. 'Such an estimate', replied Chambers, 'cannot possibly be made with any degree of certainty.'[57] As for daily wage lists 'they are of no use whatever, as they do not tend to give the least idea of the expences incurred.'[58] Hertford therefore seized upon some minor repairs at Hampton Court as a test case. He demanded fully-itemized accounts, giving separate details of prices and quantities. His action provoked a furious and very revealing outburst from the Surveyor General.[59]

'All these requisitions are without precedent, and . . . totally impracticable in the present state of the Office of Works, of which it would increase the Business Tenfold . . . If [an estimate] be made too full it cannot profit the Maker, at least in the King's Service; But if it be made too Scanty it affects his Character and Subjects him in the end to Censure, perhaps to worse Treatment. There can therefore be no Reason to Suspect any Estimate after it has been Carefully made by the Respective Clerk of the Works; and as carefully examined by Mr. Couse . . . and I confess to your Lordship that upon this present Occasion where even the Probability of Fraud cannot Exist, I do not see the Necessity, the Policy or the Justice, of Attacking the Character of Men whose Abilities cannot be disputed, whose fidelity has been proved by More than Forty Years faithful Service, and who,

---

[53] For examples of Chambers's humanity in private practice cf. H. M. Martienssen, 'Chambers as a Professional Man', *Architectural Review*, 1964, cxxxv, pp.277–83. Like Dr Martienssen's unpublished thesis (London Ph.D., 1949), this article makes no use of Chambers's official correspondence.

[54] PRO Works 6/20 f.110, 24 Mar. 1783.

[55] 22 G III c.82, clause XI.

[56] PRO Works 6/20 f.96, 15 Feb. 1783, Chambers to Herbert.

[57] PRO Works 6/20 f.132, 27 June 1783, Chambers to Keene.

[58] PRO Works 6/20 ff.134–5, 27 June 1783. For Hertford's reply, cf. Works 6/20 f.138, 3 July 1783.

[59] PRO L.C. 1/39, 26 Sept. 1783; Works 6/20 ff.166–79.

serving by His Majesty's own Immediate Appointment, should be Treated with all the deference due to so high a Patronage.'

By way of reply Hertford merely reiterated his command. 'The Letter and Spirit' of Burke's Act must be obeyed, 'whether they are without precedent or not.'[60] This peremptory order was then substantiated by a refusal to authorize the accounts for Midsummer Quarter, 1783, thus delaying the payment of tradesmen for several months.[61] But Chambers stood firm: his presentation of accounts followed the method in use 'for more than a century past', a method twice accepted since the passing of Burke's Act. As for secrecy, 'we have nothing to conceal, our books and papers will be opened to any Person duly appointed to inspect them.' And if Hertford will not give way, then extra staff must be employed; 'immediate application must be made to the Lords of the Treasury for an Additional Detachment of Clerks.'[62]

At this point, Hertford was out of town and Sir Francis Drake, who had actually ordered the work at Hampton Court, was in Devonshire. Tiring of his proxy battle with the Lord Chamberlain's Secretary, Whitshed Keene, Chambers decided to direct his fire elsewhere. He prepared an elaborate memorandum to convince the Treasury that Hertford's measures were unnecessary, and backed it up with a private letter to Edmund Burke which aimed at counteracting Keene's malign influence. Firstly, the private letter:

'The Secretary to the Lord Chamberlain has made out such an interpretation of what he calls the spirit of the regulating Act . . . as makes the Comptroller of the King's Works (what I dare say you never intended him to be) a mere footboy to the Lord Chamberlain's Office, and he . . . will, I think, very soon compleat the business he has laboured at with unremitting assiduity these four years past, which is my removal from the King's Service. At present everything in the Office of Works is thrown into confusion . . . As the correspondence [with the Treasury] is long and comes to their Lordships so weakly recommended, I have not the confidence to hope for much relief, without the interferance of some powerful friend . . . You, my dear sir, have very often honoured me with distinguishing marks of friendship and good will. I never needed your protection more than at this time . . . And setting apart my own [interest] your humanity will I am sure be cheerfully exerted in favour of many needy and many very distressed tradesmen and servants of the Crown, who, some of them, must really starve, should the embargo in the Chamberlain's Office upon their pay be long continued.'[63]

Then the official memorandum:

'However important a multiplication of Bills may at first appear towards a discovery of the Truth, it can in reality only produce additional confusion, by diverting the attention of the examiner into a hundred or five hundred channels instead of ten, and by affording an opportunity of subdividing the imposition (if such there be) into as many parts as there

[60] PRO L.C. 1/39, 26 Sept. 1783.

[61] PRO L.C. 1/39, 10 Oct. 1783.

[62] PRO Works 6/20 ff.179–83, 17 Oct. 1783.

[63] Fitzwilliam MSS, Sheffield City Library, Bk.I, f.285, 18 Oct. 1783. The letter concludes: 'P.S. If you should upon enquiry think me deserving of protection, may I flatter myself with a recommendation to your brother's favour, whose particular situation will render it of great service.' This postscript was then endorsed by Richard Burke: 'Bon – car je n'aime pas ces escrosqueries la' [Good: I don't like these swindles]. Richard Burke (d. 1794), Edmund's youngest brother, was Secretary to the Treasury (1782–3) and Recorder of Bristol (1783–94).

are separate bills . . . What I would humbly beg leave to propose . . . is that upon every occasion when the least doubt exists in the breasts of the Lords of the Treasury or the Lord Chamberlain, . . . a Person skilful in Builders' Accounts should be sent to the Office of Works, where he would find materials to trace an estimate of four lines, up to four hundred, and still upwards to the minutest article of which it is composed, and Bills whenever they were doubted might be examined in like manner: materials would be found in the Office to trace every article contained in each bill to the ten, twenty or sometimes 200 original articles of which it is composed.'[64]

Chambers won his point. The dispute ended with a Treasury directive supporting the Surveyor General.[65] Burke's influence and Chambers's experience had proved too much for Hertford's conscience and Keene's malice. Quarterly accounts were to be presented in summary form and safeguarded by the possibility of detailed investigation. Hertford received scant sympathy from the Treasury Lords.[66] After delaying the accounts for as long as five months, from July to November, he gave way. And with the change of government a few weeks later, he and his secretary went out of office, unlamented.

But this was not before they had provoked another administrative crisis which dragged on well into 1785. This time the point at issue was the Surveyor General's authority to order immediate repairs, independently of the Lord Chamberlain. Once again, victory went to Chambers. Works estimated at more than £100 had, of course, to receive the Lord Chamberlain's assent. But Chambers was determined to resist the extension of this principle to running repairs and emergency work.[67] The Lord Chamberlain countered by refusing to sanction such bills until they had been passed by the Treasury. Once more the payment of tradesmen fell into arrears. Hertford and Salisbury made much of the fact that they were 'liable to be called to account for every shilling expended.'[68] Chambers in turn emphasized the utility of his own discretionary power and the necessity of 'some little necessary elbow room.'[69] 'Some confidence', he added, 'some latitude, the nature of the service certainly requires. Parliament has given the Comptroller a great deal, His Majesty's [i.e. Gilbert's] Instructions have confined it to one tenth part. But even here the exercise of that privilege must become superfluous if the payment of what he finds necessary to order . . . is to be made optional.'[70]

This dispute ended in a compromise in Chambers's favour. He retained his discretionary control but agreed to send Salisbury weekly block estimates and retrospective reasons for every minor work. This note of co-operation was to characterize their relationship over the next ten years. We leave the contestants solving their differences by means of discus-

[64] PRO Works 6/20 ff.194–6, 30 Oct. 1783.

[65] PRO T29/54 ff.449–50, 20 Nov. 1783; Works 6/20 f.212, 28 Nov. 1783.

[66] In August 1783, for example, he was sent this brusque note: 'My Lords cannot conceive it possible that any Regulation or Instruction can exist of such an absurd Tendancy as to prevent an immediate Compliance with [Burke's request for a statement of accounts] . . . The payment of His Majesty's Civil List for the Quarter ending 5th July is exceedingly disarranged . . . [Let] the Lord Chamberlain furnish the Accounts forthwith, or show specifically what Regulation or Instruction prevents his Lordship from knowing the Expenditure of his own office for a quarter ended now a month since' (PRO T29/54 f.134, 7 Aug. 1783).

[67] PRO T29/56 f.319, 24 Mar. 1785, and f.348, 16 April 1785; Works 4/16, 17 June 1785.

[68] PRO Works 6/21 f.34, 4 May 1785.

[69] PRO Works 6/21 f.39, 17 May 1785 and ff.44–5, 27 May 1785.

[70] PRO Works 6/21 f.32, 2 May 1785.

sion. As Chambers put it, 'a few minutes . . . to explain myself' is more valuable than an hour of epistolary argument; administrative co-operation is more easily produced 'by a few words, than by many letters'.[71]

While Chambers wrangled with the Treasury Board or the Lord Chamberlain's Office, he never lost sight of the fact that administrative inefficiency often meant hardship for government employees. When official insistence on the protocol of Treasury directives delayed the settlement of bills and pensions during the hard winter of 1783–4, he reminded his superiors that while they disputed, the very livelihood of many tradesmen and pensioners was at stake. 'The keeping back of the Salaries and Compensations', he told the Treasury, 'the former of which are now three Quarters in arrear and the latter half a year in arrear, is a very great hardship upon the inferior Officers, Servants and Pensioners . . . , who having no other dependence whatever, and consequently little or no credit, are at this time absolutely in a starving condition. Their Lordships' humanity will I am confident find some speedy remedy for this evil, which is the more distressing as a great part of it falls upon very old, helpless and sick people unfit to struggle with hunger and all the other Miserys of Poverty.' Thanks to his intercession, the Treasury was moved on this occasion to pay off at least the oldest bills by distributing some £600 which still remained in the hands of Gabriel Matthias, Selwyn's ex-deputy. Chambers had begged for £900.[72]

Although subordinate to the Lord Chamberlain, the Surveyor General's control of his own department was absolute. Senior appointments were implemented by the Treasury and ratified by the King in accordance with his advice. Lesser posts formed part of his own personal patronage. As the Clerks of the Works 'are under my direction', Chambers informed Hertford in 1784, 'and I am made responsible for their conduct, they are, by virtue of His Majesty's general warrant, appointed by me.'[73] They were obliged 'to attend and receive designs and instructions from the Surveyor General, to prepare estimates and direct the execution of the works, and when compleat to measure and deliver the accounts of the same.'[74] Labourers in Trust were responsible for the daily upkeep of the royal palaces. They owed both their appointments and their prospects of promotion entirely to Chambers.[75]

However, even in the appointment of junior officers the King might occasionally intervene. In 1783 Chambers persuaded the Treasury to retain Robert Browne, snr and Richard Wetherell as Labourers in Trust at Richmond and Greenwich because they were 'well known to His Majesty'.[76] More explicitly, George III managed in 1789 to remove Thomas Tildesley from his Clerkship at Windsor and replace him first by Robert Browne, jnr and then by William Leach.[77] When in 1805 Leach in turn proved incapable, he was pensioned

[71] PRO Works 6/21 ff.44–5, 27 May 1785.

[72] PRO Works 6/20 ff.243–6, 26 Mar. 1784, 2 April 1784; Works 4/16, 26 Mar. 1784, 19 Nov. 1784; T29/55 f.161, 10 April 1784.

[73] PRO Works 6/20 f.314, 13 Nov. 1784. Clerks of the Works were formally appointed by a royal warrant, signed by the Treasury Commissioners (Works 6/13 passim).

[74] Parliamentary Papers, 1812–13, V, p.429.

[75] Parliamentary Papers, 1812–13, V, p.341. For their formal appointment cf. PRO Works 6/13 passim.

[76] PRO Works 6/20 f.76, 10 Jan. 1783.

[77] A. Aspinall, ed., Later Correspondence of George III (1962), I, no.494, George III to Pitt 15 Mar. 1789.

off at the King's direction and replaced by William Matthew, a surveyor sufficiently humble and sufficiently energetic to act as personal assistant to James Wyatt.[78]

But Tildesley's was an exceptional case. His vile temper and intemperate habits made him the stormy petrel of the department. Handling this perennial troublemaker required every ounce of Chambers's tact and patience. When in 1782 Mrs Charlotte Boyle Walsingham privately arranged for the redecoration of her apartment at Windsor, Tildesley expelled her workmen 'with very abusive language' and was officially rebuked for his incivility.[79] A year later Henry Emlyn, the resident carpenter, resigned because 'Tildesley had found fault with his Timber frivolously.'[80] Twelve months after that he was involved in a violent dispute with the local land-tax collector.[81] After his removal to Hampton Court Tildesley's accounts were discovered to be in disorder and he was involved in a furore concerning stolen lead.[82] Soon afterwards, his 'unfortunate wife and lame child . . . dreading the vehemence of his Temper, [were] forced to fly from him.' Thanks to Chambers's intercession, late in 1792, this 'Sick Child and worthy, very decent woman' were allowed £50 per annum, being the proceeds from three official houses illegally sublet by Tildesley.[83] Less than two years later, at the height of an administrative fracas over the use of stabling at Hampton Court by the King's Cavalry, Tildesley was found to be 'indisposed even to incapacity'.[84] Samuel Forrest Simmons, M.D. certified the patient as insane. Periods of mental derangement punctuated Tildesley's remaining years and only Chambers's intervention prevented his replacement in 1794 by William Tyler, RA, an established sculptor and architect patronized by the Duke of Gloucester.[85]

Chambers refused to accept Tildesley's replacement for two reasons. He was determined to prevent the 'utter ruin of an unfortunate man, his wife, and five helpless children', and he was convinced that architects like Tyler, of independent reputation or independent means, encouraged inefficiency and discontent in the department. 'My real sentiments', he told Gloucester, 'are that the Clerkships of the Office of Works will be much better served by plain Builders than by famous Architects, who deeming themselves much greater than the Comptroller will scarcely be controlled by him. Having more business of their own than they can manage they will find no leisure for that of the Crown, and having spacious town houses of their own, will scarcely quit them and their business to shift in small

[78] PRO Works 4/19, 30 May 1806; Works 6/25 f.177, Wyatt to Leach; Works 6/25 ff.53-4, 158, 162; T29/101 f.345, 25 June 1809.

[79] PRO Works 1/5 f.35, 15 Nov. 1781, and f.40, 24 Feb. 1782.

[80] PRO Works 4/16, 19 Dec. 1783.

[81] PRO Works 1/5 f.77, 17 Dec. 1784.

[82] PRO Works 4/17, 13 Aug. 1792.

[83] 'Unless the poor woman can be humanely assisted . . . both she, and her child, must throw themselves upon the Parish' (PRO Works 6/22 f.71, Chambers to Rose 5 Nov. 1792; Works 4/17, 9 Nov. 1792). Pending the sale of these houses, the Treasury permitted the continuance of this extra income after 'the difference' between Tildesley and his wife had been 'made up . . . for the benefit of [their] family' (Works 6/22 f.146, 13 Dec. 1793; Works 1/5, January 1794; Works 4/18 f.53, 24 Jan. 1794).

[84] PRO Works 4/18 f.65, 11 April 1794.

[85] PRO Works 1/5 f.131, 4 Aug. 1794; T29/67 f.171, 19 Aug. 1794; Works 6/22 f.167, 29 Aug. 1794; Works 4/18 f.198; Works 4/19, 15 May 1800. In 1797 Wyatt urged Tildesley 'to observe the strictest Oeconomy and assiduity . . . as the only chance left you of securing the situation you now hold' (Works 6/23 f.18, 17 Feb. 1797). Three years later he reiterated the need for 'steady and temperate conduct' in the circumstances of 'a Complaint like yours' (Works 6/23 f.135, 26 Sept. 1800). But this was a case of the blind leading the blind.

official habitations, and bury themselves in the Country for the inadequate reward of £150 or £200 per annum. To a common plain Builder such a reward is a powerful inducement . . . ; such a house becomes a commodious dwelling. Having been accustomed to subservience he obeys without difficulty, and having little or no business of his own, the greater part of his time will be spent in the management of the Crown.'[86]

This statement of policy was the product of sad experience. Under Chambers, therefore, the Office of Works was staffed by competent mediocrities: John Woolfe, snr and jnr, Thomas Browne, snr and jnr, William and Thomas Rice, and, worst of all, the intolerably officious Charles Alexander Craig. Only Kenton Couse and John Yenn were architects of any calibre, and they, like Chambers, were survivals from an earlier age. Robert Brettingham, appointed Resident Clerk in 1794, really belongs to the age of Wyatt. Both Yenn and Couse had been bred in the Office of Works. Both were tolerant and scupulous administrators, intensely loyal to Sir William. As Clerk of the Works at St James's, Whitehall, and Westminster, Couse had been responsible for the rebuilding of 10 Downing Street in 1766, before his promotion to administrative rank in 1782. His obituarist praised his personal qualities, and at the same time hinted at the strength of his connections in Court and Cabinet.[87] Yenn's patience was to be sorely tried over many years by his responsibilities as Clerk of the Works for Kensington Palace, Buckingham House, the Royal Mews, and Carlton House. Chambers himself described Yenn as 'an ingenious, faithful and intelligent servant.'[88] Indeed he was perhaps the Surveyor General's closest colleague, a pupil who lived to become his successor as Treasurer of the Royal Academy. But among all Chambers's assistants there was only one architect of exceptional talent, and he displayed several of the more infuriating symptoms of genius. The architect in question was the future Sir John Soane.

Chambers was usually on excellent terms with his subordinates. But Soane's behaviour was, almost from the beginning, truculent and conceited. He had been grateful enough at the time of his appointment in October 1790. Indeed, on that occasion, his letters to William Pitt and the Pittite banker Joseph Smith had been fulsome in the extreme.[89] But as his private practice grew, his reputation increased, and he cared less and less for his trivial obligations as Clerk of the Works in St James's, Whitehall, and Westminster. His discontent was magnified by Craig's promotion from Resident Clerk to Examiner. Craig was one of those industrious mediocrities whom Chambers made it his policy to favour. His chance of power was to come during Wyatt's lethargic Surveyorship; his flamboyant signature figures prominently among the chaotic records of that period. Meanwhile his presence served only to affront the pride of the Architect to the Bank of England.

As the backlog of Soane's unexecuted business accumulated during 1793, so Chambers's exasperation grew greater. In December the storm broke. Soane received an official summons from the Surveyor General:

---

[86] PRO Works 6/22 ff.163-4, 24 July 1794. In 1806 the Duke of Kent insisted that some of Tildesley's duties be delegated to Robert Browne, jnr (Works 6/24 f.51, 5 July 1806, f.53, 7 July 1806, and f.56, 26 July 1806). Tildesley died in 1808 and six years later his long-suffering wife Catherine was awarded an annuity of £75 per annum by the Treasury (Works 4/20, 26 Mar. 1812).

[87] *Gentleman's Magazine*, 1790, Pt.II, p.959.

[88] BM Add.MS 41135 f.26.

[89] A. T. Bolton, *The Portrait of Sir John Soane* (1927), p.48, 27 Oct. 1790.

'I sent last Friday to request your attendance at this Office, when a Messuage [*sic*] was returned that *you were at home if I had anything to say*. My answer was that I had, and wished to speak to you here, as it was on official Business. I remained a considerable time after at the Office, in expectation of seeing you, but you neither came nor sent any excuse, and I was of course under the necessity of giving those directions to others which should have been given to you.'[90]

Several weeks passed, and Soane made no reply. 'Though repeatedly called upon by me', Chambers complained to Rose, 'the same inconvenience still remains unremedied, the consequences of which are great delays and uncertainties in all places belonging to his Clerkship . . . His Majesty has signified to me his displeasure upon that subject.'[91]

At this point Soane decided to explain his conduct:

'I cannot attend your Board because I am particularly obnoxious to the Surveyor General, and because I cannot receive directions from an Inferior.'[92]

He went on to claim that his pointed comments on the dilatory repair of Winchester Palace[93] and on the inadequate construction of Somerset House[94] and the Fleet Prison[95] had made him personally unacceptable to Chambers. His objections to Craig were made on grounds of professional status:

'You Sir, thought proper to recommend (to a situation which requires great professional skill and practical knowledge, and therefore hitherto filled by Architects) a person who . . . has been brought up to measuring and accounts, and is now a District Surveyor . . . deeply engaged in the Lime and Coal Trade, [and] consequently, not a person by whom any regular Architect would submit to be directed . . . As you were pleased, Sir, lately to make mention of me to His Majesty, and perhaps did not recollect all the circumstances . . . , may I therefore request you to inform the King, *in my own words*, of the causes which have compelled me to adopt my present conduct.'

Chambers replied with a neat mixture of common sense and sarcasm.[96]

'In answer to your letter . . . I must beg leave to assure you that your first reason for non-attendance . . . is founded upon an entire Mistake. The Surveyor General, whose mind I ought to know, seldom or ever resents real injuries done to him, much less such trifles as are enumerated by you . . . Every free man is free to gratify his spleen, and I have only to remark that measures taken with spiteful intent however speciously they may be justified, seldom do the Assailant much service, but . . . often recoil upon himself with

---

90 PRO Works 6/22 f.143, 6 Dec. 1793.

91 PRO Works 6/22 f.144, 7 Dec. 1793 and f.147, 3 Jan. 1794. 'By reason of . . . [Soane's absenteeism] the public service received material injury' (Works 4/18 f.50, 3, Jan. 1794).

92 PRO Works 6/22 ff.150–1, 17 Jan. 1794; Works 4/18 f.52, 17 Jan. 1794.

93 During 1792–3 the buildings were turned into a reception centre for French Refugee Clergy. Soane was partly responsible for the work (e.g. PRO Works 6/22 f.74; Works 4/17, 28 Sept. 1792, 23 Nov. 1792).

94 Part of the RA Exhibition Room collapsed in December 1790. Chambers was exonerated after an investigation by James Adam, Holland, Dance, Soane, Mylne, James and Samuel Wyatt, James Johnson, Richard Norris, John Hobcroft, Richard Jupp, James White, Robert Brettingham, and S. P. Cockerell. Mylne's was the only dissentient voice (PRO T29/62 ff.444–5, 469; T29/63 ff.31, 195–6, 222). Peter Pindar made capital out of this accident:

    'Sir William! cover'd with Chinese renown,
      Whose houses are no sooner up than *down*.' (*Works* (1794), I, p.101.)

95 In December 1792 part of the boundary wall, recently rebuilt, collapsed again. This made possible several escapes (PRO T29/64 f.472; T29/65 f.217; Works 6/22 f.78).

96 PRO Works 6/22 ff.151–2, 20 Jan. 1794.

redoubled force. What squabbles may have been between yourself and Mr. Craig . . . cannot concern me. I shall neither attempt his justification, which appears to me super-fluous, nor a removal of your strong prejudice against him, which does not seem to me material to the business of this Office, but am sorry to hear from you that his great inferiority and my violent resentment prevent, and will prevent, your attendance at this Office. I have already assured you that the latter never existed, and the dangerous con-sequences of the former might I think be very much alleviated by an expedient for which the World is indebted to German Sagacity. In Germany when a great man connects with a Lady a few quarters inferior to him in rank, the great man preserves his own dignity, by performing on all connubial occasions with his left hand. The application is obvious, and I am very truly,

> Sir,
>
> Your most obedient and humble servant,
>
> William Chambers.'

The letter had its effect. Soane resigned within a fortnight. No doubt Chambers would have relished the backwoodsman's comment on the death of George Canning: 'thank God that's the last of these damned men of genius!' But this was not the only occasion when the Surveyor General was forced to act the part of disciplinarian. Office hours were normally 10 a.m. to 2 p.m. When in 1787 George Horsley, the First Assistant Clerk, and John Bankes, the Messenger and Porter, refused to attend regularly they were 'mulcted in their pay' for unpunctuality.[97]

But Horsley's recalcitrance turned out to have a deeper cause than was at first suspected. In 1790 he was suspended for persistent non-attendance, and in 1793 he was certified by Thomas Mann, M.D. as incurably insane.[98] 'Being totally unfit for business', Chambers informed the Treasury 'and sometimes so wild that the Tradesmen and other persons frequenting the Office did not think themselves in safety, I found it necessary to forbid his coming, and (that the business of the Office might not be impeded) to appoint another person to do his part . . . He is a very intelligent young man, very industrious and attentive to Business, very sober and tractable, his name is John William Hiort.'[99] Horsley's salary was increased to £80 per annum. Half this sum was for many years regularly made over to the sick man's family and half to the industrious Hiort. Architect, accountant, and inventor, Hiort became the most reliable member of the department. It was upon his versatility in a succession of different posts that the operation of the Office of Works was to depend during the Surveyorship of the negligent Wyatt.

Chambers handled cases like those of Tildesley, Horsley, and Soane with considerable tact and sympathy. His sense of humour was equal to every sort of situation. His response to one of Gilbert's less palatable reforms was this sly letter to Thomas Orde, Secretary to the Treasury:[100]

[97] They both forfeited 'one week's allowance' (PRO Works 4/17, 3 Mar. 1786, 24 Aug. 1787, 31 Aug. 1787).
[98] PRO Works 4/17, 16 Jan. 1789, 22 Jan. 1790; Works 4/18, f.22, 21 June 1793; T29/66 f.41, 11 July 1793.
[99] PRO Works 6/22 f.99, 17 May 1793; Works 4/18 f.17, 17 May 1793, and f.28, 2 Aug. 1793. In 1796 Chambers reported that Horsley 'will never be capable of returning to his duty' (Works 4/18 f.185, 24 June 1796).
[100] PRO Works 1/5 f.48, (?)5 Mar. 1783.

'The Surveyor of the Board of Works and the Officers of that Board were allowed by ancient Custom til the time of their suppression two Bucks and two Does annually; and a revival of our Places has also revived our Appetite for Vension [*sic*]. I beg leave to request in behalf of myself and Brethren, that the Allowance of the two Bucks may stil be continued to us, which will enable us to eat as well as Drink their Majesty's health on the usual days of festivity.

I am with Great Truth and Respect,

Dear Sir,

Your faithful and Obedient Servant,

William Chambers.

P.S. Mr. Secker [of the Board of Green Cloth] informs me the Secretaries of the Treasury are also Treasurers of the Vension.'

It is nice to know that Chambers received an answer which was not only favourable but appropriately elegant: Orde managed to bolster his reply 'with just enough of learning to misquote' both Vergil and Milton.[101]

As Surveyor General Chambers was also responsible for the distribution of government charity. He performed this office with common sense and humanity. Widows and other 'real objects of charity' had occasionally been recommended by the old Board of Works as worthy recipients of the Royal Maundy.[102] Chambers continued this practice, commending John Chart and Ann Gadd to the Lord Almoner, the Archbishop of York.[103] He also kept up the custom of providing a coffin and funeral expenses for deceased members of staff like Robert Churchill, an office bricklayer, and Robert Clayton, an office labourer.[104] But he did more than custom or duty required in begging generous allowances from the Treasury for disabled labourers and craftsmen. Time and time again the Treasury awarded less than Chambers demanded. In 1793 he urged that a pension of £20 to £25 be given to Jane Garrett. Her husband had been killed 'in fixing an Engine to a Well to supply a Bath for the use of His Majesty at Windsor.' The Treasury awarded a mere £12.[105] Four years previously Charles Rolfe, disabled by a fall in Scotland Yard, had been awarded 7*s* per week, although Chambers had begged for 10*s*.[106] When Edward Gurney, a carpenter, had his leg smashed by falling timber, his family's only source of income was a temporary gratuity from a Benefit Club.[107] Like Rolfe, he was given 1*s* per day. So was Christopher Codlington, a half-blind bricklayer aged seventy-seven, who had been struck by a falling

---

101 RIBA MSS 63, 9 Mar. 1783.

102 E.g. PRO Works 1/5 f.38, 22 Feb. 1782.

103 PRO Works 1/5, f.76, Christmas 1784; Works 4/16, 28 Feb. 1783.

104 PRO Works 5/75, Dec. 1786; Works 5/76, Dec. 1787; Works 4/17, 21 Dec. 1787. In 1814 similar arrangements were made for Francis Cobb, Constant Labourer, at Hampton Court, who died aged 'about ninety' (Works 6/26 f.164, 30 Aug. 1814; Works 4/21, 26 Aug. 1814). Expenses on such occasions varied between £2 and £5.

105 PRO Works 6/22 f.132, 13 Oct. 1793 and f.134, 8 Nov. 1793; T29/66 f.205, 14 Nov. 1793; Works 3/3 f.50, 5 Feb. 1794; Works 4/18 f.41, 25 Oct. 1793 and f.56, 7 Feb. 1794.

106 PRO Works 6/21 f.156, 16 May 1789; T29/60 f.373, 27 May 1789; Works 6/21 f.158, 22 May 1789; Works 4/17, 2 May 1789, 12 June 1789. For some time after Rolfe's death his allowance was illegally collected by his mistress, Mary Denby (Works 6/23 f.50, 16 Feb. 1798).

107 PRO T29/66 f.48, 11 July 1793; Works 6/22 f.86, 22 Feb. 1793; Works 4/18 f.8, 22 Feb. 1793, and f.11, 15 Mar. 1793.

tile.[108] But by means of a dramatic letter Chambers persuaded the Treasury to follow the practice of the old Board of Works and award 10s per week in one particularly tragic case, that of Henry Young. Young had been employed for fifteen years by the mason John Devall. On 8 October 1785,

'being at work in the Painted Chamber adjoining the House of Lords . . . he fell from the height of 33ft. on some wooden Steps which were broken by the violence of his fall . . . [He] had his Thigh broken in two places and two Bones of his right foot came out, and the wrist of his left hand was strained in so violent a Manner that the Surgeon says he will never have the use of it again so as to be fit for Labour. [He] has a wife and four children whose sole dependence for Maintainance and Support was on [his] industrious Labour . . . and at the time of the accident, his Wife being with Child, the fright so affected her as to turn her Milk to Water and Corruption and occasioned both her Breasts to break. The man is . . . truly an object of compassion.'[109]

As an administrator Chambers was not impeccable. In 1780, for example, he dared to by-pass the Exchequer by drawing money for the Office of Works directly from the Excise and Stamp Offices, thus depriving the Tellers of their fees.[110] By comparison with professional Civil Servants, he has even been labelled 'unquestionably extravagant and muddled in his accounts' during the pre-reform period.[111] His accounts, as Treasurer of the Royal Academy were frequently in arrears.[112] But the efficiency of the Office of Works during his period of office as Surveyor General and Comptroller contrasts markedly with the disorganization of the department before 1782 and its dislocation after 1796. He set his subordinates a high standard of dedication. During his fourteen years as chairman, he attended all but sixty-five of the 643 weekly and extraordinary meetings of the administrative board of the Office of Works.[113] His painstaking correspondence with the private occupants of royal buildings, the secretaries of government departments, the Lord Chamberlain and the Treasury, demonstrates his immediate control over every aspect of administration and finance. 'Never any business', Craig recalled, 'was better conducted than in Sir William Chambers's time.'[114] More important, every letter, every memorandum bears witness to his transparent humanity. And for this he was remembered long after his remains had been reunited in Westminster Abbey with those of his erstwhile rivals, Robert Adam and James Wyatt.

[108] PRO T29/67 ff.268-9, 4 Nov. 1794; Works 6/22 f.169, 24 Oct. 1794; Works 4/18 f.94, 24 Oct. 1794 and f.99, 28 Nov. 1794.

[109] PRO Works 1/5 f.85, Feb. 1786; T29/57 ff.477-8, 14 July 1786; Works 4/17, 28 July 1786.

[110] BM Add.MS 35402 f.240.

[111] J. Norris, Shelburne and Reform (1963), p.181.

[112] Royal Archives, Windsor, Privy Purse Accounts 1771-2, Georgian MSS 17259 and 17284.

[113] Figures compiled from Office of Works minutes 1782-96 (PRO Works 4/16-4/18).

[114] Parliamentary Papers, 1812-13, V, p.406.

Chapter 9

The *Treatise on Civil Architecture*
by Eileen Harris

Chambers's *Treatise on Civil Architecture*, or more precisely on the *Decorative Part of Civil Architecture*, meaning the five orders and their associates, may well be described as the Englishman's Palladio and Vignola. The three editions that appeared in his lifetime, and the four issued in the nineteenth century[1] bear witness to its extensive influence upon the study of architecture in this country. The wealth of practical information upon which its reputation rests speaks for itself, with little need for further comment. What is required, however, is an investigation of the theory on the more general subjects of beauty, propriety, and proportion, and the Greek, Roman, and Gothic styles, which underlies the selection and evaluation of the material he presents. With this in mind the first and third editions of the *Treatise* have been examined in conjunction with his unpublished lectures and miscellaneous notes in the Royal Institute of British Architects, and the Royal Academy.[2]

GENESIS OF THE TREATISE

It must have been as apparent to Chambers as it was to John Adam that the *Book of Chinese Designs*, with which he was to make his public debut in May 1757, could not 'raise his reputation high among the truly learned in Architecture.'[3] If he was to attract the patronage he so desperately needed to launch his career as a serious architect, it was essential that he avoid being labelled as an orientalist, and advertise his classical skills as soon as possible. Hence, on 6 April 1757, a month in advance of the Chinese book, he issued 'Proposals For publishing by Subscription, Designs of Villas, Temples, Gates, Doors, and Chimney Pieces; Composed by W. Chambers, Architect Engraved by Fourdrinier and Rooker. Conditions The Work consists of at least Sixty Large Folio-Plates, printed on the best Paper; with the necessary Descriptions and References. The Price to Subscribers to be two Guineas. One to be paid at the Time of subscribing, the other on Delivery of the Work; which is now in hand, and will be finished with all Expedition. Subscribers are taken in by the Author, next Door to Tom's Coffee House, Covent Garden, where Origi-

---

[1] See bibliography.

[2] The manuscripts of the lectures, written *c*.1770–1 for the Royal Academy and later intended for publication, are now in the RIBA and the Royal Academy (ex. late Professor A. E. Richardson Coll.). They came, through Chambers's daughter, from Halnaby Hall, Yorks; were arbitrarily split into two parts; and have now been reunited in London. Accompanying the lectures, which are for the most part written out in a fair hand with later corrections and additions, are a folder entitled 'Thoughts, Chronological Tables etc.', containing rough notes on miscellaneous subjects, e.g. beauty, grandeur, taste, and historical tables; and another group of papers headed 'Materials for a History of Gothic Architecture in England and its Origins'.

[3] Letter from John Adam to his mother, 14 September 1756. Fleming, op. cit., p.359.

nal Drawings may be seen; by A. Millar, D. Wilson, and T. Durham, in the Strand; and R. and J. Dodsley in Pall Mall.'[4] In May the *Chinese Designs* were published with a dedication to George, Prince of Wales; and before the summer was out Chambers was honoured with the appointment of tutor in architecture to the Prince, and architect to the Dowager Princess Augusta. This stroke of good fortune had a profound effect upon his future both as an architect and as an author. It was doubtlessly the tutorship that led him to abandon his proposed book of designs for a treatise. In fact, the casual relationship between the lessons and the *Treatise* is recalled by Chambers in the draft of a letter to George III, requesting permission to dedicate to him the third edition which he describes as 'a work originally written for your Majesties information . . . Your majesties Gracious indulgence and encouragement first prompted me to render publick what at first was certainly not designed for publication . . .'[5]

It was spring of 1759 when the *Treatise* appeared with a promise that if it were well received, it would be followed by a second volume on the construction and economics of architecture.[6] Its reception was very good indeed not only in London, but also in Paris, where, according to Chambers 'il m'a gagné beaucoup de réputation et quelque peu d'argent.'[7] Nevertheless, there was no second volume. Although for the next thirty years he diligently collected notes and made designs, the pressures of an extremely successful practice left him no time to 'correct and methodize' them, and in the end he had to 'relinquish the task: and consign the remainder, to the execution of some future pen.'[8] This does not mean that his writings on architecture ceased in 1759. Such was the reputation and popularity of the *Treatise* that a second edition, to which he made minor additions and corrections, was issued in 1768. Then in 1770 and 1771, when it seemed uncertain whether the ailing Thomas Sandby would be able to meet his commitments as Professor of Architecture to the newly-founded Royal Academy, Chambers resumed the mantle of architectural tutor, and began composing discourses of his own. Although the opportunity of addressing the Royal Academy students never materialized, he was stimulated by the appearance of Reynolds's *Discourses* to continue the lectures with a view to publishing them.[9]

---

[4] Munthe Letters, op. cit., quoted by Martienssen, op. cit., p.360.

[5] Royal Academy, Chambers MSS, Richardson Coll. Only the third edition was dedicated to George III. The first two were dedicated to the 3rd Earl of Bute.

[6] Chambers, *Treatise* (1759), p.84.

[7] Letter to Mons. Wargentin, Secretary of the Royal Academy of Sciences, Stockholm, 17 June 1760. See also *Treatise* (1791) p.v. The *Treatise* must have been exported to France in considerable numbers for there was never a legitimate French edition. The *Traité D'Architecture . . . Traduit de l'Anglais après la seconde Edition par Le Rouge*, Paris (n.d.) is nothing more than a selection of plates re-engraved by Le Rouge.

[8] *Treatise* (1791), p.v.

[9] Charlemont, op. cit., I, 304-5. Letter from Chambers, 30 January 1771. 'Sir Joshua Reynolds is now with me . . . He purposes [*sic*] sending you a copy of his dissertations or discourses . . . I have also an intention of making discourses on architecture. One I have finished, which I have shown to a friend or two who tell me it is very well and encourage me to go on; but I am going on so many ways at once that God knows when I shall get to the end of any of them.' Chambers's introduction to the lectures (RIBA MSS), written after 1771, begins with an explanation of their origin for the Royal Academy during Sandby's illness. Although Sandby is known to have been the first Professor of Architecture (Wm. Sandby, *The History of the Royal Academy of Arts*, I (London, 1862), p.84), Reynolds, for some unexplainable reason, wrote to Wm. Hamilton in Naples on 28 March 1768 that '. . . we have four professors Mr. Penny of Painting Mr. Chambers of Architecture Mr. Wale of Geometry and Perspective and Dr. Hunter of Anatomy each give six lectures every year – the salery [*sic*] £30 per annum . . .' Sir Joshua Reynolds, *Letters*, ed. F. W. Hilles (London, 1929), pp.22-3.

K

Two were completed: the first '. . . Pointing out the Excellencies of Architecture and . . . enumerating the Various Branches of Knowledge necessary to an Architect. The Second . . . defining the Art . . . tracing it from its origins . . . marking its progress & Periods of perfection and . . . determining the Sources whence our knowledge in its different parts was to be collected,' and a third on 'Perfection in the decorative part of Architecture'[10] was begun. But again other activities intervened and the discourses, like the promised second volume, fell by the wayside. Nevertheless, he did have a final opportunity to make use of his manuscripts in the third, augmented edition of the *Treatise*, published in 1791. As it represents his most complete and mature thoughts, it is this edition which will be considered here.

CHARACTER AND CONTENTS

The *Treatise* owes much of its character and contents to the fact that it was occasioned by the tutelage of the Prince. In it Chambers sets out, as a teacher, to provide a course of instruction on the five orders and their decorative associates. His choice of subject, though limited to only one of the several aspects of architecture, is neither unusual nor unreasonable. Not only were the orders 'the basis of the whole decorative part of architecture',[11] but they also appealed to the widest audience of professionals as well as amateurs, a practical consideration to which Chambers himself refers in defence of his failure to produce a further volume on the more technical subjects of construction and economics.[12] As for precedents, he had, in addition to Vignola, the treatises of François Blondel, D'Aviler, Le Clerc, Perrault, and other Frenchmen. In fact, it was upon the scope and arrangement of the standard French *Cours* that the *Treatise* was patterned.

More, it is true, had been written on the five orders than on any other branch of architecture. But the sheer bulk and diffusion of this material, instead of simplifying the subject, tended to make it more perplexing. The result, as Chambers observed, was 'such a multiplicity of contradictory opinions, all of them supported by plausible arguments, that it is difficult to make a choice, or to distinguish the real from that which is merely specious.'[13] Nor were the problems confronting the architectural student obviated by the recent efforts of Isaac Ware to collect in one volume 'all that is useful in the works of others.'[14] The *Complete Body of Architecture*, though the most sound and comprehensive work yet to appear in English, was encyclopaedic rather than selective, and relied solely on printed sources, which sufficed for the first generation Palladians, but not for the younger architects, like Adam and Chambers, to whom first-hand experience of the buildings of the great masters was just as important as a knowledge of their written advice. However useful Ware's book may have been to Chambers, it was neither an essential source of information nor a model for the *Treatise*.

Chambers's pedagogical approach is guided by the expert example of his own teacher,

---

[10] RIBA, Chambers MSS, Introduction to third lecture.

[11] *Treatise* (1791), p.32.

[12] Ibid., p.vi.

[13] Ibid., p.iv.

[14] Isaac Ware, *A Complete Body of Architecture* (London, 1756), Preface, p.(i).

J. F. Blondel. His aim is at once to simplify the study of architecture without sacrificing any of its richness, variety, or precision, and to cultivate taste and increase pleasure not only by providing information and examples, but also by encouraging the development of critical judgement. The method he employs to pilot the student through the labyrinth of material is the same empirical one by which he himself had been directed in Blondel's *Ecole*, and which he continued to follow in his Italian studies. He examines everything critically and impartially, constantly comparing written views with executed buildings, and accepting nothing as pre-ordained, and no one as sacred. From this he abstracts what he considers to be a series of sound precepts and good designs, supported if possible by reason, or, failing that, by universally-received opinion. His own observations of French, Italian, and English architecture and architectural literature are brought into play at every point. Indeed, the remarkable extent of his experience, apart from giving authority to his conclusions and a personal flavour to the *Treatise*, did much to broaden the horizons of English students.

Although a firm believer in the efficacy of rules, he is by no means didactic. He does not trouble to regiment minute details, nor does he ever demand absolute adherence to the rules that he does lay down. There are numerable occasions on which there is reason to admit exceptions, and these are carefully specified. His point of view tends, on the whole, to be subjective rather than objective. More importance is attached to the visual effects of an entire composition, or to practical and common-sense considerations than to theoretical correctness of detail, to reason, or propriety. He has no axe to grind, and no preconceived theory governing his decisions. This does not prevent him from discussing controversial subjects, or from committing himself to one side or the other. He is, however, highly suspicious of extremes of any kind, and wherever possible will choose a sound middle road. As a result, his *Treatise* appears to be somewhat dull and unadventurous in comparison with contemporary, and especially French, literature. Part of this conservatism may be credited to his strong sense of responsibility as a teacher. His level-headed, unbiased approach may not have stirred the imagination, but it certainly provided the soundest foundation to the study of architecture, and for that reason was unanimously accepted as the standard English text-book.

Before examining some of his views on specific aspects of architecture, it is perhaps best to reconstruct, from the *Treatise*, lectures and miscellaneous notes, his general theories of beauty, propriety, and proportion.

BEAUTY

Although Chambers never formulated anything like a complete or systematic theory of beauty, he did devote considerable thought to the subject, hastily recording his ideas in unconnected and often fragmentary notes, some of which he later incorporated in the third edition of the *Treatise*. Most of his views were provoked by the controversial theories contained in Burke's *Enquiry*, the main bone of contention being the causes of aesthetic response – how and why impressions of beauty are aroused. According to Burke, beauty is 'some quality in bodies, acting mechanically upon the human mind by the intervention of the senses', without any assistance from reason or will; so that as long as the organs of sense are operating normally, there must be a uniform response among all men.[15] Chambers, unable to share Burke's absolute faith in the power of the senses, or to accept the idea of a standard, maintains, to the contrary, that our impressions of beauty are primarily derived from associated ideas, and therefore are not uniform but diverse.

There are particular qualities in Visible Objects that Act immediately upon the organs of Vision & exact Sensations of Pain or Pleasure according to the greater or Smaller degree of tension in these organs; but far the most powerful impressions made by Visible objects are those which act upon the mind, which are the result of reasoning, & arise from an Association of Ideas. Whatever related to dimension, to Quality of light & to brilliancy of Colour is in a great meas[ure] though not totally reducible to the first of these Classes & is felt nearly in the Same manner by all persons whose Organ of Vision is Perfect.

But whatever relates to Propriety, Proportion, Symetry [sic], local Colours, Grace, dignity, imitation, Accuracy, or neatness of Execution, materials, fitness, perfection, distance may be ranged under the Second of these Classes, and owe their power Chiefly to the Ideas which we connect with them, and excite in different minds differ[ent] feelings. According as the minds are prepared for their reception.[16]

His assessment of the role of association in aesthetic experience comes close to the ideas expressed in Perrault's *Ordonnance*, 1683, and even closer to the more elaborate theories put forth by Alexander Gerard in his *Essay on Taste*, 1759.

Although Perrault does not attribute nearly so much to association, he does recognize that there are certain qualities which are considered beautiful not 'for Reasons of which everyone is a Judge, but only through Custom, and a connexion which the mind makes of two things of a different Nature, for by this Connexion, it comes to pass that the Esteem wherewith the Mind is prepossess'd, for some things whose Value it knows, insinuates an Esteem, also, for others, whose worth, it knows not, and insensibly engages it to respect them like.'[17] These qualities (proportion being the one with which he is primarily concerned) he calls 'arbitrary' beauties as distinguished from 'positive' ones, founded on 'solid convincing Reasons which please everyone', e.g. 'Richness of Materials, the Grandeur and Magnificence of the Structure, the Exactness and Neatness of the Performance' – all of which Chambers credits to association.

The theory of association had a far more radical advocate in Alexander Gerard. Influenced to some extent by Hume, Gerard stands apart from most eighteenth-century æstheticians who acknowledged the power of association to effect ideas and diversify opinion, but refused to consider it a *cause* of our ideas, and were, in fact, inclined to charge it with distorting the perceptions of the senses, which they considered to be the real cause of ideas. Not only does he maintain that there are, in addition to the pleasures derived from the effect that certain qualities have on the senses, others which result from associated ideas, but he goes even farther to conclude that *most* of the pleasures derived

[15] Edmund Burke, *Philosophical Enquiry into the Origin of our Ideas of the Sublime and Beautiful*, ed. J. T. Boulton (London, 1958), pp.92, 112.

[16] RIBA, Chambers MSS. The first sentence refers to Burke, ibid., Pt.IV, *passim*. The same argument is repeated in the *Treatise* (1791), p.108. For a more detailed study of Chambers's theories of beauty see E. Harris, 'Burke and Chambers on the Sublime and Beautiful', *Essays in the History of Architecture Presented to Rudolf Wittkower* (1967), p.209 ff.

[17] Claude Perrault, *A Treatise of the Five Orders of Columns in Architecture*, trans. John James. (London 1708), p.VI

from visible objects can be attributed to association. To him, the term 'beauty' is precisely applied 'to every pleasure which is conveyed by the eye, and which has not got a proper and peculiar name, to the pleasure we receive either when an object of sight suggests pleasant ideas of the senses; or when the ideas suggested are agreeable ones formed from the sensations of sight. In all cases, beauty is, at least in part, resolvable into association.'[18]

While Chambers is explicit enough on the function of association, he is unexpectedly vague about its handmaiden, reason. To judge from a single isolated comment, reason, by revealing the objects of beauty, acts as a guide to the senses in their reactions. 'Our approbation our love for beauty is involuntary but what then does that prove that it has no dependence on reason? Surely no. We do not love a thing til we discover it & find out its properties & when we have found it lovely we love it and cannot help loving it.'[19] This is clearly a rebuttal to Burke's contention that 'it is not by the force of long attention and inquiry that we find any object to be beautiful; beauty demands no assistance from our reasoning; even the will is unconcerned; the appearance of beauty as effectively causes some degree of love in us, as the application of ice or fire produces the ideas of heat or cold.'[20] Here, again, Chambers's reply may have been inspired by Gerard whose 'internal or reflex senses', which are responsible for aesthetic perceptions, 'do not operate, til certain qualities in objects have been perceived, discriminated from others similar, compared and compounded.'[21] These qualities having been revealed, 'it is *sense*, which is pleased or displeased . . . but *judgment* alone can determine them, and present to the sense the object of its perception.'[22]

So much for Chambers's views on the nature of aesthetic response. When it comes to defining beauty or perfection in architecture, he follows the same subjective and empirical approach. Visual appearance is his primary concern, and the universal consent of the ancients and moderns his standard. The general effect of a composition, being immediately obvious to all, must, in his opinion, take precedence over more obscure considerations of origin, reason, and fitness, which appeal mainly to the understanding, and hence are known only to a few.[23]

Like Burke,[24] he is firmly opposed to the theory that beauty consists in fitness. The two qualities 'have very little connection with each other; in architecture they are sometimes incompatible; . . . and there are many things (for example, the corinthian capital representing a basket of leaves) in that Art, which, though beautiful in the highest degree, yet in their application, carry with them an evident absurdity.'[25] Where use is the primary intention, the importance of fitness cannot be denied, '. . . but in objects merely orna-

[18] Alexander Gerard, *Essay on Taste* (London, 1759), p.45.

[19] RIBA, Chambers MSS.

[20] Burke, op. cit., p.92.

[21] Gerard, op. cit., p.90.

[22] Ibid., p.94. For a similar concept of reason as a guide to the senses, see David Hume, 'Of the Standard of Taste', *The Philosophical Works*, eds. T. H. Green and T. H. Grose (London, 1875), III, 277; and *An Enquiry Concerning the Principles of Morals*, Sect. I, *Works*, IV, 172.

[23] *Treatise* (1791), p.62.

[24] Burke, op. cit., pp.104–10.

[25] *Treatise* (1791), p.99.

mental, which are designed to captivate the senses, rather than to satisfy the understanding, it seems unreasonable to sacrifice other qualities much more efficacious to Fitness alone.'[26] Applying this distinction to pediments,[27] he fully accepts the demands of propriety on the exterior of a building where the pediment represents a roof, and therefore can appear only once at the top of the composition; but objects to an extension of such rationalism to the interior where, in his view, pediments carry no suggestion of function, and are perfectly admissible as ornaments. Even on the exterior, propriety is not the only guide to their use. Visual effects are equally important. Thus, the reason for omitting small pediments over the niches, doors, and windows of a façade, wholly or partially covered by a large pediment, is that 'wherever there is considerable difference of dimension, in objects of the same figure, both will equally suffer by it . . .', the larger appearing too heavy, and the smaller too trifling; and 'wherever the difference of dimension is inconsiderable, it will always strike the beholder as the effect of inaccuracy in the workmen, or of inattention in the contriver.'[28] This kind of aesthetic reasoning, though typical of Chambers, is rarely encountered in the writings of other architects.

By rights, Chambers's attack upon the rigorous application of fitness as a standard of beauty ought to be directed against the main advocates of that theory, Berkeley, Hume, and Hogarth. This, however, is not the case. Instead the blame is placed wholly and mistakenly upon Laugier, whose standard, as Herrmann points out,[29] is not fitness, but nature and the primitive hut. Although Chambers is guilty of a literal misinterpretation of Laugier's *Essai*, his error is not simply the result of carelessness or prejudice, and is, in fact, easily understandable. Since utility was commonly regarded as one of the guiding principles of nature, it is not unreasonable to presume that it remains a principle when nature is taken as the model of art. It seems more than likely that Chambers saw in Laugier an implication of the conclusions of Berkeley, Hume, and Hogarth. Nor was he the only reader of the *Essai* to connect nature or art, reason, use, and beauty. Isaac Ware, Laugier's first English disciple, also makes the connexion,[30] and it is almost certainly to Ware that Chambers is referring when he speaks of the 'many favourers of this writer's system who, like him, concentrate all perfection in propriety.'[31]

The analogy between beauty and fitness is in any case not the only point in Chambers's argument with Laugier. He is equally critical of his rigid adherence to the primitive hut, nature, and the origin and reason of things as standards of beauty. In his view, the primitive hut, far from being a model of perfection, as it was to Laugier, is nothing more than the first stage in an evolutionary development. 'Some pretend that an exact Imitation of the parts in the primitive hut is necessary. Laugier has written a book upon the Subject & Mansard & others have built ugly buildings upon that Idea. tis Vitruvius his doctrine yet absurd the forms in the primitive hut first suggested the principal forms in our

[26] Ibid., p.99.
[27] Ibid., pp.98–9.
[28] Ibid., p.101.
[29] Wolfgang Herrmann, *Laugier and Eighteenth-Century French Theory* (1962), p.177.
[30] Ware, op. cit., p.136. 'There is a Nobleness in architecture which is always broken in upon by ornament: therefore no ornament should be admitted but what is reasonable; and nothing is reasonable in architecture which is not founded on some principle of use.'
[31] *Treatise* (1791), p.99.

buildings & Custom has rendered them familiar but there is no reason why they should not be added to & Improved.'[32] Moreover, if deviating from the origin or reason of things (as in the placing of dentils under modillions) improves the general effect of a composition, then the practice, providing it is exercised with caution, judgement, and a due respect to the ancients, cannot be censured.[33] Similar sentiments in opposition to the rigours of Vitruvian rationalism, particularly in its application to dentils and modillions, had been expressed by Blondel, Le Clerc,[34] and others, and are summed up in Perrault's statement that 'what is found agreeable does not come from an exact imitation of the thing it represents'.[35] Chambers, however, carries the argument much further than his predecessors. To him one of the most fundamental considerations is the distinction between appearance and reality, between the image or the work of art, and the original it represents. Thus, when there is no probability of mistaking one for the other, as there ought not to be, it is ridiculous to base propriety upon the original,[36] as Cordemoy and Le Clerc do when they insist that statues of human figures should not be placed on tops of buildings, or at heights unnatural and uncomfortable to real men and women.[37]

Whatever the standard, Chambers was firmly opposed to any purely rational theory of beauty which in the extremes of its application seemed to him to neglect the pleasures of the senses, and to impose unnecessary restrictions upon the architect. Although he recognizes, in theory, the obvious advantages of an absolute standard by which to determine the merits of every work of art, he is too practical, and far too concerned with visual appearances and subjective reactions to adhere unconditionally to any single principle. He is not, however, subjective enough to do without any standard whatsoever. Perfection for him consists in mediums between extremes, which, though discovered by experience, must in the end be ratified by the universal consent of the ancients and moderns.

PROPORTIONS

Chambers's empiricism also extends to his views on the relationship between beauty and proportion. Following Perrault, he maintains that proportions in architecture, unlike musical harmonies, do not operate mechanically on the senses, and have no positive or inherent charms which please all spectators alike; but instead derive their appeal from convenience (meaning fitness to an end), custom, prejudice, or association of ideas.[38] What is more, he does not believe that beauty depends upon the simplicity or accuracy of measurements. 'The real relations subsisting between dissimilar figures have no connection with the apparent'; what is really in perfect harmony may appear discordant and vice versa. The effect of proportions varies according to the position of the spectator. For example, the ovolo of the Doric cornice appears larger than the capital of the triglyph,

[32] RIBA, Chambers MSS.

[33] *Treatise* (1791), pp.62–3.

[34] François Blondel, *Cours d'Architecture*, I (Paris, 1675), p.61; Sebastien Le Clerc, *A Treatise of Architecture* (London, 1723), p.43.

[35] Perrault, op. cit., p.viii.

[36] *Treatise* (1791), p.124.

[37] Le Clerc, op. cit., p.120; Abbé de Cordemoy, *Nouveau Traité de Toute l'Architecture*, 2nd edn. (Paris, 1714), p.96.

[38] *Treatise* (1791), p.106.

although it is, in fact, the same size; and conversely, if the ovolo was placed at an equal distance below the spectator's eye, it would appear smaller than any flat member of equal size.[39] Similarly, the double cube room, though perfectly proportioned, does not always appear so. The discrepancies between the width and length, and the difficulty of adjusting the height to both make the room seem too high when viewed from the ends, and too low when seen from the sides.[40]

In accordance with Vitruvian tradition, most architects would compensate for the changes which distance makes upon the *apparent* proportions of an object by altering its *real* proportions. But not Chambers who seems to have been convinced, at least as far as the orders were concerned, by the logic of Perrault's arguments against this practice.[41] Adjustments to the proportions of the capital and entablature of an elevated order for optical reasons are rendered unnecessary by the fact that 'the point of view being more or less distant, according to the size, or elevation of the order, the apparent magnitudes of their parts will constantly bear, nearly, the same proportion to each other . . .' Furthermore, it is only common sense that the spectator, being so far removed from the object, will be 'rather occupied in considering the general mass, than in examining its particular parts', which in any case are too far from the eye to be distinctly perceptible.[42]

Although he accepts the fact that there is no certain proportion that is invariably and universally pleasing, he is adamantly opposed to Burke's conclusion that proportion is therefore not essential to beauty. Several of his miscellaneous notes are devoted to rather lengthy but unsuccessful attempts to disprove Burke's contention that the absence of proportion in animals which are commonly esteemed beautiful (e.g. the swan and the peacock), and the diversity of proportions even within a single species indicate that proportion cannot be a cause of beauty.[43] In the first instance he argues that if proportion were not compensated by other pleasing qualities (colour, form, movement, etc.) its absence would be disgusting. But this of course does not prove that its presence would necessarily be pleasing. To explain the equal beauty of different proportions, he introduces fitness, which he claims is immediately apparent and pleasing to those who are accustomed to judging, while unfitness is always displeasing to everyone. Again, he fails to prove that the majority of individuals who are not experienced judges will necessarily derive any pleasure from either proportion or fitness. The basis of the disagreement lies in the definition of beauty. To Burke, beauty is 'some quality in bodies, acting mechanically upon the human mind by the intervention of the senses.'[44] To Chambers, whatever we call beautiful in visible objects, whether it be proportions, fitness, colour, materials, workmanship, or any other qualities, owes its merit to the ideas we associate with it, to custom, habit, or education.[45]

While he embraces, on one hand, the most revolutionary elements of Perrault's theory

[39] Ibid., p.46.

[40] Ibid., p.131.

[41] Perrault, op. cit., pp.105–19.

[42] *Treatise* (1759), p.19, also (1791), p.47.

[43] RIBA, Chambers MSS; Burke, op. cit., Pt.III, secs. ii–v. E. Harris, op. cit., p.212.

[44] Burke, op. cit., p.112.

[45] *Treatise* (1791), p.106.

– the arbitrary beauty of proportions, and the abuse of optical adjustments – and is the first English architect to do so; on the other hand, he rejects the one idea that was most commonly accepted in England – that of measuring the orders in equal parts, rather than in modules and minutes.[46] In response to the followers of the former system, who claim that it is a simpler and more accurate expression of the relations between the whole and its parts, and is easier to remember,[47] he replies first that as the real and apparent relations between dissimilar figures have no connexion, simplicity and accuracy of measurements can have no advantage as far as beauty is concerned; and secondly, that not only are modules and minutes just as easy, if not easier, to remember as complicated divisions and subdivisions of parts, but in any case it is unnecessary for the architect to overburden his memory, when a fluent knowledge of the general proportions of the orders, and recourse to figured drawings and engravings for details is perfectly adequate, and indeed much more practicable.[48] His intention is not to prove that equal parts are inferior to minutes and modules, which he happens to prefer, but rather to disprove the notion that they are any more effective in attaining perfection. Abstract mathematical ratios, however they are expressed, are of little or no importance, for to him perfect proportion is simply a visually pleasing relationship between the objects in a composition. To attain such a relationship the parts must be so contrived that the principal or essential ones 'catch the eye successively . . . according to their degree of importance in the composition, and impress their images on the mind before it is affected by any of the subservient members . . .', which should also be capable of raising distinct ideas appropriate to their particular function. The shape and position of the parts contributes something to this effect, simple and projecting forms acting faster than those that are complex and receding. But the most important quality, and the one that operates most powerfully on the mind is dimension, which cannot be accurately determined by rules, but must be discovered by experience.[49] Although such a subjective theory of proportions would seem to exclude the possibility of a standard, Chambers, like most of his contemporaries, cannot conceive of being without one, and so resorts, as he does in every other aspect of beauty, to the old standby, common consent. Thus, when the particular proportions and arrangement of a composition are found pleasing by a 'generality of judicious spectators', they are to be imitated and repeated wherever similar circumstances persist.[50] Armed with the theory of common consent, he is even able to reconcile those who seek the sources of beauty in positive qualities with their opponents who find it in association or custom, 'the maintainers of harmonick proportions, proving their system by the measures observed in the most esteemed buildings of antiquity; and the supporters of the opposite doctrine allowing, that as both artists and criticks, form their ideas of perfection upon these same buildings of antiquity; there cannot be a more infallible way of pleasing, than by imitating that, which is so universally approved.'[51]

[46] Perrault, op. cit., pp.4–5.

[47] Ibid, p.5; Ware, op. cit., pp.267, 268.

[48] *Treatise* (1791), pp.37–8.

[49] Ibid., p.46.

[50] Ibid., p.46.

[51] Ibid., p.107. For similar conclusions in French architectural literature see Herrmann, op. cit., pp.39–40.

THE ORDERS

In treating the orders Chambers endeavours to arrive at compositions which will be found visually pleasing to his 'generality of judicious spectators', and will, at the same time, convey as exactly as possible the intentions of the ancients. His preparation for this ambitious undertaking consists in having 'measured, with the utmost accuracy . . . many ancient and modern celebrated buildings, both at Rome, and in other parts of Europe; strictly copying such things as appeared to be perfect, and carefully correcting others, that seemed in any degree faulty: relying therein, not alone on his own judgment, in doubtful cases; but much on the opinion and advice, of several learned, ingenious artists of different nations, with whom he had the advantage of being intimately connected, when abroad.'[52] Most of the ingenious artists' with whom he associated were of course Frenchmen, and it is their tastes which had the greatest effect upon his judgements. His preference for Vignola's profiles and proportions is typically French. To Bosse, Cordemoy, Nativelle, or perhaps to his teacher, J. F. Blondel[53] he owes the unusual idea of representing all the orders the same height, 'by which means the gradual increase of delicacy and richness, is easily perceivable; as are likewise the relations between the intercolumniations of the different orders, and the proportions which their pedestals, imposts, archivolts, and other parts, with which they are on various occasions accompanied; bear to each other.'[54] Indeed, his whole method of composing the orders by selecting, combining, and amending the best features from a variety of sources is related, albeit in a general way, to the much more scientific procedure involved in Perrault's mean. The designs with which he emerges are thoroughly eclectic, but still quite personal. Although he has taken extraordinary pains to make them perfect, he does not in the end regard them as absolutes of perfection. Not only does he constantly refer to details in the works of other architects, that are equally suitable for imitation, but in several instances he also provides alternative designs, copied from the executed works of Palladio (which he considers far superior to his engraved designs), or from antique Roman, Renaissance, and even baroque buildings.

Having considered the form and measurements of each order as well as its application both interior and exterior, he goes on to discuss related forms (pilasters, persians, and caryatids, etc.), and decorative accompaniments (doors, windows, pediments, arches, gates, piers, niches, statues, ceilings, etc.). These subjects offer him far more opportunity to draw upon his experience, to display his erudition, and to express freely his own taste and opinions. Here we find him vehemently disputing, one by one, Laugier's objections to pilasters;[55] summoning such diverse authorities as Burke and Pierre Estève, the rather obscure author of an equally obscure work on the *Esprit des Beaux Arts*, 1753, to explain why, contrary to the laws of optics, undiminished pilasters should appear larger on top;[56]

[52] Ibid., p.47.

[53] Cordemoy, op. cit., p.69; Pierre Nativelle, *Traité d'Architecture* (Paris, 1729); Jacques-François Blondel, *Cours d'Architecture* (Paris, 1771), I, 216, pl.1; Abraham Bosse, *Traité Des Manières De Dessiner Les Ordres* (Paris, 1684), pls.XIII–XIV.

[54] *Treatise* (1791), p.36; also (1759), p.9. It was probably from Chambers that the practice was later adopted by Stephen Riou, *The Grecian Orders of Architecture* (London, 1768), p.13, pl.1; and George Richardson, *Treatise on the Five Orders* (London, 1787), p.1, pl.1.

[55] Ibid., pp.64–6.

[56] Ibid., p.67.

THE TREATISE ON CIVIL ARCHITECTURE

proposing a revival of Robert Morris's all-but-forgotten system of proportioning windows by the number of square feet on plan of the room, in preference to the widely accepted method given by Palladio;[57] juxtaposing windows by Ludovico Cigoli, Bernini, and Kent from Palazzo Ranunchini in Florence, Palazzo Bracciano in Rome, and the Horse Guards in St James's;[58] condemning Cortona's great door in S. Carlo at Corso;[59] acclaiming the plan and interior decoration of Holkham, but censuring the excessive variety of its exterior, which exhausts the eye in a 'perpetual dance';[60] or making mince of Adam's 'filigrane toy work', and his 'trifling gaudy ceilings . . . which, composed as they are of little rounds, squares, octagons, hexagons, and ovals; excite no other ideas, than that of a desert: upon the plates of which are dished out bad copies of indifferent antiques.'[61]

ROME v. GREECE

Like every architect, Chambers had his likes and dislikes, and though many of them were conservative, none was so reactionary and so vehement as his opposition to the *Gusto Greco*.

When the *Treatise* first appeared Greek studies were still too much in their infancy to be of any real concern. He knew and approved of the pioneering work of his friend Le Roy, and looked forward eagerly to the findings of his countrymen Stuart and Revett.[62] Even in the next decade, when interest in archaeology mounted, literature multiplied, and arguments over the superiority of Greek or Roman began to flare,[63] he remained unperturbed. It was only after the Society of Dilettante's publication of Chandler and Revett's *Ionian Antiquities* in 1769, following close on the heels of Major's *Paestum*, 1768, and Riou's *Grecian Orders*, 1768, that he began to take the matter seriously. In 1770 he burst forth with a stream of abuse against the abominable taste and useless expenditure of the Dilettante publication in a letter to, of all people, Lord Charlemont, a member of the Society, and one of the committee responsible for sending Revett to Asia Minor.[64] Bold and utterly tactless as this may seem, it was mild in comparison with the attack launched in his second lecture, *c.*1771.[65] Here, using the history of architecture as a virtual battlefield, he

---

[57] Ibid., p.116. Joseph Gwilt in his edition of the *Treatise* (1825), p.355, n.1, supplied Morris's name (incorrectly as James rather than Robert) and quoted in full from the *Lectures on Architecture* (London, 1734), pp.108–9.

[58] Ibid., pp.121–2.

[59] Ibid., p.129.

[60] Ibid., pp.120, 132.

[61] Ibid., pp.132, 135.

[62] *Treatise* (1759), p.36.

[63] Allan Ramsay, *The Investigator* (London, 1755; 2nd edn. 1762); J. J. Winckelmann, *Gedänken über de Nachamung der griechischen Werke* (Dresden, 1755; Trans. by Henry Fuseli, London 1765, 2nd edn. 1767); J. L. Le Roy, *Les Ruines Des plus Beaux Monuments de la Grèce* (Paris, 1758); J. B. Piranesi, *Della Magnificenze d'Architettura de' Romani* (Rome, 1761); James Stuart and Nicholas Revett, *The Antiquities of Athens*, vol.I (London, 1762); J. J. Winckelmann, *Geschichte der Kunst des Altertums* (Dresden, 1764); John Berkenhout, *The Ruins of Paestum* (London, 1767); J. B. Piranesi, *Parere su l'Architettura* (Rome, 1765). See also N. Pevsner and S. Lang 'Apollo or Baboon', *Architectural Review*, CIV, Dec. 1948, 217–79; R. Wittkower, 'Piranesi's Parere su l'Architettura', *Journal of the Warburg and Courtauld Institutes*, II, 1938–9, p.147 ff.

[64] Charlemont, op. cit., I, 298. February 1770 'The dilettante book is published, and a cursed book it is, between friends, being composed of some of the worst architecture I ever saw; there is a degree of madness in sending people abroad to fetch home such stuff. I am told this curious performance has cost the society near three thousand pounds; such a Sum well applied would be of great use and advance the arts considerably, but to expend so much in order to introduce bad taste is abominable.'

mustered every argument he could possibly conceive of – from the serious to the ludicrous – to defeat the claims of Greek superiority.

To begin with, he rejects the traditional theory that the Greeks were the inventors of architecture, maintaining, from historical evidence, that they were not only preceded by the Egyptians, who in turn may have taken their ideas from the Phoenicians, but were also surpassed by them 'in point of grandeur and extent'.[66] Nor will he credit the Greeks with the perfection of architecture. That is the honour of the Romans, there being 'more fancy, greater beauty and art and Ingenuity in Roman compositions than in Grecian buildings existing or discribed in books.'[67] A comparison of the works of Le Roy, Stuart, and Revett with those of Palladio, Desgodetz, Sandrart, and Piranesi will, he believes, provide visual proof of the deficiencies of Greek profiles, proportions, and details.[68] What he objects to most, however, is the lack of magnificence, grandeur, and richness in Grecian architecture. Armed with a sharp wit, he reduces the Temple of the Winds to a dove house, and the celebrated Lantern of Demosthenes to a sentry box in Portman Square, 'its form and proportions resembling those of a silver tankard excepting that the handle is wanting'.[69] Greek architects must have been very feeble indeed if in the building of the Parthenon three of the greatest men, Callicrates, Ictinus, and Phidias, had to 'collect themselves into a mountain merely to produce a mouse', while James Gibbs alone was able to design St Martin-in-the-Fields, a work which is not only larger, but also 'far superior to anything in Athens'.[70] The apparent distaste among the Greeks for splendour and variety must, he suggests, be the combined result of their ideas of democracy and equality, and the political subdivision and unrest in their country.[71]

The fact that Greek architecture, although known in the past, has not been imitated, is evidence to him that it is not worthy of the serious notice now lavished upon it. Roman architecture, on the contrary, has been admired and copied by all the great architects from the fourteenth century onwards. Indeed, such is the strength of the Roman tradition that it is sheer folly to suppose that it could be challenged or superseded by the Greeks. 'They might with equal success oppose a Hottentot and a Baboon to the Apollo and the Gladiator as set up the Grecian architect, against the Roman.'[72]

This fierce opposition to the *Gusto Greco,* though probably communicated to his friends, remained pent up in his lecture notes, unknown to the public, until the publication of the third edition of the *Treatise.* In the intervening twenty years the effect of Greek studies had

[65] Many of the arguments in the second lecture were inserted in the third edition of the *Treatise*. Although he claims that his observations were intended for the second edition of 1768, and were suppressed when 'after a few struggles, the Roman manner obtained a compleat victory' (*Treatise*, 1791, p.26), in fact, they were not written until two or more years after the second edition had appeared.

[66] RIBA, Chambers MSS, Lecture II, pp.12–16; *Treatise* (1791), pp.17–18.

[67] Lecture II, pp.17–18; also *Treatise*, p.18. He is, however, willing to admit that the Romans derived some of their knowledge of ornamental architecture (as opposed to construction) from the Greeks.

[68] Lecture II, p.19; *Treatise* p.19.

[69] Lecture II, pp.23–4. To add insult to injury he also compares the best of Greek taste represented in the Lantern of Demosthenes, to the 'Taste of Boromini universally & justly esteemed the most licentious & Extravagant of all the modern Italians' (Lecture II, p.24). But this is a contradiction to his general thesis that simplicity is one of the key faults of Greek architecture.

[70] Royal Academy, Chambers MSS; also *Treatise*, p.19.

[71] Lecture II, pp.27–8; also *Treatise*, pp.19–20.

[72] Lecture II, p.21.

begun to spread from the printed page, and the garden temple, where it made its first appearance, to public buildings and monuments.[73] Now that a real Greek revival seemed imminent, he considered it his duty, as leader of the profession, to publicize his views as a 'caution to stragglers'.[74]

His failure to visit Greece may have been a disappointment to him, and was certainly a disadvantage in the eyes of later architects; but it was by no means jealousy or self-defence, as Willey Reveley implied,[75] that motivated his attacks. However reactionary and biased his views may appear, he did sincerely believe that Grecian architecture, and for that matter Roman as well, was not suitable for faithful reproduction in England.[76] In this he was not alone. Ware was opposed to the use of Greek and Roman buildings as strict patterns on the grounds that 'Every country has its own particular character; and to this its buildings must be made subservient';[77] James Paine was 'satisfied that much mischief may arise from the present prevailing taste, of adopting and putting into practice, indiscriminately every example found in . . .' the publications of Stuart, Revett, and Le Roy;[78] and Gwilt, who recognized the beauties of Greek architecture and added them to his edition of the *Treatise*, also balked at the idea of Greek temples deposited in the streets of London.[79] Even Le Roy warned against copying 'sans choix, à qui a été fait par quelques architectes anciens', and admitted that, as there are some people who prefer Gothic to Greek, the beauty we admire in the Greeks 'ne peut donc passer pour une beauté essentielle, & les principes qui tendent à produire cette beauté, ne peuvent passer pour des axioms.'[80] And Pierre Patte, who like Chambers, had at first looked forward to the results of the Greek investigations, concluded after their appearance that 'Dans les ruines de la Grèce, il n'y a pas un profile, ni un détail intéressant d'Architecture dont on puisse se promettre de faire usage avec succès en exécution.'[81] However widespread anti-Greek sentiment may have been, it was the expression of such views by the leader of the architectural profession in a work as authoritative and highly esteemed as the *Treatise* that irked the younger generation of Greek revivalists most of all.

GOTHIC

An antipathy to the *Gusto Greco* might be expected from Chambers, but not an admiration of the Gothic. Although he was no more in favour of exact imitations of cathedrals than

---

[73] See David Watkin, *Thomas Hope and the Neo-Classical Idea* (London, 1968), 'Chronologies of the Introduction into England, France and Germany of Greek Doric Orders up to 1810,' pp.245–9.

[74] *Treatise* (1791), p.26.

[75] James Stuart and Nicholas Revett, *The Antiquities of Athens*, III, ed. Willey Reveley (London, 1794), p.x. Also quoted by Gwilt, *Treatise* (1825), pp.114, n.1; 115, who rejects Reveley's suggestion that Chambers, out of fear or some other purpose, withheld his condemnation of Greece until after Stuart's death in 1788.

[76] Lecture II, pp.38–9.

[77] Ware, op. cit., p.693.

[78] James Paine, *Plans, Elevations, and Sections of Noblemen and Gentlemen's Houses . . .*, I (London, 1767), p.ii.

[79] Gwilt, *Treatise* (1825), pp.116n; 136n.

[80] Julien David Le Roy, *Les Ruines Des Plus Beaux Monuments De la Grèce* (Paris, 1758), Pt.II, pp.i–ii.

[81] Pierre Patte, *Mémoirs sur les objets les plus importans de l'Architecture* (Paris, 1769), p.81. In his *Etudes d'Architecture* (Paris, 1755), p.3 he was convinced that 'C'est dans les ruines de la Grèce et d'Athènes commen dans leurs sources, qu'il seroit nécessaire de rechercher les principes de la vraye Architecture.' See Mae Mathieu, *Pierre Patte Sa Vie et Son Oeuvre* (Paris, 1940), p.110 ff.

of antique temples, and though he himself never *chose* to build in the Gothic style, he was, nevertheless, very much interested in its history, appreciated its structural merits, and considered its monuments more worthy of investigation than those of ancient Greece. It was again his second lecture on the history of architecture that set him to work on the subject. Unlike his analysis of Grecian architecture, however, most of his observations on the Gothic are neither fully worked out nor particularly original, and few, perhaps for that reason, were incorporated in the *Treatise*.

He subscribes to the belief that Gothic forms had their origin in a warm region, like India, where men worshipped in the shelter of lofty trees, and were perfected by the Arabs or Saracens, 'highly civilized people, mathematicians, and expert builders' who encouraged architecture in Spain.[82] To Gothic architects in Europe he pays tribute not only for the 'first considerable improvements in structure', but also for 'a lightness and boldness to which the ancients never arrived and which the moderns comprehend and imitate with difficulty.'[83] It is his pleasure to follow Fénelon in contrasting the efforts of the Goths to attain an *appearance* of astonishing slightness by concealing their supports with the *real* as well as apparent strength (tending towards over-solidity) sought by the Greeks.[84] Though they contain little that is new or unusual, these observations lead Chambers to issue a remarkable appeal for a greater consideration, better understanding, and higher estimation of Gothic structures in England. 'Would our dilettante instead of importing the gleanings of Greece; or our antiquarians, instead of publishing loose incoherent prints; encourage persons duly qualified, to undertake a correct elegant publication of our own cathedrals and other buildings called Gothic, before they totally fall to ruin; it would be of real service to the arts of design; preserve the remembrance of an extraordinary stile of building now sinking into oblivion; and at the same time publish to the world the riches of Britain, in the splendor of her ancient structures.'[85] Despite the fact that such projects had been recently attempted by J. H. Muntz and James Essex,[86] there seems to have been a brief moment in the 1770s when Chambers contemplated undertaking the work himself, for among his lecture notes is a folder entitled 'Materials for a history of Gothic Architecture in England and its origins.' Before this idea was incorporated in the *Treatise*, a remarkably similar plea for a study of the 'mouldering remains of Gothic genius and

[82] RIBA, Chambers MSS. 'Materials for a History of Gothic Architecture in England'. The combination of the forest and Saracen origin of Gothic forms was quite common in the seventeenth and eighteenth centuries. It was espoused by Wren, Evelyn, Florent le Compte, Felebien, Fénelon, J. F. Blondel, S. Riou, and J. F. Sobry. See Paul Frankl, *The Gothic* (Princeton, 1960), pp.364–5; Arthur O. Lovejoy, 'The First Gothic Revival And the Return to Nature' in *Essays in the History of Ideas* (New York, 1960), pp.137–40; Robin Middleton, 'The Abbe de Cordemoy and the Graeco-Gothic Ideal', *Journal of the Warburg and Courtauld Institutes*, XXV, 1962, p.303.

[83] *Treatise* (1791), p.24; also Lecture II, p.40.

[84] Royal Academy, op. cit.; François de la Motte Fénelon, *Lettre sur les Occupations de l'Académie Francaise*, 1714 in *Œuvres de Fénelon*, XXI (Paris, 1824), p.259.

[85] *Treatise* (1791), p.24; also Lecture II, p.40.

[86] James Essex, 'History of Gothic Architecture in England' (n.d. *c*.1770s) BM Add.MSS 6761–73. Essex (1722–84) was 'the first practising architect to take an antiquarian interest in medieval architecture' (H. M. Colvin, *Dictionary of English Architects*, p.197). Among the Essex manuscripts in the BM is J. H. Muntz's *Proposals For Publishing by Subscription A Course of Gothic Architecture*... London, April 12, 1760.

grandeur' was published by Soane,[87] who may well have had access to the lectures. Nevertheless, it was Chambers's professional status and the reputation of the *Treatise* that sanctioned the pioneering activities of the early Gothicists.[88]

THE RECEPTION OF THE TREATISE

Chambers's skill in channelling a wealth of information and advice through a course safe from extremes seems to have left his eighteenth-century audience speechless. Not however the garrulous Horace Walpole, whose tribute to the *Treatise* as 'the most sensible book and the most exempt from prejudices that ever was written on that science'[89] expresses what must have been the general consensus of opinion for at least the next thirty years. With the appearance of the third edition reviling the architecture of ancient Greece, the spell of silent admiration was broken. Nevertheless, even the most outraged grecophiles had to admit that it 'abounds with sound remarks'[90] and is 'certainly the only book in our language which has yet appeared worthy of being placed in the hands of the student'.[91] So great, in fact, was the demand for the third edition, in spite of its shortcomings in the historical and practical parts of architecture, that the work was brought up to date and reprinted in a smaller, more accessible form in 1825 by Gwilt, and again in 1826 by J. B. Papworth. These editions, together with Gwilt's *Encyclopaedia* incorporating a large section on the 'Practice of Architecture', extended the life of the *Treatise* almost to the end of the nineteenth century. Then, in 1896, it was taken up by Banister Fletcher, the twentieth-century successor to Gwilt, as the accepted authority on the proportions and profiles of the orders as well as on windows, doorways, arcades, colonnades, etc.[92] Strange as it may seem, thousands of architectural students throughout the world still derive their knowledge of the orders, however meagre and unimportant that may now be, from Chambers's *Treatise*.

[87] John Soane, *Plans, Elevations, and Sections of Buildings* (London 1788), p.9. James Bentham in his *History and Antiquities of the Conventual and Cathedral Church of Ely* (Cambridge, 1771), p.282, from which Chambers made notes, also recognized the need for a whole volume on the history of Gothic building in England: '. . . it would be a subject well worth the attention of an Antiquarian to investigate the Origin and Progress of Architecture in our Country; to note the various Modes of Building in different Ages; to observe the Transitions from one Style to another and the gradual advances towards Perfection, from examples that are still remaining . . .'

[88] Joseph Halfpenny, *Gothic Ornaments in the Cathedral Church of York* (York, 1795), Introduction. 'Of Gothic Architecture, Sir William Chambers speaks in terms of the highest respect . . . (quote from *Treatise*) . . . With a view to encourage and bring forward an undertaking so warmly recommended I have been induced to exhibit this selection of Gothic Ornaments . . .' Chambers's remarks are also quoted by John Britton in the opening paragraph of the preface to his *History and Antiquities of the Metropolitan Church of York* (1819), p.v.; and by T. F. Hunt, *Architettura Campestra* (London, 1827), pp.v–vi. Frankl, op. cit., using Gwilt's edition of the *Treatise* (1825) and presuming it to be the same as the 1759 edition, arrives at the strange and erroneous conclusion that Chambers's defence of Gothic 'showed the way to Romanticism'. In contrast to Joseph Halfpenny, John Britton, and T. F. Hunt, W. H. Leeds considered his edition of Chambers's *Treatise* (London, 1862, p.vi) to be the very thing 'needed to stem the rampant Gothicism of the day, which seems to affect, as its character, the veriest *sansculottism* in regard to architectural design and composition.'

[89] Horace Walpole, *Anecdotes of Painting in England*, ed. Ralph N. Wornum (London, 1888), p.xiv.

[90] James Elmes, *Lectures on Architecture* (London, 1821), p.398.

[91] Gwilt, *Treatise* (1825), p.xv.

[92] Bannister Fletcher, *History of Architecture on the Comparative Method*, 12th ed. (London, 1944), pp.842, 844.

Chapter 10

Designs of Chinese Buildings
and the
Dissertation on Oriental Gardening

by Dr Eileen Harris

It is inconceivable that Chambers, having laid the foundations of a serious architectural career, would deliberately choose to make his debut with a book of Chinese designs that he had drawn some ten years earlier, and which, as John Adam observed, would not 'raise his reputation high among the truly learned in architecture.'[1] Indeed, the choice was neither voluntary nor premeditated. The 'sketches and designs' made in Canton were, he maintains, chiefly to satisfy his own curiosity. They were never intended for publication; 'nor would they now appear, were it not in compliance with the desire of several lovers of the arts, who thought them worthy the perusal of the publick . . . .'[2] Had he, in fact, envisaged a publication when he was in China in the 1740s, there would have been no need for his frantic request in 1756 for designs of Chinese houses from his brother John in Gothenburg[3]; and the final product would surely have been more accurate and complete than it is. There can be no doubt that he was persuaded to publish by 'several lovers' of chinoiserie. Moreover, there is good reason to believe that the most persuasive of his supporters was Augusta, Dowager Princess of Wales, whose faithful pursuit of her late husband's exotic interests, in which Chambers had already been involved, led her to commission him in 1757 to lay out Kew Gardens. Obviously, the promise of royal patronage (fulfilled in the summer of 1757 when he was appointed architect to Augusta and tutor to George, Prince of Wales) outweighed any possible injuries to his future reputation as an architect. 'I cannot', he concludes, 'conceive why it should be criminal in a traveller to give an account of what he has seen worthy of notice in China, any more than in Italy, France, or any other country; nor do I think it possible that any man should be so void of reason as to infer that an Architect is ignorant in his profession, merely from his having published designs of Chinese buildings.'[4]

Contrary to the dismal predictions of John Adam, the proposals issued in 1756 brought 164 subscriptions[5] from the 'learned in architecture', friends made on the Grand Tour,

[1] Fleming, op. cit., 359.

[2] William Chambers, *Designs of Chinese Buildings, Furniture, Dresses, Machines and Utensils* (London 1757), Preface (i).

[3] RA Correspondence, 3 July 1756, letter of reply from John Chambers to William, regretting that he possessed 'no designs of the Chinese houses'.

[4] Chambers, *Designs*, Preface (iv).

[5] Among the subscribers were the Dukes of Bridgewater, Bedford, and Richmond; Lords Bruce, Charlemont, Gower, and Pembroke; Thomas Brand of the Hyde and Thomas Brand of the Hoo, Thomas Hollis, Thomas Scrope, John Hall Stevenson, Charles Turner, and Richard 'Dickie' Bateman.

future patrons, craftsmen, and architects including John and James Adam. In May 1757 the book appeared – a dignified and superbly produced folio, with a dedication to George, Prince of Wales, a supposedly authentic text, and twenty-one plates engraved by the best hands, Foudrinier, Rooker, Grignion, and Sandby. This was a far cry from the topographical accounts published by the Jesuits, Nieuhoff and Du Halde, and from the frivolous chinoiserie inventions of Halfpenny, Edwards, and Darly. Here, for the first time, Chinese architecture was presented as a subject worthy of the kind of serious study formerly reserved for western antiquity.

The opening lines of Chambers's preface, 'It is difficult to avoid praising too little or too much. The boundless panegyrics which have been lavished upon the Chinese learning, policy, and arts, show with what power novelty attracts regard, and how naturally esteem swells into admiration', have been attributed by Boswell to Dr Johnson. According to Boswell, Chambers 'whose works show a sublimity of genius, and who is esteemed by all who know him for his social, hospitable, and generous qualities', showed Johnson his manuscript to which the latter supplied 'a few lines of introduction', it wanting 'no additions or corrections'.[6] Johnson or not, and there is no proof of Boswell's assertion, Chambers goes on first to explain his reasons for publishing (the persuasion of others, and the dearth of reliable information), and second to defend the merits of his subject.

Chinese architecture is not only original, a claim that cannot be made for all western architecture, but it also possesses a 'remarkable affinity' to the 'ancients'. Similarities are detectable in the tendency for pyramidal compositions, in the diminution of bases to columns, in patterns of fretwork, in plan types such as the Ting and the peripteros, and between Chinese walling and the Revinctum and Emplecton described by Vitruvius. However interesting they may be, these chance comparisons lead nowhere, least of all to any suggestion either of a direct link or of a parity between the two styles. Chambers is honest enough to admit that the Chinese taste is 'inferior to the antique',[7] and generally unfit for most European purposes. Nevertheless, a knowledge of this singular style, apart from arousing curiosity, does have practical advantages. Architects are bound to receive a certain number of requests for such compositions, and may even introduce them with propriety in 'extensive parks and gardens, where a great variety of scenes are required', or in the inferior parts of 'immense palaces, containing a numerous series of apartments'.[8] Finally, no one could deny the pleasures of novelty and variety which had always been considered the cardinal virtues of Chinese buildings and gardens. Putting, as he often did, visual appearances over rational considerations, Chambers concludes that 'Variety is

[6] James Boswell, *Life of Johnson* (London 1953), p.1211. This was not Johnson's opinion nineteen years later. Thomas Percy's annotated copy of his *Miscellaneous Pieces Relating to the Chinese* (1762) in the Bodleian contains a note to the reprint of Chambers's *Art of Laying Out Gardens Among the Chinese*: 'August 1, 1764. The following account was drawn up by Dr. Johnson from information given him by Mr. Chambers. Mr. Johnson suspected, and at length Mr. Chambers confessed, that the conferences with Lepqua were apocryphal. Mr. Johnson even doubts whether Chambers was in China at all. I had myself some suspicions before Mr. Johnson told me this . . .' These comments are revoked in a later note 'November 10, 1770. Since I wrote the Note facing page 129 I have been in company with Mr. Chambers and also spent an evening along with him in company with Chet-qua a Chinese from Canton who is at present in England. I am now convinced Mr. Chambers has been at Canton and spent some time there . . .' 'Johnson, Percy, and William Chambers', *Bodleian Library Record*, IV, no.6, pp.291–2.

[7] Chambers, *Designs*, Preface (ii).

[8] Ibid., (ii).

L

always delightful, and novelty, attended with nothing inconsistent or disagreeable, sometimes takes place of beauty.'[9]

Chambers's intention in publishing his 'sketches and designs'[10] was 'only to give an idea of Chinese architecture'.[11] A more extensive collection of designs of particular buildings would not, he maintained, have been in the public interest. Nor, for that matter, would it have been within his abilities. As his travels in China were restricted to the environs of Canton, his observations could only be parochial. This, however, was not the way he saw it. Like most contemporary travellers, even those who did penetrate the interior, he was erroneously convinced that Chinese arts had little or no local peculiarities, and were nearly uniform throughout the country. He therefore considered it just to present Cantonese architecture as representative of the national taste.

However limited his studies of Chinese buildings may have been, the fact that they were made from an architectural point of view was in itself extremely rare. Indeed, his activities aroused considerable interest among Swedish intelligentsia. It was reported to Linneaus that Baron Harleman, Sweden's premier architect, was receiving architectural memoranda from Chambers; in particular drawings of the Chinese method of raising water, and of the columnar structure of Chinese houses. 'The proportions of the parts I dare say Mr. Chambers has also sent in'.[12] As far as we know, neither these, nor the notes and drawings that he used for publication have survived. To judge from the book, they cannot have been very detailed or comprehensive. His account of temples and towers is not only heavily dependent upon Du Halde's *Description Géographique, Historique, Chronologique et Physique de l'Empire de la Chine* . . . (Paris 1735, London 1738), but also contains startling omissions and avowed inaccuracies. One's suspicions are particularly aroused by his description of the great pagoda of Ho-nang in the southern suburb of Canton. Had he possessed an elevation of this building, which he describes as the 'most considerable' among Chinese temples, he would not have deliberately excluded it merely because 'to be of proper size it would occupy at least three Plates'.[13] The only illustration he can provide is a plan which he does not pretend to be 'very accurate', it being 'a matter of great difficulty to measure any publick work in China, with accuracy, because the populace are very troublesome to strangers . . .' In any case, he dismisses exact measurements of Chinese structures as of 'small consequence to European Artists'.[14] Perhaps he is right; certainly he is consistent in giving only general proportions even where he claims to have measured several examples. However, this may have been as much a matter of necessity (resulting from superficial observations) as of choice.

Questions of accuracy are far more pertinent to his illustrations than his text. Were Chinese buildings as regular as he depicted them? Did they really have swags on triumphal arches, and Greek key frets and friezes? Or were these his own inventions? We may well wonder. Doubtlessly his contemporaries did too. But, since the original buildings are not

[9] Ibid., (ii).
[10] Ibid., (iii).
[11] Ibid., (iii).
[12] Olaf Toren, *An East Indian Voyage* (Stockholm 1757), p.352.
[13] Chambers, *Designs,* p.2.
[14] Ibid., p.1n.

available for comparison, it is as impossible to verify his designs today as it was in the eighteenth century. Although the peculiarities of Chinese custom must have intrigued him as much as they did other western visitors, he was more seriously interested in those aspects of Chinese building that had most bearing upon his architectural studies and aspirations – houses, columns, and other ornaments and details approximating classical models. The fact that these subjects had not been treated by previous authors makes his observations all the more interesting and at the same time impossible to corroborate. If, as one suspects, the drawings and sketches that he made for his own pleasure were incomplete or inaccurate, then he would have had no choice but to omit some details and add others. It is equally possible that the buildings he selected were built in the eighteenth century under European influence. Whatever the case, his primary concern was to 'put a stop to the extravagancies that daily appear under the name of Chinese',[15] and to render real Chinese architecture intelligible to western eyes. This justified his exclusion of confusing details, and is surely the principal cause of the regular, classicizing appearance of his designs.

To assess Chambers's account on accuracy alone is to overlook the forest for the trees. That he preferred, for whatever reason, to generalize rather than to descend into particulars is neither a valid point of criticism nor a matter of great consequence. What is more important is that he provided the first account of Chinese buildings as architecture. The only misfortune is that it was published too late to have any appreciable effect upon chinoiserie in England.

Buildings in the 'Chinese taste', though never truly fashionable in the sense that chinoiserie furniture and decoration were, had their heyday in England in the late 1740s and early 1750s. A pagoda in a Chinese landscape was projected at Studley Royal in 1744;[16] in 1746 there was a Chinese hut near the Palladian bridge at Stowe;[17] by 1748 Shugborough had a Chinese summer house with adjacent Chinese bridges, and Wroxton a lodge and summer house;[18] in 1749 Chambers designed the Temple of Confucius for Frederick, Prince of Wales, who was seen that year sailing the Thames in a Chinese barge; in 1750 there were Chinese pavilions in the pleasure gardens of Ranelagh and Vauxhall, and temples at 'Dickie' Bateman's at Windsor, and at Radnor House, Twickenham; and by 1753 the Halfpennys had more or less exhausted the subject in a number of capricious pattern books.[19] Had Chambers's book appeared on the crest of the wave, in 1750 or

---

[15] Ibid. (i). Elsewhere Chambers confesses to having omitted details that would have rendered his design confused, p.6; and that the forms he saw were 'not so agreeable as that which I have represented', p.4. However, according to Frère Attiret, *A Particular Account of the Emperor of China's Gardens Near Pekin,* trans. by Sir Harry Beaumont (London 1752), p.37, 'There is this Symmetry, this beautiful order and Disposition, too in China; and particularly in the Emperor's Palace at Pekin . . . But in their Pleasure-houses, they rather chuse a beautiful Disorder, and a wandering as far as possible from all the Rules of Art.'

[16] 'Travel Journal of Philip Yorke 1744–63; ed. Joyce Godber in 'The Marchioness Grey of Wrest Park', *Beds. Hist. Rec. Soc.* CXLVII (1968).

[17] B. Seeley, *A Description of the Gardens of Lord Viscount Cobham, at Stowe in Buckinghamshire* (1746), p.18. First illustrated in George Bickham, *The Beauties of Stow* (1750), opp. p.35.

[18] Philip York, op. cit., pp.22, 27.

[19] William and John Halfpenny, *Rural Architecture in the Chinese Taste* (1750, 1752, 1755); *Chinese and Gothic Architecture Properly Ornamented* (1752); *Country Gentleman's Pocket Companion* (1753). Edwards and Darly, *New Book of Chinese Designs* (1754).

earlier, it might have wrought considerable changes, particularly in divesting the style from its rococo attachments, and perhaps even in prolonging its life. This was not the case in 1757 when interest was on the wane. Since the Chinese style was restricted to ephemeral garden buildings, there can be no accurate assessment of his influence. Nevertheless, it is surprising that there are no more than three buildings known to have been inspired by the publication. One is his own design of 1769 for a temple at Ansley, based upon one of the Canton *taas*; and the others, a late eighteenth-century version of the Canton bridge which was seen by Krafft 'on the road to Westminster',[20] and Robert Abraham's literal copy of the Canton *To-ho*, built in 1827 at Alton Towers. Of the three, only the latter survives.

If Chambers's book was wasted in England, it could hardly have been more expedient in France and Germany where the Chinese fashion did not fully flower until the 1770s and 1780s. Not only was it a unique source of practical and supposedly accurate information, but it must also have appealed to the neo-classical tastes of the time. Fortunately its influence on the continent is well documented by the architectural topographers, George-Louis Le Rouge and Johann Carl Krafft, who specialized in measuring and publishing garden buildings. In the 1770s the Ho-nang temple was used by J. A. Renard for the Duc de Penthièvre at Armanvilliers;[21] one of the *Tings* was erected at L'Hermitage by the Prince de Croy;[22] and Racine de Monville had a version of the *Pay-Leou* built as a gate to his Chinese House at Désert de Retz.[23] In Germany, Frederick II commissioned Chambers to design a Chinese bridge for Sans Souci in 1768,[24] and in the following year Gontard supplied him with a Dragon House[25] closely modelled upon the Ta-ho pagoda. At Rheinsberg,[26] a version of one of the temples belonging to the Ho-nang pagoda was built in 1771 by Von Kaphengst for Prince Heinrich of Prussia.

OF THE ART OF LAYING OUT GARDENS

No book on Chinese designs would have been complete without some mention of their art of laying out gardens which, though it did not properly belong to Chambers's profession, was much more admired than their architecture. 'Their taste in that is good, and what we have for some time past been aiming at in England, though not always with success.'[27] To assist English gardeners in their endeavours, and to gratify their interests, Chambers presents the whole of his knowledge of Chinese practices, together with his principal views on landscape gardening in general. This essay, although eclipsed by his longer and more controversial *Dissertation on Oriental Gardening*, 1772, is in fact his most substantial contribution on the subject.

It is little wonder that Chambers's predecessors did not always succeed in their aims. Until the middle of the eighteenth century their entire notion of Chinese garden design

20 J. C. Krafft, *Plans des Plus Beau Jardins Pittoresques* (Paris 1809), p.7, pl.8.

21 J. C. Krafft, *Recueil d'Architecture Civile* (Paris 1812), pl.95, no.1, near Condé, Valenciennes.

22 Georges-Louis Le Rouge, *Jardins Anglo-Chinois*, Cahier IV, pl.15.

23 Ibid., Cahier XIII, pl.10.

24 Cf. Catalogue of Works.

25 Eleanor Von Erdberg, *Chinese Influence on European Garden Structures* (Cambridge, Mass. 1936), fig.46.

26 Ibid., fig.47.

27 Chambers, *Designs,* Preface pp.iii–iv.

was founded upon a brief, second-hand report related by Sir William Temple in his essay *On the Gardens of Epicurus* (1685), 1692. According to Temple, the idea of beauty consisting in 'some certain proportions, symmetries, or uniformities', accepted by him and by most Europeans, is dismissed by the Chinese for its childish simplicity. They prefer, instead, to employ 'their greatest reach of imagination . . . in contriving figures, where the beauty shall be great, and strike the eye, but without any order or disposition of parts that shall be commonly or easily observed.'[28]

Twenty years later, Addison, in his celebrated paper *On The Pleasures of the Imagination*,[29] associated this Chinese preference for concealing art in apparent disorder with the imitation of simple nature that he recommended in place of the unnatural formalities of Temple's day. While Addison summoned the Chinese to support the natural landscape garden, Pope, in the *Guardian* of 1713,[30] enlisted the ancients for the very same purpose. The logical sequence to these equations seemed to be a relationship between the Chinese and Roman precedents. An attempt to define this relationship was made in 1728 by Robert Castell in his *Villas of the Ancients*. Drawing upon Addison, Castell credited the Chinese with the formation of the most advanced manner of laying out gardens 'whose Beauty consisted in a close imitation of nature; where the parts are disposed with the greatest Art, the Irregularity is still preserved'. The designer of Pliny's garden at Tuscum, he believes, was acquainted with this manner of 'artfull confusion' and combined it with the two earlier manners – a 'rough' manner where nature was untouched by art; and a more 'regular and exact Taste' of laying out gardens by 'the Rule and Line', where 'Art was visible in every Part of the Design'.[31] Tuscum was of immense importance, being the 'only Roman garden whose description is come down to us.' Castell's reconstruction of its plan from Pliny's letters was therefore treasured by English gardeners as an authoritative model for imitation.

Descriptions of Chinese gardens, on the other hand, were so rare as to be virtually unknown in Europe. The first visual document to arrive in England was a set of engraved views of the Emperor K'ang Hsi's palace and gardens at Jehol, made in China in 1713 by Matteo Ripa, an Italian Jesuit, and acquired from him when he passed through London in 1724 by Lord Burlington.[32] However, this extraordinary acquisition did not attract much notice, and cannot have been seen by more than a handful of Burlington's closest devotees. The fact remains that until 1752 the English knew nothing more about Chinese gardens than what was published by Temple in 1692.

In 1743, Frère Attiret, a French Jesuit and painter to Emperor Chien Hsi, sent a letter to a friend in Paris describing in detail the newly-completed complex of pleasure gardens and buildings at Yüan Ming Yüan, the Imperial summer palace outside Peking. Attiret's exclusive account, published in the *Lettres Édifiantes* of 1749 and translated into English by Joseph Spense (under the pseudonym of Sir Harry Beaumont) in 1752, became

[28] William Temple, 'Upon the Gardens of Epicurus and of Gardening in the Year 1685', *Works* (London 1770), III, 230.

[29] Joseph Addison, 'On the Pleasures of the Imagination', *Spectator,* no.414, 25 June 1712.

[30] Alexander Pope, *Guardian*, no.173, 28 September 1713.

[31] Robert Castell, *The Villas of the Ancients Illustrated* (London 1728), p.32.

[32] Basil Gray, 'Lord Burlington and Father Ripa's Chinese Engravings', *British Museum Quarterly*, XXII (1960), pp.1–2.

Europe's main source of information.[33] The first to make use of this information and to incorporate it into the landscape garden was Chambers. Although he makes no mention of Attiret, he is in fact indebted to him for numerous observations that his own visit to China did not provide. What he knew of Chinese practices – partly from the gardens he saw in Canton, which he admits were 'very small'; and chiefly from the lessons of Lepqua, a 'celebrated painter' – was hardly as sufficient as he would have us believe.[34]

His account aims, as he says, to be distinct; and that it is. Detailed, however, it is not. Particulars borrowed from Attiret are not only generalized, but also interwoven with his own ideas put into the mouths of the Chinese. In fact, his interpretation of Chinese taste is more interesting and more meaningful than the information upon which it is founded. The specific devices employed by the Chinese to achieve natural irregularity are in themselves insignificant. How they affect the mind and imagination of the beholder is what really matters to him. With the information made available by Attiret, he was able to use the Chinese example to illustrate and elaborate Addison's analysis of the 'Pleasures of the Imagination'.

He begins with the general plan of a Chinese garden, abstracted from Yüan Ming Yüan. 'The whole ground is laid out in a variety of scenes' (corresponding to the 'numerous valleys' described by Attiret) which are linked by winding passages, and are marked by some special object – a bridge, a seat, etc. 'The perfection of their gardens [as exemplified by Yüan Ming Yüan] consists in the number, beauty and diversity of these scenes.' However, when he comes to discuss the scenes themselves, fact gives way to invention paraded in Chinese disguise. It is not 'their artists' who 'distinguish three different species of scenes, to which they give the appellations of pleasing, horrid, and enchanted'.[35] It is Chambers enlarging upon Addison's distinction between the beautiful, the great, and the uncommon[36] – a theme upon which eighteenth-century aesthetics played numerous variations.

The 'enchanted' or 'romantic', like Addison's 'uncommon', though treated as a distinct species, is in effect a subdivision or counterpart of the sublime (horrid or great). Its prime effect is to excite surprise. It also, as Addison points out, 'bestows charms on a monster and makes even imperfections in nature please us'.[37] Indeed, the devices introduced by Chambers – montrous birds and animals, and sounds which are either recognizable but obscured, or are the strange results of wind directed through artfully-disposed buildings, rocks and other objects – are as terrifying as they are surprising.

His 'horrid' scenes are more clearly defined. They are also less original. The violent emotion of terror, associated with the sublime, was a frequent subject of poetry and aesthetic speculation. Mid-eighteenth-century literature is amply supplied with the

33 *Lettres Edifiantes et Curieuses, écrites des Missions Etrangères, par quelques Missionnaires de la Compagnie de Jésus,* 27 Recueil (Paris 1749), pp.1–61. English translations also appeared in: *Monthly Review,* VII (1752), pp.421–6; *Scots Magazine,* XIV (1752), pp.589–93; *London Magazine,* XXI (1752), pp.553–6; R. Dodsley, *Fugitive Pieces,* I (1765), pp.63–88; Thomas Percy, *Miscellaneous Pieces Relating to the Chinese,* II (1762), pp.148–201. See also Osvald Siren, *Gardens of China* (New York 1949), pp.117–30.

34 Chambers, *Designs,* p.14.

35 Ibid., p.15.

36 Addison, op. cit., *Spectator,* no.412, 23 June 1712.

37 Ibid.

terrible images of nature's destructive power – like the impending rocks, impetuous cataracts, dark caverns, trees blasted by tempests or lightning, and ruined buildings that Chambers describes.

To him it is 'contrast' that most powerfully affects the mind, just as to Addison it is 'variety' 'that improves what is great or beautiful, and makes it afford the mind a double entertainment.'[38] Knowing this, the Chinese 'constantly practice sudden transitions, and a striking opposition of forms, colours and shades . . . in such a manner as to render the composition at once distinct in it's [sic] parts, and striking in the whole.'[39] Horrid scenes succeed pleasing ones; limited prospects, dark caverns, or narrow walks open unexpectedly to extensive views, 'so much the more pleasing as it was never looked for.' Even the forms and colours of trees and plants are varied: some are simple, others complicated; some bright, others dark and gloomy; sometimes there are decayed trees (like those proposed by Kent for Kensington Gardens) amongst the living, and even here they are 'nice' about the form and colour of bark and moss. Concealment is another favourite device for arousing curiosity, heightening the unexpected, and stimulating the imagination. Wherever possible objects, lakes, and compositions are partially obscured by trees. Changes in movement are also a source of entertainment. From Attiret[40] come hints of narrow, noisy rivulets becoming wide and slow; of pastoral groves enlivened by agricultural activities, or by mills, hydraulic machines, and other motions of commerce. Should variety or contrast be restricted by lack of space, then a few objects are artfully disposed so that they present a different, sometimes totally unrelated appearance from different points of view.

The Chinese method of laying out gardens is comparable to the art of painting. Their gardeners, like European painters, 'collect from nature the most pleasing objects, which they endeavour to combine in such a manner, as not only to appear to the best advantage separately, but likewise to unite in forming an elegant and striking whole.'[41] They group their trees like painters do figures 'in principal and subservient masses'; and although deficient in optics, experience has taught them to form 'prospects in perspective' by lessening the size and lightening the colour of distant objects and trees. This deception they use to 'render what is trifling and limited grand and considerable in appearance.'[42]

In short, no effort is spared to entertain the mind and eye of the spectator. Taking nature as their model, the Chinese not only imitate her in all her beautiful irregularities, but they also employ a host of ingenious artifices to improve and embellish her in the most striking manner possible. This pleasurable union of art and nature, perfected at Yüan Ming Yüan, is what was admired in Pliny's garden at Tuscum, and recommended by Addison and Pope. No one, however, espoused the principle more fervently than Chambers. It was the underlying theme of his essay in the *Designs*, the merit of Kew, and finally the *cause célèbre* of the *Dissertation*.

[38] Ibid.
[39] Chambers, *Designs,* pp.15–16.
[40] Attiret, op. cit., pp.10, 24–30, 31–2.
[41] Chambers, *Designs,* p.15.
[42] Ibid., p.18.

Devoted as he was to the Chinese manner of laying out gardens, Chambers, like Temple, did not recommend it for general practice. It is, he warned, 'extremely difficult and not to be attained by persons of narrow intellect. For though the precepts are simple and obvious yet the putting them in execution requires genius, judgment, and experience; a strong imagination, and a thorough knowledge of the human mind.'[43]

The essay on garden design received far more notice than any other part of Chambers's book, particularly from the broader intellects – writers and philosophers. The *Gentleman's Magazine* carried the whole piece in May 1757,[44] exactly concurrent with its publication. In the following year Burke included it in the first volume of his *Annual Register*,[45] partly because he considered it to be 'much the best which has ever been written on the subject', but chiefly because the scenes of horror attributed to the Chinese served to demonstrate the most controversial principle of his *Enquiry* – the relation between the sublime and the terrible.[46] In 1762, the essay was again reprinted, along with Attiret's letter, in the second volume of *Miscellaneous Pieces Relating to the Chinese*,[47] edited by Thomas Percy. Lord Kames, finding the Chinese gardens 'entirely obsequious to the principles that govern every one of the fine arts',[48] concluded his discussion of gardening in the *Elements of Criticism*, 1762–3, with a 'slight view' which is clearly taken from Chambers. Robert Dodsley brings Chambers into his *Description of the Leasowes* when he compares a scene where water is heard without being seen to the 'kind of effect which the Chinese are fond of producing in what they call their scenes of enchantment.'[49] Although there can be little doubt that Chambers and Shenstone were familiar with each other's works, it is difficult to establish any interchange between them. The numerous similarities between Chambers's essay of 1757 and Shenstone's *Unconnected Thoughts on Gardening*, published in 1764 a year after his death, are the result of a mutual dependence upon Addison.[50]

While the excellence of Chinese gardens was generally acknowledged and admired, its influence was very much open to dispute. The controversy, though brought to a head by Chambers, had in fact begun before his publication. In 1755 Richard Owen Cambridge published an essay in the *World*, proudly acclaiming England's precedence in the creation of the landscape garden. 'Whatever may have been reported, whether truly or falsly, of Chinese gardens, it is certain that we are the first of the Europeans who have founded

43 Ibid., p.19.

44 *Gentleman's Magazine*, XXVII (May 1757), 216–19.

45 *Annual Register*, I (1758), 319–23.

46 See Eileen Harris, 'Burke and Chambers on the Sublime and Beautiful', *Essays in The History of Architecture Presented to Rudolf Wittkower* (1967), pp.207–13.

47 Percy, op. cit., pp.125–44.

48 Henry Home, Lord Kames, *Elements of Criticism*, II (Edinburgh 1769), p.450.

49 Robert Dodsley, 'A Description of the Leasowes' (1764), *The Works in Verse and Prose of William Shenstone*, II (Edinburgh 1768), p.xxvii.

50 Ibid., pp.94–110. In particular: p.94, Landscape gardening 'consists in pleasing the imagination by scenes of grandeur, beauty, or variety' and p.95 'Objects should indeed be less calculated to strike the immediate eye, than the judgement or well-formed imagination, as in painting. It is no objection to the pleasure of novelty, that it makes an ugly object more disagreeable. It is enough that it produces a superiority betwixt things in other respects equal . . . a series of lawn, though ever so beautiful, may satiate and cloy, unless the eye passes to them from wilder scenes; and then they acquire the grace of novelty.'

this taste.'[51] Similar sentiments were voiced by Thomas Gray in a letter of 1763[52] where he defends our style of gardening as 'the only true taste we can call our own; the only proof of our original talent in the matter of pleasure . . .' He admits that Attiret and Chambers have proved that the Chinese achieved a high degree of perfection in this art. Nevertheless, 'it is very certain we copied nothing from them nor had anything but Nature for our Model.'

These arguments are perfectly reasonable. English attitudes towards nature and the landscape garden were confirmed by the Chinese example, but they were certainly not derived from it. Indeed, nowhere is this more clearly demonstrated than in Chambers's essay, where Chinese practices, real or imaginary, are employed to illustrate and enlarge English ideas.

No sooner had Chambers expressed his views than the taste in gardening changed. Instead of the happy balance between nature and art, nature ruled supreme, with 'Capability' Brown as her champion and improver. For Chambers, the exclusion of art and association from garden after garden was painful enough. To witness it in the environs of his own houses was too much to endure.

THE DISSERTATION ON ORIENTAL GARDENING

The *Dissertation on Oriental Gardening* was published in May 1772.[53] In spite of its title, it is not a description of Chinese gardens and has no more to offer on that subject than what is contained in the previous essay, which it incorporates. The Chinese are merely the unwitting protectors of a polemic on English gardening in which Chambers pits his own views against Brown's. Unfortunately, however, the ruse backfired. His fantastic flights of imagination eclipsed his serious ideas, and ultimately discredited his authority on Chinese matters. The *Dissertation* was so utterly misunderstood that he hastened to publish a second edition in 1773, with an *Explanatory Discourse*[54] offering 'such reasons and explanations as seem necessary either to remove doubts or clear obscurities.'[55] Although he now admits that the two works are his and ought 'certainly to appear in their natural dress', to undo the elaborate Chinese disguise 'required more time than the Author can possibly spare.'[56] Hence the *Dissertation* is reprinted in its original form with minor

---

[51] *The World,* no.118, 3 April 1755.

[52] Thomas Gray to William Taylor Howe, 10 September 1763, referring to Algarotti's injustice to the English on this subject. Quoted in H. F. Clark 'Eighteenth Century Elysiums', *England and the Mediterranean Tradition* (Oxford 1945), p.169.

[53] The *Daily Advertiser,* 7 May 1772, announced the publication of the *Dissertation*.

[54] Half-title: 'An Explanatory Discourse By Tan Chet-Qua, Of Quang-Chew-fu, Gent. FRSS, MRAAP; Also MIAAF, TRA, CGHMW and ATTQ. Wherein The Principles laid down in the Foregoing Dissertation, are illustrated and applied to Practice.' Cf. Bibliography for full account of editions. The *Dissertation* and *Explanatory Discourse* are discussed together here. All quotations are therefore from the second edition of the *Dissertation*.

[55] Chambers, *A Dissertation on Oriental Gardening. The Second Edition, with Additions. To Which Is Annexed, An Explanatory Discourse, By Tan Chet-Qua, of Quang-Chew-Fu, Gent* (London 1773), p.113.

[56] Ibid., p.114. Indeed, the impressive initials following Chet-qua's name on the half-title of the *Discourse* are a clear indication of Chambers's authorship: FRSS (Fellow of the Royal Society of Sweden), MRAAP (Member of the Royal Academy of Arts, Paris), MIAAF (Member of the Italian Academy of Arts, Florence), TRA (Treasurer of the Royal Academy), CGHMW (Comptroller General of His Majesty's Works), and ATTQ (Architectural Tutor to the Queen).

alterations; and for the sake of continuity the *Discourse* is fathered upon Tan Chetqua, a Cantonese sculptor who had been in England from 1769 to 1772.[57]

'His sole aim . . . has been to point out a style of Gardening preferable to your's; and to shew how much more may be done in that Art, than has hitherto been thought on, by your or any other European nation . . .'[58] What he recommends, though certainly different from fashionable practice, and possibly even preferable to it, is not entirely original. Contrary to his claims, many of his suggestions had 'hitherto been thought on' by Thomas Whately, whose *Observations on Modern Gardening* (1770) he had read and copiously annotated.[59] Remove the Chinese veneer, and the *Dissertation* is little more than an elaboration of ideas borrowed from Whately, combined with those already presented in his essay in the *Designs of Chinese Buildings*. Few readers, however (not even Chambers himself), could spare the time 'to separate the substance from the vehicle in which it was contained.'[60] The majority mistook the 'mask for the reality', and were entertained by his Chinese extravagancies, or enraged by his attacks upon English gardening and upon Brown personally. They misconstrued the motive of his criticism as jealousy of Brown, and took little notice of the positive improvements that he recommended. Although the *Discourse* did clarify his position, it was too late to save him from the ridicule of George Mason's *Heroic Epistle*, which came out at the very same time.

Chambers is no opponent to natural gardening. Excessive partiality to it is what he condemns – first, the obstinate refusal of 'the assistance of almost every extraneous embellishment', and second, the persistence 'in an indiscriminate application of the same manner, upon all occasions, however opposite, or ill adapted.'[61] The natural style carried to such extremes is as dull and uniform as the formal one. Its religious imitation of nature, its intolerance of art, and its stress on simplicity are as unacceptable to him as the idea of the primitive hut was in architecture. There is too little variety and imagination to occupy and entertain the mind.

Nature, he agrees, should always be the general model. But resemblance to nature is not a measure of perfection. If it were, then waxworks would be superior to the sculpture of Michaelangelo.[62] Furthermore, the materials of simple nature – plants, ground, and water – are too limited, and the arrangements too familiar to excite any strong sensations in the mind, or to produce any uncommon degree of pleasure.[63] The perfect garden is one which is 'natural, without resemblance to vulgar Nature, new without affectation, and extraordinary without extravagance: where the spectator is to be amused, where his attention is constantly to be kept up, his curiosity excited, and his mind agitated by a great variety of opposite passions.'[64]

[57] For accounts of Chet-qua's (or Chit-qua) visit to England see *Gentleman's Magazine* (May 1771), p.237; *Bodleian Library Record,* op. cit.; and Rupert Gunnis, *Dictionary of British Sculptors* (London 1953), p.101.

[58] Chambers, *Dissertation,* p.119.

[59] Chambers's notes from Whately are in the Richardson Collection, Royal Academy.

[60] Chambers, *Dissertation,* p.113.

[61] Ibid., p.161.

[62] Ibid., pp.144–5.

[63] Ibid., p.16.

[64] Ibid., pp.106–7.

Novelty, variety, and effect could be produced by introducing rocks and cataracts in flat places, or plains amidst mountains. To make nature, however, is difficult, expensive, and easily exhausted.[65] It is much easier, and more effective to embellish, improve, and correct nature with the aid of art. Thus, in preference to the natural or formal styles, Chambers advocates a judicious mixture of what is best in both. This idea was by no means new. The union of regularity and irregularity had been described by Castell[66] as a Chinese invention also employed in the disposition of Pliny's gardens at Tuscum, and was recommended for English practice by Kames,[67] and Whately.[68] Although Chambers's demands for art may appear excessive, they are in fact fewer than Whately's.

The richer, more artificial manner of regular, geometrical figures, order, and symmetry is required, or at least preferable, in the grounds immediately surrounding the main house and other 'elegant structures'; in small compositions where 'the luxuriant irregularities of nature would fill up and embarrass the parts they should adorn'; near cities 'where property is much divided'; in flower gardens 'where art is much apparent in the culture'; on flats and all tame situations where the defects of nature need to be supplied quickly and efficiently.[69]

In larger gardens, straight walks are recommended as a source of grandeur.[70] Symmetrically framed by avenues of trees, they acquire an artificial infinity which Burke[71] associated with the sublime. Straight lines repeated in zig-zag pattern combine the variety and surprise of winding paths with the grandeur of plain straight ones. When the extent is vast, and the repetitions frequent, the spectator's surprise is raised to astonishment; he becomes anxious at the approach of each turn, and uncertain of where the repetition will end. His mind, in addition to being constantly occupied, is strongly impressed with ideas of the sublime. Zig-zag walks are, therefore, especially effective in scenes intended to inspire terror, veneration, or astonishment.[72] By comparison, the fashionable devices of the natural garden – the belt and the serpentine – have nothing to recommend them. The

[65] Ibid., p.17. Brown's lawns and clumps are a point in case. '. . . thousands of venerable plants, whole woods of them, have been swept away to make room for a little grass . . .', p.xi. Thomas Whately, *Observations on Modern Gardening* (London 1801), p.31, regarding clumps, 'every apparent artifice affecting the objects of nature, disgusts'.

[66] Castell, op. cit., p.32.

[67] Kames, op. cit., p.436.

[68] Whately, op. cit., p.153.

[69] Chambers, *Dissertation*, pp.17–18, 142. See also Kames, op. cit., pp.438, 439; and Whately, op. cit., pp.76, 80. Chambers also makes a bold plea for a more equitable assessment of the formal or 'artificial' style of gardening in general. The English aversion to this style is, he believes, correctly based upon the Dutch School, but unjustly extended to the French and Italian gardens. French gardens are admittedly 'all affectation: yet it is an affectation often delightful, and absurdity generally overflowing with taste and fancy: in their best works there is such a mysterious, pleasing intricacy in the disposition, such variety in the objects, so much splendour and animation in the scenery, and so much skill apparent in the execution of every part, that the attention of the spectator never flags; . . . If their Gardens are less rational than yours, they are certainly much more entertaining; and though, upon the whole, they can by no means be proposed as models for imitation, yet are there many things to be borrowed from them . . .', p.151. Italian gardens are 'less affected, less extravagant' than the French. 'There is a grandeur of manner in all their works, seldom to be met with elsewhere . . . Their vegetation too is uncommonly picturesque . . . and the venerable vestiges of ancient structures . . . add surprizingly to the dignity of the scenery', p.152.

[70] Chambers, *Dissertation*, p.57.

[71] Edmund Burke, *A Philosophical Enquiry into Our Ideas of the Sublime and Beautiful,* ed. J. T. Boulton (London 1958), pp.74–6.

[72] Chambers, *Dissertation*, pp.50–1.

circuitous belt[73] affords little variety and pleasure in proportion to its length; and the serpentine errs in the opposite extreme, pushing variety to absurdity. Although designed in imitation of nature, its 'eternal, uniform, undulating lines are, of all things, the most unnatural, the most affected, and the most tiresome to pursue.'[74]

Buildings, bridges, statues, and other objects, far from divesting a garden of its rural character, 'enrich and beautify particular prospects, without any detriment to the general aspect of the whole composition, in which Nature almost always appears predomin-ant.'[75] Indeed, there should seldom be any points with more than two or three objects; and these help to characterize and distinguish the different scenes.

It takes much more, however, than a few geometrical figures and architectural features to move the passions and gratify the senses. 'The scenery of a garden should differ as much from common nature, as an heroic poem doth from a prose relation; and Gardeners, like poets, should give a loose to their imagination; and even fly beyond the bounds of truth, whenever it is necessary to elevate embellish, to enliven, or to add novelty to their sub-ject.'[76] This bold piece of advice is unwittingly discredited by being practised as it is being preached. The bizarre fantasies of Chambers's imagination, although intended to re-inforce his plea for variety and contrast, ridicule it instead.

'The usual method of distributing Gardens in China, is to contrive a great variety of scenes . . .',[77] the more numerous and diverse, the better. These scenes are ranged by Chambers into three main categories: 'the pleasing, the terrible, and the surprizing',[78] which are an extension not only of his 1757 essay, but also of the elaborations upon it made by Whately under the influence of Burke.

The 'pleasing' scenes need little explanation. They are compositions of the gayest and most perfect productions of nature and art; where buildings, sculpture, and paintings add variety and splendour, rare animals provide amusement, and 'nothing is forgot, that can either exhilerate the mind, gratify the senses, or give a spur to the imagination.'[79]

The 'terrible' and 'surprizing or supernatural' scenes correspond to Burke's sublime.[80] The first is a veritable nightmare of dark caverns, deep valleys, impending rocks, ruined buildings, distorted trees that suggest the effects of lightning, tempest, or fire; bats, owls, and birds of prey; wolves, tigers, and howling jackals; gibbets, crosses, wheels, and the whole apparatus of torture; foundries and lime kilns belching flame and smoke from the mountain tops like volcanoes; and other images of privation, pain, danger, and destruc-tion.[81] These horrors may be excessive, but they are not entirely preposterous. Similar

[73] Ibid., p.53; and Whately, op. cit., p.114.

[74] Ibid., p.55; and Whately, op. cit., p.116.

[75] Ibid., p.82; and Whately, op. cit, p.66.

[76] Ibid., p.21; see also Shenstone, op. cit., p.95. 'I have sometimes thought that there was room for it [design] to resemble an epic or dramatic poem. It is rather to be wished than required, that the more striking scenes may succeed those which are less so. . .'; and p.102, 'Concerning scenes, the more uncommon they appear, the better, provided they form a picture, and include nothing that pretends to be of nature's production and is not.'

[77] Ibid., p.21.

[78] Ibid., p.39.

[79] Ibid., p.40.

[80] Burke, op. cit., p.57 ff.; Whately, op. cit., p.56 ff.

[81] Chambers, *Dissertation*, pp.40-1.

scenes did in fact exist, quite unplanned, at Middleton Drake near Chatsworth, and at New Weir on Wye, both described by Whately.[82]

Between the 'pleasing' and the 'terrible' are the 'surprizing or supernatural' scenes, 'calculated to excite in the mind of the spectator, quick successions of opposite and violent sensations',[83] pleasurable as well as painful. Of the three kinds of scenes, these are the most imaginative, if not outlandish. Here the spectator is submitted to extreme contrasts that startle, embarrass, or terrify him. At one moment he is led through dark passages where he is astonished by colossal statues of dragons and other horrid creatures, showers of artificial rain, sounds resembling the cries of tormented men and ferocious animals, thunder, cannons, trumpets, etc. Elsewhere he progresses from a forest where he is intimidated by parrots, apes, and cats to a flowering thicket where he is delighted by singing birds, instrumental music, arbours of jasmin, and not least 'beauteous Tartarean damsels, in loose transparent robes, that flutter in the scented air'.[84] Waterworks are employed in abundance to produce splendid and surprising effects; air to form artificial sounds and complicated echoes; and all sorts of optical illusions to vary the representation, or to render 'considerable in appearance, what in reality is trifling'.[85]

Whether the scene be pleasing, terrible, or surprising depends upon the character of the ground. Where the ground has no striking characteristics a variety of scenes can be created by disposing art and nature to accommodate the different seasons and times of day.[86] Here Whately[87] provides the natural framework to which Chambers adds a multitude of artificial diversions – some of his own invention and others borrowed from Attiret – to fill the mind with ideas of retirement (Winter), activity (Spring), exuberance (Summer), and decay (Autumn). His summer scenes, for example, are richly furnished with, amongst other things, a 'large tract for secret and voluptuous enjoyments', gaudy birds and animals, lavishly decorated pavilions for concubines, root and tree houses, and a complete city like the one at Yüan Ming Yüan.[88]

To take these tales of Oriental magnificence literally, or to attempt to imitate them is to miss the point. Of course, islands for ostriches and forests for elephants are unobtainable in England.[89] But they are not unthinkable. 'Men of genius often conceive more than it is practicable to execute; yet let them always look up to the sun and copy as much of its lustre as they can: circumstances will frequently obstruct them in their course, and they may be prevented from soaring high; but their attention should constantly be fixed on great objects, and their productions always demonstrate, that they knew the road to perfection.'[90] To Chambers, a grand and powerful style is reciprocal with genuine professionalism, and he is an inveterate champion of both. Where the standards of art are mean and insipid, it matters little who the practitioners are. Aim towards a more exalted

[82] Whately, op. cit., pp.53, 61.
[83] Chambers, *Dissertation*, p.42.
[84] Ibid., p.44.
[85] Ibid., p.46.
[86] Ibid., pp.24–39.
[87] Whately, op. cit., pp.135–9.
[88] Chambers, *Dissertation*, pp.35–7; Attiret, op. cit., pp.24–32.
[89] Ibid., p.105. This expression, added to the second edition, first appeared in a 'Letter of Sir Wm. Chambers to a Gentleman who had objected to certain parts of his Treatise on Oriental Gardening', 13 May 1772. Library of the College of Architecture, Cornell University, cf. Appendix.
[90] Ibid., p.106.

style (like the one he proposes), and gardeners will rise to the occasion and be 'men of genius, of experience, and judgment, quick in perception, rich in experience, fertile in imagination, and thoroughly versed in all the affectations of the human mind.'[91]

Convinced as he was of the need for a better style of gardening, Chambers never expected his proposals to be successfully received. Indeed, fear of censure was the ultimate cause of his downfall, for it led him not only to foster his ideas upon the Chinese, but also to frame them in jest. The Chinese disguise was a familiar literary device[92] which he presumed would be accepted and understood. It might well have been, had he not visited China. The public, informed of his travels, regarded him as an authority, and so mistook the mask, and the jokes for reality which they obviously thought ridiculous. On the other hand, his 'system' – a coalition between the natural and formal styles – which he fully expected to be misunderstood and censured[93] was not.

His pessimism, although misguided, proved on the whole to be well founded. The *Dissertation* received no ovations – only guarded reviews, outright reprehension, or ridicule.[94] The main points of criticism, apart from the Chinese fantasies, were: (1) the magnificence and expense of his recommendations, which seemed to entail a waste of land and money exceeding the rights of any democratic sovereign;[95] (2) the introduction of the terrible or horrid which was inappropriate to ornamental gardening, and a violation of nature;[96] (3) his 'wild revenge against Brown',[97] which was thought to be a jealous attempt 'to avert his royal majestie's attachment from the plan on which his garden at Richmond has been improved.'[98] These objections did not come as a surprise. Chambers had already replied to all but the last of them on 13 May 1772 (a week after the *Dissertation* was published) in a letter to an unknown gentleman[99] who had raised similar complaints after reading his manuscript. It was the unanimity of this first wave of criticism, and not

[91] Ibid., p.107.

[92] Oliver Goldsmith, *The Citizen of the World* (London 1760–1), Letter XXXI.

[93] BM Add.MS 41133, 78. Chambers to Frederick Chapman in Stockholm, 28 July 1772, 'It is a system of my own which as it was a bold attempt of which the Success was very uncertain I fathered it upon the Chinese who I thought lived far enough off to be out of reach of Critical Abuse.' See also *Dissertation*, p.112 'far from expecting at first, either applause or encouragement, he even judged artifice necessary to screen him from resentment; and cloathed truth in the garb of fiction, to secure it a patient hearing.'

[94] *Critical Review*, XXXIII (May 1772), p.143; *London Magazine*, XLI (June 1772), p.287; *Monthly Review*, XLVII (August 1772), pp.136–43.

[95] Ibid., *Monthly Review*, pp.136–7; *London Magazine*, p.287. See also letter from Voltaire to Chambers, 7 August 1772, thanking him for his gift of the *Dissertation*. 'Un Prince d'Allemagne se ruineroit en voulant être votre ecolier.' BM Add.MS 41134, 1.

[96] Ibid., *Monthly Review*, p.139.

[97] Horace Walpole, *Correspondence, Mason*, I (Yale 1955), p.34, letter from Walpole to Mason, 25 May 1772.

[98] *Monthly Review*, XLVII, op. cit., p.137. According to James Dalloway, the dispute was occasioned by Lord Clive's choice of Brown over Chambers to make alterations at Claremont. Cf. Horace Walpole, *Anecdotes of Painting in England . . .* With Additions by the Rev. James Dalloway, ed. R.N. Wornum, III (London 1888), p.106. However, Dalloway's information is clearly disproved by a letter of 28 March 1773 from Clive to Chambers, thanking him for sending a copy of the *Dissertation*. BM Add.MS 41136, 14v–15. 'I see enough to convince me, that you are master of your subject and that your garden scenes are drawn with the Pencil of a Claude. I think Mr. Brown should rather thank you for your Publication, than be offended, for he certainly may collect from your book many fine Ideas.'

[99] Cornell University Library MS, op. cit., cf. Appendix. R. C. Bald's suggestion that the 'Gentleman' was Horace Walpole is totally unconvincing; see 'Sir William Chambers and the Chinese Garden', *Journal of the History of Ideas*, XI, no.3 (June 1950), p.152. The person who 'animadverted' on Chambers's manuscript did so in 'an open and Friendly manner', which is certainly not the tone of Walpole's letter to Mason on 25 May. Walpole was convinced that the *Dissertation* was an unjust attack upon Brown. Yet there is no mention of Brown in Chambers's reply. Furthermore, the objections voiced by Walpole in his notes to Mason's *Satirical Poems* had been expressed earlier by other critics, e.g. in the *Monthly Review*. The gentleman remains unidentified.

the delayed attack in the *Heroic Epistle*,[100] that prompted him to publish a second edition with an Explanatory Discourse in 1773.

The allegations of extravagance and impracticality, being potentially the most injurious and, according to Chambers, thoroughly mistaken, merit the fullest response in the Discourse. For Europeans to be awed by the splendour of Oriental gardens is natural enough. However, to conclude that a vast expenditure of money and waste of valuable land is recommended for imitation is the result of sheer inattentive reading, coupled with a far too narrow concept of gardening. By his definition, 'Any tract of land [whether it be crossed by public roads, cultivated for use, or even barren waste] whose characteristick expressions have been strengthened by art, and in which the spontaneous arrangements of nature have been corrected, improved and adorned by the hand of taste, ought to be considered as a garden.'[101] Common paths; cornfields, orchards, and meadows interspersed with ordinary hedges or accidental plantations; farmhouses, churches, and cottages, if tastefully placed and designed, are just as ornamental and infinitely more natural than formal walks, lawns dotted with clumps, more expensive buildings, and all 'the gaudy trifling confused plantations with which all your English-made Gardens are so crouded.'[102] Given the spontaneous arrangements of England's nature, a fruitful imagination can create a stimulating garden without waste of land, and with less expense than is incurred by the present mode of gardening. Even the most dreary commons and wilds that cannot be beautified, 'may easily be framed into scenes of terror, converted into noble pictures of the sublimest cast, and by an artful contrast, serve to enforce the effect of gayer and more luxuriant prospects.'[103] Likewise, chalk pits, stone quarries, mines, etc. can be re-cast into amphitheatres, rustic arcades, peristyles, underground habitations, or grottos. 'The Great might thus have pleasure grounds, extensive and extraordinary, as those of the East.' Others would imitate them, and 'instead of spending large sums to fence and to lard a little field with twigs, to give it the name of a garden, they would beautify their whole estate.' England, by these means, 'might soon become one magnificent vast garden, bounded only by the sea.'[104]

The aversion to the terrible, being subjective rather than objective, was more difficult to dispel. The most Chambers could do to refute the idea of its being a violation of nature was to clarify its practical role as an economic and entertaining means of employing waste land. 'If any disgusting ideas are excited in the application of the terrible in decorating gardens, the fault must lie in the Composer, and not in the Objects, which are of a nature to produce the Sublime in the highest degree.'[105]

The charge against his abuse of Brown, as it could not be denied, is reversed with the utmost cunning. *On y soit qui mal y pense.* Why should Brown, whose name was never mentioned, insist upon exclusive title to criticism that was as much applicable to his brother-

[100] Arthur O. Lovejoy incorrectly described the *Discourse* as a reply to the *Heroic Epistle*, in 'The Chinese Origin of Romanticism' (1933) reprinted in *Essays in the History of Ideas* (New York 1960), p.124n. His mistake was repeated by H. F. Clark, op. cit., p.172.

[101] Chambers, *Dissertation*, p.125. See also Cornell University Library MS, op. cit.

[102] Ibid., p.130.

[103] Ibid., pp.130–1.

[104] Ibid., p.133. See also Cornell University Library MS, op. cit.

[105] Cornell University MS, op. cit. Appendix. See also *Dissertation*, pp.130–1.

hood as to him personally? Whatever has been said about English gardeners 'was with an eye to the general character of the fraternity; and by no means levelled at yon stately gentleman in the black perriwig, as he has been pleased to maintain.'[106]

In the privacy of his correspondence, Chambers confessed that his observations in China were imperfect, and that the trees and plants mentioned in the *Dissertation* had never 'appeared on Chinese paper'.[107] In public, however, he refused to do more than supply the second edition with the names of plants taken from Du Halde. He felt no need to defend the veracity of his descriptions: 'for the end of all that I have said, was rather as an Artist, to set before you a new style of Gardening; than as a Traveller, to relate what I have really seen.'[108]

The moment Chambers completed his defence, he was attacked again on the very same grounds. A week or two before the publication of the second edition with its *Explanatory Discourse* there appeared an anonymous pamphlet entitled, *An Heroic Epistle to Sir William Chambers*.[109] Its author was the poet and garden amateur, William Mason, aided and abetted by Horace Walpole.[110] On the surface, the *Epistle* is a straightforward parody of Chambers's garden theories. Underneath, however, it is a broader political squib levelled at the Tory Establishment, in which Chambers, as an intimate of the King and Comptroller General of His Majesty's Works, was a star figure, 'by Fortune plac'd to shine the Cynosure of British taste'.[111] Although the public enjoyed a good laugh at his expense, it was the political commentary that really attracted their attention, and made the *Epistle* a raging success. Its countless editions, ten in 1773 alone, were bound to have a damaging effect upon English interest in Chinese gardens, and upon Chambers's reputation as an authority on the subject. Nevertheless, in matters of architecture, he remained the 'Cynosure of British Taste'.

Chambers bore the brunt of Mason's attack with characteristic sobriety, refusing either to reply himself, or to allow his friends to do so for him. J. Leake, the proprietor of Covent Garden, was promptly discouraged from publishing some lines he had written in defence of the Dissertation 'chiefly because they would keep up the ball longer. The poem alluded to will drop of it self'; in any case, 'the great torrent of his (Mason's) wit is aimed at what doth not belong to me; that is; Peking in miniature, taken from Father Attiret's account of the Yuen Ming. With regard to the Parrots, Monkeys, whores and cats, they are all fair game; the poet may Shoot at them or eat them if he pleases; I wish him much

---

106 Chambers, *Dissertation*, p.157.

107 Cornell University Library MS, op. cit., Appendix.

108 Chambers, *Dissertation*, p.159. Note in the Designs he wished to be regarded as a traveller.

109 The preface to the *Heroic Epistle* is dated 30 January 1773, and the author claims to have written the poem the previous summer, just after the *Dissertation* appeared. Publication of the *Epistle* was first announced in the *Public Advertiser*, 11 March 1773. The second edition of the *Dissertation* with the *Explanatory Discourse* was published before 28 March 1773 for on that day Chambers received a letter from Robert Clive, thanking him for sending a copy. BM Add.MS 41136, 14v–15.

110 Mason's authorship was definitely established in the *St. James' Chronicle*, 20 February 1798.

111 [William Mason], *An Heroic Epistle to Sir William Chambers* (London 1773), p.5, lines 1–2. For a discussion of the political contents of the *Epistle* see John W. Draper, William Mason (New York 1924). Draper is in full agreement with the Walpole–Mason criticism of Chambers's gardening theories. The best defence of Chambers is given by Isabelle Chase, 'William Mason and Sir William Chambers's Dissertation on Oriental Gardening', *Journal of English and German Philology*, xxxv, no.4 (October 1936), pp.517–29.

sport, and of strong digestion. One thing is certain; his nonsense makes mine circulate.'[112] Goldsmith, encouraged by Burke, was also eager to launch a counter-attack. 'You have read no doubt a poem with some share of humour supposed to be written by a Mr. Anstye against you. Whoever the Author is he is I perceive a steddy [sic] Brownist. No matter, it will all in the end contribute to your honour. Most of the companies that I now go into divide themselves into two parties, the Chamberists and ye Brownists, but depend upon it you'll in the end have Victory, because you have Truth and Nature on your side. Mr. Burke was advising me about four days ago to draw my pen in a poem in defense of your system, and sincerely, I am very much warm'd in the Cause. If I write it I will print my name to it boldly . . . Mr. Burke you may say upon my authority as also on that of Sir Joshua Reynolds, is a profest Chamberist. He always speaks of your System with respect.'[113] The offer, heartening as it must have been, was firmly declined. '. . . for my book I shall not quarrel about it myself, nor do I wish any friend of mine should take that trouble. The poem you mention as written by Anstye, though I have heard it fathered on H. Walpole, has a great deal of humour, and will no doubt carry the laugh against me; but it is kind of humour that cannot last . . . the author whoever he is, has put me in excellent company . . . The thing is written with a Masterly hand, and is so artfully seasoned with politicks and abuse, that it cannot fail to have a great run; yet in point of real Criticism, it appears to me a Very trifle short; not worth an answer; I shall give myself no trouble about it, nor would I have you. Employ your pen my dear Doctor on better subjects; and leave my little book to fall or stand by its own strength.'[114]

Even without the *Epistle,* the *Dissertation* would never have found a sympathetic audience in England. In Europe, on the contrary, it proved to be one of the most widely-circulated and influential books on gardening of the period. The editions in French (1773) and German (1775), and the copies presented to King Gustaf III of Sweden, Count Scheffer, Voltaire, and other foreign friends and dignitaries helped not only to stimulate interest in 'Chinese' gardens, but, much more important, to set the fashion for the *Jardin Anglo-Chinois.* This was in spite of the fact that his descriptions were known or suspected to be unreliable.[115]

The paradox of Anglo-Chinese gardens without Chinese models was exposed by the German philosopher, C. C. L. Hirschfeld, in the first volume of his *Théorie de l'Art des Jardins,* 1779 (French edition of *Theorie der Garten-Kunst,* Leipzig).[116] Hirschfeld had no

[112] Chambers to J. Leake, 24 March 1773, in reply to a letter from Leake to Chambers of the same date. BM Add.MS 41134, 19–19v.

[113] Goldsmith to Chambers, BM Add.MS 41134, 21bv, 21c, 21d.

[114] Chambers to Goldsmith, after 7 April 1773, BM Add.MS 21b, 21d.

[115] Count Frederick Scheffer, as one of the most noted sinologists in Europe, must have been well aware of the fictional character of Chambers's descriptions. Yet he proposed that the gardens at Ulricksdal 'be leveled, extended on all sides, and then entirely redesigned *à la Chinoise,* or like that which Mr. Chambers describes in his recently published book on Gardens in China'. Osvald Sirén, *China and Gardens of Europe* (New York 1950), pp.168–9. Similarly, the Jesuit missionary in Peking, Pierre Martial Cibot, having completed his 'Essai sur les jardins de plaisance des Chinois', turns to Chambers for advice on their execution in the West: '. . . l'ingénieux Auteur d'un Essai sur l'architecture, a avancé depuis, qu'en faisant un heureux mélange des idées chinoises & des idées européennes, on réussiroit à avoir des jardins gais & rians'. By following such a plan one can procure 'tous les agrémens de la beauté de nos climats, & ne diminue que les dépenses pour les faire & pour les entretenir. Plus ils suivent le goût chinois, plus cela leur deviendra facile . . .', *Mémoires Concernant l'Histoire, les Sciences, les Arts, Mœurs, Usages des Chinois,* Par les Missionaires de Pe-Kin, VIII (Paris 1782), p.326.

[116] C. C. L. Hirschfeld, *Théorie de l'Art des Jardins,* I (Leipzig 1779), pp.100–18.

taste for the so-called 'Chinese' garden, and was determined to prove that the praise lavished upon it was both excessive and unwarranted. The *Dissertation* is his key witness. A careful reading firmly convinced him that the gardens described by Chambers are apocryphal. Indeed, he questions the existence of *any* gardens in China worthy of European esteem. The reputation enjoyed by the Chinese is, he concludes, entirely due to Chambers, and therefore is unmerited. If Europeans have been misled, they have only themselves to blame. Chambers was neither innocently deceived by false information, nor was he intentionally deceiving. 'Il crut que ces idées exciteroient plus d'attention, seroient mieux reçues, s'il les attribuoit à une nation éloignée qui les eût déjà mises en pratique. Il eût assez de prudence pour y mêler des choses propres au génie national des Chinois. En un mot, il planta des idées angloises dans un terrein Chinois, afin de leur donner une apparence plus frappante, et de les rendre plus séduisantes.'[117] Chambers had confessed to all of this in the *Explanatory Discourse*,[118] but Hirschfeld, it seems, was the only critic to take his confession seriously, and to appreciate its significance. The *Jardin Anglo-Chinois* was an imitation of the English landscape garden, and neither had any direct relation to the gardens of China.[119] Nevertheless, the term was justifiably applied to a landscape garden equipped with buildings and other decorative features in the Chinese style. In this context Chambers's *Designs of Chinese Buildings*, and *Plans . . . of Kew* were more influential than his *Dissertation*.

Chambers, as we have seen, had no wish to be champion of the Chinese style. It was by accident that he came to be so regarded. Nor was it his ultimate aim, as Sirén suggests, 'to call forth something that would become a synthesis'[120] of the English and Chinese landscape gardens. It is true that he demonstrated the correspondence between the two styles with remarkable efficiency, but he did so in accordance with a tradition established by Temple and Addison. It was fortuitous that Attiret's report was both available and suitable for comparison. Had he not had Attiret, or for that matter any knowledge of Chinese practice, his ideas would have been exactly the same for they were derived not from Chinese, but from English sources. Indeed, his introduction of the Chinese proved to be more of a hindrance than a help to his cause. No one realized or regretted this mistake more than he. To do him justice, one ought to heed his request, and 'gather the fruit . . . without minding the trees on which it grows.'[121]

[117] Ibid., pp.113–14. Similar conclusions were reached by J. M. Morel in his *Théorie des Jardins ou L'Art des Jardins de la Nature* (Paris 1776), see Sirén, *China and Gardens of Europe*, op. cit., pp.82–3.

[118] Chambers, *Dissertation*, pp.112–14.

[119] This was confirmed by two English visitors to Yüan Ming Yüan: John Barrow, secretary to Lord Macartney, the first British Ambassador to China, and John Francis Davis, H.M. Chief Superintendent in China. Barrow, *Travels in China* (London 1804), p.133, found Yüan Ming Yüan 'very short of the fanciful descriptions which Father Attiret and Sir William Chambers have intruded upon us as realities'. Nevertheless, he was constantly struck by the similarities between Chinese gardens and English parks. 'There is no beauty of distribution, no feature of amenity, no reach of fancy which embellishes our pleasure grounds in England, that is not to be found here.', p.130. Whether our style of gardening was copied from the Chinese or originated with ourselves, he cannot answer. There is certainly an analogy, but 'our excellencies seem to be rather in improving nature, theirs to conquer her, and yet produce the same effect . . .', p.135. Davis, *The Chinese: A General Description of the Empire of China and Its Inhabitants*, II (London 1836), p.254, concluded that 'the Chinese style of ornamental gardening, and of laying out pleasure-grounds, has been very much over drawn by Sir William Chambers, in an essay on that subject; which may be considered quite as a work of imagination in itself.'

[120] Sirén, *China and Gardens of Europe*, op. cit., p.83.

[121] Chambers, *Dissertation*, p.114

Chapter 11

The Royal Academy

Although[1] English artists had long been anxious to establish a professional body in the form of an Academy, they were never willing to submit to the kind of absolute authority which governed their French colleagues. When on 10 December 1768, the Royal Academy was finally founded, it was, as it still is, a private institution, acknowledged by the Crown, but ruled entirely by its members. In order fully to understand the circumstances surrounding the birth of the Academy, one must first review the succession of abortive efforts that preceded it.

It is no mere coincidence that the principal seventeenth-century attempts to found an Academy occurred at a time when court life and artistic production were strongly coloured by continental influence. In 1636 Charles I and his circle of courtly dilettanti organized the Museum Minervae as an aristocratic centre for the promotion of the fine arts. Meetings were held in Covent Garden at Sir Francis Kynaston's house where 'several Proffessors' taught gentlemen the 'Several Arts and Sciences, Foreign Languages, Mathematics, Painting Architecture Musick riding, fortification, &c – antiquity meddals.'[2] Perhaps Inigo Jones taught here, who knows? History is no more enlightening about Sir Balthasar Gerbier's Academy for Foreign Languages and all Noble Sciences opened at his house in Bethnal Green in 1648. Gerbier certainly lectured, but there may well be truth in the accusation that, as a convivial meeting place for royalists, the so-called Academy was perhaps more politically than culturally motivated.

The first Academy of Painting and Drawing in Great Britain was opened in 1711 – on St Luke's Day – in a house in Great Queen Street, Lincon's Inn Fields, where, according to Vertue, 'the Subscription was a Guinea for each person paid down – the place for drawing a large room ground floor', a 'great house . . . gone to decay & uninhabited'.[3] Kneller was elected its first Governor, and again Vertue tells us that the Directorate of twelve included Richardson, Thornhill, Laguerre, Pelligrini, and Francis Bird the sculptor. Top artists such as Goupy, Lens, Tillemans, Laroon, Wootton, Vanderbank, Castells, Dandridge, and Gibson, as well as a sprinkling of architects, could here share expensive equipment, study from living models, and pass the convivial hours. Thornhill who was an ambitious, socially upper-crust artist may have seen in this Academy the potential for a

[1] I am indebted to four works dealing with the history of the Academy: W. Sandby, *The History of the Royal Academy of Arts*, 2 vols, 1862; W. T. Whitley, *Artists and their Friends in England, 1700–1799*, 1928; D. Hudson, *Sir Joshua Reynolds, A Personal Study*, 1958; and S. Hutchison, *The History of the Royal Academy 1768–1968*, 1968.

[2] Vertue Notebooks, I, 156.

[3] Vertue Notebooks, VI, 168.

Royal Academy. He had unsuccessfully tried to persuade Lord Halifax to support the establishment of one in the Royal Mews, and this could have been in his mind when he succeeded Kneller as Governor in 1716. However, in 1720, he in turn was deposed when Louis Cheron and John Vanderbank led a splinter group away to St Martin's Lane. In 1722 this reformed Academy was advertised as an 'Academy for the Improvement of Painters and Sculptors by drawing from the naked'.[4] Thornhill had moved the decimated Kneller Academy to James Street, Covent Garden, where he uneventfully directed it until his death in 1735.

Thornhill's death provided the means and impetus for Hogarth, his son-in-law, to reform the St Martin's Lane Academy in new premises in Peter Court, St Martin's Lane. Of his connexion with the Academy, Hogarth wrote in 1764 'I lent to the Society the furniture that had belonged to Sir James Thornhill's Academy; and attributing the failure of the preceding Academies to the leading members having assumed a superiority which their fellow students could not brook, I proposed that every member should contribute an equal sum towards the support of the establishment and have an equal right to vote on every question relative to its affairs. By these regulations the Academy has now existed nearly thirty years, and is for every useful purpose equal to that in France or any other.'[5] Such a boast could not be substantiated. Nevertheless, from 1735 the St Martin's Lane set exercised a considerable influence upon the development of English rococo art. Its members included Hogarth, Gravelot, Roubiliac, Hayman, Moser, Cheere, Fielding, Garrick, Gainsborough, and Paine – all habitués of the nearby Slaughter's Coffee House, rightly called the convivial breeding ground for English Rococo.[6]

Frederick, Prince of Wales was the academy's principal patron. Had he not died in 1751 a royal academy might well have come into being in 1760 (when the Prince would have succeeded George II), if not earlier. The Prince was certainly party to Vertue's prescient ideas for an Academy 'for the Improvement of the Art of Delineing in this Nation' and for the establishment of drawing schools in London, Oxford, and Cambridge under the supervision of 'an Accademy settled by Publick Authority'.[7] At this time both the Prince and Vertue would have been aware of John Gwynn's *Essay on Design including proposals for erecting a Public Academy*, published in 1749, and of the meeting of a 'Grand Clubb for promoting the Arts of Drawing, painting &c',[8] possibly associated with the Society of Dilettanti, held in November 1749 'to settle the preliminarys for the Establishment of an Academy – in London'. It was certainly the Dilettanti who, by acquiring in 1753 a site in Cavendish Square upon which to build a copy of the Temple of Pola for a museum, prompted the St Martin's Lane Academy to call a meeting in this year to found a 'public Academy for the improvement of painters, sculptors and architects'. However, two years elapsed before the St Martin's Lane Committee – chaired by Hayman and including

[4] Whitley, op. cit., I, 18.

[5] Whitley, op. cit., I, 27.

[6] For an account of the birth of English rococo cf. Mark Girouard, 'Coffee at Slaughter's', *C.Life*, 13 Jan. 1966, 58–61; 'Hogarth and His Friends', *C.Life*, 27 Jan. 1966, 188–90; 'The Two Worlds of St. Martin's Lane', *C.Life*, 3 Feb. 1966, 224–7.

[7] Vertue Notebooks, I, 10.

[8] Vertue Notebooks, VI, 150.

Reynolds, Roubiliac, Hudson, Hamilton, Moser, and F. M. Newton – offered to negotiate with the Dilettanti. Neither side could resolve their differences, but as has been pointed out a set of rules anticipating in an uncanny way those of the future Royal Academy – and mistakenly attributed by Thomas Sandby to John Evelyn – might have been drawn up at this time.[9] It may not have been a coincidence that in 1755 appeared Alexander Nesbit's *Essay . . . on the Necessity and Form of a Royal Academy*. Whatever interaction there may have been, all this is sufficient proof that around 1750–5 artists were conscious of the need for an established form of royal and public recognition. Irrespective of their merits, exhibitions and academies add a gloss of status.

There had been a semi-permanent public exhibition of artists' work donated to the Foundling Hospital from 1746, and it was there, in November 1759, that 'a meeting of the artists' – mostly from the St Martin's Lane set – agreed to consider 'a proposal for the honour and advancement of the Arts', namely to promote an annual exhibition of contemporary work.[10] It was first necessary to find a suitable exhibition room, not too difficult as the Society for the Encouragement of Arts, Manufactures, and Commerce – whose interests lay away from the fine arts – had a splendid new room off the Strand, designed by Chambers. It is tempting to associate with the November 1759 meeting and the artists' first exhibition in 1760, the proposals made by Robert Wood to Lord Bute in October 1759 for a Royal Academy in a building costing 'at least £100,000', and his request to Chambers to 'throw upon paper some loose hints'.[11]

Although the first Society of Arts exhibition was a tremendous success, relations between the Society and the artists were not of the happiest. In 1761 a group of dissenting artists exhibited in Spring Gardens, calling themselves the Society of Artists of Great Britain. Those who stayed with the Society of Arts called themselves the Free Society in 1762, but broke away from the Society of Arts in 1765. They were of small consequence and ceased to exist in 1783. There was a third group who comprised some of the old St Martin's Lane artists unattached to either the Society of Artists or the Free Society. They set themselves up in Richard Dalton's Print Warehouse in Pall Mall, and it was probably through his influence that the students there were amalgamated with those at the newly-founded Royal Academy in 1768.

With Reynolds, Hogarth, Gainsborough, Wilson, Chambers, Cotes, and Sandby on its governing body, the Society of Artists was an influential body. When it received a royal charter as the Incorporated Society of Artists of Great Britain in 1765 some saw it as the parent of a Royal Academy. Indeed it was, but in a manner unexpected by many of its more conservative members. In 1768 the all too familiar internecine quarrel broke out, this time over the retirement and nomination of Directorships. On 18 October, West, Wilson, Newton, Sandby, Moser, Wilton, Penny, and Chambers (all future founder members of the Royal Academy) resigned. During the coming weeks, unknown to the Incorporated Society, clandestine meetings were being held to found a Royal Academy under the patronage of the King.

The order of events for this autumn will probably never be known. If Chambers was,

9 Sandby, op. cit., I, 19–20.
10 Whitley, op. cit., 165.
11 Robert Wood to 3rd Earl of Bute, 28 Oct. 1759 (Archives Lord Bute, Mount Stuart, Isle of Bute).

indeed, the rebel leader who saw in the October breakaway from the Incorporated Society the opportune moment to found a Royal Academy, then all honour to him. Reynolds, it is known, played no part in the penultimate phase of the secret negotiations. He had studiously avoided the acrimony in the Incorporated Society, and as late as November 1768 had declined Joshua Kirby's offer of its Presidency. According to Farington, 'West told Smirke & me that a meeting at Wilton's where the subject of planning & forming the Royal Academy was discussed, Sir Wllm. Chambers seemed inclined to (be) the *president*, but Penny decided that a *painter* ought to be the *President*. It was then offered to Mr Reynolds, afterwards Sir Joshua, though he had not attended at any of these meetings which were held at Mr Wilton's – Mr West was the person appointed to call on Sir Joshua to bring him to a meeting at Mr Wilton's, where an offer of the Presidency was made to him, to which Mr Reynolds replied that He desired to consult his friends Dr Johnson and Mr Burke upon it. This hesitation was mentioned by Sir Wllm. Chambers to the King, who from that time entertained a prejudice against Reynolds, for both Johnson and Burke were disliked by the King, the latter particularly on political grounds.'[12] Reynolds's decision to accept the secret offer may be associated with an entry in his diary under 9 December 'Mr Wilton's at 6'.[13] On 28 December a Memorial, signed by twenty-two artists, but significantly not by Reynolds, nor by Robert Adam whom Chambers banned from the Academy, had been presented to George III, explaining 'that the two principal objects we have in view are, the establishing a well-regulated School or Academy of Design, for the use of students in the Arts, and an Annual Exhibition, open to all artists of distinguished merit, where they may offer their performances to public inspection.' The King acknowledged this, asking for fuller information, and by 7 December Chambers had consulted with everyone concerned and submitted a draft to the King. This was approved of and on 10 December Chambers took the Instrument of Foundation to the King for his signature. On 14 December, in Dalton's Warehouse in Pall Mall, the new Royal Academy held its first meeting with Reynolds elected to the Presidential Chair.[14]

The part played by Chambers in these moving events is acknowledged in the *Minutes of the General Assembly of the Royal Academy* under 14 December 1768 and 2 January 1769.[15] They record 'That some time towards the latter End of November 1768, Mr Chambers waited upon the King and informed him that many artists of reputation together with himself were very desirous of establishing a Society that should more effectually promote the Arts of Design than any yet established, but that they were sensible their Design could not be carried into Execution without his Majesty's Patronage, for which they had prevailed upon him to sollicit.' In the later *Minutes* Chambers was thanked 'for his Active and able Conduct in planning and forming the Royal Academy.' Had Chambers not been the principal in this affair, he would certainly not have been singled out for special thanks. As he more egoistically wrote in his *Autobiographical Note,* the 'whole institution was planned by me and was completed through my efforts, a circumstance that affords me great

12 Farington's Diary, 12 Dec. 1804.
13 Reynold's Diary. Hudson, op. cit., 92.
14 Hutchison, op. cit., 44.
15 Archives Royal Academy.

pleasure, as in all probability this institution will cause the arts to rise as high as possible in this country.'

Did Chambers really covet the Presidency? Gossip may relate that he did, and admittedly the Academy was his child, but he must surely have been in no doubt about the rightness of choosing a painter, and the greatest one of his time. By drafting the Instrument of Foundation, however, Chambers ensured that it would be the King's prerogative to appoint the Treasurer, 'that he may have a person in whom he places full confidence, in an office where his interest is concerned.' Not surprisingly, therefore, 'His Majesty doth hereby nominate and appoint William Chambers, Esquire, Architect of his Works, to be Treasurer of The Royal Academy of Arts, to receive the rents and profits of the Academy, to pay its expences, to superintend repairs of the Buildings and Alterations & to examine all Bills. He shall be summoned to all meetings of the Council, by right of his office, and have the Liberty of giving his Opinion in all debates; but shall have no Vote, except he is of the Council for the time being. He shall once in every Quarter lay a fair State of his accounts before the Council; and when they have passed examination, he shall lay them before the Keeper of His Majesty's Privy Purse, to be by him finally Audited and the deficiency paid, if there is any. His salary shall be Sixty pounds a Year.'[16] Chambers had secured for himself a position of strength, as the personal nominee of the King responsible to no one else. We can well believe Farington who had remarked that Reynolds had told him 'that though he was President, Sir Wm was Viceroy over him.'[17]

In 1769 Chambers was in the high noon of success. He was established in a handsome town house, lived in a palatial country villa once owned by a ducal grandee, had succeeded Flitcroft as Comptroller of the Works, and was now Treasurer of the Royal Academy. His knighthood in 1770, the Somerset House commission in 1776, and the Surveyor-Generalship of the Works in 1783 but amplified the theme of worldly achievement. Such a one, who was the titular head of his profession and bred in a Parisian milieu, must have felt strongly that art and architecture could be improved by the provision of a forum for exhibition and a body of professional teachers. He was sensitive that internecine dissension had destroyed all previous attempts to found an Academy, and his paternal and autocratic handling of the Royal Academy may be excused if we see it in this light. If he has been faulted for priggishness and pomposity in the handling of his fellow academicians, then he could at least plead that these were due to principles rather than personal animosity. There is a succinct parallel here with his strict, autocratic, yet always humane control of the Office of Works. He knew that without its Regimental Sergeant Major, the Royal Academy could have gone the way of the St Martin's Lane Academy and the Incorporated Society. A reading of the *Minutes of the General Assembly* or of the *Council* evokes a picture of deep humanity. For example, he is first and foremost in his pleas for Royal Charity: In June 1769 for a 'Mr Swordfigger' architect, or in July 1775, June 1776, and June 1779 for Mary, Isaac Ware's daughter.

Posterity's opinion of Chambers and the Academy has been coloured not by events in the first twenty years, but during the 1790s when illness was dissolving his life. It was a principle that led him to oppose Reynolds's partial nomination of Bonomi as Professor of

[16] Archives Royal Academy.
[17] Farington's Diary, 10 Dec. 1804.

Perspective, and to object, as did the other Academicians, to Reynolds's attempt to exhibit Bonomi's drawings so as to curry favour. Reynolds had broken an inviolate rule. Nevertheless, it was typical of Chambers, that whereas one moment he would weigh the scales against Reynolds, the next he was anxious to restore the balance by friendship. He had once made some notes under the heading 'Wit Consists in Contrast', listing, 'Giving pain to an Object intently bent on pleasure'; or even more pertinent, of 'rendering an Object ridiculous whilst it is aiming at Importance'.[18] Reynolds had resigned the Presidency, so off went Chambers to Reynolds's house to placate him, to convey the King's wish for the withdrawal of the resignation, and to bring the great painter back to the Presidential Chair.[19]

Stricken by asthma, as the 1790s progressed, Chambers became increasingly pernickety about protocol. When Reynolds proposed special robes for the Academicians, his 'Viceroy' firmly told him 'we are in the wrong box with respect to the academy dresses';[20] or when Reynolds withdrew a picture from the 1790 exhibition, Chambers told him that this was contrary to a 'positive law of the Academy' and a 'precedent which may be Attended with very ill consequences, and a Stretch of power in you, which will be difficult to justify'.[21] Admittedly Chambers was in the right, and however one cools to his disciplinarianism, sympathetic perhaps to the painter's temperament, one can forgive him when reading his letter of justification, when he vetoed the pleas of Reynolds and West for the Academy to contribute one hundred guineas for the proposed monument to Dr Johnson in St Paul's Cathedral. It is a moving document, full of Chambersian humanity, and was read to the 'General Meeting Assembled' on 2 July 1791:

> Gentlemen, Some very particular business prevents my Attendance this Evening at the General Meeting. If nothing more were to be agitated than is mentioned in the summons, my absence, with that of half the Academicians, would be immaterial; there would still be a sufficient number to confer an empty title, but there is reason to apprehend that a proposal is to come forwards, totally foreign to the business and views of the Academy: a proposal, which if it is agreed to, must open the door to all sorts of innovation, must weaken the Academy in its revenues, & disable us from pursueing with proper Spirit and full effect, the true objects of our institution.
>
> Our business is to establish schools for the Education of young Artists; Premiums for their encouragement; Pensions to enable them to pursue their studys; an Exhibition, wherein they may set their talents to public view; and honorary titles of distinction, to be confer'd on such as are deemed to deserve them. The Royal Academy has it still farther in view, to maintain itself; to reward its Members for services done; to assist the Sick or distressed Artist; to extend its beneficence to the relief of his family; to help the Widows and Children, of such, as leave them unprovided for. – All these, I apprehend are sufficient objects for any Society to carry in view, without going astray to hunt for more. We find it very difficult to fulfill even these; our Donations do not by any means

18 RIBA Misc. Lecture Notes.
19 Cf. Hudson, op. cit., 216–21.
20 Hudson, op. cit., 126, transcribing Reynolds to Chambers 28 Jan. 1775. Cf. BM Add.MS 41135, 58; and Chambers to Reynolds 30 Jan. 1775. Cf. BM Add.MS 41135, 59.
21 Hudson, op. cit., 221.

equal the necessities of our distressed Suitors, and our Travelling Pensions are too few, for so respectable an Establishment as Ours. If therefore we judge it expedient to tap the fund of the Academy, let it flow into these, its proper channels; and let it not be spillt in useless driblets, on things absolutely foreign to the intent and Purpose of our Establishment.

The Proposal I allude to, is that made in the last Meeting of the Council, which is, I apprehend, the true cause of your being Summoned to meet this Evening. It was a Proposal made by the President, to contribute largely out of the Fund of the Royal Academy, towards the Monument of Dr Johnson, about to be erected in St Pauls. To me it seemed, I freely confess, that one might with equal propriety have proposed the Erection of a Triumphal Arch to Lord Heathfield, or a Mausoleum to the inventor of Fire Engines, or a Statue to any other person, whose pursuits, and whose excellence lay totally wide of ours. If Monuments were to be our objects, how could we without Shame and contrition, Vote one to Dr Johnson, whilst Cipriani, – Moser, – Gainsborough, – Cotes, – Wilson; and so many others of our departed Brother-Academicians, are left unnoticed and forgotten, in the dust. Let us therefore save our Credit, and spare our repentence, by Voting no Monument at all.[22]

Chambers delivered the final injustice to Reynolds in 1792 when he refused to authorize the use of the Academy for the painter's lying-in-state. Even the King saw how wrong Chambers was, and for the only time in his reign took Reynolds's side, 'that that mark of respect shou'd be shown' to the dead President.[23] Almost the last time Chambers's name appears in the Minute Books was on 10 July 1795 when in dotage he felt the Academy could not afford their annual dinner. His 'great intricacy' in 'stating his accounts' had already been commented upon by Tyler and Dance who had been appointed by the Academy to regularize its auditing. Even the King thought there was 'always something obscure' in the Treasurer's bookkeeping,[24] and in the winter of 1795 Chambers had to confess his inability to carry on with the accounting 'by reason of his advanced age and informities'.

Chambers had nursed the Academy from strength to strength. When he left it there was not the slightest doubt of its success and permanence. If he wielded the stick of rules sometimes harshly, let us not condemn him, but instead dwell upon his humanity, and believe that there were many occasions when he would vie with Boswell at composing verses[25] or sing Swedish love songs at Academy dinners.[26]

[22] *Minutes of the General Assembly.*
[23] Hudson, op. cit., 228.
[24] Farington's Diary, 14 Oct. 1795.
[25] Hutchison, op. cit., 71.
[26] Whitley, op. cit., 21, 151.

Conclusion

Trystan Edwards could ask in 1924 'Who was Sir William Chambers?' He could easily have said the same in 1964. One by one the giants of eighteenth-century architecture – Vanbrugh, Hawksmoor, Adam, and Soane – toppled to their biographers, but not Chambers. Hundreds of letters, thousands of drawings, the buildings, and the books were ample material indeed, yet no one transposed it to the printed word. The answer may be that Chambers was the *éminence grise* to so many persons, and behind so many events. He deliberately avoided the role of flamboyant actor, neither preferring the footlights, nor the social accompaniments of greatness and fame. Despite his friendship with Johnson and Boswell, Reynolds or Goldsmith, his shadow barely flits across their memoirs or letters. Similarly, his architecture was never over-stated; it expressed no personal vision; it was as conforming as his Tory politics. When Horace Walpole praised the *Treatise on Civil Architecture* as 'the most sensible book and the most exempt from prejudice that ever was written in that science', he could as easily have modified these words to describe Chambers's buildings. They are the polished reflections of an incredibly learned mind; in fact, Chambers was the supreme example of the scholar architect.

The man is revealed in his books and letters. Here he assumes the role not only of architect, but of professor, gardener, cynic, humanitarian, philosopher, or out-and-out joker. To those who have always regarded Chambers as a study in reserve and propriety, it comes as a surprise to discover his use of pornography to drive home a point in a letter, or his singing Swedish love songs at Royal Academy dinners, or vying with Boswell at composing verses. But then, his architecture reveals similar paradoxes: the Rococo State Coach, or the 'Artisan' decoration at the Hoo, or rules laid down in the *Treatise*, broken with a sense of mischief. As the first architect to return from China with measured drawings of Chinese buildings, and the first to publish them, in the *Designs for Chinese Buildings* in 1757, he changed the prevailing rococo vision of a romanticized chinoiserie. In the *Dissertation on Oriental Gardening* in 1772 his vision of gardenscape and landscape planning looked beyond the frontiers of his century, beyond even the nineteenth, to our own today. In 1763 his lavish folio in Kew Gardens may have been intended as a delight for Princess Augusta, but it was also a subtle self-advertisement for the creator of what had become a mecca for all travellers to London.

His influence as an architect was widespread. There must have been many a provincial architect inspired by a Duddingstone or a Kew in his locality; but it was Somerset House, above all, that served as inspiration and quarry for generations to come. Nash throughout his life was haunted by Chambers: 14–16 Regent Street (1822), Rockingham (*c*.1822), Westminster Fire Office (1823), Buckingham Palace (1825), are all full of Chambersian passages. The same could be said of C. R. Cockerell who synthesized Chambers in his highly idiosyncratic way who regarded him as that 'Great Golden Eagle' on his 'intellectual horizon', or of James Pennethorne whose 1852 Inland Revenue Office so handsomely carried on the Chambersian mode. Chambers's pupils and admirers imbibed his teachings and high aspirations, so there is James Gandon's recollections of his old master at the Dublin Custom House, or Thomas Hardwick at St Marylebone Church, or John Yenn at North Aston, and in his Chambersian Academy studies, recently discovered at the Royal Academy, or Sir Robert Taylor in his many villas, or James Wyatt at Dodington. Further afield one could select Latrobe and Thornton at the United States Capitol, or Bulfinch at the Massachusetts State House in Boston, where he pastiched Somerset House as early as 1787. In India the *Treatise* was on many an engineer's or draughtsman's table, and in Europe it was certainly a *sine qua non* among the essential books in architects' libraries. Soufflot, Peyre, Blondel, De Chefdeville knew and admired the book. Le Roy, Jardin, Piper, D'Argenson, Patte, and Le Geay were but a few of those who came to London to meet Chambers and to study his buildings at first hand. Looking beyond the eighteenth and nineteenth centuries to the age of Edwardian Baroque and Neo-Georgian, Chambers's presence is omnipotent. One need only take Sir Reginald Blomfield, who regarded him as a Parnassian, or Sir Albert Richardson, who saw him as one of the peaks of Georgian excellence, to appreciate how pervading his influence was 'between the Wars'. Nevertheless, despite the vast range of his accomplishments, if one portion was to be selected upon which posterity must judge him, it would be the great *Treatise* – not Duddingstone, nor Somerset House, nor Kew Gardens – but those lessons given to Prince George, and codified so brilliantly in the printed word. The aim of the *Treatise* was to provide a course of instruction on the five orders and their embellishments; its essence was selectivity; and it succeeded by direct observation, practical experience, and the use of the student's analytical judgement. Throughout the *Treatise* Chambers's method is an empirical one: he examines impartially and critically, compares written opinions with executed buildings, accepts nothing as pre-ordained and no one opinion as sacred. He abstracts what he considers to be a series of sound precepts and good designs, basing his conclusions on his own informed reason or on universally-received opinion. Direct observations of French, Italian, and English architecture and an astonishing knowledge of architectural literature, philosophies and aesthetics, are brought into play at every point. The breadth of his experience and the international flavour of his taste gave authority to his conclusions and the stamp of a unique personality to his writings. From this book thousands of architectural students throughout the world have derived their knowledge of the proportions and profiles of the orders and their decoration, and thousands more have gained insight into the sound principles and sure taste of a man who gave a new dignity to the profession of British architecture.

Appendix I

Portraits

Carl Fredrik Von Breda (1751–1818). ¾ length in RIBA, Exhib. RA 1788, no.197. A companion to Breda's portrait of Thomas Collins dated 1788 (now Dr and Mrs John Gurney Salter Coll.) and once in Collins's collection. Both portraits at Whitton in 1790.

Francis Cotes (1726–1770). Pastel, 1764, in National Gallery of Scotland; reduced version in RIBA, ex Coll. Thomas Hardwick. Oil version in Coll. Dr and Mrs John Gurney Salter. The Scottish portrait engraved in mezzotint by Richard Houston.

George Dance (1741–1825). Pencil portrait published in *A Collection of Portraits Sketched . . . Since . . . 1793* (1809). The last record of Chambers. Fuseli, 'drawling out his words', observed when looking at this portrait, 'what a *grate*, heavy *humpty dumpty*, this leaden fellow is' (J. T. Smith, *A Book For A Rainy Day*, 1861, 190).

Robert Dunkarton (1744–?) Small coloured chalk portrait, inscr. and dated 1775, in Coll. Paul Tyler, St. Mellion, Cornwall.

George Engelheart (1752–1829). Miniatures of Chambers, Lady Chambers, Cornelia Milbanke, John Milbanke, Lavinia Cottin, Selina Innes, William Innes, Charlotte Harwood, George Chambers – in Coll. Mrs Susan Scammell, East Knoyle, Wilts. Engelheart miniatures also of the Inneses in V & A Museum (P.15–16. 1958) ex. Coll. Miss E. F. E. Pebardy. Said to match 1788 sitter book record.

Peter Falconet (1741–1791). Head in relief in neo-classic frame. 1769. Several engraved versions.

Le Masson (or Le Mason). Exhib. RA 1790, no.534, bust of Chambers and medallions of two daughters.

Jeremiah Meyer (1735–1789). Miniature in V & A Museum (4044.1958), after 1769.

Charles Peart. Wax portrait medallion modelled for Wedgwood, c.1780s.

Sir Joshua Reynolds (1723–1792). Earliest portrait may be National Portrait Gallery, ¾ length, leaning on hand, ex Coll. George Chambers. Surely painted before 1760. There is no proof that a 1763 payment of £13 2s 6d in the sitter's books refers to this. Standard portrait is the RA Diploma piece, sat 1779, exhib. 1780, engraved Valentine Green. The source of many copies, the most important being the Musée Royal des Beaux-Arts de Belgique version. Head and shoulders studio version in Coll. Einer Westerberg, Stockholm, possibly that sold in von Breda sale of 1818 and therefore of Reynolds's circle provenance.

John Francis Rigaud (1742–1810). Chambers in group with Wilton and Reynolds, 1782. National Portrait Gallery.

Sir Richard Westmacott (1775–1856). Bust, exhib. RA 1797, now Sir John Soane's Museum. Oddly the only known bust portrait.

William Wyon (1795–1851). Head in profile on medal minted in 1857 for the Art Union of London, based upon the Westmacott bust.

John Zoffany (1735–1810), *see*: C. P. Dyer, *Biographical Sketches of Illustrious and Eminent Men* (1819).

Appendix II

Exhibitions

Appendix III

Bank Account

Archives Drummonds Branch, Royal Bank of Scotland, Charing Cross

The Bank Account is valuable as showing Chambers's rise to fortune from 1759 until 1775. After this date the account includes the Government moneys for the use at Somerset House; hence the considerable fluctuation in amounts. Payments to individuals are only valuable as showing the employment of artists and craftsmen. For example, of the pupils, Gandon appears in 1759, Stevens in 1762, Hardwick 1765, Yenn 1766. Some of the largest transactions were to Thomas Collins, who first appears in 1762 and is paid small amounts until 1768 when it rises to £530 in 1769. In 1770 the figure is over £1000 and in 1771 an account opens with Chambers and Collins – almost certainly an indication of speculative building, probably in St Albans Street. Payments in 1761 and 1762 are for engraving the Kew book. As a sculptor, Joseph Wilton appears regularly throughout the accounts as one of Chambers's team of craftsmen, which includes Collins, the plasterer; Benoni Thacker, joiner; Edward Gray, bricklayer; Sefferin Alken, carver; John Devall, mason; and Thomas Westcot, slater. The majority of payments are difficult to interpret: that to Gosling & Co in 1764 may be related to the projected move to Berners Street; so may the £1550 paid to T. Home between 1766 and 1768, probably for the development there. The late account under Chambers and Hume is certainly a personal one, probably for Lady Chambers's benefit when Chambers was getting advanced in age.

	Standing credit £ s. d.
1759 Account opened. Includes payment to James Gandon, Richard Langley, William Privet	470. 0. 0
1760	860
1761 Payment to James Kennedy, Fourdrinier, Samuel Cobb, Edward Rooker	660
1762 Payments to Charles Grignon and Rooker, Edward Stevens, James Basire, and Thomas Collins	1,990. 3. 0
1763 Payments to Joseph Wilton, Paul Sandby, George Warren, Solomon Brown, Rooker; Receipt of 7.18.0 from Simon Vierpyle	2,259. 1. 6
1764 Payments to Gosling & Co (272.10.0) and to Benoni Thacker, George Mercer, Edward Gray, Maria Hales, etc.	1,739. 6. 6
1765 Payments to E. Hayward. Sefferin Alken, John Gilliam, Thomas Hardwick, etc.	1,680.17.10
1766 Payments to John Yenn, Thacker, D. Campbell, W. Westcot, Richard Haywood, William Pickford, Thomas Home, Ince & Co., John Grove, George Evans, Stevens, Collins, etc., Receipt from John Drummond (208.13.7), Moses Franks (160), Collins (400)	5,038.13.10
1767 Payments to Anderson, Neal, Palmer, Snow, Gascoigne, Mercer, etc.	10,783.10. 0
1768 Payments to Norman, Richard Dalton, W. Greenell, Boyes, Drinkwater, Cole, Stark, etc.	5,496. 8. 7
1769 Payments to Ward, Christie, General Keppell, Palmer, G. Barrett, Boys, Bartolozzi, etc.	9,940. 7.11
1770 Payments to Stewart, Josiah Wedgwood, Collins, George Stubbs Jnr, Groves, etc.	6,693.17.10
1771 *Receipt* 600 from John Drummond; 500 from Edward Stevens *Account opens Chambers & Collins* *Receipt* Mayhew on Croft & Co 300; Calcraft on Lee, 1000	12,383.19. 6 6,805
1772 Payments to Deval, Gray, Wilton, Collins, etc. *Chambers & Collins*	19,952. 4. 9 5,283
1773 Payments to Oliver Goldsmith, F. M. Piper, John White, Bartoli & Co. *Receipts* 1000 from Lord Melbourne; 82.17.6 from Lord Ely; 50 from Kenton Couse *Chambers & Collins*	10,616. 7. 9 531.17. 9

1774
Payments to Cipriani, Flaxman senr,
Rebecca, Bartoli   9,053.13. 2
Chambers & Collins account closed

1775
Payments to John Cheere, John
Scott, Robert and James Adam
(1109.19.0), etc.   12,546.13.10

1776   12,879. 2. 0

1777   24,363.12. 2

1778
Payments to John Chambers,
W. Reveley, Carlini,
Cerrachi   21,712. 5. 4

1779   12,399.19.10

1780
Payments to Catherine Chambers,
William Saxon etc.   21,971.15. 3

1781
Payments to John Chambers, George
Gosling (2351.15.0)   26,147.13. 5

1782   13,171.19. 7

1783   37,081.10. 2
*Account opened Chambers & Alexander
Hume*   1,113. 5.10

1784   31,412. 9. 0
Chambers & Hume   1,966. 4. 8

1785   24,054. 4. 8
Chambers & Hume   5,441.10. 2

1786   28,200.12. 5
Chambers & Hume   2,127. 5.11

1787   47,283.11. 0
Chambers & Hume   4,948.16. 1

1788   36,695. 7. 9
Chambers & Hume   3,143.10.11

1789   27,791.19.10
Chambers & Hume   3,241. 5. 2

1790   26,015.15. 8
Chambers & Hume   2,993. 7. 8

1791   16,068.16. 6
Chambers & Hume   2,402.18. 7

1792   30,647. 9. 0
Chambers & Hume   1,049.15. 9

1793   14,479. 6.11
Chambers & Hume   3,003.15.11

1794   12,533.19. 8
Chambers & Hume   2,009. 1. 9

1795   12,016.17. 3
Chambers & Hume   13,148.13. 8

1796
Account closed on Chambers's death in
March, at £1807.19.1, examined by
executors, Collins, Robert Brown,
and George Andrews.
Chambers & Hume account   2,543. 5.10

Appendix IV

The Whitton Inventory (Royal Academy of Arts)

Valuation and Inventory of Effects at Whitton Place 30 December 1790

This valuation was probably made when Chambers sub-leased Whitton back to the Gostling family, or anticipated doing so, for after 1793 he seems not to have resided in the country. Only an abstract of the works of art is given here, for the furnishings are mostly described in the sale of 20–22 June 1796 (cf. Appendix V).

	£ s. d.
MY STUDY	
Shells & fossils value abt	150
An inlaid box by Boule	21
Ten boxes of Select antique Gems cost at Rome — duty framing & beside abt 800	21
5 Drawing framed Boucher, Blanchet, and Brown	5. 5. 0
LIBRARY	
A Medallion of Homer & frame	3.13. 6
A hymen Baccio Bandinelli & stand	6. 6. 0
5 Drawings Blanchet framed	10.10. 0
6 Do Cipriani Do	42.10. 0
4 Do Parmegiano Do	12.12. 0
6 Ant Statues Pecheux Do	18.18. 0
1 head by Boucher Do	2. 2. 0
2 Piranesi very Scarce	12.12. 0
1 Paul Sandby	6. 6. 0
1 S W Chambers Finit Cleriss	10.10. 0
1 Reisbrack	2. 2. 0
1 Doyen 6.6 One Pajou 8.8	14.14. 0
2 Painted Medici ant. Vase de Witt frame	8. 8. 0
1 Dewaillie 5.5. One Legay 5.5.	10.10. 0
1 Drawg Polidor Carravaggio	6. 6. 0
1 Rubens design for a picture in the Kings Possession by Jordans	5. 5. 0
2 Flower pieces Miss Moser	20. 0. 0
SALOON	
2 Medaillon Mason my daughter	12.12. 0
2 large Pictures Pietro Genose	52.10. 0
4 Muses by Lebrun	60.00. 0
LADYS ANTIROOM	
Migniard Picture Mars & Venus	6.16. 0
5 Picrs Catton Cradock houghton	31.10. 0
Falstaff by Hayman	10.10. 0
A horse Vandermeulen	2. 2. 0
A landscape Gainsborough	6. 6. 0
LEFT WING LADYS DRESSING ROOM	
3 Muses Le Brun	47.10. 0
2 Portraits Collins & Self (Von Breda)	21.00. 0

2 fruit Pieces vanheusen	10.10 0.
1 landscape Gainsborough	5. 5. 0
LEFT WING LADYS BEDROOM	
A portrait My son M Moser	3. 0. 0
LITTLE PARLOR	
2 Muses by Le Brun	31.10. 0
NURSERY	
A sea piece Brooking	2. 2. 0
ROOM ABOVE MY STUDY	
A picture fishes 2.2. A Do Brooking 1.1.	3. 3. 0
LUMBER ROOM UNDER LITTLE PARLR	
4 Keystone models Wilton	4. 4. 0

The total valuation at this time came to £2154.19.6. At the sale in 1796, minus certain personal effects, the contents fetched £1444.4.0.

Appendix V

Sale 20-22 June 1796

'A Catalogue Of All The Elegant Household Furniture, Capital Collection of Pictures, Drawings, and Prints', Christie, An abstract of the sale of 20 June 1796 'and Two following Days'.

NO.I ATTICS IN THE CENTRE OF THE HOUSE

Lots

1–7   Turkey and Wilton carpets, chimney glasses

NO.II THREE ROOMS, NORTH FRONT

8–20   Four-post bedstead, pier-glass, gilt frames

NO.III BED CHAMBERS AND DRESSING ROOMS, NORTH FRONT, TWO PAIR

21–27   Miscellaneous furnishing

NO.IV DINING ROOM

28   'A forty-inch cast iron Bath stove, fret fender and fire irons'

29   Window curtains, striped cotton, lined and fringed 'in the Venetian drapery taste', for three windows.

30   'One excellent oval two-flap mahogany dining table, with 6 turned legs, 5 feet 8 long by 4 feet 11 wide.'

31   'A Cross-banded circular mahogany side table, with cisterns, cellerets, drawers, &c. 6 feet 6 inches long'

32   'Twelve mahogany chairs with loose sattin horse-hair seats'

33   'A Wilton carpet 16 feet by 10 feet 6, and baize cover to ditto'

34   'An oval mahogany winde cistern and an oval pier glass 22½ inches by 31, in a partly-gilt frame'

35   'A large square mahogany two-flap dining table'

36   A ditto

37   'Celleret lined with lead, and cupboards underneath, and a carved and gilt two-light girandole'

NO.V BREAKFAST PARLOUR

38   Bath stove

39   French arm-chairs

40   Dining table, Venetian window curtains, a sopha

41   Turkey carpet

42   Pembroke table, pole screens, and 10 chimney ornaments

43   'Trou madame table'

NO.VI LADY CHAMBERS'S DRESSING ROOM

44   Festoon window curtains

45   'Square pier glasses . . gilt frames with medallions and husk ornaments'

46   'A pair of beautiful solid Sienna commode-shape pier tables, on carved bracket frames'

47   'A beautiful inlaid circular-front sattin-wood ditto with leather cover'

48   'A pair of singularly elegant bottles of the fine old olive-coloured Japan with coloured embossed flowers and a pair of old coloured Japan dishes to ditto'

49   Japan jars

50   Enamelled garden cistern

51   'old blue and white ditto'

52   Wilton carpet

53   Six beech chairs

54   'A most beautiful jaspar pier table, commode front, 5 feet long, on an elegant carved and painted plynth'

55   'An elegant bronzed urn in imitation of the verda antique, mounted in ormolu and branches to ditto'

56   'A pair of mahogany pyramid China cases glazed, mounted on frames'

57   'A superb Pagoda of 7 stories, of the fine old blue and white Nankin porcelaine, enriched with gilding, beads'

58   'Imaged enamelled eggshell jars', Two Etruscan vases

59   Scalloped bowl etc

60   Open work fruit basket etc

61   'A very capital group of 4 figures, beautifully painted'

62   Japan bowl etc

NO.VII LADY CHAMBERS'S SITTING ROOM

63   Bath stove

64   Oval chimney glass with ornaments, and a mahogany Pembroke table with drawer

65   Pair of two branch girandoles with figures

66   Festoon window curtains

67   Mahogany sopha, two arm chairs

68   Pair of card tables and pole screens

69   Two flap dining table

70   Mahogany bureau

71   Six beech chairs

72   Turkey carpet

End of Day 1

June 21, 1796

NO.XVI 'CAPITAL PICTURES, DRAWINGS
AND PRINTS, CURIOUS MARBLE
SARCOPHAGUS, URNS, BUSTOS'

1   'Eleven frames & impressions in sulphur, from antique gems'
2   'Eight frames of portrait prints of eminent French and English artists'
3   Four French aquatints
4   'Seven imitation of chalks from Bouchet and Guerchino'
5   'Two frames with ditto, and two small ditto'
6   'Four aquatint landscapes, and 2 humerous by Rowlandson'
7   'A pair in colours, the smugglers'
8   'Two heads by Bartalozzi from Angelica, and 1 in mezzotinto'
9   'Six portraits of French nobility in court dress'
10   'Three, Lord Thurlow, Lord Heathfield and Mr Pitt, fine impressions by Bartalozzi'
11   'A pair of alabaster vases'
12   'A bronze bust of a young Bacchus, and a curious carving in ivory'

IN THE LIBRARY

13   'Six drawings from antique statues in chalks, very highly finished'
14   'A frame with 2 heads, drawings by Bouchet, and 1 ditto of a ram'
15   'Five imitations of chalks, after Bouchet'

16   'Two pen drawings by Piranesi, and 1 the fall of the giants by Cipriani'
17   'A fountain and 3 other drawings in chalks'
18   'Four drawings, Parmegiano, and 4 grotesque heads'
19   'Two boquets of flowers by M Moser'
20   'A circular enamel, the Rape of the Sabines, from Raphael, a curious marble vase and 2 lionesses of Wedgewood's Etruscan ware.
21   'Two antique vases painted in oil colours, and 2 ditto in red chalk'
22   'Two drawings, a bachanalian scene, and 1 of Herodias by Doyren'
23   'Four prints in colours from Bouchet and Rogers, and 2 drawings by Rysbrack, &c'
24   'A high-finished drawing in chalks of the battle of the Centaurs, and 3 others'
25   'A high-finished drawing by Sandby, and 1 of ruins by Robert'
26   'A carved marble vase and cover, and a small whole-length statue of Hymen from the antique'

IN THE SALOON

27   'Our Saviour with his Disciples at Emaus, very capital. P. Genoese'
28   The companion, one of the Acts of Mercy, equally capital. Ditto
29   A pair, emblematic of music &c. Mignard
30   Ditto, ditto
31   'A capital bronze bust of Seneca on a marble plinth'
32   'A ditto of Socrates'
33   'A pair of tritons with candelabras'
34   'A pair of ditto of Wedgewood's manufactory'
35   'A pair of painted plaster vases and covers'

IN LADY CHAMBERS'S DRESSING ROOM

36   'Mars and Venus with nymphs and satyrs, emblematical . . . Italian'
37   'A pair of emblematical door pieces ditto'
38   'Ditto, domestic poultry Castiglione'
39   'One, a lion's den Caton'
40   'One of water fowls, a sea piece, a horse and mezzotint of Sir John Fielding'
41   'A small upright landscape. Gainsborough'
42   'One of Falstaff's humerous scenes. Hayman'
43   'One of still life, lobsters, oysters, &c. Haughton'

IN THE SITTING ROOM, ADJOINING

44   'A pair, emblematical of the muses. Mignard'
45   'One ditto. Ditto'
46   'A pair, festoons of fruit and flowers, door pieces. Van Zon'
47   'Six circles, prints in red, by Ryland, and a bust of Queen Anne, in ivory'
48   'A pair, the gambling and gipsy fortune-tellers'
49   'A small landscape and figures in oil colours Gainsborough'

IN THE BREAKFAST ROOM

50 'Two of the Muses Mignard'
51–54 Engravings etc. 'their present Majesties in wax'

IN THE DINING ROOM

55 Fruit and still life Van Utrecht
56–62 Prints by Hogarth

IN THE HOUSEKEEPER'S ROOM

63 Live fowls by 'Hondikeeter' and one of fish
64 Three portraits

IN THE HALL AND STAIRCASE

65 A pair of antique marble urns
66 'Oval marble busto on a pedestal, supporting an antique marble head'
67 'Four capitals carved in wood and artificial stone'
68 'Pair of antique marble sarcophagus'
69 'One ditto supporting an urn, in artificial stone'
70 'A pair of sarcophagus, marble, antique'
71 'A pair of war trophies, models in terra cotta'
72 'A head of the younger Brutus, Grecian marble antique'
73 'A busto of the Vestal Claudia, from the antique'
74 'A ditto of Adonis'
75 'An antique monument comprised of marble, supporting a Grecian urn of fine sculpture'
76 The shaft of a column with its base, comprised of statuary and dove-coloured marble'
77 'A pair of Ionic stone capitals and a painted plaster bust'
78 'Four marble heads in frames'

ON THE LAWN AND SHRUBBERY AND IN THE MAUSOLEUM

79 'A representation of a fountain, comprising a pillar with its pedestal, an urn, and a group of dolphins in various marbles'
79+ stone vase and pedestal
80 Garden seat etc.
81 Carved stone vases and pedestals
82 Lead figure of Mercury
83–97 Includes vases and marble medallions: 'A marble medallion of Mr Gibbs, one of Sir Christopher Wren, and one of Michel Angelo Buonarotti'; 'Couchant Venus', marble sarcophagus

MAUSOLEUM

98 Fifteen stools

POULTRY YARD

99–101

GREEN HOUSE

102–112 Orange trees and lemon trees

PLEASURE GROUND

113–116

End Second Day

22 June 1796

East Wing

NO.XVII UPPER FLOOR

1–12

NO.XVIII HOUSEKEEPER'S ROOM

13–18

Third floor, centre of the house

NO.XIX TWO ROOMS, SOUTH FRONT

19–29

NO.XX BED CHAMBERS AND DRESSING ROOMS, NORTH FRONT, TWO PAIR

30–35+

NO.XXI SALOON

36–51 Includes: 38, Wilton carpet. 40, 'Twelve India Cane Bamboo chairs'. 41. 'a ditto sopha', 42. 'ditto', 43. 'Six ditto stools'. 44. 'A pair brilliant pier glasses in two plates . . . in neat carved frames and gilt frames, with medallion head ornaments', 45. 'Mahogany pier tables on carved and painted frames', 46. 'Pair needlework fire screens, rich carved and gilt frames, on pillars and claws', 47. 'A pair of elegant large enamelled China cisterns on carved and painted tripods', 51. 'A fine-toned double-keyed harpsichord by Jacobus Kirkman 1773, in a mahogany case'

NO.XXII LIBRARY

52 Register stove
53 Wilton carpet
54 'A japanned pier table with folding wire doors, the top comprised of various specimens of spar'
55 Mahogany card tables
56 Pembroke table
57–59 includes: 'barometer & thermometer by Gatty'

NO.XXIII STUDY AND CLOSET ADJOINING

60–72 includes: 66. 'bureau & bookcase with Chinese glazed doors and green silk curtains', 67. 'A pair neat japanned cabinets with Chinese glazed doors, containing an extensive Collection of Scarce Curious Shells, Minerals and Fossils, Scientifically arranged', 68. 'An elegant Parisian cabinet composed of ebony, inlaid with brass and tutenague, and richly mounted in ormolu'

Lots 73–111 comprise Numbers XXIV–XXXIX: Wash House, Laundry, Pantry, Lumber room, Dairy (with Gothic stools and table), Cellars, Larder, Hog Yard, Kitchen garden, Coach house, stables, loft, carpenters' shop, and timber, including 'pair of capital wrought iron gates'

Total of the sale: £1444.4.0

Note: This inventory includes some of the items purchased by Chambers from the sale of the Matthew Nulty and Lord Melcombe Collections, Christie and Ansell, 27–28 March 1783:

Lots 53 'A ditto (antique marble vase) Piombeno marble, snake handles and foliage...£13.2.6'; 57 'A small ditto (Cinerary urn) with boys holding a festoon of flowers...£4'; 60 'Two medallions, marble, Lucius Verus and the elder Faustina £3'; 66 'The pedestal to ditto (a statue of Baccante), fluted grey marble £8.8'; 74 'A bust of Commodus £4'; 81 'An antique urn £1.11'; 82 'A ditto £1.11.6'; 83 'A ditto richly ornamented £4'; 85 'A ditto group of Dolphins 11s'; 90 'Two ditto (vase) fluted £3.3'; 91 'A very fine slab of petrified Turtle £2.10'; 100 'A ditto £1.10'; 105 'A capital figure of a sleeping Venus, large life £1.3'; *Second day's sale:* 91–92 'A fine Pavonazza marble, ornamented with water leaves, flat handles and open top to receive flowers, &c (and) ditto its companion £8.8'; 74 'A large Cinerary urn, with ram's heads, festoons of flowers and medusa's head in front £9.9'; 79 'An antient sepulchrale monument composed of various pieces of antiquity, put together under the direction of Cav, G.B. Piranesi £28.7'; 81 'Two medallions, Homer and Faustina ditto £3.3'; 82 'Two ditto, Seneca and Plotina ditto £3.5'; 90–93 'A ditto (bust) in alto relievo of a nobleman by ditto (Rysbrack)', 'ditto by ditto', 'ditto by ditto', 'ditto of a lady by ditto', the four lots £5.5s

A Catalogue of A Valuable Library of History, Antiquities, Architecture, &c. Late the Property of Sir William Chambers . . . Christie July 16th & 18th, 1796. A selection from 235 lots, amplified with bibliographical additions and alphabetised.

Chambers's library was certainly more extensive than this list indicates. For example, there are no books on the theory of gardening, no D'Attiret, Le Blond, or Langley. Contributions to the philosophy and theory of art are noticeably lacking, for one would have expected to find Burke *On the Sublime & Beautiful.* Obvious omissions among the architectural books are J. F. Blondel's *Cours,* an edition of Alberti or Serlio, Laugier's *Observations,* Ware's *Complete Body of Architecture,* and volumes four and five of *Vitruvius Britannicus.* It is also surprising that he may not have possessed his friend, Le Roy's *Grèce;* but not so surprising that the *Ionian Antiquities* is absent. Probably many of Chambers's books were in his office at his death, and were therefore taken by assistants, such as Brown or Yenn. A good many must also have remained in Norton Street, to be disposed of when Lady Chambers died.

ADAM, R. *Ruins of the Palace of the Emperor Diocletian at Spalatro,* London 1764.

ARGENVILLE, A. N. D. *Vie des plus fameux architectes . . . ,* 2 vols., Paris 1787.

BARBAULT, J. *Les Plus beaux monuments de Rome ancienne,* Rome 1761.

BARRY, J. *An Inquiry into the real and Imaginary obstructions to the acquisition of the Arts in England,* London 1775.

BARTOLI, P. S. *Gli Antichi sepolchri,* Rome 1697.

BARTOLI, P. *Admiranda Romanarum antiquitatum,* Rome 1693.

BELLORI, G. B. *Le Antiche Lucerne,* Rome 1691; *Gli Antichi Sepolchri,* Rome 1697; *Columna Antoniniana,* Rome 1672; *Colonna Trajana,* Rome, n.d.

BELIDOR, B. F. DE. *Architecture Hydraulique,* 4 vols., Paris 1737–53; *Nouveau Cours de Mathematiques,* Paris 1725; *La Science des ingenieurs,* Paris 1729.

BENTHAM, J. *The History and Antiquities of . . . Ely,* Cambs 1771.

BLOEMART, A. *Principes et Etudes de dessin,* Amsterdam 1740.

BLONDEL, F. *Cours d'Architecture,* 2 vols., Paris 1675–83 (now in Sir John Soane's Museum); *Résolution des quatre principaux problèmes d'Architecture,* Paris 1673.

BLONDEL, J. F. *De La Distribution Des Maisons De Plaisance.*

BRETTINGHAM, M. *The Plans . . . of Holkham,* London 1773.

BURLINGTON, LORD. *Fabbriche Antiche disegnate da Andrea Palladio Vicentino,* London 1730.

CAMERON, C. *The Baths of the Romans Explained . . . ,* London 1772.

CAMPBELL, C. *Vitruvius Britannicus,* 3 vols., London 1715–25 (now in Sir John Soane's Museum).

CAYLUS, A. C. P. COMTE DE *Receuil D'Antiquités Égyptiennes, Étrusques, Grecques et Romaines,* 7 vols., Paris 1752–67.

CLAVERING, R. *An Essay on the construction and building of Chimneys,* London 1779.

CLÉRISSEAU, C. L. *Antiquités de la France . . . ,* Paris 1778.

DAHLBERG, E. *Suecia antiqua et hodierna,* 2 vols., Stockholm 1693–1714.

D'AVILER, A. C. *Cours d'Architecture qui comprehend les Ordres de Vignole,* 2 vols., Paris 1720.

DE LA FORCE. *Description de Paris,* 8 vols., Paris 1742.

DE LA ROCHE, P. *An Essay on the Orders of Architecture . . . ,* London 1769.

DE LA RUE, J. B. *Traité de la coupe des pierres . . . ,* Paris 1728.

DÉLICES DE LA FRANCE 2 vols., Paris 1699.

DÉLICES DE L'ITALIE (by Rogissant) 4 vols., Paris 1707.

DE L'ORME, P. *Le premier tome de l'Architecture,* Paris 1567.

DERAND, F. *L'Architecture Des Voutes,* Paris 1643.

Description de Versailles, Paris 1717.

DESGODETZ, A. *Les Edifices antiques de Rome,* Paris 1682; *The Ancient Buildings of Rome . . . , Volume the First,* London 1771.

DU HALDE, J. B. *The General History of China,* London 1738.

DUMONT, G. M. *Recueil de plusieurs parties d'Architecture De Differents Maitres,* 2 vols., Paris 1768.

EMLYN, H. *A Proposition for a New Order of Architecture,* London 1781.

FICORINI, F. DE. *Le Maschere sceniche, e le Figure comiche d'antiche Romani,* Rome 1736.

FONTANA, C. *L'Anfiteatro Flavio Descritto . . .* , The Hague 1725.

FREART, L. *Parallèle De L'Architecture Antique Et De La Moderne*, Paris 1702 (now in Soane Museum).

GIBBS, J. *Bibliotheca Radcliviana*, London 1747.

GOGUET, A. Y. *De L'Origine de Loixs des Arts et des Sciences*, 6 vols., Paris 1759.

GONDOIN, M. *Description des écoles des chirugiens*, Paris 1780.

GWYNN, J. *London & Westminster Improved*, London 1766.

HALES, S. *A Description of Ventilators*, London 1743.

HAWNEY, W. *The Compleat Measurer*, London 1717.

HOWARD, J. *An Account of the Principal Lazarettos in Europe*, Warrington 1789; *The State of the Prisons in England & Wales*, Warrington 1777.

HUTCHESON, F. *An Inquiry into the origin of our ideas of Beauty and Virtue*, London 1726.

KENT, W. *Designs of Inigo Jones*, London 1728.

KIRBY, J. *Dr Brooks Taylor's Method of Perspective*, 2 vols., Ipswich 1755; *The Perspective of Architecture*, 2 vols., London 1761.

KIRCHER, A. *Arca Noe . . .* , Amsterdam 1675; *Turris Babel . . .* , Amsterdam 1679.

LAIRESSE, G. DE. *Les principes du Dessein*, Amsterdam 1719.

LAUGIER, L'ABBÉ, M. A. *Essai sur l'Architecture*, Paris 1755.

LEBRUN, C. *Méthod pour apprendre à dessiner les Passions*, Amsterdam 1702.

LE CLERC, S. *Traité D'Architecture*, 2 vols., Paris 1714.

MAJOR, T. *The Ruins of Paestum*, London 1768.

MALIE, T. *A New and Accurate method of Delineating All The Parts of the Different Orders of Architecture*, London 1737.

MAROT, D. *Oeuvres*, Amsterdam 1712.

MAWE, T. *The Gardener's Pocket Dictionary*, 2 vols., London 1786; *The Universal Gardener's Kalendar*, London 1789.

MILIZIA, F. *Le Vite de piu celebri architteti*, Rome 1768.

MITELLI, A. *Freggi Dell'Architettura*, Bologna 1645.

MONTANO, G. B. *Il Cinque Libri di Architettura*, Rome 1691.

MONTFAUCON, B. DE. *L'Antiquité Expliqué*, 15 vols., Paris 1724.

ORLANDI, P. A. *L'Abcedario Pittorico*, Venice 1753.

PAINE, J. *Plans . . . of the Mansion House at Doncaster*, London 1751; *Plans . . . of Noblemen and Gentlemen's Houses . . .* , vol.I, 1767.

PALLADIO, A. *I Quattro Libi Dell'Architettura*, Venice 1570; *I Quattro Libri Dell'Architettura*, Venice 1581.

PANVINIUS, O. *Antiquitatum Veronensium*, Padua 1648; *De Ludis Circensibus*, Padua 1642.

PATTE, P. *Mémoires sur les objets Les Plus Importans De L'Architecture*, Paris 1769.

PAUSANIAS. *Voyage Historique de la Grèce*, traduit par l'Abbé Gedoyn, 2 vols., Paris 1731.

PEYRE, M. J. *Oeuvres d'Architecture*, Paris 1765.

PILKINGTON, M. *The Gentlemen's and Connoisseurs' Dictionary of Painters*, London 1770.

PIRANESI, G. B. *Le Antichità Romane*, 4 vols., Rome 1756; *Della magnificenza de' Romani*, 2 vols., Rome 1761; *Diverse Maniere d'Adornare I Cammini*, Rome 1769; *Le Vedute di Roma*, Rome 1745–78.

PLINY. *Natural Historie of the World*, 2 vols., London 1601.

POTE, J. *The History and Antiquities of Windsor Castle*, London 1749–62.

POZZO, A. *Perspectiva Pictorum Et Architectorum*, 2 vols., Rome 1693–1700.

PRICE, F. *Salisbury Cathedral*, London 1753.

RAPHAEL, SANZO DA URBINO. *Loggie di Rafaele nel Vaticano*, 3 parts, Rome 1772–7.

RAWLINS, T. *Familiar Architecture*, London 1768.

Recueil des Maisons Royales, Paris n.d.

REVETT, N. *Ionian Antiquities*, London 1759.

REYNOLDS, SIR J. *Discourses*, London 1769–90.

RICHARDSON, G. *A Book of Ornamental Ceilings*, London 1776; *Iconology*, 2 vols., London 1779–90; *Treatise on the Five Orders of Architecture*, London 1787.

Roma Antica e Moderna, 3 vols., Rome 1750.

ROSSI, D. *Studio D'Architettura Civile*, 2 vols., Rome 1702–11.

RUBENS, P. P. *Palazzi di Genova*, Antwerp 1622.

RUGGIERI, F. *Scelta Di Architetture*, 4 vols., Florence 1755 (now in Soane Museum).

SCAMOZZI, V. *L'Idea Dell Architettura Universale*, Venice 1615; *Oeuvres D'Architecture*, The Hague 1736 (now in Soane Museum).

SGRILLI, B. S. *Descrizione . . . Di S. Maria Del Fiore*, Florence 1733.

SOANE, SIR JOHN. *Plans Elevations and Sections of Buildings . . .* , London 1788.

STUART, J. & REVETT, N. *The Antiquities of Athens*, vol.I, London 1762.

TOPHAM, J. *Account of the Collegiate Chapel of St Stephen, Westminster*, London 1795.

VARDY, J. *Some Designs of Mr Inigo Jones and Mr William Kent*, London 1744.

VITRUVIUS. *I Dieci Libri Dell'Architettura . . .* tradotti e commentari da Mons. Daniel Barbaro, Venice 1567; *Les Dix Livres d'Architecture* (Perrault), Paris 1684.

WALPOLE, H. *Aedes Walpolianae*, London 1760; *Anecdotes of Painting in England*, 5 vols., London 1762–71.

WATELET, C. H. *Essai sur les Jardins*, Paris 1774.

WILLETT, R. *A Description of the Library at Merly*, London 1785.

WOOD, J. *The Origins of Building*, Bath 1741.

WOOD, R. *The Ruins of Balbec*, London 1757; *The Ruins of Palmyra*, London 1753.

ZABAGLIA, N. *Castelli e ponti*, Rome 1743.

Sale 6 April 1799

A Catalogue of the Valuable Collection of Italian, French, Flemish, & Dutch Pictures, and Some of the English School, The Property of the Late Sir William Chambers, Dec. Together with some Valuable Drawings and Fine Prints . . . Christie. Saturday, April 6, 1799.

PRINTS AND DRAWINGS FRAMED AND GLAZED

1   A Chinese painting on glass, and 2 of birds

2   A pair of Chinese paintings (views on a river) on looking glass

3   The rake's progress 8, and the midnight conversation, Hogarth

5   Six from Claude, S. Rosa, and Both, by Brown, &c

6   The Niobe, by Woollett, and 2 from P. D. Cortona by Strange & a pair of Circles by Ryland

7   Twenty-three of the Luxembourg Gallery

8   A pair, death of General Wolfe, and Penn's treaty with the Indians

9   Two drawings of architecture

PICTURES

12   A flower piece, and an old portrait

13   Two bas-reliefs, spring and autumn, from Cipriani

14   Three ditto, from ditto

15   Monamy. A sea piece

20   Wilson. A view of the lake of Nemi, after

21   Six drawings, different orders of the French nobility

22   Four frames with prints in imitation of drawings

23   Portrait of a gentleman half length

29   Marieschi. A view in Venice

35   Cipriani. Portraits of Palladio and M. Angelo, in bas relief, and an entablature ditto

37   Italian. A pair of slips for door piece

38   Garvey. A distant view of Rome

39   V. Bloemen. A landscape with cattle

40   Paton. A high-finished sea piece with shipping, a moonlight

41   Brooking. A brisk gale

61   Rosa de Tivoli. Goats

62   Mola. A landscape and storm

65   Heemskerk. A pair of small Dutch topers

68   Spagnoletto. Portrait of Michael Angelo

69   Vlugels. The miraculous draught of fishes

71   Gainsborough. A landscape with a cottage, and asses

74   Cuyp. A man holding a white horse

75   Brooking. A sea piece, a storm

78   Borgognone. A pair of battlepieces

79   Wilson. A view near Rome

80   Barrett. A view in Wales with figures, a very beautiful and high finished picture

82   Brooking. An oval sea piece, a storm, very fine

84   Spagnoletto. Lot and his daughters, an upright oval

85   Luccatelli. A landscape with ruins, and banditti

90   Di Giannizza. Battle piece

91   Ruysdael. Sea piece

93   Gainsborough. A small high finished landscape with a corn field

95   Bamboccio. Landscape with cattle watering

96   Ferg. A pair of high finished landscapes and figures

97   Marlow. A view of London with St Magnus church, and part of London Bridge

98   Le Brun. Holy Family with Angels

99   V. der Neer. A frost piece, a view in Holland

100   Eglon V. der Neer. Danae in the golden shower

102   Marlow. A view of the Welsh bridge at Shrewsbury

103   V. de Velde. A small sea piece very beautiful

104   Blout. Beggermen, a pair

105   Teniers. Boors regaling in a cabaret

106   Domenichio. Drawing the thorn from Venus's foot, a grand composition

107   Le Brun. The Nine Muses, very capital, and well known picture of the Master, cost the late Sir William Chambers 200 guineas in Paris.

Missing lots are those belonging to other owners. Thomas Collins bought Lots 13, 39, 61, 74. Price bought 106 (£7) and 107 (£27). Lot 79 is probably the *Ariccia* in Mr Brinsley Ford's Collection, bought by Benjamin Booth.

Appendix VIII

Sale 6 June 1811

Despite the existence of several thousand drawings and designs by Chambers, out of sixty-three lots offered for sale only thirteen can definitely be traced to public or private collections. The v & A has lots 44, 65, or 66 and part of 101; the RIBA has 80, part of 96 and probably 103; the Soane has 48, part of 69, 70, 77, 83, 90, part of 104, 106; the Avery Library and the Metropolitan Museum probably share 51; and the Mellon Collection has one of 104. It is interesting to see that Soane did not buy the Somerset House drawings (106) at the sale, but only later and probably from Townly who paid the then large sum of £52 10s 0d for the collection.

A Catalogue of the Genuine and Valuable Prints and Drawings, of that Eminent Architect, The late Sir William Chambers, F.R.S. . . . etc. Christie. Thursday June 6, 1811.

PRINTS

1 Thirty-six views by Paul Sandby
2 Eighteen Views of Churches and Crosses
3 Two Portraits of Erskine and Fox
4 Ten topographical by Jukes, &c
5 Willmin Collection des Antiquities Etrusques
6 Two Portraits, Vandyke and Sir J. Reynolds
7 Two, Sir F. Reynolds and Dr Johnson
8 Fifteen Sir W. Chambers
9 Nineteen views of Oxford and Cambridge by Rooker
10 Twenty-eight large views of Greece and Italy by P. Sandby
11 Two Hogarth's Analysis of Beauty. first impression
12 Eight by Hogarth, Rake's Progress
13 Eleven Portraits, various
14 Twenty-one large Views in and about London
15 Twenty-eight various
16 Four Portraits by Wille. &c
17 Seven by Bartalozzi, Funeral Ticket of Sir Joshua Reynold, &c
18 Eighteen Foreign Prints
19 Gardner's Views on the Rhine, 8 nos
20 Gessner's Military Evolutions
21 Six Piranesi's Vases, &c and large View of the Vatican Gallery, coloured

22 Eight Blondel's Views in Churches, and eight others
23 Eight, fine, by Chambers
24 Wood's Plan and Description of Bath, and Willet's Description of Merly Library
25 Two, Woolet, Battles of La Hogue and the Boyne
26 One, Death of Lord Chatham, and Key
27 St Paul's Church on the Thanksgiving 1706/1760/; ditto in 1789, and sundry plans, illustrations
28 Two, Portraits, the King and Sir J. Banks illumination
29 Twenty-four, fine, relative to Bridges
30 Twelve, Section of St. Paul's, Interior of St Stephen's Walbrook, and Elevations. &c of St Peter's at Rome
31 Ten, Sir W. Chambers' Ornament
32 Ten Ceilings of the Barberini Palace
33 Town House of Amsterdam, with Letter-press and Views and Plans of Solomon's Temple
34 Hodges Views, large Plan of the Thames, a View of London, and sundry others
35 Twenty-six views of Cathedrals and Tower of Mecklenburgh by Hollar

ANTIQUARIAN PRINTS, *fine impressions*

36 Vertue, Nine Historical Prints, with letterpress
37 Three Historical Prints from Pictures at Cowdray
38 Encampment of Henry VIII at Portsmouth
39 Embarkation of Henry VIII at Dover
40 Procession of King Edward VI
41 Vetustae Monumenta, part of vol.2 & 3
42 London temp Queen Elizabeth, 8 Sheets, and various Plans of London, &c
43 Charles I and his Queen, Durham Cathedral, and 20 others various

DRAWINGS

44 A Portfolio with a large quantity of Italian Architectural Studies
45 A Portfolio with sundry Drawings
46 Portfolio containing sundry Drawings
47 Parcel of Gothic Ornaments for Churches &c
48 Designs in chalk
49 Portfolio of Sundry Studies
50 A Set of Roses, &c
51 A Portfolio containing forty-six Chimney Pieces
52 Parcel of French Architectural Studies

53 English Architecture, Plans of Windsor, Kew, Noblemen's Seats &c

53+ Ditto, Brewhouses, machines, &c

54 Portfolio with a quantity of Architectural Drawings

55 Original Design for Oriental Architecture

56 Nineteen various, Elevations, &c

57 Twelve Emblematical Designs for Rivers, and sixteen masters

58 A small sketch by Hollar, and eleven old masters

59 Twelve views by Gainsborough

60 Costume of the Swedish Orders of Nobility and Twelve various

61 One by Rysbrack, and one of Turkish Costume

62 Twenty-five Chinese Buildings

62+ Twenty Chinese Costume

63 A Portfolio

64 Twenty-eight Ceilings, beautifully coloured

65 Thirty-three ditto, ditto

66 Fourteen ditto, various

67 Three very beautiful and highly finished Ceilings at Woburn Abbey

68 Eleven very beautiful Ceilings of Melbourne House, highly finished

69 Ten, Elevation and Plans of Melbourne House

70 Four, Fontana di Trevi, a Casino, and Park Gate

71 Six fine by Parmegiano, Champagne &c

72 Three, Volte di Pozzuolo, and Bagni di Livia

73 Seven by Piranesi, Le Pautre &c

74 Three by Petitot, &c

75 Five by various masters

76 Sixteen, Porticos and Gates

77 Five, Mausoleums

78 Thirteen, Temples in Kew Gardens

79 Five, Temples

80 Five, Triumphal Arch at Wilton, &c

81 One, very fine, by Cipriani

82 Two ditto, the Design for the vignettes to Sir W. Chambers on Oriental Gardening

83 Two, Ornaments by Cipriani

84 One, Ditto by Ditto

85 Three, Ditto, containing 12 designs for statues

86 Ten, Ditto

87 One, Lady Montroth's Monument by Cipriani

88 One, Lady Milton's Monument by Cipriani

89+ Six Ornaments, the figures by Cipriani

89 Twenty-one, Ornamental Architecture

90 Four Designs for a new Church for St Mary-le-bone, by Sir W. Chambers, the figures by Cipriani and 3 plans

91 Seven, of Churches, &c

92 Fifteen, Lord Charlemont's House

93 Thirteen, Mr Michell's House, Sir J. Reynold's House and various

94 Six, Town Hall at Woodstock, Woburn Bridge, and Astridge, D. of Bridgewater's and 2, Blenheim Park Gates

95 Five, Richmond Lodge, Richmond Park

96 Eight, Roehampton, York House, &c

97 Eleven, York House, Goodwood, M. of Abercorn's and Lord Gower's Staircase

98 Two designs, Duddingstone House and Stables

99 Seven, Milton Abbey

100 Three, Schwatz Palace, Gothenburg Fish Market, and 1 other

101 Large Elevation of a Palace, the Dome de Starof, Dioclesian's Baths, and others

102 Elevation of a Royal Palace

103 Four Designs for a Palace at Richmond

104 Three large Views of Somerset House by Despres

104+ Four ditto, Interior of the Royal Academy, by ditto

105 Three large Elevations of the Bridge intended for Somerset House

106 Two large Portfolios, containing 33 very beautiful and highly finished . . . of Somerset House, by Sir William Chambers, the figures by Cipriani, together with all the Original Plans, Sections, smaller Elevations, &c. belonging to the Building. the Drawing of the Interior and Exterior decorations, with Manuscript observations on various parts of the Work, calculations of Values, Time, &c. the whole forming a grand and interesting series of Architecture, rarely to be met with.

107 Portfolio, containing Elevation and Plans of Whitton, sundry Anatomical Figures, and curious Architectural Manuscripts

108 A large deal case and sundry portfolios

Appendix IX

Inscription for a Monument to the Memory of Sir William Chambers

Pamphlet, printed July 1796. By Philip Norris. Soane Museum, Cupboard 2, Div.XIV, Envelope No.11.

This 'Inscription' is an over enthusiastic eulogy of Chambers, attacking Adam ('Corruptions . . . sanctioned by fashion') and Soane (The Bank . . . 'In a barbarous stile . . .'). It is printed in A. T. Bolton, *The Portrait of Sir John Soane*, 1927, 63–5, where Soane's libel action against Norris is also discussed on pp.74–7.

Near this Place are deposited
The Remains of *Sir William Chambers,*
Knight of the Polar Star,
Surveyor-General of the Board of Works,
Treasurer of the Royal Academy,
And Fellow of the Royal and Antiquarian Societies:
The Title which he bore
Was conferred upon him
By *Adolphus Frederick, King of Sweden;*
The Offices which he held
Were the Gifts
Of the *Sovereign* of *Great Britain.*
He was born in the Year M,DCC,XXII,
And died on the eighth Day of March, M,DCC,XCVI,
    aged LXXIV.
As a man
Sir William Chambers was universally beloved and
    esteemed:
As an Architect,
He merits a conspicuous place
Amongst the most excellent.
His stile of Building,
Formed on the Remains of Roman Magnificence,
And the Works of the ablest Masters
Who have flourished in Italy,
Was masculine and bold,
Enriched with all the Embellishments
Which Genius, in a long succession of Ages,
Has bestowed on Utility;
And equally free
From the ungraceful Forms
And clumsy proportions,
Of Grecian Structures,
Erected before Architecture attained maturity,
And the flimsy frippery,
By which her bloated features were covered,
In the decline of the Roman Empire.
Corruptions,
Derived from these imperfect and impure Sources,
Sanctioned by Fashion,
Or a blind partiality for Antiquity,
He saw with regret
Were, in different ways,
Debasing the Majestic Character of the Arts;
And, to prevent their baneful effect,
Composed those admirable Writings
Which have spread his reputation
Through every part of the habitable Earth.
Yet he lived to behold,
In one of our Public Buildings,
The destruction of a Work
Which had extorted the praise of Strangers,
Least inclined to do justice

To the exertions of English Art,
And a Fabric erected on its Ruins,
In a barbarous stile,
Of which, though pretending to originality,
The peculiarities are borrowed
From the examples of the dark Ages,
When Sculpture,
No longer able to give the form and grace of Nature
To the objects of her imitation,
Traced their shadows upon the stone,
And sunk the surface
With skill inferior in the carving of Egyptian
    Hieroglyphicks.
Blush, Reader,
That such disgrace should befall thy Country
At the close of the Eighteenth Century,
And during the Reign of
GEORGE THE THIRD,
Whose knowledge of Architecture,
Derived from the lessons and the labours
Of *Sir William Chambers*,
Would have distinguished him among Princes,
If it had not been eclipsed
By the splendor of those Regal Virtues
Which make him the delight
Of a brave, a faithful, and an affectionate People.
But restrain thy indignation
Against this abortive Production;
Where the finger of Scorn is directed
The voice of Taste is elevated,
And so long as it is permitted to exist,
It will stand a *memento* to Innovators
THAT CHANGE IS NOT ALWAYS IMPROVEMENT,
THAT SINGULARITY IS NOT BEAUTY,
THAT AN UNPRINCIPLED PASSION FOR NOVELTY IS
NOT GENIUS;
While *Somerset-Place*,
And other Structures erected by this great Master,
And his *Treatise*
On the Decorative Part of Civil Architecture,
Shall, in Example and Precept,
Preserve to the latest Posterity,
That manly stile of Building
Which rendered the City of Rome
The Glory of the Earth.

Genealogical Tables

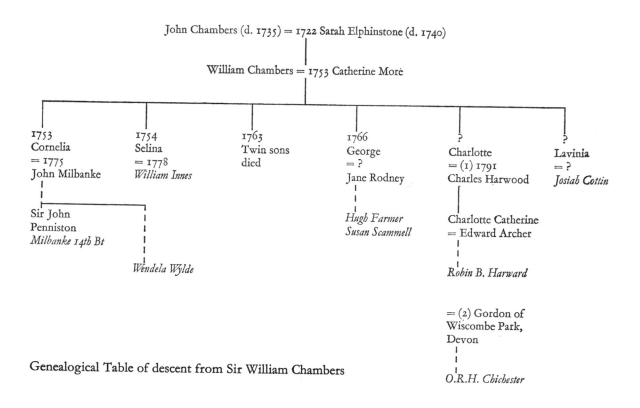

Genealogical Table of descent from Sir William Chambers

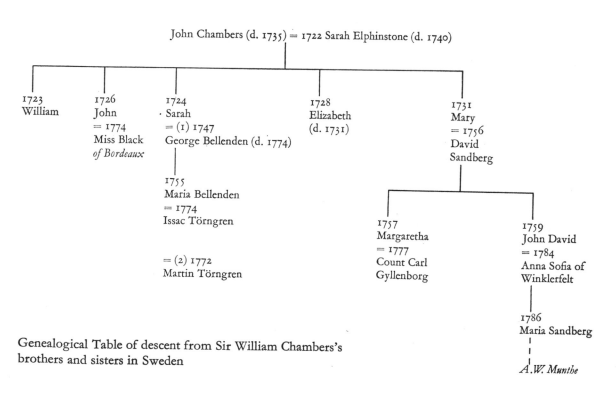

Genealogical Table of descent from Sir William Chambers's brothers and sisters in Sweden

Collections of Chambers's Correspondence

BARONSCOURT, Co Tyrone

Duddingstone correspondence, 2 Sept. 1762–Aug. 1767

BEDFORD: Bedfordshire Record Office

Bedford Papers
R. 248. Percival Beaumont to Chambers 19 Oct. 1767
R. 249. Chambers to Percival Beaumont 22 Oct. 1767
R. 798. Accounts etc 1772

Wrest Papers
10597. Chambers to Lord Grantham 13 Aug. 1773
12560. Chambers to Lord Grantham 29 April 1774

DUBLIN: Royal Irish Academy

Charlemont Papers as calendared by HMC Charlemont. Originals, however, should be consulted as calendaring is sloppy and inaccurate. Also Charlemont to Chambers 9 July 1775, and ditto undated, both about Charlemont House

FARMINGTON, Connecticut, U.S.A.: The Lewis Walpole Library

Chambers to Benjamin West 29 July 1792, and to same, undated

HOVINGHAM HALL, Yorks

Thomas Worsley's Papers
Chambers to Worsley 12 Oct. 1770, 19 Oct. 1775, 21 Oct. 1775 – all about Board of Works

LONDON: Bedford Office

BOL 13/3/4 Box 523. Chambers to Percival Beaumont 9 May 1769–16 May 1772, about Woburn and Bedford House

LONDON: British Museum

Add.MS 41133, 41134, 41135, 41136: Chambers's Letter Books (purchased Sotheby 23–26 June 1924, lot 116. In 1892 in the Collection of A. H. Heron) covering Nov. 1769 to late 1775
Add.MS 5726C, f.26. Chambers to Lord Bute 24 Dec. 1763. About gift of original drawings for Kew book (now Metropolitan Museum of Art, New York)

LONDON: India Office Library

Clive Papers. Unsorted. About Styche, Walcot and Berkeley Square

LONDON: Public Record Office

Official correspondence about Chambers and the Board of Works. *Cf.* Chapter 8

LONDON: Royal Academy

Professor Sir Albert Richardson's collection of Chambers's correspondence, ex Coll. Halnaby Hall, Yorks (Milbanke family), 1756–89; miscellaneous bills; notes for 3rd edition of *Treatise* and for lectures

LONDON: Royal Institute of British Architects

Sydney Kitson collection of Chambers's correspondence, ex Coll. Halnaby Hall, 1752–90
Henry Holland papers: Chambers to Holland 12 Sept. 1793, 25 Sept. 1793; Holland to Chambers 23 Sept. 1793. About Architects' Club and Fire prevention
Chambers to Burke 18 June 1782

LONDON: Sotheby. Sale 21 May 1968, lot 374.

Chambers to Reynolds, undated, about Reynolds's house at Richmond

SHEFFIELD: City Library

Fitzwilliam Papers
Chambers to Burke: Bk2/543, undated, about Somerset House; Bk1/115, 5 May 1782, about Board of Works; Bk1/149, 18 June 1782, about Board of Works; Bk1/285, 18 Oct. 1783, about Board of Works

STANSTEAD (Sussex)

Chambers to Earl of Bessborough, undated although after 1768

STOCKHOLM: Riksarkivet

Chambers to Count C. F. Scheffer 9 Oct. 1772, 11 June 1773, 24 Feb. 1775

STOCKHOLM: Vetenskaps Akademiens Bibliotek

Chambers to Wargentin 23 May 1768

WINDLESHAM (Surrey): Mrs Doreen Ashworth of The Paddock

Chambers to Reynolds 18 Oct. 1790 (Royal Academy matters)

WINDSOR CASTLE: Royal Library

Chambers to George III 12 March 1795 (letter of resignation from Somerset House)

The Franco-Italian Album
and the Loose Drawings of French and Italian Buildings
Victoria and Albert Museum, London

The album (accession 5172; press 93.B.21) is almost entirely devoted to those years of travel between 1749 and 1755. A few drawings of an English Palladian tour and a few sketches taken in Amsterdam and Antwerp may be the exceptions when Chambers travelled sometime between his eastern voyages during the periods 1745–8. The loose drawings are measured plans, elevations and sections, particularly details of doors and windows. The album is essentially a manual of ornamental design epitomizing Chambers's interest in decorative sculpture and embellishment, in fact, to quote from the third edition of his *Treatise*, the 'decorative part of Civil Architecture'. Although there are more than four hundred drawings or sketches in the Victoria and Albert Museum, they obviously represent but a small part of Chambers's activities during this period. For example, the loose drawings are probably the 'large quantity of Italian Architectural Studies', sold to Brown as Lot 44 at the 1811 sale, but there is no sign of the 'Parcel of French Architectural Studies' sold to Colnaghi as Lot 52. Among the loose drawings, French subjects are noticeably absent. The Museum acquired the drawings from two principal sources: C. J. Richardson's Collection, embracing those numbers between 3324 and 3435, and the dealer, E. Parsons, who sold the album in 1865 for five guineas, and over two hundred drawings (numbers in the seven thousands) in 1869 for two pounds ten shillings.

Note. Numbers refer to numerical order of drawings, or to accession numbers, not to pagination.

BELGIUM
Antwerp: 199

ENGLAND
Euston (Suffolk): 406; Highclere (Hants): 137, 416; Holkham (Norfolk): 390, 391, 392, 396, 399, 401, 402, 403, 407, 425, 426; Houghton (Norfolk): 395, 397, 405; Narford (Norfolk): 398, 400, 407, 413; Norwich Assembly Rooms: 382; Oxford Christ Church: 419, 420; Tottenham Park (Wilts): 377, 410, 412, 417; Wanstead (Essex): 389, 404, 411; Wilton: 412; Wolterton (Norfolk): 384, 408

FRANCE
Chantilly: 231, 298–303, 305–308; Maisons: 180, 228, 234; Marly: 236; Nimes: 197; PARIS: Capuchins: 119; Celestins: 192; Invalides: 264; Louvre: 61, 78, 120; Luxembourg: 128; Notre Dame de Lorette: E3274, 1934; Palais Royale: 2, 8, 9, 46, 54, 182, 226, 267, 439; Place des Victoires: 4, 5, 6, 7, 16; Pont Neuf: 196; Abbey St Germain: 50; St Sulpice: 10; Theatins: 107, 165, 213; Tuileries: 64, 91, 195, 217, 316; Versailles: 67, 80, 84, 87, 94, 95, 96, 97, 99, 100, 103, 218, 219, 451. ORNAMENTS by Saly: 13, 59, 89, 110, 232

ITALY
Caprarola: 17, 19, 23, 27, 29, 34, 35, 36, 187, 313, 317, 320, 321, and 3276; Florence: 30, 44, 104, 144, 147, 152, 193, 265, 415, 430, 492; Frascati: 145, 310, and 7074.22–24; Herculaneum: 53, and 7074.1; Rome: Capital: 3, 12, 83, 88, 93, 116, 285, 311, 324, 325, 332, 336, and 7074.26; churches: SS Apostoli: 282, 455; S. Carlo al Corso: 327; S. Ignazio: 7024.28, 7074.3, 7074.10, E. 3270; S. Luigi de' Francesi: 337; S. Maria in Campitelli: 7074.35; S. Maria del Popolo: 354, and 7074.16; SS Martina e Luca: 75; St Peter's: 163, 206, 208–214, 225, 227, 229, 233, 237, 239–240, 312, 347, and 7077.1; S. Pietro in Vincoli: 161, 162, 220–223, 241; Fontana Trevi: 155; Giardino Corsini: 193; Palaces: Altieri: 266, 270; Barberini: 45, 115, 123, 175, 271; Colonna: 85, 130; Farnese: 143, 335, 369, and E. 3268, E. 3271; Massimi: 203–204, 207, and 7074.38; Mattei: 20–22, 41, 51–52, 132, 174, 247, 290, 294, 296, 314, 371, and E. 3273, E. 3275; Spada: 156, and E. 3266, 7074.18; Pantheon: 433, and 7071.11, 7073.9, 7075.8; Porta Pia: 200, 245, 459; Porta del Popolo: 48; Vatican: 154, 244, 318, 322–323, 365, and 7074.7, 7074.8; Villas: Albani: 108, 272–273; Borghese: 149, 248, 252, 265, 269; Borsioni: 373; Corsini: 340; Doria-Pamphili: 148, 168, 170, 176–177, 255, 258, 344–346, 360; Ludovisi: 129, 262, 289, 340; Madama: 142, 153, 330, 350, 354, and 7076.1; Medici: 131, 138, 140, 158, 216, 242, 374; Negroni: 273, 367; Papa Guilia: 118, 126; Sacchetti: 151, and 7073.18, 7076.41; Venice: Redentore: 7073.19, 7073.27; Vicenza: Basilica: 7074.3, 7074.36–37, 7074.43, 7074.61, 7074.65–67, 7074.72; Villa Capra: 7073.13, 7074.77, 7074.79–80, 7076.43

Appendix XIII

Letter of Sir William Chambers
to a Gentleman who had objected to certain parts of his
Treatise on Oriental Gardening

Library of the College of Architecture, Cornell University. Bound in a copy of Chambers's *Dissertation on Oriental Gardening*, 2nd edition, 1773

Sir.

The open & Friendly manner, in which you animadverted upon my little performance flatters me highly. Had I advised with you before publication the Book would have had fewer faults, the Author fewer sins with the public, but the truth is I had not courage to trouble you.

Your definition of Gardening, though a just one, when applyed to the English Style alone; seems too confined for the more extensive system which I have ventured to describe, as it comprehends not only all the perfect parts of our English Gardening, but likewise all that deserves imitation in many other manners of culture.

'To improve Nature, & to reduce Landscape to comfortable enjoyments' (Your definition of the Art of Gardening) is indeed all that has hitherto been attempted in England, but I would endeavour to go further, & not only improve, but adorn Nature with suitable accompanyments, not only provide for the comforts, but for the most exalted pleasures of life, far from being confined to a few acres, I wish to decorate Kingdoms, even the World, & far from attending merely to the narrow views of selfish individuals, I would diffuse the comforts of cultivation to all mankind.

The justice of Your objections to the enchanted Scenery of the Chinese I will not deny, they would perhaps be unanswerable, but for one circumstance, which is that whimsical productions make only a small part of my general plan, in which great Nature, in various forms, & under various modifications, always appears triumphant, as I flatter myself you will clearly perceive upon a second reading of my little Book, if you should think it worth the while. These little sportive Episodes are introduced, & are only to be considered as Episodes in a poem or Interludes in a Drama, which serve to relieve the fatigued mind, and prepare it for something of Greater Consequence. They are chiefly contrived to amuse the curious, the vulgar, or the childish. A few inspections I grant, may satiate, perhaps disgust the owner, but they are not intended for *him*. There is

ample provision for his recreation, and he would be a churl indeed, who could not admit of nothing for the entertainment of others, Holy-day folks, as well as persons of higher condition.

A Philosopher perhaps, who has reasoned himself out of all human feeling may become insensible to praise, may even have no joy in the satisfaction of others: but there are few such philosophers, who possess Gardens, & the generality of the possessors of land being no wiser than they should be, are much affected with applause, & have great relish in giving pleasure to their neighbours.

With respect to the Terrible, it appears to me useful nay even necessary in a *large Work*, as well for the purposes of variety and contrast, as to employ many rude, & ungrateful Tracts of land, constantly intervening in extensive compositions which it is sometimes impossible to adorn, & which can never be adorned without considerable expence, a mixture of this mode would be singularly useful in most of Our English Gardens, which from a perpetual smiling sameness in all their parts, are extremely dull, & unentertaining. If any disgusting ideas are excited in the application of the *terrible* in decorating grounds the fault must be in the Composer, and not in the objects, which are of a nature to produce the Sublime in the highest degree.

I cannot give up WaterWorks, they are at present indeed exploited in England. But are the English never wrong and prejudiced? All other European nations (even those most famed for taste) still make use of & admire them. Water works are certainly productive of much pleasure, & animation in the Scenery of Gardens, where they are well contrived as those of Marli and in some of the Villas near Rome. They as well as *Electrical Effects* might (I am persuaded) be brought in to enliven our Gardens, this however I speak in a Whisper, but the Connoisseurs should hear me, who seem to have laid down as an invariable axiom that the English style of Gardening is alone right, & that whatever differs from it is absolutely absurd and wrong.

We may be puzzled perhaps in England, to find Islands large enough for Ostriches and Forests capacious enough for Elephants. Yet some such

192

spaces might perhaps offer themselves upon a nice enquiry. I am however sorry that they are not often to be met with, as I know I should delight very much to wander in scenes where the enormous Roc (Roc, a large East Indian Bird often mentioned in the Arabian nights entertainments) would figure no more than a common Tom Tit, jesting however apart, I thought it necessary to move in an exalted sphere. Our Gardeners, and I fear our Connoisseurs too, are such *tame* animals, that much sparring is necessary to keep them properly on their haunches. Do not however imagine my dear Sir, that this reflection extends to you. You are pleased to allow me some taste, & I cannot refuse you a great deal.

The Weymouth Pine is named in my work merely by way of explanation. I have indeed mentioned in it (as you remark) most of the plants known in Europe though few of them I confess have ever appeared upon *Chinese Paper*. Yet Father Du Halde assures us that the Chinese have not only all the vegetables known in Europe, but many others unknown to us, & imperfect as my observations have been in that country, they have served to convince me, that the learned Father is right. Were the Chinese to judge of our European plants by the representations they see of them upon our Painted Linens, they would imagine that no twig of their Vegetation was grew in Europe. Yet in our Herbals, there are many Chinese Vegetable productions well known and commonly cultivated amongst us.

It gives me great pleasure to hear from you, that any ideas of mine are likely to be serviceable. Great allowances will I hope be made to a man, born abroad, & unaccustomed to write & who having little licence for thinking communicates his half digested thoughts to the Public.

I am as great a friend to simplicity as any one, yet I think it may easily be carried to a blamable excess, & though in general, a close adherence to selected nature, should be recommended, yet there are many occasions where Art, nay even whim, may be admitted with propriety and success, if the contrivor be a man of taste and judgement.

I shall be happy to see your book, I am rejoiced to find that you have turned your thoughts towards gardening. I should be proud to be always of the same opinion with you, but mankind will differ, variety of opinion is useful as it seems always to settle the truth in every subject, I have the honour to be Sir, Your most humble Ser^t Wm Chambers Berners Street May 13 1772.

193

o

Catalogue of Work

This catalogue lists all Chambers's positive works; those attributable by strongly supported stylistic or circumstantial evidence; and his projects. It does not attempt to deal with the mass of minor Board of Works commissions, most of which were relegated to subordinates. An account of these will appear in the *History of the King's Works* for the relevant period by Mr H. M. Colvin and Dr J. Mordaunt Crook.

The arrangement of this catalogue is as follows: Place, Patron, Work and Date (and Plate Reference, if any, followed by E if work is still substantially existing), Listing of Designs, Listing of Manuscript Sources, Printed Books, Printed Articles, Relevant Pictorial Material, Exhibition of Designs, Sale Catalogue Reference. In many cases minor work is discussed in the Catalogue only, but when a work is discussed fully in the text, the Catalogue description is only of a summary character (e.g., Somerset House).

1 ADDERBURY (Oxon)

3rd Duke of Buccleuch

Work of unknown character (*c*.1768) (Pl.72)

Dalkeith Muniment Room: Design for 'Front of the Intended Addition'

MMA: design, for pier glass, inscr. 'for Adderbury'

Soane: 43/5[37], survey plan of house, ex. Chambers's Office

Coke, *The Letters and Journals of Lady Mary Coke*, II (1889), 28

Stroud, D., *Capability Brown*, 1957, 212

C.Life, 7 Jan. 1949, 33–5

On 12 June 1768 Lady Mary Coke wrote of the Duke of Buccleuch 'carrying on great works' at Adderbury. Unfortunately it is not known if she was referring to Brown's improvements in the park, or Chambers's to the house – perhaps both. The MMA design implies furnishings, and the Dalkeith one architectural alterations of considerable extent, which were certainly not executed to this design. Chambers's conception of his intended front was a very noble one, wholly rusticated, with four rhythmically-disposed Doric aedicules. What services he performed at Adderbury were contemporary with his extensive works for the Duke in Grosvenor Square (q.v.).

2 AMESBURY HALL (Wilts)

Duchess of Queensbury

Chinese Temple (1772) (Pl.78) E

BM. Add.MS 41133, 84 (WC to Duchess 13 Sept. 1772); 41134, 13–4 (Duchess to WC 23 Nov. 1772)

Hanway, *A Journal of Eight Days' Journey*, I (1757), 198

C.Life, 1 March 1902, 278

RIBA Jnl, 30 June 1892, 254–5

When Chambers came to Amesbury he would have found a seventeenth-century Palladian house set in a semi-formal Bridgeman landscape. There is no evidence that he had been asked to alter the house. In fact, the correspondence circumstantially hints that these alterations may have already been effected by James Paine. According to Hanway, who visited Amesbury 14 August 1755, a Chinese Temple was already in existence, having just been built: 'There is . . . an humble imitation of a Chinese house, which is well shaded and agreeable; but it consists only of one room, and is yet unfinished.' This probably ephemeral affair, was doubtless decaying by 1772, and the Duchess must have wanted it rebuilt. She therefore thought it natural to apply to the author of *Designs for Chinese Buildings* for hints and drawings.

When the surviving correspondence opens late in 1772 the temple had already been built, spanning like a bridge a narrow tributary of the river Avon. The sub-structure is of square plan, arched to allow the flow of water underneath, and surrounded above by a Chinese fret balustrade. The super-structure, or temple *cella*, composed of knapped flint arranged in patterns, is also square and here tribute is paid to China by two oval openings and a roof with deeply projecting eaves.

The Duchess's letter of 23 November 1772 concerns the finishing and decoration. She seems to have taken a lively interest, not unusual for a noted blue-stocking, in the details of her temple. Chambers is reminded that a moulding (now destroyed) was to be composed of oak leaves and acorns, rather than eggs and anchors. But much more interesting is the Duchess's recommendation that Theodore de Bruyn, a Swiss painter who had settled in England in 1760, might decorate the interior of the temple. She had apparently been attracted by paintings done by de Bruyn at Longford Castle. If he decorated Amesbury, then the paintings there have been destroyed.

'Sir William Chambers will remember most of the discourse (tho in great haste) held between him and the Dutchess of Queensbury relative to the by name Chinese house, she now puts him in mind that *Oake* leaves & Acorns were proposed instead of the Old Eggs & Anchors; she imagines Sir William will take care of the proportions, as the acorn ought just to be large enough to be seen plainly, & not big enough to disgust one, she thinks they should be painted the colour of a Acorn, & the cup a little carved, & the *Oake* leaves double or *triple* in every corner, enough to appear natural as if just gathered. Besides all the above and whatever else Sr Wm wrote down, he will remember the Dutchess told him of some things she had seen *att* Lord Radnors, by Salisbury, worth his looking *att* when it may suit, she mentioned to Sr Wm that she thought he might adapt something of that nature towards embelishing & Elegantifing the house in question. She can now acquaint him of the name and place of abode of that *Artice* sent him from abroad by the Dutchess of Norfolk. His name is de Bruyn, his dwelling place little Castle Street, Cavendish Square. Being near Sr William he will easily & soon judge by what he will shew and explain having done for Lord Radnor from Designs of Mont faucon, or whether or not any such will answer well for the Chinese house I am myself uncertain; however, Sure that if not eminently well, better not venture it at all – what I saw was in two or three colours of this man's doing, but there was a *parcell* of *Couleurs* added by a painter towards the rough finishing shocking to behold, as intollerably tawdry. Sr Wm knows that the assemblage and blending of *Couleurs* are great *Principals* of his own *Masterfull Supream* taste. The Dutchess would have nothing done in black & white, but glowing and soft, not excluding the requisite light and shade.'

AMPTHILL PARK (Beds)
2nd Earl of Upper Ossory
Addition of wings, refenestration, complete re-
decoration of interiors (1768–72) (Pl.68) E
MMA: (34.72.2 [19a]) design for a ceiling
PML: (Kauffmann Album, 22) design for a ceiling
Crichton Coll.: Plan of house made by C. R.
Cockerell
BM Add.MS 41133, IV, 2, 3, 4, 6, 7, 7v, 21v, 28v, 29
(5 Dec. 1769–2 Feb. 1770)
Neale, J. P., *Views of the Seats . . .*, VI, 1823
Stroud, D., *Capability Brown*, 1957, 144
VCH, *Beds*, III, 1912, 270–1
Walpole Society, XVI, 1928, 70

Ampthill was a late seventeenth-century house
principally designed by John Lumley and William
Winde. To this red brick, hipped-roof house
Chambers added lateral wings linked to the main
block by low corridors. He also stuccoed the brick
exteriors and redressed most of the early rooms
with characteristic Chambersian ceilings, all it
would seem, by Joseph Rose rather than by his
customary plasterer, Thomas Collins. Chambers
seems to have been beset with many labour difficulties. He complains to Rose on 5 December 1769
that 'things go on dreamingly as usual', and in the
following year was troubled by misinterpretation
of his designs for the vestibule in the hands of
Rentham the carpenter. Other correspondence of
the period concerns completion of the Hall and
Library in February and March 1770 by Mr Shaw
the joiner, and the supply of a 'Pedestal for a
figure wch is to be put up at the end of the
Gallery.'

4 ANSLEY HALL (Warwicks)
John Ludford
Chinese Temple (1767)
Bartlett, B., *Manduessedum Romanorum*, 1791, 131
Chambers, *Designs for Chinese Buildings*, 1757, pl.IV,
fig.2
VCH, *Warwick*, IV, 1947, 5–7

If Bartlett is correct, this temple was a copy of the
sacrificial temple published in Chambers's *Designs
of Chinese Buildings*, and said to have been seen in
the grounds of a pagoda in the western suburb of
Canton. Unfortunately there are no views of the
temple to substantiate Bartlett's statement. It is
the earliest instance of an engraving in the *Designs*
having been used as a source for a Chinese-style
building.

5 ASHRIDGE (Hertfordshire)
3rd Duke of Bridgewater
UNEXECUTED designs for a new house and
executed alterations to White Lodge (1770)
BM Add.MS 41133, 19 (WC to Duke 27 June 1770)
RIBA Letters: Beaumont to WC 20 June 1770
Todd, H. J., *The History of the College of Bonhommes
at Ashridge*, 1823
SALE: Christie, 6 June 1811, lot 94

According to Todd, who had access to Bridgewater papers, 'His Grace, not many years after his
accession to the title and estates, had intended to
pull down the college, and build a new mansion
and in order to do this design many fine materials
were accumulated'. The Beaumont letter refers to
the Duke's quarries – although it may refer also to
ready stone available from the Duke who was then
disinclined to proceed with a new house. White
Lodge was, in effect, the old college, and it is
shown on one of Wyatt's preliminary plans in the
RIBA (K7 Box) as a form of gatehouse, or two
largish, square rooms, symmetrically-placed each
side of an entrance way. If this was designed by
Chambers it was trifling, as stated in his letter to
the Duke on 27 June 1770: 'I have sent your
Grace's designs for the White Lodge with written
directions what is to be done . . . as it is a trifling
job I think the workmen of the country might do
it.'

ASKE HALL *see* LONDON: 19 Arlington
Street

BALDERSBY *see* NEWBY PARK

6 BARTON HALL (Suffolk)
Sir Charles Bunbury
Library (1767)
Soane: 43/68, a profile of a doorcase
Bunbury archives, Naunton Hall, Suffolk: photo-
graph of library before destruction by fire
*The Life and Letters of Lady Sarah Lennox 1745–
1820*, vol.I, 1901, 219

According to Lady Sarah, the wife of Sir Charles
Bunbury, on 12 May 1768 the Library was nearly
finished. This patronage probably emanated from
Lady Sarah rather than from Sir Charles, for she
was one of that triumvirate of sisters, all of whom
employed Chambers in the wake of their brother,
the 3rd Duke of Richmond at Goodwood (q.v.).

7 BECKETT PARK (Berks)
2nd Viscount Barrington
Work of unknown character (1766)
RIBA Letters: Barrington to WC 13 Sept. 1766
Dickins, L., and Stanton, M., *An eighteenth-century Correspondence*, 1910, 432–3
Lees-Milne, J., *The Age of Inigo Jones*, 1953, 120–1
C.Life, 10 Nov. 1900, 592–7

The correspondence between Lord Barrington and respectively Sanderson Miller and Chambers is confusing. In June 1766 Lord Barrington was discussing Miller's finishing of the stables and had 'a new plan to communicate with relation to my house.' In September he could report 'My Works go on according to the admirable Plan settled by you, but not so fast as I could wish, however my new rooms and passages are fitting up and I expect to have full use of them next summer.' Yet on 13 September he could write to Chambers, 'My friend Lord Bessborough recommended you as an assistant in some rooms which I want to fit up in an old House I have in Berkshire.' Although Beckett has been rebuilt there still remains an asymmetrically-formed watercourse spanned by a Chinese-style fret bridge, and having on its banks a rebuilt seventeenth-century pavilion. This was also given chinoiserie touches, to the extent that temple, bridge, and watercourse are an 'Anglo-Chinois' conception. Without documents it would be unwise to attribute this arrangement necessarily to Chambers's intervention at Beckett.

8 BEECHWOOD (Herts)
Sir Thomas Sebright
New dining room (1761)
Beechwood: elevations, one inscr. 'Plan of new dining Room at Beechwood 1761'
Gandon Albums II: Brewery, Laundry & Gates (in poss. Father Murphy, Robertstown, Co. Kildare)
C.Life, 12 Nov. 1938, 477, fig.8

This work for Sir Thomas Sebright is neither documented, nor has it survived. The time would place the project in the period of Chambers's work at The Hoo, a seat not far away.

9 BICKLEY HALL (Kent)
John Wells
UNEXECUTED designs for a new house (*c*.1770)
BM Add.MS 41133, 92v; 41134, 15 (29 Jan.–Feb. 1773)
Neale, J. P., *Views of Seats . . .*, II, 1819

The essentials of what Chambers had provided John Wells with are contained in a letter to the Reverend Peneck on 29 January 1773, asking him to act as an intermediary with Wells in the matter of payment for his designs. Chambers said, 'It is now a good deal above three years that I have been planning for him & what with different Designs, Journeys to his Country House & mony which I am to pay for making an Estimate . . . to say the truth I have no particular pleasure on being his Architect.' Wells was eventually persuaded to pay fifty guineas for his designs. But his house, shown in J. P. Neale's view, was not built until 1780, and then probably by Robert Mylne, whose designs are in the Richardson Collection at Ampthill.

10 BIRDSALL (Yorks)
Henry Willoughby
UNEXECUTED design for a circular temple (before 1759)
V & A: 3365, plan
Chambers, *Treatise*, 1759, pls 39–40
Le Rouge, *Jardins Anglo-Chinois*, cah.9/8

This was one of the projects included in the *Treatise* in the hope of further patronage. There is no evidence that it was executed.

11 BLENHEIM PALACE (Oxon)
4th Duke of Marlborough
Internal decorations, furniture; gateway to the kitchen garden, ornaments to the East Gate; Bladon Bridge, the Temple of Diana, the Temple of Flora, the Flower Garden; repairs to the Grand Bridge, and erection of the Bernini obelisk; the Wilton tripod, pedestals in the flower garden and great court (*c*.1766(?)–*c*.1775) (Pls 183, 193) E
Avery: (1c/2[7]), design for a chimney-piece
Blenheim Archives: Designs (2), inscr., 'Pedestal for the flower garden Blenheim'
DML: Chambers–Yenn album, 4, 6v, 10v, 11, 15 (later Yenn designs)
RA: Yenn Album, various later designs by Yenn, but including *Blenheim Gateway 1768*
RIBA: Stevens's album, 39b (kitchen garden gate)
Soane: 43/6[17], side-table with Vitruvian borders, carved by Alken and dated 12 Apr. 1768; 43/6[18], therm carved by Alken for the Temple of Diana; 43/8[5], design for Bladon Bridge
BM Add.MS 41133, 1v, 5, 5v, 72, 75, 76, 76v, 77, 84, 87v, 89, 95v, 105v, 106v, 108, 111, 111v, 112, 113, 113v, 114, 122 (Dec. 1769–Nov. 1773); 41136, 1v–2, 19, 21v (31 Jan. 1774–July 1774)
RIBA Letters: Marl. to WC, 28 May, 3 July, 29 Aug. 1773 (about East Gateway)
Chambers, *Treatise*, 3rd edn 1791, pl.52, design for tripod
Green, D., *Blenheim Palace*, 1951, 317–18
Mavor, W. F., *New Description of Blenheim*, 1789; and 10th edn *c*.1816

C.Life, 27 May 1949, 1246; 20 Apr. 1951, 118, fig.7
RIBA Jnl, 24 Aug. 1893 (abstracts of letters)
EXHIB RA 1774, 33: Tripod in gardens
SALE: Christie, 6 June 1811, Lot 94 'Blenheim Park Gates'

The 4th Duke of Marlborough, who had succeeded to Blenheim in 1758, may have first employed Stiff Leadbetter there, as had the 3rd Duke at Langley Park in 1755. It is perhaps not a coincidence that this architect died in 1766, the very year Chambers first appears under the Duke's patronage at Woodstock Town Hall (q.v.). Chambers is recorded at Blenheim at the opening, late in 1769, of the existing Letter Books, and he was still working there when they closed in 1775. For this reason Blenheim is one of the most extensively-documented of Chambers's works. There was to be found here a host of first-class artists and craftsmen: sculptors, Sir Henry Cheere, Richard Hayward, and Joseph Wilton; the mason, Thomas Stephens; the carver, Sefferin Alken and the joiner, Benjamin Thacker; cabinet makers, John Mayhew (of Ince and Mayhew) and a Mr Ansell; and a frame-maker, Mr Gasset.

Aside from his garden works, Chambers's alterations to the house must be seen as a veneer to Vanbrugh's bolder forms. As Hardwick comments in his *Memoir*, appended to Gwilt's 1825 edition of Chambers's *Treatise*, 'At Blenheim he so happily conformed to the singular style of the original architect that no discordance was produced by the additions he planned to that magnificent structure.' As far as the exterior was concerned, this work was confined to the main forecourt, where Chambers supplied pedestals with swagged disks on their faces, and the East Gate, or Vanbrugh's Great Cistern. The gate is mentioned in the correspondence of 1773, particularly in a letter from the Duke to Chambers on 29 August: 'I return you inclosed your plan for the Gateway here. I think it very handsome and wish you would order drawings for the ornaments to be made out at large; they certainly had better be made in Town. The only parts we wish to have altered in your drawing are the trophys under the cornice, we think the Lions heads in your first Sketch looked better than the Trophys.' This alteration was done and was part of a wish on the Duke's part to ameliorate the 'rude' aspect of Vanbrugh's design. Chambers must be credited with the addition of his typical rope-like swags, the fruit branch motif in the upper side panels, and probably the splendid iron gates which pick up the lion mask motif in their side pilasters.

There is some reason to believe that alterations in the nineteenth century obliterated many of Chambers's interiors to this palace, if he was indeed responsible for the decoration of rooms on the south front. He redecorated and furnished the Grand Cabinet in the south-east pavilion; supplied a chimney-piece, carved by Wilton, for the Duchess's Dressing Room adjoining her Bedchamber next to the Grand Cabinet; and right at the other end of the south enfilade, adjacent to the Long Gallery, the State Bedchamber was given its State Bed, supplied by Ince and Mayhew. This aspect of the Blenheim work is discussed in letters exchanged between Chambers and the Duke or Duchess during the middle months of 1773 when the tripartite window of the Grand Cabinet was being decorated with three lavish red silk damask drapes dependent from arched gilt cornices and divided from each other by elegant pier glasses and tables. On 25 July, Chambers had written to the Duke, 'The Glasses and tables I have bespoke of Mr Ansell, after having made the Drawings at large, he has agreed to do them for £200 but he says he cannot afford to do them in the highest perfection under £60 a pier, that is £240 for the whole. I could wish they were done as well as possible and therefore beg leave to advise the additional allowance, in which case I should also advise to have them Gilt of two coloured Gold.' In contrast to the full documentation of these pieces, the State Bed is mentioned only in a letter of 10 July 1773 when Chambers was arranging for hangings to be supplied by Mr Mayhew, of Messrs Ince and Mayhew. The early guides to Blenheim (e.g. Mavor 1789) describe the bed simply: 'The bed-posts elegantly fluted, and covered with burnished gold: their extremities adorned with military emblems. The top rises into a dome, surmounted with a ducal coronet.' In the revised tenth edition (*c*.1816), however, to this description is added 'The whole designed by Sir William Chambers.'

The Duke gave Chambers a number of commissions for a varied range of objects in the gardens and park. Nearest the house, on the western ride towards Bladon Bridge, an Ionic tetrastyle temple was set up to provide a magnificent view of Capability Brown's lake. This temple was inscribed to the 'Ionian, rural, mountain-ranging Diana', and provided with verses from the Hippolytus of Euripides. South-west of the house, on the Home Ride, Chambers was probably responsible for the whole planning of the Flower Garden. This was an oval enclosure centred by a porphyry obelisk with four white marble vases, from which radiated, spoke-like, a number of bosky paths. On the east periphery was Chambers's Temple of Flora, whose siting was discussed in a letter to the Duke on 16 August 1772. Just outside the Flower Garden could have been found the beautiful tripod illustrated in the third edition of Chambers's *Treatise*. This exquisite neo-classic object, surely the *chef-d'œuvre* of Joseph Wilton's art, has unfortunately disappeared. To complete his work on this part of the park Chambers was asked to provide an east gateway in the walls of Vanbrugh's massive Kitchen Garden just beyond the Flower Garden. For this Chambers designed a Tuscan gateway, a variation of one seen by him at the *Teatro Olympico* in Vicenza and published in his 1759 edition of the *Treatise*.

Elsewhere in the park Chambers's principal works concerned repairs to Vanbrugh's Grand Bridge (August 1772), the setting-up of Bernini's *modello* for the obelisk in the Piazza Navona (spring 1774), and the building of the New or Bladon Bridge. Both bridge and obelisk reflected the Duke's attention given to an area of the park near the widened river Glyme, south-east of the house. The Bridge was intended to carry a new ride from the Kitchen Garden to one north-west of the so-called New Garden on the other side of the river and cascade towards High Lodge. This bridge, low in outline and elegant in detail, is first mentioned in a letter to the Duke on 23 April 1773. Chambers had enquired of Thomas Carter for lead sphinxes for the terminal piers, but as his prices were excessive, sphinxes were eventually provided by Cheere who sent them to Blenheim in August of this year. For some reason, in little more than ten years, they had been replaced by low pyramidal caps put there by John Yenn who had succeeded Chambers at Blenheim in the 1780s. It is not certain if Chambers or Yenn should be held responsible for rebuilding the Bernini obelisk, for when Chambers was advising (January 1774) that 'the fountain must be repaired on the Spot where it is to be erected and built up as fast as is possible', the relevant Blenheim entries in the Letter Books come to an end. Mavor in his 1789 guide mentions the obelisk as 'newly erected' in the vicinity of the Cascade. It was later (*c*.1930) re-erected by the ninth Duke as a principal object, paired with a copy, on his Great Parterre designed by Achille Duchêne to bring formality once again to the east front of the palace.

12 CARTON (Co. Kildare)

Marquess of Kildare
UNEXECUTED designs for a new house (1762?)
Leixlip Castle, Co. Kildare: album of designs in the poss. Hon. Desmond Guinness
Kildare Archeological Soc., IV, July 1903, and pl. facing p.21
Irish Architectural Drawings, 1965, no.118

The design for Carton, inscribed, 'a house drawn, so as to be built between the collonades', is unsigned. Although the draughtsmanship is not in Chambers's hand, stylistically this appears to be a project made in the 1760s. The compilers of *Irish Architectural Drawings* date the project to 1762,

but there appears to be no date on the drawings. In fact, it is more likely, and is supported on stylistic grounds, to be a project made about 1768 when Kildare had become (1766) Duke of Leinster and was employing Chambers to redecorate interiors at Leinster House, Dublin (q.v.).

13 CASTLE HOWARD (Yorks)

5th Earl of Carlisle
Exclamation Gate and UNEXECUTED project for stables (before 1770 and 1770–2) E
Castle Howard Archives: Designs for gates and stables, latter inscr. 'principal front of the New Stable at Castle Howard'
V & A: 3352, plan of stables
BM Add.MS 41133, 21, 32v, 33–34, 36–36v, 38, 78–79 (16 Aug. 1770–July 1772)
RIBA Letters: Carlisle to WC, 1 July 17..
Jesse, J. H., *George Selwyn and His Contemporaries*, 1903, III, 27
C.Life, 25 June 1927, 1029–30

The Exclamation Gate is so called because it marks the point at which the whole breath-taking prospect of Castle Howard is suddenly brought into view. Although Chambers's design and correspondence relating to the gate are undated, they must be before 1770 when he embarked upon his abortive schemes for the stables. The design shows the piers supporting heraldic beasts, but these have since been removed. Each pier is built of frosted masonry with an entablature composed of a Greek fret architrave, garlanded frieze, and a cornice.

In August 1770 Chambers was waiting upon Lord Carlisle to discuss the proposed stables; in September he was at Castle Howard 'to settle everything'; and early in the New Year his completed designs were despatched from London. On 16 April 1771 he wrote to the surveyor, Percy Luccock, 'Lay the foundations whenever you please.' At this moment, however, economy suddenly intervened and his proposal was totally abandoned. A month later Carlisle wrote to George Selwyn informing him that he had 'made Mr Car of York give him (me) a plan for stables of a very different kind from that of Mr Chambers in point of expense.' Nevertheless, in response to Chambers's plea (July 1772) that money was 'now almost as rare as antique medals', Carlisle was obliged to settle his account for £112.15.0. Chambers's designs show a front with pavilion ends and three intermediate bays each side of a central arch.

14 CASTLETOWN (Co. Kildare)
Rt Hon. Thomas Conolly
Internal alterations and gate-piers (1759+) E
Correspondence of Emily, Duchess of Leinster, ed. B
Fitzgerald, III, Dublin, 1952, 23
The Georgian Society, V, 1913, 43–54, pls.XXVII,
XXVIII, XXI
C.Life, 3 April, 1969, 798–802; 10 April, 1969,
882–885
Irish Georgian Society Bulletin, VIII, no.3, 1965 'Sir
William Chambers, Friend of Charlemont' by
John Harris

Documentary evidence of Chambers's employment at Castletown is contained in a letter of 28
July 1759 from Lady Louisa Conolly to her sister
Lady Emily, Countess of Kildare (later Duchess of
Leinster), enquiring about the 'finishing' for the
'great room' at Castletown, which 'they (presumably the decorators) were to send the rest of it
afterwards, or else Mr. Chambers the architect,
had explained it to Mr. Verpaille.' Precisely what
these 'finishings' were is not clear, but the 'great
room' is undoubtedly the Gallery, the walls of
which were later decorated by Thomas Riley. 'Mr.
Verpaille' is of course Simon Vierpyle, the mason
who was then building the Casino at Marino to
Chambers's designs. Also Chambersian in style at
Castletown are parts of the Red Drawing room,
the Print room, the Green Drawing room, and the
Dining room. The staircase, although probably
not to Chambers's design, is contemporary with his
work as the brass balusters are signed and dated by
A. King, Dublin 1760. The gate piers on the main
drive are attributed to Chambers on the basis of
their proportions, their typical sphinxes, and other
stylistic features.

15 CHENIES (Bucks): *St Michael's church*
John Russell, 4th Duke of Bedford
Monument to the 2nd Duke of Bedford and his
Duchess (1766–9) (Pl.190) E
Bedford Office, London: Rack 13/3/4 Box 523,
Wilton to Duke's agent 25 October 1766
BM Add.MS 41133, 7 (25 March 1770)

This monument is jointly signed by Chambers and
Wilton. Although it was set up in 1769, and on
25 March 1770 Chambers had written to the
Duke's agent, Mr Beaumont, for payment of £50
for his 'trouble in designing and directing the
monument', a letter of Wilton's shows that it was
being sculpted as early as 1766. On 25 October he
wrote that 'I am very forward with my model from
which the Statues are to be executed. The Architectural part of the Monument is in great part
executed & I find Mr Chambers has not provided
Room for a long Inscription.' The monument's
style, like Chambers's slightly later Mountrath

monument in Westminster Abbey (q.v.), is still a
combination of late Roman baroque features and
neo-classic trimmings.

16 CLAREMONT (Surrey)
1st Baron Clive
UNEXECUTED designs for a new house (c.1768)

Claremont was designed by Capability Brown in
1770, but is included in this catalogue because of
the long-founded tradition that Chambers's pique
with Brown (expressed in the *Dissertation on
Oriental Gardening*) resulted from Clive's rejection
of his designs for Claremont in preference to
Brown's. The tradition goes back to Walpole as
related by James Dallaway in his *Supplementary
Anecdotes On Gardening in England*, appended to his
1826 edition of Walpole's *Anecdotes of Painting in
England*. It is certainly unusual that Clive, a faithful patron of Chambers at Styche, Walcot, and
Berkeley Square (q.v.) between 1760 and 1765,
should not have asked him for designs for Claremont. It may not be a coincidence that Claremont
is not entirely characteristic of Brown's style, for
its plan is related to Peper Harow (i.e., the English
villa-plan tradition), a type not known to have
been used by Brown elsewhere. On the other
hand, Clive's letter to Chambers on 28 March 1774
(BM Add.MS 41136, 14v–15) suggests no lack of
friendliness on the part of these two: He thought
Chambers in the *Dissertation* (2nd edn.) 'master of
your subject & that your garden scenes are drawn
with the Pencil of a Claude . . . I think Mr Brown
should rather thank you for your Publication, than
be offended, for he certainly may collect from your
book many fine Ideas.'

17 COBHAM HALL (Kent)
3rd Earl of Darnley
General restoration; provision of new rooms in
south wing, including a Library; raising of attic to
conform with the seventeenth-century pilastered
attic on west front of the Cross Wing; considerable fenestration; addition of 'Jacobethan' gables
to the north and south wings; decoration of the
Vestibule in centre of south wing; addition of a
storey to the offices on the north side of the first
office court (c.1767–70) E
Cambridge, School of Architecture Library: The
'Cobham Portfolio' containing numerous designs
by Chambers, James Wyatt, the Reptons, and
others, including for Chambers, a survey ground
plan, elevations of court fronts of north and
south wings, variant designs for the office wing
with studies for its cupola, plans and elevations
for the addition of a canted bay and new rooms at
west end of south wing, elevation for the west
front cross-wing alterations.

Atkinson, C. E. M., *The Late 18th and Early 19th Century Alterations to Cobham Hall, Kent* (unpublished Cambridge School of Architecture essay, 1968)

The 3rd Earl married in 1766 and soon after this event commissioned Chambers to attempt to bring some element of modernity to this old-fashioned late-Elizabethan pile. His work may have extended from 1767 until 1770 or even 1771. In 1770 he was paid twenty pounds for a journey to Cobham. Although the decoration of the Gilt Hall – with splendid panels of Frenchified trophies – has been attributed to Chambers, in fact the designs are neither in his hand nor in that of any of his known assistants. If it is, indeed, by Chambers, then he was working here as late as 1776, and it must be regarded as a *chef-d'œuvre* in any account of his decorations. An odd aspect of Chambers's work here concerned his addition of an extra storey to the office wing on the north side of the office court. His additions were in a sixteenth-century style and incorporated a 'Decorated'-style porch. Most of Chambers's work was destroyed by either James Wyatt or the Reptons. However, in the transverse passage across the centre of the south wing, his masculine and unaffected ornamentation may be discerned. In Lady Darnley's Garden is a temple modelled upon that of Augusta at Kew, but with a fluted order. This was designed by Chambers not for Cobham, but for Ingress Abbey, Kent (q.v.) from whence it was brought in 1820 by the 4th Earl of Darnley.

18 COLEBY HALL (Lincs)
Thomas Scrope
Temple of Romulus and Remus (1762) (Pl.82) E
BM Add.MS 41135, 35b, c+verso; 41136, 19v–20, 21–21v, 35 (29 June–29 July 1774)
RIBA Letters: Scrope to WC 20 June 1774
Dugdale, James, *The New British Traveller*, III, 1819, 608
RIBA Jnl, 27 Oct. 1892

On 29 June 1774 Thomas Scrope, writing to Chambers, a long-standing friend with whom he had 'viewed old Rome', recalls his building the Temple of Romulus and Remus 'about twelve years ago.' The approximate date, 1762, seems accurate enough, for had the temple been designed before 1759 Chambers would certainly have included it in his *Treatise*. In addition to Chambers's temple, there is also at Coleby a small, half-domed rotunda dedicated to Pitt which Scrope himself had designed.

The remainder of the correspondence between the two friends is concerned with Scrope's request for a 'gateway to be an Object Seen from a Temple of Yours and Mine, which I have built, and in which I now write this. I would not have the gateway expensive but truly elegant and chaste, you know my taste, it will be the main entrance to my gardens', which he delightedly describes as his 'hobby horse.' However, 1774 was a most inappropriate moment to ask for such a Commission, as Chambers was then in Paris preparing for Somerset House on the horizon. He therefore replied, stressing 'Business in the Building kind', which he wished he could suspend, 'but tis vain', he pleaded, 'this year I have insensibly been drawn into so much, of one sort or the other, that I do not know how or where to turn, tout est en désordre et je ne sais ou donner de la tête. There is a man near you whose head is in much better order, one Carr, dwelling at York, and once Lord Mayor there. He has built for Mr Lascelles and many other worthy gentlemen in the North, and would I think shine at Coleby. Some business will take me into Yorkshire about the time of the York races; I shall take a day or two of the sport, and hope to meet you there, when we will talk the matter over. I will endeavour to put you in a way, though I can undertake nothing myself.' But Scrope continued to plead, 'No Carr for me; in short you must see Coleby . . . this place must not be cobled [*sic*] it must be either you or Wyatt; but I had much rather had an old friend and an acquaintance . . . pray send me a sketch for my gateway and for the epergne . . . I beg we may meet and have some fun here; tis the very seat of the Gothic Empire. Sr Cecil Wray, the Solomon of these parts, I much fear is doing all he can to pull down the finest Roman antiquity in the Island, a Roman Arch belonging to the old Roman Station Lindum, near Lincoln, and all this to break a pieces [*sic*] to mend the turnpike roads. If he carries his point, I'll hand him down to posterity with Attila, Alaric, &c, in some strong English or Latin inscription on some building at Colby, on the old Roman road straight from Sandwich across the Humber through your Lordship.'

There is no evidence that Chambers designed any building at Coleby during this period, but Scrope had an imitation of the Lincoln Arch (the Newport Arch) built in his grounds. Possibly Chambers handed Scrope's request over to John Yenn, for Yenn's connexion with Coleby is proved by his Royal Academy exhibit of 1792: 'a gentleman's mansion to be executed at Coleby.' Engravings show that the east front of Coleby was Georgianized about this time. However, a design in the Yenn Albums, RA, inscr. *Elevation of the South Front an Addition to the House of Thomas Scrope esqr at Colby near Lincoln*, may be in Chambers's hand.

19 CULHAM COURT (Berks)
Richard Michell
UNEXECUTED designs for a new house (1770)
Passages From the Diaries of Mrs Philip Lybbe Powys,
ed E. J. Climenson, 1899, 123
SALE: Christie, 6 June 1811, Lot 93: 'Mr Michell's
house'

Richard Michell is probably to be identified with
the Richard Mitchel who subscribed to the *Designs
for Chinese Buildings*, and the Richard Michel who
subscribed to the *Treatise*. Mrs Lybbe Powys,
visiting Culham Court on 13 July 1771, describes
it as 'Mr Michell's new house . . . not finished.'
The house is of the villa type, built of brick. *In
Seats and Mansions of Berkshire*, 1880, however, the
house is described as having been built from 'a
design by Sir Thomas Taylor [*sic*]', and this
assumption is almost certainly correct.

20 CULWORTH (?Northants)
Designs for a stable
Gandon Album 2 (in poss. Father Murphy,
Robertstown, Co. Kildare)

The ascription to Culworth, Northamptonshire,
is only tentative. The work was possibly executed
by Gandon when in Chambers's office.

21 CULZEAN CASTLE (Ayrshire)
Sir Thomas Kennedy
UNEXECUTED design for a pavilion (before
1759)
Soane: 43/4², plan inscr. 'the situation commands
four fine views for which reasons have made the
dining open on all four sides'
Chambers, *Treatise*, 1759, pl.45
Le Rouge, *Jardins Anglo-Chinois*, cah.9/13

This temple was probably meant for a prominent
site on the cliffs overlooking the sea. In 1771
Thomas Kennedy, then 9th Earl of Cassillis,
made considerable alterations to the old Castle of
Culzean, but it is not known whether Chambers
was employed at this time. It was under the 10th
Earl that the castle was rebuilt by Robert Adam
in 1777.

22 DANSON HILL (Kent)
John Boyd
Internal alterations, including chimney-pieces;
the Temple, and a 'Palladio' bridge (late 1760s–
c.1770) (Pl.184) E
MMA: (49.56.19) design for a chimney-piece, inscr.
'Eating Room' and 'to draw the Vase for Mr
Boyd'
Soane: 42/38: detail, 'Profile & ornaments for the
frames over Mr Boyd's doors'

BM Add.MS 41133, 17V, 102; 41134, 24V–25 (12
June 1770–26 May 1773)
RA: Letters, Boyd to WC, 11 and 12 June 1770
Copper Plate Magazine, vol.1 (view of 'Palladio'
bridge)
Harrison's *Views*, 1787
C.Life, 2 March 1961, 458 (letter with illustration)
C.Life, 6 July 1967, 17–21, 'The Villas of Sir
Robert Taylor – I', by Marcus Binney

Danson is a villa designed for John Boyd by
Sir Robert Taylor in 1756 or 1759, but for reasons
unknown the interior seems never to have
been completed, for the remarkably sumptuous
chimney-pieces are clearly by Chambers, an attribution based not only upon style, but upon the
identity of the Dining Room chimney-piece to the
Metropolitan Museum design. Chambers's responsibility for other parts of the interior is proven
by the Soane design which may relate to the
Octagon Room, where the ceiling is Chambersian.
The correspondence describes the latter phase of
this patronage when Boyd's attentions had been
directed to the gardens, then recently 'improved'
by Brown. Chambers designed a 'Palladio' bridge
and small Doric temple. The Bridge is first
mentioned by Boyd in a letter to Chambers
written on 11 June 1770, when the foundations
were ready for this timber structure. Boyd also
asked Chambers to send the design for the
Temple. To this letter Chambers promptly replied
the following day, 'Excessive hurry . . . has
prevented my doing your designs. I am just a
going into Hertfordshire for some days and on
my return will immediately do your temple. In the
mean time I have sent you a design of a Bridge
whc has scarcely any rise at all. It is a thought of
palladios and provided you have it framed by a
skilful carpenter will do very well and look very
handsome.' The type of bridge, copied from a
model in the third book of Palladio's *I Quattro
Libri*, was a popular garden ornament, and
Chambers had designed one earlier at Kew
Gardens.

The tone of the correspondence gives the impression that Chambers and Boyd were close
friends. Boyd was never billed for designs and had
to remind Chambers on 14 May 1773 'that I am in
your debt for the Drawings of my Temple, which
is finished, and when your leisure will permit,
should be glad you would come to see it, and
spend a day at Danson with your Ladys.' To this
Chambers replied, 'If the temple pleases you it
will make me happy.' This little temple with a
tetrastyle Doric portico has been removed to
Waldenbury, Hertfordshire.

23 DUBLIN: CHARLEMONT HOUSE
(Pl.93; Fig.7)
1st Earl of Charlemont
Town house and furnishings (1762–75) E
MMA: (34.78.2 [11]) design for hall chimney-piece
V & A: 2216.28, detail of moulding; 4969.1910,
chimney-piece inscr. 'Ld Charlemont's Eating
Room'; 7078.31, moulding inscr. 'String for a
Stair Earl Charlemont's hs in Dublin'; 2216.25,
ceiling Back Drawing room; 2216.29, ceiling
Small Front Drawing room
BM Add.MS 41133, 75 (13 June 1772); 41135, 64–
64v, 71–72 (WC to Charlemont 17 Apr. 1774;
3 Aug.1775)
RIA, Dublin: MSS Charlemont letters, reported in
HMC Twelfth Report, App Pt X, vol.1, 1891; and
two unreported letters, Charlemont to WC Jan.
1768 and 9 July 1775
Chambers, *Treatise*, 3rd edn., 1791, plate of
'utensils'
Craig, M., *The Volunteer Earl*, 1948, 126–33
The Georgian Society, IV, 1912, 23–33, pls.VII–XI
The Irish Builder, 1903, XXXVI, 121
Irish Georgian Soc. Bull., VIII, no.3, 1965 'Sir
William Chambers, Friend of Charlemont', by
John Harris
Office of Public Works, Dublin: plans (measured
1917) of house before conversion
Pool, R., and Cash, J., *Views . . . in the City of
Dublin*, 1780
RIA, Dublin: Photographs of house before con-
version
Ware, Isaac, *Compleat Body of Architecture*, 1756,
no.43, 433; 40, 404, for sources

In 1762 Lord Charlemont provided Chambers
with his first opportunity to design a town house,
on the north side of Rutland Square and on a long
narrow plot. Chambers utilized his space to great
advantage, for he not only erected a standard
frontage to the Square, but at the end of the
garden built a magnificent Library wing linked to
the house by an interesting corridor which was
punctuated in the centre by a square vestibule to
allow an easy transition from a lower to a higher
level. As would be expected from one who was
then refining the English Palladian tradition for
his villas, Charlemont House is also firmly based
upon such precedent; and in particular Isaac Ware
is laid under tribute for the façade. Charlemont
was not a rich man, and as at the Casino, he seems
to have adopted a leisurely attitude towards building, because in 1775 there were still finishing
works in progress. When the Dublin Corporation
took over Charlemont House for a Municipal
Gallery in 1929 they unwisely demolished everything north of the main block, including, of
course, Charlemont's famous library.

However much the destruction at Charlemont
House is to be regretted, the disappearance of

furniture and furnishings, much of it designed by
Chambers, is an even greater loss. The finest piece
was undoubtedly the medal cabinet, first mentioned by Chambers in a letter to Charlemont on
25 August 1767, wherein he apologizes for the
bronze founder, a Mr Anderson, 'who had the
bronzes in hand hath laid at the point of death for
some time and there is no hope of his recovery; so
that as soon as I can get the models I must employ
some other person to do the work, both for the
medals cases and the Tritons. Alken (Sefferin) has
carved one of the little heads for the corner of the
doors of the medal cases. It is very fine, but as he
tells me he cannot do them under three guineas
and a half a head, I have stopped his further
progress till I hear from your lordship, and I
think antique patterns or nails which will cost but
a trifle will answer the purpose almost as well. Be
pleased to send me the inscriptions which are to
be on the shields of the medal cases, for Mr
Anderson has lost the former ones.' The progress
of this work is further reported in letters on 12
September and 2 October of the year, and on 9
February and 12 March 1768. In the following
October Anderson was reported dead, 'but I find
that the ornaments for the medal cases are cast and
his man will finish them as well as he could have
done himself', and together with the 'Triton
candle-branches', also cast in bronze, were expected on 12 March 1768 to be imminently available.
In this year 'side-boards for the French room' are
mentioned on 15 September, and girandoles for
the Library Anti-Room on 19 December. The
quality and beauty of Chambers's designs in this
material have never been appreciated. With the
originals lost, some idea may be gained from a
plate of 'ornamental utensils' in the third edition
of the *Treatise* and from two designs for candlesticks in the National Gallery of Scotland (Inv.
no.D.944, 945). The work of Mr Anderson requires further investigation, but he is probably
Diedricht Nicholas Anderson. He exhibited a tripod
designed by James Stuart at the Free Society of
Artists in 1761, and, to judge by the tripods
attributed to him at Althorp, was an artist in
bronze and ormolu comparable to the more
famous Matthew Boulton (Cf. Eileen Harris, *The
Furniture of Robert Adam*, 1963, 65, 105).

24 DUBLIN: LEINSTER HOUSE
1st Duke of Leinster
Redecoration of apartments on first-floor garden
front (1767)
Charlemont Letters, I, 283 (WC to Charlemont
25 Aug. 1767)
Mac Criosta, M., *Leinster House*, 1955
The Georgian Soc., IV, 1912, 43–61, pls XVIII–XLIX
Irish Georgian Soc. Bull., VIII, no.3, 1965, 'Sir

William Chambers, Friend of Charlemont', by John Harris

When Leinster House was designed in 1745 by Richard Castle for the 20th Earl of Kildare it was known as Kildare House, and from 1747 its Countess was Lady Emily Lennox, the sister of Lady Louisa at Castletown (q.v.) and of Lady Sarah at Barton Hall (q.v.). Although Chambers's designs for Lady Emily at Carton (q.v.) were not executed, here at Leinster House he seems to have provided a suite of newly-decorated parade apartments on the first floor of the garden front, a decision that followed Kildare's elevation to the Dukedom of Leinster in 1766. In fact it is probably related to a comment made by Chambers to Charlemont on 25 August 1767: 'I shall with great pleasure obey her grace's commands on this and on all other occasions on which she shall please to honor me with them.' As at Castletown, the designs at Leinster House have been provincialized in execution by Dublin craftsmen. In one room a Jonesian type of chimney-piece is similar to that at Milton Abbey (q.v.) and in another room a ceiling is almost identical to one at Castletown.

25 DUBLIN: MARINO HOUSE
1st Earl of Charlemont
Alterations, additions and gate-piers (c.1758–c.1775)
Richardson-Houfe Coll., Ampthill: Design for a Cold Bath Pavilion
V & A: 7074.45, unexecuted design for a Doric gate, inscr. 'Lord Charlemont'
Charlemont Letters, I, 283, 285 (WC to Charlemont 25 Aug. 1767; 9 Feb. 1768)
Bowden, C. T., *A Tour Through Ireland*, 1791, 78
Chambers, *Treatise*, 3rd edn., 1791, 136
Craig, M. J., *The Volunteer Earl*, 1948, 123
The Georgian Soc., V, 1913, CXVI, CXVII, CXXI
Irish Georgian Soc. Bull., VIII, no.3, 1965, 'Sir William Chambers, Friend of Charlemont', by John Harris

Marino House was unfortunately demolished without adequate measuring and surveys, with the result that it is difficult to understand the nature of Charlemont's additions. It had originally been built c.1750 and in 1755 was known as Donneycarney. The Georgian Society show an incoherently-arranged plan and a front obviously of 1750. In fact it is quite clear that Charlemont preferred to spend his money upon the Casino, the park, and his Dublin town house. Nevertheless, there were rooms here redecorated by Chambers and a temple to exhibit statuary was incorporated into one side of the building. This is commented upon in the third edition of the *Treatise* when describing

Henry Willoughby's rotunda, a design 'afterwards considerably augmented in its plan, and contrived for the reception of statues and other valuable antiquities, belonging to the Earl of Charlemont's collection at Marino.' On 9 February 1768 Chambers wrote to Charlemont enclosing 'Cipriani's drawing for the dragons of the gate at Marino.' This partly remains, although the outer piers with surmounting antique tripods have disappeared, and the dragons have been removed to another site in the grounds.

26 DUBLIN: MARINO HOUSE: THE CASINO
1st Earl of Charlemont
Temple called The Casino (1758–76) (Pls 52–54, 84; Fig.2) E
MMA: (53.521.8) designs for chimney-pieces
RA: Diploma submission March 1773 (red chalk perspective in ruined state)
Richardson–Houfe Coll., Ampthill: Elevation of Casino
V & A: 3342, 43–44 and 46 (plans and elevations)
BM Add.MS 41133, 27v–28 (31 Jan. 1771)
Charlemont Letters, I, 283–6, 291, 304, 314–15, 337–8
Chambers, *Treatise*, 1759, pls 35–6
Craig, M. J., *The Volunteer Earl*, 1948, 134–42 and Appendix III, 264–5
The Georgian Soc., V, 1913, pls.CXIX–CXX
Irish Georgian Soc. Bull., VIII, no.3, 1965, 'Sir William Chambers, Friend of Charlemont', by John Harris
EXIB S of A 1765, 203; RA 1773, 47

It has always been said that the first stone of the Casino was laid in 1761 or 1762, but an assessment of the evidence makes it clear that the beginnings lie in 1758. Chambers's *Treatise*, compiled at the latest in the autumn of 1758, appeared in March 1759, and then the Casino was described as 'building.' Walpole, writing to Montagu on 30 December 1761, could ask 'is his villa finished? I am well pleased with the design in Chambers'. The Casino was probably habitable in 1765 but, like Charlemont House, for financial reasons the project was not hurried in any way.

The relationship between Chambers and Charlemont was the rare one of complete understanding. Because of this, the Casino is the perfect expression of Chambers's creative ability in small-scale design and his inclinations towards the neo-classic plan and elevation. There can be little doubt that the Casino is cradled among Chambers's Franco-Roman experiences of the early 1750s.

27 DUBLIN: TRINITY COLLEGE

Theatre, Chapel and UNEXECUTED project for a tower (1775–*c.*1797) (Pls 149–51) E

Charlemont Letters, I, 349–50 (WC to Charlemont 20 May 1779)

RIBA Letters: WC to Anon, referring to Myers

Trinity College: Minutes of the Board, 4 March, 6 Dec. 1775, 28 May 1777; Register IV, 315, 331, 373

Payne, J., *Universal Geography*, Dublin, 1793, 197

Pool, R., and Cash, J., *Views in the City of Dublin*, 1780

Wright, C. N., *An Hist. Guide to Ancient & Modern Dublin*, 1821, 33–4

Irish Georgian Soc. Bull., VIII, no.3, 1965, 'Sir William Chambers, Friend of Charlemont', by John Harris

Trinity, I, 1949, 30, 'The College in 1780', by G.F.M.

Trinity, II, 1959, 14–16, 'The West Front of 1759', by M. Craig

The early history of this project is not fully documented, but on 6 December 1775 Chambers had agreed 'to undertake the business of drawing plans for the intended new buildings of the College, and having proposed to engage himself to furnish all the necessary designs for the workmen of every sort, figured, drawn out at large and accompanied with such instructions as will enable any intelligent clerk of the work to conduct the buildings with as much precision as if he were on the spot himself, in consideration of his receiving 3 per cent upon the amount of the bills, this proposal was this day accepted.' On 28 May 1777 it was 'Order'd that the intended new buildings on the South Side (consisting of the Theatre, with Lodgings for Fellows on the right and left of it) be forthwith begun.' The initiative may well have come from Lord Charlemont, or from one of the Irish circle of Chambers's friends. It is improbable that once Chambers embarked upon Somerset House he would have relished attending to such a public commission in Dublin; in fact we know that the designs provided were executed under the superintendence of Graham Myers, an extremely competent Irish builder. This is quite clearly stated by Chambers in his letter to Lord Charlemont on 20 May 1779, 'A couple of years ago I was requested to make designs for some very considerable additions to the buildings of Trinity College which I readily agreed to on a supposition that in the course of these works I might have an excuse for a voyage to Ireland, but the great difficulty attending the vast work I am now about, and the perplexed measures sent me from Dublin, obliged me to desist; and all I could do was to give a general disposition of what I intended, from which as I have since learnt the buildings are now executing. If there be any merit in the general intention I may claim some little share in it; but the whole detail, on which the perfection of these works must greatly depend, is none of mine and whatever merit that has is Mr Myers who I understand is the operator.'

Although no designs for this project have survived, the two engravings by Pool and Cash, published March 1779, are important documents, for they undoubtedly show Chambers's original scheme. Passing beneath the 1759 west front, the visitor to the College would have seen two projecting wings of identical composition: that on the north side containing the Chapel, and that on the south containing the Theatre. In the middle of the east side of the court would have been Chambers's obelisk tower, taken over literally from his unexecuted project for St Marylebone church (q.v.) and surmounting the rebuilding of an earlier structure by Castle. Pool and Cash, of course, anticipate for, according to Samuel Byron's axiometric view, exhibited in 1780 (and now lost), only the Theatre on the south side was built by then, although it was not completed internally for another six years. The Chapel had hardly been begun and was not complete in 1793 when Payne could yet hope that the 'beautiful steeple from a design of Sir William Chambers' would be built. Alas it never was.

28 DUDDINGSTONE (Edinburgh)

8th Earl of Abercorn

New house, stables and temple (1762–7) (Pls 62, 85–86; Fig.4) E

Soane: 42/9[7], chimney-piece inscr. 'No.5 1764 Ld Abercorn's drawing-room Alken £5·18'; 43/4[24–25], two plans showing staircase divided from hall by colonnade

Abercorn Papers, Baronscourt S.A.1/3; 1/4: Correspondence 2 Sept. 1762–29 Aug. 1767; Letter Books, vol.7 (I.K./7): progress reports by Key the mason, to Abercorn

RA: WC to Sandberg, 13 May 1763

RIBA Letters: Abercorn to WC 19 July, 25 Aug. 1763; 1 July 1764

Baird, W., *Annals of Duddingstone and Portobello*, Edinburgh, 1898, 84–6

RCHM, *Scotland*, 1951, 237–8

Statistical Account of Scotland, 1796, XVIII, 364

Vitruvius Britannicus, IV, 1767, pls.14–17

C.Life, 24 Sept. 1959, 358–61

The correspondence at Baronscourt, between James, 8th Earl of Abercorn, negotiating with Chambers for a new house, opens in September 1762. It is important accurately to date the inception of Duddingstone because of the relationship of its portico to that by Robert Adam at Shardeloes, building a little later. In terms of a stylistic synthesis of Palladian villa forms, Duddingstone must surely be Chambers's ultimate villa, for it is difficult to imagine any further evolution without the distortion of an accepted architectural vocabulary. In fact, by the elision of his basement, bringing the piano-nobile to ground level, and by the attachment of his splendid portico, Chambers almost converted the house into a temple. It is quite clear that the similar portico at Shardeloes was designed (1763) after Duddingstone, but the manner of linking the stables to the house at Shardeloes certainly preceded Duddingstone, for Adam's stable design in the RIBA is dated 1760. In quality and character, however, the Duddingstone stables are a masterpiece worthy of European regard.

Inside Duddingstone practically all Chambers's attention was directed towards the Hall, the most important compartment in the house. It contains a staircase which rises by a single central flight, dividing to right and left, and returning back upon itself, not to a connecting gallery, but to balconied platforms. There has been a certain alteration made to the stairs in the nineteenth century, and it seems almost certain that a gallery opened out to them from the wall above the mid-landing. The interior is notable for the absence of any order, except on chimney-pieces, and this may reflect a certain lip-service to Laugier. It is also known, for example, that Chambers originally wanted the Doric order of the stable colonnades to stand without bases. Except for the splendid ceiling of the Hall, an essay in circles, ovals and hexagons moulded by Thomas Collins, the decoration is so sparse and restrained that it is more in character with late eighteenth-century France than with mid-Georgian England. The mason and clerk of works, brought from Lord Bessborough's at Roehampton, was a Mr Key, and the carver was Sefferin Alken, mentioned by Chambers when writing to Abercorn on 15 May 1764 'Alken has done the Model for the arms & I think very well' (Abercorn Papers). According to Baird the house was finished in 1768 at a cost of £30,000.

29 DUNTISH COURT (Dorset)
Walter Fitz-Foy
New House (1760) (Pl. 60; Fig.3a)
Soane: 43/4²⁷, basement plan
V & A: 3366, basement plan; 7076, ground plan
Hutchins, John, *The History . . . of Dorset*, ed. Gough, III, 1813, 259
Oswald, A., *Country Houses of Dorset*, 1959, 164–5
Vitruvius Britannicus, V, 1771, 61–3

It is a pity that documentation on this early villa is lacking. Although Foy was of obscure Dorset landed gentry he must have spent a considerable sum building this grand country house in miniature, then named Castle Hill. There is no evidence

that Foy appeared in any of the circles patronized by Chambers, nor is the date of Duntish certain. 'About 1760' is given by Hutchins, and there is probably no reason to doubt this. In fact it would not be surprising if Duntish was found to be Chambers's first villa. At the time of writing the house was being demolished; but in any case, the roof was raised, the staircase rebuilt, and the cupolas on the flanking lateral pavilions altered, in the nineteenth century. The interiors here were the epitome of Chambers's decorative style for ceilings and chimney-pieces, and were of unusually high quality.

30 EAST BARNET (Herts): St Mary's Church
ATTRIBUTED monument to John Sharpe (after 1756) E
Cass, F. C., *East Barnet*, 1885–92, 111–12

This attribution is based on grounds of comparison with the almost identical monument to Sir Hans Sloane in Old Chelsea churchyard (q.v.). Sloane died in 1753 and Sharpe in 1756. It seems unlikely that Joseph Wilton, the sculptor of the Sloane monument, was capable of such markedly advanced neo-classic forms. These are impressive funerary monuments: a base decorated with typically Chambersian rope-like garlanded panels, and an urn standing free beneath an open-arched baldachino with low pyramidal cap.

31 EDINBURGH: ST ANDREW SQUARE: DUNDAS HOUSE (now Royal Bank of Scotland)
Sir Laurence Dundas
Town house (1771–4) (Pls 105–108; Fig.10) E
Royal Bank archives (on loan from Zetland papers): 2 plans, elevation of garden front, and section; part site plan and plan for laying out the garden
BM. Add. MS 41133, 38–38v, 53–53v, 115v (18 April 1771–27 Jan. 1774)
Arnot, Hugo, *The History of Edinburgh*, 1788, 319
RCHM, *Scotland*, Edinburgh, 1951, 188–9
Royal Notes, Royal Bank of Scotland Staff Mag. Spring 1965, no.29, 37–41, 'The Dundas Mansion' by C.W. and W.M.L.
Smith, John, *Notes on Sir Laurence Dundas Bart. His Mansion Dundas House, St Andrew Square*, MS 1917, 37–58 (in poss. Royal Bank of Scotland)

The building of the Dundas house must be seen against the background of James Craig's 1767 plan for laying out the New Town: George Street terminating at the west end by Charlotte Square with St George's church placed on the west axis, and St Andrew Square with an intended St Andrew's church to complete the east axis. Sir

Laurence already owned a site behind the proposed site for the latter church and in 1768 he had extended his property nearer to the site. The next step was clear and later in 1768 Sir Laurence must have acquired the whole church site giving him a superb position for his intended new house. In this year he at once began enquiring for plans; on 23 September John Carr, who had been altering Aske for Sir Laurence, received 'Twenty pounds on account of the Edinburgh Plan', and before or after this payment James Byers, a Scotsman living in Rome and an artistic agent for Sir Laurence, provided a set of Roman designs (now RIBA, ex archives Aske). Neither project seemed to suit Dundas and for some reason he shelved the scheme for several years, until 18 April 1771 when Chambers refers to one or both of these projects in a letter to Sir Laurence, saying that *his* designs would propose a 'much more convenient house in less space than the design wch Sir Laurence brought from the North'. Very soon after this the house was begun and on 30 October 1773 Chambers could 'hear your House in Scotland advances fast'. The final bills were settled on 27 January 1774.

We know from Arnot that the mason of the superbly-detailed house was William Jamieson, later to perform a similar task for Robert Adam at the Register House, and this is confirmed by Jamieson's signature to the designs in company with those of a Jo Pringle (solicitor) and Charles Dundas, Sir Laurence's brother.

Chambers has attempted here a more ornamented front than hitherto, and this accords with the trend of his style after 1770, culminating in Somerset House. The source for the front is the English villa, particularly Marble Hill. By great fortune the surviving section, combined with the floor plans, is enough to show that the staircase was derived directly from its near contemporary in Melbourne House. It is sad that both these remarkable stairs should have been destroyed. The decoration of the interiors was probably never lavish and the ceiling remaining in the present Board Room is by George Richardson, published in *Ornamental Ceilings*, 1776. The two periods of alteration which radically affected Chambers's interiors are 1828 when the house opened as a bank and an ill-conceived porch was slapped onto Chambers's façade, and 1858 when the domed banking hall was added at the rear and the staircase area gutted. We have no proof that the garden plan was executed although there is no reason to suggest it was not. The area and shape of the ground fit the site today perfectly. As a proposal it is a rare document for, apart from Kew, no other plan by Chambers for a garden exists. Like Kew the interest and colour are kept to peripheral walks. At Ladykirk, Berwickshire, is an almost identical version of the Dundas front, designed not by Chambers, but by Archibald Elliot in 1796.

32 EDINBURGH: 26 ST ANDREW SQUARE
Gilbert Meason
New house (1769) E
BM Add.MS 41133, 6, 12–12v (18 Feb.–5 May 1770)
Drummonds Bank Account: Meason to WC
£10.10. paid in February 1770
Kirkwood's 1817 map of Edinburgh
RCHM, *Scotland*, Edinburgh 1951, 191–2

While Dundas House is the central feature of the east side of St Andrew Square, Gilbert Meason's house at no.26 on the north side is but one of a variegated terrace. It has been refaced and altered but retains its original proportions of five bays and three storeys. Meason was a merchant of Leith, upon whom Chambers drew ten guineas in February 1770, 'due to me by you on acnt of the designs for your house'. In March he was sending Meason 'handsome patterns of flock paper' and advising that the parlours be painted a stone colour.

33 ENVILLE (Staffs)
5th Earl of Stamford
UNEXECUTED designs for a new house (*c*.1770)
RIBA: J4/38¹⁻², designs for two fronts
BM Add.MS 41133, 78v; 41134, 4v (28 July 1772)
Architectural Review, Sept. 1953, 'A New Design by Chambers', by G. Beard

In place of the untidy pseudo-medieval pile existing at Enville, Chambers proposed a new house with one front of nine bays and two main storeys with a three-bay pedimented centre, and another of nine unbroken bays copied from his 1762 design for refacing the Queen's House (q.v.). Lord Stamford, however, was much more interested in gardening than architecture, and it is not surprising, in view of his taste for Gothic follies and garden trivia, that he was unattracted by Chambers's simple and sedate designs. On 28 July 1772 Chambers wrote to the Earl asking, 'If it be not inconvenient to your Lordship I should esteem it a very particular favor at this time if you would order Payment of my Bill sent in some time ago amounting to £80.12. I am involved in so many building schemes that I am always in want of Money and more so now than ever for Guineas are now grown scarce as Othos, and my builders as greedily bent on collecting the one, as the first Virtuosi in Europe are in search of the other.'

34 ESHER (Surrey)
Richard Barwell
Work of unknown character (*c*.1763?)
MMA: (46.56.24) design for a chimney-piece inscr.
'Mr Barwell Esher'

Surrey CRO: list of Freeholders for Surrey 1762–71
Barwell was a freeholder in Esher from 1763 until
1767, and Sheriff of Surrey in 1768. The location
of his house is not known.

35 GOODWOOD HOUSE (Sussex)
3rd Duke of Richmond
South wing of house, stables, and gate-piers
(1757–60) (Pl.48) E
Gandon Albums: 1. 'Kitchen from that of Duke
of Choiseul, Paris' (in poss. Father Murphy,
Robertstown, Co. Kildare)
RIBA: J4/20, inscr. 'Principal Entrance', dated 1760
V & A: 3352, plan for stables not as executed;
7074.51, design for gate-piers, inscr. 'Goodwood
WC'
West Sussex CRO: Richmond Papers, Box 30/7
(bills)
Goodwood Sussex, A Guide, 1960 (reproducing a
plan of the house)
Jacques, D., *A Visit to Goodwood*, 1822
Mason, W. H., *Goodwood*, 1839
C.Life, 9 July 1932, 38–44
SALE: Christie, 6 June 1811, 97

The Richmond bills for 1757 and 1758 include
'Various designs for building at the Stud Apr
1758', 'Designs for the Stables at Goodwood now
Executing', and for 'finishing the large room.'
The extensive stables situated at the south-west
angle of the house must certainly have dwarfed
the modest early eighteenth-century hunting box
which remained from a large late seventeenth-
century house and which was only enlarged to its
present size after 1800 by James Wyatt.

The enigmatic 'large room' mentioned in the
accounts may be the room immediately behind the
south front of the house at right angles to the east
front of the stables. This is a small five-bay
(1–3–1) villa façade once the front of a projecting
wing but now squashed between circular towers
added by Wyatt. Goodwood may therefore possess
Chambers's first attempt at a villa design and, if
earlier than the attributed front to Osterley (q.v.),
his first 'front'. The decoration of rooms in this
wing is now predominantly of the 1770s, but the
large Library, once the 'large room', retains an
earlier entablature of Chambersian style. The gate-
piers designed for Goodwood have disappeared.

36 GOTHENBURG (Sweden)
UNEXECUTED design for a Fish Market
(*c*.1766)
EXHIB S of A 1767, 226–7
SALE: Christie, 6 June 1811, 100

The whereabouts of these designs, sold to Thomas
Hardwick in 1811, is now unknown. They were
probably drawn *c*.1766 perhaps at the instigation
of either David Sandberg or of John Chambers.
The Gothenburg City archives do not reveal any
proposals for a Fish Market at this time.

GOTHENBURG *see also* PARTILLE SLOT

37 GUNNERSBURY PARK (Middlesex)
Princess Amelia
ATTRIBUTED garden temple *c*.1760s. E

In 1761 Princess Amelia, daughter of George II
and aunt of George III, bought Gunnersbury, a
house designed in 1663 by John Webb. As the
princess was in close touch with her nephew at
nearby Kew, it is surely likely that she would have
borrowed his architect for any works she might
have undertaken. All that survives is an ambitious
temple with a tetrastyle Doric portico, in stone,
opening into a T-shaped brick cell behind. Its size
is larger than the Temple of Bellona at Kew, and
its Doric was based upon that of the Temple of
Pan there. At Gunnersbury there were further
allusions to Kew as there once existed a Temple of
the Sun, of the Baalbec kind.

38 HAREWOOD HOUSE (Yorks)
Edwin Lascelles
UNEXECUTED designs for a new house (1756)
(Pls 43–45)
Harewood archives: plans of ground and first
floor; elevations of one front and of the stables
RIBA Letters: John Hall Stevenson to WC 3 Nov.
1755; Lascelles to WC 20 June 1756

When Chambers was invited to 'compete' for
Harewood, the biggest plum on the country-
house market around the mid-eighteenth century,
he had designed nothing in England. His blunder
was to submit a set of uncompromisingly neo-
classic designs in the style of what we might
suppose was being produced at the French
Academy in Rome at the time. Edwin Lascelles
was unimpressed, influenced perhaps by the Earl
of Leicester to whom the designs had been shown.
Harewood would have been an astonishing house
if Chambers had been its architect. Parts of it were
very fine: the 'Louvre' portico or the columnar
pavilions, but it was undoubtedly, in its lack of
cohesion, a youthful essay not worthy of a York-

P

shire maecenas. One must regret that Chambers's nobly-rusticated stables were not built. There is no basis for the attribution of the present stables at Harewood to Chambers. They were, in fact, being built when Chambers was paid off for his rejected designs in 1756. In later years Harewood became a quarry for a number of designs: the portico turns up at Svarstjo, and in a simplified form at Lucan; the pavilions were utilized for the Casino at Marino. From the stables, Chambers took the entrance gateway and it became Thomas Brand's 'Rustic Tuscan Gate imitated from Inigo Jones York-Stairs', published in the *Treatise* in 1759, and finally the Water Gate for Somerset House.

39 HEADFORT (Co. Kildare)
1st Earl of Bective
UNEXECUTED designs for a new house (1765)
Headfort archives: album of designs
C.Life, 21 March 1936, 303

The architectural history of Headfort reflects Lord Bective's inability to decide upon what designs he should choose for his new house. Eventually those by Robert Adam were executed, with modifications, from 1771. Chambers's designs were submitted in 1765, as revealed by Lord Bective writing on them, 'this plan was drawn for me in London by Mr Chambers, anno 1765, for which I paid him Forty Guineas'. The idea of a high-pedimented centre rising above lower flanks was taken over for the garden front of Stanmore Park in 1769. Chambers had also suggested for Headfort quadrant colonnades linking the main block to pavilions.

40 HEDSOR LODGE (Bucks)
2nd Baron Boston
New house (1778) (Fig.3b)
Soane: 43/4¹⁴⁻¹⁸, plans inscr. 'Lord Boston's Plans'
WCRL: PA3, two sets of plans and elevations for variant scheme
RIBA Letters: Lord Hardwicke to WC 18 May 1767, *verso*, MS description of Hedsor
RIBA MSS: description of Hedsor and Cliveden
Ambulator, 1811, 136
Boydell, J. and J., *An History of the River Thames*, I, 1794, p.274 (plate)
Britton, J., and Brayley, E. W., *Beauties of England and Wales*, I, 1801, 387
Florence, George (Lord Boston), MS *History of Hedsor*, 1899
Passages From The Diaries of Mrs Philip Lybbe Powys, ed. Climenson, 1899, 202

Chambers probably knew the old house at Hedsor

long before 1778, for until 1764 it served as a minor 'accommodation' for Augusta, Dowager Princess of Wales when she was staying at nearby Cliveden. Lord Boston's new villa forms one of that small group, with the Poston Casina and Trent Place, of post-Somerset House projects. Boydell shows a three-storey brick villa with four bays on the side flanks and five bays (1–3–1) with canted projections on the adjacent front. From the preliminary plans it is possible to deduce that the canted projection was repeated on the opposite front. Mrs Lybbe Powys wrote, 'tho not to be styled large or magnificent (it) is altogether the most elegant one I've seen for a vast while . . . my lady's dressing room octagon, the corners fitted up with the cleverest wardrobes in inlaid woods'. Hedsor was demolished in 1865.

41 THE HOO (Herts)
Thomas Brand
Alterations and interior decoration; bridge, temple, gateway; designs for stables, boat-house, gate-piers (c.1762) (Pls 81, 188)
RIBA: Hoo Album containing designs for bridge, temple by the bridge, stables, boat-house, dairy, ceilings, bookcases, etc.
Soane: 43/6¹⁹, design for an overmantel, inscr. 'Done for Thos Brand at the Hoo . . . the woodwork by Thacker and the carving very well done by Alken'.
V&A: 3383, design for a proposed gate as published in the *Treatise*
RIBA Letters, Brand to WC 1 July 1764
T. Crowther and Son, hall chimney-piece and interior fragments
Chambers, *Treatise*, 1759, pl.49, design for gateway
Neale, J. P., *Views of the Seats*, ser.2, V, 1829
Vitruvius Britannicus, IV, 18, 1767: engraving of the bridge, inscr. on proof engraving (RIBA) 'Plan & Elevation of a Bridge at Thos Brand's Esqr of the Hoo in Hertfordshire', J. Gandon delin.M.Darly sc

To avoid confusion it is first of all essential to distinguish between Thomas Brand of The Hoo and his cousin Thomas Brand of The Hyde in Essex. Brand of The Hyde assumed the name of Brand-Hollis after the death of his friend Thomas Hollis, in 1774. Brand of The Hoo died in 1770 and was succeeded by his son, yet another Thomas, who employed Chambers in St James's Square (q.v.).

Chambers began working at The Hoo at the latest in 1762. The RIBA Album contains his designs for ceilings and bookcases; a bridge and a temple by the bridge; a dairy, boat-house, stables and gate-piers. He also supplied chimney-pieces as is evident from the Soane design and from the superbly carved (possibly by Hayward or Wilton) hall chimney-piece and other fragments acquired by Messrs Crowther when the house was demolished.

The most interesting aspect of Chambers's work here is his deliberate use of old-fashioned motifs. This is easily explained by the fact that the existing Hoo was one of a group of Hertfordshire houses built during the Protectorate in an artisan mannerism style. Chambers's efforts to attain some stylistic continuity may be seen in the broken scrolled pediment of the Alken-Thacker chimney-piece, the half-pilaster dependent from an eared architrave and scrolled at its base, and the curious gable on the Bridge temple.

The one surviving letter concerning The Hoo was written by Brand to Chambers, 1 July 1764. Not only does this date the gate but, even more interesting, it also reveals that Brand was then contemplating building a Mosque like the one at Kew. He writes, 'I have been looking over the Estimate you gave me in relation to the Gate I this year built, & find that the Mason contracted to do the Stone work of the Gate including fifteen feet of Coping on each side of it for 36£. now I find there is none of the Coping done & the bills left unpaid in the Country of Carriage for the Tools backwards & forwards & Iron Cramps, all of which in works contracted for are to be paid by the person who agrees to set up the Building. I have ordered the Wall to be coped by a Country Workman & have paid the bill for Cramps but I have left unpaid the Carriage of the Man's Tools. I thought you ought to be acquainted with these Particularly that you may know what to expect from that Mason in great things, that plays such Tricks in these Trifling works. the Accounts stands that I am to pay five pounds three shillings more for the Stone work than I had contracted to pay, a Seventh part of the Mason's bill. I am ready to reproduce the written Estimate if the Man should deny the Agreement. I beg the favor of you to let me know how many Bricks would be wanted to build the Turkish Mosque which you designed for the Princess's Gardens at Kew supposing all the Walls to be made of Brick till the beginning of the Domes. I hope you are by this time perfectly recovered & that you will take care not to sit too much as nothing can be worse for your Complaint . . .'

42 HOTHFIELD PLACE (Kent)
8th Earl of Thanet
Discussions for a new house (1773)
BM Add.MS 41133, 105, 106v (July–Aug. 1773)

This project never reached the design stage for Thanet imposed the unreasonable condition that Chambers should purchase the old house for

materials before building a new one. To this breach of etiquette Chambers obviously demurred!

43 HOUGHTON CONQUEST (Beds)
Marquis of Tavistock
Restoration and alteration (1765)
RIBA: plan for suggested restoration by Mr Musman
Russell, P., and Price, Owen, *England Displayed* . . . by a Society of Gentlemen, I, 1769, 355

According to Russell and Price this Jacobean house, said to have been altered a little later by Inigo Jones, 'in the year 1765, underwent another reformation, under the inspection of the celebrated Mr Chambers'. In this now gutted ruin there is now no evidence of Chambers's work. The Marquis is said to have taken up residence in 1764. If indeed Chambers was employed here, then his presence at the Marquis's father's house at Woburn in 1766 after Leadbetter's death is explained. According to Mr Musman's plan, Chambers created an octagonal room in the south tower.

44 HOVINGHAM HALL (Yorks)
Thomas Worsley
UNEXECUTED design for a Corinthian temple
Chambers, *Treatise*, 1759, pl.43
WCRL: Chambers's portfolios: drawing for the *Treatise* plate

Thomas Worsley, Surveyor General of the King's Works from 1760 until his death in 1778, was an enthusiastic amateur architect and a good friend of Chambers. The latter's publication of the design for a temple dedicated to Worsley may be interpreted as a token of friendship rather than a hoped-for commission. A similar temple may have been designed for Lord Fitzwilliam at Milton Park (q.v.).

45 HULL (Yorks): Trinity House Chapel
Corporation of Trinity House (1772)
BM Add.MS 41133, 79v–80, 97; 41134, 4 (1 Aug. 1772–March 1773)
Georgian Society of East Yorks Trans., II, Pt.iv, 1948–9
Tickell, John, *Hist. of Kingston Upon Hull*, 1796
RIBA Jnl, 7 Apr. 1892, 254

Because the Chapel of Trinity House, Hull, was destroyed in 1844, and is only partially shown in Tickell's book of 1796, it is impossible to make any critical judgements. It appears to have had a long and narrow pedimented front with a window flanked by a tall Doric order. In August 1772 their building was already completed and

Chambers was agreeing to 'make any alteration the Corporation pleases in their plans with Regard to painted windows. They are when well done very handsome but they seem to be properer for Gothic Buildings than for yours. They are very expensive & darken the inside considerably.' In March 1773 he thanked the 'gentlemen of Trinity House' for 'a few hams, &c, Yorkshire produce, and a cask of the best ale the country affords.' Some of the correspondence in the Royal Academy suggests that the Chambers family had trading interests in Hull, an obvious port for Anglo-Swedish exchange.

46 THE HYDE
Thomas Brand
Hall and staircase (1761) (Pl.91) E
Disney, J., *Memoirs of Thomas Brand-Hollis*, 1808, 5; pls. inscr. 'Section of the Hall and staircase at The Hyde, near Ingatestone Essex Sr Wm Chambers Archt, 1761', and 'Section of one end of the Hall . . .'

The Hyde was built by Timothy Brand in 1721 and improved in 1761 by Thomas Brand (who changed his name to Brand-Hollis in 1774). Needing additional space to house his collection of antique sculpture in more appropriate surroundings, Thomas called upon his old friend Chambers to provide a new hall and staircase. The latter is skilfully placed behind a screen of superimposed columns, and is thus spatially part of the hall, but does not obtrude upon it. The ceiling is a pattern of enriched diagonal cross-beams.

47 INGRESS ABBEY (Kent)
John Calcraft
Work of unknown character, including a Doric tetrastyle temple to house a collection of Roman altars (before 1770)
BM Add.MS 41133, 82v (4 Sept. 1772)
MMA: drawing attributed to Thomas Carter, inscr. 'A Frieze in a chimney piece at Calcrafts Kent'
Brayley, E. W., *The Beauties of England and Wales* (Kent), 1808, 574–5, and plate
Hasted, E., *History of Kent*, I, 1778, 263–4

On 4 September 1772 Chambers wrote to the agent of the Ingress estates whose owner, John Calcraft, had recently died, 'I have a debt due to me of £74 part of a pretty long-standing for designs of things executed at Ingress'. The Earl of Bessborough had sold Ingress to Calcraft immediately after Lady Bessborough's death in 1760. It seems probable therefore that Calcraft similarly employed Chambers about this time, although it should be borne in mind that Adam had proposed additions in 1765 (Soane, *Adam Drawings*, II, 121;

31.120–2). Hasted, the Kent historian, comments upon Bessborough's improvements at Ingress, and says that Calcraft extended the plantations and gardens and, 'had he lived, Ingress would most probably have been one of the greatest ornaments of this century'.

The house was spectacularly sited on a low plateau facing the Thames just west of Gravesend. Brayley's engraving of 1808 shows the centre with an oddly-proportioned semi-circular domed portico, flanked by projecting canted bays and topped by sphinxes. If the £74 were for designs supplied, then considerable alterations must have been made to Ingress. Brayley also refers to an 'elegant summer house' where Calcraft kept his collection of Roman altars. This temple, a fluted version of the Temple of Arethusa at Kew, is now at Cobham Hall, Kent (q.v.) where it was installed by the 4th Earl of Darnley in 1820.

48 KEW GARDENS (Surrey)
Frederick, Prince of Wales
ATTRIBUTED House of Confucius (1749) (Pl.23)
MMA: (25.19) drawing by Chambers for Kew book
Sandbeck Archives: Account book Frederick, Prince of Wales 1750
Chambers, *Plans . . . Of . . . Kew*, 1763
Apollo, Aug. 1963, 'Exoticism at Kew', by John Harris

The circumstantial evidence for Chambers's participation in the design of this important chinoiserie building is strong enough to warrant an attribution to him. Although he was working at Kew only six years after it was built, employing the same craftsmen who had been employed by the Prince, and patronized by the Prince's widow, he seems in the *Plans* to have deliberately confused the authorship of this temple. He was vague as to whether Joseph Goupy designed it, although Goupy was then alive; attributes the furniture to Kent, whom he knew had died in 1748, and yet, as if by a slip of the engraver's burin, his name appears below the plate as the architect, whereas elsewhere in the book buildings not by him are correctly ascribed. This attribution cannot be considered in separation from the genesis of the Alhambra, built in 1758 but based upon a drawing made for the Prince in 1750 and almost certainly in the hand by J. H. Muntz who was possibly in Paris in this year. A plausible explanation is that Chambers visited Kew between his return from the East in July 1749 and his visit to Paris in either October or November. There can be little doubt that his interest in Chinese architecture had permeated to countries outside of Sweden, and this interest would certainly have appealed to a

Prince who was himself around this time fascinated by the exotic and rococo. If Chambers designed this temple, then there is a good reason for his wish to disguise the fact, for it is detailed in a typically Western manner (such as the comparable Chinese House at Shugborough of *c*.1747), in a radically-different style to the Chinese houses presented by Chambers in his 1757 *Designs for Chinese Buildings*. Perhaps the most telling clue to Chambers's participation in the Prince's interests in 1749 is the fact that he prepared many designs for the Prince's Mausoleum in 1751 when living in Rome as, virtually, an Anglo-Swedish student. No one else made such designs.

49 KEW GARDENS (Surrey)
Augusta, Dowager Princess of Wales
UNEXECUTED designs for a mausoleum for Frederick, Prince of Wales (1751–2) (Pls 4–7; Fig.1)
RA: Yenn Albums, MS description of the allegorical programme
Soane: 17/7, nos.716. Elevation inscr. 'Mausol. L. Wales WC'; no.717. Plan. no.718, Elevation inscr. 'Mausoleum Prince of Wales 1751 WC'
V & A: 3339, section inscr. 'February 1752 Section of the Mausoleum for the P. of Wales'; 3340, elevation; 3341, plan
Essays in the History of Architecture Presented to Rudolf Wittkower, 1967: 'Le Geay, Piranesi and International Neo-classicism in Rome 1740–50', by John Harris
SALE: Christie, 6 June 1811, 77

These designs are intimately related to the columnar inventions of the French Academy in Rome in the decade of the forties, by such architects as Le Geay, Piranesi, Le Lorrain, Challe, Petitot, Dumont, and Jardin. It is difficult to separate the interchange of ideas, for this circle of architects seem to have been on familiar terms with each other. There is, however, no doubt as to their obsession with the mausoleum as an ideal form of neo-classic monument.

50 KEW GARDENS (Surrey)
Augusta, Dowager Princess of Wales and George III
Bridge or sub-structure to House of Confucius (1757); Gallery of Antiques (1757); Orangery (1757–61); Temple of Pan (1758); Temple of Arethusa (1758); Alhambra (1758); Garden seats (1758); Porter's Lodge (1758); Stables (1758); Temple of Victory (1759); Ruined Arch (1759); Theatre of Augusta (1760); Temple of Bellona (1760); Menagerie (1760); Exotic Garden (1760); Mosque (1761); Temple of the Sun (1761); Pagoda (1761–2); Temple of Peace (1763, un-

completed); Temple of Eolus, Temple of Solitude, Palladian Bridge (all before 1763); Dairy, and alterations to Kew House for George III, (1772) (Pls 22–40) E
BM: King's Maps XL.46M, plan of Kew 1763; XL.46 O 1, plan of Kew 1785; and survey of Kew by T. Richardson, 1771
J. Harris Coll., London: Section of the Mosque with proposed decorations
Mr and Mrs Paul Mellon Coll.: Design for a monument to Pope; design for Peace
MMA: (25.19), MSS and drawings for Plans . . . of Kew; (34.78.2 [31]), design for ceiling in Alhambra
MPL: design for temples, mostly by Thomas Hardwick and John Yenn
RIBA: J4/19$^{1-2}$, drawing, attributed to J. H. Muntz, of a Hispano-Moresque building, and the model for 1758 Alhambra; J4/19^3, Elevation of Temple of Peace; E3/61, design for the Pagoda
Soane: 43/4$^{12-13}$, floor plans of Kew House; 43/7^6, mausoleum to Pope and Gay; 43/7$^{7-8}$, Temple of Peace; 43/7^9, copy of design for Temple of Arethusa; 43/7$^{17-18}$, plan and elevation of Theatre of Augusta
V & A: 3384, 3386, projects for Pope, Gay mausoleum
WCRL: PA4, plan of Kew House for alterations in 1772; designs for Augusta, Pan and a classical version of the Ruined Bridge
BM Add.MS 5726 C, 26: WC to Lord Bute, 24 Dec. 1763; Add.MS 41133, 11v–12, 13–13v, 14, 16, 69 (2 May 1770–12 March 1772)
Duchy of Cornwall Office: Accounts Dowager Princess of Wales, XLI(1) Vouchers – XLVIII(1) Vouchers (Oct. 1757–Jan, 1764)
PRO: works 4/14 Minutes and Proceedings Jan. 1767–Oct. 1772; works 4/15 Oct. 1772–April 1778
RA: Robert Wood to WC, 22 Aug. 1757
RIBA Letters: WC to W. Seward, 15 Nov. 1790
WCRL: Archives 55537, account for journeys to Kew, 1768–9; 55564, account for Solomon Brown's work, 1768–9; 55507, bill for 'sundry expences' £546.7.7 on account of the Pagoda, including £27.19.8 to John Chant, carpenter
Chambers, *Plans . . . of Kew*, 1763; edition by P. Norbury and G. Bickham, between 1763 and 1769
Gentleman's Magazine, XLII, 1772, 400 (descriptions of the Mosque)
Hirschfeld, C. C. L., *Théorie de l'Art des Jardins*, III, Leipzig, 1781, 76–81
Le Rouge, *Jardins Anglo-Chinois*, cah.6/4–5, 6/30; 8/28
Papendick, G. E., *Kew Gardens: a series of Twenty-four Drawings on Stone* (*c*.1820)
Sirén, O., *China and Gardens of Europe . . .* , New York, 1950
Walpole, H., 'Journal of Visits to Country Seats', *Walpole Soc.*, XVI (1928), 23–4, 38

Apollo, Aug. 1963, 'Exoticism at Kew', by John Harris
C.Life, 31 May 1930, 'Sir William Chambers and Kew', by A. Oswald
C.Life, 28 May 1959, 'Fate of the Royal Buildings', by John Harris
The Burlington Magazine, 'Richard Wilson's Views of Kew', by D. Cooper
EXHIB SofA 1762: The Ruin and Temple of Victory
SALE: Christie, 6 June 1811, 53, 78; Sotheby, 23 May 1951, 26

In contrast to the profusion of designs, there are hardly any documents for the buildings at Kew. Although the Duchy of Cornwall accounts are complete for day-to-day work, they concern only the Orangery (called the New Room), Porter's Lodge, Stables, and re-siting of the House of Confucius and repairing School House. It seems possible, therefore, that most of the buildings were paid out of a Privy Purse account, which has not survived. Chambers's work begins in September 1757, soon after he had been appointed architect to the Princess. His main output was recorded in the lavish folio of 1763, paid for by the King, but he continued to supervise Kew until the death of the Princess in 1772. Immediately George III gave orders for the workmen at Kew to be in readiness for alterations to the palace, as there was then a pressing need to accommodate his growing family, and on 12 August 1772 an estimate for £4982 was presented to the Office of Works (Works 4/14), and a further one of £4130 on 16 October the same year (Works 4/15). G. E. Papendick shows the Clock Tower built then.

In 1757 a number of craftsmen who had worked for Prince Frederick before 1751 and for the Dowager Princess between 1751 and 1756 came under the supervision of Chambers. They included Andrews and William Jelfe, masons; John Devall, mason; George Warren, carpenter; Francis Engleheart, plasterer; and Solomon Brown, bricklayer. Other recorded craftsmen are Samuel Cobb, painter; Thomas Davies, paviour; Ralph Taylor, bricklayer; Joseph Wilton, sculptor; Charles Frime, carver; William Greenel, joiner; and Charles Chapman and Aubrey Keene, decorative(?) painters, and John Chant, carpenter.

After 1772 Brown, Warren, Engleheart, and Cobb are still recorded at Kew along with the newcomers, Sefferin Alken and Thomas Hardwick. The few years covered by the Letter Books provide a fascinating commentary upon the unending chapter of repairs and renovations. For example, on 2 May 1770 Chambers found it necessary to rebuke the plumber, Mrs Hillman, because 'the repairs done in the kitchen garden at Kew by her men are very ill done'; and on 13 May 1770, Warren was desired to put up the minaret at the Mosque, to pitch gutters on the exotic stove, to repair the capitals of the Temple of Arethusa, and to check whether the rail has been put around the top storey of the Pagoda. We find Cobb working on the Flower Garden, the Aviary, and the Temples of Sun and Pan; and likewise, Engleheart is ordered to repair the plasterwork at the Alhambra.

Out of twenty-five buildings and objects erected at Kew between 1757 and 1763 only five survive: the Orangery, the Ruined Arch, the Pagoda, and the rebuilt temples to Bellona and Eolus.

51 KIRKANDREWS (Cumberland): Church of St Andrew
ATTRIBUTED design of church *c*.1774 E
Gibb, Sir Alexander, *The Story of Telford*, 1935, 322

Sir Alexander Gibb relates that after 1774 Telford helped Robin Hotson to build this church 'designed by Sir William Chambers.' Chambers is unlikely to have accepted a country job like this in 1774, and less likely in 1776. The church is, however, a London-styled one, and is perhaps by Thomas Hardwick, hence the Chambers association.

52 KIRKLEATHAM HALL (Yorks)
Charles Turner
Gallery (*c*.1765)
Young, A., *A Six Months' Tour through the North of England*, II, 1770, 107–8

On the basis of style alone it is difficult to accept the Gallery at Kirkleatham as a work by Chambers. The attribution by Arthur Young is worded ambiguously, made in the course of describing the doorcases, and therefore may not refer to the room as a whole. But Young also states that the chimney-pieces were carved by Wilton who was, of course, habitually employed about this time by Chambers, and hardly ever by John Carr, known to have been working at Kirkleatham in 1765. Young's report, together with the known relationship between Chambers and Turner, through a cousin in Ripon, suggests that Chambers probably supplied designs altered by Carr, for Carr's style is evident in the Gallery. There is no basis for the traditional attribution of the gate-piers to Chambers, for they only remotely resemble his style.

53 LIVERPOOL (Lancs)
Theatre Royal (1772)
Lancs CRO: Holt–Gregson Papers, v.12, 9
Broadbent, R. J., *Annals of the Liverpool Stage*, Liverpool, 1908

Brooke, R., *Liverpool in the last quarter of the 18th century*, 1855

Chaffers, Robert, Engraving of the painting made of the Theatre front, published 12 May 1773

According to information supplied by Mr S. A. Harris, of Liverpool, the Holt–Gregson papers contain the statement by John Holt, a promoter of the Theatre, that Chambers was the architect. This is the source for the attribution in both Broadbent and Brooke. If a fact, then designs must have been submitted in 1771 or 1772, for the Theatre was officially opened in June of the latter year. There is, however, no mention of this project in the very complete Letter Books covering the years from 1769 to 1775. The front is a provincial rendering of the Town Hall at Woodstock, in brick not stone, with the addition of a central Venetian window and the triplicate of entrances, and must surely be the work of a local builder interpreting Chambers's designs. It no longer exists, having been rebuilt in 1802.

54 LLANAERON (Cardiganshire)
John Lewis
UNEXECUTED project for a villa (*c.*1761?)
(Pl.61)
B. Pardoe Coll: design for the portico front, inscr. 'FRONT ELEVATION llanerchaern'
Meyrick, S. R., *The Hist. & Antiqs of Cardigan*, 1808, 286–7
Nicholas, T., *Annals of the County Families of Wales*, I, 200–1

Unfortunately very little is known about the genesis of this important design which may be considered as penultimate to Duddingstone. It would be especially interesting to know, for example, how the obscure John Lewis (like Foy of Duntish) came to employ Chambers. Llanaeron was rebuilt late in the eighteenth century by John Lewis's heir, Colonel William Lewis.

55 LONDON: 19 ARLINGTON STREET
Sir Laurence Dundas
ATTRIBUTED alterations of unknown character (1772)
BM Add.MS 41133, 77v, 81, 115v (27 July 1772–30 Oct. 1773)

On 22 July 1772 Chambers wrote to Sir Laurence, 'Your Rooms are now dry enough to finish be pleased therefore to give directions about the choice of your Paper or hangings & I should be glad to meet your paperman.' Although Chambers was still concerned with Dundas House in Edinburgh (q.v.) this letter, having been written in London and addressed to Edinburgh, must surely be referring to work either in London or at

Sir Laurence's country houses at Moor Park, Hertfordshire, or Aske Hall, Yorkshire. As there are no indications of alterations to Moor Park at this period, and as Aske seems to have been under the superintendence of John Carr, we may conclude the letter refers to minor alterations to 19 Arlington Street where Sir Laurence had previously employed Robert Adam. The fact that both Chambers and Carr were employed by Sir Laurence suggests that he may not have been entirely happy in his relationship with Adam. Chambers's letter of 30 October 1773 says, 'Your floors were relaid a great while ago and all the other little jobs you ordered done.'

56 LONDON: 21 ARLINGTON STREET
3rd Viscount Weymouth
New house (1769) E
Avery: (1C/219) design for a chimney-piece, inscr. 'Lady Weymouth'
BM Add.MS 41133, 29 (Feb. 1770)
WPL: Rate Books

In February 1770 Chambers requested Lord Weymouth to settle his bills delivered late in 1769 for work executed the previous summer. The outstanding payment then due to Chambers was £275.11.0. This, the Avery design, and the fact that Lord Weymouth was rated for a new house from 1770, clearly indicates that Chambers was the architect of 21 Arlington Street. Although a mansard attic has been added, and the ground-floor windows altered, it is still possible to discern Chambers's simple, finely-proportioned front of four bays and three storeys, built of smoothly-detailed brick.

57 LONDON: BEDFORD HOUSE
4th Duke of Bedford
Alterations and minor redecoration; alteration of gates (*c.*1769–*c.*1772)
Bedford Office, London: 13/3/4, box 523 (20 Nov. 1769–16 May 1771)

On 27 June 1766 Stiff Leadbetter had obviously been employed upon extensive work here, for his painting bill came to £600 (BRO R.327), and presumably after his death Chambers took over, as at Woburn. There is no evidence, however, that Chambers was responsible for substantial work.

58 LONDON: 45 BERKELEY SQUARE
1st Baron Clive
Internal decorations (1763–7) E
IOL: Clive MSS, bills, letters and receipts, unsorted (Boxes 77, 79, 80, 81, 82)

Prescott, P. M., *45 Berkeley Square*, 1967
C.Life, 2 Jan. 1937, 14–18

Between February and July 1763 Clive was
searching for a town house and to this end
Chambers surveyed for him 'Ld Grenville's
house', 'Mr Dunche's house in Scotland Yard',
'Mr Frederick's house in Grosvenor Street', and
'Lord Hertford's house' on Park Lane.

According to the bills, work at Berkeley Square
began about July 1763 and extended until 1767.
Although these accounts are not complete, an
abstract of expenditure in 1766–7 records the sum
of £3718.5.5. In the two previous years Chambers had himself been credited with £700 and
£800, so it is fairly clear that the refashioning of
this early-Georgian town house, almost certainly by Flitcroft, cost Clive about £6000. Later
alterations have obliterated much of Chambers's
work, but there remains the splendid ceiling and
doors of the first-floor Saloon; the ceiling of the
back reception room; and chimney surrounds
principally in the ground-floor apartments. On
22 November 1766 Charles Catton was paid £40
'To painting Ornaments in gold and colours –
pasting pictures in the ovals – & gilding a carved
soffit on a ceiling'. The ceiling referred to has disappeared, although the inset pictures may have
been by Augustin Brunias who was paid £14.14
for paintings in 1766–7. Payments to Thomas
Westcot, the slater, indicate that Chambers probably also added a low attic-storey to this house.
The other craftsmen recorded here are the mason
George Mercer; the bricklayer, Edward Gray; the
carver, Sefferin Alken; the plasterer, Thomas
Collins; the carpenter, Benjamin Thacker; the
smith, James Palmer; a painter and gilder, George
Evans; and the plumber, William Chapman.

59 LONDON: BERNERS STREET Numbers 13–
22; 44, 45(?), 46–47, 48–53(?), 54–58
Houses for himself and for speculation (1764–70)
(Fig.11)
MMA: (34.78.2 [23]), copy of V & A ceiling 2216.27
RIBA: J4/30, inscr. 'Ceiling for the front Room 1 pr
of Stairs Mr Colling's large house'; Collins'
Album: 4 inscr. 'Cornice round the Screen in
Yard Mr Collins's large house'; 20 inscr. 'Sky
Light' and 'Large house'; 29 inscr. 'Ceiling for Mr
Collins's Back Room One pr stairs at his house
now Building on the East side of Berners Street
Apr 1770'; 30 inscr. 'Elevation of Door for Mr
Collins's small house'; 31 inscr. 'Elevation of the
door for Mr Collins's large House'
Soane: 43/2³, ground floor plan of 13–15 inscr.
'Parlour floor of Mr Chambers' houses in Berners
Street'; 43/69⁻¹⁰, detail for 13 inscr. 'String for my
Stair'
V & A: 7076.10, cellar plan of 19–20; 7078.4, oval

mirror inscr. 'For my Eating room'; 7078.7 inscr.
'ceiling in front room of the small house'; 2216.27
inscr. 'No 12 ceiling In Mrs Chambers's Drawg
Rm W Chambers Invent 1765'
BM Add.MS 41133, 4v, 31–31v, 51v–52, 66v (28
Dec. 1769–Jan. 1772)
St MPL: Rate, lighting and paving books; deeds
Horwood, R., Plan of the Cities of London and
Westminster, 1799
Moore, N., and Paget, S., *The Royal Medical and
Chirurgical Society of London Centenary*, 1905
LCC: Survey of London Photographic Collection
(Photos of 19–21, 56)
NMR: Photographs of 46 and 56

Chambers began developing Berners Street in
1764–5 when he designed the first house, 13, for
himself.

From the evidence of the Rate Books building
progressed northwards on this, the east side of
the street. 14 was for James Lacy; 15 for Thomas
Rouse; 16 for Major-General Keppel; 17 is an
attributed house, but clearly by Chambers; 18 was
for William Green; 19 for John Gordon; and 20
was the 'large house' building in April 1770 for
Thomas Collins, a partner in this speculation, and
also a partner in a temporary bank account (1770–
3) at Drummonds. Berners Street, in fact, put
Collins on the road to a great fortune leading him
to larger-scale speculation which culminated in his
development of the Portland Estate with John
White.

On the west side of the street, progressing
southwards, Collins is found in 1768 at 44, his
'small house'. Then 46–47 and 53–58 were all
probably by Chambers.

The Letter Books document two of the Berners
Street leaseholders. William Green was informed
on 28 December 1769 that his house at 18 'seems
to me very fit for reception whenever the up-
holsterers have finished and the house cleaned'
(Add.MS 41133, 4); Robert Gregory's interest can
be followed from design to completion. In February 1771, Chambers writes, 'I have made as near
calculation as I can find that the house you wish to
treat with me for will cost £2700 when finished in
a neat manner like the other houses I have built in
the same street any of which I can show you'; and
on 31 August 1771, 'I expect to have your house
finished in a months time . . . if you have any particular fancy about the painting your principal
rooms, my intention is to finish the whole of a
fine stone colour . . . excepting the eating parlour
which I propose to finish pea green with white
mouldings & ornaments' (Add.MS 41133, 51–52);
finally in December 1771 Gregory is sent his
insurance policy and the bill for work done.

It is possible to ascribe to Chambers the design
and building of nineteen houses in this street. If
he was responsible for 45 and 48 to 54 (as is

probable), then the sum may be increased to about twenty-six houses. These were, without exception, of dignified proportions, with external decoration restricted to fine doorcases, variants of which were later to appear at Somerset House. The excellent plasterwork inside was by Collins. Although in Berners Street Chambers indulged successfully in speculation, he employed none of the usual speculator's gimmicks for making easy money. Even in their smallest details his houses revealed the best of craftsmanship and materials.

The most tantalizing account of Chambers's own house comes from Charles Bielefeld (*On the Use of the Improved Papier-Mâché In Furniture, in the Interior Decoration of Buildings, and In Works of Art*, new edn 1850, 7, 11) who tells us that in the eighteenth-century chimney-pieces were 'very effectively decorated in Papier-Mâché, as was formerly much practised by Sir William Chambers and others', and that 'Chambers's own house in Berners Street . . . has the Papier-Mâché which enriched the *fanciful* (author's italics) architecture at the back of the house in perfect preservation'; and the *Literary World* for April 1840 tells us 'The Papier-Mâché decorations distributed in the ornamental parts of houses erected from designs of Sir William Chambers, and supplied from the workshop of his friend Wilton, the statuary, appear, on a late inspection, to be in a perfectly sound condition'. Can we perhaps believe that Chambers's 'fanciful' façade to his house was in some exotic style, a papier-mâché Chinese veneer painted and varnished?

60 LONDON: BLACKFRIARS BRIDGE

Competition (1759) (Pl.140)
W. J. Harvey Collection (1893): plans, elevations and sections, inscr. 'The Front of a Design for the Intended Stone Bridge at Black Fryars by W. Chambers, Architect to the Prince of Wales' Mylne, R. S., *The Master Masons to the Crown of Scotland*, Edinburgh, 1893, pl. facing p.264 and p.265 (reproducing elevation of centre)
EXHIB S of A 1761, 182

Chambers's design was one of sixty-nine submitted by various architects in the competition for Blackfriars Bridge which was won by Robert Mylne. According to Gwilt (*Memoir* in 1825 edition of Chambers's *Treatise*), Mr Paterson, 'an opulent city merchant', encouraged Chambers to submit his designs. It is not surprising that they were rejected by the Committee as being too magnificent for execution, for not only are they in the 'Grand Prix' tradition, but they do not attempt to solve any of the structural or engineering problems posed by the task, and solved by Mylne.

61 LONDON: BUCKINGHAM PALACE

(formerly Buckingham House, then Queen's House)
King George III and Queen Charlotte
Rebuilding of main block, addition of north and south wings, west and east libraries; the Octagon Library, interior decorations and the Riding House (1762–76) (Pls 113–120)
BM: Crace Views XIII, 14. Showing works in construction 1768
RA: Yenn Albums, elevation by Cipriani(?), of window wall of Saloon
RIBA: G3/1, design for ceiling in Second Drawing Room, by Chambers and Cipriani, inscr. 'Costs/ Cipriani for painting 17 Pictures & 4 Genii Ls 225/Catton for painting in Gold & colour all/ the ornaments and the four angles & moulds 120/ Norman for pasting up the work 12.12.0' £375.12.0'
Soane: XXIV/5, section through stairs and saloon; Adam volume 22, nos 56–8, designs for chimney-pieces dated 1761
V & A: N18. Section through staircase and saloon (copy of Soane, XXIV/5)
WCRL: Portfolio *Royal Palaces*, folder inscr. '3 Elevations of the Queens Palace'; folder inscr. 'The Queens Palace', with survey plans; designs by Capability Brown for the gardens. P.A.4, folder 'The Royal Apartments at . . . Queens House' with four plans showing proposed and executed additions.
WPL: Gardner Coll., 39/15–18, 31, 39 (copies of plans submitted to George III 23 March 1776; 39/12 (elevation for refacing main block); 39/23–5 (designs for Octagon Library); 39/11a (design for stair wall to Saloon); 39/30 (Yenn's plan and elevation of the Riding House)
Worsley Coll., Hovingham: design for a doorcase by George III; unexecuted design dated 1762 of Robert Adam's refronting of the palace
Abercorn Papers, Baronscourt: WC to Abercorn 2 Sept. 1762
PRO: *Works Minutes*, 4/13, 4/14; 5/63
WCRL: *Buckingham Palace, History and Plans of the Grounds . . .*, 1762
Adam, R. and J., *The Works in Architecture*, I, no.v (1778) pl.IV, chimney-piece in great saloon; pl.VII, ceiling in Japanned room
Journals of the House of Commons, XXXV, 320: expences 1762–1774=£72,627.0.1½
Pyne, W. H., *The History of the Royal Residences*, II, 1819
Smith, E. Clifford, *Buckingham Palace*, 1931
Vitruvius Britannicus, I, 1715, 43–4
Walpole, H., 'Journal of Visits to Country Seats', *Walpole Soc.*, XVI (1928), 78 (1783 refers to Cipriani)
C.Life, 12 July 1962, 'The Sheffields at Buckingham House', by John Cornforth
Principal craftsmen and artists employed:
Benjamin Carter, sculptor

Charles Catton, painter
Sir Henry Cheere, sculptor
G. B. Cipriani, painter
Thomas Clark, plasterer
Richard Cobbett, glazier
John Devall, mason
John Devall, plumber
William Hogarth, painter
William Jelfe, mason
James Moss, joiner
Samuel Norman, gilder
Philip Nind, ironmonger
William Oram, painter
James Palmer, smith
John Philips, carpenter
Joseph Pratt, bricklayer

In 1702 John Sheffield, Earl of Normanby and soon to be Duke of Buckingham, acquired the site of his future Buckingham House. By 1705 his new house was nearly complete, designed by Captain William Winde who may have been following designs already supplied by William Talman. What arose on the edge of Westminster was a great country house. William Fitch contracted to build the brick carcase, Laguerre supplied a splendidly-colourful interior, and the great Tijou some of his best ironwork. As Edward Hutton could comment in his *New View of London* in 1708, here was a 'seat not to be contemned by the greatest monarch'. It was therefore appropriate that when the legality of the seventeenth-century leases were subjected to enquiry about 1760, and the house was found to be standing partly upon Crown lands, it was purchased for £28,000 in 1762 for Queen Charlotte. After this it was sometimes called Buckingham House, but more often The Queen's House.

The Board of Works sanctioned repairs from July 1762, and on 2 September Chambers could mention to Lord Abercorn 'designs to be made for various alterations in the Queen's house'. Until at least 1776 hardly a year passed without the Board being instructed, or giving instructions, for some alteration to this royal mansion, beloved of George III. In general the King was given the ground-floor apartments and the Queen those on the first floor; and as a generalization it could be said that the former were designed with an eye to utility and the latter for display. Chambers's first tasks were to encase and give a face-lift to the old 1705 front, which he considerably modernized and refined. The forecourt was raised, Winde's pilasters and bucolic swags were disposed of, and the fenestration was sashed. But the principal structural addition comprised two balancing wings to the garden front, each of seven bays with a slight centre break of five bays. Paradoxically, although there are dozens of views of the entrance front, there is none showing these wings facing the garden.

The accommodation required in the northern wing was mainly domestic, but in the southern block apartments were added for the King's growing library. First to be built between 1762 and 1766 was the Great or West Library, 60 feet by 30 feet; then between 1766 and 1768 followed the South Library and the Octagon; and finally in 1772 and 1773 the East Library was squeezed in between the Octagon and the south end of the house. Above the South Library was a Gallery in which to keep the royal collection of drawings and medals, and in 1774 the walls of the East Library were heightened to form a gallery known as the Marine Gallery, where the King displayed his models of British ships and harbours. As Capability Brown's designs for laying out the gardens show, the north wing was added slightly later than the southern one, and the accounts pin it down between 1766 and 1768. It was further extended around 1776 for the Prince of Wales by a wing projecting eastwards and having a semi-octagonal termination. By 1776 The Queen's House had cost £72,627.0.1½.

Chambers's most notable interiors were the Saloon and the Octagon Library, although had he had his way the staircase would have been re-modelled grandly. As built by Winde the stairs were arranged around three sides of a well, and the visitor to the Saloon would, on reaching the top landing, have turned into two front-garden rooms before being able to enter the Saloon on the court front. There was then no direct access to this Saloon from the staircase. Chambers altered this. From the top landing he broke through the Saloon wall, destroying one of Laguerre's murals, but substituting for it a grisaille composition painted by William Oram as a *trompe-l'œil* exhedra around the new doorway. In 1776 Chambers had proposed a grand 'Imperial' stair here, but this was not carried out as perhaps too expensive. It was left to James Wyatt to design the staircase shown by Pyne – and so, in all probability, to execute a design by a master whom he revered.

Thus through this aggrandized doorway we would have entered the Queen's Saloon, in effect her Throne Room, and appropriately the richest of the state apartments. Oram probably collaborated with Cipriani to decorate the walls with grisaille bas-reliefs, and also to help with the ceiling. Two other rooms possessed paintings by Cipriani, one designed by Chambers and the other by Adam. It is now quite clear that Adam's part in this rejuvenation of an older house was minimal. Although Joint Architect to the King, he was not liked by that monarch and one must suspect that Chambers helped to keep him at bay. In fact all he is known to have designed, apart from the Cipriani ceiling, is the Saloon chimney-piece (now in the Queen's Presence Chamber at Windsor

Castle), possibly the Queen's Dressing Room, and perhaps a grandiose door.

The one other main addition built under Chambers's auspices was the Riding House built between 1763 and 1766 at a cost of £5726.15.7. This building, 264 feet in length, is substantially the Riding House today refaced by Nash who added to its pediment Theed's relief of Hercules taming the horses of Diomedes. As there are many designs for stables by his Office of Works's colleagues in Thomas Worsley's collection at Hovingham, it must be presumed that this great equestrian gave his advice over this building.

At first the Queen's House was not strictly maintained by the Office of Works, and was probably built from verbal discussions that took place between the King and his two friends Chambers and Worsley – who was his Surveyor General and therefore Chambers's immediate superior. In April 1769, however, the building came under Treasury jurisdiction and William Robinson was appointed Clerk of Works there.

62 LONDON: BUCKINGHAM PALACE
King George III
Astronomical Clock (1768) (Pls 131–133) E
Soane: 43/7^{22}, design for one face of clock
Lord Chamberlain's Office: Pictorial Inventory of George IV, vol. B, 3, drawing showing clock on its caryatid stand
The Letters and Journals of Lady Mary Coke, ed. Hume, 1889, XI, 180–1

The clock is in the form of a domed temple, reminiscent of the Casino at Marino. Two Corinthian fluted columns and a pilaster are grouped at each angle; in front of each face stand neo-classic urns draped with rope-like swags; and urns surmount the cornice. It is made of tortoise shell with ormolu and silver mounts, and the four dials with chased silver faces show the time of day and solar time, tides at principal ports, signs of the Zodiac and sidereal time, and a planetarium with a thermometer. It was made by Christopher Pinchbeck with the assistance of John Merigeot and Edward Monk. On 29 January 1768 Lady Mary Coke went to Mr Pinchbeck's shop to see 'a very fine clock that was just finisht for his Majesty. Twas well worth seeing. The Clock itself is very curious, but too complicated a piece of workmanship to be easily described', and she commented, the design was 'partly His Majesty's and partly Mr Chambers his architect'. Made originally for the Queen's House, the clock was later removed to Windsor Castle when it was detached from its caryatid stand (now lost). The style of this clock should be compared with the eight-day clock in the Queen's Private Sitting Room at Windsor Castle (q.v.) also designed by Chambers.

63 LONDON: BUCKINGHAM PALACE
King George III
State Coach (1760–2) (Pls 134–138) E
Buckingham Palace, Royal Mews: Design inscr. *WC The Kings State Coach figures J. B. Cipriani 1760*; engraving of a design by S. Butler and J. Linnell
WCRL: 13999, the hinder part of the coach; 14000 inscr. *The Fore part of the State Coach*; 17969, 17970, designs by Cipriani for the painted panels
Soane: 43/6^{23}, design for the front part, inscr. *Lord Clare's Carriage*
London Museum: Wax model of the coach made by Capezzuoli and Voyez
PRO: AO1/1455 Roll 71. *Bills and other Disbursements discharged and laid out by His Grace The Duke of Rutland, Master of the Horse, betwixt the 1st of Oct 1765 and 31st December following*
Royal Mews: *Journal of the Clerk of the Stables of the Master of the Horse*
Description of Her Majesty's State Coach, 1954
Smith, C. Clifford, *Buckingham Palace*, 1931
Smith, J. T., *Nollekens and his times* (ed. Stonier 1949), 12
Straus, R., *Carriages and Coaches*, 1912, 185–7
Walpole, Horace, *Correspondence*, ed. W. S. Lewis and others. v.22 Mann VI (1960), 104
C.Life, 17 Apr. 1937, 422–3
C.Life, Coronation Issue 1953, 84–7 'Three Famous State Coaches', by E. Croft-Murray
Daily Advertiser, 25 Nov. 1762
Lloyd's Evening Post, 24 Nov. 1762
London Chronicle, 20–3, 25–7 Nov., xii, 501–2, 513
London Evening Post, 25–27 Nov. 1762
The Motor, 20 May 1953, 'The State Coach of England'
SALE: Christie, 8 June 1811 (presumed sale), bought Colnaghi, sold 12 June 1811 to Prince Regent

King George II died on 25 October 1760, George III was crowned in September 1761 and appeared in his new state coach for the opening of Parliament in November 1762. Because the design is dated 1760 it is logical to assume that this magnificent and most opulent of all Chambers's designs took just two years to build. The existence of an engraved design by Samuel Butler and John Linnell is proof that the commission must have been cherished by others. The coach is of characteristic and traditional type, technically similar to the Lord Mayor's coach built by Butler a few years earlier. There can be little doubt that Chambers's design was revised in the light of Butler's great experience of coach building. To some, Chambers's authorship of this rococo design may seem an anachronism; but of course it was too early for neo-classic geometricality to be applied to a coach whose lines favoured the curvaceous motifs of the rococo.

The account in the Public Record Office lists

the artists and craftsmen and the payments made to them: Samuel Butler, coachmaker, £1673.15.; Joseph Wilton, 'for making a Model of the ffigures and Ornaments on the State Coach executing the same in Wood..'£2.500.; Henry Pujolas, 'for Painting Varnishing and Gilding', £933.14.; Giovanni Batista Cipriani, 'for Painting the Pannels', £315.; Bryant Barrett, laceman, 'for Rich Cartizane Trimming of Gold. Gold Rare ffringe', £737.10.7.; George Coyte, chaser, 'for Chasing and Gilding Buckles', £665.4.6.; William Ringsted, harnessmaker, 'for a set of Morocco Leather Harness', £385.15.; Thomas & William Hinchcliffe, mercers, 'for flowered and Genoa Velvet', £202.5.10½.; William Kerr, bitmaker, 'for Pattern Gilt Bitts, Bosses, Stirrups', £99.6.6.; Jane Mott, milliner, 'for Rich Blue Ribband', £31.3.4.; John Blake, sadler, 'for a Saddle', £10.16.6.; James Mann, Woolen draper, 'for Crimson serge and Green baize', £4.3.6.; James Campbell, cover maker, 'for Baize and Wadding', £3.9.6.; George Cole, Upholsterer, 'for Pully Rods, Green Baize for Curtains', £14.14.; Joseph Haynes, 'for Charcoal', £6.10.; Philip Nind, ironmonger, 'for a hot Stove, ffender Poker and Shovel', £4.11. A total of £7,587.19.9½.

Description of the coach
Eight palm trees contain the framework of the body. The four corner trees support trophies commemorating Britain's victories. Supporting the body of the coach by means of braces are four Tritons, those in the front holding shells, thus announcing the approach of the Monarch of the Ocean, those in the rear carry the Imperial Fasces topped with tridents. In the centre of the coach roof three boys represent the Genii of England, Scotland, and Ireland, and support the Imperial Crown of Great Britain. They hold in their hands the Sceptre, Sword of State, and Ensigns of Knighthood. They are adorned with laurel festoons linking with the angles of the coach. The Driver's footboard is a large Scollop shell; the Pole is a bundle of lances; the Splinter bar is a rich moulding issuing from beneath a voluted shell, each end terminating in the head of a dolphin; the Wheels are imitations of those on a triumphal chariot. The paintings by Cipriani may be explained as follows: FRONT PANEL: Victory presents a Garland of Laurel to Britannia who is seated on a throne, holding a staff of Liberty, and attended by Religion, Justice, Wisdom, Valour, Fortitude, Commerce, and Plenty. In the background may be seen St Paul's Cathedral and the River Thames. RIGHT-HAND DOOR: Industry and Ingenuity presenting a cornucopia to the Genius of England. RIGHT-HAND PANELS: History recording the reports of Fame, and Peace burning the implements of War. LOWER BACK PANEL: Neptune and Amphritite, attended by the Winds, Rivers,

Tritons, Naiads, etc. issuing from their palace in a triumphal car, drawn by sea horses. They bring the tribute of the world to British Shore. UPPER BACK PANEL: The Royal Arms. LEFT-HAND DOOR: Mars, Minerva, and Mercury supporting the Imperial Crown of Great Britain. LEFT-HAND PANELS: The Liberal Arts and Sciences protected.

64 LONDON: 14 CECIL STREET
Dr Elliott
Interior work (*c.*1772)
RIBA Letters: Lord Pembroke to WC 20 August 1772, *verso* sketch for a ceiling, inscr. 'Make a design for a Ceiling 34.1½×22.10, to be sent before Wednesday morning to Dr Eliott Cecil Street Strand'
WPL: Rate Books

Elliott's house was the next to the last at the south end of the east side of Cecil Street. As the houses on this street were predominantly of the late-seventeenth century, Chambers's ceiling, if executed, would have been part of a modernizing scheme. Cecil Street has now been swallowed up by the Savoy Hotel development.

LONDON: CHARING CROSS: ANDREW DRUMMOND'S HOUSE, *see* **STANMORE PARK**

65 LONDON: CHELSEA: ALL SAINTS' CHURCH
ATTRIBUTED monument to Sir Hans Sloane (after 1755) E
V & A: D386, 1890. John Carter sketch-book, containing detail of impost moulding, and inscription ascribing this monument to Wilton
Faulkner, T., *An Historical and Topographical Description of Chelsea*, 1810, 67
LCC: *Survey of London*, VII, 1921, Pt.III, 77 and pl.88

Faulkner confirms the attribution to Wilton, and also adds the information that the commission was due to Sloane's daughters, Lady Elizabeth Cadogan and Lady Sarah Stanley. The fact that the monument is almost identical to John Sharpe's in East Barnet churchyard (q.v.) suggests that it too may have been initially designed by Chambers.

66 LONDON: 6 CHEYNE WALK
Dr Bartholomew de Dominiceti
Water Bath (*c.*1768)
BM Add.MS 41133, 50, 66 (19 Aug. 1771-2 July 1773)
Faulkner, T., *An Historical and Topographical*

Description of Chelsea, 1810, 427–9
LCC: *Survey of London*, 11, 1927, 42–9
The Reminiscences of Henry Angelo, 1, 1904, 101 and note on 414

Dr Dominiceti acquired 6 Cheyne Walk in 1765, and 'In the garden and communicating with the house, he constructed a building which contained his famous baths, fumigating stones, and sweating bed chambers' (Angelo). According to Faulkner the baths were housed in a brick building 100 by 16 feet in area which appears on Richardson's map of 1769 as an addition extending the whole length of the east side of the garden. Dominiceti entered this venture, on which he is said to have spent £37,000, in partnership with his friends Karl Friedrich Abel, the viol da gamba player, Domenico Angelo Malevolti Tremamondo, the fencing master, and Johann Sebastian Bach, the composer.

From the Letter Books it seems that Chambers was requested to provide designs for the bath around 1768. His bill for £26.5.0 was unpaid in August 1771 and in July the following year he was still awaiting the doctor's share of £6.11.0.

67 LONDON: CLEVELAND ROW: ERRINGTON (later Warwick) HOUSE
Henry Errington
New house (*1770–1*) E
BM Add.MS 41133, 3v–4, 10v, 14–14v, 19v, 22v, 24, 31v, 51v, 54, 61v–62, 118v (24 Dec. 1769–Dec. 1773)
PRO: LRRO 63/88, p.46 (plan of 1798)
LCC: *Survey of London*, XXX, 1963, 506–7 and pls. 232, a, b
Sheppard, E., *Memorials of St James's Palace*, 1894, 1, 54

In 1770 Henry Errington called upon Chambers to design and build for him a small town house on a newly-acquired plot facing St James's Park on the west, abutting onto Kent's Queen's Library on the south, and with access to Stable Yard on the east (later in the century Stornaway House was built against the north side filling in a tongue of land that extended much farther into the park than the row of buildings in line with Spencer House).

The 1798 plan reveals a simple compact house with four bays facing the park and access in the second bay leading through a garden room to the staircase which rose around the curved face of a D-shaped compartment. In the south-west angle was the dining room with the painted ceiling by Cipriani (described by Sheppard). Surprisingly enough, behind the present French Renaissance façade and other additions of 1827, 1853, and 1860, Chambers's house still exists. The north-west room on the ground floor contains one of the fine chimney-pieces carved by John Walsh, and the staircase has elegant S scroll balustrades. Unfortunately, Cipriani's ceiling, which survived until as late as 1894, has now been destroyed.

In April 1770 Chambers explained to Errington that the cost would be 'about £4000 including the expense of three handsom ceilings and three good marble Chimney pieces for the best rooms'. Although pleased by this estimate Errington requested that the chimney-pieces be patterned upon those by James Paine. To this preposterous breach of etiquette, Chambers firmly replied, 'I cannot give designs for them without breaking through an established rule: they are inventions of Mr Payne's and he must be applyd for them, and as I have no connections with him myself I must entreat the favour of you to make application. He lives in Salisbury Street in the Strand and will not only furnish you with designs but likewise with the chimney pieces and keeps statuary for the purpose and works I believe, as well and upon easy terms as any other Tradesman.' Errington immediately withdrew his request, whereupon Chambers wrote to suggest his own sculptor, John Walsh, whose 'proposals about the chimney piece are reasonable, and if he will send me the size of the tablet I will make a drawing for it. In a day or two I shall have the drawings done for your other two chimney pieces and I will then send for Mr Wash [*sic*] to hear his proposals. I think he will execute them very well.' Later, on 29 August 1771, he writes with reference to Cipriani's ceiling: 'I have 6 Pictures by me for your Ceiling which are copys of Things found at Herculan. I will require 7 more which I will get done for you if you please on reasonable terms.'

68 LONDON: 62 CURZON STREET (formerly 1 Bolton Row)
Agmondesham Vesey
Interior alterations, probably of minor extent (before June 1773)
BM Add.MS 41134, 27 (4 June 1773)
Brocklebank family, Christmas card and pamphlet for 1938, with history of the house

The submitted bill for 'Drawings for finishing the Rooms, such as Cornices door Entablatures Window Architraves Bases surbase &c £6.6.0', probably refers to work in this London house rather than at Lucan (q.v.). 62 Curzon Street has been demolished, but photographs show the interiors to have been extensively redecorated in the late eighteenth century, in an Adamesque rather than Chambersian style.

LONDON: GLOUCESTER HOUSE *see*
LONDON: UPPER GROSVENOR STREET

69 LONDON: COTTON GARDEN

King George III

Kitchen for the Coronation (1762)

Soane: 43/5[19], plan inscr. 'Plan of temporary Kitchens in the Cotton Garden Westminster for the Coronation of Geo 111'

PRO: *Works* 4 Minutes & Proceedings, 13 (Bricklayer's bill)

This was one of the many Coronation tasks that came under the jurisdiction of the Board of Works. After the festivities, the kitchens were demolished.

70 LONDON: 15 GEORGE STREET

2nd Earl Fauconberg

Alterations including Doric entrance doorway

BM Add.MS 41133, 130v (late Apr. 1774); 41135, 47 (20 Sept. 1774); 41136, 17v (14 Apr. 1774)

Lord Fauconberg, a friend and neighbour of Thomas Worsley, living at Newborough, near Hovingham, Yorkshire, engaged Chambers to bring his London (George Street) house up-to-date. Apart from the probable stucco facing of the Early-Georgian brickwork, the only obvious Chambersian addition is the dignified Doric doorcase of the entrance. On 14 April 1774 Chambers wrote, 'all things are going on briskly', and on 20 September in the same year, received £600 from Fauconberg. The house was rated as the largest in the street, and still exists.

71 LONDON: 20 GROSVENOR SQUARE

3rd Duke of Buccleuch

Alterations and interior decoration (1767)

V & A: 2216.36, design for a ceiling inscr. 'No 32 D Buccleuch WC'

Dasent, A. I., *A History of Grosvenor Square*, 1935

Horwood, R., *Plan of the Cities of London & Westminster*, 1792–9

EXHIB RA 1769, 16

SALE: Christie, 6 June 1817, 7: 'Ornamental Designs for Ceilings &c at the Duchess of Buccleuch's by Sir William Chambers & richly coloured (5)'

Horwood gives a plan of this Grosvenor Square house, then (1792) in the possession of Thomas Coke, showing it on the north side doubled up with an adjoining one in North Audley Street. There seems to be little doubt that the conjoining was done by the 3rd Duke of Buccleuch who acquired his lease of no.20 in 1767. A guide to the extent of Chambers's work may be judged by the five ceiling designs sold in 1817; but alas, apart from one design now in the V & A there is no record of these demolished interiors. It is worth

remembering that Buccleuch had also been employing Chambers at Adderbury (q.v.).

72 LONDON: 25 GROSVENOR SQUARE

8th Earl of Abercorn

Alterations (1762)

Abercorn Papers, Baronscourt: WC to Abercorn 21 July 1763; Abercorn to WC 16 Aug. 1763

Dasent, A. I., *A History of Grosvenor Square*, 1935

Lord Abercorn acquired the lease of no.25 Grosvenor Square, on the west side, in 1763, a year after he had begun to employ Chambers at Duddingstone (q.v.). The fact that the London work was finished by the summer of this year, suggests that it was probably limited to a simple refurbishing of the earlier house built in 1728. This conclusion is supported by Chambers's letter to Abercorn on 21 July 1763:

'Your Lordship's house in Grosvenor Square will be entirely finished this week there being now only a part of the great stair to clean and one small room on the ground floor to Paper for whc the Paper will be ready in a day or two. I have had nothing done to the Lattice work on the garden as it is rotten & not worth Painting but I have ordered Your Lordship's Gardener to trim the trees & nail them up where it is wanted to prevent their being blown down and torn to Pieces by the Wind. I am now abt measuring the work in order to Settle the bills wth the Workmen'.

73 LONDON: 51 GROSVENOR STREET

Charles Turner

Alterations of unknown character (1774–5) E

BM Add.MS 41133, 53v (22 Sept. 1771); 41135, 70 (28 July 1775)

WPL: Rate Books, St George's Parish, C321, 3

Although in 1771 Chambers advised Charles Turner of Kirkleatham against altering his house at 51 Grosvenor Street, in 1775 he is found writing to his cousin William Chambers, a surgeon, at Ripon, 'if they, or you, should see their cousin Charles Turner; pray let him know his Erection is in a fair way, and that all things will stand as they ought to do when he and Mrs Turner come to town'. Chambers, as revealed in a letter to Sandberg, his brother-in-law, was distantly related to Turner by the marriage of a second cousin to a first cousin of Turner's. Today 51 Grosvenor Street presents a five-bay, three-storey front in a Georgian style, but of the nineteenth century. Like Lord Fauconberg's house in nearby George Street, Chambers may here have only been concerned with alterations to an early Georgian fabric, although 'Erection' suggests a new, or almost wholly new, house.

74 LONDON: 25 HARLEY STREET
New house (1770s?)
MMA: (46.56.21) design for a chimney-piece, inscr. '69 Harley Street'

25, formerly 69, Harley Street is a plain but well-proportioned three-bay brick house. It is not altogether certain that the house was designed by Chambers, for the speculators on this estate were Thomas Collins and John White. Unfortunately, the extent of Chambers's participation in this post-Berners Street speculation is not known. As it belonged to the Somerset House years his interest may have been negligible.

75 LONDON: KNIGHTSBRIDGE
John Calcraft
New house (1770–2)
Soane: 43/4⁵, ground floor plan
V & A: 7076.8; 7076.12, two floor plans, one inscr. 'Calcraft'
BM Add.MS 41133, 15, 38v, 39v, 42–43v, 44v–45, 48v–49, 56, 58–58v, 64, 67v, 71v, 74v, 77, 84v (22 May 1770–4 Sept. 1772)
RA: Thomas Williams to WC 31 Aug. 1772
RIBA Letters: Calcraft to WC 10 Apr. 1770

John Calcraft's house probably stood adjacent to Rutland House, facing the park in what is now designated Rutland Gate. In plan it was square with five windows to the front and five to the garden, with a handsome staircase, and a small number of rooms suitable to the needs of a bachelor. Although there are no views or descriptions of the house, one presumes its outward appearance was as simple and unprepossessing as its plan. It was probably demolished around 1838 when Rutland Gate was laid out. Calcraft was a difficult client who delayed signing his contract, a joint one with Chambers and Thomas Collins, and quibbled over Chambers's charges for 'a Great Number of Drawings which I made for different-sized houses by your Desire, none of which you Chose afterwards to execute, but fixed upon another design'. Nevertheless the house progressed rapidly. On 2 May 1771 the carcase was well advanced and by March the following year Collins was ready to put up the ceilings. Unfortunately, however, Calcraft died that summer leaving the house nearly completed and a debt of £2250 owing to the craftsmen.

76 LONDON: LEICESTER SQUARE: LEICESTER HOUSE
Augusta, Dowager Princess of Wales
Minor alterations and maintenance (1757+)
Duchy of Cornwall Office: Accounts XLII(i)

vouchers Jan. 1758–Jan. 1759; XLIII(i) vouchers Jan. 1759–Jan. 1760
GLC, *Survey of London*, XXXIV, 1966, 451

Leicester House, which stood on the north side of Leicester Square, is best shown in Sutton Nicholl's view of 1721, three years after it had become the residence of George, Prince of Wales, later George II. Frederick, Prince of Wales died here in 1751. The accounts, examined by Chambers, are for minor repairs a few years previous to the accession of George III. The Dowager Princess left here in 1764 for Carlton House (q.v.).

77 LONDON: 47 LEICESTER SQUARE
Sir Joshua Reynolds
ATTRIBUTED painting room and gallery; sitter's chair, stool and bench (c.1760–2) (Pl.182)
RA: Sitter's Chair
GLC, *Survey of London*, XXXIV, 1966, 508–9
Hudson, D., *Sir Joshua Reynolds*, 1958, 70–5
Furniture History, II (1966), 'Early Neo-Classical Furniture', by John Harris

When Reynolds acquired his house in Leicester Square in 1760 he commissioned the building of an octagonal painting room and a gallery. Despite the fact that James Paine published a chimney-piece from this house in 1783, there is no evidence that it belonged to the first phase of alterations. Indeed, in 1760 Chambers was more likely to have been employed than Paine. Around 1762 when the house was paid for, Reynolds acquired a new set of studio furniture. In the portrait of Emma, Countess of Mount Edgecumbe (1762) the chair can be seen; in Mrs James Paine and daughters (1765) a stool or bench; and in Mrs Baldwin (1782) an arm-stool. All have in common the straight tapering legs of square section and a seat rail with Doric frieze complete with triglyphs. Like the Society of Arts's President's chair the lower parts of Reynolds's chair are uncompromisingly neo-classical, whereas the arms and back are designed for the sitter's comfort. Whoever designed this suite of furniture was in advance of his time, for the arm-stool can only be matched by Adam's window stools designed for Croome Court in 1764.

78 LONDON: LINCOLN'S INN(?)
Thomas Hollis
Work of unknown character (?1760s)
Avery: (1C/2⁶) Study for the MMA – chimney-piece
MMA (46.56.18): design for a chimney-piece and overmantel inscr. 'Hollis, late of Lincoln's Inn'
Memoirs of Thomas Hollis, 1780 (for the life of Hollis)

Thomas Hollis was the friend of Thomas Brand of The Hyde, Essex (q.v.), whom he accompanied on travels through France and Italy, where they probably met Chambers sometime between 1750 and 1754. Although Hollis's principal lodgings were in Lincoln's Inn, he also lived for some time in Bedford Street, and possessed a farmhouse at Corscombe in Dorset.

79 LONDON: LOMBARD STREET
Mr Blachford
Alteration to a Drawing Room
Gandon Album 2 (in poss. Father Murphy, Robertstown, Co. Kildare)

The Gandon album was discovered too late to be studied in any depth. Some of the drawings were made by Gandon when in Chambers's office (Goodwood, q.v.).

80 LONDON: MARLBOROUGH HOUSE
4th Duke of Marlborough
Addition of attic, interior alterations (1771–4) (Pl.186) E
Avery: (1C/2⁹) design for a chimney-piece in the State Drawing room
DML: Chambers–Yenn album, 1v, 3, 6v, 12v, 13, 28v, 30v, 31 (details of furniture, perhaps designed by John Yenn, in Saloon, Ante-Drawing room; and designs, also by Yenn, for the Observatory)
Soane: 43/6², 43/8⁴, details, inscr. 'Mahogany doors for Marlborough house'
BM Add.MS 41133, 39, 40–40v, 47, 52, 59v–60, 79, 112v (April 1771–3 Feb. 1774)
RIBA Letters: Marlborough to WC 3 July 1773
BM *Crace Views*, XII, 19 (view by John Buckler in 1827)
Charlton, John, *Marlborough House*, 1962
C.Life, 17 Apr. 1937, 441–2 figs 4, 5

This work at Marlborough House follows upon the Duke's patronage at Woodstock Town Hall and Blenheim Palace (q.v.). A comparison of the engraving in the first volume of *Vitruvius Britannicus* (1715) of the original house of 1708, with John Buckler's view in 1827, shows that Chambers replaced Wren's balustraded parapet by a low half-storey attic, which was again raised to its present height in 1865. The two principal rooms redecorated by Chambers, the State Dining Room and the Drawing Room, were also radically altered in 1865, but fortunately Pennethorne retained the sumptuous Chambers chimney-pieces. The southwest room is the most complete survival, however, with typical doorcases and a fine restrained ceiling. Upstairs are several chimney-pieces, also in our architect's style.

From the correspondence one learns that, as at Woburn (q.v.), the project had been in the hands of Stiff Leadbetter before his death in 1766. In April 1771 Chambers wrote to the Duke about 'an estimate of the Intended attick at Marlborough House according to Mr Leadbetter's Plan', costing £4,467, and closed his correspondence on 3 February 1774 hoping 'most of the smell will be gone before your Grace arrives in town'. The Delaware Album is almost certainly a record of John Yenn's later alterations and furnishings.

81 LONDON: MARLBOROUGH STREET
Lady Midleton
Repairs (?)
BM Add.MS 41133, 118v (2 Dec. 1773)

In the British Museum letter Chambers writes to Lady Midleton about her smoky chimneys and some form of settlement in the house, defects he promises to put right. Cf. also Peper Harow (q.v.).

LONDON: MARYLEBONE LANE: COURT HOUSE *see* LONDON: ST MARYLEBONE CHURCH

82 LONDON: 85 NEWMAN STREET
Mr Gray
New house (*c.*1769)
RIBA: Collins's Album, 5, design for the chimney flank of a wall, inscr. 'Chimney Breast Mr Grays front Parlor'
St MPL: Rate Books 1770

Chambers's responsibility for this house is suggested by the proximity of Newman Street to Berners Street where he and Collins were at the peak of their speculating in 1770. The design belongs to an album that seems apparently to be entirely devoted to this area. The overmantel of the chimney flank has an elaborate plasterwork panel supporting a tripod, similar in style to others in Berners Street executed by Collins.

LONDON: PADDINGTON STREET: BURIAL GROUND *see* LONDON: ST MARYLEBONE CHURCH

83 LONDON: PALL MALL: CARLTON HOUSE
Augusta, Dowager Princess of Wales; George Prince of Wales (later George IV)
Maintenance (1757–61); Porter's Lodge and remodelling of entrance passage (*c.*1761); alterations for reception of Prince George (1783–6)
BM: Crace, XII, *Plans*, 8. Plan of the courtyard inscr. *The Plan was made for the Dowager Princess of*

Wales 1761 WC; Crace, x, *Views*, 28, perspective
of porter's lodge and courtyard
DML: Chambers–Yenn Album, 2v. Elevation of
porter's lodge
PRO: Works 4/13 Oct. 1761–Dec. 1766
RIBA Letters: Col. G. D. Hotham to WC 25 Oct.,
1 Nov. 1783
WCRL: Georgian MSS 35053 *Estimate of Expences on
Building & Alterations at Carlton House:* Work
under WC to 6 March 1786 spending £9046.6.6;
Georgian MSS 35221–5. Dispersal of £60,000
grant for work 1783–4
Great Britain: Parliamentary Reports: *A Return ...
of all sums issued on account of Carlton House ...*, 30
May 1791
LCC: *Survey of London*, XX, 1940, 19, pls 55–6, fig.72

Carlton House was an old friend of Chambers, for
it had been under his jurisdiction since 1757 when
he was appointed architect to the Dowager
Princess of Wales. His 1761 plan for remodelling
the entrance approach may not have been executed in its entirety, but the existence of the drawing in the DML album suggests he built the lodge.
The large payments itemized in Works's accounts
between midsummer and Christmas 1763, when
£12,893 was spent, relate to designs supplied by
William Robinson and executed without the
proper authority of the Board of Works, an im-
proper move to which Chambers strongly objected
(cf. BM Add.MS 41135, 28v, 29). Two decades later,
in 1783, Carlton House was prepared for the
reception of George Prince of Wales at his
coming-of-age. As a Board of Works's representative Chambers was receiving considerable sums of
money at this time: according to Hotham's letter
£3277 as 'half the Abstract Amount' in 1783, and
according to the WCRL estimate £9046.6.6 had
been spent to 6 March 1786. We shall probably
never know if Chambers supplied actual designs,
for it is clear that the Prince's architect was Henry
Holland who is first referred to on 12 October
1784 in an 'Estimates of the Several Works carrying on and ordered to be done under the direction
of Henry Holland' (WCRL 35014). The explanation
may be that as Surveyor-General Chambers had a
controlling hand in the dispersal of money and in
the scrutiny of estimates. For example, in the 1791
Return Holland's *Estimate* for completing works
submitted in May 1787 was reported upon by
Chambers, K. Couse and C. A. Craig for the
Works and Treasury. There is perhaps one significant point worth commenting upon: Holland's
staircase (Pl.169) is quite atypical of his work and
fits in perfectly with the complex stairs designed
by Chambers at Melbourne House and Somerset
House. It may simply be, however, that Holland's
staircase was based directly upon his first-hand
knowledge of those of Chambers.

84 LONDON: PALL MALL: YORK HOUSE
Edward Augustus, Duke of York and Albany
UNEXECUTED designs for a new house (1759)
(Pl.94; Fig.6)
RIBA: J4/26, section inscr. (by another hand)
'Section of York House W Cambers Ao 1759'
Soane: 43/4³¹⁻³⁴, plans of ground and first floors
WCRL: PA3 Section (as at RIBA) without staircase
LCC: *Survey of London*, XXX, 1963, 364–5, pl.212
EXHIB SofA 1761, 184
SALE: Christie, 6 June 1811, 91, 97

Chambers's loss of the commission for York
House, which would have been his first town
house, may be compared with his disappointment
at Harewood a few years earlier. The cause of his
failure is evident in his section, where, once again,
he attempted to introduce an unfamiliar Franco-
Italian style in place of the traditional, and of
course, acceptable, Palladian one. By far the most
interesting and important element of this abortive
project is the staircase, an early manifestation of
remarkable originality, and a worthy prelude to
those at Parksted, Gower House, Melbourne
House, Dundas House, and Somerset House. The
York House design was exhibited in 1761 at the
Society of Artists where it must have been seen by
James Paine whose staircase at Wardour Castle is
a direct paraphrase. But it is even more intriguing
to speculate upon the influence of this York
House staircase on the French architect, Charles
de Wailly, whose staircase at the Château les
Ormes (q.v.) may well have been based on a
model already supplied to the owner of that
château by Chambers himself.

85 LONDON: PARK LANE: MILTON HOUSE
1st Baron Milton
Additions, entrance gates and screen (1769–71)
BM Add.MS 41133, 23v, 56v, 57v (27 Oct. 1770–
22 Oct. 1771)
Coutts Bank Archives: Milton Bank Account
WPL: Rate Books, C345, 16
Carter, John, *Builder's Magazine*, 1774, II, pl.x (of
entrance gates and screen)
Horwood, R., *Plan of the Cities of London & West-
minster*, 1792–9

After John Vardy's death in 1765 Chambers succeeded him as architect to Lord Milton at Milton
House and then at Milton Abbey. The extent of
his additions and alterations to the London house
is difficult to define. We know from John Carter's
engraving that he designed the entrance screen
and gates. From the correspondence it appears that
he also added a new wing which may be identified
with a south-easterly extension shown on Horwood's map. This addition was evidently well-
advanced by 27 October 1770 when Chambers

Q

wrote to inform Lord Milton 'We go on with all possible expedition in Town the whole new building is covered in and the roof over the stairs will be done in three or four days . . . ' Then exactly a year later, he reported, 'The carver has already done a good part of the carving in the new rooms . . . Ansell has not yet been able to make out his Estimate for the Gilding. I find it is to be like some Gilding done by Norman for the Queen's House.' At least two payments in Milton's bank account may refer to Milton House: 10 Oct. 1770 of £500, and 1 Dec. of £600.

When Lord Milton, whom Chambers described as 'this noble imperious Lord, who treats me, as he does everyone else, ill', was raised to the Earldom of Dorchester, the name of the London house was changed to Dorchester House. It was demolished in 1851 to make way for Vulliamy's palazzo, which in turn was replaced in 1929 by the Dorchester Hotel.

86 LONDON: 79 PICCADILLY
4th Earl Fitzwilliam
Alterations and additions of attic storey (1770–1)
BM Add.MS 41133, 44v, 54–55, 67v, 87v (2 July 1771–22 Oct. 1772)
Dasent, A. I., *Piccadilly*, 1920, 68

Chambers's work at 79 Piccadilly, like that at Milton Park, Northants, was occasioned by Lord Fitzwilliam's marriage in 1771. When the correspondence opened in July 1771 the new attic had been covered in, and when it closed on 22 October 1772 the painters were 'near finished in Piccadilly . . . but none of the ornaments in my Lady's dressing room is yet done'. The house stood lengthwise in Stratton Street with a narrow frontage to Piccadilly. It was demolished in 1929.

87 LONDON: PICCADILLY: MELBOURNE HOUSE
1st Lord Melbourne
New House (1771–6) (Pls 96, 97, 99, 103; Fig.9) E
Albany Archives: plan of principal floor; sections of Eating room, Ante-room, and staircase; two designs for screens; design for ceiling of Eating room; design for office wing
MMA: (34.78.2 [13]), design for a chimney-piece and instructions as to 'Round Room'
Royal Academy, Stockholm: (Pi-e-2), ground plan by J. M. Piper, July 1773
RIBA: J4/25, basement plan
Soane: 43/3¹, Chambers's copy of Adam's design for Lord Holland; 43/3²⁻³, ground floor plans; 43/3⁴, basement plan; 43/3⁵, principal floor plan; 43/3⁶⁻⁷, variants of principal floor plan; 43/3⁸⁻⁹, upper floor plans; 43/3¹⁰⁻¹², plan and section of stairs; 43/7²⁰⁻²¹, elevations of south front; 17/7,

nos.4–5 drawings of entrance screen and ironwork
V & A: 2216.40, Dressing room ceiling; E.839.1916, Eating room colonnade; 3422, Staircase section; 3432, Screen to Piccadilly; 7074.1, Central window on first floor south front; 7078.36.
Beds RO: Wrest Papers 1059 (Chambers–Grantham letter)
BM Add.MS 41133, 65, 76v, 79–79v, 80, 80v, 82, 90, 97v, 107, 114, 115, 116v, (2 Nov. 1771–Nov. 1773); 41134, 33 (13 Aug. 1773); 41135, 8, 21v–23, 50v–52v (26 Feb.–Nov. 1774); 41136, 9v–10 (26 Feb. 1774)
RIBA Letters: Melbourne to WC 13 Nov. 1774
Trustees Albany: Deed of Purchase, 31 March–1 April 1771
Badderly, S., *Memoirs of Mrs S. Badderley*, 11, 202–4
Birkenhead, Sheila, *Peace in Piccadilly*, 1958
Bolton, A. T., *The Architecture of Robert and James Adam*, 1921, I, 62
Chambers, *Treatise*, 3rd edn 1791, pl.53
LCC, *Survey of London*, XXXII, 1963, 367–89 and pls. 111–19
Paine, James, *Plans . . . of . . . Gentlemen's Houses*, pt.2, 1783, pl.XCIX
EXHIB RA 1773, 48
SALE: Christie, 6 June 1811, 68–9

After considering rebuilding his house in Piccadilly to designs by Adam, Lord Holland decided instead to sell it to Lord Melbourne for £16,500. Melbourne completed the purchase on 1 April 1771 and almost immediately contracted with Chambers to build a new house on the site for £21,300. By October 1773 building expenses had mounted to £22,958.19.11 bringing the total cost of this grandiose London establishment to approximately £40,000.

Chambers's letter to Lord Melbourne on 29 October 1773 provides a most informative account both of the extent and progress of the work and of the craftsmen employed. The whole of the second floor was then nearly completed, 'My Ladys Ceiling is done & the drawing room Ceiling is in great forwardness, the Plaisterers are entirely out of the House, the Eating room Chimneys up & Mr Payne promises the others very soon & we are putting up some other Chimneys, the front Entrance is finished & all the Offices done – Cipriani has finished all the paintings for the great room.' He also adds that Thomas Collins was 'very pressing for money'. Collins was undoubtedly responsible for modelling the plaster ceilings which received decorative paintings by Cipriani, probably in the form of 'insets', including those for the 'great ceiling in the Saloon'. In addition William Marlow executed two paintings, probably architectural landscapes, which were set in stucco frames in the Eating room. Although Birkenhead also mentions Biagio Rebecca among the artists working here, there is no evidence to confirm her statement.

The presence of James Paine at Melbourne House is explained by the fact that he had built Brocket Hall in 1760 for Lord Melbourne's father, Sir Matthew Lamb, and was employed from 1768 to 1770 by Lord Melbourne (then Sir Peniston Lamb) to complete the house in a more fashionable style.

Another major contributor to the decoration of Melbourne House was Thomas Chippendale. On 14 August 1773 Chambers writes to Melbourne, 'Chippendale called upon me yesterday wth some Designs for furnishing the rooms wc upon the whole seem very well but I wish to be a little consulted about these matters as I am really a Very pretty Connoisseur in furniture'; and a year later, on 13 October 1774, Chippendale was again advising about the 'round room', a vestibule or boudoir on the first floor, for which he appears to have supplied sofas and mirrors for the niches. Chambers had explained to Melbourne on 22 October 1774 that the brilliancy of gilding in this room 'will set the plainess of the rest off to perfection'.

There can be little doubt that the *pièce de résistance* of Melbourne House was its superb staircase (with a cast-iron flyer), designed with spatial ingenuity in a square top-lit well. In complexity its peer was only the oval staircase at Somerset House. It seems inexcusable that Henry Holland could have destroyed one of the finest staircases in London when he converted Melbourne House into residential apartments between 1803 and 1810. By this time, of course, Lord Melbourne no longer lived there, for he had exchanged Melbourne House for York House (Whitehall) in 1791.

LONDON: QUEEN'S HOUSE *see* LONDON: BUCKINGHAM PALACE

88 LONDON: ST ALBAN'S STREET
New house on east side of street (1770)
MRO: Register of Building Affidavits. Return of 29 Nov. 1770

It is not clear from the Return, required by the new Building Act of 1764, whether this house was in Westminster or Lambeth, but probably the former. This was undoubtedly a speculation, for the Return is entered jointly under Chambers and Collins.

89 LONDON: ST JAMES'S PALACE
Frederick Papendiek
Internal decorations (late 1760s)
Court and Private Life in The Time of Queen Charlotte: Being the Journals of Mrs Papendiek, ed. Broughton, 1887, I, 46

Mrs Papendiek records in her diary, 'Sir William Chambers; who with every other attendant at the palace was partial to my father, repaired these apartments for him, and made them as ornamental and convenient as the nature of them would permit.' As these were grace and favour apartments their redecoration would have come under the jurisdiction of the Office of Works.

90 LONDON: 3 ST JAMES'S SQUARE
Thomas Brand junior
Minor alterations (1771)
Soane: Drawer 36, Set II, no.79 (plan of 1799)
BM Add.MS 41133, 41, 44, 52, 59v–60, 75v, 79v (23 May 1771–18 June 1772)
LCC, *Survey of London*, XXIX, 1963, 180–1; XXX, 1963, pl.133a, b (view of 1815)

This late seventeenth-century house on the Square was purchased in May 1749 by Thomas Brand of The Hoo, who lived in it until his death in 1770, whereupon it passed to his son, Thomas Brand, junior. Just as elder Brand had employed Chambers at The Hoo, so the son employed him upon his small town house. Although sums of £400, £500, and £800 are mentioned in the correspondence, it is clear from the view of the house taken in 1815 that Chambers did nothing to substantially alter the character of the early brick front. Brand had apparently suggested that the front be colour-washed, for in May 1771, Chambers advised, 'Upon Examination I find it a very neat piece of Brickwork like Marlborough House; it would therefore be better only to clean it and point the Joynts as any Colour that can be laid upon it will wash off in a few Years and will even at first look but very indifferently, whereas the red brickwork is very perfect in its kind and will be kept in countenance by the Queen's house Marlborough house etc.' This work was under way in June, and in December Chambers thought it looked 'vastly well'. If the three individual payments were cumulative, then an expenditure of at least £1700 suggests that Chambers altered the interior. Presumably this work was of a decorative nature for the plan of 1799 shows no apparent late Georgian additions. The house was demolished in 1847 to make way for the Army and Navy Club.

91 LONDON: ST MARTIN'S LANE
Henry Fougt
Design for a shop sign (*c.*1767)
V & A: 7078.50, inscr. 'Alken Broad Street dufour court'
Kidson, Frank, *British Music Publishers*, 1900, 49–50

This spirited design shows the old pediment over the main door to Fougt's shop surmounted by the new sign of the 'Lyre and Owl', ornamented with a lyre in a garlanded medallion and an owl perched upon musical instruments, and inscribed 'Henry Fougt Musical Typographer'. The sign was presumably carved by Sefferin Alken, who is known, as the inscription on the design implies, to have lived in Dufour Court, off Broad Street.

92 LONDON: ST MARYLEBONE CHURCH
UNEXECUTED designs for a new church; alterations to the Court House, and laying-out of the Burial Ground (1770–4) (Pls 144–147; Fig.15)
V & A: 3433, elevation scheme A; 3435, sketch elevation scheme A; 3434, plan scheme B; 3363, section scheme B; 3429, elevation scheme C; 7072.17, section scheme C
Soane: Drawer XVII, Set 7, elevations scheme A; Drawer XLII, Set 9, sections scheme A; 43/9[16], plan scheme B
BM Add.MS 41133, 20, 22, 73v–74, 93–93v, 125 (3 Aug. 1770–16 Feb. 1774); 41136, 2–2v (Feb. 1774)
Soane: Dw 41/5, memorandum of 26 Apr. 1776, to 'Make application to friends for Marybone. Collins, Mercer, Wilton, Newton'
St MPL: Vestry Minutes 1772–4, 28, 69 (Court House)
Sheppard, F. H. W., *Local Government in St Marylebone, 1688–1835*, 1958
Soane, Sir John, *Lectures*, ed. A. T. Bolton, 1929, pls.56–7
RIBA Jnl, 24 Aug., 28 Sept. 1893 (abstracts letters)
SALE: Christie, 6 June 1811, 90

The long correspondence about this abortive scheme opens on 3 August 1770 after Chambers had been asked by the Reverend John Harley (representing the Vestry or Church Committee) to supply designs for a new parochial church. In his first letter Chambers speaks of two alternative schemes, one with a dome and the other with a spire: 'I have estimated the different designs for Marybone church and find that the Dome will exceed the sum you Purpose laying out considerably & the solidity of the Work requires so many Precautions which affect the Conveniency of the Building that I do not think the Dome so proper a design as the other. The design with the Spire

will as near as I can Determine upon rough calculation Amount to £16,109 inclusive my commission of 5 p cent.' Turning a deaf ear to Chambers's advice, and to the inability of the sponsors to find enough money, or even to decide upon a suitable site, the Vestry decided in favour of the dome scheme. It is therefore not surprising to find Chambers complaining nearly two years later, 'I have already made five if not six different designs some of them very considerable ones. I have also made several estimates of this Building & in the whole been at a Good deal of Expense & had a great deal of trouble' (8 June 1732. Add.MS 41133, 73v, 74). Even on 15 February 1773 he was still making 'the new plan of Marybone church'. In recompense for all this trouble Chambers was offered the paltry and insulting sum of £100. From his understandably angry note of February 1774 (Add.MS 41136, 2–2v) the fact emerges that he had already altered or designed the Court House (now destroyed) in Marylebone Lane, and laid out the Burial Ground (N. side of Paddington Street), besides making '6 different sets of designs for the intended church & 3 exact estimates'. The Vestry must have remained adamant in their attitude because the Soane memorandum, dated as late as 26 April 1776, is obviously an attempt to rally his friends who lived, or had influence, in the parish.

Chambers's project was the first 'great' church to be proposed after the 1711 Church Building Act. Although three Acts (1770, 1772, 1773) were obtained for its erection, it was not until 1818 and the passing of two additional Acts, that it was finally built by Chambers's pupil, Thomas Hardwick, on the St Marylebone Road.

For sources for both his spire and dome design Chambers turned, as he had done a few years earlier at the German Lutheran Chapel of The Savoy (q.v.), to James Gibbs. His detail, however, especially for the interior, is decidedly Franco-Italian. The dome design had been adumbrated by an unexecuted scheme for a large domed temple, possibly proposed for Kew Gardens, now among the theoretical drawings at Windsor Castle; and the spire design was literally transposed in 1775 as the intended centre-piece for the east court wing of Trinity College, Dublin (q.v.), but this also remained a paper dream; and then for the abortive Woodstock Church spire (q.v.).

93 LONDON: THE SAVOY
Duchy of Lancaster and The Crown
UNEXECUTED projects for Barracks (1776–88) (Pl.178)
Soane: 43/1[2–4], 43/1[24–26] (designs by William Robinson); 41/1[5–21, 25, 27] (Chambers's designs)
PRO: Treasury Minutes T29/56, 6; T29/56, 221
Soane: 41/5, MSS agreements 28 May 1774

Somerville, Robert, *The Savoy*, 1960

Robinson had submitted his mundane schemes for the Savoy in May 1774. He and posterity were relieved of them when he died in 1775. Although a royal warrant was issued for barracks at the Savoy on 25 December 1775, Chambers was far too busy with the preliminaries at Somerset House to think seriously about the projected buildings. Fire destroyed the old barracks on 2 March 1776, and Chambers presented plans to the Duchy on 5 February 1777. In 1782 and 1788 the Duchy were still considering plans and on 10 August 1795 Chambers could plaintively (now he was old and infirm) tell the Treasury about his 'complete set of designs' that had 'in general been approved of'. Only an optimist could have believed in a repetition of Somerset House next door. With his experience and second stylistic wind, Chambers would certainly have risen to the occasion. His 'ideal' perspective, fragmentary as it is, is nevertheless a noble conception, and ranks, with Adderbury and the Prince of Wales's Mausoleum, as one of Chambers's unexecuted masterpieces.

94 LONDON: THE SAVOY: GERMAN LUTHERAN CHAPEL
Committee for the Vestry
Chapel (1766) (Pls 142–143)
V & A: 248.90, elevation; 7073.17, preliminary section; 7073.20, 22, sections; 7074.44, studies for west and east ends of interior
WPL: 90/7, approved plans and sections; 90/8 (1–31), bills of work; 90/9, book of accounts
Somerville, R., *The Savoy, Manor: Hospital: Chapel*, 1960 and pl.IV

A Royal Warrant 'for rebuilding and enlarging our Lutheran church in the Savoy' was obtained on 28 February 1766 and was recorded in the Vestry Minutes the following 25 July. Presumably the approach to Chambers was made between these dates. Because the new Chapel was finished by the end of 1767 work must have progressed rapidly.

The exterior of the Lutheran Chapel as shown in Somerville's view of 1875 suggests that the building was little more than a simplification of Chambers's Gibbsian elevations, modelled after the latter's Harley Chapel. According to the surviving bills, however, the elegant galleried interior may well have been executed to Chambers's satisfaction. Many of the craftsmen employed here were also currently engaged upon Clive's house in Berkeley Square (q.v.), such as James Pickford, mason; Edward Gray, bricklayer; James Palmer, smith; William Chapman, plumber; and John Westcot, slater. Other craftsmen were Oliver Alken, an otherwise unrecorded carver; William

Rhodes, measurer; John Johnson, carpenter; Thomas Clark, plasterer; Samuel Cobb, painter; and William Cobbald, glazier.

95 LONDON: SOMERSET HOUSE
New Public Offices (1776–96) (Pls 155–168, 170–176) E
Designs
Mellon Coll. (U.S.A.): Perspective by Desprez of the river-front
MMA: (46.56.20) design for a chimney-piece, inscr. 'Mr Moser'
Royal Institute of British Architects
J4/1ᵃ⁻ᶜ, three plans as executed: ground plan of Strand block; ground plan of blocks enclosing south-west angle of quadrangle and of the westermost block; ground plan of the blocks enclosing the south-east angle of the quadrangle, showing basement plan on the courtyard side. J4/2: half plan at two levels of the portico in centre of north elevation, court front, of Strand block. J4/3: ground floor plan of Strand block. J4/4ᵃ⁻ᵇ: plan and section of water front at embankment level. J4/4ᶜ⁻ᵈ: section of water front at embankment level. J4/5ᵃ: plan of balustrades inscr. 'Back Building Center break Balustrades'. J4/5ᵇ: elevation of end break on east elevation, facing courtyard of west block. J4/5ᶜ: elevation of other end of break on east elevation, facing courtyard of west block. J4/5ᵈ: elevation of end break of south façade, facing river of river block, inscr. (on frieze) 'E. Hatton's Drawings No.1'. J4/6ᵃ: elevation of west façade of the west quadrangle block. J4/6ᵇ: half elevation and half section of end, north, façade of west quadrangle block. J4/6ᶜ: section of west quadrangle block towards south. J4/6ᵈ: elevation of two bays of west façade of the west quadrangle block. J4/7: north elevation, courtyard front, river block. J4/8: elevation of pavilion, end break, of south façade to courtyard of Strand block. J4/9: west elevation of return front to wings of Strand block. J4/10: elevation of the central pavilion of façades on east or west courtyard fronts. J4/12ᵃ: elevation and details of cornice of door casement in Strand vestibule. J4/12ᵇ: elevation of doorway to wings of courtyard fronts of Strand block. J4/12ᶜ: elevation of a semi-circular headed archway with a rusticated composite order. J4/12ᵈ: elevation of a triangular-pedimented doorway to central pavilions of east and west courtyard fronts. J4/13ᵃ: elevation of composite capital for a window. J4/13ᵇ: triangular-headed window for central feature and pavilions, first floor, of façades facing quadrangle. Detail of cornice and balustrade. J4/13ᶜ: triangular-headed window for central part of south façade, courtyard, Strand block. Elevation and details of cornice. J4/13ᵈ: details of mouldings. J4/14: copy by Robert Browne, March 1810, of J4/1ᶜ.

Sir John Soane's Museum
*Drawer 41/1*c1–34, preliminary projects to 'approved' scheme, plans only
Scheme A: (5) A river front of 6–7–9–7–6 bays with bridges to right and left linked to adjacent fronts of unequal length. The site behind occupied by three massive courtyard blocks, one off-axis, two forming the base of an oval courtyard opening at its apex into vestibules on the Strand front. The blocks inter-linked and bridged by elaborate niched and columnar vestibules. This is called the 'Ideal' plan. *Scheme B*: (3) A river front of 5–13–5 bays, the centre recessed, and bridges to right and left. One main north–south oblong court opening to the Strand and river by columnar vestibules. (4) An elaboration of 3. The river wing split longitudinally into narrow parallel blocks and a more intricate columnar treatment. *Scheme C*: (2) Two courtyards on axis, to the north circular, to the south, oblong. Divided by cross-wings with columnar vestibules. Probably a development of 5. *Scheme D*: (25–27) A square court formed by two Ls back to back. The base of the L on the river linked by a thin wing with a recess the width of the court. *Scheme E*: (6) Two E-shaped wings flanking a court open to the river and linked to the Strand wing. Vestibule through to Strand opens into a semi-circular screened niche. River front of 639 feet. (7) Variation of 6. (8) The court now closed to river and the E reduced to straight north–south wings with courts to right and left. (22–24) A development from 8. A court closed to the river where the front includes the circular Seamen's Waiting Hall, intended to support a largish dome. The disposition of the apartments now close to the 'approved' set of designs. (29) A pencil sketch of numbers 22–24.
Approved Schemes: (9) Apartments still to be decided, but plan fixed. (16–18) Lateral wings joined to Strand block by pairs of arched screens. (19–21) The 'approved' set drawn by an Office hand, probably for Government submission. (28) Final plan. Seaman's Hall with columnar treatment as executed. (30–33) Office set of plans, as executed. (34) Plan to large scale, as executed.
Drawer 41/2(1–32): *Working drawings*
(1) RA stair ceiling. (2) RA stair. Sketch of basement plan. (3) RA stair. Cellar plan. (4) RS stair. Principal floor plan. (5) RS stair. Mezzanine plan. (6) RS stair. Ground-floor plan. (7) Part plan RA principal floor. (8) Strand vestibule, vault plan. (9) RS Principal floor plan. (10) Copy of no.9. (11) RS Mezzanine floor plan. (12) Strand block, garret-floor plan. Inscr. (by Chambers) 'These Plans were approved of at the treasury board with the Elevations belonging to them July 3rd 1777. Present Lord North, Lord Onslow. Mr Cornall & Lord Westcot.' (13–30) Complete set and duplicate plans of Strand block. (31–32) Working details. Cornices, basement, back of Strand block.

Drawer 41/3(93–180)
(93–104) Plans of Offices for the Sick and Wounded. Approved 9 August 1777. (105–172) Plans of Navy Pay Office. Two sets, one small, one larger. One set approved summer 1776. Larger set approved 14 February 1777. (173–180) Plan of Stamp Office. No approval date.
Drawer 41/4(1–92)
(1–6) Plans of Audits of Imprest and Pipe Office. (7–12) Plans Surveyor General of the Crown Lands. (13–18) Plans Privy Seal and Signet. (19–24) Plans 'Various Duplicates'. (25–30) Plans Tax Office. Inscr. 'Examined these Plans and found them well calculated for carrying on the Business of this Office', 25 March 1777. (31–39) Plans, Duchy of Lancaster. Accepted March 1777, rejected May 1777. (40) Plan of Lottery Office. Dated 24 May 1776. (41–46) Plans of Ordnance Office. (47–64) Plans of House of the Treasurer of the Navy. (65–71) Plans of house for a Commissioner of the Navy. (72–92) Plans of Victualling Office. Dated 14 February 1777. With plans of 'new' Victualling Office, probably post-Chambers.
Drawer 41/5(1–40)
MSS documents. Victualling Office requirements, 13 March 1776. Sick and Wounded requirements, 18 and 19 February 1777. Navy Office, Tax Office, Pipe Office, Stamp Office, all n.d. Pay Office, 1 March 1777. Duchy of Cornwall, 29 March 1776. Royal Society n.d. Plans of the former Offices: Lottery (Palace Yard, Whitehall). Salt Office (York Buildings) 1771. Hawker's Office (Grays Inn). Stamp Office (Lincoln's Inn). Old Navy Office 25 May 1769. Pay Office (Broad Street). MS of Navy Board. William Robinson, 18 February 1774.
Drawer 41/6 (1–6)
Plans of Duchy of Cornwall Office. By Soane 1795.
Drawer 41/7(91–4)
'Plans and Section of the Embankment Wall'. Two other plans, cf. SAVOY.
Drawer 41/8(1–3)
Old plans of the Victualling Office and Navy Office. Probably William Robinson.
Drawer 42/1 (1–28)
Strand front, detailed sections; RA Great Stair, details; design for rusticated doorway with blocked Ionic pilasters; south elevation of wings of Strand block; basement plan of RA stair, dated 17 May 1779; elevations of terrace front at river level; sections of vestibule of Strand block; part elevation of Strand front; part elevation of embankment of river-front terrace; design for entrance doors to the court wings of the south front of the Strand block; detail of court front, first-floor windows of Strand block; design for first-floor windows on return fronts of Strand block.

Drawer 42/2[(1–48)]
Details of the Royal Academy, Royal Society and Society of Antiquaries' apartments. Ante-room Royal Academy 'ex[d] March 12, 1779', and Royal Society stair dated 22 May 1779.

Drawer 42/3 [(1–44)]
Large scale details (1–43) of Strand block. Design for a vase (44) by Coade and Sealy, dated 24 January 1786.

Drawer 42/4 [(45–100)]
Miscellaneous decorative and working details. No.100 inscr. 'Profile for Chimney Pieces' and 'Grenelle Arrow Allen Lawrence Dec 6 1778'.

Drawer 42/5 [(101–131)]
Miscellaneous decorative and working details. No.131 for the heads on pilasters to cove of RA exhibition room ceiling, inscr. 'Wilton'.

Drawer 42/6 [(1–24)]
Design for chimney-pieces. RS Library, S of A Meeting room (by Wilton), RA Lecture room (by Wilton), RS Meeting room (Wilton, 2 July 1780), Garret chimney-pieces (by Gilliam), plain chimney-pieces (by Wilton).

Drawer 42/7 [(1–19)]
Designs for ceilings, mostly RS Meeting room and Ante-room. Nos.2–3 for Strand Watch House – Two elevations of variant designs.

Drawer 42/8 [(1–7)]
Details of doors and windows.

Victoria and Albert Museum
E.527.1910, detail of pilaster panel (Strand apartments), inscr. 'Approved of 9 May 1778'; 3248, elevation, inscr. 'Entrance to the Wings of the Strand Building Settled feb.28, 1778 WC'; 3348, elevation three bays of ground-storey windows, court front of Strand block; 3353, section of RA staircase; 3388, elevation of south court front, river wing, inscr. 'Elevation of the Back front Mr Clarkes Examd Jany 24th 1777 WC'; 3390, elevation of the Strand Watch House, in front of St Mary le Strand; 3391, half-elevation of the main block river front with terrace; 3394, detail of a cornice; 3405, detail inscr. 'Royal Societys Meeting room Guilloch frame'; 3407, detail of a cornice, inscr. 'Royal Academy lecture room and Royal Societys meeting room'; 3411, design for a doorway with banded Doric order and frieze with bucrania; 3412, design for a chimney-piece, inscr. 'Royal Exhibtion Antiroom', and dated 6 December 1778; 7078.42, detail of a cornice.

BM Add.MS 41135, 28b, 39v (22 June, 13 Sept. 1774)
PRO: *Declared Accounts*, A.O.I.: 1244; 2495, 412–16; 2496, 417–21; 2497, 422–6; 2498, 427–31. *Treasury Minutes*, T.29/54/59/60/61
RIBA: Building Accounts in three volumes, 1776–96
RIBA Letters: WC to Lord North, 1 Nov. 1775
Sheffield University Library: Fitzwilliam MSS

BK2/5434 WC to Burke undated
WCRL: Archives, letter WC to George III, 12 March 1795
Baretti, J., *A Guide Through the Royal Academy*, 1781
Brewer, J. N., *An . . . Account of . . . Palaces and Public Buildings*, 1810, 1–29
Britton, J., and Pugin, A., *Illustrations of the Public Buildings of London*, II, 1828, 16–31
Clarke, C., *The Plaisterer's Bill for . . . Somerset House*, 1783
Copies of the Minutes and Proceedings . . . for carrying on the Buildings at Somerset House, 1788
Copies of the Several Reports made by the Board of Works respecting the work done under the Direction of Sir William Chambers at Somerset House 1788 (House of Lords Record Office Abbot Papers 564)
The Correspondence of King George The Third, ed. Fortescue, III, 1928, 207
Hutchison, S.C., *The History of the Royal Academy, 1768–1968*, 1968; *The Homes of the Royal Academy*, 1956
Journals of the House of Commons, XXXV, 321 (27 Apr. 1775); XXXVII, 788–9 (14 Apr. 1780); XXXVII, 818–19 (3 May 1780); XXXVIII, 944 (23 Apr. 1782); XXXIX, 836 (20 June 1783); XLI, 1099 (23 June 1785); XLII, 691–2 (27 Apr. 1787); XLIII, 432 (30 Apr. 1788); XLV, 116 (24 Feb. 1790)
Journals of the House of Lords, XXXIV, 407, 451a, 454b, 456b, 458b, 461b, 462b, 465b, 466a, 480b (12 Apr.–26 May 1775)
Needham, R., and Webster, A., *Somerset House Past and Present*, 1905
Parliamentary History, XVIII, 12 (26 Apr. 1775)
Apollo, Jan. 1969, 11–21, 'Decorative Painting for Lord Burlington and the Royal Academy', by Edward Croft-Murray
Architectural Review, Sept. 1954, 163–7, 'Old Somerset House', by N. Pevsner
C.Life, 16–23 Nov. 1967, 'Somerset House, London', by John Harris
Gentleman's Magazine, 1788, II, 985; and 1812 (ed. Gomme, 1891, Pt.II, 61)
SALE: Christie, 6 June 1811, 106

Somerset House created a unique situation for Chambers – a situation that for a much younger man would have marked a radical cross-roads in the development of his style and taste. The responsibility of organizing and controlling a public work of such vast size and importance cut him off, more or less permanently, from private practice at the peak of his architectural career. The effect of this sudden but welcome challenge, combined with his study during May and June of 1774 of new building in Paris, was to accelerate his stylistic development, bringing it to an early climax in the Strand façade and the 'Gabriel'-styled façades of the court. It must not be imagined that the planning and designing of Somerset House was an easy or straightforward task. The necessity to provide for a multitude of wholly independent offices and to adjust the large formalized complex to an irregular site was an immensely intricate and limiting problem to which Chambers provided a solution both logical and full of clarity, answering the real requirements but perhaps not all the ideal architectural expectations. Space limitations precluded the grand approach; the radical difference in length, width and depth between the court and river fronts of the Thames prohibited a satisfactory placing of a dome (better omitted); and an unyielding site also dictated the unsatisfactory shape of the Strand block plan and its unusual room divisions which in turn throw the entrance vestibule off axis.

Like Inigo Jones's Whitehall projects, the virtues of Somerset House lie in its parts, not all fully integrated, but each of polished sophistication. Indeed, there is a valid parallel between Somerset House Strand block and the Whitehall Banqueting House. In both the inspiration may be found in the Italian Renaissance, but its sources are transmuted in such a way that the result is purely English. One can detect throughout Chambers's career his longing for his first and principal love, Parisian architecture of the mid century – the architecture of De Wailly, Peyre, and Soufflot, his friends and contemporaries. At Somerset House he cast aside the trappings of English Palladianism, acknowledging its existence, it is true, but rendering his façades and details in the pure style of neo-classic Paris. Take an unknowing Frenchman (blindfold) into the Somerset House court, and upon seeing it he would imagine himself in the courtyard of a Paris palace or public building. Somerset House is even more than this, for despite its French detailing and management, it is the classic text-book on Georgian craftsmanship. Enrolled in its account books are the very finest sculptors, carvers, craftsmen and artists that London could produce. The Great Fire of London, especially St Paul's Cathedral, resulted in a renaissance of English craftsmanship; similarly, the works upon Somerset House from 1776 until well beyond Chambers's death in 1796, provided a unique training and apprenticeship for hundreds of younger men.

By 1790 it was obvious to Chambers that his masterpiece would never be completed; in fact, at his death the whole of the east colonnade and Palladian Bridge on the river front had yet to be built, and was completed by Sir Robert Smirke only from 1829. In any case a work the size of Somerset House would have taken years in any country, but unfortunately government parsimony after 1780 and the wars with France and Spain in 1796 and 1798 frustrated any hopes that it might have been completed within the century.

96 LONDON: STRAND: LITTLE DENMARK COURT: SOCIETY OF ARTS

'Great Room' and adjacent apartments, together with President's Chair and furnishings (1759–60) (Pls 139, 181)

RIBA: J4/24B, plan inscr. 'Plann of a Building for the Society of Arts manufactures and Commerce'
V & A: Forster Coll., Baker-Arderon Correspondence, IV, 130, 190
Mount Stuart, Bute Papers: Letter Robert Wood to Lord Bute 28 Oct. 1759
Royal Society of Arts: Loose Archives A/8, J. William 1759; Ledger 1760; Society and Committee Minutes 1759–60
Allan, D. G. C., *The Houses of the Royal Society of Arts*, 1966
Hudson, D., and Lockhart, W. K., *The Royal Society of Arts, 1754–1954* (1954), 19–20
Wood, H. T., *A History of the Royal Society of Arts*, 1913, 54–6
J. Roy. Soc. Arts, Apr. 1962, 'A Plan by Sir William Chambers for the Society of Arts', by John Harris

The Great Room, designed by Chambers and used for the exhibition of contemporary works of art, was destroyed in the later eighteenth century and is now known only from documentary information contained in the leases and inventories of the Society. Although (according to the Baker-Arderon correspondence) there seems to be some question as to the exact size of the room, the official leases and specifications describe a double cube of $80 \times 40 \times 40$ feet (in other words a double cube one third larger than the famous one at Wilton) with a 'Palladian' ceiling and a large oval dome supported upon four Corinthian columns. Below this, on the ground floor, was a smaller double cube 36×18 feet serving as a 'Repository', a Committee Room, and a staircase also lit from the top by a dome. These apartments ceased functioning in 1772 when the Society moved to a larger building in John Street designed by Robert Adam. The RIBA plan may be dated between 1757 when Chambers was elected to the Society and 1759 when the new apartments were built. Because of the great size of the plan it was undoubtedly made in the spirit of an ideal essay. Perhaps the most surprising information revealed by the Committee Minutes is that the furniture of the Great Room was also designed by Chambers. On 7 November 1759 'a Drawing of a chair for the President was produced for the Society by Mr Chambers', and a week later the Committee ordered 'the said chair' as well as 'the Tables and Benches drawn by Mr Chambers' and 'five Chandeliers after the above Drawing' (by Chambers) to 'be forthwith made'. Unfortunately the chandeliers, costing £121, tables and benches have disappeared. The President's Chair, however, is still in use. Its style is an early but tentative approach to neo-classicism, for straight-tapered legs and a seat rail ornamented with Vitruvian scroll are combined with a rococo back and arms. There would seem to be little doubt that the neo-classical elements are a reflection of Chambers's experiences in Paris, for in his Franco-Italian album (p.60) may be found the drawing (pl.180) of a chair measured and seen by him between 1749 and 1755. Both have straight tapered circular legs and a straight seat rail.

97 LONDON: UPPER GROSVENOR STREET: GLOUCESTER HOUSE
Duke of Gloucester
Unspecified alterations and project for a new house (?c.1770) (Pl.177)
Grosvenor Estate Office, London: elevation of an entrance front; Bedford Lemere photographs of the interiors of Grosvenor House

The Duke of Gloucester acquired his house in 1761. He married in 1766, after which year he might have contemplated improvements to his house – if not earlier. Gloucester House became Grosvenor House, and in the Bedford Lemere photographs, the Dining Room is quite clearly a room of *c.*1770. It had, in fact, a very fine compartmented ceiling with rinceau and other ornamentation perfectly in accord with the best of Chambers's work. If Chambers can, stylistically, be associated with decoration in Gloucester House, this would explain the presence in the Grosvenor archives of this design by Chambers. It is a very noble project, surely nearer to 1775 – or even 1780 – than to 1770. On the other hand, as at Adderbury (q.v.) Chambers had reached a new stage of maturity of style by 1770. The idea of a raised belvedere (if it was one) can be paralleled in the late 1770s designs for the Savoy (q.v.) but perhaps more pertinently with the ill-fated Harewood design (q.v.) – an elevation very similar (high centre and low wings) to Gloucester House. No exact source has been ascertained for the Mannerist arched windows in the wings.

98 LONDON: WESTMINSTER ABBEY: ST JOHN'S CHAPEL
Earl and Countess of Mountrath's monument (1771) (Pl.191) E
BM Add.MS 41133, 40v (WC to Wilton 23 May 1771, asking for £50 on account)
SALE: Christie, 6 June 1811, 87; 6 June 1817, 55: 'Design for a monument erected to the Memory of Lady Monteath [*sic*] by Sir William Chambers, grand compositions in bistre' (by Cipriani)

The Countess is seen depicted against an architectural framework surmounted by two neo-classic urns, kneeling on a sarcophagus and ready to be conducted to Heaven by an attendant angel. The group should be compared with the slightly earlier Bedford monument at Chenies (q.v.), also carved by Wilton; and with Wilton's own monument to Lady Anne Dawson erected after 1770 in Dawson's Grove, Co. Cavan. This latter monument includes an identical angel.

99 LONDON: WESTMINSTER ABBEY
UNEXECUTED design for a monument to General Wolfe (1760)
HWC: 21, Mann, 1 (1960), 428

The evidence for Chambers's submission of a design for Wolfe's tomb is contained in a letter written by Walpole to Sir Horace Mann on 1 August 1760: 'Apropos to Wolfe, I cannot imagine what you mean by a design executed at Rome for his tomb. The designs have been laid before my Lord Chamberlain several months; Wilton, Adam, Chambers, and others all gave their drawings immediately.' In fact nothing transpired from this competition, and it was not until 1771 that the commission was eventually placed in Wilton's hands.

100 LONDON: WHITEHALL: GOWER HOUSE
2nd Earl Gower
Town house (1765–74) (Pls 95, 98, 100–102; Fig.8)
MMA: design for a trapezoidal panel, probably for octagon room ceiling
PML: M. Pergolesi album: 74, frieze inscr. 'Lord Gowe – Leibrary'; 80, copy of MMA panel; 82, frieze inscr. 'Lord Gower Leibrary'
GLC: drawings by C. J. Richardson (1819) and J. P. Emslie (1885)
NMR: photographs taken by Bedford Lemere prior to demolition
Soane: 42/2³⁶, section of staircase; 43/6²⁰, section of Drawing Room (later Ball Room), inscr. 'Walsh a large glass see it'; 17/7, measured elevations of façades; 17/3, Basevi lecture diagram of staircase
V&A: E.3244.1934 'Earl Gower's Elevation Towards the Street Whitehall'; 3377, possibly preliminary design for staircase; 7076.9, 20–21, 27, 29, five floor plans
WPL: Gardner Coll. 39.13, section of Drawing Room
BM Add.MS 41133, 11–11v, 24–24v (28 Apr. 1770–19 Nov. 1770); 41135, 33v, 50, 50v (9 July 1774–20 Oct. 1774)
RIBA Letters: Gower to WC 12 Oct. 1774
Chancellor, E. B., *Eighteenth-Century London*, 1920, figs 122–3
Ellwood, G. M., *English Furniture and Decoration*, 1933, 100–1, 102–3

Lenygon, *Decoration in England, 1660–1770*, 1914, figs 84, 150–1, 215
LCC, *Survey of London*, XVI, 1935, 176 ff., pls.94–5
Richardson, A. E., and Eberlein, H. D., *The Smaller English House of the Later Renaissance 1660–1830*, 1925, fig.247
Tipping, A., *English Homes*, per. VI, 1926, figs vii, viii, ix, x
The Builder, 9 August 1884, 190, 196, 201; 10 April 1886, 558; 24 April 1886, 628
Westminster and Lambeth Gazette, 10 April 1886
EXHIB S of A 1767, 228; RA 1769, 17; RA 1770, 37
SALE: Christie, 6 June 1811, 97

Gower House although frequently illustrated and evidently one of the most highly-esteemed London town houses, nevertheless fell victim to demolition in 1886. Fortunately, surviving plans, diagrams, old drawings, and photographs make it possible to reconstruct the staircase, the Drawing (or Ball) Room, the Eating Room, and the general character of the remaining interior decoration.

A lease of the site on the corner of what is now Horse Guards Avenue, facing the north flank of the Banqueting House in Whitehall, was granted to the 2nd Earl Gower on 5 March 1765. The earliest mention of the newly-projected house does not occur, however, until the following year. The *London Chronicle* for 9–12 March reported 'A large handsome house is going to be built at Whitehall for Lord Gower', which suggests that Chambers's designs were known. As no building accounts survive, the progress of this house can only be ascertained from exhibited designs and the fragmentary correspondence in the Letter Books. In 1767 drawings of terms for the Eating Room were shown at the Society of Arts; in 1769 the ceiling for Countess Gower's Dressing room was at the Royal Academy where in 1770 the famous Gower House staircase was also exhibited. On 29 April 1770 Chambers asked Lord Gower to settle an account of £2012.11.6 and repeated the request on 19 November, noting that 'money is at this time a Very scarce Commodity'.

There is no further mention of building activities in the correspondence until July 1774 when finishing touches were being made to the Great Drawing Room (later called the Ball Room), which was apparently still incomplete on 20 October (Add.MS 41135, 50v).

Unrelated as they may be, these dates indicate that the building of Gower House extended over a period of at least nine years, four more than Melbourne House and unusually long for any town venture.

The plan of the house is an ingenious solution to an irregularly-shaped site. There are two main fronts, a Whitehall 'parade' façade of five bays and two and a half storeys, with a central bay containing a tripartite window below and a Palladian one above; and a narrow Privy Garden façade with a tripartite door and window side by side on the ground floor and three windows over them lighting the Great Drawing Room.

Breaking with tradition Chambers placed the entrance in this secondary front, which contained his Hall and Eating Room on the ground floor, while the Whitehall wing was given over to an enfilade of reception or private rooms. Between these two suites of apartments, squarely in the centre of the L-shaped house, was the splendid staircase which Chambers synthesized in a remarkable manner from Longhena's famous stair in the Convento of S. Maria Maggiore, Venice. The walls of the stair were decorated with neo-classic compositions of ravishing beauty, almost certainly modelled by Thomas Collins. The most important rooms were the Great Drawing Room and the Eating Room, both of which were panelled in the French manner with ornamented pilaster strips dividing the wall into large compartments. This new mode of decoration had been introduced by Chambers into England in the Saloon of Buckingham House in 1763. He employed it again at Peper Harow and at Somerset House, and it anticipates the more familiar style of Henry Holland's interiors by nearly 15 years.

Fortunately the dearth of contemporary documentation is balanced by Bedford Lemere's invaluable photographic record of the most notable interiors made in 1886. Publications of the period perpetuate the Staircase, Eating Room, Hall and Great Drawing Room. It is obvious that one of Chambers's associates, probably Cipriani or Biagio Rebecca, contributed 'insets' to the ceiling of the Great Drawing Room and probably also the Eating Room and Countess Gower's Dressing Room. At the sale of 1886 the finer chimney-pieces were purchased by Lords Carrington and Hillingdon, the former installing his – with many other fragments from the house – at Buckinghamshire, where they remain.

101 LONDON: WHITEHALL: GRANTHAM HOUSE
Sir Thomas Robinson, 1st Baron Grantham
Alterations of unknown extent (?1760s)
Newby Hall (N.R. Yorks) archives: 'Ceiling for the Boudoir'; 'Plan of the Staircase at the Rt Honble Lord Granthams at Whitehall'; section of the staircase; 'Profiles for the Chimney piece'; 'Base & Surbase for the room'
LCC, *Survey of London*, XIII, 1930, 160–1

The inscription on one of the designs indicates that they were made for Thomas Robinson after he became Baron Grantham in 1761. They must be related in time to Chambers's designs for Newby Park (Baldersby) (q.v.) also in the archives at nearby Newby Hall. Unfortunately this Whitehall work was never recorded before the house was demolished about 1896. After Grantham's death in 1770 his son employed John Yenn for further alterations, possibly after his marriage in 1780. Yenn's designs are in the University of Delaware.

102 LONDON: WHITEHALL: PEMBROKE HOUSE
10th Earl of Pembroke
Internal decorations (1760), Riding House (1773) (Pl.92)
MMA: design for Gallery ceiling
V & A: 2216.24, design for Gallery ceiling dated 1760; 2216.47, design for Saloon ceiling dated 1760
BM Add.MS 41133, III, 111v–12, 116, 117–18 (Sept.–Oct. 1773); 41135, 14 (27 March 1774); 41136, I–IV, 11–12, 12–13 (Jan.–March 1774)
RIBA Letters: Lord Bruce to WC 15 July 1756
Wilton Archives: Bill. Jan. 1760 'designs for fitting up some rooms at Whitehall £42.0.0'
LCC, *Survey of London*, XIII, 1930, 167–75
C.Life, 19 Sept. 1936

The V & A designs, like the Wilton bill and the Autobiographical Note, all limit Chambers's work at Pembroke House to 'diverse ceilings' without suggesting, as the *Survey of London* does, that he was responsible for the design of the house as well. That Chambers was not the architect is perfectly clear from Lord Pembroke's letter of 27 March 1774 informing him the house had been built by a Mr Evans. Thus, when Chambers was advised by Lord Bruce as early as 1756 to try to attract Pembroke's attention with a view to gaining this commission, Evans, or some other architect, had already been chosen. Nevertheless Chambers did manage, probably with the aid of Lord Bruce, to gain employment at Wilton in 1757 and it was surely his worth there that induced Pembroke to finish the main apartments (Gallery & Saloon) of his town house in the latest Chambersian style visible at Richmond House, also in Whitehall (q.v.) and at Roehampton (q.v.).

In 1773–4 Chambers was again altering Pembroke House and adding a Riding House, for which his friend the Marquis de Voyer d'Argenson may also have supplied designs (at Wilton, initialled VD).

Pembroke House was demolished in 1913 and the Saloon ceiling is preserved and incorporated in the new Government Offices.

103 LONDON: WHITEHALL: RICHMOND HOUSE
3rd Duke of Richmond
Gallery, Greenhouse, Gate to Privy Garden, and a Therm (1759–60)
MMA: (49.56.51) detail for a moulding inscr. 'Duke of Richmond's Greenhouse', together with a note about Joseph Wilton sending to Carrara for marble; (34.78.2 [17]) design for a Therm. inscr. 'Therm for his Grace the Duke of Richmond executed at Whitehall'; (34.78.2 [33]), design for the Gallery ceiling
Soane: 43/6¹, design for a ceiling inscr. 'A Ceiling for the Duke of Richmond's Gallery Wthall' and dated 1760
West Sussex CRO: Richmond Papers Box 36/7, estimate (£84.4.0) for the Privy Garden gate, dated February 1759
Annual Register, 1758, 84–5
Chambers, *Treatise*, 1759, pl.50. Gate to the Privy Garden
LCC, *Survey of London*, XIII, 1930, 247–8

Chambers's additions from 1759 to Richmond House, which by then had been partially rebuilt by Lord Burlington, are contemporary with his work for the Duke at Goodwood (q.v.). All that we know of the London house, which was totally destroyed by fire in 1791, are the Privy Garden gate published in the *Treatise* and designed in February 1759; a detail for stone carved by Joseph Wilton that points to the building of a Greenhouse in a garden (perhaps at Goodwood?); and the decoration of the Gallery designed in 1760. There may well be some connection between Chambers's decoration of the Gallery and the Duke's generous offer to allow artists access to his collection of classical sculpture and casts, an access granted to the Incorporated Society of Artists in 1758 and the actual opening of the room in 1760.

104 LUCAN HOUSE (Co. Dublin)
Agmondesham Vesey
Design for a new villa (1773–5) (Pl.70) E
Dublin: National Library: Survey plans and designs by Stapleton and James Wyatt
BM Add.MS 41133, 99, 103v (Jan.–19 June 1773); 41134, 27 (4 June 1773); 41135, 17v–18 (28 March 1774); 41136, 16–16v (28 March 1774)
RIBA Letters: Vesey to WC 3 Jan. 1773
HMC Twelfth Report, *Charlemont*, App. Pt.x, 1, 1891, 332
Milton, Thomas, *The Seats and Demesnes of . . . Ireland*, 1, 1783, Pl.III
C.Life, 31 Jan. 1947, 278–81
Irish Georgian Soc. Bull., VIII, no.3, 1965, 'Sir William Chambers, Friend of Charlemont', by John Harris

The Connoisseur, Sept. 1965, 'An Irish Villa for an Italian Ambassador', by John Hunt

Vesey's decision to rebuild the house at Lucan, near Dublin, is first expressed in a letter to Chambers dated 3 January 1773. 'I have got this landskip of Lucan & its environs & wish to shew you the Situation & aspects of a place which I am persuaded will receive great Embellishments from your hands.' To this Chambers replied on 5 May 'I have been out of town else your Elevation should have been done & Plans altered sooner. I wish the Elevation may please you. I think it is not amiss, & as you mean to build wth stone the Additional Expence will be trifling.' A month later, on 4 June, Chambers sent Vesey his bill 'more in compliance with your desire than my inclination' for 'Drawings for finishing the Rooms, such as Cornices door Entablatures Window architraves Bases surbase &c £6.6.0' and 'Various Plans Elevations Sketches & Designs for a Villa £26.5.' The drawings for finishing the rooms were in all probability not intended for Lucan which Vesey was then considering rebuilding, but for another commission, perhaps minor work in Vesey's London house (q.v.). Of the 'Various' 'Designs for a Villa' Chambers provides a more detailed description in a letter of 19 June. 'There are four plans, the Elevations and the Section, the windows do not come perfectly regular on one side but I have contrived it so that the difference will scarcely be perceptible' (Add.MS 41133, 103v). This letter provides an interesting link between Chambers's lost designs and the executed villa in which the windows are in fact irregular on one side, proving furthermore that Vesey must have incorporated some part of his old house in the new fabric.

The final form of the projected (new) villa was rather long in the making. After six months of discussion several features still remained unsettled. On 28 March 1774 Vesey wrote to Chambers 'I am much more intent in finishing the South front of your Plan at Lucan this summer ... I pray You'll give me any rough sketch for a portico of four Columns that commands a long view of the river, is situated near a pretty brook and opposite to an open grove. You have taught me to think pediments but common architecture by substituting newer and more pleasing ornaments in their place at Lord Charlemonts & in other works, but this I leave absolutely and implicitly to you, if I am to have a pediment the lower Greek one will suit the Situation best, if you turn over that elegant magazine of drawings, the book which I have often admired, you'll find Several designs there which will suit me, and you may depend both on my friendship & my pleasure in executing any work of yours, that it shall be finished ad Unguem.'

Building activities do not seem to have been begun, however, until the following summer or autumn, for visiting Lucan on 25 June 1775 Lady Louisa Conolly wrote, 'The house ... is almost pulled down, and I hear wont be habitable these two years.' It was 1780 or 1781 before the new villa was completed, in time to be included in Thomas Milton's *Seats ... of Ireland* (vol.I, 1783).

The executed façade of Lucan is typically Chambersian, its pedimented central portico projecting above lower flanks being a feature of the abortive Harewood and Svartsjo designs (q.v.). But neither plan nor the details are characteristic. It is perhaps significant that Edward Stevens is mentioned by Chambers in answer to an enquiry about slating at Lucan, for it was Stevens who signed the Svartsjo design now in Stockholm. It is also necessary to consider Vesey's own abilities as an amateur architect, who according to Boswell 'understood architecture very well and left a very good specimen of his knowledge in that art by an elegant house built on a place of his own at Lucan'. And no doubt for that reason Vesey was the Professor of Architecture in Dr Johnson's Utopian university.

Although Chambers's designs for Lucan no longer exist, there are in the National Library of Dublin a survey plan and numerous interior designs by Michael Stapleton, a Dublin master builder and plasterer, and designs for the oval room by James Wyatt. To this latter London architect has been attributed the 'tortoise' monument in the gardens.

MANRESA HOUSE, *see* ROEHAMPTON: PARKSTED

105 MARLBOROUGH (Wilts)
4th Duke of Marlborough
UNEXECUTED proposals for a new inn
RIBA Letters: Thomas Walker to WC 17 Oct. 1769

The idea of a new inn at Marlborough seems to have been suggested by Chambers, but was rejected by Walker, the Duke's auditor, because of its 'costly' expense.

106 MILTON ABBEY (Dorset)
1st Baron Milton
New house; Porter's Lodge; Gothicizing of the west front of the Abbey church (1769–75) (Pls 64–66) E
RIBA: G4/16. Plan of grounds before removal of village; G4/19. Design for Gothic gates; G4/20–21. Designs for chimney-pieces by Chambers and Thomas Carter; K9/20. John Vardy's proposals for a Gothic or classical house

Soane: 43/6[15], details of Gothic profiles and a study for a Gothic door

BM Add.MS 41133, 23v, 25, 25v–26v, 30–31, 32–32v, 32v–33, 36v, 38v, 42v–43, 45v–46v, 46v–48, 52–53, 57, 59v, 60, 60v, 60v–61, 62–64, 66v–67, 68v, 70–70v, 75–75v, 77v, 87, 88, 90v, 94v, 95, 96, 96v, 97v, 102, 109v, 111, 112–113, 115v, 118, 120, 125, 127v, 129, 129v, 130 (Dec. 1769–16 June 1774); 41134, 20v–21 (17 Apr. 1773); 41135, 12–13v, 15v–16, 68v (24 March 1774–9 July 1775); 41136, 13v–14, 14v (Apr. 1774)

Coutts Bank Archives: Lord Milton's bank account

RIBA Letters: Milton to WC 3, 9 June 1775

Buck, S. and N., Engraving of view of the Abbey taken in 1733

Hutchins, J., *Hist. & Antiqs . . . County of Dorset*, IV, 1815, 217–18

Neale, J. P., *Views of Seats*, 2 ser., IV, 1828

Oswald, A., *Country Houses of Dorset*, 1959, 108–13

Rooker, E., Engraving of *The North West View of Milton Abbey*

Stroud, D., *Capability Brown*, 1957, 81–2

Watts, W., *Seats of the Nobility and Gentry*, 1781

C.Life, 29 May, 5 June, 1915; 16, 23, 30 June 1966; 21, 28 July 1966

SALE: Christie, 6 June 1811, 99; Fairbrother, Clark & Lye, 30 June 1852

Chambers's activities at Milton Abbey followed close upon his work in 1768 or 1769 at Lord Milton's Park Lane house (q.v.). The demolition of the medieval abbey, or what remained of it less the Great Hall, was begun in January 1771 under the direction of Stephen Carpenter, a master mason from the nearby town of Blandford. Between February and April the foundations were laid for the east front and kitchen wing and for the south front that enclosed the Great Hall. From then on, however, work progressed slowly. Plans for the north front were produced in October 1771, but the wing was not finished until November 1773, by which time Chambers was beginning to feel the brunt of Milton's irascible moods. In May 1773 they argued over Milton's refusal to pay travelling expenses, that were, Chambers explained, 'Allowed to every Architect of reputation here. I know Mr Wright, Mr Taylor, Mr Adam always charge their expences' (BM Add.MS 41133, 97v). But Milton apparently remained unconvinced, forcing Chambers to reply in exasperation, 'I have considered the conditions insisted upon, and now see in a stronger light than before, the impropriety of complying with them. I can by no means consent to an arrangement which must disgust all my other employers, and fix upon me a character which I have so long studied to avoid; I have hitherto acted upon liberal principles, and must not now fall off. The conditions I require are not

of my invention. They were in use long before my arrival in England. They still continue so, and all things considered, are far from being extravagant, even in your Lordship's case. You have, my Lord, often mentioned Mr Paine as being much more moderate in his charges; I do not find that to be the case; as will appear by the enclosed letter from him. I ask no more than Mr Paine, or any other man of character; and there is, I presume, no reason why I should accept of less' (BM Add.MS 41133, 109v–110). This exchange ultimately resulted in a complete break with Milton, whom Chambers later described as an 'unmannerly imperios Lord who has treated me as he does everybody ill'. Maltreated as he was, Chambers nevertheless insisted upon departing honourably. On 29 March 1774 he wrote 'whether we part or not, the laying of the new foundations (*west wing*) must necessarily be done by me (BM Add.MS 41135, 15v–16). As it turned out, Chambers's association with Milton lasted longer than he had anticipated. Builders' bills for £4070 13s and his own fee of £365 11s, were sent in on 15 January 1775, and even on 9 July Milton was enquiring of Chambers about plans, to which Chambers replied that they might have been left with Joseph Rose the plasterer (who according to the bank account was paid £200 on 5 August 1776 and £100 on 19 December 1778).

The completion of Milton Abbey after Chambers's departure was the work of two architects, to a lesser extent Capability Brown, and to the greater, James Wyatt. Brown had been called in to landscape the park between 1764 and 1770, and was called in yet again between 1773 and 1774 to execute the model village (q.v.) and eventually to landscape those parts of the park south of the house and abbey church where stood the old medieval village. It is possible that Brown made some alterations or completion works to the interiors and, when he did so, incorporated certain elements of Chambers's designs. The ground-floor rooms – Staircase, Ante-Room, Dining Room, Library – nearest the south-west tower are in Chambers's style, and it is known that these rooms were completed first. The Dining Room, for example, has a characteristic Chambersian ceiling related to one in the Dining Room of Milton Park, Northamptonshire (q.v.). The designs for Wyatt's work date from 1776 and include decoration of the upper rooms of the west front, except for the spacious barrel-vaulted Saloon or Gallery not completed until about 1793 or 1794.

Chambers had little respect for this type of 'associational' style and designed only one other Gothic building, a little Dairy and Tea Room for his friend Thomas Hyde of The Hoo, Hertfordshire (q.v.). It would seem that the choice of style at Milton was his lordship's or John Vardy's, for not only do the earlier Vardy proposals exist, but his plans are mentioned in several contexts in the Chambers's correspondence. It is therefore quite clear that Chambers was executing and modifying a Vardy design. To these facts must be added the rider that Rooker's view of the Abbey is of a building differing in many details from the executed one. The windows, for example, are rococo-Gothic, and in style the north front of Milton, to which must be added the ogee cupolas now demolished, is a child of Kent's Esher. On the other hand Chambers gave to Milton something that Vardy never could: the excellence of its stonework and the crispness of its details. It is precisely in these that Milton stands apart as the work of a neo-classic architect trained in Paris.

107 MILTON ABBEY: Village (Milton Abbas)
1st Baron Milton
Planning of new model village (1773) (Pl.197) E
BM Add.MS 41133, 97v and v
Stroud, D., *Capability Brown*, 1957, 81–2
C.Life, 29 Sept. 1966, 'Market Town Into Model Village', A. Oswald

When Lord Milton, as Joseph Damer, bought Milton Abbey in 1752 the village lay to the south of the Abbey Garden. Right from the first Milton must have had it in his mind to remove the village. However, he did not succeed until 1773, by which time his relationship with Chambers was beginning to break up. On 3 April 1773 Chambers sent 'a plan of a part of the intended Village & an Elevation', and a description of his proposed layout. Although Chambers did not cease work at Milton until the end of 1774, no further mention was made of the village. Capability Brown had visited Milton in 1773 and 1774 and Milton had paid him £105 for plans for the village. It is clear, however, from Chambers's description, that the layout of the village was his, although it was modified in execution. In fact, it is doubtful if the Vicarage was built before Brown's departure, and the church, built about 1774, was in charge of Stephen Carpenter, Chambers's clerk of works at Milton Abbey and a local builder from nearby Blandford. There is certainly no comparable model village before 1774. Whatever Brown's responsibilities in the affair, to Chambers must go the credit for this humanitarian layout. It accords perfectly with his championship of the working classes.

108 MILTON PARK (Northants)
4th Earl Fitzwilliam
Alteration and interior decoration. Garden temple (1770–6) (Pls 87, 89) E
MMA: (34.78.2 [8]), designs for saloon chimney-piece
V & A: 7076.37 (survey plan)
BM Add.MS 41133, 23, 34–35, 35–36, 37–37v, 39–39v, 50v, 54v–55, 56v, 61–61v, 64–64v, 65–65v, 67, 67v, 76, 82, 83, 86, 110v, 115–15v (18 Oct. 1770–30 Oct. 1773); 41134, 8 (22 Oct. 1772)
RIBA Letters: Fitzwilliam to WC 31 Aug. 1773, 17 Aug. 1776
Northants RO: Fitzwilliam (Milton) Vouchers 114, 115
C.Life, 18 May 1961, 1148–51; 25 May, 1210–13; 1 June 1270–4

Lord Fitzwilliam, anxious to improve his suite of apartments at Milton Park, in preparation for his marriage to Lady Charlotte Ponsonby, called in Chambers on the advice of Lady Charlotte's father Lord Bessborough, who had employed him at Roehampton (q.v.).

Milton at the time could be described as nothing short of a muddle. Although the south front had been rebuilt in a Palladian style by Flitcroft in the 1750s, the north side remained primarily of the sixteenth century, with the result that the floor as well as roof levels were uneven. Furthermore, as Flitcroft's work was never completed due to lack of funds, the only Palladian rooms in the house were the North Hall, Main Staircase, and Pillared Hall on the ground floor. To these Chambers added a new Dining Room (now the Smoking Room) on the north front and on the first floor, also on the north front, the Peterborough Dining Room, Tea Room, and Green Library. His most splendid addition, however, was undoubtedly the Gallery which he built into the shell left by Flitcroft in the centre of his south front. Chambers accepted the existing tripartite division of the area, as well as the openings for doors, windows and chimney-pieces, but provided barrel vaults to the end bays and a shallow dome on pendentives over the centre. The detailing of these rooms is most unconventional and may be said to reflect the 'other face' of our architect. Pilasters are tucked into the angles, a practice condemned in the *Treatise* and the barrel vaults are banded *à la Borromini*, whose work is always Chambers's target for attacks.

The correspondence relating to Chambers's work at Milton dates from October 1770 to October 1773. This identifies the plasterer as Thomas Collins and the sculptors of the chimney-pieces as William Tyler (described by Chambers as 'poor as a tube') and Edward Bingham of Peterborough.

The foreman in the initial stage was Robert

Smith who was soon dismissed after being reprimanded by Chambers for 'always tripping about with your coat and waistcoat on & instead of finding your Head clear and capable of receiving directions or of giving a reasonable answer to my questions, I found you always confused and unfit for anything' (Add.MS 41133, 65–65v). His successor Mr Roby, a joiner by profession, who proved an 'admirable workman, most civilized and obliging', was eventually employed by Chambers at Melbourne House.

Chambers's last task at Milton was the design for a Corinthian temple to be a present from Lord Bessborough to his son-in-law. It was planned in October 1773 and built by Edward Bingham, but has since been dismantled. The size and superb quality of the remaining fluted marble columns suggest a resemblance to the temple dedicated to Worsley and published in the *Treatise*.

109 NEWBOROUGH PRIORY (Yorks)
2nd Earl Fauconberg
Work of unknown character (1774)
BM Add.MS 41135, 37 (WC to Thomas Worsley Aug. 1774)
RIBA Letters: Thomas Worsley to WC 3 July 1774
C.Life, 11 Nov. 1905, 666–76

On 3 July 1774 Worsley could ask Chambers 'Do you visit L. Fauconberg here, does he intend buildings? If you do I hope to see you'; and in reply Chambers could inform him in August of his imminent departure for the York Races, accompanied by the Marquis de Voyer D'Argenson. They intended to call at Coleby (q.v.) and afterwards at Hovingham, 'then on to Lord Fauconberg where I shall be employed some days'. It seems hardly possible that Chambers would have gone out of his way for as long as three days for any minor task, nor can this diversion refer to his work for Lord Fauconberg at his London house in George Street (q.v.) where everything was 'going on briskly' in April 1774. Newborough has been considerably altered and the only later eighteenth-century work observable there is Gothic windows to the Great Kitchen and a typically Chambersian columnar recess in one of the rooms.

110 NEWBY PARK (West Riding Yorkshire)
Sir Thomas Robinson, 1st Baron Grantham
Pheasantry and Menagery and alterations to the house of unknown extent (?c.1760s) (Pls 75–77)
Newby Hall (N.R. Yorks) archives: 'Elevation of the Pheasant pens & Entrance to the Pheasantry'; 'Front of the Pavillion in the Pheasantry'; designs for Chinese-styled fret finials, inscr. 'Mr Chambers for Menagery Paling'; 'A design of a Section for

Newby The Seat of the Right Honble Lord Grantham'

This house, designed by Colen Campbell was gutted by fire in the nineteenth century. Nothing therefore remains of what Chambers may have done to the interiors. The Pheasantry and Menagery have also gone. His section indicates a complete interior redecoration. There exist designs made by Robinson (himself an amateur architect) in 1764, an approximate date for Chambers's intervention. Confusingly, the family owned both Newby Park (now known as Baldersby) as well as nearby Newby Hall.

111 ORMES (Touraine): Château les Ormes
Marquis de Voyer d'Argenson
Staircase (*c*.1770)
RIBA: Parisian Album, 10: plan and section of 'de Wailly's stair'
BM Add.MS 41133, 122v (8 Feb. 1774); 41134, 14 (25 Oct. 1772)
Jnl Soc. Archtl. Histrns GB (Architectural History), 6 f, 1963, 'Sir William Chambers and his Parisian Album', by John Harris

When de Voyer d'Argenson wrote to Chambers on 25 October 1772, saying 'mon escalier est finie', he was referring to works undertaken at his Château les Ormes, designed by Charles de Wailly. But it would seem that as far as Chambers was concerned the staircase was executed to *his* design, a fact conveyed in a letter to Le Roy on 8 February 1774 a few weeks before departing for Paris. Chambers asked Le Roy to enquire from de Wailly 'que je ne manquerai pas d'aller voir l'Escallier surprenant qu'il dit avoir bati en l'air aux Ormes la première fois que j'irai en France. Il y a deux ans que j'envoyais des Desseins d'un Escallier a Mon sieur de Voyer pour être erigé aux Ormes & il m'a ecrit depuis qu'il l'avait fait construire, mais celui la quoique fort leger ne se pouvoit pas suspendre en l'air comme le tombeaux de Mahomet. de Wailly aura apparament rencheri sur ma construction ou inventé une nouvelle de sa facon dont les architectes jusqu'à présent n'ont eu aucune Idée de l'autre coté.' It would seem almost certain that Chambers's record of 'de Vaillies stair' in his Parisian Album only three months after this letter is, in fact, the one at les Ormes. Unfortunately this famous staircase was destroyed in 1823. There is a very distinct relationship between both architects' conceptions of staircase design. Dr Robin Middleton has verbally pointed out the resemblance between de Wailly's stair in the Château de Montmusard (1760s) and James Paine's at Wardour Castle (1770s). But Paine's is directly derivative from Chambers's unexecuted design for his York House stair (q.v.)

exhibited at the Society of Artists in 1762. The les Ormes stair may well be by Chambers out of de Wailly. D'Argenson was an intimate and old friend of Chambers and would surely have informed him had he executed another's design.

112 OSTERLEY PARK (Middx)
Francis Child
ATTRIBUTED north wing including Gallery (before 1761) (Pl.49)
Avery: design for a chimney-piece in the Gallery
Soane: Adam Drawings v.43/92, a plan of 1761; Adam Drawings v.22/201, a design for the Hall chimney-piece (unexecuted) by Joseph Wilton
Ward-Jackson, P., *Osterley Park, A Guide*, 1959
C.Life, 20 Nov. 1926, 782–90; 27 Nov. 1926, 818–26

It is clear from Adam's plan of 1761 that the rebuilding of the Elizabethan Osterley was already in progress when he arrived on the scene. Precisely when the work was begun is not known, but 1756, the year of Francis Child's coming-of-age, may be put forward as a likely date. By 1761 the new north front of nine bays with a slightly projecting pedimented centre (entrance and staircase added later by Adam, and the refacing of the end towers also by him) and the Gallery behind it were completed. Although the authorship of this work is not documented it may safely be attributed to Chambers on several accounts. First, the pair of therm chimney-pieces in the Gallery are patently characteristic of his style and are in fact similar to one of his unspecified designs in Avery Library. Wilton's signed design for a Hall chimney-piece also suggests the presence of Chambers, for the two artists had returned together from Italy in 1755 and worked in a mutual partnership. The slowly-modulated proportions and immaculately-detailed red brick of the exterior are likewise Chambersian, providing the keynote for the remainder of the refacing by Adam.

113 OXFORD: MAGDALEN COLLEGE
Dr George Home
UNEXECUTED designs for the President's House (1768)
BM Add.MS 41133, 67v–68 (21 Jan. 1772)

On 21 January 1772 Chambers sent his second reminder for payment of £51.9.0: 'Dr the Society of Magdalen College Oxen to Wm Chambers Esq of Berners Street 1768 Augt 1st To a journey to Oxford to survey & receive directions excluding Expence £14.14/to plan Elevation Sections & Estimate for a House for the President £36.15', ending his letter 'Sir the above is a Copy of my Bill sent in 2 years ago & also last Year. I take the liberty of sending a 3rd copy as I apprehend the two former ones have been forgot, when it is convenient I shall be glad to have the money.' Unfortunately the designs do not survive and there appears to be no documentation, other than this letter, of any need for the President to have a new house in 1768, the year he was elected.

PARKSTED see ROEHAMPTON

114 PARTILLE SLOTT (Sweden)
David Sandberg
New Villa (1770) (Pl.73)
BM Add.MS 41134, 23v (Sandberg to WC 12 May 1773)
Gothenburg University Library: 19/8 MS Diary (entry 1782)
RA: Sandberg to WC 18 July 1770
Baeckström, A., *Studier i Göteborgs byggnadshistoria före 1814*, Stockholm, 1923

It was to be expected that Chambers should be called upon by his brother-in-law, David Sandberg, to rebuild Partille, an old timber house acquired in 1763 outside Gothenburg. Proposed rebuilding is first mentioned in 1770, but although a wooden model seems to have been constructed immediately from Chambers's designs, the foundation of the new house had not yet been laid when Sandberg wrote on 12 May 1773 and progress on the whole appears to have been much slower than usual, for as he said 'we build slowly here and require much time to collect our materials'. Partille was almost certainly built by the young architect Carl Wilhelm Carlberg, to whom may be attributed the interiors (which have in any case been otherwise radically altered) and a pair of forward-placed pavilions, now destroyed.

115 PEPER HAROW (Surrey)
3rd Viscount Midleton
Alterations to old house(?), offices, Bath House, new villa; interior completion of the villa (1760?, 1762, 1765–7, 1773–6) (Pls 59, 88, 189; Fig.3d)
Grinke Collection, London:
Design for 'A Bath for Lord Middleton'
Richardson–Houfe Coll., Ampthill: plans (2) and an elevation for an unexecuted house
Soane: 42/9⁵,⁶,⁹,¹²,¹⁴,²³: designs for chimney-pieces, two dated 1761, one dated 1760
V & A: E.3234. 1934; E.3238. 1934: front and side elevations approved 11 March 1765; 3393, design for a chimney-piece inscr. *Brodric*
BM Add.MS 41133, 25–25v, 109, 110v, 118, 129 (24 Dec. 1770–19 Apr. 1774)
RA: Midleton to WC 3 Aug 1763

RIBA Letters: Midleton to WC 27 Dec. 1761; 12
Jan., 25 July, 10 Aug. 1763
Hussey, C., *English Country Houses, Mid-Georgian*,
1956, 111–14
Prosser, G. F., *Select Illustrations of the County of
Surrey*, 1828
C.Life, 26 Dec. 1925, 1002–9

The building programme of Peper Harow is a
complicated one which tends to be confused
rather than simplified by the relevant designs and
documents. The Soane Museum chimney-piece
designs of 1760 and 1761 are inscribed 'Broderick'
and could be either for Midleton's Marlborough
Street house in London or for Peper Harow. If the
latter, then Chambers was first employed here for
interior alterations to the old house. Capability
Brown was landscaping the park *c*.1760 and must
then have made his design for rebuilding the old
house (Richardson–Houfe Coll., Ampthill); probably Chambers made his first design then, proposing a two-storey front of seven bays with an
attached three-bay Corinthian portico. Chambers's
next task according to the RIBA letters was
'offices' or stables, for which he prepared designs
in 1762 and they were built a year later. The Bath
House, a small pedimented temple with an arched
opening, overlooking the lake also belongs to this
period. It was not until several years after this
phase that Midleton decided to rebuild the whole
of his house. On 11 March 1765 designs submitted
by Chambers were approved and a few months
later Midleton died. Although the 4th Viscount was
only eleven years old building activities seem to
have continued as planned for on 25 August 1773
Chambers wrote to the Dowager Viscountess
Midleton informing her that the house was by
agreement to have been finished in three years,
but took only two. In this letter, which was perhaps occasioned by plans for the Viscount's
coming-of-age in 1775, Chambers also states his
expenses from 11 March 1765 to 8 February 1768
as £8189.19.11. Additional accounts were in
existence in 1925 when Christopher Hussey first
wrote up the house for *C.Life*, but have now unfortunately disappeared, leaving the question of
costs rather confused. Mr Hussey describes an
estimate dated 1775 for £8180.14.0 and an
account sheet dated from 1777 for a total expenditure of £9912.10.5½. Allowing for small discrepancies, there can be little doubt that the figure
£8189.19.11 given by Chambers in 1773 and the
£8180.14.0 given in 1775 represent the same
work which must have been the erection of the
carcase of the house exclusive of interior decoration between 1765 and 1768. This work is, as I
see it, repeated again in the 1777 account for
£9912 'To the amount of the contract for the
Offices £3200/Do for thr Chambers, Garret and
Basement of House £2585/Do for finishing Prin-

cipal Floor £2340 (totalling £8125)'. The remaining £1788.0.5½ refers only to the work done
between 1775 and 1777. This is described as
'extras' and includes payments to Joseph Wilton
(£202), Richard Hayward (£186.12), Sefferin
Alken (£294.14.9), John Westcott (£292.11.3),
and Thomas Collins (£975.18.0) as well as general expenses for carpentry, plumbing, etc. The
total cost of the house would therefore have been
in the vicinity of £10,000.

If the interiors date from 1775 to 1777, then the
Gallic pilaster strips in the hall post rather than
pre-date the similar decorations of *c*.1763 in
Buckingham House and *c*.1766 in Gower House
(q.v.). Although Chambers's interiors have remained more or less intact, Peper Harow has had
many later additions and alterations. John Yenn
did work in the Drawing Room in 1791, C. R.
Cockerell added the entrance porch in 1843, and
the house was drastically raised by an attic storey
in 1913. In the gardens a conservatory was built
by James Wyatt in 1797.

116 POSTON COURT (Herefordshire)
Sir Edward Boughton
The Casino (1760s)
Robinson, *Mansions and Manor Houses of Hereford-
shire*, 1873, 275
Trans. Woolhope Naturalists Field Club, 1933, XXIX

According to Robinson, Poston was a 'very
curious Round House or Casino built by Sir Ed.
Boughton, after designs by Sir W. Chambers'
c.1780. If this were correct, then Poston would be
one of the very few private commissions following Somerset House. But as Sir Edward succeeded
to the estate in 1760, the Casino may well be an
early rather than a late work. This is certainly
suggested by the style of the building which
belongs with the early theoretical designs included in the *Treatise*, and to such temples as the
1762 one at Coleby (q.v.).

Although flanked by nineteenth-century wings
Poston still retains its tetrastyle Doric portico of
some nobility and a domed circular room with
three windows commanding expansive views of
the Herefordshire plain.

117 RATHFARNHAM CASTLE (Co. Dublin)
Henry Loftus, later Earl of Ely
Partial casing of exterior(?) and interior decor-
ation (1770–1)
RIBA: J4/37, parlour floor plan; J4/38, ground
floor plan
BM Add.MS 41133, 11, 26v–27, 43v–44, 69v, 95v–
96 (22 Apr. 1770–11 March 1773)
The Georgian Soc., V, 1913, 77–8 and pls LXXXI–
LXXXVIII

Irish Georgian Soc. Bull., VIII, no.3, 1965, 'Sir William Chambers, Friend of Charlemont,' by John Harris

When Rathfarnham came into the possession of Henry Lord Loftus in 1769 it was basically a sixteenth-century castle with square towers at the angles. Although the house may have been re-faced before that date, it is clear from the Letter Books that the later Georgian interiors, e.g., the Gilt Room, Breakfast Room, Gallery and other minor rooms, were commissioned by Lord Loftus and executed with modifications to Chambers's designs.

The first phase of work was almost complete by 22 April 1770, the date of the first letter. Having been received by Lord Loftus designs were entrusted to Irish workmen who apparently found them difficult to understand and execute. In a letter of 29 January 1771 Chambers comments 'I am apt to think your Lordships workmen all rather careless in perusing the designs and seldom read what is written upon them. which occasions their difficulties.' The problems, however, were settled, and in March 1772 Chambers wrote to thank Loftus (then Earl of Ely in the 2nd creation) for payment of his bill of £82.17 saying 'It would make me happy to visit Ireland on many accounts & whenever it happens I shall certainly not fail to pay my respects to your Lordship. In the meantime it gives me great Pleasure to hear that the Execution of the Designs answers your Lordship's Expectations.'

Owing no doubt to the poorly supervised or second-rate workmanship, the rooms designed by Chambers look provincial. The one exception is the Gallery or Drawing Room with a ceiling which once had painted insets dubiously attributed to Angelica Kauffmann.

118 RICHMOND (Surrey): WICK HOUSE
Sir Joshua Reynolds
New House (1771)
Gandon Albums: 2 'Sir J.R.', details (in poss. Father Murphy, Robertstown, Co. Kildare)
Soane: 43/4²², possibly the ground-floor plan before addition of bay
BM Add.MS 41133, 55–55v, 64, 71, 85v, (13 Oct. 1771–15 Oct. 1772)
Hudson, Derek, *Sir Joshua Reynolds*, 1958, 108–12, 223
RIBA Jnl, 24 Aug. 1893 (abstract of letters)
SALE: Christie, 6 June 1811, 93

The building of Wick House seems to have been plagued by the strained relationships between Reynolds and Chambers. Not only were the two at odds in the Royal Academy, but it is possible that Reynolds had recently employed James Paine in preference to Chambers for architectural assistance on his London house.

The earliest mention of the Richmond villa occurs in a letter of 14 October 1771 concerning two windows which had settled as a result of both the steep slope of the site towards the Thames and Reynolds's last-minute decision to have a canted-bay front.

Subsequent correspondence reveals that Solomon Brown, who built the Pagoda in Kew Gardens, was the bricklayer; a Mr Bell of Richmond was the joiner; and Francis Engleheart of Kew Green was the plasterer. The most interesting of all the letters, however, is one of 15 October 1772 in which Chambers submits his bill for £1655.1.4½ (of which Reynolds had already paid £940), together with a case history. 'I herewith send your Bills for the House at Richmond which you will find exceed what you proposed to lay out there chiefly owing to the changes that have from time to time been made in the 1st Design. You may remember that your 1st intention was only to have one large room which was to be on the Parlour Floor & only to have atticks over it. You then desired to have the large room upstairs & an eating Room upon the Parlour floor & this was done & attended wth some additional Expense. When finished however your friends thought there was not elbow room enough, so a good part of what was done was demolished & a large Eating room wth a Bow Broke out was made at considerable expense. Your little Garden wth the Pales that enclose it has likewise cost something.' It is apparent, and even understandable, that the magnificent views of the Thames which were afforded from the site led Reynolds to sacrifice practical for aesthetic considerations.

119 RICHMOND GARDENS (Surrey)
King George III
Projects for a royal palace (1762, 1764, 1769, 1775)
Project 1 (1762)
Kielmansegge, Frederick, *Diary of a Journey to England In The Years 1761–2*, 73–4
Walpole Soc., XXVII (1939), 63
EXHIB S of A 1762, 173
Project 2 (1764) (Pls 109, 111; Fig.12)
BM: Kings Maps, CXXIV, 59–60, plan and elevation
Kew Gardens Library: Brown's plan of Richmond Gardens dated 10 Dec. 1764
PRO: Works 32/96, undated Brown plan for Richmond
RIBA: plan of ground floor
Soane: Dance Cabinet Slider 3, set 7, no.7
WCRL: PA2, 9 plans and 4 elevations
RIBA Archives: photographs of the wooden model, destroyed by the Ministry of Works in 1922
WCRL: inserted in survey of Richmond, 'Estimate

of a Palace to be erected in the Royal Gardens at Richmond', together with an 'Estimate of the Expence of building the Royal Palace at Richmond' of £89,320.17.11

C.Life, 19 Nov. 1959, 'Two Lost Palaces', by John Harris (as for projects 3 and 4)
Court Mag., 1765, 801
Home Counties Mag., Jan., Apr., Jun., Oct. 1905, 'The Royal Gardens at Kew', by W. L. Rutton
SALE: Christie, 6 June 1811, 95, or 102, 103
Project 3 (1769) (Pls 110, 112)
BM: Kings Maps, XLI, 16i 'Plan of Richmond and Kew Gardens', 1771
WCRL: Portfolio 58, plan of part of Richmond Garden
BM Add.MS 41134, 30 (Worsley to WC 19 July 1773)
RIBA Archives: photographs of the wooden model (for project 4), destroyed by the Ministry of Works in 1922
Uppsala University Library: Chambers's Autobiographical Note, 1770
Letters and Journals of Lady Mary Coke, ed. J. A. Horne, III (1892), 268–9
The Journals of Mrs Papendiek, ed. V. Delves Broughton, I (1887), 42–3
Lysons, S. and D., *The Environs of London*, I (1810), 329
EXHIB RA 1769, 18
Project 4 (1775) (Pls.110, 112)
RIBA: E3/6, elevation of penultimate quadrant scheme
WCRL: PAI, 6 groups of plans and elevations
BM Add.MS 41135, 72–72v (WC to Worsley 4 Aug. 1775)
Gough, J., *British Topographer*, I (1780), 357
SALE: Christie, 6 June 1811, 95, or 102, 103

Proposals for building a dignified royal residence in Richmond Gardens were many. Ormonde (later Richmond) Lodge had been bought by George, Prince of Wales in 1719, and throughout his reign as George II, and his grandson's as George III, it functioned as a summer retreat. Before 1733 Sir Edward Lovett Pearce had been commissioned to design a grand Palladian palace, projected more likely soon after 1727; then between about 1734 and 1737 William Kent had the pearwood model (now in the Dutch House at Kew) made in the style of a Holkham. Neither was accepted, and although Richmond Lodge continued to receive alterations and minor additions, nothing more in the palace way was contemplated until George III's accession in 1760.

In October 1761 Count Kielmansegge was told that the King 'has decided to begin the building of an entirely new palace in February' 1762, but its site was yet to be settled. Chambers was, of course, the obvious choice of architect, and his 'North front of a villa for a particular situation near London', exhibited at the Society of Artists in 1762, was recognized by Walpole as for this project I. Nothing more was heard about it. Then in December 1764 Brown's plan for Richmond Gardens shows the site of a palace measuring 400 by 200 feet, which roughly equates with the first of the two wooden models destroyed in 1922, and with the estimate of £89,320. According to the *Court Magazine* for 1765 the model was made by Benoni Thacker and presented to the King in that year. Its style was a rather monotonous interpretation of Holkham, although very much larger: 328 × 225 feet in contrast to Holkham's 160 × 110 feet. Unfortunately in 1765 the King was in no position to spend nearly £90,000. However, for Chambers's reputation it was perhaps fortunate, for it was not a good design, and had none of the sophistication of his third try.

In 1769 Chambers exhibited at the Royal Academy an 'Elevation of one of the flanks of a royal palace'; Mrs Papendiek commented that the King 'was greatly occupied in digesting plans with Sir William Chambers'; and in January 1770 Chambers wrote in his Autobiographical Note that he was 'at present engaged on the plans for a Royal Palace in Richmond'. The foundations were laid in the summer of 1770 and Lady Mary Coke reported its frontage as 140 feet 'built on arches in order, as I suppose, to command a greater prospect' – meaning, as did Lysons much later, a vaulted basement or rusticated arcades. Lady Coke estimated the cost at 'no more than five and twenty thousand pounds'. It was ominous that she mentioned the slowness of the work, and in 1773 Worsley makes it clear that work had ceased. There seem to be no designs for this palace, but Mrs Papendiek, writing from recollection, identified this palace with the second model which has a main block and quadrant colonnades linked to detached wings, in the manner of Nostell or Kedleston. There is no doubt, however, that this is the model commented upon by Gough in 1775 as having been made by Mr Goldsmith of Rose Street, Covent Garden.

It seems logical that the 1775 model, commented upon in this year by Chambers, was the 1769 project aggrandized by the addition of wings. In fact, the decorative detailing of the wings shows Chambers in the spirit of Somerset House, that is *after* he had visited Paris in 1774. The façade of the main, 1769, block, however, adumbrates that of the Strand Block of Somerset House, but not in detailing. The ground-floor arcading and the one-and-a-half storey pilastered elevation above could have been taken from Leoni's Queensbury House.

In 1772 the royal family had moved into Kew House, the Princess Dowager Augusta's late residence. Even there they were overcrowded, and it must have been this situation that prompted

R*

resuscitating the 1769 project in 1775. The decision to build the enormous Queen's Lodging at Windsor Castle (q.v.) in 1778 must have come directly from this same predicament. It was about this time that Windsor began to succeed Kew in the King's affections.

120 RICHMOND GARDENS (Surrey)
King George III
Observatory (1768) (Pl.125)
BM: King's Maps, XLI/16R (early view before alterations)
BM Add.MS 41133, 5v (WC to S. T. Demainbray 29 Jan. 1770)
WCRL: 55656–7, George III accounts, for John Devall, plumber; Mary Hartley, smith; James Arrow, carpenter; and Solomon Brown, bricklayer, for £204.11.1
PRO: Works 5/66: account 1778 for three stone obelisks supplied by Edward Anderson for £157
Académie royale de Belgique, Classe des Sciences, *Mémoires*, XXXIV, Fasc.5, Brussels 1964, 'Astronomical Observatories in the 17th and 18th Centuries', by M. C. Donnelly
Proc. Royal. Soc., 39 (1885), 37–86, 'History of Kew Observatory', by S. H. Scott

The Observatory was begun in 1768 to enable George III to watch the Transit of Venus in 1769, after which it was occupied by His Majesty's Observer, Stephen Demainbray. In spite of its importance as a royal project, the building is, for some unexplainable reason, very poorly documented. The only surviving accounts are for work done by James Arrow carpenter and Solomon Brown bricklayer. The fact that these are among the papers of the Dowager Princess of Wales at Windsor suggests that the project was financed by her and perhaps presented as a gift to her son, or was paid for out of The King's Privy Purse.

Chambers conceived the design in terms of a small villa – in fact, a simplification of the Tanfield Casine (q.v.) design – with canted bays on the north and south fronts creating a pair of conjoined octagon rooms on one axis. Apart from the raising of the side roofs to the level of the observing chamber sometime after 1884 the building remains unaltered.

James Arrow's interior joinery is a noteworthy example of the best of Georgian craftsmanship. Both octagons are fitted with elaborately-glazed book and model cases and the north octagon has a timber gallery with Chinese fret balustrades.

121 RICHMOND GARDENS (Surrey)
King George III
Pavilion for the reception of Christian IV of Denmark on 24 September 1769 (Pl.126; Fig.14)
Soane: 43/4²⁹, plan of the pavilion; Adam Drawings, XXXIV, 114, Adam's plan for a ballroom on the site
WCRL: PA3, two preliminary plans and a finished elevation
Gentleman's Magazine, October 1768, 490

Fortunately we have two reliable and highly-detailed descriptions of the temporary pavilion built by Chambers in the vicinity of the Observatory around an earlier unused pavilion designed by Robert Adam for Queen Charlotte. The first is a note written by Chambers on his plan (now in the Soane): '... placed near where the Observatory now Stands and Surrounded with a broad fosse to keep out the populace. It was framed with wood and covered with Canvas, the inside elegantly painted and Gilt in a Whimsical but agreeable Style. The center part had been Contrived for the Queen some years before by Mr Adam but never used, the remainder was added by me to Whom his Majesty Committed the whole Management. On the entrance side on the banks of the fossee was erected a Most Magnificent transparent Illumination painted by Messrs Cipriani, Richards and other assistants, consisting of three triumphal arches decorated with emblems of Various sorts and connected by Continuous pedestals ranging with those of the Arches, on which were placed the figures of Rural deities with Nymphs & Satyrs holding festoons of flowers suspended from one figure to the other between the Arches, the whole admirably painted in transparency by the above mentioned Artists. The festival Consisted of an Elegant Supper preceded with grand fire Works.' To this may be added the account of the entertainment published in the *Gentleman's Magazine* in October 1768: 'A most elegant structure was erected, in the centre of which was a large triumphal arch about 40 feet high of the Grecian order, decorated with figures and trophies and other embellishments from which on each side was a range of statues, supporting festoons of flowers in proper colours: at the termination of each side were two lesser arches through which appeared emblematical pictures alluding to the arts and sciences, the whole in extant 200 feet. These were all transparencies with such outside illuminations as the design would admit. The great arch led into a very superb enclosed pavilion in the centre of which was a dome supported by eight columns wreathed with flowers and ornamented with gold: from the centre the plan extended four ways, with apartments within for a band of music, sideboards and the whole decorated with paintings.'

122 ROEHAMPTON (Surrey): PARKSTED (now Manresa House)
2nd Earl of Bessborough
New villa (1760) (Pls 55, 57, 83; Fig.3c)
Gandon Albums: 2. 'Lord Bessborough's Roof' (in poss. Father Murphy, Robertstown, Co. Kildare)
MMA: (35.73.4) design for hall chimney-piece
Soane: 43/4[10], elevation of portico front; 43/4[11], two floor plans inscr. 'Bessborough W Chambers Wm Wilton'
V & A: 3355, preliminary design for portico front; 2216.30, Hall ceiling 1763; 2216.41, Library ceiling 1763; 2216.42, China Room ceiling 1761; 7078.26, impost of passage; 7078.34, Library cornice
Abercorn Papers, Baronscourt: WC to Abercorn 30 Sept. 1762
Bessborough Papers, Stanstead: WC to Bessborough, after 1768
BM Add.MS 18559, 42: Sir Richard Kaye's anecdotes
Vitruvius Britannicus, IV, 1767, 11–13
SALE: Christie, 6 June 1811, 96

Lady Bessborough died 20 January 1760 and Lord Bessborough decided to leave Ingress Abbey (q.v.) immediately and build himself a small villa nearer to London. Ceilings are dated 1761 and 1763, and on 30 September 1762 Chambers reported to Lord Abercorn that the villa was 'not yet covered in'. Finally, the Bessborough letter indicates final completion around 1768–9. Roehampton, or Parksted as it was called in the eighteenth century, was probably the first of Chambers's villas. Although Sir Richard Kaye reported on 28 April 1781 that Chambers had told him that 'Roehampton was Lord Bessboroughs own Design', this is not borne out by the facts. The villa fits in perfectly with Chambers's permutations of Palladian villas at Duntish, Duddingstone, and Peper Harow. Despite later additions and the complete rebuilding of the wings, the central body of the villa is well preserved, and its interiors display Chambers's early style of decoration better than anywhere else now that Duntish has been demolished. The staircase has, however, been altered. Within its central well there was originally an octagonal servants' stair – an idea copied from John Webb's Amesbury Hall. The Clerk of the Works was a Mr Key (later to go to Duddingstone), Rogers was a carpenter or joiner, and so perhaps was Webb. William Wilton was Joseph Wilton's father and cited here as both mason and ornamental plasterer. He appears in the Styche (q.v.) accounts linked with Thomas Collins. Joseph probably carved the Hall chimney-piece – a singular composition resembling three others by Chambers in Peper Harow (q.v.) Charlemont House, Dublin (q.v.), and Duntish (q.v.). The

fluted Doric tetrastyle temple has been removed to Mount Clare, Surrey (*C.Life*, 26 Jan, 1935, 93)

123 ROXBOROUGH (Co. Tyrone)
1st Earl of Charlemont
UNEXECUTED designs for a Hunting Lodge (1768) (Pl.69; Figs 5c, d)
RIBA: J4/36, inscr. 'Lord Charlemont's hunting seat' and Plan for project A
Soane: 43/4[23], plan project A
V & A: 3370, 3371, 3419, plans project A; 3418, elevation project A; 3420, 3450, 3372, plans project B; 3354, 3420, elevations project B
HMC: *Charlemont*, I, 285–86, WC to Charlemont 15 Apr. 1768; *Charlemont*, II, 372, Charlemont to WC (1768)
Irish Georgian Soc. Bull., VIII, no.3, 1965, 'Sir William Chambers, Friend of Charlemont,' by John Harris
EXHIB RA, 1769, 15

It is perhaps difficult to believe that Charlemont could seriously contemplate another building project at a time when his finances were being drained by the Casino, Charlemont House, and Marino House. Nevertheless, he must have asked Chambers for designs as he acknowledged receiving them early in April 1768, to which Chambers replied on 15 April with a letter discussing the required modifications. The project was definitely a passing whim which ended here for it is never again mentioned in the correspondence and is not known to have been executed. The 'lodge' mentioned by Charlemont is in all probability the same as the designs, some of which are inscribed 'Lord Charlemont's hunting seat'. There are two projects both for a three-bay two-storey house with slightly recessed lower single-bay wings on each side. Project A is the largest version with a more complicated and interesting plan built on columnar themes, using screens in the Saloon and Staircase Hall, columnar aedicules or surrounds to the windows, and an external colonnade on the bow of one front.

Although Charlemont did not specify where he intended to build his hunting lodge, the only place would have been Roxborough which was his remaining country estate.

124 SANDON HALL (Staffs)
Lord Archibald Hamilton
UNEXECUTED designs for a new house (*c.*1769)
BM Add.MS 41133, 78v (28 July 1772)
Vitruvius Britannicus, V, 1771, 99 (the house as built)

On 28 July 1772 Chambers wrote to Lord Hamilton requesting payment of an outstanding bill for

£45.3.0 which presumably refers to designs for a new house submitted some years earlier. If Chambers made his designs around 1769 they would fit perfectly well with what we know of the architectural history of Hamilton's new country house, Sandon Hall. It was published in 1771 in *Vitruvius Britannicus* as the work of Joseph Pickford, whose designs must have been accepted in preference to Chambers's by 1770. Ironically, Pickford first appeared on the architectural scene in 1766 as a mason in Chambers's employ at Berkeley Square (q.v.). A year later he was in Staffordshire working for Josiah Wedgwood.

125 SANSSOUCI (East Germany): NEW PALACE
Frederic II
UNEXECUTED designs for Chinese bridges (1763) (Pl.42)
Berlin, Hohenzollern Haus Archive: receipt signed by WC, dated 6 June 1763
Sanssouci archives: design (now mislaid) for Chinese Bridge, inscr. no.2
Kurth, Willy, *Sanssouci, Ein Beitrag zur Kunst des deutschen Rokoko*, Tübingen, 1964
Huth, Hans, 'Chambers and Potsdam', in *Essays in the History of Architecture Presented to Rudolf Wittkower*, eds. D. Fraser, H. Hibbard, and M. J. Lewine, 1967, 214–16

Chambers was first introduced to Frederic II in 1752, for on 3 February, whilst in Rome, Chambers had been negotiating with a John Forbes to enter the King's service as an architect. Nothing, of course, came of this. In 1763, with *Designs for Chinese Buildings* and his Kew book to his credit, Chambers was an obvious source for designs for anyone interested in chinoiserie buildings. The drawing he produced for Frederic was based upon two of his Canton Tings (plates II and III in the *Designs*, cf. Pl.41). In his receipt Chambers writes of three drawings and three plans 'à la Chinoise', the bridge to be executed in brick, stone or wood, but the superstructure in painted or lacquered wood. He also suggests that the roof be covered either in linen, enamelled brick or thin lacquered tin sheets.

126 SHERBORNE CASTLE (Dorset)
6th Baron Digby
UNEXECUTED(?) design for an entrance gate (*c*.1758) (Pl.79)
RIBA: J4/23[1–2], plan and elevation inscr. 'Lord Digby's park gate WC'
Architectural Review, July 1957, 122, 'A Note on the Egyptian Revival', by John Harris

The design for the Doric gate, although similar to the Duke of Richmond's Privy Garden gate in the *Treatise* of 1759, is distinguished, and perhaps put in a class of its own, by the seated Egyptian figures in the niches flanking the arch. The use of these figures seems to have no explanation. They have no counterpart in Chambers's work and do not reflect any known interest of Lord Digby's in Egyptology. This may also be the earliest example of a decorative form of Egyptian Revival in England. Unfortunately the design is undated, but if Lord Digby's interest in architectural embellishment at all related to the landscaping of his estate, then the most likely date would be *c*.1758 when Capability Brown's first scheme was nearly completed. This, of course, would fit in perfectly well with the Duke of Richmond's gate and the period of Chambers's interest in the exotic at Kew Gardens.

127 SKELTON CASTLE (Yorks)
John Hall Stevenson
Work of unknown character and an UNEXECUTED design for an octagonal temple (*c*.1770 and *c*.1759)
BM Add.MS 41133, 37 (WC to Stevenson 2 Apr. 1771)
Chambers, *Treatise*, 1759, pl.42
VCH, *Yorks NR*, 1923, 405–6

The temple was probably dedicated to Chambers's close friend, John Stevenson, in gratitude for his attempts to intervene with Edwin Lascelles over the designs for Harewood (q.v.). Although the work referred to in 1771 is unspecified, it must have been of sufficient merit to justify the employment of Benjamin Thacker, a first-class London joiner, rather than a local man from, for example, York. Thacker apparently died shortly after work was completed, for Chambers had written, 'I received your letter & sent the draughts to Thacker's executors the poor man himself is dead', and he concluded his letter with the friendly comment. 'I cannot send you any Bill for what I have done for you, never having kept any account of it, but it is a trifle not worth mentioning.'

128 SLANE CASTLE (Co. Meath)
Henry, Viscount Conyngham
Work of unknown character (?1760s)
Avery: (1C/2⁵), design for a chimney-piece inscr. 'General Burton'
Slane Archives: plans of Slane Castle, 1783, containing (no.5) an elevation of the principal front and (no.6) inscr. 'Proposed Elevation's .*WC*
Irish Georgian Soc. Bull., VII, no.1, 1964, 16–19, 'Georgian Castles in Ireland – 1', by A. J. Rowan
Irish Georgian Soc. Bull., VIII, no.3, 1965, 'Sir William Chambers, Friend of Charlemont', by John Harris

The confused chronology of events at Slane prohibits any valid assessment of what Chambers may have proposed there. Henry (Burton) Conyngham had been raised to the barony of Mount Charles in 1753 and made Viscount Conyngham in 1756. He was not made an Earl until January 1781. It is not entirely clear when Henry Conyngham could have been titled General, unless it was at some time after being made a Captain of the Horse in the Irish Establishment. In the eighteenth century military titles changed frequently, and James Gandon could address Henry as Colonel on a design at Slane dated 1773, as could James Wyatt on an undated ceiling design in the Metropolitan Museum of Art. In the late 1750s Slane was an old castle partly classicized, and to this Capability Brown added the present Gothic-style stables in the sixties. James Gandon's design of 1773 should be mentioned, and so should Wyatt's designs for a classical hall made in September 1775. All this work was incorporated, revamped, or obliterated, in Wyatt's total rebuilding of the castle from 1785.

129 SOUTHILL (Beds)
4th Viscount Torrington
Work of unknown character, perhaps alterations and staircase (c.1768)
Whitbread Archives, Southill: Album inscr. 'Old Plans Southill' containing two designs attributed to Chambers, inscr. respectively, 'Section of the Great Stair' and 'New Stair Case for Southill'
BM Add.MS 41133, 79; 41134, 5, 22; 41135, 16v, 40–40v; 41136, 3–3v (30 July 1772–14 Sept. 1774)

Between 30 July 1772 and 11 February 1774 Chambers made three requests to Torrington to pay a bill of £68.13.6. Torrington finally replied on 28 October 1774 and then had the effrontery to ask for a design for a lodge or gate 'of the cheapest and plainest design', adding that 'most of the first plans have never been executed nor were they proper.' Two of these unexecuted plans may be linked with the designs in the Southill Album for the 'New Stair Case'. Whatever their description Chambers's designs were, of course, intended for the older Palladian house, not the Southill built by Henry Holland from 1795.

130 STANMORE PARK (Middx)
Andrew and John Drummond
Completion of work upon a new house designed by John Vardy for Andrew Drummond (*obit* 1769) and the addition of a new front and wing for John Drummond (c.1763–70) (Pl.67)
Middlesex PRO: PR 17/67, view of the garden front
Soane: 42/9²,¹⁰, designs for chimney-pieces dated 1763, 1764, inscr. 'Drummond', and one inscr. 'Alken £6.15'

BM Add.MS 41133, 4, 15v–16 (Dec. 1769–12 Oct. 1770)
Drummond's Branch of the Royal Bank of Scotland, Charing Cross: Bank account under *Estate at Stanmore*: entries 1763–6
RIBA Letters: John Drummond to WC 25 Dec. 1769
Bolitho, H., and Peel, D., *The Drummonds of Charing Cross*, 1967, 111
Brewer, J. N., *Beauties of England and Wales*, X, Pt.IV, 1816, pl. opp. 630
Druett, W. W., *The Stanmores and Harrow Weald*, 1938, 203–7
Keate, W., *Beauties of Middlesex*, 1850, 134, 138

The section of Andrew Drummond's bank account (at Drummond's Bank) entitled *Estate at Stanmore* is the most complete guide to the architectural history of Stanmore Park. Records of building begin in 1763 with payments to John Vardy in 1764 and 1765. Then in 1766 Chambers suddenly enters the scene to receive sums of £600 and £208.13.7, a turn of events which must be explained by Vardy's death in May 1765. Whether these payments include the Soane Museum chimney-piece designs dated 1763 and 1764 and inscribed 'Drummond' is not known. Of course, these designs may have been made not for Stanmore, but for Drummond's town house at Charing Cross. From Brewer's view of Stanmore in 1816 showing a typical Palladian front attributed to Vardy, one can conclude that Chambers was initially called in only to complete what had been begun by Vardy. This, however, was not the end of the building programme at Stanmore. In 1769 Andrew Drummond died and was succeeded by his son John. From December of that year the Letter Books record a new chapter of events opening with a letter from Chambers to Drummond. Although this may sound like the demolition of the newly-built Vardy house, a comparison of Brewer's view with an early nineteenth-century watercolour in the Middlesex Record Office reveals that Vardy's front was either a single wing on an earlier house or was never fully executed owing to the death of Andrew Drummond. In any case, what Chambers provided was a new garden front, a tall three-bay centre of two amply-proportioned storeys and an attic storey, with lower three-bay, three-storey wings on each side, a paraphase of the 1765 unexecuted designs for Headfort (q.v.).

131 STRATTON PARK (Hants)
4th Duke of Bedford
Dismantling (c.1767–72)

Minor references occur to Stratton in the Bedford Estate Office, London, archives. For example, on 21 May 1769 Wilton wrote to Percival Beaumont to know 'what is to be done at Stratton'. Some of John Sanderson's chimney-pieces, designed *c*.1732, were removed to Woburn.

132 STYCHE HALL (Salop)
1st Baron Clive
New house and stables (1762–6)
V & A: E.3278.1934, design for stables
IOL: Clive MSS, box 76 (accounts 24 Sept. 1762–11 Feb. 1764); box 77 (Misc. accounts 1763–4); box 79 (accounts 1765)

In response to Clive's well-known taste for simplicity Chambers, early in his career, provided at Styche an entirely unassuming brick façade of seven bays and two-and-a-half storeys. Unfortunately, however, the plain, well-proportioned appearance of this work was ruined in 1796 by the addition of canted bays on each side of the entrance. The brick stables (foundations laid February 1763) were executed to Chambers's design now in the V & A. Among the craftsmen employed here was Joseph Wilton who supplied two chimney-pieces for £175.15.3, receipted 19 February 1763; his father William Wilton and Thomas Collins, both probably engaged upon the plasterwork; William Steel who was Clerk of the Works; John Shropshire and Charles Trubshaw, both masons; Matthew Glasham a carpenter; and a Mr Eyken who seems to have been responsible for carving the fine doorcases, and who may be identified with Roger Eyken, a little-known sculptor of Wolverhampton.

133 SVARTSJÖ (Sweden)
Dowager Queen Louisa Ulrica
UNEXECUTED design for a palace and for laying out the park (*c*.1769–74) (Pls 127, 128)
National Museum, Stockholm: THC 2296, design for a front s. *Edw. Stevens Arct Anno 1769*
Stockholm: Byggnadstyrelsen archive, survey plan of 1814
V & A: 3362, design for a front; 7076.16–17, two designs for laying out the park, one inscr. *Idée Générale des Jardins de Swartsio WC Invt*
BM Add.MS 41135, 37–37v (16 Aug. 1774); 41136, 2v, 24v (Feb.–Apr. 1774)
Selling, G., *Svenska herrgårdshen under 1700-talet*, Stockholm, 1937, 80–7
Stavenow, Å., *Carl Hårleman*, Upsala, 1927, 149–57
EXHIB RA 1775, 57–8
SALE: Christie, 6 June 1811, 100

In 1775 Chambers exhibited at the Royal Academy a design for the Dowager Queen Louisa Ulrica's palace near Stockholm. There is no correspondence relating to this design (described by Horace Walpole as 'handsome and simple'), but it is reasonable to assume that it was projected at a time when the Queen became interested in extending a palace built between 1734 and 1739 by Carl Hårleman. In fact, the palace was extended by Adelcranz between 1770 and 1774, and there is no reason to believe that Chambers's design was ever utilized. It may, however, have prompted his knighthood in 1770. Stevens's participation was probably as both architect and draughtsman. He was obviously much thought of by Chambers, who was always anxious to advance his brighter pupils. The Stockholm design is drawn by Stevens but based upon the V & A design which was probably the exhibited one. Both relate to the abortive projects for Harewood.

When Adelcranz's additions were complete Chambers's interest was sought for laying out the park. Early in 1774 he sent to Baron von Nolcken, the Swedish Envoy in London, 'the designs of the gardens of Swartsio wherein he has preserved a great part of the old, & introduced a Style of new that may be executed at a moderate expence according to her Majesties intention'. Although he sent fuller instructions to Count Scheffer in Sweden, and received the Count's acknowledgement on 16 August 1774, the project appears to have been dropped. Although parts of an 'English Garden' were eventually laid out at Svartsjö, little of it can be attributed to Chambers.

134 TANFIELD HALL (Yorks)
Thomas, Lord Bruce
UNEXECUTED design for a hunting pavilion (before 1759), executed(?) with modifications *c*.1776
Chambers, *Treatise*, 1759, pls.38–9
RIBA Letters: Bruce to WC 5 June 1776
Tanfield Lodge Archives (Major J. A. Bourne-Aston): copy of 1804 survey and Norton ditty

Tanfield was a hunting seat of Lord Bruce. In the 1759 *Treatise*, Chambers says of his design 'Elevation of the principal Front of a Casine, designed by me for Lord Bruce to be erected at Tanfield Hall, his Lordship's Seat in Yorkshire'; then in the 1791 edition the same design is described as 'designed many years ago'. Bruce was an intimate friend of Chambers and was employing him for minor alterations to Tottenham Park (q.v.) in 1770 and 1771. When Bruce's lodge at Tanfield was built is not known, but it was no ordinary or utilitarian building as a ditty written by Thomas Norton, a builder or joiner, indicates:

'This fair Fabrick you may call
Yorkshire's wonders Gotham's hall
Fixed where nobody can find it
And when finished none will mind it
Built not for pleasure nor for use
But by the fancy of Lord Bruce'

The reference to Lord Bruce dates the ditty before he acquired the Earldom of Ailesbury on 10 June 1776. The 1804 survey shows the building as of rectangular plan with a projection on the north front, in fact a plan similar to the 'Casine' minus its canted bay. The survey describes it as built of stone, of three storeys (as was the Casine), and with a hall, dining room, six bedrooms, and offices and stabling for fourteen horses. It was said to have been demolished in 1816. It is tempting to associate this building with the letter sent by Bruce to Chambers 5 June 1776, crediting him with £200 and with a further £150 if needed.

135 TEDDINGTON GROVE (Middx)
Moses Franks
House, greenhouse and temple (c.1765) (Pl.63)
v & a: 7079.34, preliminary design for a front, inscr. *Mr Penn for Franks*
bm Add.ms 41133, 117v, 123; 41136, 3v, 3v–4, 4 (Dec. 1773–Feb. 1774)
Drummond's Bank Account: Receipt £160 in 1766
The Ambulator, 1811, 247–8 (no entry in 1st, 1774, edition)
Loudon, J. C., *The Gardener's Magazine*, v, NS,1839, 425

The attribution of this villa to Chambers in the *Ambulator* (1811) and in Loudon's *Gardener's Magazine* (1839) are now amply confirmed not only by the appearance in Chambers's Bank Account of a payment from Moses Franks in 1766, but also by a bill for work done between 1767 and 1769 submitted to Franks but not paid until February 1774. The fact that this bill covers a 'Journey to Teddington to inspect Kitchen & Scullery' (£3.3) on 16 May 1767; 'Plans & elevation for a Greenhouse & for a temple (£9.9) on 10 July; and another journey to Teddington (£3.3) on 30 September 1769 suggests that the villa may have been complete by 1766.

From the description of the house and gardens provided by Loudon it is apparent that the v & a design showing a front modelled after one of Palladio's villas was an earlier rejected idea which must have been superseded by another. Loudon presumes the grounds to have been laid out by Chambers, and comments that, because of their flatness, surface variety was provided by hollowing and raising different parts of the garden (as had been done at Kew). He describes the villa as 'a square mass, completely isolated, without the appearance of offices of any kind, and with nothing in it, or about it, not even a servant's window in the basement which requires to be concealed. We could fancy it a temple in a wood, from the absence of every thing like offices . . . The principal floor is 6 or 8 feet higher than the level of the lawn; and, in the centre of the lawn front, a portico projects from the centre drawing-room window, and opens to a double flight of steps, which adds to the temple-like effect.' Were it not for Loudon's admiring description we would know nothing of this house which was demolished some time in the past without any record of its appearance having survived. Unfortunately Loudon's promises to publish plans and views of the house and garden were not fulfilled.

136 TERLING PLACE (Essex)
John Strutt
Work of unknown character (1767–8)
bm Add.ms 41133 6v (2 March 1770)
Essex C.R.O.: Strutt Papers t/b 181/2/1; WC to Mr Branston; t/b/181/2/2, original of bm letter

On 2 March 1770 Chambers sent to John Strutt, M.P., 'my little bill' a reminder of an unpaid one sent in eighteen months earlier for work executed about 1767–8. Strutt purchased Terling in 1761, but what may have been done here by Chambers was destroyed in the 1772 rebuilding. According to Essex RO t/b/181/2/1, Chambers was introduced to Strutt by a Mr Branston who, in this letter, was apparently questioning the bill, at Strutt's request(?). The work must therefore have been of small account.

137 TOTTENHAM PARK (Wilts)
Thomas, Lord Bruce
Work of unknown character (1770–6)
v & a: Franco–Italian Album, 377, 410, 412, 417
bm Add.ms 41133, 21, 53v (16 Aug. 1770–22 Sept. 1771)

The rebuilding of Tottenham in a grandiose classical style by Thomas Cundy in 1825, and the consequent destruction of much of the eighteenth-century house designed by Lord Burlington, adds considerable importance to the sketches of hall and staircase included in Chambers's Franco–Italian Album. Although an old friend from the Grand Tour days, Lord Bruce was a decidedly minor patron. Chambers had published a design for a hunting pavilion at Tanfield (q.v.) in the *Treatise*, but it was only at Tottenham between 1770 and 1771 that we have firm evidence for his employment by Bruce. Even then the commission was not particularly large or interesting. In 1770–1 he appears to have been concerned with a pantry, kitchen and outbuildings. Chambers's work was swept away in the 1825 rebuilding.

138 TRENT PLACE (Middx)
Sir Richard Jebb
Small lodge or villa (*c*.1777) (Pl.74)
Soane: Reveley Drawings AL/8C, 21, inscr. 'Sketch of a lodge on Enfield chase altered by Sir W Chambers for Sir R Jebb'
The Ambulator, 1811, 255–6
Brewer, J. N., *The Beauties of England and Wales*, 1816, pl. facing p.734
Great Britain, Parliament Acts: *Act for Dividing Enfield Chace*, 1777
Lysons, D., *Environs of London*, 11, 18, 291

In 1777 the remainder of the ancient forest of Enfield Chace was divided by Act of Parliament and lots were auctioned by the Duchy of Lancaster. Among the purchasers was Dr Richard Jebb who had attained a certain fame for having cured the Duke of Gloucester at Trent in the Tyrol. It has been said that when the King knighted Jebb in 1778 he bestowed the name of Trent upon his estate. The drawing made by Willey Reveley when in Chambers's office is of special value as the only view of this villa before the extensive alterations made in the early nineteenth century. The *Ambulator* describes it as Reveley drew it, 'this elegant villa, in imitation of an Italian loggia, with a music room'. Reveley's inscription 'altered by Sr W Chambers' suggests that Jebb's Trent was a neo-classical embellishment of an Early Georgian keeper's lodge.

139 WALCOT HOUSE (Salop)
1st Baron Clive
Remodelling of earlier house (1764–7)
RA: Yenn Albums. Designs for chimney-piece details, inscr. *Mr Alken is desired to get these done with all possible expedition Mr Gilliams of Piccadilly must do the marble work*
BM Add.MS 41133, 1 (16 Nov. 1769)
IOL: Clive MSS Box 79: Sefferin Alken, 10 March 1764, mason's work £13.17.1½; Duncan Campbell, clerk of works, bills June–Oct. 1764; Richard Hayward, Dec. 1764, for 2 pair 'Vulterra' vases, £8.11.6; Thomas Stephens, 24 March 1764, mason's work for Alken, £1.19.5; Benjamin Thacker, 24 March 1764, joiner's work for Alken, £4.15.11½; Joseph Wilton, bill including 'Two alabaster urns £4.4.0'; and 'plain; flatt chimneys', etc; Box 80: Duncan Campbell, account 1765, £1257.19.6; Box 81: To WC 1766–7; and Gilliam for chimney-pieces £29.10.0; letters WC to Campbell etc. 11 June 1764–15 July 1766
National Library of Wales: Clive MSS, 88. Joiner's bill Aug.–Nov. 1765
RA: Campbell to WC 25 Sept. 1764
Salop CRO: Bank payments Clive to WC in Clive MSS
Leach, Francis, *The County Seats of Shropshire*, 1891, 43–8

C.Life, 14 Oct. 1939, 388–92

Here the comparatively humble tastes of Clive during this period in his career are as evident as they were at Styche (q.v.). The latter was, of course, the old house of the Clive family. Walcot, on the contrary, was purchased in 1764 from John Walcot and was almost immediately rebuilt with long low brick elevations unornamented except for simple balustrading. All the familiar craftsmen were employed here: Sefferin Alken, carver; Benjamin Thacker, joiner; and Richard Hayward, Joseph Wilton, and John Gilliam, sculptors. Several of these men had already worked at Styche and were called in again, after Walcot, for Clive's town house in Berkeley Square (q.v.).

140 WANSTEAD (Essex)
2nd Earl Tylney
UNEXECUTED design for a Doric temple (before 1755)
Soane: 43/7[11], the drawing for Chambers's engraving(?)
Chambers, *Treatise*, 1759, pl.41
Le Rouge, *Jardins Anglo-Chinois*, cah.9/12

According to Chambers's text this temple, with its pairs of free-standing Doric columns on the diagonal sides of the octagonal plan, was designed in Florence, probably in 1754 or 1755 when he would have met Lord Tylney. It was obviously made in the hope of future employment at the great house of Wanstead. This, however, was not forthcoming for after the completion of Wanstead in 1730 no further architectural work was undertaken until the house was demolished in 1824.

141 WHITTON PLACE (Middlesex)
Sir William Chambers
Redecoration and probable alterations to an earlier villa; an imitation of a Roman Bath; Greenhouse; Temple of Aesculapius (1789); Mausoleum (1765–90) (Pl.198)
Soane: 43/4[26], unexecuted designs for a new house inscr. 'Plans of a Villa for W.C.'; 43/7[15–16], unexecuted designs for new stables
RA: 'Valuation and inventory of Effects at Whitton', dated 30 Dec. 1790; Account for repairs and gardens 1782–3; 'Various purchased at Whitton Place' (?from 1796 sale by Lady Chambers)
The Ambulator, 1811, 286–7
Brewer, J. N., *The Beauties of England and Wales*, X, Pt.V 1816, 431–2
Robertson, A., *A Topographical Survey of the Great Road*, 1792, Pt.I, 49
Ross, J. Maclaren, 'The Life, Work, and Influences of Sir William Chambers', *Architectural Association Prize Essay*, 1900 (A.A. Library)
SALE: *A Particular of the Noble Large House . . . of*

the late Duke of Argyle situate at Whitton (17 July 1765) (Guildhall Library Fo. Pam. 1330)

Christie, 21 May 1795: *Particulars . . . of a Spacious and Elegant Roman Villa . . . called Whitton Place*

Christie, 20–22 June 1796: *Elegant Household Furniture, Capital Collection of Pictures*

Christie, 16–18 July 1796: *A Catalogue of a Valuable Library*

Christie, 6 April 1799: *A Catalogue of the Valuable Collection of Italian, French, & Flemish & Dutch Pictures*

Christie, 6 June 1811: *A Catalogue of the Genuine and Valuable Prints and Drawings*

Cobb: 29 July 1898: sale of the Gostling estate

Whitton was designed from about 1727 by Roger Morris, for Archibald Campbell, Earl of Islay (later 3rd Duke of Argyll). The Duke died in 1761 and on 17 July 1765 the house was auctioned and sold to a Mr Gostling. It seems that, perhaps by prior arrangement, Gostling immediately sold or leased the villa and the major portion of the pleasure grounds to Chambers, retaining for himself Gibbs's Orangery, converted into a house. The Soane designs suggest that Chambers at first contemplated a new house, although it should be pointed out that the designs are not inscribed for Whitton. Probably, Chambers furnished, rather than altered, this Palladian villa. The 1795 sale catalogue mentions, for example, rooms painted by Andien de Clermont. We must believe the compiler of *The Ambulator* that 'In his improvements of this delightful spot, Sir William appears to have had in view the decorations of an Italian villa', for, he continues, 'Temples, statues, ruins, and antiques, are interspersed'. There was an imitation of a Roman Bath, a Mausoleum, the upper storey of Inigo Jones's screen removed from the Chapel of old Somerset House, and a Temple to Aesculapius. The last-named was built to celebrate Dr Willis's cure of the King. Surprisingly, this temple survived until at least 1901, for a drawing of it is included in Maclaren Ross's A.A. Prize Essay. It had a four-column Ionic portico and fluted pilasters to the back wall. On top of the portico was some form of antique bas-relief, and another relief surmounted the doorway. The most attractive and evocative description of the gardens is to be found in the 1795 sale catalogue: 'The Approach to the House, divides the Estate; is terminated at each End by the Common, and passes by the Kitchen Garden and Close of Meadow Ground, containing a beautiful Octagon Summer House on a Mount, inclosed by a sunk Fence to the Left, and to the right by the beautiful Menagery, containing Two elegant small corresponding Buildings, crowned with similar Pigeon Houses, decorated with Tablets &c. The Buildings are divided by a small stream and Sheet

of Water, to contain a Cow House with Calves Pens, &c. Chicken and Duck Houses. The whole inclosed by substantial close Paling, and (the Pigeon Houses excepted) screened by Plantations from the House. The Approach leads into the Pleasure Ground through handsome Iron Gates, with corresponding Iron Rails and handsome Stone Piers in the Fence of the Meadow on the opposite side of the road. The Gravel Walk leads from the Gate to the Right along the Menagery over a Small Bridge decorated with Great Taste, by an elegant Green House to the Mausoleum, by the road in front of the House; containing an admired Figure of the sleeping Venus in white Marble, and numerous Sarcophaguses, Medallions, Busts and Urns; inscribed to the mighty Dead Of Greece and Rome, and returns along the Sheet of Water by the Cenotaphs, containing white marble Medallions of Bernini, Gibbs, &c, and Busts of Sir Christopher Wren and Beunoroti, and by handsome Garden Seats, Antique Statues and other Decorations, to an Elegant Ionic façade of the Temple of Aesculapius; near which stands a capital Lead Figure of Mercury, and on the opposite Side of the Lawn a Ditto of Endymion on handsome pedestals.'

It is not at all clear why an inventory should have been necessary in 1790, but it is just possible that in old age Chambers sub-leased the villa back to the Gostling family. The later history of the villa is a sad one. It was demolished about 1847, but the large and handsome Orangery existed as late as 1898 and, as has been mentioned, the Temple to Aesculapius, even later. Today, Whitton is remembered only by a place name in a wilderness of subtopia.

142 WILTON HOUSE (Wilts)
10th Earl of Pembroke
Triumphal Arch, Casina, Rock Bridge, Library, Tennis Court, and miscellaneous work (1757–74) (Pls.46–47)
RIBA: J4/22¹⁻², measured drawings of the Palladian Bridge by John Yenn; J4/21¹⁻⁶, drawings of Maçon's Tennis Court in Paris; J8/5¹⁻², design for the Triumphal Arch, inscr. 'Triumphal Arch at Wilton WC'
Soane: 43/8⁴, measured drawing of Palladian bridge, Office of WC
V & A: 3373–4, measured drawing of Palladian Bridge by Yenn, 1774; 3387, design for the Casina; 7076.25, design for the Rock Bridge
Wilton archives: design for the Triumphal Arch; drawings of Maçon's Tennis Court; unexecuted design for the 'Saw-Mill' bridge inscr. 'to be erected on the river Nadir'
BM Add.MS 41133, 70v, 74–74v (Apr.–June 1772); 41134, 6v–7, 16, (Sept. 1772–Jan. 1773); 41135,

1a (9 Jan. 1774); 41136, I, I–IV, 11–12, 12V–13 (Jan.–March 1774)

RIBA Letters: James Kennedy to WC 23 Sept. 1766; Pembroke to WC 20 Aug. 1772

RIBA MSS: description of Wilton by WC

Wilton archives: bill for works completed, 16 Dec. 1762

Chambers, *Treatise*, 1759, pls.37, 48 (Casina and Triumphal Arch)

J. Hanway, *A Journal of Eight Days' Journey*, I (1757), 64

Le Rouge, *Jardins Anglo-Chinois*, Cah.8/14, Cah.9/10

C.Life, 28 Jan. 1944, 158, fig.4

C.Life, 9, 16, 23 May 1963; 25 July 1963; 1, 8 Aug. 1963

EXHIB Arch. S of A 1761, 183; Casina, S of A 1765, 202

SALE: Christie, 6 June 1811, 80; Triumphal Arch

Perhaps through the instigation of Lord Bruce, Chambers was introduced to Lord Pembroke late in 1756 or early the following year. This introduction followed rather than preceded the Earl's decision to employ 'Mr Evans' to build or design his Whitehall house, to which Chambers contributed interiors in 1759. Although Chambers says in his description of Wilton that the 'Arch was the first work of Stone I executed in England', his memory may have been at fault, for the Goodwood work could have been slightly earlier. Our architect publishes the Arch and the Casina in his *Treatise* and billed Lord Pembroke in 1759–60 for these and other works: '1759 To the Amount of two Buildings Erected at Wilton/in Contract 1500/1760 Jan. To Various designs for fitting up some rooms/at Whitehall with Attendance and trouble in/ directing the Execution 42.0./August. Designs for a Rock bridge at Wilton wth/a Journey to Wilton. Expenses included and model/ 21.0.0/October 16. To, paid for Glass sent to Wilton/by Mr Kennedy's desire 1.6.8/Nov. Various Sketches and designs for fitting up/a library at Wilton 5.5.0/(total) 1569.11.6/1758 July 17 . . . but having executed the Buildings which I contracted for cheaper than I expected I make a Voluntary Abatement of two hundred pounds. Recd Dec 16 1762 Witness E. Stevens.'

Both Arch and Casina were placed on the hill opposite the south front of the house in an area that had already been formally planted in the later seventeenth century. On the evidence of Knyff (c.1720) and Rocque (1746) there existed here a triumphal arch supporting the Marcus Aurelius. Chambers's task therefore was to replace the earlier, probably timber, arch with his own handsome stone one, supporting the seventeenth-century equestrian group. Around 1800 James Wyatt removed the Arch to act as a prelude to the main forecourt of the house, adding flanking lodges to his own design. Perhaps C. R. Cockerell

had this arch in mind when he commented in his diary for 16 April 1821 'Sir W. Chambers would make a Triumphal arch for a duck to swim under'. The Casina, however, remains where Chambers placed it, a tetrastyle Vignolesque Doric loggia raised upon a rusticated basement and built of exquisitely-cut Chilmark stone. The third project at this time, for the Rock Bridge, can be seen in one of Richard Wilson's paintings of the southern area of the gardens. It was a cascade intended to dam the river and create a stretch of more placid water. Finally, the Library is commented upon by Hanway who visited Wilton on 10 August 1755, He wrote, 'We were told, that the present young lord intends to build a library, or to convert one of his apartments to that use; in the mean while the books sleep in their huge chests, of which a large room was full.'

Between 1772 and 1774 Chambers was called once again to Wilton to design a Tennis Court (now demolished) based upon drawings of Maçon's famous court in Paris, and to build or furnish a Greenhouse. This last task raised a good deal of bantering interchange between Chambers and his friendly patron, such as Pembroke's letter about the man who came to install heating stoves: 'Mr Stove my dear Sir has been here, and is so honest and so modest a gentleman that I have kept two of his Stoves, though they throw out less heat than any in Europe. However, since the pipe has been kept within doors, instead of without, the environs are not quite so cold as an ice house. Mr Stove went over to see Mr Grenvilles, which do vastly well and consume little fuel, but by a selfish calamity attached to human nature, he returned full of contempt for them & full of admiration for his own expensive glaciery.'

143 WINDSOR CASTLE (Berks)
George III and Queen Charlotte
The Queen's Lodge and Lower Lodge (1778–82) (Pls 121–124) and UNEXECUTED project for fitting-up the Horn Court

WCRL: PA3, preliminary studies in both a castellated and uncastellated style

PRO: Works 34/164–169

PRO: Works 4/15, 5/64, 5/65

Chambers, *Treatise*, 3rd edn 1791, pl.53 (a chimneypiece)

Farington, J., *Diary*, 8 June 1794

Horwood, T. E., *Windsor Old and New*, 1929, 94

Papendiek, *Court and Private Life* . . . , 1887, I, 92

St John Hope, W. H., *Windsor Castle*, I, 1933, 347

Cooper, Richard, View of castle from the south, engraved by S. Alken 1799

Robertson, George, View of lodge from northwest (H.M. The Queen)

West, Benjamin, portrait of Queen Charlotte and her Children (H.M. The Queen)

In Sandby's view of the castle from the Long Walk (Oppé, Sandby Cat. no.82) may be seen a seven-bay house and adjacent to it a fourteen-bay one. These were the Seventeenth Century House and Nell Gwynn's House, rebuilt by Chambers into one composition comprising the Queen's Lodge and the Queen's Lower Lodge. Views of the resultant rebuilding are conflicting in what they portray, but basically there was a thirteen-bay block with four-storey towers at each end, and east of this stretched an interminably-long, lower, nineteen-bay wing. Then behind the tower block, on its south side, was a seven-by-seven-bay block. It looked, in Walpole's words, 'plain even to meanness', but it was intended as an economical lodging. With its simple arched windows and castellated parapets, it imitated the style of Hugh May's seventeeth-century work in the Upper Ward, and it formed an admirable foreground building to the silhouette of a castle unrestored by Wyattville. The Board of Works began to account for work on 28 November 1776, and between March 1777 and June 1782 £49,754 had been spent. It was an expensive lodging that lasted only forty years.

144 WINDSOR CASTLE (Berkshire)
King George III
Eight day clock (c.1770–1) (Pls 129–130)
Lord Chamberlain's Office: Pictorial Inventory of George IV, vol.B, 26, design for the clock
Boulton Coll., Birmingham: Matthew Boulton to Thomas Wright 14 Feb. 1771
C.Life, 13 June 1963, 1386–7, 'Elegance For The Mantlepiece', by M. Archer
The Connoisseur, Dec. 1967, 213–21, 'Matthew Boulton's Geographical Clock', by N. Goodison

This clock forms part of a *garniture de cheminée* of two candelabrum and two urns, now at Windsor Castle but originally in Queen Charlotte's Drawing Room in the Queen's House. Archer (fig.2) shows this garniture. The design in the Pictorial Inventory shows sphinxes on a flat base and a different form of urn termination. The movement was made by Thomas Wright 'Watchmaker to the King', and Boulton's letter to him implicates Chambers as the initial designer. The same urns and ram's-head mounts with rope-like swags were used almost simultaneously by Boulton on the case of his Geographical Clock made for a private patron in February 1771.

145 WOBURN ABBEY (Beds)
4th Duke of Bedford
Rebuilding of south wing; interiors including Eating Room and Library; unascertainable work in Tower Room and Anti-Room; Basin Bridge (1767–72) (Pls 71, 80, 90)
Richardson Coll., Ampthill: design for Library ceiling
Soane: 43/6[18], elevation of wall inscr. 'Chimney side of the tower room on the principal floor at Wooburn' and 'best of the two therm chimneys wch came from Stratton Park'
V & A: 2826, detail of bridge with arch centring; 3375–6, elevation and section of bridge; 7076.11, Leadbetter's design for rebuilding south wing dated Sept. 1765
BM Add.MS 41133, 2, 3v, 6v, 7, 7v, 12v, 14v–15, 16v, 17–24v, 28v–30, 43v, 45v, 50v, 54–55v, 60v, 70–72, 74, 75 (5 Dec. 1769–13 Sept. 1772)
Bedford Office, London: 13/3/4 Box 523 (Chambers to P. Beaumont etc., 9 May 1769–July 1771)
PRO: R.327, Leadbetter to P. Beaumont 27 June 1766; R.425, Leadbetter to the Duke 24 July 1766; R.248, R.249, R.798 (Chambers to P. Beaumont 19 Oct. 1767, 22 Oct. 1767, 26 May 1772)
RIBA Letters: Beaumont to WC 20 June 1770 and 11 Nov. 1771
EXHIB RA 1770, 38 (Library ceiling); 1777, 55 (the bridge)
SALE: Christie, 6 June 1811, 67, 94

Chambers's work at Woburn has never received due attention. In 1765 Stiff Leadbetter prepared designs for rebuilding the south wing, and was corresponding about this on 24 July 1766, less than a month before he died. In 1765 Chambers had been consulted by the Duke's son at Houghton Conquest (q.v.) and late in 1766 by the Duke about the Chenies monument (q.v.). On 19 October 1767 the Duke wished 'to consult you about the Rebuilding one of the Wings' of Woburn, i.e. the south wing. There is no doubt that this is precisely what Chambers set about, and it confirms the Autobiographical Note that (by 1770) he had built 'a front and parade apartments'. This front is substantially what exists today, an expanse of thirteen bays with two bays projecting slightly forward at each end. When Holland accounted for the work he had done in 1788–9 he specified 'Alterations of South Front'. By raising the terrace to the level of Chambers's piano nobile he needed to give the front some form of stability, and so he set Chambers's first-floor windows in the projections into arched recesses. The fact that Holland only billed for £297 in 1788 is an indication of just how little he altered Chambers's work.

The principal room decorated by Chambers was the Library in Flitcroft's south-west tower. It seems incredible that with its ceiling painted by

Cipriani and Rebecca, costing no less than £597, it could have been destroyed barely eighteen years later. Richard Hayward supplied the chimney-piece in this room in 1771.

Chambers designed the Bridge in June 1770 and with the initial help of William Jelfe, the mason, had it complete by September 1772. In 1771, however, both the Duke and Jelfe died, and the Duchess was persuaded to finish the bridge with the help of a Woburn mason named Cowley. This most elegant structure, adorned with obelisks and with keystones carved by Wilton, has been most drastically rebuilt and shorn of its ornamentation.

146 WOODSTOCK (Oxon)
Thomas Walker
Interior work to a new house (c.1769?)
RIBA Letters: Walker to WC 17 Oct. 1769

As the Duke of Marlborough's Auditor, Walker would have been known to Chambers who had been in the Duke's employ since 1766. He wrote to our architect on 17 October 1769 asking 'if you will let me know how much I am in yours or any other persons debt for the Chimney pieces and other things I have troubled you about concerning my New house'. Either Chambers designed Walker's new house or, as is more likely, he supplied some chimney-pieces of his design to a house that had recently been built.

147 WOODSTOCK (Oxon): CHURCH OF ST MARY MAGDALENE
Church Vestry
UNEXECUTED proposal for rebuilding tower (1776) (Pl.148)
Bodleian MS Oxford Dioc. Pps.a.I.f21ᵃ: Elevation of tower design
V & A: 3369, plans of five floors of tower design
Oxford Arch. Soc. Rpt, 87 (1949), 9–14: 'The Rebuilding of Woodstock Church Tower', by H. M. Colvin

On 29 April 1770 the Vestry of Woodstock church decided to apply to Chambers for a survey of the old medieval church tower. If he made his survey, such is not recorded and the Vestry took no further action until November 1776 when a number of local builders were applied to for designs for a new tower. Although Chambers's name does not occur in the Minutes of the Vestry at this time, his design in the Bodleian Library is inscribed 'Plan of Woodstock Tower in 1776 by Sr Wm Chambers'. Unbeknown to the Vestry this was Chambers's third attempt to get such a tower built. He had proposed a similar one for a St Marylebone project (q.v.), and had transferred

that to the proposed designs for Trinity College, Dublin, tower (q.v.).

148 WOODSTOCK (Oxon)
4th Duke of Marlborough
Town Hall (1766) (Pl.141)
Blenheim Archives: bill 1767–8 for £497.14.4½
Green, D., *Blenheim Palace*, 1951
EXHIB S of A, 1768, 225
SALE: Christie, 6 June 1811, 94

It may have been to this project that the Duke first summoned Chambers to work for him, and there is every reason to suppose that Chambers was continuously employed at Blenheim Palace from at least 1767. Hardwick describes the town hall in his *Memoir of Sir William Chambers* in terms of 'simplicity' and 'appropriate character', attributes that few would deny today. This handsome building is not, however, exactly as Chambers left it in 1768, for in the nineteenth century the open, airy arcades were filled in to provide extra closed accommodation.

149 WREST PARK (Beds)
2nd Earl of Hardwick
ATTRIBUTED Chinese Pavilion (c.1766)
RIBA Letters: Hardwick to WC 18 May 1767
Edwards, E., *Anecdotes of Painters*, 1808, 40
Von Erdberg, E., *Chinese Influence on European Garden Structures*, 1936, 188, fig.52

This painted Chinese pavilion with a double curved roof, a dragon and bells, was decorated by Peter Falconet between 1766 and 1769. It is therefore tempting to associate its design with Lord Hardwick's call to Chambers on 18 May 1767 to come to his town house in St James's Square and 'settle with him'. It may be pertinent that Edward Stevens was working at Wrest in 1770. According to Mr Peter Curnow who has examined accounts in the Bedfordshire Record Office, on 31 August 1770 Stevens submitted a bill for work upon the Cascade Bridge and the Cold Bath, costing a total of £288.6.4½. These are in the north-eastern area of the garden (behind Cléphane's Orangery). The Cold Bath can only be described as a curious primitive structure of obscure derivation.

150 UNIDENTIFIED LOCATION

Mr Bradshaw
Design for a cottage (after 1770)
RIBA Letters: Bradshaw to WC

'. . . Mr Bradshaw means to go into *the Island*, the beginning of the week after next, & as he could wish to examine the plan, Sir Wm Chambers is so good as to promise him upon the spot, he will take it as an additional favor, if he could let him have a Sketch of his *very small Cottage*, before that time, in which Mr. B. hopes Sir Wm will take care that there is a room, that he will like to lie in, whenever he comes into the Island, & that he will always make the Cottage his Inn.' Bradshaw may have meant an island on the Thames, or perhaps even the Isle of Wight. An eminent cabinet maker at this time was George Smith Bradshaw.

151 J. R. Gittius
Provision of a new vestry to an unlocated church (1766–7)
RA: J. R. Gittius to WC 25 Sept. 1766

The Gittius letter, written from Bedford Street, refers to his congregation's decision to accept Chambers's proposals for improved vestry accommodation (to be behind the altar), and for Chambers to execute them.

152 Mr Kenwick
Undescribed designs (?1771)
BM Add.MS 41133, 69v–70 (WC to Kenwick 13 March 1772)

Chambers's letter reveals he had made designs for Mr Kenwick who was not satisfied with them, and had got one of his friends to produce a plan which had been altered by Chambers. 'It is a little extraordinary that you should decline paying me', demanded Chambers.

153 Mr Kirby
Design for a chimney-piece
RIBA: Collin's Album. Chimney-piece inscr. *Mr Kirby*

The presence of this design in the Collins Album suggests it was intended for Berners Street or its vicinity. It is probably not for John Joshua Kirby, at Kew or in Half Moon Street, for that perspectivist would surely have designed his own architectural alterations or decorations.

154 Mr Steward
Designs for interior decoration, perhaps the completion of a town house
RIBA: Collins's Album, 17, 18, 19, details inscr. 'Sections of Mr Steward's front Parlor'

Because this design is among those belonging to Berners Street, it is almost certainly for a town house, perhaps on this small estate. The name Steward was spelt variously in the eighteenth century as, for example, Stuart or Stewart. His Parlour was terminated by a wide, shallow, coved niche flanked by Ionic pilasters.

155 Mr Waterman
Designs for interior decoration, perhaps the completion of a town house
RIBA: Collins's Album, II, detail inscr. 'Profile of the Cornice &c for Mr Waterman's Chimney peice'

Like Mr Steward's design this is probably for the area of Berners Street, and is inscribed to the effect that Edward Stevens was handling the management of this project, and that the sculptor was a Mr Mason, an otherwise unrecorded sculptor.

UNIDENTIFIED PROJECTS

156 Design for a concert or assembly room
Soane: 43/2¹⁵⁻¹⁶; 43/7¹⁹, plan and sections

This was proposed as an addition to an earlier building on an irregular site at the meeting of two streets. The main assembly room was intended to be aisled, of nine bays and two storeys, and was fitted up with elegant decoration.

157 Survey sketches of an existing house, possibly prior to rebuilding
V & A: E.837.38–1916, two plans

The house shown is an irregular one with a main front of ten unequally-spaced bays and an attached tetrastyle portico probably above a three-bay arcade at ground level. Beyond the Hall was a five-bay loggia on the garden front between projecting wings. Above the loggia was a Gallery 42 feet long and 12 feet high.

UNLOCATED OR DESTROYED FURNITURE

158 Satinwood Table made by Georg Haupt
Burlington Magazine Monographs, 1929, III, 'Georgian Art', 54
Burl. Mag., Nov., 1969, 648 'Christopher Fuhrlogh, as Anglo-Swedish cabinet-maker,' by John Hayward

This table, perhaps a *table à café,* last recorded in a sale in 1912, was inscribed *Cette table a été Commandée et Dessinée par Mr Chambers Premier Architect de sa Majesté Britannique et executée par son très humble serviteur George Haupt, Suedois, London le 4 de Février 1769.* It was a satinwood table with one drawer, inlaid with laurel festoons. The top was inlaid with nine specimen plaques of coloured marbles; the legs were tapering, the stretcher X shaped, and it was 16¾ inches square. Haupt was in England from early 1768 until late in 1769. The inscription on the table might suggest it was made for Chambers personally. Hayward suggests that

Haupt received his appointment was *Ebéniste du Roi* through Chambers, and the latter's friendship with the Swedish Ambassador, Baron Gustav Adam von Nolcken.

159 Combined Bureau, Dressing Table, Jewel Case and Organ (1793)
Charles IV of Spain
Edwards, R., and Jourdain, M., *Georgian Cabinet Makers*, 1955, 80
Partridge, Lewis, and Simmons, *Specimens of Old English Furniture* (n.d.), item 37
Robinson, F. S., *English Furniture*, 1905, title page and plate CLVII
EXHIB London: Franco–British Exhibition, 1908

The ascription to Chambers of what must have been one of the most remarkable pieces of furniture produced in the eighteenth century is unfortunately without foundation. According to an inscription it was designed by him, made by the firm of Seddon and Shackleton, and signed by the chief cabinetmaker James Newham. The oval and octagonal panels were painted by William Hamilton. It was never delivered to the King and after many vicissitudes was eventually broken-up in New York. It may in all probability have been reduced to a sideboard.

Bibliography

CHAMBERS'S WORKS

Designs of Chinese Buildings, Furniture, Dresses, Machines, and Utensils, Engraved by the Best Hands, From the Originals drawn in China by Mr Chambers . . . to which is annexed A Description of their Temples, Houses, Gardens, &c. Published for the Author 1757; edition in French published by J. Haberkorn, 1757; plates pirated by G. L. Le Rouge, *Jardins-Anglo-Chinois*, cah.2, pl.4; cah.4, pl.15; Garden essay reprinted in *Gent's Mag.*, May 1757, 216–19; Annual Register, 1758, 317–23; Bishop Percy, *Miscellaneous Pieces Relating to the Chinese*, 1762; in Russian, St Petersburg, 1771

A Dissertation On Oriental Gardening, W. Griffin, 1772; 2nd edition 1773; edition in French 1773; in German, 1775

Plans, Elevations, Sections, and Perspective Views of The Gardens And Buildings At Kew in Surry, The Seat of Her Royal Highness The Princess Dowager of Wales, J. Haberkorn, 1763; plates pirated by G. L. Le Rouge, *Jardins-Anglo-Chinois*, cah.4, pls.24–6; cah.6, pls.4, 5, 30; cah.8, pl.28

A Treatise On Civil Architecture, In Which The Principles of that Art Are laid down, and Illustrated by A great Number of Plates, Accurately Designed, and Elegantly Engraved by the best Hands, J. Haberkorn, 1759; 2nd edition by J. Dixwell, 1768; plates pirated *c.* 1772 by G. L. Le Rouge as *Traite D'Architecture Contenant les Principes de L'Art . . . Traduit de l'Anglais apres la second Edition*, Paris, Charles Dien; plates pirated again by Le Rouge, *Jardins-Anglo-Chinois*, cah.2, pls. 1–3, 5, 6; cah.8, pl.14; cah.9, pls.8–13; 3rd edition, considerably revised, published as *A Treatise On The Decorative Part of Civil Architecture. Illustrated By Fifty Original, and Three Additional Plates*, Joseph Smeeton, 1791. Posthumous editions; by Joseph Gwilt, *With Illustrations, Notes, And an Examination of Grecian Architecture,,* Priestley and Weale, 1825; revised and edited by W. H. Leeds, 1860, 1862. By John B. Papworth, called the *Fourth Edition, to which are added Copious Notes, And An Essay On The Principles of Design in Architecture*, J. Taylor, 1826, 5th edition, 1835–36. Reprint ed. J. Harris, Blom, NewYork, 1968. Chambers's *Treatise* was abbreviated, and the plates redrawn, by J. Landmann: *A Course of the Five Orders of Civil Architecture. The Five Orders all taken from Mr Chambers's Elegant Treatise on Civil Architecture*, 1785, 2nd edn., 1806.

SELECT BIBLIOGRAPHY

Architectural Publication Society, *Dictionary of Architecture*, ed. Wyatt Papworth, 1848–92

Bald, R. C., 'A Note From Oliver Goldsmith', Cornell University Library *Bulletin*, Winter 1945

Bodleian Library Record, 'Johnson, Percy and Sir Wm Chambers', IV, no.6, 291–2

The Builder, 1 (1843), 540. 'British Architects', Sir William Chambers.

The Builder, 82 (1902), 2–7, 'Sir William Chambers'

Busby, J. H., *Thomas Collins of Woodhouse, Finchley and Berners Street*, unpublished typescript 1965, copies deposited with the author, the Royal Institute of British Architects, and Sir John Soane's Museum

Boulton, J. T., *Edmund Burke, A Philosophical Enquiry Into Our Ideas Of The Sublime And The Beautiful*, 1958

Chase, I. W., 'William Mason and Sir William Chambers's Dissertation On Oriental Gardening', *Jnl Eng. & Ger. Philosophy*, xxxx, Oct. 1936, 517–27

Clark, H. F., 'Eighteenth Century Elysiums', *England and The Mediterranean Tradition*, ed. Warburg and Courtauld Institutes, Oxford, 1945

Clark, Sir K., *The Gothic Revival*, 1964

Colvin, H. M., *A Biographical Dictionary of English Architects, 1660–1840*, 1954

Country Life, weekly articles on country houses, indexed annually

Craig, M. J., *The Volunteer Earl*, 1958

Edwards, A. T., *Sir William Chambers*, 1924

Farington, J., *The Farington Diary*, ed. J. Grieg, 8 vols., 1922–8 and typescript of complete mss in British Museum Print Room

Fleming, J., *Robert Adam and his Circle*, 1962

Gandon, J., *The Life of James Gandon*, ed. T. J. Mulvany, Dublin 1846. Reprint ed. M. J. Craig, 1970

Hardwick, T., 'Life of Sir William Chambers', prefaced to J. Gwilt's edition of the *Treatise*, 1825

Harris, E., 'Burke and Chambers on the Sublime and Beautiful', *Essays in the History of Architecture Presented to Rudolf Wittkower*, ed. Fraser, Hibbard and Lewine, 1967

Harris, J., 'Chambers's Pagoda', *RIBA Jnl*, Nov. 1966, 530

Harris, J., 'Early Neo-Classic Furniture', *Jnl of the Furniture History Soc.*, II, 1966

Harris, J., 'Exoticism at Kew', *Apollo*, Aug. 1963, 103–8

Harris, J., 'Le Geay, Piranesi and International Neo-Classicism in Rome 1740–1750', *Essays in the History of Architecture Presented to Rudolf Wittkower*, ed. Fraser, Hibbard and Lewine, 1967

Harris, J., 'Sir William Chambers and His Parisian Album', *Architectural History*, 6, 1963

Harris, J., 'Sir William Chambers Friend of Charlemont', *Irish Georgian Bull.*, July–Sept. 1965

Hilles, F. (ed.), *Letters of Sir Joshua Reynolds*, Cambridge, 1929

Hilles, F., *The Literary Career of Sir Joshua Reynolds*, Cambridge, 1936

Hirschfeld, C. C. L., *Théorie de L'Art Des Jardins*, Leipzig, 1779

Hodgson, J. E., and Eaton, F. A., *The Royal Academy and its Members 1768–1830*, 1905

Hudson, D., *Sir Joshua Reynolds, A Personal Study*, 1958

Hussey, C., *English Gardens and Landscapes 1700–1750*, 1967

Hutchison, S., *The History of the Royal Academy 1768–1968*, 1968

Huth, H., 'Chambers in Potsdam', *Essays in the History of Architecture Presented to Rudolf Wittkower*, ed. Fraser, Hibbard and Lewine, 1967

Kaufman, E., *Architecture in the Age of Reason*, Harvard, 1955

Lovejoy, A. O., 'The Chinese Origin of a Romanticism', *Essays in the History of Ideas*, New York, 1948

Malins, E., *English Landscaping and Literature 1660–1840*, 1966

Manwaring, E. W., *Italian Landscape In Eighteenth Century England*, 1965

Martienssen, H. M., 'Chambers as a Professional Man', *Arch. Rev.*, April 1964

Martienssen, H. M., *Sir William Chambers*, unpublished University of London thesis 1949

Mason, W., *Heroic Epistle to Sir William Chambers*, 1773, 11th edition before end of year, 14th edition 1777

Mason, W., *Heroic Postscript to the Public, occasioned by their favourable reception of the late Heroic Epistle to Sir William Chambers*, 1774, 8th edition before the end of the year

Papworth, Wyatt (Account of Chambers's Letter Books), *RIBA Proc.* NS 8, 1892, 371–3, 398–9

Pevsner, N., 'The Other Chambers', *Arch. Rev.*, June 1947

Ross, J. M., 'The Life, Work, and Influences of Sir William Chambers', Architectural Association Prize Essay, 1900, in *A. A. Notes*, XVI, Jan.–Dec. 1901 (refer to original in A.A. Library)

Sandby, W., *The History of the Royal Academy of Arts*, 2 vols., 1862

Sirén, O., *China and Gardens of Europe*, New York, 1950

Smith, J. T., *Nollekens and his Times*, 1949

Stroud, D., *Capability Brown*, 1965

Summerson, Sir J., *Architecture in Britain 1530–1830*, Harmondsworth, 1963

Summerson, Sir J., 'The Classical Country House in 18th Century England', *Jnl. Roy. Soc. of Arts*, July 1959

Von Erdberg, E., *Chinese Influence on European Garden Structures* (ed. B. W. Pond), Harvard, 1936

Walpole, H., *Correspondence* (ed. P. Toynbee), 1903–1925, and *Correspondence* (ed. W. S. Lewis and others), Yale edition, continuing

Whitley, W. T., *Artists and Their Friends In England 1700–1799*, 2 vols., 1928

Plates

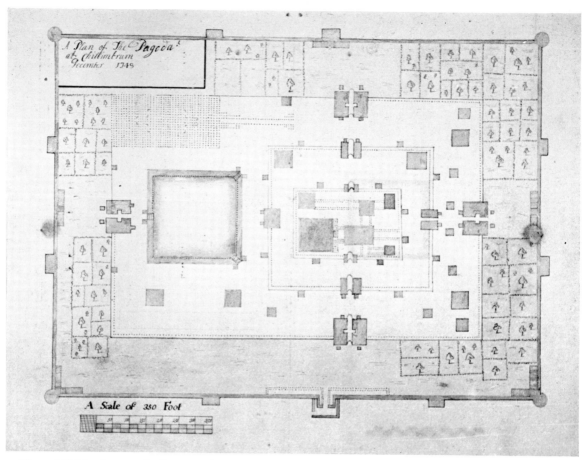

1 Plan of Chidambarum, India. 1748 (RIBA)

2 A frame by Oppenord, Palais Royal, Paris (V & A)

3 A candelabra by Oppenord, Palais Royal, Paris (V & A)

4 Frederick, Prince of Wales's Mausoleum (Sir John Soane's Museum)

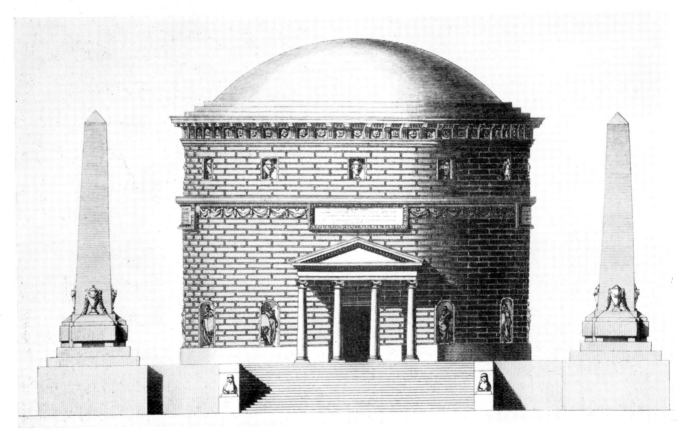

5 Frederick, Prince of Wales's Mausoleum. Plan (V & A)

6 Frederick, Prince of Wales's Mausoleum (V & A)

7 Frederick, Prince of Wales's Mausoleum as a ruin (V & A)

9 *Mausoleo antico* (from Piranesi's *Opera Varie*)

8 Plan of a gigantic church. Chambers after Le Geay (RIBA)

10 J. L. Le Geay. Title page of *Vasi Invention*

11 G. B. Piranesi. Composition from *Parere su l'architettura*

12 Francesco Preziado. Design for the *Festa della Chinea*, 1746

13 Louis Le Lorrain. Design for the *Festa della Chinea*, 1745

14 Louis Le Lorrain. Design for the *Festa della Chinea,* 1746

15 Louis Le Lorrain. Design for the *Festa della Chinea,* 1747

16 N. H. Jardin. Triumphal Bridge

17 N. H. Jardin. Mausoleum

18 G. P. M. Dumont. Temple of the Arts

19 M. A. Challe. Imaginary Composition (Mrs Phyllis Lambert, Chicago)

21 E. A. Petitot. Triumphal Bridge

20 E. A. Petitot. Design for the *Festa della Chinea*, 1749

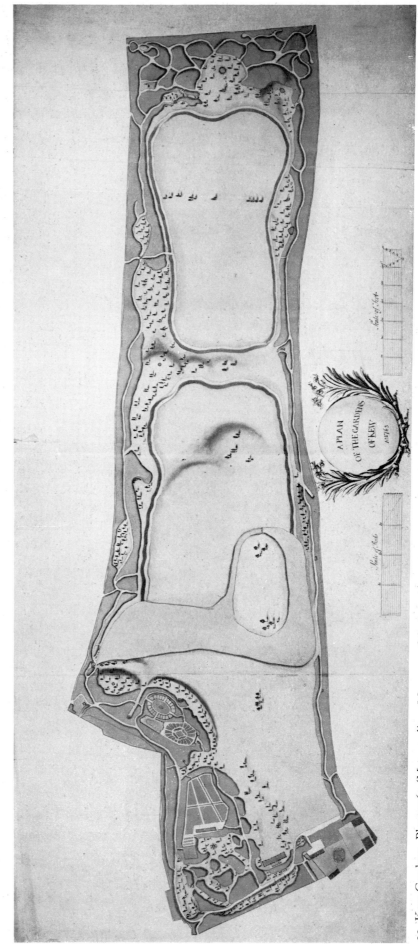

22 Kew Gardens. Plan 1763 (Metropolitan Museum of Art)

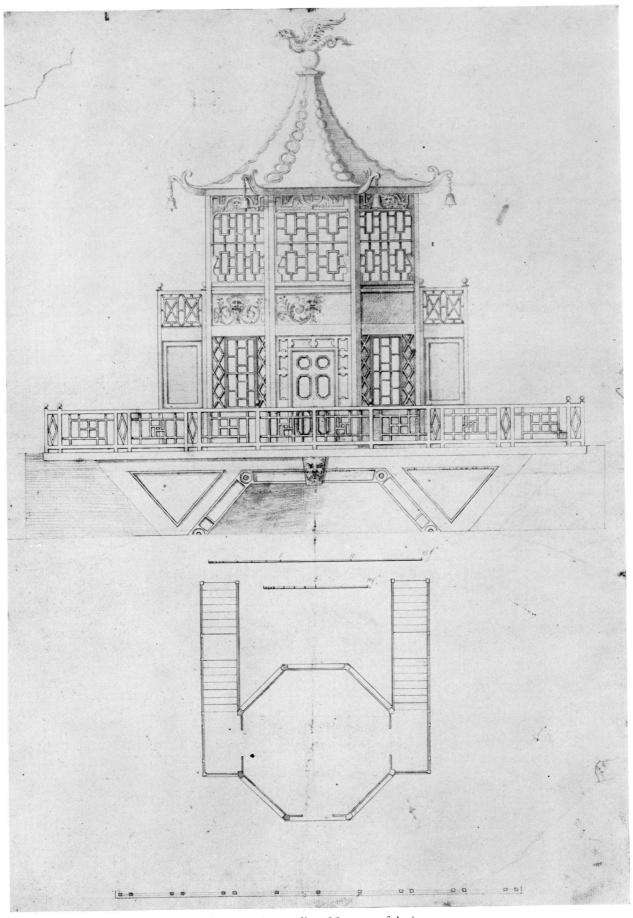

23 Kew Gardens. The House of Confucius (Metropolitan Museum of Art)

24 J. H. Muntz. Design for an Alhambra (RIBA)

25 Kew Gardens. The Alhambra

26 Kew Gardens. The Orangery

27 Kew Gardens. View of the Menagery (Metropolitan Museum of Art)

28 Kew Gardens. Temples of Solitude and Eolus

29 Kew Gardens. Temple of Bellona

30 Kew Gardens. Temple of Victory

31 Kew Gardens. The Ruined Arch

T

32 Kew Gardens. View of the Wilderness (Metropolitan Museum of Art)

The Mosque

33 Kew Gardens. The Mosque

34 Kew Gardens. Design for decoration of Mosque (John Harris Collection, London)

35 Kew Gardens.
Design for the Pagoda (RIBA)

36 Kew Gardens. Gallery of Antiques

37 Kew Gardens. Theatre of Augusta

38 Kew Gardens. Temple of the Sun

The Temple of Peace

39 Kew Gardens. Temple of Peace

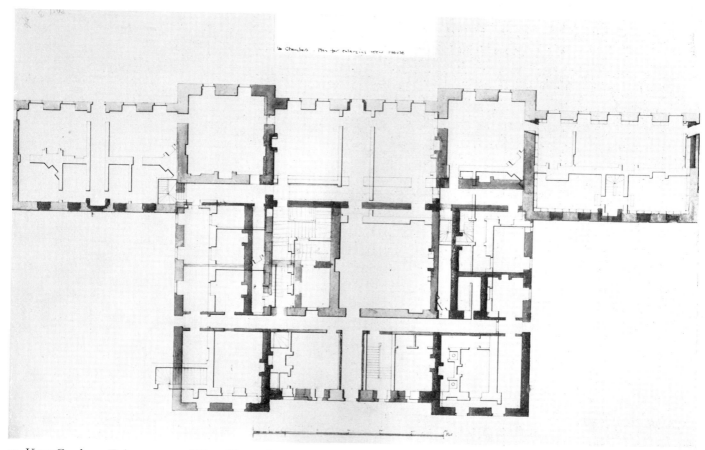

40 Kew Gardens. Enlargement of Kew House (By gracious permission of H.M. The Queen, Windsor Castle)

41 Court elevation of a Cantonese Pagoda. *Chinese Designs*

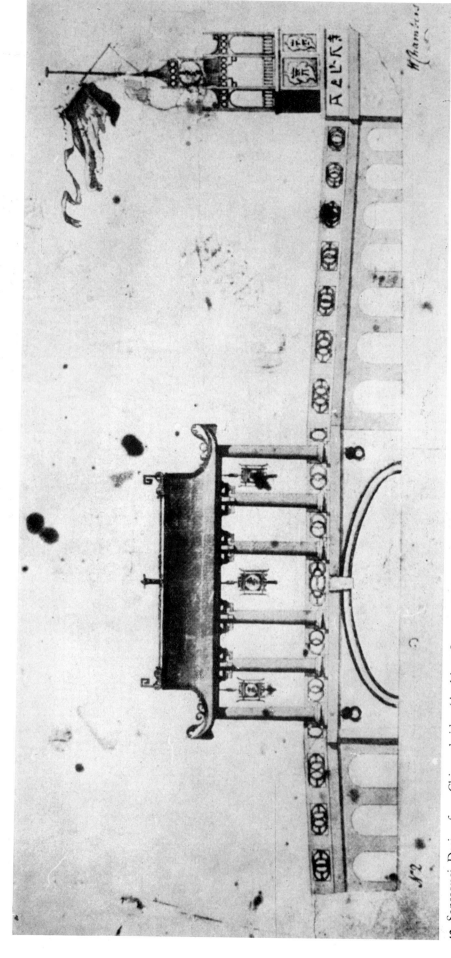

42 Sanssouci. Design for a Chinese bridge (Archives Sanssouci)

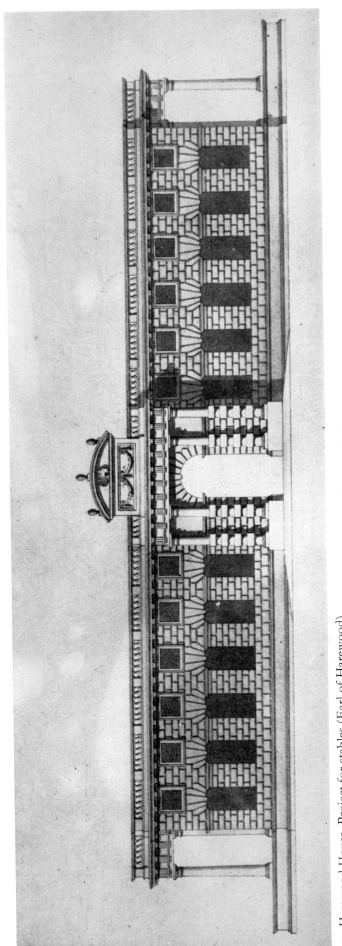

43 Harewood House. Project for stables (Earl of Harewood)

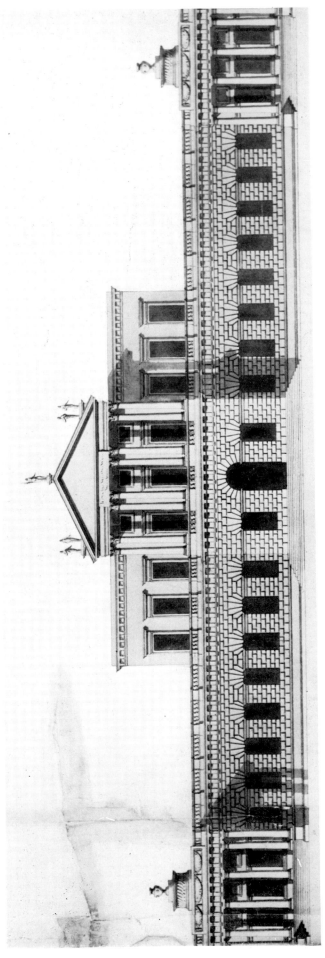

44 Harewood House. Project for house (Earl of Harewood)

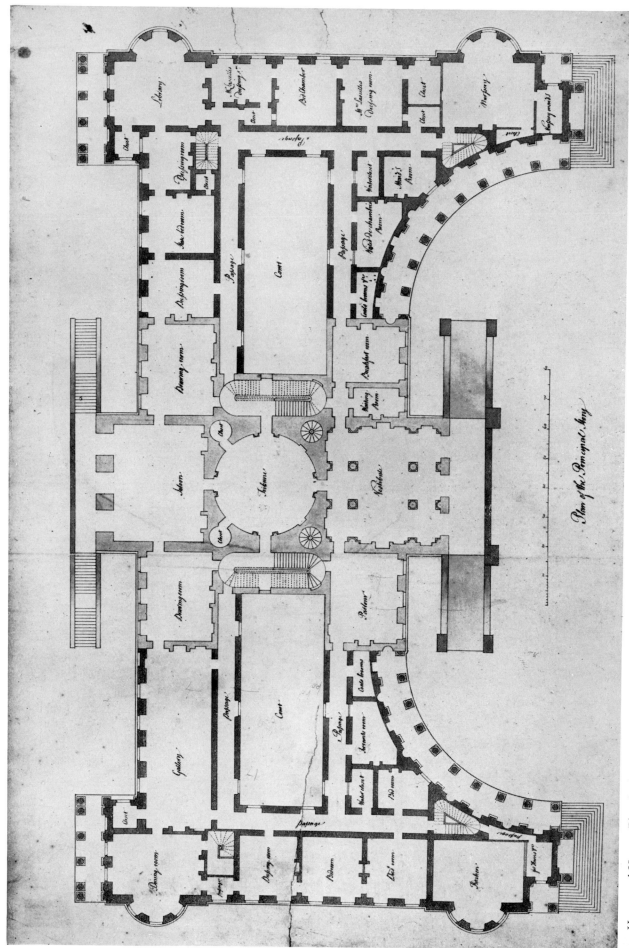

45 Harewood House. Plan for house project (Earl of Harewood)

46 Wilton House. The Casina. Copyright *Country Life*

47 Wilton House. The Triumphal Arch

48 Goodwood House. The stables

49 Osterley Park. The garden front. Copyright *Country Life*

50 Casino at Marino, Dublin

51 J. L. Le Geay. Drawing of the Casino (Miss Lambart John)

52 Casino at Marino. Urns

53 Casino at Marino. Detail of pedestal decoration

54 Casino at Marino. Detail of podium urn

55 Roehampton House, Portico front

56 Foots Cray (from *Vitruvius Britannicus*)

57 Roehampton House. Portico front (from *Vitruvius Britannicus*)

58 Wrotham Park (from *Vitruvius Britannicus*)

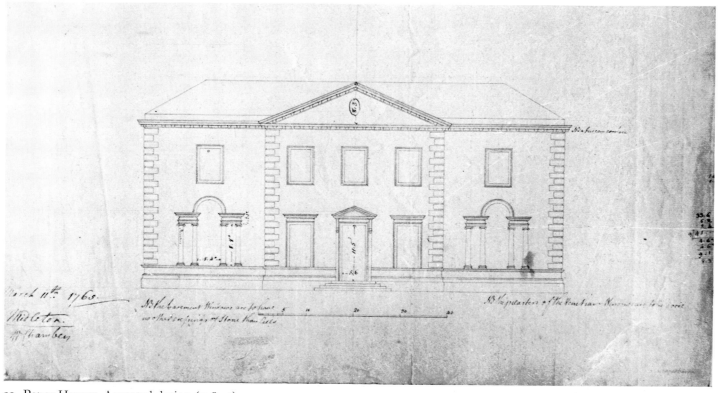

59 Peper Harow. Accepted design (V & A)

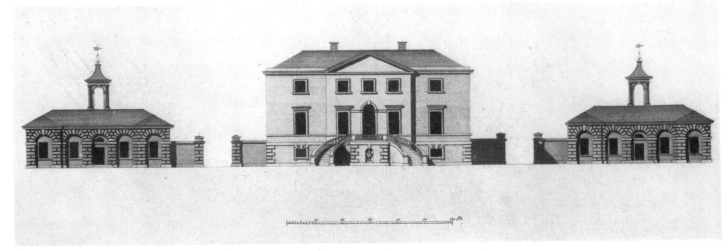

60 Duntish Court (from *Vitruvius Britannicus*)

61 Llanaeron. Project for a villa (B. Pardoe Collection)

62 Duddingstone. Porticoed entrance front

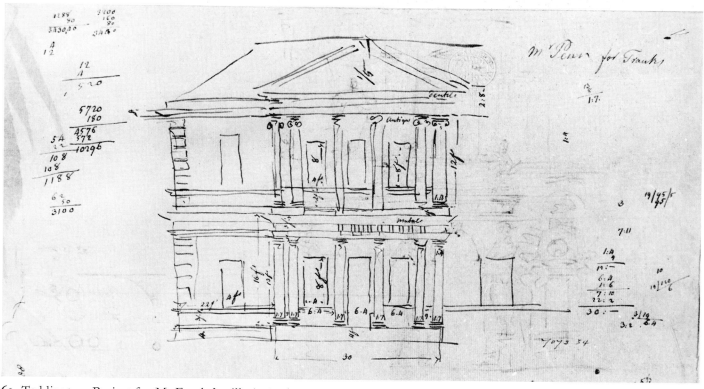

63 Teddington. Project for Mr Franks's villa (V & A)

64 Milton Abbey. West front and abbey church

65 Milton Abbey. North front (from Neale's *Seats*)

66 Milton Abbey. Entrance of north front. Copyright *Country Life*

67 Stanmore Park. Garden front (Greater London Record Office)

68 Ampthill House. Garden front (from Neal's *Seats*)

69 Roxborough. Project for a hunting lodge (V & A)

70 Lucan House. The entrance front

71 Woburn Abbey. The south front. Copyright *Country Life*

Front of the Intended Addition

72 Adderbury. Intended addition (Duke of Buccleuch, Dalkeith Palace)

73 Partille Slot, Gothenburg

Sketch of a lodge on Enfield chase altered by Sir W Chambers for Sir J Jebb.

74 Trent Place, drawn by Reveley (Sir John Soane's Museum)

75 Newby. Proposed redecoration. Section (Major E. R. Compton, Newby Hall)

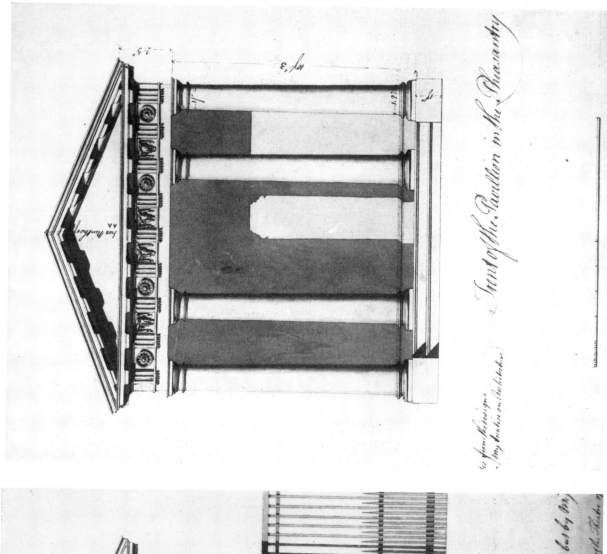

Front of the Pavilion in the Pheasantry

77 Newby. Pavilion in the Pheasantry (Major E. R. Compton, Newby Hall)

Elevation of the Pheasant pen Entrance to the Pheasantry

76 Newby. Entrance to the Pheasantry (Major E. R. Compton, Newby Hall)

78 Amesbury. The Chinese Temple

79 Sherborne Castle. The Doric Gate (RIBA)

80 Woburn Abbey. The Basin Bridge (v & a)

81 The Hoo. Design for a ruined bridge (collection unknown)

82 Coleby. Temple of Romulus and Remus

83 Roehampton House. The garden hall

84 Casino at Marino. Bedroom or China Closet ceiling

85 Dudingstone. Hall ceiling

86 Duddingstone. Staircase and hall

87 Milton Park. Peterborough Dining Room. Copyright *Country Life*

88 Peper Harow. Entrance hall. Copyright *Country Life*

89 Milton Park. The Gallery

90 Woburn Abbey. Design for Library ceiling (Richardson Collection, Ampthill)

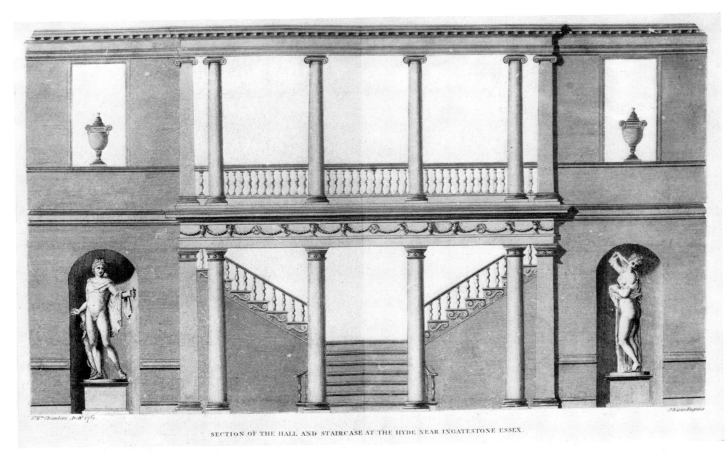

SECTION OF THE HALL AND STAIRCASE AT THE HYDE NEAR INGATESTONE ESSEX.

91 The Hyde. Hall and staircase (engraving by J. Basire)

92 Pembroke House, Whitehall. Gallery ceiling (V & A)

93 Charlemont House, Dublin. Front to Square

Drawing of York House. November 1760.

94 York House, Pall Mall. Section (RIBA)

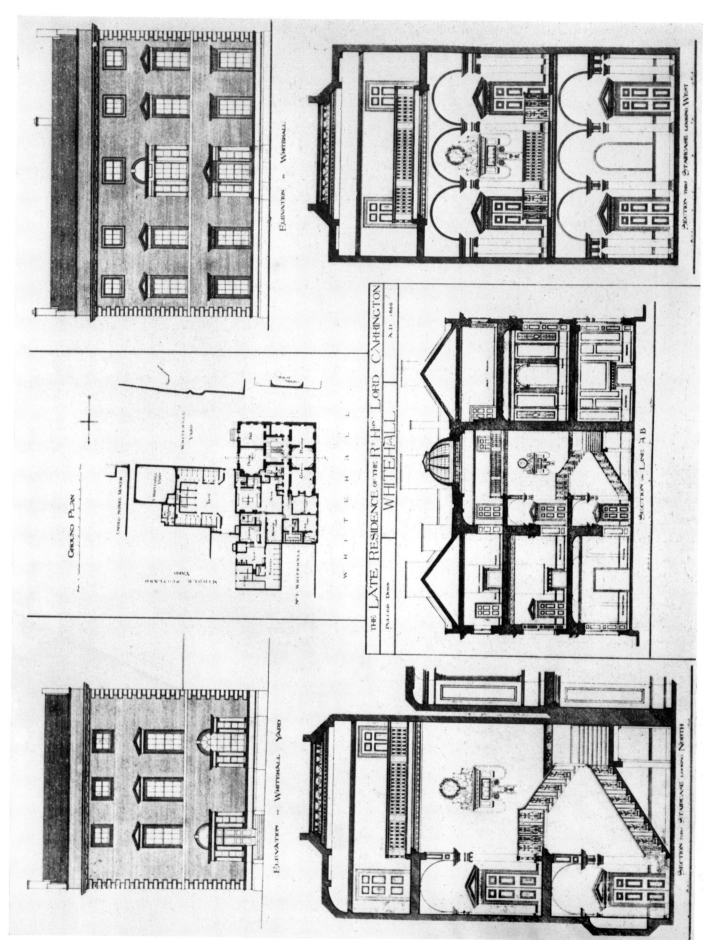

95 Gower House, Whitehall (from *The Builder*)

96 Melbourne House, Piccadilly (Sir John Soane's Museum)

97 Melbourne House. Entrance gates (V & A)

98 Gower House, Whitehall. Staircase (Sir John Soane's Museum)

99 Melbourne House, Piccadilly. Staircase (V & A)

100 Gower House, Whitehall. Saloon (Sir John Soane's Museum)

101 Gower House, Whitehall. Staircase

102 Gower House, Whitehall. Staircase

103 Melbourne House, Piccadilly. Entrance front

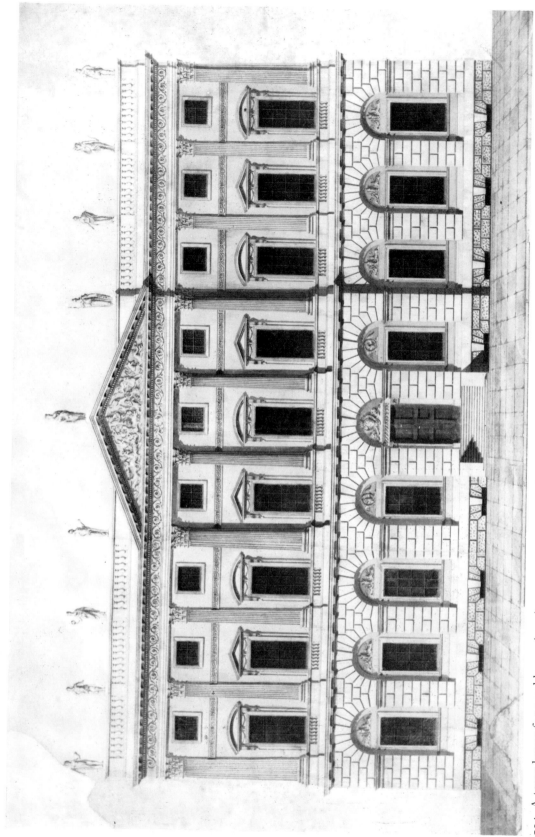

104 A town house for a nobleman (RIBA)

105 Dundas House, Edinburgh. Front to square

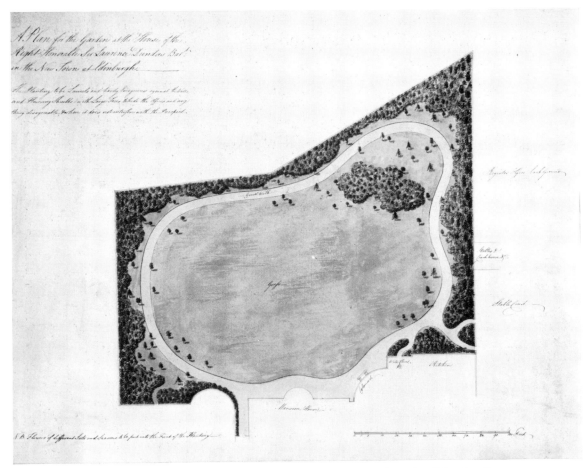

106 Dundas House, Edinburgh. Plan for the garden (Archives Royal Bank of Scotland).
By kind permission of the Most Honourable The Marquis of Zetland

107 Dundas House, Edinburgh. Design for the back front (Royal Bank of Scotland)

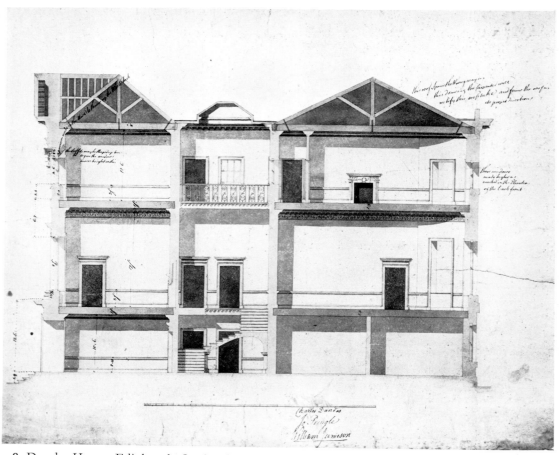

108 Dundas House, Edinburgh. Sectional design (Royal Bank of Scotland)

109 Richmond Palace project 2 model (Archives RIBA)

110 Richmond Palace project 4 model (Archives RIBA)

Geometric Elevation of the Principal Front

111 Richmond Palace project 2 design (By gracious permission of H.M. The Queen, Windsor Castle)

112 Richmond Palace project 4 design (RIBA)

W

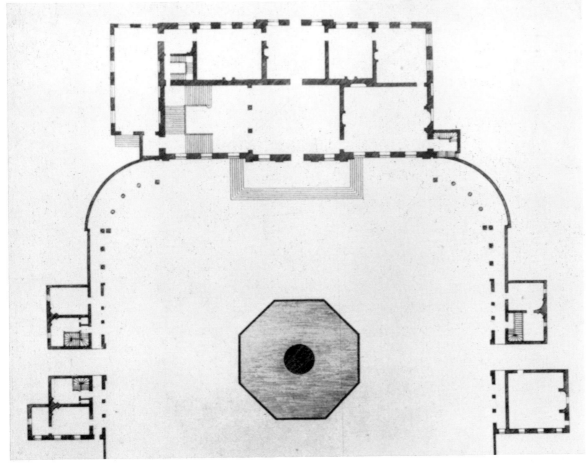

113 Buckingham House, London. Plan in 1715 (from *Vitruvius Britannicus, 1*)

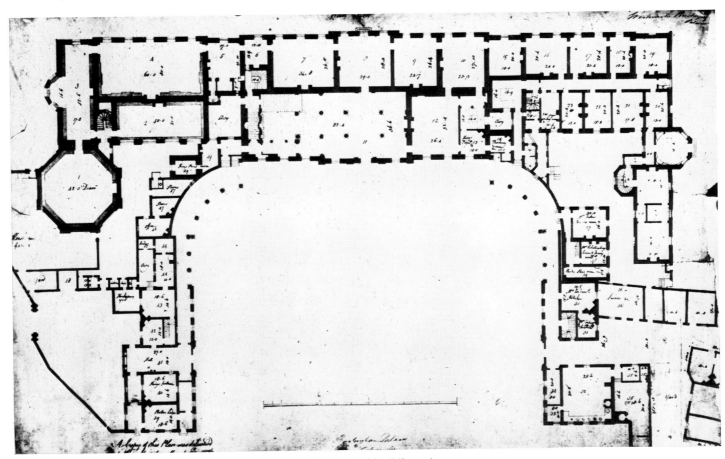

114 Buckingham House, London. Plan in 1776 (Westminster Public Library)

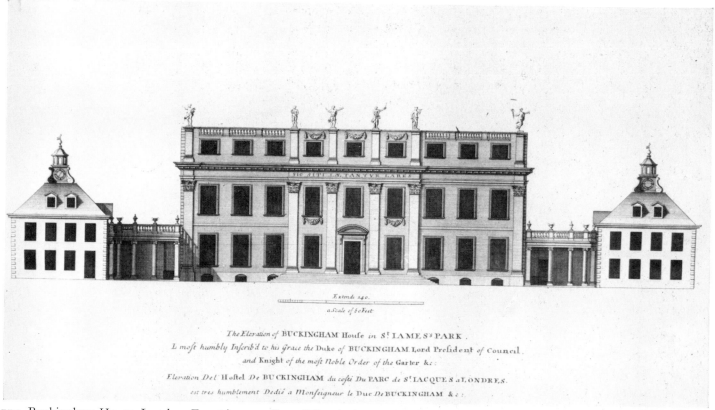

115 Buckingham House, London. Front in 1715 (from *Vitruvius Britannicus,* 1)

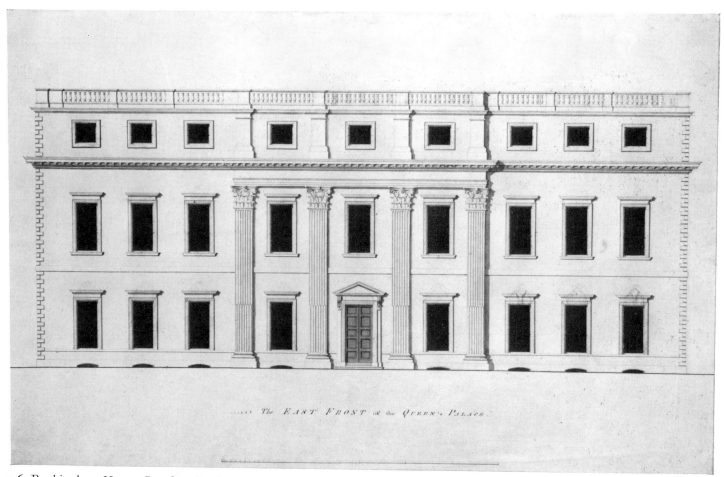

116 Buckingham House, London. Design for refacing of front (Westminster Public Library)

117 Buckingham House, London. The Saloon (from Pyne's *Royal Residences*)

118 Buckingham House, London. The Octagon Library (from Pyne's *Royal Residences*)

119 Buckingham House, London. Second Drawing Room ceiling (RIBA)

120 Buckingham House, London. The Riding House (Westminster Public Library)

121 Windsor Castle. The Queen's Lodge. Design (By gracious permission of H.M. The Queen, Windsor Castle)

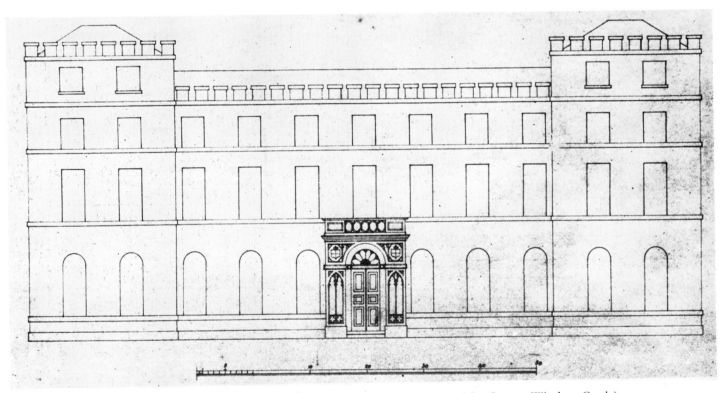

122 Windsor Castle. The Queen's Lodge. Design (By gracious permission of H.M. The Queen, Windsor Castle)

123 Windsor Castle. The Queen's Lodge (By gracious permission of H.M. The Queen, Windsor Castle)

124 Windsor Castle. The Queen's Lodge. Detail from painting by Benjamin West (By gracious permission of H.M. The Queen, Windsor Castle)

125 Richmond Observatory (Mr and Mrs Paul Mellon)

126 Richmond Gardens. King of Denmark's Fête Pavilion (By gracious permission of H.M. The Queen, Windsor Castle)

127 Svartsjö, Sweden. Palace drawn by Edward Stevens (Nationalmuseum, Stockholm)

128 Svartsjö, Sweden. Chambers's Royal Academy exhibit of palace (V & A)

130 Eight-day clock at Windsor Castle (By gracious permission of
H.M. The Queen)

129 Design for an eight-day clock at Windsor Castle (By gracious permission of
H.M. The Queen)

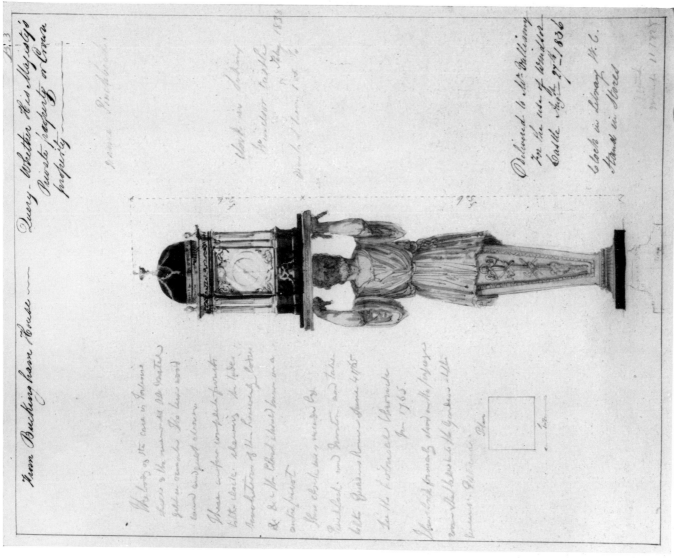

131 Design for Astronomical Clock (Sir John Soane's Museum)

132 Astronomical Clock and stand (By gracious permission of H.M. The Queen)

133 Astronomical Clock at Buckingham Palace (By gracious permission of H.M. The Queen)

134 Design for the State Coach (By gracious permission of H.M. The Queen)

135 The 'Wilton' model for the State Coach (London Museum)

136 The State Coach. Copyright *Country Life*

137 The State Coach. Detail. Copyright *Country Life*

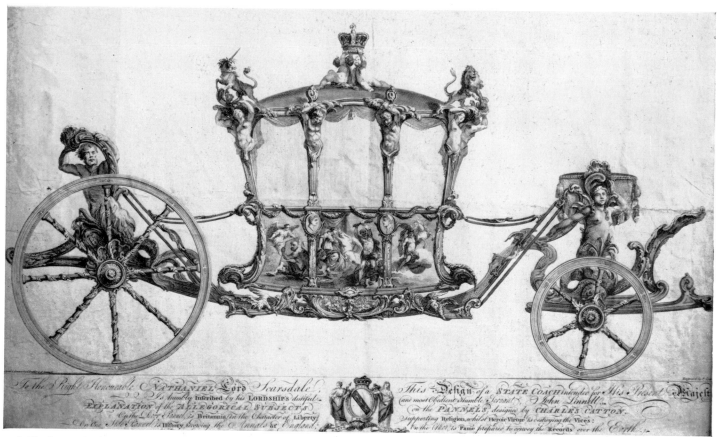

138 Butler and Linnell's design for a State Coach

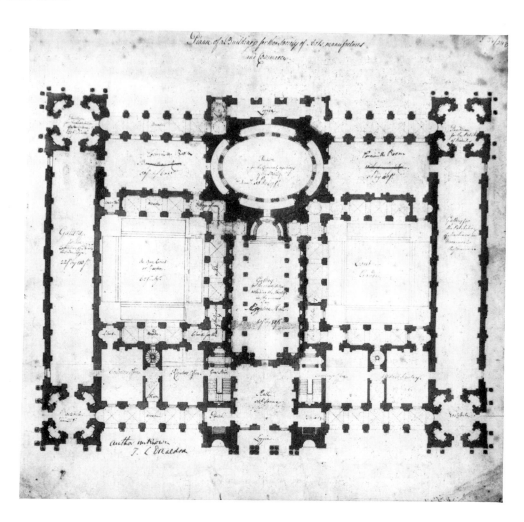

139 Plan for the Society of Arts (RIBA)

140 Blackfriars Bridge competition design

141 Woodstock Town Hall

X

142 The Savoy, London. German Lutheran Chapel (V & A)

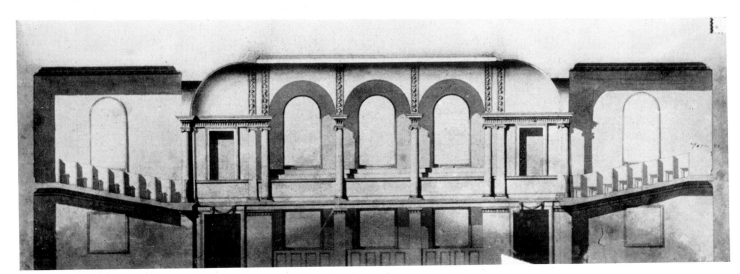

143 The Savoy, London. German Lutheran Chapel. Section (V & A)

144 Marylebone parish church. Dome elevation (v & a)

145 Marylebone parish church. Dome section (V & A)

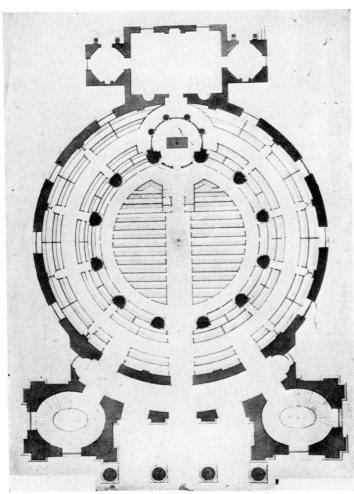

146 Marylebone parish church. Dome plan (V & A)

147 Marylebone parish church. Spire elevation (V & A)

148 Woodstock parish church.
Spire design (Bodleian Library)

149 Dublin. Trinity College.
Spire design
(Engraved for Pool and Cash)

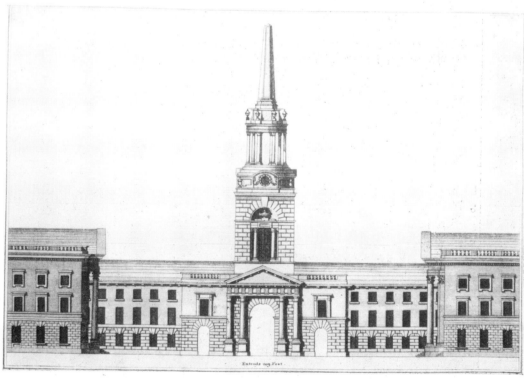

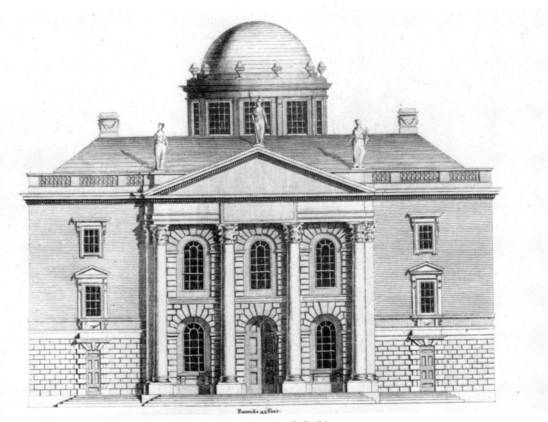

150 Dublin. Trinity College. Theatre (Engraved for Pool and Cash)

151 Dublin. Trinity College. Chapel

152 Paris. Details of Place de la Concorde and Hotel d'Uzez (RIBA)

153 Paris. La Monnaie (RIBA)

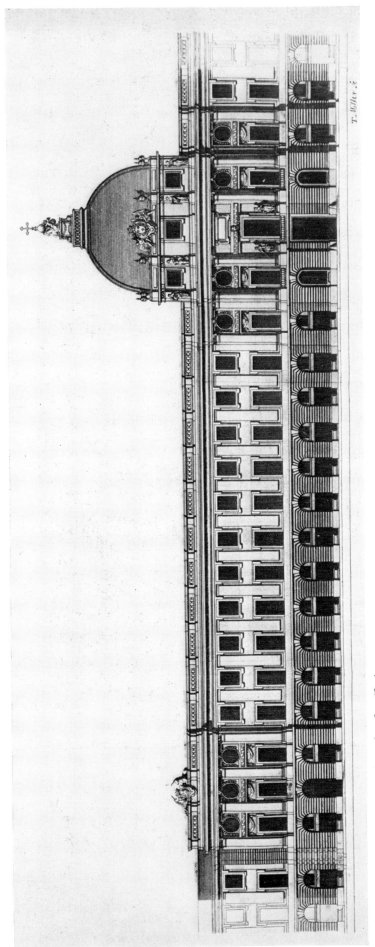

154 Lyons. Hôtel Dieu (Engraving after Soufflot)

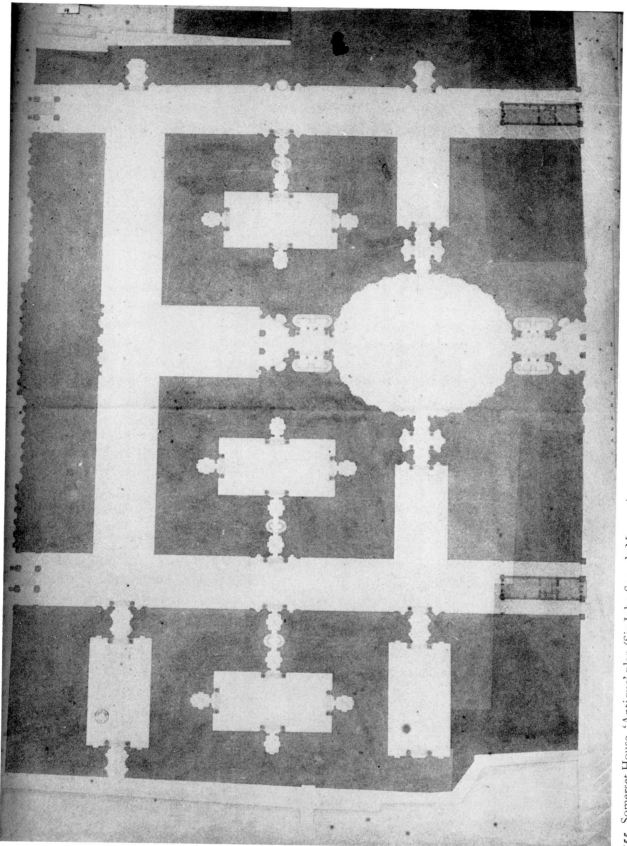

155 Somerset House. 'Antique' plan (Sir John Soane's Museum)

156 Somerset House. Strand front

157 Somerset House. Detail of vestibule

158 Somerset House. Attic to court front, Strand Block

160 Somerset House. Vestibule towards court

159 Somerset House. Doorway in court wings of Strand Block.
Copyright *Country Life*

161 Somerset House. Centre east side of court

162 Somerset House. Towards south-east corner of court

163 Somerset House. South side of court

164 Somerset House. *View of court side Strand Block* (aquatint by Malton)

165 Somerset House. The Court, drawn by Desprez (Sir John Soane's Museum)

Y

166 Somerset House. River front from Blackfriars Bridge

167 Somerset House. River front idealized by Desprez (Mr and Mrs Paul Mellon)

168 Somerset House. The Navy Staircase

169 Carlton House. Holland's staircase (from Pyne's *Royal Residences*)

170 Somerset House. The Navy Staircase. Detail

171 Somerset House. Staircase in Strand Block. Detail. Copyright *Country Life*

172 Somerset House. Staircase in Strand Block. Detail

173 Somerset House. Royal Society Council Room ceiling. Detail

174 Somerset House. Royal Society Library

175 Somerset House. Royal Society Library ceiling

176 Somerset House. The Exhibition Room (aquatint after Rowlandson)

177 Gloucester House. Project for a new house (Grosvenor Estate Office, London)

178 The Savoy Barracks. 'Ideal' study (Sir John Soane's Museum)

179 An urban palace for the king (RIBA)

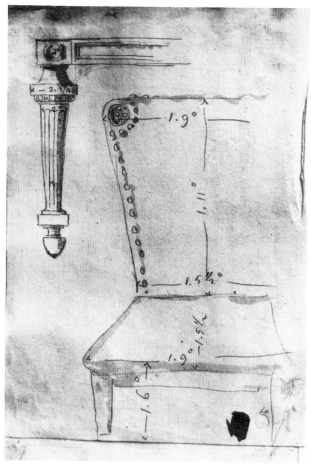

180 Drawing of a chair seen in Paris (V & A)

181 Royal Society of Arts. President's Chair

182 Sir Joshua Reynolds's Sitter's Chair (Royal Academy)

183 Blenheim Palace. State Bed. Copyright *Country Life*

185 Design for a chimney-piece (Avery Library, Columbia University)

Eating Room

184 Danson Hill. Design for a chimney-piece (Metropolitan Museum of Art)

186 Marlborough House. Saloon chimney-piece (Avery Library, Columbia University)

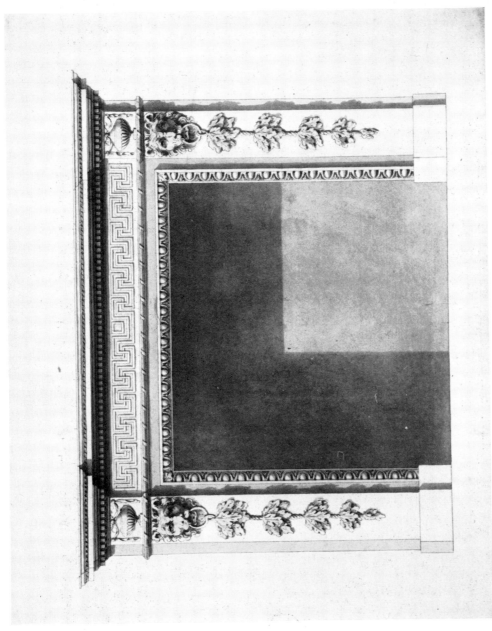

187 Design for a chimney-piece (Avery Library, Columbia University)

188 (right) The Hoo. Chimney-piece in the Hall (whereabouts unknown)

190 Chenies church. Bedford monument

189 Peper Harow. Hall chimney-piece. Copyright *Country Life*

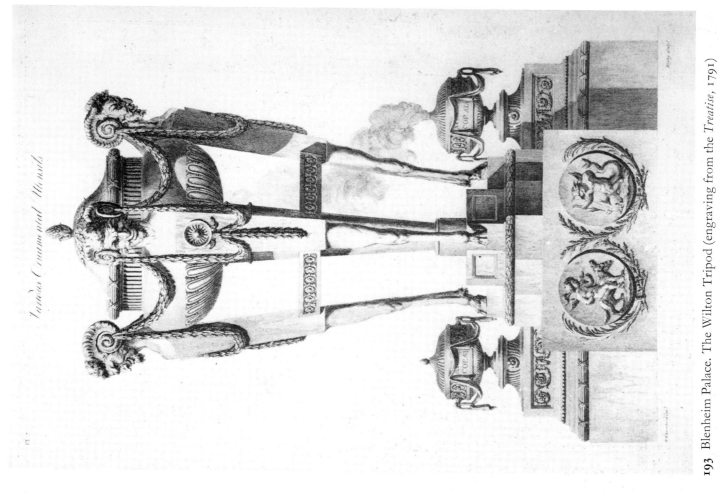

Various Ornamental Utensils.

193 Blenheim Palace. The Wilton Tripod (engraving from the *Treatise*, 1791)

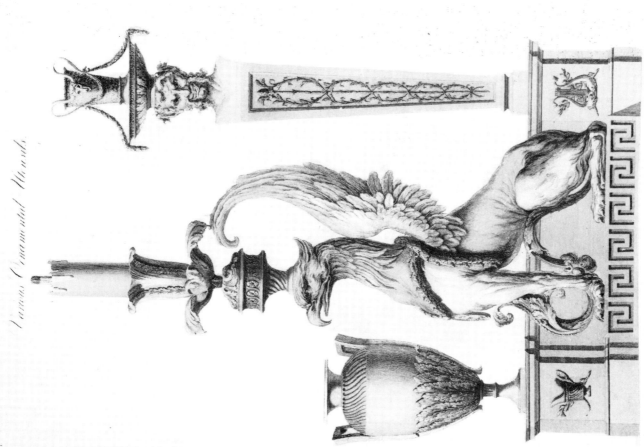

Various Ornamental Utensils.

192 Various ornamental utensils (engraving from the *Treatise*, 1791)

194 Design for a candlestick (National Gallery of Scotland)

195 Design for a candlestick (National Gallery of Scotland)

196 A primitive hut (By gracious permission of H.M. The Queen, Windsor Castle)

197 Milton Abbas in the nineteenth century

198 Whitton Park. Chambers's country house (from Harrison's *Seats*)

199 Lady Catherine Chambers, by Sir Joshua Reynolds (Iveagh Bequest, Kenwood)

Index

Bandinelli, Baccio, 177

Bankes, John, 125

Banks, Sir Joseph, 14 n.57, 185

Banks, Thomas, 103, 103 n.45

Baretti, Giuseppe, 67, 97, 101 n.39, 102, 104

Baronscourt, Co. Tyrone, 206(28)

Barracks, *see* London, Savoy

Barreau de Chefdeville, François-Dominique, 6, 41, 41 n.2, 42, 90, 171

Barret, George, 175, 184

Barrett, Bryant, 220(63)

Barrington, 2nd Viscount, 55, 198(7)

Barrow, John, 162 n.119

Bartlett, B., 197(4)

Bartoli and Co., 175, 176

Bartolozzi, Francisco, 15 n.61, 175, 179, 185

Barton Hall, Suffolk, 197(6), 205(24)

Barwell, Richard, 209(34)

Basire, James, 175

Bateman, Richard, 144 n.5

Beaumont, Sir Harry *see* Spence, Joseph

Beaumont, Percival, 190, 197(5), 201(15), 247(131), 253(145)

Beckett Park, Berks, 55, 198(7)

Bective, 1st Earl of, 210(39)

Bedford, 2nd Duke of, 201(15)

Bedford, 4th Duke of, 57, 91, 144 n.5, 201(15), 215(57), 247(131), 253(145), 254(145)

Bedford, 5th Duke of, 57

Beechwood, Herts, 198(8)

Belanger, Joseph, 12, 12 n.43

Bell, Mr, 242(118)

Bellenden, George, 189

Bellenden, Maria, 189

Belle Vue, Essex?, 5 n.10

Bellucci, Antonio, 84

Bengal, 4

Bentham, James, 143 n.87

Bentley, Richard, 34

Berkeley, Bishop, 134

Bernini, Gian Lorenzo, 22, 56, 63, 94, 139, 200(11), 251(141)

Bessborough, 2nd Earl of, 46, 56, 190, 198(7), 207(28), 212(47), 238(108), 239(108), 245(122)

Bessborough, Lady, 46, 212(47), 245(122)

Bickley Place, Kent, 198(9)

Bielefeld, Charles, 73, 217(59)

Bingham, Edward, 238(108), 239(108)

Bird, Francis, 163

Birdsall, Yorks, 198(10)

Bjornstahl, Jacob J., 12 n.44

Blanchford, Mr, 224(79)

Blake, John, 220(63)

Blanchet, Thomas, 177

Blandford, Dorset, 237, 238(107)

Blenheim Palace, Oxon, 12, 13, 56, 57, 75, 91, 94, 174, 186, 198(11), 224(80), 254(148), (Pls 183, 193)

Bloemen, Jan Frans van (Orizonte), 184

Blomfield, Sir Reginald, 171

Blondel, François, 18, 130, 135

Blondel, Georges François, 185

Blondel, Jean François, 5, 11, 14 n.54, 18, 19, 20, 30, 131, 138, 142 n.82, 171

Bloot, Pieter de, 184

Board of Works, *see* Office of Works

Bonomi, Joseph, 167, 168

Booth, Benjamin, 184

Borgognone, 184

Borromini, Francesco, 22, 23, 56, 140 n.69, 238(168)

Bosse, Abraham, 138

Boston (USA), Mass. State House, 171

Boston, 1st Baron, 50, 210(40)

Boston, 2nd Baron, 14, 50

Boswell, James, 145, 169, 170, 236(104)

Both, Jan, 184

Boucher, François, 177, 179

Boufflers-Reverel, Countess of, 14 n.54

Boughton, Sir Edward, 241(116)

Boulle, A. C., 177

Boullée, Etienne-Louis, 19, 26

Boulton, Matthew, 174, 204(23), 253(144); his geographical clock 253 (144)

Boutcher, William, 7, 7 n.21

Boyd, Sir John, 38 n.25, 46, 203(22)

Boyes, Mr, 175

Braad, Christopher, 5 n.9

Bradshaw, Mr, 254(150)

Bradshaw, George Smith, 255(150)

Brand, Thomas of the Hoo, 37 n.23, 54, 55, 103, 103 n.44, 144 n.5, 210(41), 227(90)

Brand, Thomas of the Hyde, 21, 54, 55, 144 n.5, 210(41), 212(41), 223(78)

Brand, Thomas Jnr, 210(41), 227(90)

Brand, Timothy, 212(46)

Branston, Mr, 249(136)

Raphael, 179

Rathbone, Richard, 103, 103 n.45

Rathfarnham Castle, Co. Dublin, 241(117)

Reed, John, 11 n.41

Rebecca, Biagio, 104, 176, 227(87), 234(100), 254(145)

Renard, J. A., 148

Rentham, carpenter, 197(3)

Reptons, the, 55, 201(17), 202(17)

Reveley, Willey, 11 n.41, 50, 100, 141, 141 n.75, 176, 250(138)

Revett, Nicholas, 139, 140, 141

Reynolds, Sir Joshua, 6, 6 n.12, 13, 14, 15, 15 n.61, 42, 104, 129, 129 n.9, 161, 165, 166, 167, 168, 170, 173, 185, 186, 190, 223(77), 242(118)

Rheinsberg, 148

Rhodes, William, 229(94)

Rice, Thomas, 123

Rice, William, 123

Richards, John Inigo, 85, 244(121)

Richardson, Sir Albert, 170, 190

Richardson, C. J., 191, 233(100)

Richardson, George, 138, n.54, 208(31)

Richardson, Jonathan, 163

Richardson, Thomas, 38, 79

Richmond, 3rd Duke of, 9, 10, 41, 42, 42 n.7, 62, 144 n.5, 197(6), 209(35), 235(103), 246(126)

Richmond, Surrey, 32; Wick House, 186, 190, 242(118)

Richmond Gardens, Surrey, 12, 32, 78, 114, 158, 186; Hermitage, 32; Fete Pavilion, 12, 33, 85, 244(121), (Pl.126, Fig.14); Merlin's Cave, 32; Observatory, 12, 33, 78, 79, 85, 244(120), (Pl.125); Old Palace or Lodge, 12, 32, 33, 39, 85, 86, 186, 242(119), 243; Palace projects, 33, 70, 77–80, 89, 101, 174. Specifically: I, 78; II, 78, (Pls 109, 111), (Fig.12); III, 78–80, 80 n.8, 107; IV, 79–80, 80 n.8, (Pls 110, 112); Queen's Cottage, 79

Richmond Green, Surrey, 32

Riddarhuset, 4

Riding Houses, 217(61), 235(102)

Rigaud, John Francis, 15, 104, 173

Ringsted, William, 220(63)

Riou, Stephen, *Grecian Orders,* 138 n.54, 139, 142 n.82

Ripa, Matteo, 149

Ripley, Richard, 11 n.41, 114, 117

Ripon, Yorks, 3, 4, 214(52)

Robert, Hubert, 6, 14, 20, 179

Robertson, George, 252(143)

Robinson, William, 14, 96, 97, 98, 105, 106, 107, 219(61), 225(83), 228(93), 229(93), 230

Roby, Mr, 239(108)

Rockingham, 2nd Marquess of, 110, 170

Rockingham Whigs, 110, 113

Roque, John, 33

Rodney, Jane, 15, 15 n.62, 189

Rodney, 1st Baron, 15

Roehampton (once Parksted), Surrey, 10, 46, 47, 51, 52, 53, 57, 63, 70, 186, 225(84), 235(102), 238(108), 245(122), (Pls 55, 57, 83, Fig.3c)

Rogers, Mr, 179

Rogers, carpenter, 245(122)

Rolfe, Charles, 126, 126 n.106

Rome, 6, 21–31, 35 n.17; Archivio del Vicariato, 6 n.18; Capitol, 191; Fontana Trevi, 100, 186, 191; French Academy, 7, 24–31, 90; Giardino Corsini, 191; Pal. Altieri, 191; Pal. Barberini, 191; Pal. Bracciano, 139; Pal. Colonna, 28, 191; Pal. Farnese, 28, 191; Pal. Massimi, 191; Pal. Mattei, 191; Pal. Spada, 191; Pantheon, 25, 191; Porta Pia, 191; Porta del Popolo, 191; Tomb of Cecelia Metella, 25; S. Andrca al Quirinale, 94; SS. Apostoli, 191; S. Carlo al Corso, 139, 191; S. Ignazio, 191; S. Luigi de' Francesi, 191; S. Maria in Campitelli, 191; S. Maria del Popolo, 191; SS. Martina e Luca, 191; St Peters, 27, 191; S. Pietro in Vincoli, 191; SS Trinita dei Monti, 63; Strada Felice, 6; Vatican, 191; Villa Albani, 191; Villa Borghesi, 191; Villa Borsioni, 191; Villa Corsini, 191; Villa Doria-Pamphili, 191; Villa Ludovisi, 191; Villa Madama, 191; Villa Medici, 191; Villa Negroni, 191; Villa Papa-Guilia, 191; Villa Sacchetti, 191

Rondlet, Jean-Baptiste, 19

Rooker, Edward, 58, 128, 145, 175, 185

Roper, Mr, 43 n.10

Rosa, Salvator, 184

Rosa de Tivoli, 184

Rose, Mr, (Office of Works), 122 n.83, 124

Rose, Joseph, 58, 60, 93 n.15, 197(3), 237

Rose, William, 17 n.71, 100

Roslin, Alexander, 90, 90 n.4

Roubiliac, Louis François, 164, 165

Rouse, Thomas, 73, 216(59)

Rowlandson, Thomas, 179

Roxborough, Co. Tyrone, 52, 174, 245(123), (Pl.69, Figs.5c, d)

Royal Academy, 12, 129, 163–9, 186, 190; Genisis, 163–6; Chambers's part described in *Minutes of General Assembly*, 166–7; his humanity in, 167; his insistence upon protocol, 168–9; exhibitions, 174

Royal Bank of Scotland, *see* Drummonds's Bank

Royal Botanical Gardens Library, 33 n.4

Rubens, Peter Paul, 177

Rudd, John, 11 n.41

Rutland, 3rd Duke of, 219(62)

Ruysdael, Jakob van, 184

Ryland, William, 179, 184

Rysbrack, Michael, 36, 177, 179, 181

St Martin's Lane Academy, 164, 165, 167

St Petersburg, 30

Salisbury, Bishop of, 39

Salisbury, 1st Marquess of, 117, 117 n.49, 120

Salter, Dr John Gurney, 6 n.15, 173

Salvi, Nicola, 22, 100, 100 n.38

Saly, Jacques-Francois-Joseph, 15 n.61, 27 n.23

Sandberg, David, 4, 13, 49, 189, 206(28), 209(36), 222(73), 240(114)

Sandberg, John David, 189

Sandberg, Margaretha, 189

Sandberg, Maria, 189

Sandberg, Mary, *see* Chambers, Mary

Sandby, Paul, 10 n.34, 15 n.61, 145, 175, 177, 179, 185, 253(143)

Sandby, Thomas, 111, 112, 114, 129, 129 n.9, 165

Sanderson, John, 95

Sandon Hall, Staffs, 245(124)

Sandrart, 140

Sangallo, Antonio de, 54

Sans Souci, German Democratic Republic, 77, 148, 246(125), (Pl.42)

Saragossa, 35

Saxon, Samuel, 100

Saxon, William, 176

Scammell, Susan, 189

Scamozzi, Vicenzo, 22

Scheffer, Count Carl Fredrik, 5, 6, 13 n.47, 18, 87, 161, 161 n.115, 190, 248(133)

Scott, John, 176

Scrope, Thomas, 144 n.5, 202(18)

Sebright, Sir Thomas, 198(8)

Secker (of Board of Green Cloth), 126

Seddon and Shackleton, 256(159)

Selwyn, George Augustus, 112, 112 n.22, 114, 121, 200(13)

Serlio, Sebastiano, 25, 27

Servandoni, Jean-Jerome, 20

Seward, William, 36 n.19, 213(50)

Shaftesbury, 3rd Earl of, 77

Shardeloes, Bucks, 47, 47 n.20, 52 n.29, 206(28), 207(28)

Sharpe, John, 9, 207(30), 220(65)

Shaw, joiner, 197(3)

Shelburne, 2nd Earl of, 110, 110 n.14

Shenstone, William, 152, 156 n.76

Sherborne Castle, Dorset, 24, 55, 57, 62, 246(126), (Pl.79)

Sheridan, Richard Brinsley, 114

Shoebury Castle, Essex, 86

Shropshire, John, 248(132)

Shugborough, Staffs, 34 n.10, 147, 213(48)

Simmons, Samuel Forrest, 122

Skelton Castle, Yorks, 246(127)

Slane Castle, Co. Meath, 246(128), 247(128)

Slaughter's Coffee House, 164

Sloane, Sir Hans, 9, 207(30), 220(65)

Smeaton, William, 14 n.57

Smirke, Sir Robert, 105, 105 n.51, 166, 232(95)

Smith, Consul, 83

Smith, Joseph, 123

Smith, J. T., 81

Smith, Robert, 238(108), 239(108)

Snow, Mr, 175

Soane, Sir John, 15, 21 n.8, 123, 124, 124 n.91, 124 n.93, 124 n.94, 125, 143, 170, 187, 230; - Chambers's letter to Stevens given to him, 21–2; his behaviour in the Office of Works, 123–5

Sobry, J. F., 142 n.82

Society for the Encouragement of Arts, Manufactures and Commerce, 165

Society of Arts of Great Britain, 9, 63, 75, 78, 87, 165, 166, 167, 174, 235(103), 240(111), 243

Society of Arts, 89, 90

Society of Dilettante, 139, 164

Soufflot, Jacques-Germain, 6, 14 n.54, 20, 100, 103, 171, 232(95)

Southill, Beds, 55, 69, 247(129)

Spagnoletto, 184

Spain, drawings of building in, 5

Sparre, Fridrik, 6 n.13

Spence, Joseph (pseud. Sir Harry Beaumont), 149

Spencer, Lord Charles, 112 n.20

Stables, 200(13), 203(20), 206(28), 240(115), 248(132)

Staircases, Gower House: 68–9; Melbourne House: 70, 227(87); York House: 225(84); Château les Ormes: 239(111)

Wille, Johann Georg, 185

William III, 32, 77

Williams, Thomas, 223(75)

Willis, Dr, 251(141)

Willoughby, Henry (later 5th Baron Middleton),
6 n.17, 53, 198(10), 205(25)

Wilson, D., 129

Wilson, Richard, 38, 165, 169, 184, 252(142)

Wilton, Joseph, 15, 21, 23, 34 n.12, 38, 42, 53,
56, 62, 63, 66 n.12, 75, 81, 93, 101, 101 n.39,
102, 102 n.40, 105 n.48, 165, 166, 173, 175, 177,
199(11), 201(15), 207(30), 211(41), 214(50),
214(52), 220(63), 220(65), 228(92), 231, 233(98),
233(99), 235(103), 240(112), 245(122), 247(131),
248(132), 250(139)

Wilton, William, 53, 245(122), 248(132)

Wilton House, Wilts, 10, 11 n.40, 41, 63 n.6, 89,
174, 186, 191, 232(96), 235(102), 251(142),
(Pls 46–7)

Winchester Palace, clerkship of, 113, 114, 124

Winde, William, 83, 197(3), 218(61)

Windsor (Old), Berks: Bateman's house, 147

Windsor Castle Berks, 114; Queen's Lodge,
14, 78, 86, 244(119), 252(143), (Pls 121–4);
Seventeenth Century House and Nell Gwynn's
House, 253(143); Eight Day Clock, 253(144),
(Pls 129–30)

Winklerfelt, Anna Sofia of, 189

Witney, Oxon, 13

Woburn Abbey, Beds, 12, 57, 58, 91, 174, 186,
190, 211(43), 215(57), 224(80), 253(145),
(Pls 71, 80, 90)

Wolcot, Dr J. J., *see* Peter Pindar (pseud.)

Wolfe, General, 184, 233(99)

Wolterton, Norfolk, 191

Wood, Robert, 8, 32, 36, 165, 213(50), 232(96)

Woodstock, Oxon, church tower, 92, 94–5,
228(92), 254(147), (Pl.148); town hall, 12, 56, 90–1,
174, 186, 199(11), 215(53), 224(80), 254(148),
(Pl.141); Thomas Walker's house, 254(146)

Woolfe, John, Sr, 123

Woolfe, John, Jr, 123

Woollett, William, 184, 185

Wootton, John, 163

Worsley, Thomas, 14, 78, 79, 83, 97, 109, 112,
112 n.24, 113, 113 n.30, 190, 211(44), 219(61),
222(70), 239(108), 239(109), 243

Wray, Sir Cecil, 202(18)

Wren, Sir Christopher, 75, 77, 85, 112, 142 n.82,
180, 224(80), 251(141)

Wrest Park, Beds, 254(149)

Wright, Stephen, 82, 109, 111, 237

Wright, Thomas, 253(144)

Wrotham Park, Middx, 48, (Pl.58)

Wroxton Abbey, Oxon, 147

Wyatt, James, 17, 40, 41, 55, 59, 69, 84, 86, 87,
106 n.53, 109, 111, 116, 116 n.44, 117 n.48, 122,
122 n.78, 122 n.85, 123, 124 n.94, 125, 171, 197(5),
201(17), 202(17), 209(35), 218(61), 235(104),
236(104), 237, 241(115), 247(128), 252(142)

Wyatt, Samuel, 124 n.94

Wyattville, Sir Jeffry, 86, 253(143)

Wycombe Abbey, Bucks, 69 n.21

Wylde, Wendela, 189

Wyon, William, 173

Yenn, John, 11, 11 n.41, 15 n.62, 16, 17 n.71,
49, 75, 100, 105 n.49, 123, 171, 175, 182, 200(11),
202(18), 213(50), 217(61), 224(80), 235(101),
241(115), 251(142)

York, Archbishop of, 126

York, Edward Augustus, Duke of, 225(84)

York Races, 14

Yorke, Philip, 34 n.10

Yorktown, USA, 110

Young, Henry, 127

Index to the distribution of designs in collections

BEECHWOOD, Herts: Sebright papers, 198(8)

BLENHEIM, Oxon: Marlborough papers, 198(11)

CAMBRIDGE: School of Architecture, 201(17)

CASTLE HOWARD, Yorks: Carlisle papers, 200(13)

CRICHTON Coll. Isle of Anglesey: 193(3)

DELAWARE MEMORIAL LIBRARY, University of Delaware, USA: 198(11), 224(80), 225(83)

DUBLIN: National Library, 235(104)

EDINBURGH: Royal Bank of Scotland, 207(31)

GRINKE Coll. London: 240(115)

HAREWOOD, Yorks: Lascelles papers, 209(38)

W. J. HARVEY Coll. 217(60)

KEW GARDENS, Surrey: Royal Botanical Gardens, Library, 242(119)

GUINNESS Coll. Leixlip, Ireland: 200(12)

LONDON:
—Albany archives, 226(87)
—British Museum, 224(83), 242(119)
—Buckingham Palace, 219(63)
—Greater London Council, 233(100)
—Grosvenor Estate Office: Westminster papers, 233(97)
—Minet Public Library, 213(50)
—Public Record Office, 242(119)
—Royal Academy, 202(18), 205(26), 212(48), 250(139), 252(143)
—Royal Institute of British Architects, 198(11), 208(33), 209(35), 210(41), 211(43), 213(50), 216(59), 217(61), 224(82), 225(84), 226(87), 229(95), 236(106), 239(111), 241(117), 242(119), 245(123), 246(126), 251(142), 255(153), 255(154), 255(155)
—Sir John Soane's Museum, 196(1), 197(6), 198(11), 203(21), 203(22), 206(28), 207(29), 210(40), 210(41), 213(49), 213(50), 216(59), 217(61), 219(62), 219(63), 222(69), 223(75), 224(80), 225(84), 226(87), 227(90), 228(92), 228(93), 229(95), 233(100), 235(103), 237(106), 240(112), 240(115), 242(118), 242(119), 244(121), 245(122), 247(130), 250(138), 250(140), 250(141), 251(142), 253(145), 255(156)
—Victoria and Albert Museum, 200(13), 204(23), 205(25), 205(26), 207(29), 209(35), 210(41), 213(49), 213(50), 216(59), 217(61), 220(65), 222(71), 223(75), 226(87), 228(91), 228(92), 229(94), 231(95), 233(100), 235(102), 238(108), 240(115), 245(122), 245(123), 248(132), 248(133), 249(135), 249(137), 251(142), 253(145), 254(147), 255(157)

—Westminster Public Library, 217(60), 229(94), 233(100)

MR and MRS PAUL MELLON Coll. Upperville, USA: 229(95)

FATHER MURPHY Coll. Robertstown, Ireland, 198(8), 203(20), 209(35), 224(79), 242(118), 245(122)

NEWBY HALL, Yorks: Grantham papers, 234(101), 239(110)

NEW YORK:
—Avery Library, Columbia University, 215(56), 223(78), 224(80), 240(112), 246(128)
—Metropolitan Museum of Art, 196(1), 197(3), 203(22), 204(23), 205(26), 209(34), 212(47), 212(48), 216(59), 223(74), 223(78), 226(87), 229(95), 233(100), 235(102), 235(103) 238(108), 245(122)
—Pierpont Morgan Library, 197(3), 233(100)

OXFORD: Bodleian Library, 254(147)

MR and MRS B. PARDOE Coll. Ottershaw, Surrey: 215(54)

RICHARDSON-HOUFE Coll. Ampthill, Beds: 205(25), 240(115), 253(145)

SANS SOUCCI, Potsdam: 246(125)

SLANE CASTLE, Ireland: Conyngham papers, 246(128)

SOUTHILL, Beds: Torrington papers: 247(129)

STOCKHOLM:
—Byggnadstyrelsen archiv, 248(140)
—National Museum, 248(133)

WINDSOR CASTLE, Royal Library: 210(40), 211(44), 213(50), 217(60), 219(62), 225(84), 243(119), 244(121), 252(143)

WILTON HOUSE, Wilts: Pembroke papers: 251(142)

WORSLEY Coll. Hovingham, Yorks: 217(60)

397